*A Practical
Approach to
Arbitration Law*

To
Alexander James Tweeddale

A Practical
Approach to
Arbitration Law

Andrew Tweeddale MSc *(Prop), LLB (Hons), Dip. Arb., FCI Arb.*
Solicitor and Non-practising Barrister in the Construction and Engineering Group of Norton Rose

and

Keren Tweeddale MSc *(Prop), BA (Hons), Dip. Arb., FCI Arb.*
Non-practising Barrister

**BLACKSTONE
PRESS LIMITED**

This edition published in Great Britain 1998 by Blackstone Press Limited, Aldine Place, London W12 8AA. Telephone (020) 8740 2277 www.blackstonepress.com

© Andrew Tweeddale, Keren Tweeddale, 1999

ISBN: 1 85431 974 4

British Library Cataloguing in Publication Data
A CIP catalogue record for this book is available from the British Library

Typeset by Style Photosetting Ltd, Mayfield, East Sussex
Printed by Ashford Colour Press, Gosport, Hampshire

Contents

Preface

The Arbitration Act 1996 represents one of the most significant developments in English arbitration law. The fact that it is so new and so radical means that even two years after its introduction we are still having to interpret, for the first time, particular sections of the Act. Since 1996 there has been a plethora of new cases to which we have referred, including a number of Court of Appeal decisions which we have analysed. We have also incorporated the Civil Procedure Rules 1998 in so far as they affect arbitration proceedings. *A Practical Approach to Arbitration Law* is primarily intended for students of arbitration law and practitioners who are perhaps coming to the subject for the first time, whether they are claims consultants, solicitors or parties. It is therefore intended to give a complete overview of the arbitration system and includes a detailed examination of the law as well as procedure. We have also included an introduction illustrating the history and development of arbitration in England, a résumé of the main principles involved in international arbitrations, a guide to various administered schemes and a section of precedents to assist those who are involved in the arbitral process.

Our special thanks to Irene Eres for two years of baby-sitting and for putting up with all our moods and to Zev Eres for helping to look after Alex.

Thanks to everyone at Corbett & Co. and especially Edward Corbett, Anne Holmes and Richard Dillon. Thanks to Andrew White QC, Jonathan Gaisman QC and James Robinson for providing us with recent cases on arbitration. Thanks also to Derek French for his invaluable editing and authors notes and to Alistair MacQueen, Jeremy Stein, Heather Saward and Jo Herbert at Blackstone Press for all their help.

Andrew Tweeddale
Keren Tweeddale

Table of Cases

Table of Statutes

Table of Statutory Instruments

Table of International Conventions

Table of Arbitration Rules

1 Introduction

1.1 DEVELOPMENT OF ARBITRATION LAW

Dispute resolution by way of arbitration in England has existed for as long as the common law. However, it is only recently that there has developed a distinct branch of jurisprudence termed arbitration law. The development of arbitration law in England can be described as falling into six distinct periods:

(a) Common law until the statute 9 & 10 Will 3, c. 15 (1698).
(b) From the statute 9 & 10 Will 3, c. 15, to the Common Law Procedure Act 1854.
(c) From the Common Law Procedure Act 1854 to the Arbitration Act (AA) 1889.
(d) The Arbitration Acts 1889 to 1934.
(e) The Arbitration Acts 1950 to 1979.
(f) The Arbitration Act (AA) 1996.

Arbitration is a consensual process. Although it is possible to arbitrate without any interference from the court system, several practical and theoretical difficulties arise if such a course is adopted. One practical difficulty is that the enforcement of an arbitration agreement becomes impossible and it is all too easy for one of the parties to frustrate the arbitral process. On a theoretical level it renders uncertain any commercial contract. An arbitral tribunal, which is not subject to any form of review, may apply or ignore principles of law.

The courts and the legislature have therefore at times involved themselves with the consensual process of arbitration. The courts have taken the view that, although an arbitral tribunal has a quasi-judicial function, arbitration should be considered as an area of private law, and as such be subject to their overriding control. Not all countries have strictly adopted this approach. In examining what are the rights, duties and powers of the arbitral tribunal the court begins by examining the arbitration agreement. Arbitration law in England is therefore dominated by English contract law.

1.2 COMMON LAW UNTIL THE STATUTE 9 & 10 WILL 3, C. 15 (1698)

References to arbitration, or as it was termed until just after the turn of the twentieth century arbitrament, can be found in the yearbooks and cases from the reigns of Elizabeth I and James I. Arbitrament was defined in *Termes de la Ley*, p. 50, as being: 'an award, determination or judgment which one or more makes at the request of two parties at the least for and upon some . . . controversie had between them . . . and they that make the award or arbitrament are called . . . arbitrators'. These essential characteristics which define what an arbitration is still exist today.

The use of arbitration as a system of dispute resolution can be traced back to classical Greek and Roman times. However, to think of arbitration as being invented is to misunderstand the process of arbitration. In primitive societies justice was dispensed by the family head or by the elders of the tribe. This primitive form of justice is as much the keystone to arbitration as it is to the development of the courts. This method of dispensing 'rough justice' is in many ways more akin to arbitration than to court systems.

To understand how England developed a system of arbitration one must remember that even as far back as the Middle Ages England was a trading nation. The royal court system was slow, arduous and gave no recourse to parties who were not resident in England. There was a complicated system of finance and trade during the Middle Ages that spread from England across Western Europe and was centred around the import and export of goods as wide ranging as wool, cloth, silks, tin, pewter, silver, furs and wines. The financing of international trade as far back as 1484 by English merchants is discussed by Fifoot in *History and Sources of the Common Law* (London: Stevens, 1949).

The royal courts were not suited to afford protection to the merchants who traded in England. The writs that could be issued out of the royal courts were designed in this period to deal with disputes about land and issues affecting the King's peace. The writs that one could issue out of the royal courts were therefore limited and rarely would have encompassed matters such as commercial trade. The procedure to issue a writ out of the royal courts was also slow so that merchants passing from fair to fair would find themselves out of the jurisdiction within a short period. Finally, the royal courts would not enforce judgments where one of the parties was a foreigner.

The lack of the ability of the royal courts to dispense justice led to the development of international and local courts. In England there developed the courts of the borough, of the fair and of the staple. These courts, unlike similar ones in Europe, were not run by commercial men but often by the grantor of the franchise where the market or fair was held. The courts of the fair, which were termed the courts of piepowder, 'to commemorate the pedlars who trailed their dusty feet from market to market' (Fifoot, op. cit., p. 295) were controlled by the officer of the borough. However, the law that was applied was often declared by the merchants themselves. The strict formalities of these courts were often waived or set aside with the idea that 'the law should be speedily administered in commercial causes' (Lord Parker of Waddington, *The History and Development of Commercial Arbitration* (Jerusalem: Magnes Press, 1959)). In the staple courts matters relating to the quality of goods sold were tried not only by the mayor but also by 'merchant strangers'.

In addition to these courts the guilds administered arbitration tribunals which determined mercantile problems affecting guild members. It was therefore in the fifteenth century that England first saw the development of what can be seen as 'modern' arbitration, that is, arbitration independent of the courts of law.

One of the first recorded arbitrations is to be found in the rolls of the Mayor's Court of the City of London in 1424. The case involves a claim for medical negligence in the treating of a wound to the thumb. The record states:

> The Arbitrators, having diligently considered and fully understood the matter, on the evidence of the parties, and the sworn testimony of John Parker, a barber admitted for the practice of surgery only, and also of other trustworthy persons having knowledge of the course of the aforesaid treatment, found that the complainant William Forrest on 31 January last past, the moon being consumed in a bloody sign, to wit, Aquarius, under a malevolent constellation, was seriously wounded in the said muscles, and on the 9 February, the moon being in the sign of Gemini, a great effusion of blood took place; that Simon Rolf staunched the blood first time, and that afterwards John Harwe, with the assistance of John Dalton, skilfully stopped the flow, which broke out six times in dangerous fashion, and that on the seventh occasion, the wounded man preferring a mutilated hand rather than death, the said John Harwe, with the consent of the patient, and for lack of other remedy, finally staunched the blood by cautery, as was proper, and thus saved his life.

The arbitral tribunal stated that this course was correct and continued: 'any defect, mutilation or disfigurement of the hand was due either to the constellations aforesaid or some defect of the patient or the original nature of the wound'. Although the decision was based more on astrology than good medical practice, the medical practitioners who were asked to arbitrate were no doubt more skilled in determining the cause of the injury than would have been a court of law.

The courts of staple, borough courts and fair courts disappeared over the next few centuries as the society of England changed. The international society of the Middle Ages disappeared with the advent of nation States and the agricultural and industrial revolutions. The guilds all but disappeared and were replaced by entrepreneurs and joint-stock companies. Although independent arbitration was still desired by commercial men, the courts and government sought to intervene to control and regulate how trade could be done.

With the dissolution of the 'merchant' courts and guilds a void was left which was filled during the Stuart and Tudor reigns. The Court of Star Chamber was created to deal with disputes between merchants whatever their nationality. The Court of Star Chamber realised that there was a desire for commercial disputes to be referred to commercial men for arbitration and therefore would refer ordinary disputes to arbitration. Potter, *Historical Introduction to English Law and its Institution*, 2nd ed. (1943), p. 160, quotes the Chancellor of the Star Chamber saying in 1475:

This dispute is brought by an alien merchant . . . who has come to conduct his case here, and he ought not to be held to await trial by 12 men and other solemnities of the law of the land but ought to be able to sue here from hour to hour and day to day for the speed of merchants.

In line with the need to deal with international disputes the common law courts and the courts of Admiralty developed the rule of notional venue in England, which gave jurisdiction to the courts to deal with international disputes. However, the criticism of the English court system, that it was slow and that there was no understanding of mercantile customs, remained. The criticism was succinctly expressed by W. Cole, *A Rod for the Lawyers* (1659):

Having often discoursed with lawyers and others about the delays, burdens and uncertainties of trials at law, I very seldom found any averse to Merchants' courts . . . for what a ridiculous thing is it, that judges in Chancery must determine of merchants' negotiations, transacted in foreign parts, which they understood no better than the seats they sit on.

Although, the courts developed a jurisdiction to deal with international commercial disputes this still did not address the complaint of the merchants that it was far better for merchants to deal with mercantile problems. The merchants therefore took the lead in developing their own requirements for dispute resolution by incorporating into their own charters the privilege of settling disputes arising among themselves. The charter of the African Company (1672), for example, established a court consisting of 'one person learned in civil laws and two merchants', who were to try cases 'according to the rules of equity and good conscience and according to the laws and customs of merchants'.

The conflict between the courts, which wished to retain their control over all matters legal, and the merchants, who wanted a dispute resolution system that catered to their needs, was finally addressed by Parliament. An Act of 1571 gave jurisdiction to a tribunal comprised partly of lawyers and partly of merchants to deal with bankruptcy matters. An Act of 1601 established a court of merchants and lawyers to deal with the settlement of insurance matters in London. Parliament was, however, reluctant to establish courts of *lex mercatoria*. This may be explained by the debt owed by Parliament to the common law courts for siding with it during the Civil War.

Contemporaneously to these developments in the court structure a basic system of arbitration law also developed. The yearbooks and some reports record early arbitrations: *Anonymous* (1468) YB 8 Edw 4 f. 11; and *Blake's Case* (1606) 6 Co Rep 43b. These arbitrations were conducted in almost a judicial character with the need for finality and certainly. By 1670 the principles of arbitration law could be stated from a small body of case law in the *Consuetudo vel Lex Mercatoria* by Gerard de Malynes:

First, that the Award be given up in writing within the time limited, by the bonds of compromise made between the parties.

Second, that there be limited and appointed by the Award some reciprocal Act to be done by each party to the other, which the Law requireth to be quid pro quo, albeit never so final.

Third, that they make a final end, and so determine upon all the points or differences produced before them by specification or otherwise, if they be required so to do and authorised thereunto.

Fourth, that they do not award any of the parties to do or perform any unlawful act or thing prohibited and against the law.

Fifth, that they do award anything whereby any matter, already determined by Decree in Chancery, or Judgment at Common Law or any sentence judicially given in the cause be infringed or meddled withal.

The extent of the power that the arbitral tribunal had was in some respects greater than that of the courts. The point is made clear in West's *Symboleographie* (1647), part 2, p. 164. The 'power is larger than any power of any ordinary judge . . . for the arbitrator hath power to judge according to the compromise after his own mind as well of the fact as of the law, not observing the form of law'.

From this position in the mid seventeenth century the courts began to intervene in the exercise of the power of the arbitral tribunal. Lord Parker of Waddington, *The History and Development of Commercial Arbitration* (Jerusalem: Magnes Press, 1959) at p. 13 has assessed the reasons:

There are various theories:

    1.   The natural desire of the courts to keep all adjudications within their sphere;

    2.   The fear of the growth of a new system of law;

    3.   The fact that litigants in arbitrations needed the assistance of the courts who in turn exacted a price for such assistance.

However, the arbitration procedure was unsatisfactory in that it relied upon the good faith of the parties. Awards could not be enforced as judgments of the courts, but only by an action on the award so that a party obtaining an award in its favour was forced to bring a fresh action for breach of covenant. For the purposes of achieving an enforceable result the award might not be worth the paper it was written on.

The reference to arbitration could be complicated further in that either party could withdraw from the reference up until the time that the award was published. Up until that time the courts took the view that the reference to the arbitrator was a revocable authority that could be withdrawn at any time prior to the award. The effect of this was threefold. First, the arbitration agreement was not a submission to arbitration. It was the actual appointment of the arbitrator that determined the submission to arbitration. Secondly, an action in the courts could be brought in defiance of the arbitration agreement. Any agreement that sought to exclude the jurisdiction of the courts was seen to be contrary to public policy: *Doleman and Sons* v *Ossett Corporation* [1912] 3 KB 257 at p. 267. Thirdly, even when the arbitration hearing had been held a party could, fearing that the award would be against him, revoke the authority of the arbitrator before the award was made.

Further problems could arise if the arbitrator died or refused to proceed with the reference. Also, if one of the parties failed to agree to the appointment of the arbitrator, there was nothing that the other party could do to enforce the arbitration agreement.

Several methods were developed to counter these difficulties. First, the parties could, by indenture, covenant to stand by the award of the arbitrator. However, enforcement of the award could only be achieved by a fresh action for breach of covenant. Secondly, the obligation to abide by the award could be secured by a bond given under seal. Again this had to be enforced by a separate action on the bond. Thirdly, the parties could make a parol contract, which again needed a fresh action if enforcement was required.

A partial answer to these problems was evolved in the Court of King's Bench when Sir John Kelyng was Chief Justice during the reign of Charles II. Where a dispute was submitted to an arbitrator under the inherent jurisdiction of the court or by consent of the court then to revoke the consent given to the reference was considered a contempt of court and could be enforced by attachment of the contemnor's property: *Forster* v *Brunetti* (1696) 1 Salk 83. This rule was perhaps the most important development in the laws of arbitration prior to 1698 and its importance was realised by Parliament which gave statutory force to it in the statute 9 & 10 Will 3, c. 15.

1.3 THE STATUTE 9 & 10 WILL 3, C. 15 TO THE COMMON LAW PROCEDURE ACT 1854

In enacting the statute 9 & 10 Will 3, c. 15, Parliament realised the significance of arbitration to trade. The preamble to the Act stated:

Now for promoting trade, and rendering the awards of arbitrators the more effectual in all cases, for the final determination of controversies referred to them by merchants and traders, or others, concerning matters of account or trade, or other matters . . .

The Act took steps to remedy inherent problems within the body of case law applicable to arbitrations. It made it possible to enforce a written arbitration submission by an action for contempt. The Act stated that it is:

lawful for all merchants and traders, and others desiring to end any controversy . . . for which there is no other remedy but by personal action or suit in equity, by arbitration, to agree that their submission of their suit to the award or umpirage of any person or persons should be made a rule of any of His

Majesty's courts of record, which the parties shall choose, and to insert such their agreement in their submission.

It was therefore not a mandatory requirement of the Act that a submission to arbitration should contain a provision that it be made as a rule of court. Where there was proof of such an agreement the Act stated that 'a rule shall thereupon be made by the said court, that the parties shall submit to, and finally be concluded by the arbitration or umpirage which shall be made . . . pursuant to such submission' on pain of contempt.

In *Lucas* d *Markham* v *Wilton* (1759) 2 Burr 701 Lord Mansfield CJ explained the significance of this development. His lordship stated that it was made 'to put submissions to arbitration in cases where there was no cause depending, upon the same foot as those where there was a cause depending'. In other words the effect was to give references made on covenant, or on obligation, the same status as if they were made by reference by the courts.

A second section of the Act gave the Court power to set aside an award which had been procured by fraud or undue means. In the commentary to *Veale* v *Warner* (1669) 1 Saund 326 at p. 327 the learned editor stated that:

Nor could an award, where the submission was by bond or other writing, or by parol, be in any other manner set aside at common law for the misbehaviour of the arbitrators, until the statute 9 & 10 Will 3, c. 15, gave relief, where the submission is by bond or other writing; for the law seems to be still the same in this respect, where the submission is by parol, it being held that the statute does not give the courts authority to make a submission by parol a rule of court.

Oral agreements to refer matters to arbitration are still outside the scope of the statute governing arbitration, which is now the Arbitration Act 1996.

The principle that a submission to arbitration was made as a rule of court lasted in excess of 200 years. The Civil Procedure Act 1833 (3 & 4 Will 4, c. 42) developed this theme further in that it supplemented the process of contempt by making the appointment of the arbitral tribunal irrevocable except where the leave of the court was given. However, the result was that arbitrations required the support of the courts and with this support the courts now had the opportunity to review and scrutinise the conduct of the arbitration.

This development in the power of the courts to review and scrutinise an award can be clearly illustrated in the development by the courts of their right to refuse to enforce an award. Prior to 1698 the only ground for the courts refusing to enforce an award were on the jurisdictional merits of the case, that is, whether the arbitral tribunal had acted within the submission. On questions of law and fact the decision of the arbitral tribunal was not reviewable. The courts would not even review the merits of the award where questions of natural justice were raised. In *Matthew* v *Ollerton* (1693) 4 Mod 226, the courts refused to overturn an award made by the arbitrator who was in fact one of the parties in dispute. Reference was made in *Matthew* v *Ollerton* to the unreported case of *Sergeant Hards*. The court held that, although in litigation natural justice dictated that a party should not be a judge in his own cause, this rule was inapplicable to arbitrations because of their consensual nature. If one party chooses the other party to settle matters between them then he must be bound by that choice.

In *Morris* v *Reynolds* (1703) 2 Ld Raym 857 there was a division of judicial view about the above principle. The case before the court was that the arbitral tribunal, who had been chosen by the parties, had misconducted the arbitration in that they refused to hear from the defendant. The court was divided on whether it had power to set aside the decision of the arbitrators on this ground. Holt CJ was of the opinion that to do so was 'contrary to all practice that he had known in his experience which was that in such case the integrity of the arbitrators shall never be arraigned, no more than the integrity of any judge'. However, the remaining three judges thought that to give credence to the arbitral tribunal's actions would be 'abominable'. Again in *Harris* v *Mitchell* (1704) 2 Vern 485 the election of an umpire by the arbitral tribunal by throwing cross and pile (an act similar to throwing dice) was set aside by the Master of the Rolls, who stated: 'An election or choice is an act, that depends on the will and understanding; but the arbitrators followed neither in this case, and it is distrusting of God's providence to leave matters to chance'.

Although the courts were prepared to review an award where principles of natural justice had been breached they were not so ready to re-examine questions of fact and law. The development of the courts' power to review an award where there was an error on the face of the award is somewhat obscure. In *Corneforth* v *Geer* (1715) 2 Vern 705, the Lord Chancellor stated: 'If it appears that the arbitrators went upon a plain mistake, either as to the law, or in a matter of fact; the same is an error appearing in the body of the award, and sufficient to set it aside'. However, in *Anderson* v *Coxeter* (1720) 1 Str 301 the Court of King's Bench held: '. . . nothing is a ground within that statute for us to set aside an award, but manifest corruption in the arbitrators. We will not unravel the matter, and examine into the justice and reasonableness of what is awarded.'

The development of the power to review can, however, be seen to be emerging in the case of *Lucas* d *Markham* v *Wilton* (1759) 2 Burr 701. Here the Court of King's Bench indicated that it would be prepared to allow a limited review but only in certain circumstances. Lord Mansfield stated that 'the court will not enter at all into the merits of the matter referred to arbitration; but only take into consideration such legal objections as appear on the face of the award, and such objections as go to the misbehaviour of the arbitrators'. In the commentary to *Veale* v *Warner* (1669) 1 Saund 326 at p. 327 reference is made to *Anonymous* (1700) 1 Salk 71 in support of the learned editor's view that:

But where the submission to arbitration was by rule of court, which was often the case, the conduct of the arbitrators, and of the parties to the submission, might, as it still may, be examined into, and if, on examination, it appeared that the arbitrators had been partial and unjust, or had mistaken the law, the court would not enforce a performance of the award.

Although the above cases appear contradictory most of them can be reconciled by drawing a distinction between cases in which an error by the arbitral tribunal was not apparent on the face of the award and those where it was apparent. It would appear that the courts would not look behind the award, but they would not enforce an award that on its face was patently wrong. In *Anderson* v *Coxeter* (1720) 1 Str 301 it was held that the court cannot set aside an award if made in pursuance of the statute on any ground other than fraud or corruption in the arbitrators. In *Hutchins* v *Hutchins* (1738) Andr 297 it was held that though the courts cannot set aside the award upon any other ground but fraud or corruption, yet if there was any illegality or defect on the face of it, the court would refuse to enforce the award by attachment, but leave the party to an action on the bond, or on the award itself.

The power to review a factual error was clearly stated to be beyond the power of the courts by 1788. Lord Commissioner Wilson stated in *Morgan* v *Mather* (1792) 2 Ves Jr 15:

It would be a melancholy thing, if, because we differed from the arbitrators in points of fact, we should set aside awards. The only grounds for that are, first, that the arbitrators have awarded what was out of their power; secondly, corruption, or that they have proceeded contrary to the principles of natural justice, though there is no corruption, as if without reason they will not hear a witness; thirdly, that they have proceeded upon mere mistake, which they themselves admit. I am of opinion, that when any thing is submitted to arbitration, the arbitrators cannot award contrary to law; as that is beyond their power; for the parties intend to submit to them only the legal consequences of their transactions and engagements.

The effect of this *obiter dictum* is wide ranging. Challenges to an award which is contrary to the law can, if not suitably restricted, frustrate the very purpose of the arbitration. Almost any dispute, save possibly for some determinations by experts of quality or price, involves some legal principle. Any dispute arising from a breach of contract involves a determination that there was in fact a contract. The finding that a contract exists; that there is an offer, acceptance, consideration, intention to create a legal relationship, capacity etc. involves determinations of questions of law. To allow all these matters to be opened up and revised by an appellate court would frustrate the purpose of a quick and speedy resolution of a dispute.

It is therefore not surprising that the courts curtailed this power of legal review. In *Kent* v *Estob* (1802) 3 East 18 it was argued that there was no power by the courts of review where the arbitral tribunal had made an award which was not in accordance with the strict rule of law. The court in this case admitted the practice of review on a point of law but held that this power only existed where the mistake of law was apparent on the face of the award or from a statement of reasons given in writing by the arbitrator at the time of giving the award. This principle was affirmed in *Hodgkinson* v *Fernie* (1857) 3 CB NS 189, although one of the members of the court disapproved of the court's jurisdiction to review even on errors of law on the face of the award. Lord Parker of Waddington, *The History and Development of Commercial Arbitration* (Jerusalem: Magnes Press, 1959) at p. 18 has sought to explain this reaction against court intervention as a fear by some members of the judiciary of developing a body of rules which could be termed 'arbitration law'.

1.4 FROM THE COMMON LAW PROCEDURE ACT 1854 TO THE ARBITRATION ACT 1889

The Common Law Procedure Act 1854 greatly revised the law of arbitration. It has been said that during this period the developments within arbitration law 'transmuted the practice of commerce into an effective part of the ordinary law of the land, and brought the commercial tribunal under the control of the ordinary courts': Lord Parker of Waddington, *The History and Development of Commercial Arbitration* (Jerusalem: Magnes Press, 1959). However, although the Common Law Procedure Act 1854 has been described as the foundation of the modern law of arbitration the Act was in fact predominantly concerned with reforms in the administration of justice rather than with arbitration: Mustill and Boyd, *Commercial Arbitration*, 2nd ed. (London: Butterworths, 1989), p. 440. Section 17 of the 1854 Act provided that all written submissions were made rules of court, and the right of attachment was applied, unless a contrary intention was expressed within the written submission. The effect of s. 17 and the provisions of 3 & 4 Will 4, c. 42, was that a submission to arbitration was irrevocable except by the leave of the court.

The Common Law Procedure Act 1854 also created new powers. A right was given to the parties to seek to apply for a stay of legal proceedings brought in contravention of the arbitration agreement. The court retained its inherent jurisdiction to refuse or to allow a stay where it was thought equitable to do so. This power to seek a stay has remained one of the fundamental principles of arbitration, though, as will be seen, the AA 1996 has severely limited the court's right to refuse a stay.

The power to stay litigation to arbitration arises from the court's stance that the agreement of the parties should be honoured. However, this power to stay only arises where there is a dispute between the parties. An arbitration agreement is an agreement to refer present or future disputes to arbitration. Although an analysis of the meaning of the word 'dispute' will be undertaken subsequently in chapter 4 it is enough to state at present that without a dispute there can be no reference: *Collins* v *Collins* (1858) 26 Beav 306.

Sections 12 and 13 of the Common Law Procedure Act 1854 gave the court power, in certain circumstances, to appoint an arbitrator or umpire, and empowered a party to an arbitration where two arbitrators are to be appointed to substitute a new arbitrator where the election of one of the arbitrators fails. A power was also given to one of the parties to appoint his own arbitrator as sole arbitrator where one of the parties failed to elect an arbitrator.

The power to remit an award back to the arbitral tribunal was another new power given under s. 8 of the Common Law Procedure Act 1854 and the now much discredited power to state a case was given under s. 25. Although the Common Law Procedure Act 1854 was subsequently repealed it is not understating the matter to say that its effect can thereafter be seen in every subsequent Arbitration Act up until and in some respects including the AA 1996.

As England's position as a major trading nation developed in the mid 1880s the law of arbitration developed also to meet the needs of commercial men. Arbitration law developed for both domestic and international arbitrations during this period. International trade was the lifeblood of many industries and the problems with the enforcement of judgments abroad and the problems with the conflict of laws arising from private international law led to sophisticated developments in arbitration law.

1.5 THE ARBITRATION ACTS 1889 TO 1934

The various Acts that were passed between 1889 and 1934 were:

(a)   The Arbitration Act 1889 (52 & 53 Vict, c. 53).
(b)   The Arbitration Clauses (Protocol) Act 1924 (14 & 15 Geo 5, c. 39).
(c)   The Arbitration (Foreign Awards) Act 1930 (20 & 21 Geo 5, c. 15).
(d)   The Arbitration Act 1934 (24 & 25 Geo 5, c. 14).

From the commencement of the Arbitration Act 1934 the above Acts were to be known collectively as the Arbitration Acts 1889 to 1934.

Although mainly declaratory the AA 1889 repealed the rule which made a submission to arbitration a rule of the court. Instead s. 1 of the AA 1889 deemed references to arbitration to be made as if made by a rule of the court. The word 'submission' was defined to include all agreements for arbitration whether or not completed by the appointment of an arbitrator. By s. 12 of the AA 1889 Act enforcement of an award could be made by leave of the court in the same way as a judgment. Statutory effect was given to the court's inherent power to remove an arbitrator for misconduct. The courts were also given the power to compel the arbitrator to state a case. This enabled the courts to adjudicate on any point of law arising in the reference.

The increased control over all matters of law arising in an arbitration put added burdens on the court system. Arbitrations required the courts to deal with legal submissions put to them quickly and efficiently. However, because of the expansion of commerce in England and the rapid development of the common law, the inadequacies of the courts quickly became apparent. The fusion of equity and the common law in this period also failed to solve the problems that the courts had with delays and over technical rules. In 1883 major amendments to the Rules of the Supreme Court were implemented to resolve these problems, but by 1895 some 7,000 decisions had been made on points of practice.

Criticisms were again levelled by commercial men that arbitrations should be left in the hands of those most able to deal with arbitration, by which they meant anyone other than the courts. It was not only the forum that was criticised. Criticism was also levelled at the judiciary, who were once again accused of having little or no knowledge of the commercial matters that they were being asked to decide upon. This failing was, however, something that the judiciary accepted. As Scrutton LJ said in *Butcher, Wetherly and Co. Ltd* v *Norman* (1933) 47 L1 L Rep 324:

> One of the objects of justice is to satisfy the litigants that their cases are fairly and properly heard, and unfortunately some classes of commercial case are so complex in their nature that a judge who is not conversant with that class of commercial business has to have a great many explanations made to him in the course of the case as to matters with which he is quite unfamiliar, and so with every judge.

The inability of some judges to deal with commercial matters was blindingly apparent. In particular Mr Justice J.C. Lawrance, nicknamed 'Long Lawrance', has been severely criticised. In *Rose* v *Bank of Australasia* (1892 unreported) his lordship had to rule on a complex matter of general average. Lord Justice MacKinnon (1944) 60 LQR 324 described 'Long Lawrance' as knowing 'as much about the principles of general average as a Hindoo about figure skating' and his decision in *Rose* v *Bank of Australasia* appears not to be based on any assessment of the merits of either of the parties' cases. It is not without coincidence that in 1894, in the light of severe criticisms by commercial men, a 'Commercial Court' was set up as part of the Queen's Bench Division. In fact Scrutton LJ mockingly stated that 'Long Lawrance' was 'the only begetter of the Commercial Court'.

The Arbitration Clauses (Protocol) Act 1924 and the Arbitration (Foreign Awards) Act 1930 created new powers in dealing with non-domestic arbitrations. Under the 1924 Act a power was given to the court to stay proceedings brought in breach of an agreement to refer to arbitration if an international Protocol set out in the schedule to the Act (the Geneva Protocol) applied to the agreement. The Arbitration (Foreign Awards) Act 1930 dealt with the enforcement of foreign awards where the country in which the award was made had reciprocal provisions for enforcement with England and Wales.

The AA 1934 made numerous important changes to arbitration law as a result of recommendations of the MacKinnon Committee in 1927. Q.M. Hogg, *The Law of Arbitration* (London: Butterworths 1936) p. 6, lists the more striking reforms that were introduced by the 1934 Act:

(1)   Death is no longer a revocation of a written submission (s. 1).

(2)   There is now provision for the bankruptcy of a party to a submission (s. 2).

(3)   The power of the court to appoint an arbitrator or umpire is extended (s. 3).

(4)   The court is given in certain circumstances the power to rescind an arbitration agreement, whether or not it contains a *Scott* v *Avery* clause (ss. 3 and 14).

(5)   References to three arbitrators, one to be appointed by each party, and one by the two so appointed, are now to be treated as references to two arbitrators and an umpire; in other cases of references to three arbitrators a majority decision is to bind (s. 4).

(6)   The court may now order an umpire to proceed with the reference at any stage and notwithstanding the terms of the submission (s. 5).

(7)   The provisions in the implied terms of reference that the award is to be made in a limited time are repealed; instead an arbitrator or umpire is to use reasonable dispatch, on pain of removal by the court and the loss of his fees (s. 6).

(8)   The implied terms of reference are extended by the addition of power to the arbitrators to order specific performance of contracts other than contracts relating to land, and power to make an interim award (s. 7).

(9)   The court is given power to make or vary interlocutory orders in the arbitration (s. 8).

(10)   An award in the form of a special case can now be directed by the court, and the provision with regard to appeal in the two types of special case are assimilated (s. 9).

(11)   Judgment can now be entered in the terms of an award (s. 10).

(12)   An award now carries interest like a judgment (s. 11).

(13)   An agreement for the reference of future differences making the costs or part of them payable by a party in any event is void (s. 12(1)).

(14)   Where an arbitrator makes no provision as to costs in his award the parties may apply direct to him for an addition to his award (s. 12(4)).

(15)   Application may be made to the court for taxation of the arbitrator's fees if he seeks to enforce them by means of his lien (s. 13).

(16)   Parties to a submission of future differences may complain of an arbitrator's bias, although they knew or ought to have known about it at the time the submission was made and where fraud is alleged even a *Scott* v *Avery* clause may be ignored (s. 14).

One other effect of the AA 1934 was a change in terminology. Prior to the Act the 'arbitration agreement' was known as 'the submission to arbitration'. Although the phrase 'submission to arbitration' is still used in international arbitrations it is usually a reference to the referral rather than the arbitration agreement itself.

2 Arbitration Law from 1950 to 1996

2.1 INTRODUCTION

This chapter gives only a brief overview of the Arbitration Acts of 1950, 1975 and 1979 because the AA 1996 has repealed Part I of the AA 1950, the whole of the AA 1975 and the AA 1979. However, the previous legislation still applies to all arbitration proceedings commenced prior to 31 January 1997.

The AA 1950 was designed to consolidate the existing legislation as described in chapter 1. As such the Act was not intended to alter the law, though in the drafting of the legislation unintended changes did occur affecting the existing law. These changes were relatively minor and to all intents and purposes the AA 1950 appeared as a continuation from the AAs 1889 to 1934. The AA 1950 came into force on 1 September 1950. It was not retrospective and did not apply to arbitrations already in existence, or pending, as at 1 September 1950.

The AA 1975 was enacted to give effect to the New York Convention on the Recognition and Enforcement of Foreign Arbitral Awards. The AA 1975 was applicable to England, Wales, Scotland and Northern Ireland. The AA 1975 applied where there was a non-domestic arbitration agreement and where the applicant had not taken a step in the action. The courts had a mandatory obligation to stay any court proceedings to arbitration unless satisfied that the arbitration agreement was null and void, inoperative or incapable of being performed or that there was no dispute between the parties. This provision is reflected in s. 9 of the AA 1996 save that the reference to 'no dispute between the parties' is omitted. Section 5 of the AA 1975 (refusal of enforcement) is also to be found substantially re-enacted in s. 103 of the AA 1996.

The AA 1979 received royal assent on 4 April 1979 and was effective from 1 August 1979. The AA 1979 applied to arbitrations commenced after 1 August 1979 but also applied to arbitrations commenced prior to that date with the agreement of the parties. The AA 1979 set out a new regime in respect of appeals on points of law. Section 8(3)(b) of the AA 1979 repealed s. 21 of the AA 1950, which dealt with stating an award or a point of law in the form of a special case. Sections 3 and 4 of the AA 1979 dealt with exclusion agreements and s. 5 dealt with interlocutory orders. The AA 1979 was applicable only to England and Wales.

The following specific matters will be reviewed in this chapter:

(a)   What is an arbitration agreement?
(b)   What is a dispute?
(c)   When will court proceedings be stayed?
(d)   What are powers and jurisdiction?
(e)   How can an award be challenged?

These specific areas have been chosen because the AA 1996 has altered the relevant law in respect of these areas.

2.2   OVERVIEW OF THE ARBITRATION ACTS 1950 TO 1979

Many of the provisions of the AAs 1950 to 1979 were applicable only if the parties failed to express a contrary intention in their arbitration agreement. Arbitration is a consensual process and the arbitral tribunal derives its jurisdiction and, in many cases, its powers from the arbitration agreement. The AAs 1950 to 1979 were therefore not intended to apply a code under which arbitrations were to be conducted but rather they acted in a default manner to support and to give substance to the arbitration agreement if required. If the parties did not wish for the arbitral tribunal to have a power to order specific performance the parties were required to state this, otherwise such a provision would be deemed to exist (AA 1950, s. 15).

One of the main complaints regarding the AA 1950 was that there was little logic in the format of the legislation. The meaning of an arbitration agreement was dealt with at s. 32 of the AA 1950 whereas the irrevocability of the authority of the arbitrator was dealt with in s. 1. Although the AA 1950 contained the main framework of relevant legislation, it was not the only statute applicable to arbitrations. In addition there was a huge body of case law which expanded the meaning of much of the legislation. England as a forum for arbitration was therefore not the first choice for many parties wishing to resolve international disputes.

2.2.1   Arbitration Act 1950

Part I (ss. 1 to 34) of the AA 1950 deals predominantly with domestic arbitrations whereas Part II (ss. 35 to 43) deals with the enforcement of foreign awards. Sections 1 to 5 deal with the irrevocability of the authority of the arbitrator, the death and bankruptcy of the parties, the staying of court proceedings and the reference of interpleader issues to arbitration. Section 1 of the AA 1950 made the authority of the arbitrator irrevocable except with the leave of the court. As Mustill and Boyd, *Commercial Arbitration*, 2nd ed. (London: Butterworths) 1989, state, at p. 529: 'The purpose of s. 1 and its predecessors was to protect the interest of the parties who had contracted for the resolution of their disputes by an arbitrator from having the arbitrator's mandate promiscuously revoked'. Section 23 places the power of revocation into the hands of the parties and also sets out a default position, where there is no agreement between the parties in regard to the revocation.

Sections 6 to 11 of the AA 1950 deal with references to a single arbitrator, to three arbitrators, an umpire or a judge of the Technology and Construction Court, and the power of the parties to fill a vacancy. Every arbitration agreement is deemed to provide that the reference shall be to a single arbitrator unless a contrary intention is expressed in the agreement: s. 6 of the AA 1950. Section 12 of the AA 1950 deals with the conduct of the proceedings.

Sections 13 to 17 of the AA 1950 deal with the time for making the award, interim awards, specific performance, finality of the awards and the power to correct slips. Sections 18 to 20 deal with costs, taxation of the arbitral tribunal's fees and interest. There have been some major changes in regard to interest on awards brought about by the AA 1996 which will be discussed in following chapters. Sections 21 to 26 of the AA 1950 deal with the power to order that a case be stated, the power to remit or set aside an award and the removal of the arbitrator. Section 21 of the AA 1950 was repealed by s. 8(3) of the AA 1979 and is discussed at 2.6.1. The power to set aside an award for misconduct is dealt with at 2.7.

Sections 26 to 34 of the AA 1950 are a miscellany of provisions including: the enforcement of an award, the power of the court to extend the time for commencing arbitration proceedings, terms as to costs, that the Crown is to be bound and the meaning of 'arbitration agreement'. By s. 30 the Crown was bound by the AA 1950 save where the arbitration was of an international character and caught within the provisions of Part II of the AA 1950 or the AA 1975.

Part II (ss. 35 to 43) of the AA 1950 relates to the enforcement of certain foreign awards. There are two schedules to the AA 1950 which deal with foreign awards. The AA 1996 does not repeal Part II of the AA 1950 (apart from s. 42(3)) or the two schedules.

2.2.2   Arbitration Act 1975

The preamble to the AA 1975 stated that it was: 'An Act to give effect to the New York Convention on the Recognition and Enforcement of Foreign Arbitral Awards'. Section 1 of the AA 1975 made it mandatory for the courts to stay court proceedings relating to a dispute which was the subject of an arbitration agreement which was not a domestic arbitration agreement. Section 1(4) provided that an arbitration agreement was a domestic arbitration agreement if: (a) it did not provide for arbitration in any other State than the United Kingdom; and (b) no party to the arbitration agreement was resident or incorporated outside the United Kingdom at the time the proceedings sought to be stayed were commenced.

The definition implies that the status of the arbitration would not change even if a party subsequently became resident outside the United Kingdom after proceedings were commenced. From this it is also implied that a non-domestic arbitration could not become a domestic arbitration if, after the proceedings were commenced, the parties then became resident in the United Kingdom.

Section 3 of the AA 1975 makes a Convention award (meaning an award made in an arbitration in a State, other than the United Kingdom, which is a party to the New York Convention) enforceable by virtue of s. 26 of the AA 1950. Section 4 of the AA 1975 sets out the evidence required if a party wishes to enforce a Convention award. Section 5 of the AA 1975 sets out the grounds on which a court may refuse to enforce a Convention award. This section mirrors the grounds for refusal as set out in the New York Convention and is substantially re-enacted as s. 103 of the AA 1996.

2.2.3 Arbitration Act 1979

The AA 1979 was brought into force to stem mounting criticism from abroad of the arbitration process in England and especially the problems that had arisen relating to the requirements to state a case under s. 21 of the AA 1950. Arbitration in England and Wales and Northern Ireland is a major source of invisible export earnings. The problems associated with the procedure of case stated are analysed in 2.6.1. In brief, the main criticism from abroad was that the procedure could be used to tie up the arbitration process by continually insisting that the arbitral tribunal refer any question of law to the courts. In this way the arbitration process could be brought to a halt while court time was found to hear these questions.

In the mid 1970s a governmental committee was established to examine the problems with the case stated procedure. The options open to the committee were to leave the case stated process in place, make all decisions of the arbitrator final and binding and not subject to review, or steer a middle course. The committee chose the middle course, and this is reflected in the AA 1979. Section 1 of the AA 1979 provided the court with the power to review awards on points of law only and provided that a party seeking to appeal on a point of law would have to show that it was one that substantially affected the rights of the parties to the agreement. Section 2 gave a power to the parties, by agreement, to request the courts to give a determination of a preliminary point of law, but provided that the courts should only hear points that substantially affected parties' rights or in order to produce substantial savings in costs.

Sections 3 and 4 of the AA 1979 dealt with exclusion agreements. Section 5 attempted to solve a problem that many arbitral tribunals had faced where one of the parties failed to comply with orders that it had made. It entitled the arbitral tribunal, or any party, to apply to the court to have the arbitral tribunal's powers extended to those of a judge of the High Court where one of the parties had failed to comply with an order of the arbitral tribunal. There is no equivalent section in the AA 1996 as the arbitral tribunal is now provided with a power under that Act to make peremptory orders. Section 42 of the AA 1996 does, however, allow for a party to apply to the court to enforce a peremptory order and that section of the AA 1996 is perhaps the most analogous to s. 5 of the AA 1979.

2.2.4   Supreme Court Act 1981 and Administration of Justice Act 1982

Sections 18 and 148 of and sch. 5 to the Supreme Court Act 1981 made minor amendments to both the AA 1950 and the AA 1979. Section 148 of the Supreme Court Act 1981 was expressly repealed by the AA 1996. However, by implication s. 18(1)(g) of the Supreme Court Act 1981 will also become redundant when arbitrations started before the AA 1996 came into force have been completed. The amendments made by sch. 5 to the Supreme Court Act 1981 were to s. 38 of the AA 1950 in respect of evidence required in enforcing a foreign award. This section of the AA 1950 remains in force.

The Administration of Justice Act 1982 added a new s. 19A to the AA 1950, but this has now been repealed by the AA 1996. The new section involved a major change to the powers of the arbitrator to award interest on a sum in dispute which had been paid after arbitration proceedings had been commenced but before the award had been made.

2.2.5   Limitation Acts

Legislation relating to limitation (the Limitation Acts 1939, 1963 and 1980) applies to arbitration proceedings as it does to litigation. A referral to arbitration after the limitation period has expired will not prevent a party relying on the Limitation Acts at the hearing of the matter: *Re Astley and Tyldesley Coal and Salt Co. and Tyldesley Coal Co.* (1899) 68 LJ QB 252. Under s. 29 of the AA 1950 an arbitration was deemed to commence when one party requested the other by notice to appoint an arbitrator or to refer the matter to a designated arbitrator under the contract. It is this notice to refer which stops the limitation period running. The parties, however, may under contract confer a shorter period than that allowed for under the Limitation Acts to start the arbitration.

The limitation periods are six years for contracts under hand and 12 years for contracts of speciality, that is, contracts made by deed. There are other limitation periods which may be applicable where the claim is brought in negligence, especially where the damage caused arises from a latent defect. Where an award is made in arbitration proceedings there is also a six-year limitation period for enforcement of the award. The date when the time limit for this begins to run is from the date of the award.

2.2.6   Courts and Legal Services Act 1990

Sections 99 to 103 of the Courts and Legal Services Act 1990 made some major amendments to the existing law of arbitration. Sections 99, 101, 102 and 103 of the Courts and Legal Services Act 1990 were repealed by the AA 1996. Section 102 of the Courts and Legal Services Act 1990 deals with inordinate and inexcusable delay and has been substantially re-enacted in s. 41(3) of the AA 1996.

Section 100 of the Courts and Legal Services Act 1990 has not been repealed. It states:

In any cause or matter proceeding in the High Court in connection with any contract incorporating an arbitration agreement which confers specific powers on the arbitrator, the High Court may, if all parties to the agreement agree, exercise any such powers.

The section was implemented to deal with the problems which had arisen following *Northern Regional Health Authority* v *Derek Crouch Construction Co. Ltd* [1984] QB 644. In that case the court held that where the contract provided that an arbitral tribunal had the power to open up, review and revise the certificates of an architect it did not follow that the court had a similar power. If the parties elected an architect or engineer to decide the value of works done then it was not the role of the court to review that decision.

The effect of this case was that unless the parties agreed to give the power to a court to open up, review and revise a certificate a party was almost precluded from starting proceedings in the courts on matters involving a re-examination of a certificate. As a result of the case references to official referees acting as arbitrators became more common under s. 11 of the AA 1950, because an official referee sitting as an arbitrator had the power to exercise all the non-judicial functions that an arbitrator would be able to exercise under the contract including the power to review a certificate.

Under s. 11 of the AA 1950 as originally enacted the official referees were bound to hear and determine disputes referred to them, unless the High Court or one of its judges transferred the matter or determined otherwise. Because of the large increase in official referees' business after *Northern Regional Health Authority* v *Derek Crouch Construction Co. Ltd*, s. 99 of the Courts and Legal Services Act 1990 replaced s. 11 of the AA 1950 making the power to accept an appointment by an official referee (now a judge of the Technology and Construction Court) discretionary.

In *Tarmac Construction Ltd* v *Esso Petroleum* [1997] CILL 1290 Judge Lloyd QC distinguished *Northern Regional Health Authority* v *Derek Crouch Construction Co. Ltd*, holding that in the case before him the wording of the contract did not intend that the engineer's decision was to be final and binding and therefore the decision could be reviewed by the court. The wording of the contract also required that a dispute would proceed by litigation rather than arbitration. The learned judge held that in reviewing and revising a certificate a court would not be doing anything other than enforcing the parties' rights, which was within its jurisdiction and something which the court regularly did.

In *Beaufort Developments (NI) Ltd* v *Gilbert Ash NI Ltd* [1999] 1 AC 266 the *Crouch* decision was overruled. According to the headnote of the report cited the House of Lords held that: 'the court's jurisdiction was unlimited; that, therefore, the fact that power to open up, review and revise was expressly conferred upon the arbitrator but not upon the court could not be construed as removing the court's power'. The rationale for this change was provided by Lord Hoffmann, who held at p. 281 that: 'cases since *Crouch* show that the decision has caused such uncertainty and even injustice that its dicta should be disapproved'. *Beaufort Developments (NI) Ltd* v *Gilbert Ash NI Ltd* has removed the original reason for the enactment of s. 100 of the Courts and Legal Services Act 1990.

2.3   THE ARBITRATION AGREEMENT

Under the AA 1950 an agreement to refer a dispute to arbitration may be made before or after the dispute has arisen. In building and engineering contracts clauses referring future disputes to arbitration are the norm. For an arbitration agreement to come within the terms of the AA 1950 it was required to comply with s. 32 of the Act, which stated:

> In this Part of this Act, unless the context otherwise requires, the expression 'arbitration agreement' means a written agreement to submit present or future differences to arbitration, whether an arbitrator is named therein or not.

This section must be read with a considerable body of case law to fully understand its meaning. An arbitration agreement that is not in writing is not void. The fact that it is not in writing only means that the provisions of the AA 1950 are inapplicable. Parties may, if they so choose, arbitrate under a verbal agreement. If the parties are so minded and each honours the award then such an arbitration can be as successful as if made under the provisions of the AA 1950. The problems arise if one of the parties seeks to delay matters or refuses to be bound by the decision of the arbitrator. Chapter 1 gives a brief analysis of the common law rules in relation to arbitrations and illustrates how one party may frustrate the arbitration agreement if that party so chooses.

An arbitration agreement can be as simple as 'arbitration to be settled in London' (*Tritonia Shipping Inc.* v *South Nelson Forest Products Corporation* [1966] 1 Lloyd's Rep 114) or extremely detailed. The AA 1950 was not intended to provide a system under which the arbitration was to be conducted but rather to give powers to the arbitrator for the conduct of the reference. As will be discussed in later chapters arbitrations are often conducted under institutional rules and in such cases it is these rules which set out the procedure under which the arbitration will be conducted. The Construction Industry Model Arbitration Rules (CIMAR), for instance, envisage three varying ways under which the arbitration can be conducted and the parties have the power to choose which of the modes will be appropriate for the conduct of the reference.

Q.M. Hogg *The Law of Arbitration* (London: Butterworths, 1936), at pp. 8–13, noted that there were prerequisites that determined when there was an arbitration rather than an expert's decision or other ruling. Mr Hogg, at p. 16, stated that:

> arbitration is the reference for binding judicial determination of any matter in controversy capable of being compromised by an agreement by way of accord and satisfaction or rendered arbitrable by statute between two or more parties to some person or persons other than a court of competent jurisdiction.

This definition was given prior to the AA 1950 but is applicable to it and is equally applicable to the AA 1996.

The scope of an arbitration agreement, or as it was known before the AA 1950 'arbitration clause', was analysed in *Heyman* v *Darwins Ltd* [1942] AC 356, in which it was held that if a contract containing an arbitration clause was determined by something arising outside the contract, such as a *force majeure* event, the arbitration clause would be determined as well. If the contract was determined from something directly arising out of itself, such as one party repudiating the contract by refusing to proceed with it, then the arbitration clause would still operate: *Metropolitan Water Board* v *Dick, Kerr and Co.* [1918] AC 119. This position was altered when in *Harbour Assurance Co. (UK) Ltd* v *Kansa General International Insurance Co. Ltd* [1993] QB 701 the court held that a contract that was void *ab initio*, by reason of a fraudulent representation about a company's ability to trade, did not necessarily determine the arbitration clause, which was held to be separate from the main contract. The AA 1996 has now incorporated the principle set out in *Harbour Assurance Co. (UK) Ltd* v *Kansa General International Insurance Co. Ltd* and is discussed at 5.2.1.

2.4 THE DISPUTE

For there to be a reference to arbitration there needs to be a dispute. The position under the AA 1950 was that where there was no dispute that was capable of compromise by accord or satisfaction there could be no reference to arbitration. This fundamental principle is important when consideration is given to s. 4 of the AA 1950, which gave a discretion to the court to refuse to stay litigation to arbitration. The word 'dispute', as applied to the AA 1950, is given its ordinary common-sense meaning. If a party admits a claim then this is something which is incapable of being compromised by accord, and therefore there is no 'dispute'. In such a case a party cannot refer the matter to arbitration because there is no dispute to found the jurisdiction of the arbitral tribunal: *Cannan* v *Fowler* (1853) 14 CB 181; *Bede Steam Shipping Co. Ltd* v *Bunge y Born Ltda SA* (1927) 43 TLR 374. In *London and North Western Railway Co.* v *Jones* [1915] 2 KB 35 there was an Act referred to which entitled the railway company to make additional charges for the detention of wagons. The Act contained an arbitration clause. Jones refused to pay the additional charge levied by the railway Company. Rowlatt J said, at p. 38: 'It does not, however, follow that the courts cannot be resorted to without previous recourse to arbitration to enforce a claim which is not disputed but which the trader merely persists in not paying' (*Halki Shipping Corporation* v *Sopex Oils Ltd* [1998] 1 WLR 726 and *Davies Middleton and Davies Ltd* v *Toyo Engineering Corporation* (1997) 85 BLR 59 have effectively reversed this position).

A distinction is to be drawn between referring a dispute to an arbitral tribunal and referring a question in order to prevent a dispute. A mere valuation or appraisement is not a matter that generally can be referred to arbitration. However, the distinction between 'arbitration' and 'mere valuation' cannot be put in simple terms such as 'dispute' versus 'mere valuation'. What establishes the difference is the process that is adopted to arrive at the decision. A valuation which is arrived at by the process of judicial enquiry may therefore be an arbitration: *Re Hopper* (1867) LR 2 QB 367.

2.5 STAYING PROCEEDINGS

Mustill and Boyd, *Commercial Arbitration*, 2nd ed. (London: Butterworths, 1989) at p. 467, summarise the requirements for an application to stay proceedings in favour of arbitration under s. 4 of the AA 1950. The person applying must prove the existence of an arbitration agreement, that there are legal proceedings commenced in a court brought by a party to the arbitration agreement, and that the person applying for the stay is itself a party to the arbitration agreement. The court will also have to be satisfied that the 'applicant was and is ready and willing to do all things necessary to the proper conduct of the arbitration; [and] there is no sufficient reason why the dispute should not be referred to arbitration'. Where these requirements are met there is a prima facie right to stay under s. 4 of the AA 1950 unless there are good reasons why the stay should not be granted.

Many of the requirements of s. 4 of the AA 1950 appear and are repeated in s. 9 of the AA 1996. See further discussion at 4.5.

Section 4(1) of the AA 1950 allows for a party to apply to the court to stay legal proceedings in any court where there is an arbitration agreement in a contract between the parties and where the party making the application has not taken any step or delivered any pleading. The court has a discretion to refuse the stay of those legal proceedings where there are sufficient reasons why the matter should not be referred to arbitration in accordance with the agreement. This discretion, however, is only applicable to domestic arbitrations. In regard to non-domestic arbitration agreements there was a mandatory requirement to stay under s. 1 of the AA 1975 save where the arbitration agreement was null and void, inoperative or incapable of being performed or there was not in fact any dispute between the parties.

There is no equivalent discretionary power to refuse to stay litigation in favour of arbitration under the AA 1996, as s. 86 of the AA 1996 has not been brought into force. Certain aspects of s. 4 of the AA 1950 are echoed in s. 9 of the AA 1996. For instance, under both sections a party must take the appropriate procedural step to acknowledge the legal proceeding but must not take a step in those proceeding to answer the substantive claim. A step in the proceedings is an act such as an application to the court. Talk and the writing of letters between solicitors will not amount to the taking of a step: *Ives and Barker* v *Willans* [1894] 2 Ch 478 at p. 480; *Brighton Marine Palace and Pier Ltd* v *Woodhouse* [1893] 2 Ch 486; *Blue Flame Mechanical Services Ltd* v *David Lord Engineering Ltd* [1992] CILL 760.

An applicant for a stay under s. 4(1) of the AA 1950 must show that 'at the time when the proceedings were commenced' and at the time of the application he is 'ready and willing to do all things necessary to the proper conduct of the arbitration' (see *Dew and Co.* v *Tarmac Construction* (1978) 15 BLR 22). There is no similar provision in s. 9 of the AA 1996. The fact that the time limits to begin an arbitration have expired will not preclude a party from averring that he is ready and willing to proceed: *W. Bruce Ltd* v *J. Strong* [1951] 2 KB 447. To allow otherwise would mean that one party could defeat the arbitration agreement by waiting for the time limits to expire before bringing proceedings in court. There are many cases which illustrate when the courts have found the applicant unready and unwilling to refer the dispute to arbitration: see, for example, *Davis* v *Starr* (1889) 41 ChD 242; *Parry* v *Liverpool Malt Co.* [1900] 1 QB 339; and *Hodson* v *Railway Passengers' Assurance Co.* [1904] 2 KB 833. Where the time limits have expired the appropriate course is for an application to be made under s. 27 of the AA 1950 for an extension of time for commencing the arbitration proceedings.

A party who makes an application under s. 4(1) of the AA 1950 must prove by means of affidavit evidence that he is ready and willing to proceed: *Piercy* v *Young* (1879) 14 ChD 200, at p. 209; *Willesford* v *Watson* (1873) LR 8 Ch App 473. A party attempting to show that he intends to proceed must satisfy the court that he does not intend to postpone or delay the arbitration. The court can take into account facts such as whether the party has indicated his unwillingness to appoint an arbitrator and can look at any delay attributable to the applicant.

The court is also entitled to look at whether the applicant wishes to have the matter resolved by arbitration rather than by having it resolved by any other means. The court would be entitled to refuse a stay if the applicant had started court proceedings in another jurisdiction and it was clear that the reason for the application was merely to prevent the English courts from having jurisdiction.

An application to stay proceedings is usually made at an early stage and therefore the applicant will usually have to do no more than indicate his willingness to proceed with the arbitration by showing an intention to appoint an arbitrator. Where delay by the applicant subsequently occurs then the other party may make an application to the court requesting the lifting of the stay, though such an application has rarely been granted.

For a stay to be granted there must be legal proceedings in respect of any matter agreed to be referred to arbitration. These requirements also appear in s. 9 of the AA 1996 and will be discussed in chapter 4. Section 4(1) of the AA 1950 refers to a party to an arbitration agreement or any person claiming through or under him. Section 9 of the AA 1996 refers only to a party to an arbitration agreement. However, s. 82(2) of the AA 1996 defines, party to include any person claiming under or through a party to the agreement. Further discussion of who can be a party to an arbitration is undertaken in chapter 6. However, the change to s. 9 of the AA 1996 is one of common sense. Mustill and Boyd, *Commercial Arbitration*, 2nd ed. (London: Butterworths, 1989) at p. 471 make the point that s. 4 of the AA 1950 is illogical in that a person applying to stay proceedings will be the person receiving the claim and therefore 'it is not easy to see how he can be said to be "claiming under" the party to the arbitration agreement'.

2.5.1 Application to the court

In the High Court the application for a stay is made before a judge in private, a master or the Admiralty registrar. The application is made on notice of application. An appeal lies to a judge from the decision of a master or Admiralty registrar. An appeal to the Court of Appeal can be made from the decision of a judge in private but leave is required.

It is for the court to determine how the costs of an application are to be borne. In *Belfield* v *Borne* [1894] 1 Ch 521 the practice was developed of directing that the costs of the stay should be dealt with by the arbitrator. However, there is doubt about whether the arbitrator would have the power to deal with this matter. In *Ballast Nedam BV* v *Vulcan Aquatec* (1995 unreported) Judge Lloyd indicated that he took the view that the question of costs incurred in the application to stay was not a matter that the arbitrator could deal with and made an award of costs following the normal rule that costs follow the event.

2.5.2 Discretion

The underlying principle which the court will apply is that where the parties have entered into an arbitration agreement they should be compelled to carry out that agreement. In *Wickham* v *Harding* (1859) 28 LJ Ex 215 Martin B stated that: 'A bargain is a bargain, and the parties ought to abide by it, unless a clear reason applies for their not doing so'. Therefore if a party can show that there is a valid and subsisting arbitration clause, the onus falls on the other party to show why the matter should not be stayed: *Bristol Corporation* v *John Aird and Co.* [1913] AC 241 at p. 259; *Heyman* v *Darwins Ltd* [1942] AC 356 at p. 388. The case law on this point is only indicative of when the courts will apply that discretion and sometimes appears contradictory. A vast amount of case law exists on the exercise of the discretion and this illustrates that particular factors have had some bearing on the exercise of the court's discretion.

2.5.2.1 Expense The possible extra cost to a party in bringing arbitration proceedings over court proceedings is generally considered not to be a proper ground for ordering a stay: *Ford* v *Clarksons Holidays Ltd* [1971] 1 WLR 1412. However, where the impoverished plaintiff would be able to get legal aid to bring court proceedings, and the reason for his impoverishment was the action of the other party, a stay of the proceedings may be refused: *Fakes* v *Taylor Woodrow Construction Ltd* [1973] QB 436.

2.5.2.2 Fraud Where a question of fraud arises the court is not required to order a stay of the proceedings (s. 24 of the AA 1950). This principle extends also to questions of professional incompetence (*Charles Osenton and Co.* v *Johnston* [1942] AC 130) and dishonesty (*Radford* v *Hair* [1971] Ch 758). To give effect to this power the court also has power to treat a *Scott* v *Avery* clause as being ineffective: *Permavox Ltd* v *Royal Exchange Assurance* (1939) 64 Ll L Rep 145.

The discretion to refuse to stay litigation in favour of arbitration arises not only from the provisions of s. 24 of the AA 1950 but also under the inherent jurisdiction of the court. Where there is no evidence that shows a fraud has been committed, the court is not obliged to refuse an application for a stay. A mere allegation of fraud is treated in the same way: *Cunningham-Reid* v *Buchanan-Jardine* [1988] 1 WLR 678.

2.5.2.3 Delay   Delay in certain circumstances will form a ground whereby the court will decline to order a stay. If one of the parties has acted to its detriment expending time and money to bring a claim then this may be a material factor in deciding whether or not to order a stay. Delay in certain circumstances may also be seen as evidence of a waiver of the arbitration clause: *The Elizabeth H* [1962] 1 Lloyd's Rep 172. However, the mere fact that the claimant would be out of time for bringing a claim in an arbitration would not in itself be grounds for refusing to order a stay.

2.5.2.4 Issues of law   The fact that there is an issue of law in the dispute will not be in itself a ground for refusing to order a stay. In *Re Phoenix Timber Co. Ltd's Application* [1958] 1 Lloyd's Rep 305 a stay was ordered even though the court accepted that the dispute was suitable to be heard by the court. If the only issues in dispute are questions of law, the court may exercise its discretion and refuse to order a stay: *Heyman* v *Darwins* [1942] AC 356 at p. 391. Each question will have to be examined on its own merits: *Bonnin* v *Neame* [1910] 1 Ch 732.

2.5.2.5 Scott v *Avery clauses*   A *Scott* v *Avery* clause is a clause in a contract which does not permit an action under the contract until an award in an arbitration is first given. A stay where such a clause exists will almost always be granted otherwise any claim made would be countered with the defence that the condition precedent of the claim had not been met. However, a stay may be refused notwithstanding the *Scott* v *Avery* clause where one party alleges fraud, or argues that there has been a waiver of the clause or that the requirements for a stay, as set out above, have not been met.

2.5.2.6 Multiplicity of proceedings   Where disputes have arisen concerning several interrelated contracts, a stay of one of the proceedings in favour of arbitration will usually be refused so as to avoid the same issues being heard by different tribunals: *Heyman* v *Darwins Ltd* [1942] AC 356. The courts have shown themselves more willing to refuse a stay on this ground than any other, although the onus is on the party opposing the stay to show why the stay should be refused: *Bulk Oil (Zug) AG* v *Trans-Asiatic Oil* [1973] 1 Lloyd's Rep 129; *Berkshire Senior Citizens Housing Association* v *Fitt* (1979) 15 BLR 27 (CA); *University of Reading* v *Miller Construction Ltd* (1994) 75 BLR 91. The rationale for not staying proceedings in these circumstances is that where the same issues are to be heard by different tribunals there is the risk that on the same facts the different tribunals will come to differing decisions: *The Eschersheim* [1974] 2 Lloyd's Rep 188. In *Great Ormond Street Hospital* v *Wates Construction Ltd* [1997] CILL 1295 Wates sought to have its dispute with the hospital referred to arbitration. The hospital however wanted the matter heard at the same time as other disputes that it had with other consultants. The court exercised its discretion and refused to stay the proceedings on the ground that there would be multiplicity in the proceedings.

The courts will also examine whether there are some aspects of the dispute that fall outside the scope of the arbitration agreement. The courts will refuse a stay where part of the dispute would be dealt with by the arbitrator and part would have to be dealt with by the court: *Ives and Barker* v *Willans* [1894] 2 Ch. 478.

2.5.3 Terms of the stay

The court has jurisdiction to order that the matter be stayed with conditions attached. These conditions may involve the applicant giving security for costs, to abandon a particular claim or to set down a timetable. The court may also decide to stay only part of the claim: *Radio Publicity (Universal) Ltd* v *Compagnie Luxembourgeoise de Radiodifusion* [1936] 2 All ER 721. Examples of where this has occurred can be seen in cases where there are discrete issues of fact and law such as *Hyams* v *Docker* [1969] 1 Lloyd's Rep 341 and *Re Carlisle, Clegg* v *Clegg* (1890) 44 ChD 200. However, the court will generally not take this course where the point of law is one which will be required by the arbiter of fact for its decision. Although the grant of a stay will usually place the whole matter within the ambit of the arbitration the court may, if it thinks fit, take back the dispute into its own hands. Such a situation will occur if the court can be persuaded that the arbitration has foundered: *Digby* v *General Accident Fire and Life Assurance Corporation Ltd* [1940] 2 KB 226. Furthermore, under the inherent jurisdiction of the court, the court may amend such terms under which a stay has been granted.

2.5.4 Mandatory stay

The position under the AA 1975 is somewhat different to that under s. 4(1) of the AA 1950. Section 1(1) of the AA 1975 states:

> If any party to an arbitration agreement to which this section applies, or any person claiming through or under him, commences any legal proceedings in any court against any other party to the agreement, or any person claiming through or under him, in respect of any matter agreed to be referred, any party to the proceedings may at any time after appearance, and before delivering any pleadings or taking any other steps in the proceedings, apply to the court to stay the proceedings; and the court, unless satisfied that the arbitration agreement is null and void, inoperative or incapable of being performed or that there is not in fact any dispute between the parties with regard to the matter agreed to be referred, shall make an order staying the proceedings.

Section 1 of the AA 1975 applies in situations where there is not a 'domestic arbitration agreement'. Section 1(4) of the AA 1975 defines a 'domestic arbitration agreement' as being:

an arbitration agreement which does not provide, expressly or by implication, for arbitration in a State other than the United Kingdom and to which neither—
(a) an individual who is a national of, or habitually resident in, any State other than the United Kingdom; nor
(b) a body corporate which is incorporated in, or whose central management and control is exercised in, any State other than the United Kingdom; is a party at the time the proceedings were commenced.

As under s. 4(1) of the AA 1950 the application to stay may be made at any time after an appearance but before the delivery of pleadings or taking a step in the action.

Once the requirements of s. 1 of the AA 1975 are made out the court must stay the proceedings: *Nova (Jersey) Knit Ltd* v *Kammgarn Spinnerei Gmbh* [1977] 1 WLR 713; *Associated Bulk Carriers Ltd* v *Koch Shipping Inc* [1978] 1 Lloyd's Rep 24; *Paczy* v *Haendler & Natermann GmbH* [1981] 1 Lloyd's Rep 302. Under s. 1 a stay must be refused if the arbitration agreement is null and void (see, for example, *AB Bofors-UVA* v *AB Skandia Transport* [1982] 1 Lloyd's Rep 410) or is inoperative: (*Lonrho Ltd* v *Shell Petroleum Co. Ltd* [1981] 2 All ER 456) or is incapable of being performed (*The Rena K* [1979] QB 377); or where there is in fact no dispute (*Associated Bulk Carriers Ltd* v *Koch Shipping Inc.* [1978] 1 Lloyd's Rep 24; *Nova (Jersey) Knit Ltd* v *Kammgarn Spinnerei Gmbh* [1977] 1 WLR 713).

2.6 POWERS AND JURISDICTION

The distinction between the jurisdiction and the powers of the arbitral tribunal is not always easy to define. The jurisdiction of the arbitral tribunal derives solely from the arbitration agreement. This may be found in the underlying contract between the parties or in a separate ad hoc agreement where the underlying contract does not contain an arbitration clause. In an ad hoc agreement the parties may agree to refer a number of specific matters to the arbitral tribunal for determination. If subsequent matters arise, the arbitral tribunal will not have jurisdiction to decide on these unless the parties extend the arbitral tribunal's jurisdiction. If the arbitral tribunal attempts to decide these new matters without the consent of the parties, it acts outside its jurisdiction and commits what was termed 'misconduct' under s. 23 of the AA 1950. Conversely, if the arbitral tribunal has had submitted to it a number of matters, it has jurisdiction to deal with all of them and a failure to do so is again misconduct as it is again acting outside of its jurisdiction. The rationale for this can be explained in that the arbitral tribunal has agreed for reward to deal with the matters submitted to it. It should do no more or no less.

An arbitral tribunal may exercise powers within the jurisdiction that is possesses. Therefore, if a dispute relating to the final account under a building contract was referred to an arbitral tribunal, it would have the power to order disclosure of documents relating to that dispute or, if the parties have so agreed, order that the claimant provide security for the defendant's costs. If the parties have not agreed to give to the arbitral tribunal the power to order security for costs, it would act in excess of its powers if it tried to do so.

It is impossible to set out every power that an arbitral tribunal may possess. Each case will be dependent on the terms of the arbitration agreement. The common law implies a number of powers into the arbitration agreement. Examples of common law powers include: the power of an arbitral tribunal to delegate the performance of acts of a ministerial nature (*Thorp* v *Cole* (1835) 2 Cr M & R 367) and the power to order inspection of property owned by a party to the arbitration (*Vasso (Owners)* v *Vasso (Owners of cargo lately laden on board* [1983] 3 All ER 211). Where an arbitration agreement incorporates for example, the Construction Industry Model Arbitration Rules (CIMAR) certain powers over and beyond those that exist at common law or are provided by statute are incorporated into the agreement.

2.6.1 Awards in the form of a special case

Section 21 of the AA 1950 enabled the arbitral tribunal to state any point of law, or an award, in the form of a special case. Where a point of law arose in arbitration proceedings the arbitral tribunal could, and was obliged to if ordered by the court, give its decision on that point of law which would then be reviewed by the court. An arbitral tribunal could also be ordered to state the award in the form of a special case which would then be reviewed by the court. A party to an arbitration also had the right to request that the arbitral tribunal state a case on any question of law. If the arbitral tribunal refused to do so then that party could apply to the court to require the arbitral tribunal to state a case. In *Halfdan Grieg & Co. A/S* v *Sterling Coal and Navigation Corporation* [1973] QB 843 the court held that where there was a clear point of law to decide, the arbitral tribunal should state a case and would be ordered to do so unless there were special reasons.

Although s. 21 of the AA 1950 was subsequently repealed by the AA 1979, and few if any arbitrations presently proceeding in England and Wales or Northern Ireland incorporate this power, the power to state a case is worthy of some mention because of its applicability to arbitrations under foreign laws. The Gibraltar Arbitration Ordinance, for example, still includes the power for the arbitral tribunal to state a case.

Section 21 of the AA 1950 sets out three situations where the arbitral tribunal may state a case. First, on any question of law arising in the reference. Secondly, on an award or any part of an award. Thirdly, on an interim award. Where a party requests that the arbitral tribunal state a case and the arbitral tribunal refuses to do so, this will not amount to misconduct where the request has been made after the award has been published. However, where the request is made prior to the award and in plenty of time the arbitral tribunal's refusal will amount to misconduct: *Giacomo Costa Fu Andrea* v *British Italian Trading Co. Ltd* [1963] 1 QB 201. The arbitral tribunal is entitled to refuse to state a case in a number of circumstances: where a party makes a request simply to delay the arbitration or where an arbitral tribunal's decision on a question of fact renders the requirement to state a case redundant. Where the only question for the arbitral tribunal to decide is one of law it has been held that it would not be misconduct for the arbitral tribunal to refuse to state a case: *Re Canadian Line Materials Ltd, Dominion Cutout Co. Ltd and Southern States Equipment Corporation* (1960) 22 DLR (2d) 741. The rationale for this decision is that to order the arbitral tribunal to state a case would be in effect to impose a determination by the court on a matter that the parties have agreed should be referred to arbitration. The right to state a case could not be excluded by the agreement of the parties: *Czarnikow* v *Roth Schmidt and Co.* [1922] 2 KB 478.

2.7 CHALLENGES TO THE AWARD

Under the AA 1950 an arbitration award could be challenged on a number of grounds including: that the arbitral tribunal has exceeded its jurisdiction, that it has had its authority revoked, or that it has committed misconduct. Many of these grounds of challenge are equally applicable under the AA 1996. The case law, under the AA 1979 involving challenges on points of law has now been given statutory effect under the AA 1996 and is discussed in chapter 12 as are claims that the arbitral tribunal has exceeded its jurisdiction. However, one of the notable changes in the AA 1996 was to give a ground for challenge by reason of 'serious irregularity'. This new ground replaces the old ground for remitting or the setting aside of an award for 'misconduct' under ss. 22 and 23 of the AA 1950.

There is no all-embracing definition of misconduct and the courts have approached what is or is not misconduct on a case-by-case basis. The test that has been applied in regard to setting aside for misconduct is set out by Ackner LJ in the *Ardahalian* v *Unifert International SA* [1984] 2 Lloyd's Rep 84:

Do there exist grounds from which a reasonable person would think that there was a real likelihood that [the arbitrator] could not, or would not, fairly determine [the issue in the arbitration] on the basis of the evidence and arguments to be adduced before him?

There are, however, some grounds which seem to be treated as misconduct per se. The failure by the arbitral tribunal to conduct the reference in accordance with the agreement of the parties would be an example of this type of misconduct. The courts have held that to act in a way contrary to public policy would amount to misconduct as would acting contrary to the rules of natural justice. In *Fox* v *P.G. Wellfair Ltd* [1981] 2 Lloyd's Rep 514 the court removed the arbitral tribunal under s. 23 of the AA 1950 on the basis that it had used its own specialised knowledge rather than basing its award on the evidence before it. The word 'misconduct' does not necessarily imply bad faith but rather refers to any action which the arbitral tribunal does which is contrary to that which it is legally obliged to do. However, an error of law or fact is not misconduct. An award by the arbitral tribunal based on an error of law must be challenged under s. 1 of the AA 1979. There will be no remedy if the arbitration agreement excludes the right to appeal an award for an error of law: *Danae Air Transport SA* v *Air Canada* (1999) *The Times*, 31 March. In *Fairclough Building Ltd* v *Vale of Belvoir Superstore Ltd* (1990) 56 BLR 74 the arbitral tribunal was removed when the court held that it had misapplied the rules of evidence. A recent case where the arbitral tribunal was removed for misconduct is *D.F. Mooney* v *Henry Boot (Construction) Ltd* (unreported 11 April 1995), in which Henry Boot applied for the removal of the arbitral tribunal and/or to have the arbitral tribunal's award set aside on the grounds, *inter alia*, that the arbitral tribunal had acted in excess of jurisdiction or otherwise was guilty of misconduct. The grounds of challenge included the fact that the arbitral tribunal had been asked to supply further reasons for its award in the form of answers to questions which had been put to it but failed to answer all the questions. Judge Lloyd QC stated, at page 5 of the transcript, that:

> . . . an arbitrator who does not comply with the court's order for further reasons not only fails to provide the court with the material that it requires but also fails to honour its obligations to the parties to the reference and does them a disservice. Such occasions must be rare but it should clearly be understood by arbitrators that an order for further reasons is to be observed like any other order of the court.

The learned judge concluded at p. 41 that:

> Remission is inappropriate because the arbitrator's failure to deal properly with this section of the dispute, his failure to heed the warning given by Boot's solicitors, and his failure to comply with the court's order mean that there are serious and well-founded grounds for Boot to believe that the arbitrator does not have the ability to determine this part of the dispute judicially or competently. For the same reasons Boot are in my judgment correct in submitting that an order for the removal of the arbitrator is also appropriate.

Arbitral tribunals have often been sensitive to the word 'misconduct' and to mitigate this sensitivity the courts created two separate forms of misconduct: 'misconduct of a personal nature' and 'technical misconduct'. Although there are numerous references in case law to either technical or personal misconduct nothing turns on the distinction and the powers of the court in respect to either type of misconduct are the same. Where misconduct has occurred in the proceedings a court can remit the award back to the arbitral tribunal (s. 22 of the AA 1950), set aside the award or remove the arbitral tribunal (s. 23(1) and (2) of the AA 1950).

3 Background to the Arbitration Act 1996

3.1 INTRODUCTION

London has for centuries been a predominant centre for international arbitration. However, with the rapid expansion of international trade in the post-war era and the adoption by many countries of more sophisticated arbitration rules the choice of London as an automatic seat of an arbitration was being threatened by what was perceived to be England's antiquated arbitration law.

The AA 1950 was a consolidating statute in respect of the AAs 1889 to 1934 and therefore did not address flaws in the existing legislation. The main criticisms of the English arbitration procedure were that it enabled the court to review the content of an award or review matters of law by way of the case stated procedure (see chapter 2) or by setting aside an award by reason of technical misconduct. This frustrated the aims of the parties to the arbitration who desired a quick and final method of resolving their dispute by an arbitral tribunal of their own choice. The case stated procedure was open to abuse. It enabled one of the parties to the arbitration to refer matters of law to the court which had the effect of delaying the making of an award and increasing the costs of the arbitration. The procedure was, however, an established part of English arbitration law and its removal was a controversial issue: *Universal Cargo Carriers Corporation* v *Citati* [1957] 1 Lloyd's Rep 174. In the mid 1970s a number of 'supranational disputes' occurred leading to numerous questions of law being referred from arbitrations to the courts. The excessive delays that occurred resulted in renewed criticisms of the case stated procedure. The need to remove the case stated procedure from English arbitration law was no more clearly stated than in a letter from the general counsel of a major US company which was subsequently read in the House of Lords by Lord Hacking (Hansard HL, 18 May 1978, col. 91):

> The purpose of utilising arbitration in lieu of litigation is generally thought to be that arbitration proceedings will be speedy, inexpensive, and private. Perhaps they are private, but they are certainly neither inexpensive, nor speedy in the United Kingdom. . . . While I recognise that some of the delays might be attributable to the specific arbitrators appointed by the parties, I am told that even when arbitrators with a sense of urgency are handling the case, defendants may delay proceedings by frequent appeals back to the judicial system.

The case stated procedure was subsequently removed from English arbitration law by s. 1 of the AA 1979.

The court's power to set aside an award for error on the face of the award was based on an established common law principle that the courts had control over all civil law disputes within their jurisdiction and such jurisdiction could not be ousted by the agreement of the parties. Although not so widespread in its use this power was also removed from the courts by s. 1 of the AA 1979. Section 1(2) of the AA 1979 contained a new statutory power whereby only appeals on points of law could be made and the right to appeal was subject to restrictions.

The AA 1979 went a long way in assuaging the criticisms which had been levelled at the AA 1950. Section 3 of the AA 1979 also allowed for arbitrations of a non-domestic nature to exclude the right to appeal. Following the enactment of the AA 1979 London's position as a leading centre for international arbitration seemed secure. However, in the late 1980s and early 1990s a number of decisions of the courts relating to security for costs and the court's intervention with the conduct of the arbitral tribunal seemed once again to threaten that position. Further, the UNCITRAL Model Law was being adopted by a number of countries and many commentators took the view that this offered a fresh approach to arbitration without the delays and unnecessary court intervention which were prevalent in many common law jurisdictions.

The criticisms that were made largely arose as a result of the House of Lords decision in *Coppée-Lavalin NV* v *Ken-Ren Chemicals and Fertilizers Ltd* [1995] 1 AC 38. The case involved a dispute under the ICC Rules of Arbitration regarding the construction of a chemical plant. The seat of the arbitration was in England. The claimant applied to the English court for an order that the respondent provide security for its costs on the basis that Ken-Ren was an insolvent company which was being supported in the arbitration by the Kenyan government. The ICC Rules governed the conduct of the arbitration and it was argued by Ken-Ren that therefore the English courts had no power to order it to provide security. Coppée-Lavalin responded that there was a residual power of the court to order security although it conceded that such a power should only be used in 'exceptional circumstances'. The House of Lords held by a majority that it did have the power to order the respondent to provide security and that there were 'exceptional circumstances' that justified such an order being made. The active role of the English courts in international arbitrations was criticised strongly on the Continent.

Under s. 23(2) of the AA 1950 the courts had a reviewing power in respect of arbitration awards and the conduct of the reference. Section 23(2) stated: 'Where an arbitrator or umpire has misconducted himself or the proceedings, or an arbitration or award has been improperly procured the High Court may set the award aside'. Prior to the AA 1996 the court was criticised for exercising its powers too freely under this provision: *Fox* v *P.G. Wellfair Ltd* [1981] 2 Lloyd's Rep 514; *D.F. Mooney* v *Henry Boot (Construction) Ltd* (1995 unreported). During that time there was a general perception that the increasing amount of court intervention in arbitration proceedings was undermining the fundamental principle of party autonomy upon which English arbitration law was founded. A new statute was required to modernise and restate English arbitration law in line with the requirements of commercial parties.

The principle of party autonomy is stated in s. 1 of the AA 1996 alongside the other principles upon which Part I of the AA 1996 is founded. These other principles are the fair resolution of the dispute by an impartial tribunal without unnecessary delay and expense and that the court should not intervene in the arbitration proceedings except as provided for in Part I of the Act.

3.2 THE DEPARTMENTAL ADVISORY COMMITTEE

UNCITRAL adopted its Model Law on International Commercial Arbitration (the UNCITRAL Model Law) in 1985. The United Kingdom government then set up a Departmental Advisory Committee (the DAC) to review the UNCITRAL Model Law. The DAC was chaired by Mustill LJ. In June 1989 the DAC published its first report. The DAC's brief was to consider whether to adopt the UNCITRAL Model Law. It strongly recommended that the UNCITRAL Model Law should not be adopted in England but made the following recommendations, at para. 108, for a new and improved Arbitration Act.

(1)   It should comprise a statement in statutory form of the more important principles of the English law of arbitration, statutory and (to the extent practicable) common law.

(2)   It should be limited to those principles whose existence and effect are uncontroversial.

(3)   It should be set out in a logical order, and expressed in language which is sufficiently clear and free from technicalities to be readily comprehensible to the layman.

(4)   It should in general apply to domestic and international arbitrations alike, although there may have to be exceptions to take account of treaty obligations.

(5)   It should not be limited to the subject matter of the Model Law.

(6)   It should embody such of our proposals for legislation as have by then been enacted: see paragraph 100 [of the 1989 report].

(7)   Consideration should be given to ensuring that any such new statute should, so far as possible, have the same structure and language as the Model Law, so as to enhance its accessibility to those who are familiar with the Model Law.

The DAC took the stance that the existing state of English arbitration law was not defective per se but rather that there were fundamental problems in the presentation of that law. Although the June 1989 report strongly advised against the adoption of the UNCITRAL Model Law it approved of the logic and presentation of it. The June 1989 report found that there was much uncertainty and confusion in English arbitration law. This finding has been echoed by Saville LJ, *The Arbitration Act 1996. Keynote Address,* IBC Conference, 4 July 1996, where his lordship stated that:

Our law has built up over a very long time indeed. In the main the developments have come from cases, but in addition, from as early as 1698, Parliament has passed legislation dealing with the law of arbitration. To a large degree this legislation has been reactive in nature, putting right perceived defects and deficiencies in the case law. Thus it is not easy for someone new to English arbitration to discover the law, which is spread around a hotchpotch of statutes and countless cases.

In 1990 work had begun on preparing a new Act to replace the existing legislation. However, the Parliamentary drafter thought that the principles recommended at para. 108 of the June 1989 report were incapable of being put into legislative form. Instead the drafter recommended that there should be a consolidating statute bringing together the three main Arbitration Acts, the AA 1950, the AA 1975 and the AA 1979. It was further recommended that an accompanying handbook should be issued giving guidance to these Acts but having no force of law. This concept was almost instantaneously rejected as failing to accord to what the DAC, now under the chairmanship of Lord Steyn, wished. At the same time as this work was being undertaken Mr Basil Eckersley, formerly a leading maritime arbitrator, had prepared his own draft as a possible statute incorporating the policy expressed in para. 108 of the June 1989 report (see A.L. Marriott, 'The new Arbitration Bill' (1996) 62 Arbitration 100).

The 'Eckersley draft' was sent out for an informal consultative process in 1991 and received favourable comments from interested parties both in England and abroad. In 1991 it was passed to another parliamentary drafter, Miss Furlonger. By March 1993 she had prepared her first draft and this was submitted to the DAC with the Eckersley draft by a private working group who recommended the Eckersley draft. Opposition to the Eckersley draft, however, meant that the DAC had to proceed with the Furlonger draft.

In February 1994 the DAC put out for consultation the Furlonger draft after it had been redrafted. It received strong criticism in that it appeared also to consolidate the existing statutes, the AA 1950, AA 1975 and AA 1979. Brian Davenport QC, a former law commissioner, criticised the draft in strong terms and concluded that it was like half a loaf, better than none but full of stones (*Arbitration International*, vol. 10, No. 2). The defects and deficiencies of the existing law were simply repeated. Although the Furlonger draft was severely criticised, one effect was that those interested in arbitration responded with a vast amount of carefully considered criticism. It was at this point that Saville LJ took over the chairmanship of the DAC. Saville LJ and a junior barrister, Toby Landau, prepared what was to become known as the 'illustrative draft'. The 'illustrative draft' was published for consultation in April 1995.

Geoffrey Sellars, one of the most respected Parliamentary drafters, then undertook the job of preparing a draft Bill and altered and improved the draft in consultation with all those in the DAC who had worked on its preparation.

The draft Bill contained in excess of 100 clauses bringing together all the main principles of English arbitration law. Consideration had been given as to whether there should be two statutes, one dealing with domestic arbitrations and the other dealing with international arbitrations. This approach was rejected in favour of an all-encompassing statute. The Bill passed through Parliament with very few amendments and was enacted as the AA 1996 and came into force on 31 January 1997.

The AA 1996 is made up of four parts. Part I sets out the major provisions of the Act. Part II includes provisions relating to 'domestic arbitration agreements' (not brought into force), consumer arbitrations and statutory arbitrations. Part III gives effect to England's treaty obligations under the New York Convention and Part IV sets out a number of general provisions. There are also four Schedules.

The extent of time and effort of those involved in drafting the AA 1996 may seem to be out of proportion to the subject matter. For those who deal on a day-to-day basis with arbitration law, as arbitrator, lawyer, expert or claims consultant, the reason why such effort was put in is clear. Arbitration is a form of alternative dispute resolution (ADR) but stands alone from other forms of ADR methods such as conciliation or mediation. Those who elect to have their disputes resolved by mediation or conciliation may walk away from the process. They may decide not to follow an agreement reached or choose at any time to exercise their rights to bring proceedings by way of litigation. An arbitration agreement is, however, binding on the parties and once the arbitration procedure has started there is no unilateral right or election to refuse to proceed. An arbitral award legally made will be enforceable by the court and will have the same status as an order of the court. In many respects arbitration is more similar to litigation than any other form of ADR. Arbitration therefore has been said to 'exist in the shadow of public coercion': Professor W.W. Park (1996) 12(2) Arbitration International.

Although the intent of the AA 1996 was to put within one statute all law relating to English arbitration it should be noted that it has not repealed all previous legislation relating to arbitrations. In chapter 2 the extent of the repeal of the previous law has been discussed. In subsequent chapters the effects and extent of the pre-existing law will be analysed.

The AA 1996 is probably the most radical piece of legislation in the history of English arbitration law. It contains an almost complete statement of principles relating to the law of arbitration. It uses straightforward and logical language to explain those principles and presents them in a chronological format starting with the principles affecting the arbitration, the seat of the arbitration, the formation of the arbitral tribunal and ending with the recognition and enforcement of an award. Although at its conception it was agreed that the AA 1996 would not enact without modification the UNCITRAL Model Law it is clear from the use of language and format that that Law has played a major part in the shape that the Act has taken.

The AA 1996 does not stand alone. The DAC report issued in February 1996 provides a commentary on each of the sections of the AA 1996 explaining its intended use. Although the report has no legislative status it remains a useful guide to help in the interpretation of the AA 1996. Further help for the user of the AA 1996 was also given by the drafter by using a cross-referencing system within the Act helping both lawyer and lay person to find other sections of the Act relevant to the matter in dispute.

Although by no means perfect it is generally thought that the AA 1996 rectifies many of the problems with the arbitration process that existed before its commencement. During the debate on the second reading in the House of Lords of the Bill which was enacted as the AA 1996 Lord Hacking stated that: '. . . it measures up to some of the great statutes at the end of the nineteenth century, the Bills of Exchange Act 1882 or the Sale of Goods Act 1893': Hansard HL, 18 January 1996, col. 769.

The test of whether the AA 1996 will live up to its expectation will be in its use. Theoretical anomalies that exist within the AA 1996 may remain as such. Whether technical arbitrators will use the powers that they are now provided with remains to be seen. One major factor for the success of the AA 1996 will be whether the users of the arbitration process use arbitration as an alternative to litigation giving a speedy and inexpensive method of dispute resolution. If the parties to the arbitration process continue to proceed as if the matter were litigation, producing long and complex pleadings, the arbitration process may never be shortened even with the most proactive of arbitrators. Lord Hacking, 'Arbitration law reform: the impact of the UNCITRAL Model Law on the English Arbitration Act 1996', *Arbitration* (November 1997), p. 299, makes this point and refers to the case of *Mylward* v *Weldon* (1596) cited in R.E. Megarry, *Miscellany at Law* (London: Stevens, 1955), p. 41, as a warning to lawyers who treat arbitration simply as litigation in suits. In this case the plaintiff had drawn up a pleading occupying: 'Six score sheets of paper, and yet all the matter thereof which is pertinent might have been well contrived in 16 sheets of paper'. The court would have none of this truck and sharply brought the pleader's attention to the error of his ways. They ordered him to be committed to the Fleet Prison! But there was more punishment in store for him. The warden of the Fleet Prison was then directed to take him to Westminster Hall at 10.00 a.m. on the following Saturday:

> . . . and then and there shall cut a hole in the midst of the same engrossed replication which is delivered unto him for that purpose, and put the said [pleader's] head through the same hole, and so let the same replication hang about his shoulders with the written side outward, and then, the same so hanging, shall lead the said [pleader] bareheaded and barefaced round about Westminster Hall, whilst the courts are sitting, and shall show him at the bar of every of the three courts within the Hall, and then shall take him back again to the Fleet, and keep him prisoner until he shall have paid £10 to Her Majesty for a fine, and 20 nobles to the defendant for his costs in respect of the aforesaid abuse.

3.3   SOURCES FOR PART I OF THE ARBITRATION ACT 1996

It was originally intended that the AA 1996 should comprise a statement in statutory form of the more important principles of the English law of arbitration. As enacted the AA 1996 has done far more than this. It has not only taken the existing English law of arbitration but also supplemented it with many principles from the UNCITRAL Model Law. It has created new rights and obligations. It has also set out general principles under which it is to be construed. The AA 1996 radically altered the existing English law of arbitration — although at the same time preserving many perceived benefits of English arbitration law that have developed over centuries.

Table 3.1 is intended to indicate the sources from which sections of the AA 1996 were derived. It should be emphasised that it was not the intent that the AA 1996 should re-enact the AAs 1950 to 1979 in a logical format. Changes have been made in almost every section, some minor and some radical. Accordingly, the full text of the AA 1996 should be referred to when considering its provisions.

Section of the AA 1996	Subject matter	AAs 1950 to 1979, other legislation and case law	UNCITRAL Model Law
1	General principles		Articles 5, 19(1).
2	Scope of application of provisions		Article 1(2).
3	The seat of the arbitration		
4	Mandatory and non-mandatory provisions		
5	Agreements to be in writing	AA 1950 s. 32. AA 1975 s. 7(1).	Article 7(2).
6	Definition of arbitration agreement	AA 1950 s. 32. AA 1975 s. 7(1).	Article 7(1), (2).
7	Separability of arbitration agreement	*Harbour Assurance Co. (UK) Ltd* v *Kansa General International Insurance Co. Ltd* [1993] QB 701.	Article 16(1).
8	Whether agreement discharged by death of a party	AA 1950 s. 2(1), (3).	
9	Stay of legal proceedings	AA 1950 s. 4(1). AA 1975 s. 1.	Article 8.

Section of the AA 1996	Subject matter	AAs 1950 to 1979, other legislation and case law	UNCITRAL Model Law
10	Reference of interpleader issue to arbitration	AA 1950 s. 5.	
11	Retention of security where Admiralty proceedings stayed	Civil Jurisdiction and Judgments Act 1982 s. 26.	
12	Power of court to extend time for beginning arbitral proceedings, etc.	AA 1950 s. 27.	
13	Application of Limitation Acts	Limitation Act 1980 s. 34. Foreign Limitation Periods Act 1984 s. 5.	
14	Commencement of arbitral proceedings	Limitation Act 1980 s. 34(3).	Article 21.
15	The arbitral tribunal	AA 1950 ss. 6, 8, 9.	Article 10(1).
16	Procedure for appointment of arbitrators		Article 11(2), (3).
17	Power in case of default to appoint sole arbitrator	AA 1950 ss. 7(b) and 10(3B).	
18	Failure of appointment procedure	AA 1950 s. 10.	Article 11(4).
19	Court to have regard to agreed qualifications		Article 11(5).
20	Chairman	AA 1950 s. 9.	Article 29.
21	Umpire	AA 1950 s. 8(2), (3).	
22	Decision-making where no chairman or umpire		Article 29.

Section of the AA 1996	Subject matter	AAs 1950 to 1979, other legislation and case law	UNCITRAL Model Law
23	Revocation of arbitrator's authority	AA 1950 s. 1.	Article 14.
24	Power of court to remove arbitrator	AA 1950 ss. 13(3), 23(1) and 24(1).	Articles 12 to 14.
25	Resignation of arbitrator		Article 14.
26	Death of arbitrator or person appointing him	AA 1950 s. 2(2).	
27	Filling of vacancy, etc.	AA 1950 s. 25.	Article 15.
28	Joint and several liability of parties to arbitrators for fees and expenses		
29	Immunity of arbitrator		
30	Competence of tribunal to rule on its own jurisdiction		Article 16(1).
31	Objection to substantive jurisdiction of tribunal		Article 16(2), (3).
32	Determination of preliminary point of jurisdiction		
33	General duty of the tribunal		Article 18.
34	Procedural and evidential matters	AA 1950 s. 12(1) to (3).	Articles 19, 20, 22 to 24.
35	Consolidation of proceedings and concurrent hearings		
36	Legal or other representation		

Section of the AA 1996	*Subject matter*	*AAs 1950 to 1979, other legislation and case law*	*UNCITRAL Model Law*
37	Power to appoint experts, legal advisers or assessors		Article 26(1).
38	General powers exercisable by the tribunal	AA 1950 s. 12(1) to (3).	Article 17.
39	Power to make provisional awards		
40	General duty of parties		
41	Powers of tribunal in case of party's default	AA 1950 s. 13A.	Article 25.
42	Enforcement of peremptory orders of tribunal		
43	Securing the attendance of witnesses	AA 1950 s. 12(4), (5).	Article 27.
44	Court powers exercisable in support of arbitral proceedings	AA 1950 s. 12(6)(d) to (h).	Article 9.
45	Determination of preliminary point of law	AA 1979 s. 2.	
46	Rules applicable to substance of dispute		Article 28.
47	Awards on different issues, &c.	AA 1950 s. 14.	
48	Remedies	AA 1950 s. 15.	
49	Interest	AA 1950 ss. 19A and 20.	
50	Extension of time for making award	AA 1950 s. 13(2).	
51	Settlement		Article 30.
52	Form of award		Article 31.

Section of the AA 1996	Subject matter	AAs 1950 to 1979, other legislation and case law	UNCITRAL Model Law
53	Place where award treated as made		Article 31(3).
54	Date of award		
55	Notification of award		
56	Power to withhold award in case of non-payment	AA 1950 s. 19.	
57	Correction of award or additional award	AA 1950 ss. 17 and 18(4).	Article 33.
58	Effect of award	AA 1950 s. 16.	
59	Costs of the arbitration		
60	Agreement to pay costs in any event	AA 1950 s. 18(3).	
61	Award of costs	AA 1950 s. 18(1).	
62	Effect of agreement or award about costs		
63	The recoverable costs of the arbitration	AA 1950 s. 18(1), (2).	
64	Recoverable fees and expenses of arbitrators	AA 1950 s. 19.	
65	Power to limit recoverable costs		
66	Enforcement of the award	AA 1950 s. 26(1).	Article 35.
67	Challenging the award: substantive jurisdiction		Articles 16, 34.
68	Challenging the award: serious irregularity	AA 1950 ss. 22, 23.	Article 34.

Section of the AA 1996	Subject matter	AAs 1950 to 1979, other legislation and case law	UNCITRAL Model Law
69	Appeal on point of law	AA 1979 ss. 1, 3. *Pioneer Shipping Ltd* v *BTP Tioxide Ltd* [1982] AC 724.	
70	Challenge or appeal: supplementary provisions	AA 1950 s. 23(3). AA 1979 s. 1(5), (6).	
71	Challenge or appeal: effect of order of court	AA 1950 s. 22(2). AA 1979 s. 1(8).	
72	Saving for rights of person who takes no part in proceedings		
73	Loss of right to object		Article 4.
74	Immunity of arbitral institutions, etc.		
75	Charge to secure payment of solicitors' costs	AA 1950 s. 18(5).	
76	Service of notices, etc.		Article 3.
77	Powers of court in relation to service of documents		
78	Reckoning periods of time		
79	Power of court to extend time limits relating to arbitral proceedings		
80	Notice and other requirements in connection with legal proceedings		
81	Saving for certain matters governed by common law		

Section of the AA 1996	*Subject matter*	*AAs 1950 to 1979, other legislation and case law*	*UNCITRAL Model Law*
82	Minor definitions		
83	Index of defined expressions: Part I		
84	Transitional provisions		

4 Aspects of Arbitration Proceedings

4.1 UNDERLYING PRINCIPLES OF ARBITRATION

An arbitration is a private process of dispute resolution between parties to an arbitration agreement. The subject matter of the arbitration may be an existing or potential dispute but it cannot be a claim for a mere valuation. The award of the arbitral tribunal is final and legally binding and must be made in the light of the evidence and arguments submitted to it. Arbitration is therefore a quasi-judicial process.

The main principles of arbitration law are set out in s. 1 of the AA 1996:

(a) the object of arbitration is to obtain the fair resolution of disputes by an impartial tribunal without unnecessary delay and expense;

(b) the parties should be free to agree how their disputes are resolved, subject only to such safeguards as are necessary in the public interest;

(c) in matters governed by this Part [i.e., Part I of the AA 1996] the court should not intervene except as provided by this Part.

Section 1 of the AA 1996 requires that the provisions of the Act should be applied purposively. Where there is doubt within any section within the AA 1996 then regard should be had to these principles. Section 1(a) of the AA 1996 defines the objective of an arbitration. The words 'without unnecessary delay and expense' were added following complaints of the lengthy, expensive and slow arbitration process under the previous arbitration legislation. Section 1(a) of the AA 1996 should be read alongside s. 33, which imposes positive duties on the tribunal to adopt procedures to avoid unnecessary delay and expense. Section 1(b) of the AA 1996 puts into statutory form the fundamental principle of arbitration law that the parties are autonomous in deciding how the arbitration should proceed subject only to matters of public interest, for example, the parties cannot agree terms which contravene principles of natural justice. The section does not use the word 'shall'. Therefore the principle established in s. 1(b) of the AA 1996 is only a principle of intention. This is because the AA 1996 includes mandatory sections, which cannot be excluded by the parties. The parties have autonomy only in respect of the conduct of the proceedings and not in respect of all matters to do with the arbitration. Section 1(c) of the AA 1996 gives further effect to the principle of autonomy by limiting the court to intervening only where permitted by the AA 1996.

The main advantages of arbitration proceedings over litigation are preserved by s. 1(a) to (c) of the AA 1996. The parties can choose who should hear their dispute and what powers the arbitral tribunal should have to conduct the proceedings. The parties can choose an expert in a particular field related to the dispute. This has the advantage that the person who is to resolve the dispute is already familiar with the subject matter of the dispute. Another benefit of the arbitral process is that there is flexibility in the rules to be applied compared to litigation. The arbitral tribunal may tailor the arbitral process to fit the dispute. The use of document-only arbitrations and fast-track arbitrations can provide a speedy resolution to disputes. A further advantage of arbitration over litigation is that arbitration proceedings are conducted in private.

However, since the introduction of the Civil Procedure Rules, many of the perceived benefits of arbitration over litigation may no longer be as great. The underlying principles as set out in s. 1 of the AA 1996 are now all but mirrored in the Civil Procedural Rules. This point was emphasised in *Jitendra Bhailbhai Patel* v *Dilesh R Patel* [1999] BLR 227, 229, where Lord Woolf stated:

If it appropriate for me to say so, the underlying spirit of the new Arbitration Act in very much in accord with the underlying spirit of the new procedural rules which will be applicable to the civil courts in this jurisdiction from 26 April 1999.

4.2 DISPUTES

4.2.1 Definition of dispute

It is a fundamental aspect of the arbitral process that only disputes can be referred to arbitration. This is embodied in s. 1(a) of the AA 1996: 'the object of arbitration is to obtain the fair resolution of disputes'. The definition of the word 'dispute' is crucial in deciding whether a matter can or cannot be referred to arbitration. Section 6(1) of the AA 1996 defines an arbitration agreement as 'an agreement to submit to arbitration present or future disputes (whether they are contractual or not)'. The recent case of *O'Callaghan* v *Coral Racing Ltd* (1998 unreported) suggests that a dispute that has no legal content, such as a wagering transaction, cannot be the subject of an arbitration.

Section 32 of the AA 1950 defined an arbitration agreement as 'a written agreement to submit present or future differences to arbitration'. Prior to the enactment of the AA 1996 the distinction between 'dispute' and 'difference' was an important one. In *Sykes* v *Fine Fare* [1967] 1 Lloyd's Rep 53 Danckwerts LJ stated at p. 60: 'The word "differences" seems to me to be particularly apt for a case where the parties have not agreed'. Viscount Dunedin said in *May and Butcher* v *The King* [1934] 2 KB 17, '. . . a failure to agree . . . is a very different thing from a dispute. But it seems to me that the word "difference" is particularly apt to describe that situation.' However, in contrast, in *Hayter* v *Nelson* [1990] 2 Lloyd's Rep 265 at p. 267 Saville J stated that it was assumed in practice that a 'dispute' was much the same thing as a 'difference'. The current trend is for the court to give words their natural meaning as Judge Gilliland QC stated in *Cruden Construction Ltd* v *Commission for the New Towns* [1995] 2 Lloyd's Rep 387 at p. 393:

> The words dispute or difference are ordinary English words and unless some binding rule of construction has been established in relation to the construction of those words in clause 35 of the JCT contract I am of the opinion that the words should be given their ordinary everyday meaning.

The distinction between a 'dispute' and a 'difference' is no longer as important as it was before the AA 1996 came into force as 'dispute' is now defined in s. 82(1) of the AA 1996 as including 'any difference'. The DAC at para. 41 of their February 1996 report stated that 'dispute' within s. 6(1) of the AA 1996 reflected Article 7(1) of the UNCITRAL Model Law and provided 'a more informative definition than in s. 32 of the 1950 Act'. The word 'disputes' was used in s. 6(1) of the AA 1996 because it has a narrower meaning than the word 'differences' as the DAC explained in para. 41:

> We have used the word 'disputes' but this is defined in clause 82 as including 'differences' since there is some authority for the proposition that the latter term is wider than the former; see *F. and G. Sykes (Wessex) Ltd* v *Fine Fair Ltd* [1967] 1 Lloyd's Rep 53.

The court, prior to the AA 1996, made a distinction between the words 'disputes' or 'differences' as used in arbitration agreements and the word 'claim': *Woolf* v *Collis Removal Services* [1948] KB 11. The issue recently came before the Court of Appeal in *Halki Shipping Corporation* v *Sopex Oils Ltd* [1998] 1 WLR 726, in which the question was whether an indisputable claim, a claim where there was no arguable defence, was still a dispute. It was held by the Court of Appeal that whether a defence was genuine or not and whether a dispute existed was a matter for the arbitral tribunal to decide rather than the court. The facts of the case were that Halki Shipping had chartered to Sopex a vessel under a charterparty for the carriage of goods from the Far East to Europe. Halki Shipping issued a writ in the High Court claiming demurrage in respect of Sopex's breach of contract for failing to load and discharge the vessel within the agreed laytime. Sopex did not admit liability and applied for a stay of the court proceedings under s. 9 of the AA 1996, as the agreement between the parties contained an agreement to refer any dispute to arbitration. Halki Shipping argued that the word 'dispute' meant a genuine or real dispute, and a claim which was indisputable because there was no arguable defence was not a dispute and so s. 9 of the AA 1996 could not apply. Sopex argued that the word 'dispute' meant any disputed claim which therefore covered any claim which was not admitted as due and payable. The Court of Appeal found in favour of Sopex. The Court of Appeal upheld the decision of Clarke J, the judge at first instance, that where parties agree to refer disputes under a contract to arbitration, any claim which thereafter arises out of the contract which one of the parties does not admit is a dispute, even if there is no arguable defence to all or part of the claim. The Court of Appeal relied on *obiter dicta* from Saville J in *Hayter* v *Nelson* [1990] 2 Lloyd's Rep 265 at p. 268:

> In my judgment in this context neither the word 'disputes' nor the word 'differences' is confined to cases where it cannot then and there be determined whether one party or the other is in the right. Two men have an argument over who won the University Boat Race in a particular year. In ordinary language they have a dispute over whether it was Oxford or Cambridge. The fact that it can be easily and immediately demonstrated beyond any doubt that the one is right and the other is wrong does not and cannot mean that that dispute did not in fact exist. Because one man can be said to be indisputably right and the other indisputably wrong does not, in my view, entail that there was therefore never any dispute between them.

Henry LJ in his judgment in *Halki Shipping Corporation* v *Sopex Oils Ltd* [1998] 1 WLR 726 referred to and relied on a substantial body of case law to support the view that an indisputable claim was still a dispute, including *Ellerine Brothers* v *Klinger* [1982] 1 WLR 1375. In *Ellerine Brothers* v *Klinger* the Court of Appeal had followed *Tradax Internacional SA* v *Cerrahogullari TAS* [1981] 3 All ER 344, in which it was held that where a claim was made but the defendants had done nothing about it, silence did not mean that they admitted the claim and Kerr J stated that until the defendant admits that a sum is due and payable there is a dispute within the meaning of the arbitration clause. In *Ellerine Brothers* v *Klinger* it was held that a dispute arises once a claim is made which is either ignored or met with prevarication. Templeman J said, at p. 1381:

> . . . if letters are written by the plaintiff making some request or some demand and the defendant does not reply, then there is a dispute. It is not necessary, for a dispute to arise, that the defendant should write back and say 'I don't agree'. If, on analysis, what the plaintiff is asking or demanding involves a matter on which agreement has not been reached and which falls fairly and squarely within the terms of the arbitration agreement, then the applicant is entitled to insist on arbitration instead of litigation.

In *Halki Shipping Corporation* v *Sopex Oils Ltd* [1998] 1 WLR 726 Swinton Thomas LJ concurred with Templeman LJ's view that '. . . there is a dispute once money is claimed unless and until the defendants admit that the sum is due and payable'.

4.2.2 When a dispute arises

The issue of when a dispute arises was considered recently at first instance in *Secretary of State for Foreign and Commonwealth Affairs* v *Percy International and Kier International* (1998) judgment ORB No. 635. It was submitted by the defendants that the prerequisites for a dispute were that:

(a)   a claim was made;

(b)   comprised in that claim was an allegation that the other party was liable for some or all of that claim; and

(c)   there was a denial by that other party that it was so liable or a refusal or failure to answer the allegation made.

In respect of point (a) above the defendants relied on *Monmouthshire County Council* v *Costelloe and Kemple Ltd* (1994) 5 BLR 83, in which Lord Denning said: at p. 89:

> The first point is this: Was there any dispute or difference arising between the contractors and the engineer? It is accepted that, in order that a dispute or difference can arise on this contract, there must in the first place be a claim by the contractor.

In respect of points (b) and (c) above the defendants relied on *Cruden Construction Ltd* v *Commission for the New Towns* [1995] 2 Lloyd's Rep 387. It was held in this case that, where a party serves a notice of arbitration and the other party merely asks for further information, a dispute cannot be said to have arisen. Judge Gilliland QC said, at p. 394:

> In my judgment it cannot properly be said as a matter of ordinary English that the plaintiff and defendant were in dispute or that a dispute had arisen between them when the notice of arbitration was served. The plaintiff had not denied any liability. It had not ignored the letter of Oct. 7. No details had been given by the defendant to enable the plaintiff to make any kind of informed decision in relation to any of the matters which were being alleged by the housing association let alone how those allegations affected the plaintiff. I accordingly hold that no dispute or difference existed between the plaintiff and the defendant within the meaning of cl. 35 when the notice of arbitration was served and accordingly that notice was in my judgment ineffective to commence a valid arbitration.

In *Secretary of State for Foreign and Commonwealth Affairs* v *Percy International and Kier International* Judge Bowsher QC found for the plaintiff that a dispute arose when he served a notice to concur in the appointment of an arbitrator.

The learned judge held that for a dispute to arise it was not always necessary for a claim to be made, nor does the making of a claim necessarily mean that there is a dispute. The judge referred to Mustill and Boyd, *Commercial Arbitration*, 2nd ed. (London: Butterworths, 1989), at p. 128 in support of his view: '. . . just as a claim is not necessary to the creation of a dispute, neither is it sufficient in itself'. The judge distinguished the cases of *Monmouthshire County Council* v *Costelloe and Kemple Ltd* (1994) 5 BLR 83 and *Cruden Construction Ltd* v *Commission for the New Towns* [1995] 2 Lloyd's Rep 387 from the case before him and stated that they were correct on their own facts.

4.2.3 'Dispute' in applications to stay court proceedings

Under the AAs 1950 and 1975 it was established practice for a defendant's application for a stay of proceedings and a plaintiff's application for summary judgment under RSC, ord. 14 (now CPR, Part 24) to be heard jointly. This was described by Lord Mustill in *Channel Tunnel Group Ltd* v *Balfour Beatty Construction Ltd* [1993] AC 334 at p. 356 as opposite sides of the same coin. If the court decided that there was no dispute between the parties, it would generally give summary judgment for the plaintiff. If on the contrary the court decided that there was a dispute, the matter would generally be stayed. Under s. 4 of the AA 1950 the court had a discretion whether to order a stay of proceedings or not. Under s. 1 of the AA 1975 it was mandatory for the court to order a stay of proceedings unless it was satisfied that one of the exceptions stated in s. 1 applied. One of these exceptions was that the court did not have to order a stay of proceedings if it was satisfied that there was 'not in fact any dispute' between the parties. This exception is omitted from s. 9 of the AA 1996, which has replaced s. 4 of the AA 1950 and s. 1 of the AA 1975. Prior to the AA 1996 the court in considering whether it was satisfied that there was 'not in fact any dispute between the parties' for the purposes of s. 1 of the AA 1975 held that indisputable claims should be dealt with by way of summary judgment and were not 'disputes' within the context of an arbitration agreement which should be referred to arbitration: (*Nova (Jersey) Knit Ltd* v *Kammgarn Spinnerei Gmbh* [1977] 1 WLR 713 (CA); *Ellis Mechanical Services Ltd* v *Wates Construction Ltd* [1978] 1 Lloyd's Rep 33. In contrast the majority of the Court of Appeal (Hirst LJ dissenting) held in *Halki Shipping Corporation* v *Sopex Oils Ltd* [1998] 1 WLR 726 that indisputable claims are 'disputes' within the context of an arbitration agreement and should be referred to arbitration. This decision was based on the following points:

(a)   The words 'not in fact any dispute' in s. 1 of the AA 1975 had a different meaning to the general meaning of the word 'dispute'.

(b)   The policy reason for the court's decision in the pre AA 1996 cases no longer applied.

(c)   Parliament in enacting s. 9(4) of the AA 1996 without the s. 1 of the AA 1975 qualification intended to stop the practice of indisputable claims being dealt with by way of summary judgment.

Swinton Thomas LJ made a distinction between the phrase 'any dispute' in its general context of an arbitration agreement, which has a broad meaning, and the phrase 'not in fact any dispute' as contained in s. 1 of the AA 1975, which has a restricted meaning. The grounds for imposing a stay of legal proceedings in s. 1 of the AA 1975 derived from s. 1 of the Arbitration Clauses (Protocol) Act 1924 as amended by s. 8 of the Arbitration (Foreign Awards) Act 1930. The distinction between the two phrases comes from Saville J's *obiter dicta* statement in *Hayter* v *Nelson* [1990] 2 Lloyd's Rep 265 at p. 270 in which he considered s. 8 of the Arbitration (Foreign Awards) Act 1930. Henry LJ in *Halki Shipping Corporation* v *Sopex Oils Ltd*, at p. 748, agreed with the conclusion of Saville J:

> . . . in the 1930 amendment requiring the court to refuse a stay where satisfied that 'there is not in fact any dispute between the parties with regard to the matter agreed to be referred', the word 'dispute' had to be given a different (i.e. more restricted) meaning from the word used in ordinary arbitration clauses: it must be read as meaning 'there is not in fact anything disputable'.

Swinton Thomas LJ stated in *Halki Shipping Corporation* v *Sopex Oils Ltd* that the distinction between the two phrases 'is of central importance in understanding what underlies the cases that preceded the 1996 Act' and that the historical reason for the decisions in past cases was to a large extent a matter of policy to ensure a speedy remedy by way of summary judgment. It was considered that it would cause unnecessary delay to claimants to refer the matter to arbitration. Since the enactment of the AA 1996, which has given the arbitral tribunal powers to conduct the arbitration without unnecessary delay, the attitude of the court is to allow the matter to be dealt with by the tribunal chosen by the parties. Henry LJ, concurring with Swinton Thomas LJ, said, at p. 750:

> I take s. 1 in general and s. 1(b) [of the AA 1996] in particular as emphasising the importance of the fact that the parties have chosen an alternative form of dispute resolution, namely arbitration, and should not be limited in that preference unless 'such safeguards . . . are necessary in the public interest'.

In considering parliament's intention for omitting the s. 1 of the AA 1975 qualification from s. 9(4) of the AA 1996 the Court of Appeal referred to para. 55 of the DAC report of February 1996 on the Arbitration Bill, which stated that:

> The Arbitration Act 1975 contained a further ground for refusing a stay, namely where the court was satisfied that 'there was not in fact any dispute between the parties with regard to the matter agreed to be referred.' These words do not appear in the New York Convention and in our view are confusing and unnecessary, for the reasons given in *Hayter* v *Nelson* [1990] 2 Lloyd's Rep 265.

Henry LJ in *Halki Shipping Corporation* v *Sopex Oils Ltd* considered what the DAC meant by 'unnecessary' and agreed with Clarke J, who, in the same case at first instance ([1997] 1 WLR 1268), had said:

> It seems to me that, when the DAC report said that the words were unnecessary, it must have meant that there was no need for the court to have jurisdiction since, as Saville J said in the third of the three general points referred to above, courts should not be doing what the parties have agreed should be done by the chosen tribunal and, as his first point made clear, arbitrators have ample powers to proceed without delay, as for example by making interim awards.

The decision in *Halki Shipping Corporation* v *Sopex Oils Ltd* will in practice stop cross-applications for summary judgment in applications for stay of legal proceedings under s. 9(4) of the AA 1996 unless the arbitration agreement is null and void, inoperative or incapable of being performed. The current trend, which endorses the spirit of the AA 1996, appears to be that if parties have made an arbitration agreement to settle disputes then the word 'dispute' should be construed widely so that the matter can be referred to arbitration. This attitude can be seen in the Court of Appeal decision of *Davies Middleton and Davies Ltd* v *Toyo Engineering Corporation* (1997) 85 BLR 59 and the first-instance decision of *Al-Naimi* v *Islamic Press Agency* [1998] CILL 1443.

In *Davies Middleton and Davies Ltd* v *Toyo Engineering Corporation* a dispute arose, in the final account stages of the contract for the installation of pipework, about the value of the work which had been undertaken by Davies Middleton and Davies. The parties in a letter headed 'Procedure to settle final account' and signed by both of them agreed that Toyo would make certain payments to Davies Middleton and Davies as a gesture of goodwill pending the final resolution of the position and that each party should appoint an expert to resolve the dispute in respect of the remaining sums. Toyo never paid the sums agreed in its undertaking. A further dispute arose over the matters that the experts were to address. Toyo removed its expert and made an application to stay legal proceedings under s. 9 of the AA 1996. Davies Middleton and Davies made an application for summary judgment or an interim payment in the alternative. At the hearing for the application for a stay of legal proceedings Davies Middleton and Davies argued that their contracts with Toyo did not include an arbitration agreement. Judge Thornton agreed that Toyo should be permitted to submit additional evidence on this issue but that the letter headed 'Procedure to settle final account' would not be subject to the arbitration clause in the original contract in any event. Davies Middleton and Davies's application for summary judgment was adjourned. Toyo appealed. The Court of Appeal found in Toyo's favour. The Court of Appeal held that the letter headed 'Procedure to settle final account' did not impose a separate dispute resolution and remitted back to the judge the question whether an arbitration agreement was incorporated in the original contracts. The Court of Appeal further held that if the original contracts did incorporate an arbitration agreement then the refusal to comply with the expert's decision was a dispute which should be referred to arbitration and the legal proceedings would be stayed. It appears from Phillips LJ's judgment that although Toyo had already agreed to pay certain sums to Davies Middleton and Davies the fact that these sums had not been paid meant that this was also a dispute, which should be referred to arbitration. Phillips LJ stated, at p. 76:

> If these sums remain unpaid they should, subject to any defence of which I am unaware, be susceptible to relatively speedy recovery, whether by court or arbitration proceedings, dependent upon the manner in which Judge Thornton resolves the issue that is being remitted to him. In my judgment the approach in *Halki Shipping Corporation* v *Sopex Oils Ltd* [1997] 1 WLR 1268 applies as much to these sums as it would have applied to the final account.

The facts of *Al-Naimi* v *Islamic Press Agency* [1998] CILL 1443 were that Al-Naimi was a builder who contracted with Islamic Press Agency, under a JCT Minor Works Contract, to do certain alterations to a property in East Burnham. The JCT Minor Works Contract contained an arbitration clause. Conversations subsequently took place about the extent of the works that would be required. A dispute arose between the parties. Al-Naimi claimed that the conversations with the Islamic Press Agency created a second contract, 'the oral contract'. Al-Naimi claimed that there were therefore two contracts and only one of them had an arbitration agreement. The Islamic Press Agency alleged that all the works were covered by the JCT Minor Works Contract. Judge Bowsher QC held that: 'To be entitled to a stay, the defendant must show that there is an arbitration agreement and that there is a relevant dispute concerning that arbitration agreement: that dispute may be a dispute whether the arbitration agreement is relevant to the cause of action'. He further held that:

> I am satisfied on the evidence before me there are genuine disputes concerning the construction of the contract of 12 July 1996 and other matters related to that agreement. In using the words, 'genuine disputes', I bear in mind the decision of the Court of Appeal in *Halki Shipping Corporation* v *Sopex Oils Ltd* [1998] 1 WLR 726.

The legal proceedings were stayed in favour of arbitration with a direction to the arbitral tribunal that the first matter was to construe the original agreement. The judge said that if the arbitral tribunal held that the arbitration agreement did not cover the dispute then the stay could be lifted.

4.2.4 Form of wording

The arbitration agreement gives the arbitral tribunal the jurisdiction to conduct the arbitration. The form of wording within the arbitration agreement is crucial in determining the issues that can be referred to arbitration. As stated previously a dispute or difference is required if there is to be an arbitration. However, the wording of the arbitration agreement may restrict or widen the issues which are caught by the arbitration agreement. The arbitration agreement may refer to 'disputes', 'differences' or 'claims'. In determining whether a matter falls within the arbitration agreement the courts have had to analyse the meaning of these words. The current approach is to give these words their natural meaning. These words are given a wide interpretation but they must be interpreted within the context of the subject matter of the arbitration agreement. As stated previously the word 'difference' is included within the definition of 'dispute': s. 82(1) of the AA 1996. However, the word 'claim' is different from a difference or dispute. As stated by Judge Bowsher QC in *Secretary of State for Foreign and Commonwealth Affairs* v *Percy International & Kier International* (1998 judgment — ORB No. 635) there need not be a claim for a dispute to arise, nor does the existence of a claim mean that there is a dispute. The undertaking given by Toyo to pay the sum owed in *Davies Middleton and Davies Ltd* v *Toyo Engineering Corporation* (1997) 85 BLR 59 would result in a claim being made if Toyo breached the undertaking. If Toyo failed to make payment on the undertaking then there might not be a dispute or difference between the parties as Toyo, by their undertaking, have accepted that the sum is due. This gives rise to a possible distinction between undisputed and indisputable claims.

Where the words 'in connection with' and 'in relation to' appear within an arbitration clause they are generally given a broad interpretation if the context of the contract allows. For example, in *A & B* v *C & D* [1982] 1 Lloyd's Rep 166, the Court of Appeal held that the words 'in connection with the contract' covered disputes arising from a second contract which related to the original contract which contained the arbitration clause. In *Ashville Investments Ltd* v *Elmer Contractors Ltd* [1989] QB 488 the Court of Appeal held that these words were wide enough to cover a claim for the rectification of a contract and a claim for damages against a party which had induced the other party to enter into the contract by an innocent or negligent misrepresentation. These claims could therefore be referred to arbitration. At first instance Sir Neil Lawson stated:

> I have also a strong feeling that the climate has grown wider in relation to arbitration during the last 45 years. This is demonstrated by the changes in the statute law and by the trend of modern cases concerning arbitration. I am therefore confident that now it is right to adopt a broad and liberal approach to the construction of submission clauses and, where the dispute is about what should properly be paid to a building contractor by the building owners in respect of work which has been fully completed and carried out within an acknowledged contractual situation and not otherwise, to hold that such a dispute is not in connection with the contract because the parties were not *ad idem* as to what the contract in every respect actually provided for would be too narrow and legalistic an approach.

This broad interpretation, although not endorsed by the Court of Appeal at that time, subsequently found favour with the courts: *Sudbrook Trading Estate Ltd* v

Eggleton [1983] 1 AC 444; *Queensland Electricity Generating Board* v *New Hope Collieries Pty Ltd* [1989] 1 Lloyd's Rep 205.

The words 'arising out of' are generally given a very broad interpretation. Prior to the AA 1996 it was held that this form of wording would cover almost every dispute except a dispute about whether there was ever a contract in existence: per Pilcher J in *H.E. Daniels Ltd* v *Carmel Exporters and Importers Ltd* [1953] 2 QB 242. A dispute relating to the existence of the contract could now be covered by this form of wording, by reason of s. 7 of the AA 1996, if the arbitration agreement is valid. The reason for this is that the arbitration agreement and the underlying contract are treated as being separate and questions relating to the validity of the underlying contract fall within the arbitral tribunal's jurisdiction. As Swinton Thomas LJ stated in *Halki Shipping Corporation* v *Sopex Oils Ltd* [1998] 1 WLR 762, '. . . the court no longer has to consider whether there is in fact any dispute between the parties but only where there is a dispute within the arbitration clause of the agreement'. What is not covered by this form of wording is a dispute relating to whether the proper form of notice has been given in an appeal from an award of other arbitral tribunals since the dispute does not arise out of the contract but the award itself: *Getreide-Import GmbH* v *Contimar SA Compania Industrial Comercial y Maritima* [1953] 1 WLR 207.

4.2.5 Future disputes

The arbitral tribunal has the jurisdiction to hear any dispute which has arisen between the parties up until the arbitration commences: *Cathiship SA* v *Allanasons Ltd* [1998] 3 All ER 714 and *Alfred McAlpine Construction Ltd* v *RMG Electrical* [1998] ADRLJ 53. In order for the arbitral tribunal to have the jurisdiction to hear matters relating to disputes which have arisen after the arbitration has started, the parties would have to extend the jurisdiction by agreement. Institutional rules which the parties may have adopted may deal expressly with this situation. In some circumstances the arbitral tribunal may consider a future dispute which flows from the issues in dispute at the time of its appointment: *Rederij Lalemant* v *Transportes Generales Navigacion SA* [1986] 1 Lloyd's Rep 45.

4.3 RELATIONSHIP WITH THE COURT

Section 1(c) of the AA 1996 sets out the general principle that: 'in matters governed by this Part the court should not intervene except as provided by this Part'. This general principle is derived from Article 5 of the UNCITRAL Model Law, although a slight difference in wording exists. Article 5 of the UNCITRAL Model Law states: 'In matters governed by this Law, no court shall intervene except where so provided in this Law'. In the final consultative paper on the Arbitration Bill, published in July 1995, the word 'shall' rather than 'should' was used. The amendment to the wording was made without notification to arbitration practitioners.

There has been some debate about the effect of the change from the imperative 'shall' to the permissive 'should'. In *Arbitration*, August 1996, at p. 236, Professor Michael Needham concluded that the change from the imperative to the permissive will allow the courts to intervene in matters not otherwise expressly within their ambit. Professor Needham argues that the change leaves the inherent jurisdiction of the court to review an arbitral tribunal's award intact. In contrast, however, Mr Bruce Harris argues that there is no such thing as imperative or permissive principles (*Arbitration*, February 1997, p. 76). Principles are, he suggests, just that, principles. Although the change of wording has opened up greater scope for argument, the fears expressed by Professor Needham are likely to be unfounded.

If the courts do have an inherent power to intervene in the arbitral process, that power will be limited to matters arising from an award. The courts do not possess an inherent jurisdiction over arbitral proceedings. However, this was not always thought to be the position. In *Japan Line Ltd v Aggeliki* [1980] 1 Lloyd's Rep 288 Lord Denning stated that the court has, as well as its statutory powers, an inherent jurisdiction to supervise the conduct of an arbitral tribunal, This was doubted in *Bremer Vulcan Schiffenbau und Maschinenfabrik* v *South India Shipping Corporation* [1981] AC 909 where the House of Lords held that the proposition that the High Court had a general supervisory power over the conduct of an arbitral tribunal, more extensive than that which was conferred upon it by the Arbitration Acts, would be rejected. If the courts do possess an inherent jurisdiction to intervene with matters arising from an award by reason of the permissive 'should' rather than 'shall', then such power will be limited.

4.4 EXCLUDING THE COURT'S JURISDICTION

It is misleading to talk about the AA 1996 excluding, as a general proposition, the court's jurisdiction, because not all of the court's power can be excluded. The parties are, however, free to exclude the jurisdiction of the courts in regard to specific matters. In regard to an appeal on a point of law, under s. 69(1) of the AA 1996, the parties are free to exclude the jurisdiction of the court. Such an exclusion can occur either by the agreement of the parties that there will be no appeal on a point of law arising from an award or that the parties agree that reasons need not be included within the award. The latter option is considered to be an agreement to exclude the court's jurisdiction under s. 69(1) of the AA 1996.

The AA 1996 is divided into mandatory and non-mandatory sections. The mandatory provisions are listed in sch. 1 to the Act. The mandatory sections have effect notwithstanding any agreement by the parties to the contrary (s. 4(1) of the AA 1996). The effect of this is that the parties are unable to contract out of the mandatory sections. A term of an agreement which attempts to exclude any of the mandatory sections is invalid. The parties are therefore unable to exclude the court's powers in relation to the following items:

(a) ss. 9 to 11 (stay of legal proceedings);

(b)   s. 12 (power of the court to extend agreed time limits);
(c)   s. 13 (application of Limitation Acts);
(d)   s. 24 (power of the court to remove arbitral tribunal);
(e)   s. 31 (objection to substantive jurisdiction of tribunal);
(f)   s. 32 (determination of preliminary point of jurisdiction);
(g)   s. 40 (general duty of the parties);
(h)   s. 43 (securing the attendance of a witness);
(i)   s. 56 (power to withhold an award in the case of non-payment);
(j)   s. 66 (enforcement of award);
(k)   ss. 67 and 68 (challenging the award: substantive jurisdiction and serious
irregularity), and ss. 70 and 71 (supplementary provisions; effect of order of the
court) so far as relating to those sections;
(l)   s. 72 (saving for rights of person who takes no part in proceedings); and
(m)   s. 75 (charge to secure payment of solicitor's costs).

The parties are free to exclude the non-mandatory provisions of the AA 1996 by
written agreement. Section 4(2) of the AA 1996 therefore states that:

> The other provisions of this Part ('the non-mandatory provisions') allow the
> parties to make their own arrangements by agreement but provide rules which
> apply in the absence of such agreement.

Agreements to replace the non-mandatory rules may be made expressly between
the parties, for instance, in the arbitration agreement itself. The non-mandatory
rules may also be replaced by agreeing to the application of institutional rules
(s. 4(3) of the AA 1996). Further, if the parties choose a law other than English
law such law will override the non-mandatory provisions.

4.5   STAY OF LEGAL PROCEEDINGS

Section 9 of the AA 1996 deals with the power of the court to stay legal proceedings
in favour of arbitration. It is a mandatory section and cannot be excluded by the
parties to an arbitration agreement. The court may only grant a stay in respect of
issues in dispute between the parties which are covered by the arbitration agreement.
It was held in *Ellerine Brothers (Pty) Ltd* v *Klinger* [1982] 1 WLR 1375 that issues
which arise after the legal proceedings have been commenced should not be stayed.
The trend of the court has been to stay most issues between the parties to arbitration
since the enactment of the AA 1996: *Halki Shipping Corporation* v *Sopex Oils Ltd*
[1998] 1 WLR 672; *Wealands* v *CLC Contractors Ltd* [1998] CLC 808; *Grimaldi
Compagnia di Navigazione SpA* v *Sekihyo Line Ltd* [1998] 3 All ER 943.
    Section 9(1) of the AA 1996 states:

> A party to an arbitration agreement against whom legal proceedings are brought
> (whether by way of claim or counterclaim) in respect of a matter which under

the agreement is to be referred to arbitration may (upon notice to the other parties to the proceedings) apply to the court in which the proceedings have been brought to stay the proceedings so far as they concern that matter.

The court has no power to grant an application for a stay of legal proceedings unless a party to an arbitration agreement makes an application under s. 9 of the AA 1996. The arbitration agreement must be in writing (s. 5(1) of the AA 1996) and it must be valid (s. 9(4)). The court will not stay proceedings to arbitration where the question in dispute relates to the validity of the arbitration agreement. In such a case the court will determine whether there is a valid arbitration agreement or not and if it concludes that there is a valid agreement it will only then stay the proceedings to arbitration: *Birse Construction Ltd v St David Ltd* [1999] 1 BLR 194. The party making the application under s. 9 of the AA 1996 has the onus of showing that the legal proceedings to which the application applies deal with a dispute which can be referred to arbitration under the arbitration agreement. Once the court has granted a stay of legal proceedings this does not mean that the dispute automatically becomes the subject of an arbitration, it means that the claim can now be pursued only through arbitration: *Channel Tunnel Group Ltd v Balfour Beatty Construction Ltd* [1993] AC 334. Equally if a dispute is referred to arbitration this does not amount to a justifiable reason for extending time to issue a claim outside the limitation period: *Hydro Agri Espana SA v Charles M Willie & Co. (Shipping) Ltd* [1998] All ER (d) 64 (CA). It is now clear that only a party against whom proceedings are brought can apply to stay those proceedings. Section 4(1) of the AA 1950 empowered any party to the proceedings to apply for a stay. This meant that if a party issued a writ and subsequently changed its mind then that party could apply to have the proceedings stayed. A party is defined in s. 82 of the AA 1996 as including any person claiming under or through a party to an arbitration agreement (see chapter 6.1 for a definition of this term). 'Legal proceedings' are defined in s. 82 of the AA 1996 and include 'civil proceedings in the High Court or a county court'. 'Notice' is also a defined term within s. 80 of the AA 1996 and refers to notice of the originating process as is required by the rules of court.

Section 9(2) of the AA 1996 states: 'An application may be made notwithstanding that the matter is to be referred to arbitration only after the exhaustion of other dispute resolution procedures'. This section gives effect to the common law rule that an application to stay can be made notwithstanding that there is some other form of dispute resolution procedure that must be proceeded with as a prerequisite to commencing arbitration: *Channel Tunnel Group Ltd v Balfour Beatty Construction Ltd* [1993] AC 334. Parties who wish to have their dispute finally decided by an expert or adjudicator should take note of the fact that if they do not provide a complete procedure for the determination of that dispute the matter may be thereafter referred to arbitration: *Davies Middleton and Davies Ltd v Toyo Engineering Corporation* (1997) 85 BLR 59 at p. 62.

Section 9(3) of the AA 1996 states that:

An application may not be made by a person before taking the appropriate procedural step (if any) to acknowledge the legal proceedings against him or after he has taken any step in those proceedings to answer the substantive claim.

The language used in s. 9(3) of the AA 1996 is different to that used in s. 4(1) of the AA 1950, although there is no radical change to the pre-existing law. The defendant must, under the AA 1996, acknowledge the service of the claim form but apply for the stay prior to serving a defence. Under the AA 1950 the taking of any procedural step in the legal proceedings prevented the court from ordering a stay: *Chappel* v *North* [1891] 2 QB 252; *Blue Flame Mechanical Services Ltd* v *David Lord Engineering Ltd* (1992) CILL 760. A claimant may, under the AA 1996, take a procedural step in the proceedings and still apply for a stay as long as that procedural step does not have the effect of answering the substantive claim: *Jitendra Bhailbhai Patel* v *Dilesh R. Patel* [1999]1 BLR 227. Section 9(3) of the AA 1996 therefore follows Article 8(1) of the UNCITRAL Model Law. For further cases relating to taking a step in the proceedings under the AA 1950 see chapter 2.5.

Section 9(4) of the AA 1996 provides:

> On an application under this section the court shall grant a stay unless satisfied that the arbitration agreement is null and void, inoperative, or incapable of being performed.

The court is no longer required to consider whether there is in fact any dispute which can be referred to arbitration, as was the case under s. 1(1) of the AA 1975. For a further discussion on this point see 4.2.3. An arbitration agreement will not be considered incapable of being performed if one party is impoverished: *Paczy* v *Haendler & Natermann GmbH* [1981] 1 Lloyd's Rep 302.

Section 9(5) of the AA 1996 provides:

> If the court refuses to stay the legal proceedings, any provision that an award is a condition precedent to the bringing of legal proceedings in respect of any matter is of no effect in relation to those proceedings.

This section deals with what is commonly known as a *Scott* v *Avery* clause: *Scott* v *Avery* (1856) 5 HL Cas 811. A *Scott* v *Avery* clause is one which makes arbitration proceedings a condition precedent to the bringing of legal proceedings. Section 9(5) of the AA 1996 now makes a *Scott* v *Avery* clause ineffective where a court refuses to grant a stay of litigation in favour of arbitration. This subsection does not, however, apply where there is a statutory arbitration (s. 97(c) of the AA 1996). The rationale behind this is that there is no arbitration agreement in the context of statutory arbitration and therefore the subsection is not applicable.

4.6   SECTIONS 85 TO 87 AND THE EC TREATY

The AA 1996 was brought into force with the issue, by the Secretary of State, of a statutory instrument (SI 1996/3146) under s. 109 of the AA 1996. This statutory instrument brought into force the whole of the AA 1996 from 31 January 1997 save for ss. 85 to 87. Sections 85 to 87 provide separate rules where the arbitration is of a domestic character. Section 85 defines what is meant by a domestic arbitration. Section 86 of the AA 1996 provides that where the arbitration is domestic in character then the court has a discretion to refuse to stay litigation to arbitration. Section 87 of the AA 1996 restricts the parties' rights to exclude the court's jurisdiction.

The reason for the omission of these sections was that it was considered that they might breach European law in treating nationals of England and Wales and Northern Ireland differently from other European nationals. The DAC, in their report of February 1996 at paras 317 to 331, took the view that these sections were not beneficial to the arbitral process and although they included them in the AA 1996 they strongly criticised their inclusion.

The view that ss. 85 to 87 of the AA 1996 might in fact breach European Community law was not arrived at until the second informal consultative process of the draft Arbitration Bill. Certainly, no one had considered that the previous legislation could be contrary to the United Kingdom's Treaty obligations. Article 6 of the Treaty of Rome, however, provides that:

> Within the scope of application of this Treaty, and without prejudice to any special provisions contained therein, any discrimination on the grounds of nationality shall be prohibited.

In *Collins* v *Imtrat Handelgesellschaft mbH* (cases C-92 and 326/92) [1993] ECR I-5145 Advocate General Jacobs described this principle as 'the single most important principle in Community law. It is the leitmotiv of the EEC Treaty.' The question whether there was a conflict between Community law and English domestic law was addressed by the Court of Appeal in *Philip Alexander Securities and Futures Ltd* v *Bamberger* (1996) 22 YB Com Arb 872. The Court of Appeal held that the exclusion of non-domestic arbitration clauses from the protection of the Consumer Arbitration Agreements Act 1988 was a restriction on the freedom to provide services to nationals of other member States of the European Community. It therefore follows that s. 4 of the AA 1950 (and s. 86 of the AA 1996) would also probably contravene Articles 6 and 59 of the EC Treaty and possibly also Article 220.

4.7 REFERENCE OF INTERPLEADER ISSUES TO ARBITRATION

Section 10(1) of the AA 1996 states:

> Where in legal proceedings relief by way of interpleader is granted and any issue between the claimants is one in respect of which there is an arbitration agreement between them, the court granting the relief shall direct that the issue be determined in accordance with the agreement unless the circumstances are

such that proceedings brought by a claimant in respect of the matter would not be stayed.

Section 10 is one of the mandatory provisions of the AA 1996. No definition is provided within the AA 1996 of what are interpleader proceedings. Interpleader proceedings occur where a person who holds money or goods belonging to another is sued by two or more persons for the return of the money or the goods. If the person has no interest in the money or goods, that person can apply to the court for relief by way of interpleader. An interpleader hearing occurs where the rival claimants to the money or goods are made to interplead between themselves as to the ownership of the property. An example of where interpleader proceedings may occur is when the employer in a building contract has taken possession of the contractor's equipment for completion of the works under the provisions of the contract (for example, clause 63 of FIDIC's Red Book). At the end of the works the employer receives a claim from the contractor for the return of the equipment and another claim from a third party who claims ownership of the equipment. The employer may then apply to the court for relief by way of interpleader. The rights of the rival claimants to the equipment are then determined.

If there is no arbitration agreement between the rival claimants, the court will determine who has ownership of the goods or money. If, in the above example, the rival claimant was a subcontractor, and an arbitration agreement existed between the contractor and subcontractor, then the court, on an application to stay the legal proceedings, would be bound to refer the dispute about ownership of the equipment to arbitration, unless the exceptions in s. 9(4) of the AA 1996 applied.

The last sentence of s. 10(1) of the AA 1996 implies that there are circumstances where the court would not refer the dispute to arbitration. This section was drafted when it was anticipated that s. 86 of the AA 1996 would also be enacted. Section 86 of the AA 1996 would have given the court a discretion not to refer the matter to arbitration where the dispute was domestic in character as defined by s. 85. Reference should now be made to s. 9 of the AA 1996 for the circumstances in which the courts are permitted to refuse to stay a matter in favour of arbitration. There is therefore almost no circumstance in which the court will refuse to grant a stay in favour of arbitration where there is a valid arbitration clause between the rival claimants.

Section 10(2) of the AA 1996 deals with the effect of a *Scott* v *Avery* clause in the arbitration agreement. A *Scott* v *Avery* clause is one which makes arbitration proceedings a condition precedent to the bringing of legal proceedings. Section 10(2) now makes a *Scott* v *Avery* clause ineffective where a court refuses to grant a stay of interpleader proceedings.

4.8   EXTENSION OF TIME LIMITS

Section 12(1) of the AA 1996 states that:

> Where an arbitration agreement to refer future disputes to arbitration provides that a claim shall be barred, or the claimant's right extinguished, unless the claimant takes within a time fixed by the agreement some step—

(a)   to begin arbitral proceedings, or

(b)   to begin other dispute resolution procedures which must be exhausted before arbitral proceedings can be begun,

the court may by order extend the time for taking that step.

Section 12 of the AA 1996 is a mandatory provision. The power to extend time limits applies to those time limits that are set out in contracts, not to those set out in statutes. Section 12(1) applies only to the starting of the arbitral proceedings or other dispute resolution procedures. It should be read alongside s. 14 of the Act, which deals with the commencement of proceedings. Section 12(1) of the AA 1996 is, however, not applicable to provisions within the contract that have the effect of making decisions of third parties, such as architects or certifiers, final and conclusive rather than simply barring the claim: *Crown Estates Commissioners* v *John Mowlem* (1994) 70 BLR 1. In that case Crown Estates employed Mowlem as the building contractor for a retail outlet at Kensington Barracks. On 2 December 1992 the architect issued the final certificate under the JCT 80 form of contract. Clause 30.9.1.1 of the JCT 80 form of contract provided that notice of arbitration should be given within 28 days of the issue of the final certificate, otherwise the final certificate would be conclusive evidence that the quality and standard of works was in accordance with the contract. It was not until April 1993 that the Crown Estates gave notice of arbitration which was well outside the 28 days provided for under the contract. The Crown Estates made an application for an extension of the 28 day period to begin the arbitration under section 27 of the Arbitration Act 1950 (the equivalent to s. 12 of the AA 1996).

At first instance Judge Fox-Andrews gave an extension of the 28 day period and found that the certificate was conclusive only to the quality of standards expressly left to the satisfaction of the architect. Mowlem appealed the decision. The Court of Appeal held that there was no power under section 27 of the AA 1950 to extend the 28 day period and that the final certificate was conclusive as to the quality of all materials and standards of workmanship. This would be equally applicable to an application made under s. 12 of the AA 1996. Even if an extension of time could be given to commence the arbitration proceedings, the fact remains that the certificate had become conclusive as to the quality and standards. The commencing of an arbitration would not have an effect on the certificate and there would therefore be no cause of action to pursue. In addition to the court's power in s. 12(1) of the AA 1996 to extend the time for commencing the arbitration, the court also has a general power to extend the time limits agreed by the parties relating to the arbitral proceedings at any time during the course of the arbitration proceedings, under s. 79 of the AA 1996. The court is also given a specific power under s. 50 of the AA 1996 to extend the time limit agreed by the parties for making the award.

In *Vosnoc Ltd* v *Trans Global Projects Ltd* [1998] 1 WLR 101 Judge Jack QC was required to consider what step was required to commence an arbitration. Judge Jack said, at p. 110:

English law has taken the approach that something more must be done than to request that the matter be referred to arbitration. A step must be taken towards getting the arbitration under way, a step towards the appointment of the tribunal.

Judge Jack considered *Nea Agrex SA* v *Baltic Shipping Co. Ltd* [1976] QB 933 and Lord Denning MR's statement that:

> In such a case the arbitration is deemed to commence when the one party, expressly or by implication, requires the other party to appoint his arbitrator. If he simply says: 'I require the difference to be submitted to arbitration in accordance with our agreement' that is sufficient to commence the arbitration: because it is by implication a request to the other to appoint his arbitrator.

Judge Jack also considered *Surrendra Overseas Ltd* v *Sri Lanka* [1977] 1 Lloyd's Rep 653, in which it was held that words implying that an arbitration would commence at some time in the future were insufficient to commence the arbitration. Judge Jack considered that the question of what was required to start an arbitration was 'undecided' and therefore concluded that he could 'apply the law as he found it to be'. Judge Jack held that what was required before an arbitration could be treated as having been commenced was for one party to serve on the other a notice which not only required the other party to arbitrate, but which also required it to appoint an arbitrator. Judge Jack held that a notice, which did no more than state that the dispute was referred to arbitration, was insufficient to commence arbitral proceedings because it did not by implication request the recipient to appoint an arbitrator.

This approach was not followed in *Charles M Willie & Co. (Shipping) Ltd* v *Ocean Laser Shipping Ltd* [1999] 1 Lloyd's Rep 225 or *Allianz Versicherungs AG* v *Fortuna Co. Ltd* [1999] 2 All ER 625. In *Allianz* Judge Moore-Bick held that the case of *Nea Agrex SA* v *Baltic Shipping Co. Ltd* [1976] 2 Lloyd's Rep 47 was binding authority. Judge Moore-Bick held that it was widely accepted that a notice of arbitration, though technically incorrect under the Limitation Act 1980, s. 27(3), was sufficient to commence arbitration proceedings if it made clear, by whatever language, that the arbitration agreement was being invoked and required the other party to take steps towards the constitution of the arbitral tribunal.

Section 12(2) of the AA 1996 provides that:

> Any party to the arbitration agreement may apply for such an order (upon notice to the other parties), but only after a claim has arisen and after exhausting any available arbitral process for obtaining an extension of time.

An application to the court for an extension of time must therefore be given on 'notice' (which is defined in s. 80 of the AA 1996). The applicant must also have exhausted any possible application for an extension of time under the arbitral process: see *Grimaldi Compagnia di Navigazione SpA* v *Sekihyo Line Ltd* [1998] 3 All ER 943. An application cannot be made until after a claim has arisen. A person cannot therefore apply for an extension of time as a protective measure where there is only a possibility of a claim arising.

Section 12(3) of the AA 1996 provides two grounds when the court shall make an order extending the time for beginning the arbitration proceedings:

> The court shall make an order only if satisfied—
> (a) that the circumstances are such as were outside the reasonable contemplation of the parties when they agreed the provision in question, and that it would be just to extend the time, or
> (b) that the conduct of one party makes it unjust to hold the other party to the strict terms of the provision in question.

These conditions are different from the condition of undue hardship in s. 27 of the AA 1950 and the old case law no longer applies. In *Harbour and General Works Ltd v Environment Agency* [1999] 1 BLR 143, Coleman J stated that 'to hold otherwise would be to create out of section 12 something akin to the benevolent regime of section 27 which the 1996 Act set out to abolish'. In *Vosnoc Ltd v Trans Global Projects Ltd* [1998] 1 WLR 101 Judge Jack held that s. 12(3)(b) of the AA 1996 was not applicable on the facts but s. 12(3)(a) was applicable and provided a two-stage test. The first stage is whether the circumstances before the court were outside the parties' contemplation. In *Vosnoc Ltd v Trans Global Projects Ltd* the learned judge expressed the opinion that, although not present in the instant case, the following matters would also be relevant on the question whether circumstances were outside the contemplation of the parties:

(a) whether the damage was latent;

(b) whether the loss was originally thought to be trivial but subsequently turned out to be substantial; and

(c) whether there was illness on the part of the person handling the claim for the claimant.

Judge Jack was of the view there is no limit to the grounds which the court is entitled to consider. Section 12(3)(a) is expressed to come into operation only if the circumstances were outside the reasonable contemplation of the parties when they agreed the provision in question: *Cathiship SA v Allanasons Ltd* [1998] 3 All ER 714. The approach adopted by Judge Jack in *Vosnoc Ltd v Trans Global Projects Ltd* [1998] 1 WLR 101 was, however, criticised by Coleman J in *Harbour and General Works Ltd v Environment Agency* [1999] 1 BLR 143. Coleman J stated that he did not think that a request for arbitration that was made just after the limitation period had expired was 'relevant to the question whether the circumstances were outside the parties' mutual contemplation'. Judge Jack took the view that if one party obstructed or misled another party then this would be a circumstance outside the reasonable contemplation of the parties. In *Cathiship SA v Allanasons Ltd (The Catherine Helen)* [1998] 3 All ER 714, 729 Geoffrey Brice

QC held that mere silence or the failure to alert the claimant to the need to comply with a time bar cannot in itself render the barring of a claim unjust. Section 12(3) of the AA 1996 therefore makes changes to the pre-existing law. Factors that were considered relevant in *Graham H. Davis (UK) Ltd* v *Marc Rich and Co. Ltd* [1985] 2 Lloyd's Rep 423, such as the length of the delay and the amount at stake, appear to be excluded from the court's consideration under s. 12(3) of the AA 1996. In *Fox and Widley* v *Guram* [1998] 1 EGLR 91 Clarke J, in examining s. 12(3)(a) and (b) of the AA 1996, held that the fact that one party might obtain a windfall was not in itself a ground for extending time under s. 12 of the AA 1996. However, in *Cathiship SA* v *Allanasons Ltd* [1998] 3 All ER 714 it was held that the 'circumstances', as referred to in s. 12(3)(a) of the AA 1996, were all those placed before the court, and the court had to consider those circumstances as a whole and focus on those that appeared particularly relevant.

The second stage of s. 12(3)(a) identified by Judge Jack in *Vosnoc Ltd* v *Trans Global Projects Ltd* [1998] 1 WLR 101 is whether it would be just to extend the time for commencement. The learned judge found that the following three factors were relevant to his consideration on this point:

(a)   That the mistake made by Vosnoc was based on their ignorance of what was required in English law to commence an arbitration and that there was no authority on this point.

(b)   That Vosnoc had clearly shown their intention to give notice of arbitration.

(c)   That the claim was substantial.

It may be that future claimants will not be able to rely on ignorance of what is required to commence an arbitration, as the point has now been settled. In *Metalfer Corporation* v *Pan Ocean Shipping Co.* [1997] CLC 1574 the High Court refused to grant an extension of time under s. 12 of the AA 1996. Further, Colman J in *Harbour and General Works Ltd* v *Environment Agency* [1999] 1 BLR 143, 151 doubted whether this ground should have been considered when assessing whether to extend time. His Lordship stated, 'On whether the conclusion arrived by Judge Jack cold be justified on the basis of the perceived uncertainty of the law as to when an arbitration was commenced I entertain very considerable doubt but I express no concluded view'.

In *Fox and Widley* v *Guram* [1998] 1 EGLR 91 Clarke J was asked to extend the time in which a tenant could serve a counter-notice in respect of a rent-review clause. A rent-review notice had been served on the tenant by the landlord whereby the landlord sought to increase the rent on the premises from £4,750 per annum to £14,000 per annum. Evidence was adduced that the actual rent should be £3,500 per annum. Clarke J held that it was not unjust to hold the tenant to the strict terms of the agreement where there had only been a simple overstatement of rent by the landlord.

Section 12(4) of the AA 1996 provides that where the court makes an order extending time it may do so for such period and on such terms as it thinks fit. This subsection also makes clear that the power of the court to extend the time for the commencement of the arbitration can be exercised whether or not the time limit agreed by the parties has expired. Section 12(5) makes clear that nothing in s. 12 affects the operation of the Limitation Acts. Section 12(6) of the AA 1996 provides that leave of the court is required for an appeal from a decision of the court under s. 12.

In *Grimaldi Compagnia di Navigazione SpA* v *Sekihyo Line Ltd* [1998] 3 All ER 943 an application for declaratory relief and alternatively for an extension of time under s. 12 of the AA 1996 was stayed to arbitration by Mance J. Grimaldi sought certain declarations from the court which, if granted, would mean that the Hague Rules would not bar them from commencing arbitration proceedings against Sekihyo for loss or damage. Grimaldi also applied, as an alternative to the declarations, for an order under s. 12(3)(a) to extend the time limit to begin arbitration proceedings. Sekihyo issued a cross-application for an order under s. 9 to stay the proceedings. Mance J said, at pp. 950–1, that the issues on which Grimaldi sought declaratory relief were:

> all matters which the parties must be taken to have assumed would normally be investigated before arbitrators rather than the court. It is difficult to see why, unless both parties are content, they should suddenly become matters for the court to determine, merely because the claimant may, if he is wrong on them, need to seek the court's exercise of discretion under s. 27 [of the AA 1950] or now s. 12 [of the AA 1996].

His lordship held that an interrelationship existed between ss. 9 and 12 of the AA 1996 whereby the arbitral tribunal could initially decide whether an extension of time should be granted. If the arbitral tribunal refused to grant the extension of time then an application could thereafter be made to the court. Mance J stated that where the parties agreed that the application for an extension of time under s. 12 of the AA 1996 should be made to the court then the matter should and could be determined by the court. However, where no agreement was made then the court would stay the application for an extension of time if one of the parties insisted that the matter be determined by the arbitral tribunal.

4.9 APPLICATION OF LIMITATION ACTS

Section 13(1) of the AA 1996 states: 'The Limitation Acts apply to arbitral proceedings as they apply to legal proceedings'. In relation to England and Wales, 'the Limitation Acts' means the Limitation Act 1980, the Foreign Limitation Periods Act 1984, and any other Act that sets out limitation periods for commencing an action, such as the Carriage of Goods by Sea Act 1971 and the Consumer Protection Act 1987. If there is no contractual time bar provision within the arbitration agreement then the time limits in which the arbitration proceedings may be commenced will be governed by the Limitation Acts.

There are two important points to note in regard to the limitation periods. First, time ceases to run in regard to the limitation periods from the time when the parties to an arbitration have either agreed when the arbitral proceedings are to be regarded as commenced (s. 14(1) of the AA 1996), or, in the absence of such an agreement, when a valid notice to commence arbitration proceedings has been served (see s. 14(2) to (5) of the AA 1996). There are conflicting authorities as to whether the default provisions in s. 14(2) to (5) are exhaustive. In *Vosnoc Ltd* v *Trans Global Projects Ltd* [1998] 1 WLR 101 Judge Jack held that an arbitration could only be commenced as stated in s. 14 of the AA 1996. However, the court took a broader view in *Allianz Versicherungs AG* v *Fortuna Co. Ltd* [1999] 2 All ER 625; *Charles M Willie & Co. (Shipping) Ltd* v *Ocean Laser Shipping Ltd* [1999] Lloyd's Rep 225; and *West of England Ship Owners Mutual Protection and Indemnity Association (Luxembourg) Ltd* v *Hellenic Industrial Development Bank SA* (1998 unreported). These cases are discussed further at 4.10. If the parties have agreed a procedure for commencing the arbitration then that procedure must be carried out for the arbitration to have validly commenced. Secondly, if the limitation period has run out before the arbitration has validly commenced then this will not prevent an arbitration notice being served. However, unless the claimant can argue that the case is one in which an extension of the period of time should be granted, then the respondent will have an incontestable defence to the claim. Section 12(1) of the AA 1996 only provides the court with the power to extend the time limit for commencing an arbitration, which has been agreed by the parties. There is no provision within s. 12 of the AA 1996 to extend the periods of time provided by the Limitation Acts.

The limitation periods for actions founded in simple contract or in tort are six years from the date when the cause of action arose in contract (s. 5 of the Limitation Act 1980) and six years from the date when the damage occurred in tort (s. 2 of the Limitation Act 1980). In contract the cause of action will arise when the contractual duty is breached. In tort damage may occur at a date considerably later than when there was a breach of duty. It may therefore be beneficial to a defendant if a claim is brought in tort rather than contract.

An exception to the six-year limitation period in contractual disputes occurs where a contract between the parties is in a deed. In such cases the limitation period in respect of a claim arising out of the contract will be 12 years, unless a shorter limitation period is specifically referred to in the contract (s. 8 of the Limitation Act 1980). In a claim for a contribution by a defendant against another party, in separate proceedings to those which established the defendant's liability, the limitation period is two years from: (a) the date on which the judgment against the defendant was given or the arbitration award made; or (b) the earliest date on which the amount of compensation was agreed (s. 10 of the Limitation Act 1980). In an action which involves an element of personal injury the limitation period is three years. This date runs from the date of breach or the date of knowledge, whichever is the later (s. 11 of the Limitation Act 1980).

The Foreign Limitation Periods Act 1984 is applicable where the arbitral tribunal will have to apply foreign law to the contract. This will occur where the seat of the arbitration is England but the contract is subject to a different law. In such a case the limitation period is that provided for under the foreign law. English law will, however, be the *lex arbitri* (the law of the arbitration). The Foreign Limitation Periods Act 1984 does create exceptions to the above general rule where undue hardship would be involved or where the application of the rule would be contrary to public policy.

Section 13(2) of the AA 1996 provides for a further exception to the general rules regarding limitation periods. Where an award or part of an award is set aside or declared to be of no effect then the court may order that the period of time, between the commencement of the arbitration and the order setting aside the award, shall be excluded from any reckoning of time in respect to limitation. This exception prevents any undue hardship for a party where the award has been set aside.

Section 13(3) of the AA 1996 relates to *Scott* v *Avery* clauses. Where a *Scott* v *Avery* clause has been included in the contract then a party may seek to argue that the limitation period should not run until there is a valid award. The effect of s. 13(3) is to make such an argument ineffective. Time will be deemed to have started to run when the cause of action arose.

In *International Bulk Shipping and Services Ltd* v *Minerals and Metals Trading Corporation* [1996] 1 All ER 1017 the Court of Appeal had to consider when the limitation period for the enforcement of an arbitral award began. The Court of Appeal held that time ran from when the claimant was entitled to enforce the award as this was when the claimant's cause of action arose.

4.10 COMMENCEMENT OF PROCEEDINGS

Section 14 of the AA 1996 deals with the commencement of arbitral proceedings. Section 14(1) of the AA 1996 states that: 'The parties are free to agree when the arbitral proceedings are to be regarded as commenced for the purposes of this Part and for the purposes of the Limitation Acts'. In the absence of such an agreement s. 14(2) provides that s. 14(3), (4) and (5) apply. Section 14 of the AA 1996 is not a mandatory provision and the election by the parties of a law other than English law or the adoption of procedural rules may have an effect on exactly when an arbitration is considered to have been commenced. Under the UNCITRAL Model Law, for instance, the mere reference to arbitration in the arbitration notice is sufficient to commence proceedings. In contrast, under s. 14 of the AA 1996, the default provisions provide that in order to stop time running the arbitration notice must require a step to be taken which is more than just the requirement that the arbitration commences.

Any agreement between the parties under s. 14(1) of the AA 1996 as to when the arbitral proceedings are to be regarded as being commenced must be in writing (s. 5(1) of the AA 1996). The effect of this subsection could provide the parties with the ability to opt out of the AA 1996 by agreeing that the arbitration commenced before the AA 1996 came into force. However, an anomalous position would arise in that s. 14(1) of the AA 1996, which permits the parties to agree a date when the arbitral proceedings are commenced, would not be in force. It is doubted whether the courts would permit such a circular argument to succeed.

Section 14(3) of the AA 1996 provides that:

> Where the arbitrator is named or designated in the arbitration agreement, arbitral proceedings are commenced in respect of a matter when one party serves on the other party or parties a notice in writing requiring him or them to submit that matter to the person so named or designated.

An arbitration agreement is defined in ss. 6(1) and 6(2) of the AA 1996 (see chapter 5.1). By s. 76(6) 'notice' includes 'any form of communication in writing', which includes a communication recorded by any means' (s. 5(6)). Section 14(3) also refers to 'a matter' being referred to arbitration. 'Matter' is a term which is wider than 'dispute' and will also include 'claims'.

In *Vosnoc Ltd* v *Trans Global Projects Ltd* [1998] 1 WLR 101 Judge Jack QC considered the conflicting cases of *Nea Agrex SA* v *Baltic Shipping Co. Ltd.* [1976] QB 933 and *Surrendra Overseas Ltd* v *Sri Lanka* [1977] 1 WLR 565 on when an arbitration is commenced. The learned judge considered that the question of what was required to start an arbitration was 'undecided' and therefore concluded that he could 'apply the law as he found it to be'. He held that a notice that did no more than state that a dispute was referred to arbitration in accordance with an agreement was insufficient to commence the arbitration under s. 34(3)(a) of the Limitation Act 1980, now superseded by s. 14 of the Arbitration Act 1996. Such a notice did not carry with it by implication a request that the recipient appoint an arbitral tribunal. This approach was not followed in *West of England Ship Owners Mutual Protection and Indemnity Association (Luxembourg) Ltd* v *Hellenic Industrial Development Bank SA* (1998 unreported). Clarke J held in this case that it was conceivable that an arbitration could be started without strict adherence to the provisions in what is now s. 14 need not apply to commence an arbitration. In *Allianz Versicherungs AG* v *Fortuna Co. Ltd* [1999] 2 All ER 625 it was held that a notice of arbitration, which failed to comply with the Limitation Acts because of a technicality, was sufficient to commence arbitration proceedings if it made clear that the arbitration agreement was being invoked and required the other party to take steps towards appointing the arbitral tribunal. Further, Rix J held in *Charles M Willie & Co. (Shipping) Ltd* v *Ocean Laser Shipping Ltd* [1999] 1 Lloyd's Rep 225 that the default provisions within s. 14 of the AA 1996 were not exhaustive and if even if they were exhaustive an implied request for the appointment of the arbitral tribunal was sufficient to comply with s. 14 of the AA 1996.

Section 14(4) of the AA 1996 provides the default position where the arbitral tribunal or arbitral tribunals are to be appointed by the parties. The arbitral proceedings are commenced when one party serves on the other a notice requiring that party to appoint an arbitral tribunal or to agree to the appointment of an arbitral tribunal. In *Dew Group Ltd* v *Costain Building and Civil Engineering Ltd* 1997 SLT 1020 a dispute arose between a contractor and subcontractor, who agreed to approach a named person to act as the arbitral tribunal. The subcontractor approached the named person, who informed him that he would not be able to hear the matter for at least a year. The subcontractor suggested to the contractor that they find an alternative arbitral tribunal because the named person was extremely busy. It was held that the parties had 'agreed an arbitral tribunal' under the provisions of the contract (Institute of Civil Engineers form of contract clause 18(3)) and the contractor could not therefore prevent the arbitration from continuing. Lord Weir held in this case that: 'What mattered as between the parties was that they had agreed upon a person who might be approached to act. Once that had happened the agreement was binding and the parties moved inexorably down the path towards arbitration.' By analogy this case would be equally applicable to s. 14(4) of the AA 1996. If the parties have agreed to the appointment of an arbitral tribunal, the fact that the named person cannot act as arbitral tribunal will not prevent the arbitral proceeding from being commenced.

Section 14(5) of the AA 1996 provides the default position where the arbitral tribunal is to be appointed by a third party. Arbitral proceedings are commenced in respect of a matter when one party gives notice to that third party 'requesting him to make the appointment in respect of that matter' (but see the cases above). A claimant should, however, be careful to ascertain whether there is an agreement to commence arbitration proceedings or whether the default position is applicable. An agreement to refer a matter to arbitration under the ICC Rules of Arbitration would, we suggest, be an agreement under s. 14(1) of the AA 1996. Under Article 4 of the ICC Rules the first step in commencing the arbitration procedure is to send a Request for Arbitration (the 'Request') to the Secretariat. Article 4(2) of the ICC Rules states that: 'The date on which the Request is received by the Secretariat shall, for all purposes, be deemed to be the date of the commencement of the arbitral proceedings'. Notice sent to the ICC is not the same as being received by the Secretariat. When limitation periods are relevant a claimant must ensure that there has been strict compliance with the requirements for commencement of the arbitration agreement.

4.11 TERMINATING THE ARBITRATION

The arbitration may be terminated by the consent of the parties. This requires a separate agreement to the underlying contract. If the underlying contract ceases to exist this will not terminate the arbitration agreement (see chapter 5.2). The agreement to terminate need not be in writing: s. 23(4) of the AA 1996. This is in direct contrast to an agreement to arbitrate, which must be in writing: s. 5 of the AA 1996. There is a difference between an agreement to terminate the arbitral proceedings and an agreement to stay those proceedings. An agreement to stay the proceedings leaves the arbitration agreement subsisting. A valid agreement to terminate the arbitration means that neither party can start a new arbitration in respect of the issues in the terminated arbitration. An agreement to stay the arbitration does not prevent the parties from agreeing to resolve a new dispute by arbitration which may refer back to unresolved matters in the previous arbitration: *Wakefield (Tower Hill Trinity Square) Trust* v *Jason Green* Properties (1998) *The Times*, 20 July. Whether the agreement to terminate the arbitration is valid is determined on contractual principles. There must be an offer and acceptance to terminate the arbitration: *Villa Denizcilik Sanayi ve Ticaret AS* v *Longen SA, The Villa* [1998] 1 Lloyd's Rep 195. Inactivity by either the claimant or the respondent in pursuing its claim or counterclaim is not usually regarded as an offer or acceptance to terminate the arbitration agreement: *Thai-Europe Tgpioca Service Ltd* v *Seine Navigation Co. Inc* [1989] 2 Lloyd's Rep 506.

5 The Arbitration Agreement

5.1 DEFINITION AND VALIDITY

Section 6(1) of the AA 1996 defines an arbitration agreement as 'an agreement to submit to arbitration present or future disputes (whether they are contractual or not)'. Section 6 of the AA 1996 derives in part from s. 32 of the AA 1950, from s. 7(1) of the AA 1975 and from Article 7 of the UNCITRAL Model Law. The definition is intended to reflect the pre-existing law. The word 'dispute' is defined by s. 82 of the AA 1996 as including any difference. The meaning of 'dispute' is analysed in chapter 4. The agreement to submit disputes to arbitration may be contained in the underlying contract between the parties from which the dispute arises or it may be contained in a separate agreement. The reference in an agreement to a written form of arbitration clause constitutes an arbitration agreement if the reference is such as to make the arbitration clause part of the agreement: s. 6(2) of the AA 1996.

5.1.1 Agreement in writing

Whether the arbitration agreement is in the underlying contract, or in a separate agreement, or is incorporated by reference, it must be in writing in order for the provisions in Part I of the AA 1996 to apply: s. 5(1) of the AA 1996. Subsections (2) to (6) of s. 5 deal with what is meant by 'agreement in writing'. The term 'in writing' includes any means in which an agreement can be recorded, such as by a tape recording as well as electronic transmissions: s. 5(6). Equally, any other agreement between the parties as to any matter in the arbitration is only effective for the purposes of Part I of the AA 1996 if it is in writing: s. 5(1). If the parties wish to oust any of the default provisions in the non-mandatory parts of the AA 1996, they have to agree to do so in writing. The one exception to this requirement is an agreement to terminate the arbitration agreement: s. 23(4). The DAC, in para. 40 of their February 1996 report, were of the view that it was impractical to impose a requirement that an agreement to terminate the arbitration should be in writing. The DAC stated that: 'Parties may well simply walk away from the proceedings, or allow the proceedings to lapse, and it could be extremely unfair if one party were allowed to rely upon the absence of writing at some future stage'.

The written agreement need not be signed by the parties for Part I of the AA 1996 to apply to it. It may simply be made by an exchange of communications in writing, such as letters and faxes: s. 5(2)(b) of the AA 1996; *Birse Construction Ltd* v *St David Ltd* [1999] 1 BLR 194. In fact the agreement need not itself be in writing. It is sufficient for the purposes of the AA 1996 if it is evidenced in writing, for example, in a memorandum: s. 5(2) of the AA 1996. An agreement is evidenced in writing if it is recorded by one of the parties, or a third party, with the authority of the parties to the agreement: s. 5(4). The DAC in their February 1996 report at para. 37 stated that the purpose of s. 5(4) of the AA 1996 is to maintain the parties' flexibility to agree matters of procedure during a hearing. The DAC stated that: 'Given that this third party could of course be the tribunal, the parties are free during a hearing to make whatever arrangements or changes to the agreed procedure they wish, as long as these are recorded by the tribunal'.

An arbitration agreement, if it is to be valid, must be written in clear and certain terms. It is an agreement like any other contract and will therefore be void for uncertainty if its meaning is so ambiguous as to be incapable of being construed to give the agreement certainty. However, the courts have tried, where possible, to support the parties in their intention. In doing so the courts will sometimes attempt to resolve the ambiguity that exists within the agreement. In *Mangistaumunaigaz Oil Production Association* v *United World Trade Inc.* [1995] 1 Lloyd's Rep 617 the arbitration agreement stated: 'Arbitration, if any, by ICC rules in London'. The respondents argued that the phrase 'if any' rendered the arbitration agreement too vague. The judge took the view that the phrase was meaningless and could be ignored or alternatively it could be construed as meaning an abbreviation for 'if any dispute arises'. On either conclusion the judge held that the arbitration clause was not uncertain. In contrast in *J.F. Finnegan Ltd* v *Sheffield City Council* (1988) 43 BLR 124 a contract contained the provision that it was a matter for further discussion whether disputes under the contract were to be referred to arbitration. It was held that this was too vague.

5.1.2   Oral agreement

Part I of the AA 1996 will apply to an oral agreement if it refers to terms which are in writing, such as a reference to a standard form of contract which contains an arbitration clause: s. 5(3) of the AA 1996. This subsection was inserted into the AA 1996 to cover common business practices such as exist in salvage operations.

An allegation by one party of an oral agreement or of an implied agreement to arbitrate which is contained in an exchange of written submissions in legal or arbitral proceedings can constitute an agreement in writing as between those parties. However, this is only the case if the other party responds to the submission which contains the allegation without denying it: s. 5(5) of the AA 1996. Certain anomalies in the arbitration proceedings may arise from this provision. The use of the word 'proceedings' indicates that a claim or some other application to the court has been made or alternatively that a notice to commence arbitral proceedings has been served. If a party to an oral arbitration agreement brings legal proceedings against the other party alleging the existence of the arbitration agreement and the other party does not deny the existence of that arbitration agreement, but denies the claim, then a written arbitration agreement will come into effect. However, the party making the claim cannot apply to have the matter stayed to arbitration because that party is not a party against whom legal proceedings are brought: s. 9(1) of the AA 1996. Similarly the person who has failed to deny the existence of the oral arbitration agreement, but denies the claim, cannot apply to have the matter stayed because, by denying the claim, that person has taken a step in those proceedings: s. 9(3) of the AA 1996.

Equally it is difficult to see how two persons can agree to have a purely oral arbitration agreement which will not be caught by s. 5(5) of the AA 1996. As soon as either party makes any form of written statement setting out that there was an oral arbitration agreement, the other party must deny it. If the statement is not denied then the arbitration proceedings would appear to be caught by all the provisions of the AA 1996. It follows that any such denial would thereafter bring the jurisdiction of the arbitrator into question. It also follows that in an arbitration pursuant to an oral arbitration agreement the parties must either agree not to mention the oral arbitration agreement in any proceedings or conduct the arbitration orally.

An oral arbitration agreement, which is not evidenced in writing, is not invalid. However, an arbitration under an oral arbitration agreement is not subject to the AA 1996. The requirements of s. 5 of the AA 1996 now make it difficult for an arbitration to be conducted which is outside the scope of the AA 1996. Where both the arbitration agreement and the underlying contract are oral then it is also likely that the very existence of these agreements would be called into doubt: *E. Turner and Sons* v *Maltind Ltd* (1985) 5 Const LJ 273.

5.2 SEPARABILITY OF THE ARBITRATION CLAUSE

Where the parties have entered into a contract, whether orally or in writing, which incorporates by reference a written form of arbitration clause, this will constitute an arbitration agreement (s. 6(2) of the AA 1996). However, the arbitration clause and the contract which incorporates it are two distinct contracts. The arbitration clause contains the parties' agreement to resolve present and future disputes by arbitration. The contract, which incorporates the arbitration clause by reference, is the underlying contract. The dispute between the parties arises from the underlying contract and is the subject of the arbitration. The doctrine of separability of the arbitration agreement is set out in s. 7 of the AA 1996:

> Unless otherwise agreed by the parties, an arbitration agreement which forms or was intended to form part of another agreement (whether or not in writing) shall not be regarded as invalid, non-existent or ineffective because that other agreement is invalid, or did not come into existence or has become ineffective, and it shall for that purpose be treated as a distinct agreement.

Section 7 applies where the law of the arbitration agreement is that of England and Wales or Northern Ireland even if the seat of the arbitration is outside these locations or has not been designated or determined (s. 2(5)). It is a non-mandatory section.

5.2.1   Position at common law

Section 7 of the AA 1996 gives statutory effect to the common law rule in *Harbour Assurance Co. (UK) Ltd* v *Kansa General International Insurance Co. Ltd* [1993] QB 701 that an arbitration agreement within a contract is separate from that contract. In *Harbour Assurance Co. (UK) Ltd* v *Kansa General International Insurance Co. Ltd* the Court of Appeal held that even though the underlying contract was void for illegality the arbitration clause could still survive as the illegality of the underlying contract did not impeach the arbitration agreement. The arbitration agreement and the underlying contract need not rise and fall together. However, where a contract is void *ab initio* because one of the parties is a minor then this ground would also affect the arbitration agreement. An arbitration agreement is as much a contract as any other contract. The requirements of offer and acceptance, consideration, capacity and the intention to create a legal relationship apply to the arbitration agreement as to any other contract.

The concept that an arbitration agreement was separable from the underlying contract is not recent. In *Heyman* v *Darwins Ltd* [1942] AC 356 the House of Lords held that an arbitration agreement is not terminated by a breach of the underlying contract. The House of Lords held that neither the repudiation of the underlying contract by one of the parties nor the acceptance of that repudiation will determine the arbitration agreement. Lord Macmillan held, at p. 374, that the non-defaulting party can insist, in such circumstances, that the matter be referred to an arbitral tribunal for its determination:

> . . . what is commonly called repudiation or total breach of contract . . . does not abrogate the contract . . . though all further performance of the obligations undertaken by each party in favour of the other may cease. It [the contract] survives for the purpose of measuring the claims arising out of the breach, and the arbitration clause survives for determining the mode of their settlement.

However, in *Heyman* v *Darwins* a distinction was drawn between the effect on the arbitration clause contained in the underlying contract if the contract was wrongfully terminated by one of the parties and the effect on the arbitration clause if the underlying contract was void. In the former case the House of Lords held that the arbitration clause would not be impeached but that in the latter case it would be, following the case of *Joe Lee Ltd* v *Lord Dalmeny* [1927] 1 Ch 300. The Court of Appeal in *Harbour Assurance Co. (UK) Ltd* v *Kansa General International Insurance Co. Ltd* [1993] QB 701 drew a further distinction between the effect on the arbitration clause if the underlying contract was void for initial illegality and if it was void *ab initio*. In the former case the Court of Appeal held that the arbitration clause could survive but that in the latter case it could not. The Court of Appeal stated that it was a question of fact whether the type of illegality affected both the underlying contract and the arbitration clause.

5.3   SEPARABILITY AND *KOMPETENZ-KOMPETENZ*

The doctrine of *Kompetenz-Kompetenz* derives from German law, in which the term is used to express the concept of the jurisdiction to rule upon jurisdictional matters. The DAC at para. 138 of its February 1996 report stated that the advantage of giving the arbitral tribunal the power to rule upon its own jurisdiction would be that a recalcitrant party could not delay 'valid arbitration proceedings indefinitely by making spurious challenges to its jurisdiction'. Whether the arbitral tribunal has the substantive jurisdiction to conduct the arbitration depends *inter alia* on the existence of a valid arbitration agreement: s. 30(1)(a) of the AA 1996. If a party alleges that the underlying contract is void, the question of whether the arbitration clause within it has been impeached is now a matter for the arbitral tribunal to decide. Section 30 of the AA 1996 provides for the arbitral tribunal to rule upon its own jurisdiction. It is a non-mandatory section and the parties are free to exclude it from their arbitration agreement. In this respect the AA 1996 differs from Article 16 of the UNCITRAL Model Law.

Section 30 of the AA 1996 states:

(1)   Unless otherwise agreed by the parties, the arbitral tribunal may rule on its own substantive jurisdiction, that is, as to—
(a)   whether there is a valid arbitration agreement,
(b)   whether the tribunal is properly constituted, and
(c)   what matters have been submitted to arbitration in accordance with the arbitration agreement.
(2)   Any such ruling may be challenged by any available arbitral process of appeal or review or in accordance with the provisions of this Part.

If a party wishes to challenge the decision of the arbitral tribunal then it is the courts that have the final say as to whether the arbitral tribunal does in fact have jurisdiction: s. 30(2) of the AA 1996. As Saville LJ stated in a speech at Middle Temple Hall on 8 July 1996:

Questions of the jurisdiction of the tribunal cannot be left (unless the parties concerned agree) to the tribunal itself, for that would be a classic case of pulling oneself up by one's own bootstraps.

Prior to the AA 1996 the common law position was that the arbitral tribunal was entitled to make enquiries as to whether or not it had the jurisdiction to proceed with the arbitration. In *Christopher Brown Ltd* v *Genossenschaft Oesterreichischer*

Waldbesitzer Holzwirtschaftsbetriebe Registrierte Genossenschaft mbH [1954] 1 QB 8 Devlin J held at pp. 12–13 that:

> It is clear that at the beginning of any arbitration one side or the other may challenge the jurisdiction of the arbitrator. It is not the law that arbitrators, if their jurisdiction is challenged or questioned, are bound immediately to refuse to act until their jurisdiction has been determined by some court which has power to determine it finally. Nor is it the law that they are bound to go on without investigating the merits of the challenge and to determine the matter in dispute, leaving the question of their jurisdiction to be held over until it is determined by some court which had power to determine it. They might then be merely wasting their time and everybody else's. They are not obliged to take either of those courses. They are entitled to inquire into the merits of the issue whether they have jurisdiction or not, not for the purpose of reaching any conclusion which will be binding upon the parties — because that they cannot do — but for the purpose of satisfying themselves as a preliminary matter whether they ought to go on with the arbitration or not. . . . They are entitled, in short, to make their own inquiries in order to determine their own course of action, and the result of that inquiry has no effect whatsoever upon the rights of the parties.

Section 30 of the AA 1996 extends this common law principle. Under s. 30 the arbitral tribunal is given the power to rule on its own substantive jurisdiction, unless the parties have agreed otherwise. The arbitral tribunal's decision is, however, subject to any process of appeal or review which is permitted under the AA 1996.

5.4 OBJECTING TO THE ARBITRAL TRIBUNAL'S LACK OF SUBSTANTIVE JURISDICTION

Section 31 of the AA 1996 deals with objections to the substantive jurisdiction of the arbitral tribunal. It is a mandatory section and cannot be excluded by the parties' agreement. Any objection to the arbitral tribunal's lack of substantive jurisdiction must be made within the time stipulated in this section. The DAC, at para. 145 of their February 1996 report, were of the view that the mandatory nature of these time limits was 'highly desirable by way of support for the object of arbitration' as set out in s. 1 of the AA 1996. Section 31 of the AA 1996 does not apply to a party who refuses to take part in the proceedings. Such a party may bring a court action to question whether there is a valid arbitration agreement, whether the arbitral tribunal is properly constituted or what matters are capable of being submitted to arbitration in accordance with the arbitration agreement (s. 72(1)(a) to (c) of the AA 1996).

Having appointed or having participated in the appointment of the arbitral tribunal does not preclude a party from raising an objection to the arbitral tribunal's lack of jurisdiction (s. 31(1) of the AA 1996). An objection that the arbitral tribunal lacks substantive jurisdiction will include a claim that the arbitration agreement is void or that the arbitral tribunal has not been appointed in accordance with the arbitration agreement. If the objection is raised at the outset of the proceedings then it must be raised by a party: 'not later than the time he takes the first step in the proceedings to contest the merits of any matter in relation to which he challenges the tribunal's jurisdiction' (s. 31(1) of the AA 1996). The use of the word 'proceedings' indicates that any step taken before the notice of arbitration will not count as a step in the proceedings. If a party takes a step to contest merits then the right to object to substantive jurisdiction is lost subject to the arbitral tribunal's discretion given by s. 31(3) of the AA 1996. An act outside the proceedings such as a request by one solicitor to another for an extension of time to deliver a defence will not be a step in the proceedings: *Ives and Barker* v *Willans* [1894] 2 Ch 478; *Brighton Marine Palace and Pier Ltd* v *Woodhouse* [1893] 2 Ch 486; *Blue Flame Mechanical Services Ltd* v *David Lord Engineering Ltd* [1992] CILL 760; see also *Jitendra Bhailbhai Patel* v *Dilesh R. Patel* [1999] 1 BLR 227.

A party which objects that the arbitral tribunal is exceeding its substantive jurisdiction during the course of the arbitral proceedings must make its objection as soon as possible after the matter which raises the issue of jurisdiction appears: s. 31(2) of the AA 1996. An objection under this section would include claims that the arbitral tribunal was dealing with matters outside the arbitration agreement. The arbitral tribunal may admit an objection later than the time specified in s. 31(2) if it considers the delay is justified: s. 31(3). However, there must be some material basis on which the arbitral tribunal should exercise its discretion if it is to extend the time limits: *Ratnam* v *Cumarasamy* [1965] 1 WLR 8; *Lewis* v *Haverfordwest Rural District Council* [1953] 1 WLR 1486; *Savill* v *Southend Health Authority* (1994) *The Times*, 28 December. If there is no such basis then the arbitral tribunal should refuse the application to extend the time limits: *Civil Service Co-operative Society Ltd* v *General Steam Navigation Co.* [1903] 2 KB 756.

Section 31(4) of the AA 1996 provides that if an objection is made to the substantive jurisdiction of the arbitral tribunal and the arbitral tribunal has the power to rule on its own jurisdiction it may, subject to the parties agreeing otherwise:

(a) rule on the matter in an award as to jurisdiction, or
(b) deal with the objection in its award on the merits.

The arbitral tribunal must make its choice in accordance with its duty under s. 33 of the AA 1996. However, if the parties agree on the course to be taken then the arbitral tribunal must follow that course. Under s. 31(5) of the AA 1996 the arbitral tribunal has the discretion to stay the proceedings whilst an application is made to the court under s. 32 (determination of preliminary point of jurisdiction). However, the arbitral tribunal must stay the proceedings if this is what the parties have agreed: s. 31(5).

A question of substantive jurisdiction may be ruled upon by means of an interim award, or dealt with in an award on the merits. In either case an appeal may be brought under s. 67 of the AA 1996. A challenge to the substantive jurisdiction may also be made under s. 32 of the AA 1996. A challenge to the arbitral tribunal's substantive jurisdiction may involve questions of law and facts. Therefore any finding by the arbitral tribunal on fact and law may be challenged under s. 67 of the AA 1996. This was stated to be the case by the DAC in their February 1999 report at para. 143.

5.5 DETERMINATION OF A PRELIMINARY POINT OF JURISDICTION

If a valid arbitration exists between the parties and the seat of the arbitration is in England and Wales or Northern Ireland, any party who wishes the court to determine any question as to the substantive jurisdiction of the arbitral tribunal must do so under the AA 1996: *ABB Lummus Global Ltd* v *Keppel Fels Ltd* (1998) 12 CLN 1. A party, during the course of the arbitration, may object that the arbitral tribunal lacks substantive jurisdiction under s. 31 of the AA 1996 and apply to the court to determine the issue under s. 32(1) of the AA 1996. Alternatively a party may challenge an award under s. 67(1)(a) of the AA 1996 on the ground that the arbitral tribunal lacked substantive jurisdiction. The parties' rights under ss. 32 and 67 of the AA 1996 may be lost if a party is dilatory in making its objection: s. 73 of the AA 1996. This changes the pre-existing law under which a challenge to the substantive jurisdiction of the arbitral tribunal could be made at any time.

Section 32 of the AA 1996 is a mandatory section which provides for a determination of a preliminary point of jurisdiction as an alternative to requesting an award from the arbitral tribunal on the issue under s. 30 of the AA 1996. It would be appropriate for a party to apply under this section only in exceptional circumstances, for instance, where an issue of jurisdiction is raised and a party thereafter refuses to proceed with the arbitration. It will, in such circumstances, be quicker and cheaper to proceed by this route rather than proceed *ex parte* to an award, which would thereafter be challenged. Section 32 of the AA 1996 includes restrictions on a party's right to apply to the court. It is clear that this section is not intended to defeat the doctrine of *Kompetenz-Kompetenz* by allowing parties to apply to the courts in regard to every challenge to the substantive jurisdiction of the arbitral tribunal.

A party which requires the court to determine a preliminary point of jurisdiction during the arbitration must make its application to the court on notice to the other parties: s. 32(1) of the AA 1996. The court then has the discretion to determine any question as to the arbitral tribunal's substantive jurisdiction: s. 31(1) of the AA 1996.

The importance of making an application under s. 32 of the AA 1996 quickly is stressed in the Act. Section 40(2)(b) of the AA 1996 is a mandatory section which requires a party to take any necessary steps without delay to obtain a decision of the court on a preliminary question of jurisdiction. Section 32 must therefore be read alongside s. 31, which deals with timescales in challenging the substantive jurisdiction of the arbitral tribunal. In addition, unless the applicant has complied with the requirements of s. 73 it may lose its right to object: s. 31(1). Section 73(1) requires a party, which continues with the arbitration, to make its objection forthwith or within such time limits as the arbitration agreement, the arbitral tribunal or Part I of the AA 1996 permits. The objection may not be raised later before the arbitral tribunal or the court unless the party objecting can demonstrate that, at the time it continued with the arbitration, it 'did not know and could not with reasonable diligence have discovered the grounds for the objection': s. 73(1). Furthermore, where the arbitral tribunal has ruled upon its own jurisdiction a party wishing to challenge this decision must do so within the time permitted in the arbitration agreement or Part I of the AA 1996. Where no such objection is raised then that party may not object later on any ground which was the subject of the arbitral tribunal's ruling on jurisdiction: s. 73(1). This rule applies whether the challenge is to be made during the arbitration under s. 32 or as a challenge to the award.

The court will not consider the application under s. 32 unless the conditions in s. 32(2) are satisfied, which are that:

(a)   the application is made with the agreement in writing of all the parties to the proceedings, or

(b)   it is made with the permission of the tribunal and the court is satisfied:

(i)   that the determination of the question is likely to produce substantial savings in costs,

(ii)   that the application was made without delay, and

(iii)   that there is good reason why this matter should be decided by the court.

A substantial saving of costs might occur where oral and expert evidence is required to ascertain whether the arbitral tribunal has substantive jurisdiction. In *Azov* v *Baltic Shipping* [1999] 1 Lloyd's Rep 68 Azov alleged that it was not a party to a contract with Baltic Shipping and therefore that it was not bound by an arbitration agreement. In order to ascertain whether or not there was a contract, oral evidence and expert evidence were required. A hearing lasting three days took place before the arbitral tribunal. The arbitral tribunal found in favour of Baltic Shipping and Azov challenged the award under s. 67 of the AA 1996. Rix J held that the court, in reviewing the decision of the arbitral tribunal under s. 67 of the AA 1996, should not be in a worse position than the arbitral tribunal and that Azov was entitled to have a complete re-hearing. The judge then stated, by way of *obiter dicta*, that this perhaps was a case where the parties should have come straight to the court for a determination of this issue. The judge continued that if agreement by the parties had not been reached on this course of action, then the arbitral tribunal may have been willing to consent to such a course because of the nature of the challenge.

Section 32(2)(b)(ii) requires evidence that a party complied with its duty under s. 40(2)(b) in making the application without delay. There is no guidance given within the DAC Report as to what is a 'good reason' for the purposes of s. 32(2)(b)(iii), but matters which will persuade the court are likely to include a saving of time or questions of bona fides. Unless the court gives leave, no appeal lies from a decision of the court as to whether the conditions specified in s. 32(2) are met: s. 32(5).

The grounds on which an application to the court is made under s. 32 of the AA 1996 should be set out, unless the application is made with the agreement of all the parties: s. 32(3). Unless the parties agree otherwise, the arbitral tribunal may continue the arbitral proceedings and make an award while an application to the court under s. 32 is pending: s. 32(4). However, it would be usual for the arbitral proceedings to be stayed. If the parties agree that the arbitral proceedings should be stayed then the arbitral tribunal should follow the wishes of the parties and agree to stay the proceedings while the application is heard. If the arbitral tribunal insists on proceeding with the arbitration then the parties may apply to the court, at the same time as making their application, for an injunction suspending the arbitration proceedings: s. 32(4).

The decision of the court on the question of jurisdiction is treated as a judgment of the court for the purposes of an appeal: s. 32(6). There are two possible grounds for appeal under s. 32 of the AA 1996. The first is an appeal as to whether the conditions in s. 32(2) have been met. The second possibility for appeal is from a decision of the court as to the substantive jurisdiction of the arbitral tribunal. In either case leave of the court making the decision is required: s. 32(6). Where an appeal is made in regard to a decision of the court as to the substantive jurisdiction of the arbitral tribunal, leave will only be given where the court: 'considers that the question involves a point of law which is one of general importance or is one which for some other special reason should be considered': s. 32(6). It is doubtful whether the quantum of a claim could ever amount to a special reason: *British Gas plc* v *Dollar Land Holdings plc* [1992] 1 EGLR 135; see also *Babanaft International Co. SA* v *Avant Petroleum Inc.* [1982] 1 WLR 871.

5.6   INCORPORATING THE ARBITRATION AGREEMENT

Sections 6(2) and 5(3) of the AA 1996 give the only indication regarding when the incorporation of an arbitration agreement by reference may occur. The DAC in their February 1996 report at para. 42 examined the question of when incorporation would occur:

> In English law there is at present some conflicting authority on the question as to what is required for the effective incorporation of an arbitration clause by reference. Some of those responding to the July 1995 draft Clauses made critical comments of the views of Sir John Megaw in *Aughton Ltd* v *M.F. Kent Services Ltd* (1991) 57 BLR 1 (a construction contract case) and suggested that we should

take the opportunity of making clear that the law was as stated in the charterparty cases and as summarised by Ralph Gibson LJ in *Aughton*. (Similar disquiet has been expressed about decisions following *Aughton*, such as *Ben Barrett and Sons (Brickwork) Ltd v Henry Boot Management Ltd* [1995] CILL 1026.) It seems to us, however, that although we are of the view that the approach of Ralph Gibson LJ should prevail in all cases, this was really a matter for the courts to decide. The wording we have adopted certainly leaves room for the adoption of the charterparty rules in all cases, since it refers to reference to a document containing an arbitration clause as well as reference to the arbitration clause itself. Thus the wording is not confined to cases where there is specific reference to the arbitration clause, which Sir John Megaw (but not Ralph Gibson LJ) considered was a requirement for effective incorporation by reference.

The question whether an arbitration agreement can be incorporated by reference where the reference is to a set of contract conditions therefore remains uncertain. In *Aughton Ltd v M.F. Kent Services Ltd* (1991) 57 BLR 1, *Co-operative Wholesale Society Ltd v Saunders and Taylor Ltd* (1994) 39 Con LR 77 and *Ben Barrett and Sons (Brickwork) Ltd v Henry Boot Management Ltd* [1995] CILL 1026 the arbitration agreement was held not to have been incorporated. The facts of *Ben Barrett and Sons (Brickwork) Ltd v Henry Boot Management Ltd* were that Ben Barrett was employed as a specialist subcontractor to do brickwork and blockwork at a University of Manchester hall of residence. Works commenced in December 1993 and in December 1994 Ben Barrett left site. Ben Barrett claimed that the works were done under a letter of intent and that no formal contract was signed. Further, Ben Barrett claimed that they were therefore entitled to be paid on a *quantum meruit* basis, that is, a reasonable sum for the materials supplied and the work that they had undertaken, which was claimed to be £339,605. In the alternative Ben Barrett claimed that if there was a contract then they would be entitled to recover this sum for breach of contract.

Henry Boot claimed that the letter of intent, signed by the parties, constituted a contract between the parties. As an alternative Henry Boot alleged that in undertaking the works Ben Barrett had accepted an offer made in the letter of intent and therefore the contract had come into being on that basis. Henry Boot maintained that there was an arbitration agreement within the contract, as reference was made in the invitation to tender to Works Contract/1, which included an arbitration clause. The court found that the letter of intent made no reference to the arbitration agreement. The letter of intent, however, did make reference to the documents, which incorporated the contract conditions of which the arbitration clause was part. The court followed the *obiter dictum* of Sir John Megaw in *Aughton Ltd v M.F. Kent Services Ltd* (1991) 57 BLR 1 that:

If the self-contained contract is to be incorporated, it must be expressly referred to in the document which is relied on as the incorporating writing. It is not incorporated by mere reference to the terms of the conditions of contract to which the arbitration clause constitutes a collateral contract.

Following this rationale the court held that the arbitration agreement was therefore not incorporated into the contract.

In *Alfred McAlpine Construction Ltd* v *RMG Electrical* [1999] ADRLJ 53 Judge Hedley took an opposite view. The facts of the case were that McAlpine were the main contractors on a hospital project in Wrexham. RMG were the specialist mechanical and electrical (M & E) subcontractors. The contract between McAlpine and RMG was to be on an amended DOM/1 form of contract although no formal contract was ever signed. An order was sent to RMG which referred to DOM/1. A dispute arose and McAlpine terminated the contract and called on a performance bond for £100,000. RMG gave notice to McAlpine of its intention to commence arbitration under clause 38 of the DOM/1 conditions. An arbitral tribunal was appointed by the Royal Institute of Chartered Surveyors and McAlpine challenged the arbitral tribunal's jurisdiction at a preliminary meeting. The court found that the contract was a letter sent to RMG on 11 February 1993 which made reference to the DOM/1 form of contract. There was, however, no express reference to the arbitration clause on the face of the letter of 11 February 1993. The court held that the parties were familiar with the terms of DOM/1. The letter referring to DOM/1 was in effect a type of shorthand whereby DOM/1 need not be reproduced in whole. As it was in effect a form of shorthand all clauses of DOM/1 were incorporated as if they were set out in full including the arbitration clause. A similar conclusion was reached in the case of *Extrudakerb (Maltby Engineering) Ltd* v *Whitemountain Quarries Ltd* [1996] NI 567.

The question of incorporation of an arbitration agreement was analysed in *Secretary of State for Foreign and Commonwealth Affairs* v *Percy International & Kier International* (1998 Judgment ORB No. 635). The case involved a dispute, which was governed by the AA 1950 although the matter came before the court after the AA 1996 had been enacted. The defendants submitted that an arbitration agreement cannot validly be incorporated into an agreement by express reference in that agreement to a written set of conditions which contains the arbitration clause in question, but without express mention of the arbitration clause itself. This followed the *Ben Barrett and Sons (Brickwork) Ltd* v *Henry Boot Management Ltd* [1995] CILL 1026 line of argument. Judge Bowsher QC rejected this argument and held:

> Depending always on the words used in the individual transaction under consideration, an arbitration clause can validly be incorporated into an agreement by express reference in that agreement to a set of conditions which contains the arbitration clause in question, but without express mention of the arbitration clause itself.

Judge Bowsher then referred specifically to s. 6(2) of the AA 1996 and stated:

> Because it was not in force at the relevant times, that subsection does not apply to the present summonses. It does in any event leave it to the courts to decide

in the individual case what reference validly incorporates an arbitration clause into an agreement. The older law will remain a guide.

The judge then considered older authorities. He reviewed both the first and second editions of Mustill and Boyd and *Chitty on Contracts* (1994 edition) making reference to paragraph 15–011 of *Chitty*:

> An arbitration clause may be incorporated in a contract by reference, e.g. to the standard form of a trade association, or by course of dealing between the parties. . . . It is a question of construction in each case whether words in a bill of lading which incorporate some or all of the terms of the charterparty into the bill will have the effect of incorporating into the bill an arbitration clause contained in the charterparty.

The judge also referred to *Roche Products Ltd* v *Freeman Process Systems Ltd* (1996) 80 BLR 102, in which Hicks J had examined the authorities on this point and concluded that specific reference to an arbitration clause was not required, but that an arbitration clause could be incorporated into a contract by general words. This was considered to be 'a statement of first principles'. Hicks J stated that there was substantial and binding authority on him to conclude this in the case of *Modern Buildings Wales Ltd* v *Limmer and Trinidad Co. Ltd* [1975] 1 WLR 1281. Judge Bowsher referred to *The Annefield* [1971] P 168. This was a decision of the Court of Appeal approving Brandon J's decision at first instance. Judge Bowsher quoted from Brandon J's judgment: '. . . it is not necessary, in order to effect incorporation, that the incorporating clause should refer expressly to the arbitration clause. General words may suffice.' Judge Bowsher, however, expanded on the *ratio decidendi* of Brandon J:

> . . . where the arbitration clause is one of a set of standard conditions written especially for the purpose of incorporation in contracts of a certain type, general words in a contract of that type incorporating those terms as a whole will usually bring the clause into the contract so as to make the arbitration clause applicable to disputes under the contract.

The approach suggested by Judge Bowsher in his *obiter dicta* in *Secretary of State for Foreign and Commonwealth Affairs* v *Percy International & Kier International* (1998 Judgment ORB No. 635) was not, however, followed by Judge Jack in *Trygg Hansa Insurance Co. Ltd* v *Equitas Ltd* [1998] 2 Lloyd's Rep 439. In that case a contract of primary insurance contained an arbitration clause. The reinsurance contract entered into by the parties contained a clause that the reinsurance 'follow the same terms . . . as the policy of primary insurance'. Trygg Hansa therefore argued that the arbitration clause had been incorporated into the reinsurance contract by, reference. Judge Jack held that it had not. The learned judge stated that, in the absence of special circumstances, general words of incorporation were not effective to incorporate an arbitration clause under s. 6(2) of the AA 1996. The learned judge distinguished the arbitration clause from other contractual provisions and stated that there had to be some express indication for the incorporation of an arbitration clause. Judge Jack considered *Aughton Ltd* v *M.F. Kent. Services Ltd* (1991) 57 BLR 1 and followed *Excess Insurance Co. Ltd* v *C.J. Mander* [1997] 2 Lloyd's Rep 119. It therefore remains uncertain as to when an arbitration clause will be deemed to be incorporated into a contract by reference. Certainly the DAC indicated that they hoped general words would suffice. A restrictive approach to incorporation tends to be against the spirit of the AA 1996. It is hoped that the Court of Appeal will soon give clear guidance on this particular issue.

5.7 AD HOC AGREEMENTS

The phrase 'ad hoc' agreement or 'ad hoc' submission has two distinct and separate meanings. First, it may mean an agreement to refer a subsisting dispute to arbitration. Secondly, it may mean an agreement to refer a dispute to arbitration without an arbitral institution providing the procedural rules. The second of these definitions is more commonly found in international arbitrations.

The distinction between present and future disputes was of some importance where a distinction was made between domestic and non-domestic arbitrations. Since ss. 85 to 87 of the AA 1996 have not been brought into force the distinction has to a great extent been removed. Under the AA 1950 the courts had power to revoke an arbitration agreement to refer a future dispute which involved a question of fraud. This power did not exist where there was an agreement to refer an existing dispute. Under the AA 1996 this distinction has now been removed and an arbitral tribunal may deal with a dispute that involves a question of fraud irrespective of whether it arises from an agreement to refer a future or present dispute to arbitration.

5.8 CONDITIONS PRECEDENT

A condition precedent is something that makes arbitration proceedings conditional on an event occurring. The event may be as simple as the works of the underlying contract having been completed or may involve an examination of the dispute by an independent third party. In *Smith* v *Martin* [1925] 1 KB 745 the court approved the view that where the underlying contract containing the arbitration clause stated that the 'reference shall not be opened until after the completion of the works' any award will be invalid if the works have not yet been completed.

In civil engineering contracts the use of an adjudicator, dispute adjudication board or dispute review board to initially determine the dispute is becoming common. The impetus for this change is to be found in the Latham Report of 1994, as implemented by the Housing Grants, Construction and Regeneration Act 1996. The NEC Engineering and Construction Contract 2nd edition was the first civil engineering contract in England to use adjudication as a first tier in dispute resolution. Previously, many civil engineering contracts required that the dispute be first submitted to the engineer for its decision. When providing a decision the engineer was to act impartially.

The new FIDIC (International Federation of Consulting Engineers) contracts all use a form of dispute adjudication board. It was not, however, until the late 1980s and early 1990s that there was any impetus to provide for independent review by a separate body and therefore deprive the engineer of this cherished role. FIDIC's 'Orange Book' and the supplement to the 'Red Book' 4th edition both provide for the use of a dispute adjudication board (DAB) (see E.C. Corbett, *FIDIC 4th: A Practical Legal Guide: A Supplement* (London: Corbett & Co., 1993). The use of the DAB has, however, now been accepted as a positive step forward and its role is confirmed in the new editions of the FIDIC contracts. The decision of the DAB is final and binding unless and until overturned by arbitration.

The Housing Grants, Construction and Regeneration Act 1996 (HGCR Act 1996) now provides that in all construction contracts there is a requirement that as a condition precedent to the bringing of arbitration or litigation the matter be first submitted to adjudication. A 'construction contract' is, however, given a limited definition under the HGCR Act 1996. The adjudicator must act impartially (s. 108(2)(e) of the HGCR Act 1996) and may take the initiative in ascertaining the facts and law (s. 108(2)(f) of the HGCR Act 1996).[1]

5.8.1 Enforcement of an adjudicator's decision

Where a party has obtained a favourable adjudicator's decision then it may need to enforce that decision if the other party does not comply with it. In *Macob Civil Engineering* v *Morrison Construction Ltd* (1999) CILL 1470 a party sought to enforce an adjudicator's decision by way of court proceedings. The underlying contract contained an arbitration agreement. Dyson J in the Technology and Construction Court held that the court was not precluded from enforcing the adjudicator's decision even though the underlying contract contained an arbitration clause. Dyson J further held that the Adjudication Scheme in the HGCR was intended to provide a speedy mechanism for settling disputes in construction contracts on a provisional interim basis. Further, the adjudicator's decision had to be treated as binding and enforceable until any challenge to it was finally determined. The fact that a challenge existed did not mean that the decision was not enforceable.

The decision in *Macob Civil Engineering* v *Morrison Construction Ltd* (1999) CILL 1470 was distinguished in part in the case of *Project Consultancy Group* v *Trustees of the Gray Trust*, (1999 unreported). In this case the adjudicator issued a decision which was challenged on the basis that the adjudicator lacked initial jurisdiction. This was distinguishable from the facts of *Macob* where the challenge arose on the basis of a lack of jurisdiction because of a procedural error. The court held that a contract entered into before 1 May 1998 would not be caught by the provisions of the HGCR and, therefore, an adjudicator's decision would not be binding on the parties. Whether the courts will stay applications for the enforcement of an adjudicator's awards to arbitration where no challenge to the authority of the adjudicator is made remains unclear. However, the indications in *Macab Civil Engineering* v *Morrison Construction Ltd* (1999) CILL 1470 are that in such a case the court may stay the matter to arbitration.

---

[1] There are various adjudication schemes now in place. Each of these differ slightly and each must be examined to ascertain its precise requirements.

6   The Parties

6.1   DEFINITION OF A PARTY

Section 82 of the AA 1996 defines a range of terms which are used in Part I of the Act. Section 82(2) provides the following definition of the term 'party': 'References in this Part to a party to an arbitration agreement include any person claiming under or through a party to the agreement'.

The words 'any person claiming under or through a party to the agreement' are derived from s. 4(1) of the AA 1950 and s. 1(1) of the AA 1975. 'Person' does not only refer to individuals but includes any body of persons corporate: see s. 61 of the Law of Property Act 1925. The words 'any person claiming under or through a party to an agreement' appear to cover circumstances where the interest of a party to an arbitration has passed to some other person through death, bankruptcy, voluntary assignment, agency law or, for example, by 'name borrowing' (see 6.5.6). Unless it is otherwise agreed by the parties, any arbitration award is final and binding both on the parties and also on any persons claiming through or under them: s. 58 of the AA 1996.

6.2   CAPACITY OF A PARTY

The capacity of a party to enter into an arbitration agreement is governed by contract law principles. The general common law principle is that all persons should be bound by the contracts that they make. This general rule is subject to a number of exceptions. Persons under the age of 18 and mentally ill persons have a qualified capacity. Corporate bodies, partnerships, individuals and public authorities will generally all be bound by arbitration agreements that they make. Corporate bodies are bound by contracts even where the purpose of the contract is outside the company's memorandum of association (s. 35A(1) of the Companies Act 1985). The arbitration clause can be enforced by any person who deals with the company in good faith. Once a company has ceased to exist, any arbitration to which it is a party comes to an end: *Baytur SA* v *Finagro Holding SA* [1992] QB 610. A corporate body that has been created by statute also has the capacity to enter into an arbitration agreement subject to any provision expressed in its constitution to the contrary.

Where there is a partnership, any partner who enters into a contract which contains an arbitration clause binds the whole partnership: ss. 5 and 6 of the Partnership Act 1890. A distinction has to be drawn, however, between future and existing disputes. A partner cannot enter into an arbitration agreement to refer an existing dispute to arbitration, only a future dispute. To refer an existing dispute to arbitration the other partners would need to adopt or agree to the arbitration, either expressly or impliedly by their conduct: *Thomas* v *Atherton* (1878) 10 ChD 185.

An unincorporated body has no legal identity and therefore cannot be a party to a contract such as an arbitration agreement, unless it is given express or implied authority by statute such as in the case of trade unions (s. 10(1)(a) of the Trade Union and Labour Relations (Consolidation) Act 1992). Any member of an unincorporated body who enters a contract without the authority of the other members is bound by it, but it does not bind all the persons who from time to time are members of the association: *Bradley Egg Farm Ltd* v *Clifford* [1943] 2 All ER 378. However, if some of the members expressly or impliedly authorised the entry into the contract then the contract is binding on them under the principles of agency law.

6.2.1 Capacity of the Crown

There are no special rules relating to the Crown in regard to domestic arbitrations. The AA 1996 provides that the Crown has the capacity to be a party to an arbitration agreement. This follows s. 30 of the AA 1950 and makes no change to the pre-existing law. The Crown is bound by the agreement as any other party. Section 106(1) of the AA 1996 states that Part I of the AA 1996 applies to any arbitration agreement to which the Queen or the Duke of Cornwall, i.e., the Prince of Wales, is a party. Part I of the AA 1996 deals with domestic arbitrations only.

The Crown is bound by the arbitration agreement to which it is a party whether the agreement has been entered into by the Queen in the right of the Crown or of the Duchy of Lancaster or by the Queen or the Duke of Cornwall in their personal capacity. The law under the previous Arbitration Acts has been extended to apply where the Queen is acting in her personal capacity. Therefore if a dispute arises in a royal household it can now be resolved privately by arbitration away from the media spotlight.

Where the Queen has entered into an arbitration agreement in the right of the Crown for a government department, the arbitration will proceed in the name of that department and will be conducted by appointed solicitors. Where the Queen has entered an arbitration agreement in the right of the Duchy of Lancaster Her Majesty can be represented by the Chancellor of the Duchy or any person that the Chancellor may appoint: s. 106(2)(a) of the AA 1996. Section 106(2)(b) of the AA 1996 provides that in any other case, where the Queen has entered an arbitration agreement other than in the right of the Crown, Her Majesty may be represented by any person appointed by Her Majesty in writing. Similarly, where the Prince of Wales has entered an arbitration agreement as the Duke of Cornwall, s. 106(3) of the AA 1996 states that he may be represented in the proceedings by any person he may appoint. Therefore, the Queen and the Prince of Wales can enter an arbitration agreement in their personal capacities but need not take part in person in the actual proceedings.

The Crown was not bound by foreign awards under Part II of the AA 1950. That part of the AA 1950 is not repealed by the AA 1996 and therefore nothing within the AA 1996 changes the position that foreign awards do not bind the Crown. However, if the award were registered as a judgment then enforcement may be possible under s. 25 of the Crown Proceedings Act 1947.

6.2.2   Capacity of foreign States

A foreign State can be a party to an arbitration agreement if its constitution permits. Enforcement of an arbitration award in the courts of England is permitted against a foreign State under s. 1 of the State Immunity Act 1978. Section 9 of the State Immunity Act 1978 does, however, provide exceptions. A foreign State will not be bound by an arbitration award if the parties have so agreed or if the arbitration is between two States. If an award is made against a State then the State may seek to protect itself by pleading that it has immunity from execution. In order to overcome this problem a State would have had to agree to exclude this right to immunity in the arbitration agreement or alternatively the party claiming will have to show that the funds which it seeks to claim are funds held for a commercial purpose: s. 13(2)(b) and (4) of the State Immunity Act 1978; *Alcom Ltd* v *Colombia* [1984] AC 580.

6.3   PRIVITY OF CONTRACT

Arbitration agreements are subject to the doctrine of privity of contract. There are two aspects to the doctrine of privity: only a party to a contract can acquire rights under it and only a party can be subjected to liabilities under it (*Tweddle* v *Atkinson* (1861) 1 B & S 393). Only the party named in the underlying contract which contains the arbitration clause or in the arbitration agreement can be a party to the arbitration subject to the exceptions below. The arbitration award is only binding on the parties or on any person claiming through or under them (s. 58 of the AA 1996). The Law Commission has recommended that the doctrine of privity be reformed but as yet the recommendation has not yet been followed by legislation: Law Commission, *Privity of Contract: Contracts for the Benefit of Third Parties* (Consultation Paper No. 121) (London: HMSO, 1991).

6.4   THIRD PARTIES

An arbitration is a consensual procedure, between two parties, to resolve some matter or difference between the parties: *Collins* v *Collins* (1858) 26 Beav 306. Persons who are not parties can be excluded from the proceedings: *Oxford*

Shipping Co. Ltd v *Nippon Yusen Kaisha* [1984] 2 Lloyd's Rep 373. However, there are situations where third parties are also involved in the proceedings. For example, a third party may be a person claiming under or through a party to an agreement; the contract may have been novated to a third party; the third party may be a guarantor or the arbitration may involve multiple parties. In such cases those third parties will have a right to attend at the hearing.

6.4.1 Novation

Novation occurs when two parties to a contract agree that a third party shall stand in the place of an original party. The two original parties and the new party enter a tripartite contract. The original contract comes to an end and a new contract is created. This is different to an assignment, where benefits under the contract are transferred to a third party. As a novation creates a new contract, contractual law principles apply. It is therefore necessary to obtain the consent of all the parties and for consideration to be provided for the new contract by the new party: *Tatlock* v *Harris* (1789) 3 TR 174 at p. 180.

In the context of arbitration proceedings once the novation has taken place the new party must comply with the arbitration clause. The new party is treated as if it was an original party to the contract: *Smith* v *Pearl Assurance Co. Ltd* [1939] 1 All ER 95. The original party is no longer bound by the arbitration clause and cannot be a party to the arbitration proceedings.

Novation may also arise by statute such as the Third Parties (Rights against Insurers) Act 1930. Under this Act when the rights of an assured person under an insurance policy are subrogated to a third party, the third party is bound by the arbitration clause in the insurance policy: *Smith* v *Pearl Assurance Co. Ltd* [1939] 1 All ER 95.

6.4.2 Guarantor, surety and indemnifiers

A party to a contract containing an arbitration clause may have entered a separate contract of guarantee, surety or indemnity. Where a guarantee or indemnity has been entered into, the arbitration award against the principal will usually not be binding on the guarantor. In *Re Kitchin, ex parte Young* (1881) 17 ChD 668 the guarantee was expressed as follows: 'I undertake and guarantee that all wines supplied to them by you shall be duly paid for. . . . I undertake and guarantee that the agreement shall be otherwise duly performed in all respects.' The guarantor had guaranteed to pay any debt owed by the principal debtors and the performance of the contract. The guarantor had not agreed to be bound by an award against the principal debtors. The guarantor was not a party to the arbitration and was therefore not bound by the award. The Court of Appeal held that in the absence of a specific agreement by the guarantor to be bound by an award made against the principal debtors such an award does not bind the guarantor. The rationale was that general words are insufficient as otherwise a serious injustice may occur. For example, an award may result from an admission of liability by the principal debtor without the authority of the guarantor: *Bruns v Colocotronis* [1979] 2 Lloyd's Rep 412.

Where, however, the guarantee contains an obligation to honour an award then the guarantor will be bound by the award of the arbitral tribunal. In *Compania Sudamericana de Fletes SA* v *African Continental Bank Ltd* [1973] 1 Lloyd's Rep 21 Mocatta J held that:

(a)   the obligation on a party to a contract containing an arbitration clause to meet an award was an obligation which arose out of the contract; and

(b)   therefore a guarantee of 'due fulfilment of any obligation' in respect of the contract included a guarantee of the obligation to discharge an award.

If the guarantor is to be bound by an award against the principal debtor then clear words imposing that liability must be in either the arbitration agreement or in the guarantee. Lush LJ said in *Re Kitchin, ex parte Young* (1881) 17 ChD 668 at p. 674: 'You must find explicit words to make a person liable to pay any amount which may be awarded against a third person'. Where no such clear words appear then an arbitration award is not evidence against the guarantor in an action against him by the creditor. The guarantor is entitled to have the liability proved as against him in the same way as the principal debtor. The position was summed up succinctly by Lord Diplock in *Moschi* v *Lep Air Services Ltd* [1973] AC 331, at p. 349:

. . . whenever the debtor has failed voluntarily to perform an obligation which is the subject of the guarantee the creditor can recover from the guarantor as damages for breach of his contract of guarantee whatever sum the creditor could have recovered from the debtor himself as a consequence of that failure. The debtor's liability to the creditor is also the measure of the guarantor's.

The consequence of this is that the creditor may have to bring two claims in order to have a binding award against the principal debtor and a judgment against the guarantor. Parallel or consecutive proceedings such as these are costly and can lead to inconsistent results. Findings of law or fact in one set of proceedings are irrelevant to the other set of proceedings. A solution is for the guarantor to agree to be bound by the findings of the arbitral tribunal: *Roche Products Ltd* v *Freeman Process Systems Ltd* (1996) 80 BLR 102. However, in practice the guarantor will only do this if it is in its interest.

The case of *Alfred McAlpine Construction Ltd* v *Unex Corporation Ltd* (1994) 70 BLR 26 involved the construction of a substantial office building in Cambridge. McAlpine were employed by Panatown Ltd to construct the building. Unex entered a parent company guarantee to indemnify McAlpine if Panatown defaulted on the contract and its obligations. Disputes arose between McAlpine and Panatown, which were referred to arbitration. However, during the course of the arbitration McAlpine sought to enforce the parent company guarantee and commenced an action in the High Court. Unex applied for a stay of proceedings under the inherent jurisdiction of the court. Judge Esyr Lewis QC dismissed the application and Unex appealed. On appeal it was held that Unex's rights and obligations were separate from the rights and obligations under the contract between McAlpine and Panatown. The liability of Unex to McAlpine was a primary liability and did not rely on the liability of Panatown to McAlpine. There were no explicit words making Unex liable to pay any amounts awarded by the arbitrator against Panatown. The Court of Appeal on the facts of the case dismissed the appeal and refused to grant a stay to the litigation.

Glidewell LJ held that while the arbitration determined the liabilities between McAlpine and Panatown it was irrelevant to determining the liabilities of Unex. However, he held that, because of the wording of the indemnity, an arbitration award did have one effect on the indemnifier. An arbitration award provided the maximum liability of Unex to McAlpine. The Court of Appeal finally addressed the question of whether the litigation should be stayed. Evans LJ held that as Unex had not made or offered any formal admission of liability under the parent company guarantee so that they could raise new matters not canvassed in the arbitration, a stay of the litigation proceedings should be refused. This case should be compared with *Roche Products Ltd* v *Freeman Process Systems Ltd* (1996) 80 BLR 102 where Judge Hicks QC ordered a stay of litigation. The case is, however, distinguishable in that the guarantor offered to be bound by the findings of the arbitral tribunal.

The creditor is also unable to issue a claim against both the principal debtor and the guarantor. Section 9 of the AA 1996 requires that litigation be stayed to arbitration where there is a valid arbitration clause. If the principal debtor therefore applied to the court, in which the claim was issued, to stay the proceedings, that court would be obliged to stay the litigation against the principal debtor except where the arbitration agreement was shown to be null and void, inoperative or incapable of being performed. Once again the creditor would have to succeed in two sets of proceedings.

A distinction should be made between a guarantee and an indemnity. A guarantor is said to have a secondary obligation. An indemnifier is said to have a primary obligation. The distinction between a primary and secondary obligation is this: where there is a secondary liability then if the principal debtor is not liable the guarantor will not be liable either; where there is a primary liability then an action may proceed against the indemnifier even though the creditor has no enforceable rights against the principal debtor. The distinction between primary and secondary obligations has been criticised for having 'raised many hair-splitting distinctions of exactly that kind which bring the law into hatred, ridicule and contempt by the public': *Guild and Co.* v *Conrad* [1894] 2 QB 885, at p. 892.

6.4.3 Multiple parties

Arbitration agreements are essentially bilateral agreements, which concern two parties. However, there are situations where it would be appropriate that arbitration proceedings involve more than two parties. First, a claimant in an arbitration may have a claim arising out of the same set of facts against one or more other persons. It is not uncommon, for example, for an employer, in a construction contract, to have a claim against a contractor and subcontractor. Secondly, a party against whom a claim is made in an arbitration may wish to bring a third party into the arbitration. For example, the contractor may seek compensation from the subcontractor who undertook the work which is the subject of the dispute. However, with arbital proceedings unlike court proceedings, there is no mechanism in arbitration proceedings for making claims against third parties, except with the agreement of all the parties. Thirdly, a multi-party arbitration may be appropriate where there exists a 'string' contract. This is where there is a series of contracts, each of which passes liability down to the final contract.

Section 35(1) of the AA 1996 states that the parties are free to agree to consolidate in one arbitration other arbitral proceedings or to hold concurrent hearings. Such agreement must be in writing between the parties, either in each contract from which the disputes have arisen or in a later separate contract. The arbitral tribunal has no power to order consolidation of proceedings or concurrent hearings unless the parties have conferred such a power on it: s. 35(2) of the AA 1996. This confirms the position at Common Law: *Oxford Shipping Co.* v *Nippon Yusen Kaisha* [1984] 2 Lloyd's Rep 373. But see also *Aquator Shipping Ltd* v *Kleimar NV, The Capricorn I* [1998] 2 Lloyd's Rep 379.

The question of multi-party disputes was one of the issues that the Society of Construction Arbitrators addressed when drafting the Construction Industry Model Arbitration Rules (CIMAR). The CIMAR expressly provide that the arbitral tribunal may order concurrent proceedings where it is appointed in two or more related disputes which involve common issues. The concurrent proceedings may relate to the whole claim or any issue in the dispute. The parties need not be the same. The arbitral tribunal may, however, only order consolidated proceedings if the parties to those proceedings agree: r. 3.9 of CIMAR. Where there are concurrent proceedings then separate awards are required for each dispute unless the parties otherwise agree: r. 3.8 of CIMAR. Where there are consolidated proceedings then only one award is required unless the parties otherwise agree: r. 3.10 of CIMAR. Other institutional rules adopt similar approaches to circumvent the problems of duplicated proceedings; see, for example, the GAFTA Arbitration Rules.

In each case the parties must agree to the consolidation of the disputes in the one arbitration or that they should be run concurrently (s. 35(1)(a) and (b) of the AA 1996). If the parties do not agree to this then the court cannot intervene to prevent the duplication of proceedings. Although s. 35 of the AA 1996 does not specifically state that the court has no such power this is implied by the fact that no mention is made of the court and s. 1(c) of the AA 1996 makes it clear that the court should not intervene except as provided for in Part I of the Act. However, there is no reason why the court or other appointing authority may not appoint the same tribunal to hear the various disputes consecutively (*Abu Dhabi Gas Liquefaction Co. Ltd* v *Eastern Bechtel Corporation* [1982] 2 Lloyd's Rep 425), though the court has no power to make the parties acquiesce in this.

In contrast to arbitration the High Court and county courts always have a power to consolidate actions. Although there are obvious advantages to the joining of actions, such as saving time and costs, providing a mandatory power to order consolidation of arbitration proceedings was not recommended by the DAC in their report on the Arbitration Bill of February 1996 at para. 180:

> In our view it would amount to a negation of the principle of party autonomy to give the tribunal or the court power to order consolidation or concurrent hearings. Indeed it would to our minds go far towards frustrating the agreement of the parties to have their own tribunal for their own dispute. Further difficulties could well arise, such as disclosure of documents from one arbitration to another. Accordingly we would be opposed to giving the tribunal or the court this power. However, if the parties agree to invest the tribunal with such a power, then we would have no objection.

One example, given by the DAC, of institutional rules allowing consolidated or concurrent hearings is the Rules of the London Maritime Arbitrators Association, which include a provision along these lines.

6.5 PERSONS CLAIMING THROUGH OR UNDER A PARTY TO AN ARBITRATION AGREEMENT

6.5.1 Trustees and personal representatives

Personal representatives are the executors nominated in a valid will or the appointed administrators of the deceased's estate where the deceased has died intestate. Trustees and personal representatives have the statutory power, under s. 15(f) of the Trustee Act 1925, to be a party to an arbitration and to enter arbitration agreements in respect of any dispute which arises from the estate or trust in their control. This statutory power may, however, be limited or even abrogated by the trust deed: s. 69(2) of the Trustee Act 1925. Trustees or personal representatives will not incur any personal liability as long as they have acted in good faith: s. 15 of the Trustee Act 1925.

Unless otherwise agreed by the parties, if a party to the arbitration dies, the arbitration agreement still survives. The personal representatives of the deceased may enforce that agreement or have the agreement enforced against them: s. 8(1) of the AA 1996. This reverses the common law position and is the case so long as the substantive cause of action is not extinguished by the death of a party. A substantive cause of action will be extinguished if it is personal to the deceased, as in the case of a defamation claim: s. 8(2) of the AA 1996. This provision applies where the applicable law to the arbitration is the law of England and Wales or Northern Ireland, even if the seat of the arbitration is outside this jurisdiction or the seat has not yet been designated or determined: s. 2(5) of the AA 1996.

The matter is complicated where a party dies during the course of an arbitration. Until the personal representatives are appointed and made parties to the arbitration there will only be one party in the arbitration proceedings. The problem is less acute if one of the parties dies prior to the appointment of the arbitral tribunal. In such a case the personal representatives will act as that party and the claim will be made either by them or against them. Where the party dies during the course of the arbitration the person named as executor will wish to investigate both the estate and the claim. Notice of a party's death should be given to both the arbitrator and the other party in the arbitration. It may be that the person named as executor will wish to renounce the office of executor, especially where the estate would be unable to meet an award made against it. In such a case the claimant can apply to the Probate Registry for a grant of representation for nominee representatives such as the Official Solicitor to be appointed. On the death of a party to the arbitration it would, in almost every case, be advisable for the arbitral tribunal to stay the proceedings pending the appointment of a personal representative.

6.5.2 Trustee in bankruptcy

A contract that has been entered into by a bankrupt is binding as against the bankrupt but not as against the bankrupt's estate. A bankrupt can therefore be a party to an arbitration but not in order to put his creditors at a disadvantage: *Re an Arbitration between Milnes and Robertson* (1854) 15 CB 451. The bankrupt's estate passes to the bankrupt's trustee in bankruptcy and is subject to the Insolvency Act 1986, Parts VIII to XI.

At common law an arbitration agreement is not discharged by an order for bankruptcy: *Hemsworth* v *Brian* (1845) 14 LJ CP 134. Paragraph 46 of sch. 3 to the AA 1996 repeals s. 3 of the AA 1950 and inserts s. 349A in the Insolvency Act 1986. The provisions in this section only apply where a party to a contract, which contains an arbitration clause, becomes bankrupt after entering into that contract: s. 349A(1) of the Insolvency Act 1986. In such a case the arbitration agreement is only enforceable by or against the trustee in bankruptcy in respect of matters arising from or connected with the contract if the contract is adopted by the trustee in bankruptcy: s. 349A(2) of the Insolvency Act 1986. If the contract is not adopted by the trustee in bankruptcy and a matter to which the arbitration agreement applies requires to be determined in connection with or for the purposes of the bankruptcy proceedings, the trustee in bankruptcy, with the consent of the creditors' committee, or any other party to the agreement, may apply to the court: s. 349A(2)(a) and (b) of the Insolvency Act 1986. The court may, if it thinks fit in all the circumstances of the case, order that the matter be referred to arbitration in accordance with the arbitration agreement.

Once the bankruptcy order has been made, the bankrupt has no power to enter into any agreements which affect any of the property which has been frozen by the bankruptcy order: s. 284 of the Insolvency Act 1986. However, if the court or the creditor's committee agree, the trustee in bankruptcy may be a party to an arbitration agreement in respect of any claims which remain outstanding against the bankrupt: s. 314(a) and sch. 5, para. 6 of the Insolvency Act 1986. Once a bankruptcy order has been made or bankruptcy proceedings commenced, the court may stay any outstanding arbitration proceedings which may exist against the bankrupt: s. 285(1) of the Insolvency Act 1986. A party wishing to proceed with the arbitration before the bankruptcy order is discharged must obtain the permission of the court: s. 285(3) of the Insolvency Act 1986.

6.5.3 Administrator, administrative receiver or liquidator

Once a company has ceased to exist any arbitration to which it is a party comes to an end: *Baytur SA* v *Finagro Holding SA* [1992] QB 610 at p. 619. Lloyd LJ in this case held that: 'An arbitration requires two or more parties. There cannot be a valid arbitration when one of the two parties has ceased to exist.' Further, once a company has ceased to exist the arbitration cannot be revived. In *Foster Yates and Thom Ltd* v *HW Edgehill Equipment Ltd* (1978) *The Times,* 29 November 1978 Megaw LJ in the Court of Appeal held:

> Apart from authority, I should have taken the view that when a corporate body is dissolved as a result of winding up, any action which is pending at the date of dissolution ceases, not temporarily and provisionally, but absolutely and for all time. . . . That is the view which I should have taken on this issue as a matter of principle. It is confirmed in my judgment, inferentially, by reference to the Rules of the Supreme Court; and also, much more importantly, by reference to the decision of the House of Lords in *Morris* v *Harris* [1927] AC 252.

In *Newcastle Protection and Indemnity Association* v *Assurance Foreningen Gard Gjensidig* (24 May 1998 QBD Commercial Court unreported) a claim was made by a shipowners' P & I club on a letter of guarantee provided by a charterers' P & I club. The letter of guarantee provided that issues under it would be resolved through the arbitration procedure in a time charter agreement. The charterers were subsequently irretrievably dissolved and for all purposes ceased to exist. Colman J held that because any arbitration between the charterers and owners had now been rendered impossible by the dissolution of the charterers, the requirement that issues under the guarantee be resolved through the arbitration procedure in the time charter agreement had also been rendered impossible. His lordship held that in such a case the agreed procedure for the resolution of the disputes was discharged and it was appropriate for the court to determine the issues in dispute instead of an arbitral tribunal.

The dissolution of a company should not be confused with the administration or liquidation of a company. Once an administration order has been made against a company, no other proceedings or legal processes may be commenced or continued against it during the period that the order is in force: s. 11(3)(d) of the Insolvency Act 1986. However the administrator of the company has the power to refer any question affecting the company to arbitration: s. 11(3)(d) and sch. 1, para. 6 of the Insolvency Act 1986. Where a company is being wound up by the court, the liquidator may, with the sanction of the court, bring or defend proceedings: s. 167 and sch. 4, para. 4 of the Insolvency Act 1986. Under s. 178(2)(a) of the Insolvency Act 1986 a liquidator may, by giving notice, disclaim any onerous property such as unprofitable contracts, and thereby disclaim any arbitration agreements within them. For the effect this may have on an interested party, see s. 181(3) and (4) of the Insolvency Act 1986. Once the company has been made subject to a winding-up order or a provisional liquidator has been appointed, no new proceedings can be commenced except with leave of the court: s. 130(2) and (3) of the Insolvency Act 1986.

6.5.4 Assignee

A party to a contract which contains an arbitration clause can assign its rights under the contract to a third party (the assignee). The assignee will then be bound by the arbitration clause: *Shaylor* v *Woolf* [1946] Ch 320; *Montedipe SpA* v *JTP-RO Jugotanker* [1990] 2 Lloyd's Rep 11; *Schiffahrtsgesellschaft Detler von Appen GmbH* v *Voest Alpine Intertrading GmbH* [1997] 2 Lloyd's Rep 279. Assignment in its legal sense means a transfer of the rights of a party arising out of a contract, or part of those rights, to another person who is a stranger to the contract. An assignment may occur in two ways: by operation of law or by the party to the contract passing its rights to the third party by a contractual assignment. A valid assignment will allow the third party to sue under the contract in respect of the rights assigned to it.

An assignment by operation of law occurs, for example, on the death of a party to a contract, when the rights and liabilities of non-personal contracts will vest in the executors. On the bankruptcy of a party the rights and liabilities of non-personal contracts vest in the trustees in bankruptcy.

It is only the benefit of a contract which can be assigned and the contract must not be of a personal nature: *Tolhurst* v *Associated Portland Cement Manufacturers (1900) Ltd* [1902] 2 KB 660. The burden of a contract cannot be assigned: *Tolhurst* v *Associated Portland Cement Manufacturers (1900) Ltd* [1902] 2 KB 660; *Nokes* v *Doncaster Amalgamated Collieries* Ltd [1940] AC 1014. However, the burden of a contract may be performed by a third party where there is a novation of the contract or where vicarious performance of the contract is permitted. If the contract includes an effective non-assignment clause, the assignee is not bound by the arbitration clause: *Bawehem Ltd* v *MC Fabrications* (1998 unreported).

An assignment may be legal or equitable. A legal assignment under s. 136 of the Law of Property Act 1925 enables the assignee to sue under the contract in its own name. If the assignment is only equitable then the assignee must sue in the assignor's name or, if the assignor refuses to be joined as a claimant, must add the assignor as a respondent: *William Brandt's Sons and Co.* v *Dunlop Rubber Co. Ltd* [1905] AC 454; *Weddell* v *J.A. Pearce and Major* [1988] Ch 26. Alternatively, the assignee may perfect the assignment by giving notice of the assignment to the other party in writing, thereby complying with s. 136 of the Law of Property Act 1925.

The assignee may then bring new proceedings in its own name. The difference between a legal and equitable assignment is therefore predominantly a matter of procedure. If an equitable assignee sues in his own name without joining the assignor as a party then the proceedings will be a nullity.

Section 136 of the Law of Property Act 1925 states that for an assignment to be legal it must fulfil the following conditions. First, it must be an absolute assignment and cannot be by way of charge only. Secondly, the assignment must be in writing. Thirdly, express notice must be given to the other party to the contract. The assignee will then have all the rights of the original party to the contract.

An equitable assignment need not be in a particular form (apart from an equitable assignment of an equitable interest, which needs to be in writing: s. 53(1)(c) of the Law of Property Act 1925) but a clear intention is required. If there is a clear intention to assign a right under the contract but one of the requirements of s. 136 of the Law of Property Act 1925 has not been satisfied then an equitable assignment will arise. Where an equitable assignment has taken place but the other party has had no notice of it and pays or settles with the assignor, that party will have no liability to the assignee. An equitable assignment was held to have arisen in *Herkules Piling* v *Tilbury Construction* (1992) 61 BLR 107. In the course of an arbitration Herkules' assets and undertakings were purchased by a third party. Tilbury was not given any notice of this and only became aware of the purchase at the disclosure state of the proceedings. The court stated that the only right that the equitable assignee possesses in such circumstances is the right against the assignor, who will become the trustee of such sums of money as are paid to it.

An arbitration agreement in a contract is assignable before and after the arbitration has started. However, where there is an arbitration in progress, neither a legal assignee nor an equitable assignee will automatically become a party to the arbitration. Hobhouse J clarified the position of a legal assignee in *Montedipe SpA* v *JTP-RO Jugotanker* [1990] 2 Lloyd's Rep 11. His lordship stated that before a legal assignee can become a party to a pending arbitration there are two steps to be taken. First, notice must by given by the assignee to the other side. Secondly, the assignee must also give notice to the arbitrators. His lordship said, at p. 18:

> Once these steps have been taken both the practical and conceptual difficulties are, or can be, resolved. The right to arbitrate is assignable; that assignment is completed and becomes legally binding upon the other persons concerned by the service of the notice. The service of the notice and the intervention in the arbitration provide as effective and satisfactory method of carrying on the proceedings as that which is provided in relation to litigation by RSC, ord. 15, r. 7(2).

This was cited with approval by Lloyd LJ in *Baytur SA* v *Finagro Holdings SA* [1991] 4 All ER 129, which concerned the position of an equitable assignee in arbitration proceedings where no notice of the assignment had been given to the other side or to the arbitral tribunal. The facts of the case were that the plaintiff had contracted to sell goods to the buyer, a French company, in 1985. The plaintiff did not ship any goods so the buyer claimed damages. The dispute was referred to arbitration pursuant to the contract. However, in 1986 a *traité de scission* (a demerger under French law) took place and the buyer company was dissolved. The buyer's rights and obligations under the contract and on the pending arbitration were transferred to the defendant. In 1989 the arbitral tribunal made an award in favour of the buyer. In May 1989 the plaintiff gave notice of appeal. In August 1989 the plaintiff received notice that the buyer had been dissolved in 1986. The plaintiff sought a declaration that the arbitrator's award was null and void because one party to the arbitration had ceased to exist and that the arbitrators had in consequence no jurisdiction to make the award. At first instance this declaration was granted. The defendant appealed.

The defendant argued that an assignee's rights and obligations in arbitration proceedings arise out of the contract of assignment and are transferred whether or not notice is given under s. 136 of the Law of Property Act 1925. The plaintiff refuted this argument and said that there was a crucial distinction between having an equitable right and exercising it.

On appeal Lloyd LJ agreed with the plaintiff. At p. 615 his lordship said: 'The fact that the defendants might have applied to become a party to the arbitration does not mean that they were already a party. They had, in Mr Leigh-Jones's vivid phrase, bought a ticket. They had not yet joined the train.' Lloyd LJ followed the rationale in *Montedipe* SpA v *JTP-RO Jugotanker* [1990] 2 Lloyd's Rep 11 and held as follows, at p. 617:

> I would decide the present case on this simple ground. An assignee does not automatically become a party to a pending arbitration on the assignment taking place in equity. Something more is required. He must at least give notice to the other side, and submit to the jurisdiction of the arbitrator.

As the defendant had not given notice to the plaintiff of the assignment, to bring it within s. 136 of the Law of Property Act 1925, it could only pursue the action in the name of the assignor. However, it was impossible to proceed with the action as the assignor had ceased to exist. The arbitration therefore lapsed.

Lloyd LJ raised an interesting point in his judgment by way of *obiter dicta*. His lordship questioned whether a mere submission to the jurisdiction of the arbitral tribunal would be sufficient for an assignee to become a party to the arbitration or whether the other party to the arbitration and the arbitral tribunal first had to consent to the assignee becoming a party. The point is relevant where the assignor no longer exists and the question of costs arises. In *Montedipe* SpA v *JTP-RO Jugotanker* Hobhouse J had stated that the assignor would remain liable for costs already incurred in the arbitration and that the assignment added another party who was potentially liable for those costs. In the present case the assignor had ceased to exist. Therefore the burden of the costs solely fell on the assignee. This raises a possible conflict with the principle that an assignor cannot transfer the burden of a contract to an assignee. Lloyd LJ considered what would have happened if the plaintiff had had a counterclaim in the arbitration. His lordship stated at p. 138 that:

> There would be scope for great injustice if an insolvent assignor could assign away the benefit of a claim in arbitration to an associated company, while remaining solely liable for the burden of the respondent's counterclaim. This has led me to question whether a *mere* submission is enough. Because of the nature of arbitration, as a consensual method of settling disputes, it may be that the consent of the arbitrator, and the other party to the arbitration, is required. If this is the correct analysis, then the only exception might be where the foreign law creates a universal successor, as in *National Bank of Greece and Athens SA* v *Metliss* [1958] AC 509.

Lloyd LJ did not go further in attempting to answer this question. His lordship stated that the 'argument was not fully developed before us, and must therefore wait another occasion'. His lordship, however, implied that in such circumstances there was doubt as to the soundness of the 'independent doctrine of pure benefit and burden'. However, a legal or equitable assignee takes the benefit: 'subject to all rights of set-off and other defences which were available against the assignor': *Roxburghe* v *Cox* (1881) 17 ChD 520 at p. 526. So an assignee of a claim takes subject to any counterclaim by the other party to the contract arising out of the contract. In such circumstances there is unlikely to be the scope for injustice foreseen by Lloyd LJ.

6.5.5 Agents

The general principle of law is that an agent may enter into an arbitration agreement on behalf of its principal. The agency agreement may be created expressly or impliedly. There need not always be a contract between agent and principal and in some situations the relationship of agent and principal will arise by reason of the conduct of the parties or by operation of law.

As a general proposition it may be said that where an agent, on behalf of its principal, has entered into a contract with a third party the contract is between principal and third party. If a dispute arises out of the contract then the parties to that dispute are the principal and the third party. The agent cannot sue or be sued. Therefore where an arbitration agreement is within the contract the agent cannot be a party to the arbitral proceedings. This general proposition is, however, subject to a number of exceptions.

The first and major exception to the above general proposition is where the agent has acted for an undisclosed principal. This is where the agent does not disclose to the third party the fact that there is an agency agreement and the third party genuinely believes that it is contracting with the agent. In such a case the principal may still sue or be sued on the agreement, though the third party would also have a right of action against the agent: *Public Trustee* v *Taylor* [1978] VR 289. Where principal and agent are both potentially liable the third party must elect whether to proceed against the principal or agent. Having elected to bring proceedings against either principal or agent the third party loses its right to bring proceedings against the other. Although there is no clear authority on this point it is likely that in such a case the third party could elect to issue a notice to arbitrate against either the principal or the agent. Such authorities as there are on who the third party has contracted with are contradictory. In *Keighley, Maxsted and Co.* v *Durant* [1901] AC 240 at p. 261 the House of Lords gave the opinion that it was a contract with the principal. However, in *Higgins* v *Senior* (1841) 8 M & W 834 the court had held that the third party could not be deprived of its right to bring proceedings against the agent if it so desired and therefore treated the contract as being with the agent.

6.5.6 Subcontractors

Certain forms of contracts in the construction industry permit subcontractors to bring an action against the employer in the name of the contractor although there may be no dispute between the contractor and the employer. This is commonly known as 'name borrowing'. In practice the subcontractor tends to 'name borrow' when the employer makes a decision which puts the subcontractor at a disadvantage.

This type of action appears to have the effect of circumventing the privity of contract rule, which only permits the parties to a contract to sue or be sued under the contract. The arbitration agreement is in the main contract and is between the contractor and the employer. The subcontractor is not a party to either the main contract or the main contract arbitration agreement. However, where name borrowing occurs the main contract will be incorporated into the subcontract by reference. In *Trafalgar House Construction (Regions) Ltd* v *Railtrack plc* (1995) 75 BLR 55 at p. 79 the court held that although the main contract and the subcontract were legally separate, they were 'plainly connected with each other both commercially and in their terms'.

In *Birse Construction Ltd* v *Co-operative Wholesale Society Ltd* (1997) 84 BLR 58 the contractor brought arbitration proceedings against the employer on behalf of the subcontractor. The action was for loss and expenses incurred by the subcontractor due to the employer having breached the main contract. The arbitrator made an award of damages in the name of the contractor on behalf of the subcontractor against the employer. The employer went into liquidation without paying this sum. The subcontractor relied on the arbitrator's award and sought to recover the damages from the contractor. The Court of Appeal held that although no actual moneys had been paid by the employer to the contractor, the contractor was still obliged to comply with the arbitrator's award and pay the damages to the subcontractor. In coming to this decision Phillips LJ said at p. 71 that:

> It is common ground that, in addition to his duty to lend his name to the subcontractor for name-borrowing arbitrations in accordance with the specific

provisions of the subcontract, the main contractor can also be obliged to pursue an arbitration for the benefit of the subcontractor pursuant to clause 8(c) and clause 12 of the subcontract.

Further, Phillips LJ accepted the submission of Mr Fernyhough QC that:

> . . . it is implicit that where, in an arbitration under the main contract, the arbitrator makes an award of a sum which should have been certified as due in respect of the subcontract works, that sum falls to be treated in the subcontract as a sum duly certified, so that, in that respect, the award is binding on the subcontract.

Phillips LJ continued that if the arbitral tribunal's award was not to have an effect on the subcontract then this would lead to an absurd result. The subcontractor could insist on borrowing the main contractor's name in order, by arbitration, to challenge a certificate of the architect but the decision of the arbitrator would then not have a direct effect on the subcontract.

7 The Arbitral Tribunal

7.1 ROLE AND FUNCTION OF THE ARBITRAL TRIBUNAL

The role and function of the arbitral tribunal is to determine the dispute between the parties based on the evidence and facts that are submitted to it in a judicial, fair and impartial manner. In this respect the function of the arbitral tribunal is similar to that of a judge. However, in other respects the role of the arbitral tribunal differs fundamentally from that of a judge in so far as the jurisdiction of the arbitral tribunal arises solely from the parties' arbitration agreement and not from the State. The arbitral tribunal cannot exceed the authority given to it by the parties. It is the right of the parties to decide how their dispute should be resolved (s. 1(b) of the AA 1996). This includes under s. 46 of the AA 1996 the freedom of the parties to choose the law to be applied in resolving the dispute. However, the arbitral tribunal's role is also determined by the AA 1996. The arbitral tribunal has to abide by the mandatory sections contained within the AA 1996, particularly s. 33, which sets out the general duty of the arbitral tribunal:

(a)   to act fairly and impartially as between the parties, giving each party a reasonable opportunity of putting his case and dealing with that of his opponent, and

(b)   to adopt procedures suitable to the circumstances of the particular case, avoiding unnecessary delay or expense, so as to provide a fair means for the resolution of the matters falling to be determined.

The AA 1996 also provides the arbitral tribunal with certain powers, principally in ss. 34 to 39 and ss. 41 to 44. These sections apply where the parties have not made a contrary agreement. These powers give the arbitral tribunal a wide discretion in the conduct of the proceedings. See chapters 8 and 9 for a further discussion of the arbitral tribunal's duty and powers.

7.2 COMPOSITION OF THE ARBITRAL TRIBUNAL

7.2.1   Number of arbitrators

The arbitral tribunal may be composed of one or more arbitrators. The parties are free to agree on the number of arbitrators to form the arbitral tribunal and whether there is to be a chairman or umpire: s. 15(1) of the AA 1996. If there is no agreement on the number of arbitrators, the arbitral tribunal shall consist of a sole arbitrator: s. 15(3) of the AA 1996. In *Villa Denizcilik Sanayi Ve Ticaret AS* v *Longen SA* [1998] 1 Lloyd's Rep 195 it was held that the court had no jurisdiction to appoint more than one arbitrator where s. 15(3) of the AA 1996 applied.

Once a request is made by one party to the other to appoint an arbitrator then the parties have 28 days thereafter to make a joint appointment of a sole arbitrator: s. 16(3) of the AA 1996. If the parties fail to agree on a joint appointment then the matter of the appointment is resolved by any default procedure agreed by the parties: s. 18(1) of the AA 1996. If the parties do not concur in the appointment of the sole arbitrator and they have not agreed a default procedure, a party can apply to the court under s. 18(2) of the AA 1996 for it to exercise its powers under s. 18(3)(a) to (d) of the AA 1996.

If parties have not specified a particular number of arbitrators but have referred in the arbitration agreement to a resolution of the dispute by 'arbitrators' then, if there is no evidence to the contrary, a presumption exists that the arbitral tribunal shall consist of two arbitrators: *Fletamentos Maritimos SA* v *Effjohn International BV* [1995] 1 Lloyd's Rep 311. An arbitral tribunal consisting of two arbitrators could find themselves at in impasse. To prevent this problem arising, s. 15(2) of the AA 1996 provides that a further arbitrator be appointed to act as chairman.

7.2.2   Chairman or umpire

The parties are free to agree that their dispute be resolved by an arbitral tribunal consisting of two arbitrators or any even number. Where the arbitral tribunal is made up of an even number of arbitrators then problems could arise where the arbitral tribunal is unable to reach an agreement. The AA 1996 therefore provides that unless otherwise agreed by the parties an additional arbitrator must be appointed to act as chairman of the arbitral tribunal where the arbitral tribunal is made up of an even number: s. 15(2) of the AA 1996. Alternatively the parties can agree to appoint a third arbitrator to act as an umpire.

The use of an umpire in arbitral proceedings is a peculiarly English concept. It is, however, rare. The umpire may be appointed by the arbitral tribunal at any time during the reference and shall be appointed before the substantive hearing or forthwith if they cannot agree. If the arbitral tribunal refuse a request by the parties that an umpire be appointed before a disagreement has occurred then the parties should agree in writing to vary the arbitration agreement: *Taylor* v *Denny, Mott and Dickson Ltd* [1912] AC 666.

If the parties have agreed that there should be an umpire, they are free to agree what the functions of the umpire should be: s. 21(1) of the AA 1996. It is particularly important to decide whether the umpire is to attend the proceedings and when the umpire is to replace the other arbitrators as the arbitral tribunal with power to make decisions, orders and awards: s. 21(1) of the AA 1996. Where the parties have not agreed these functions the umpire shall attend the proceedings and be supplied with the same documents and other materials as the other arbitrators are to be given: s. 21(3) of the AA 1996. The umpire shall only have the power to make decisions, orders and awards in place of the other arbitrators in cases where they cannot agree on a matter relating to the arbitration: s. 21(4) of the AA 1996.

Where the arbitral tribunal cannot agree they must immediately give notice in writing to the parties and the umpire of that disagreement. The umpire's jurisdiction to replace the arbitral tribunal arises when notice is received of the disagreement from all members of the arbitral tribunal. If the arbitral tribunal, or any one of them, fails to notify the umpire of the disagreement then s. 21(5) of the AA 1996 enables any party to apply to the court: 'which may order that the umpire shall replace the other arbitrators as the tribunal with power to make decisions, orders and awards as if he were sole arbitrator'. The party making the application should first give notice of the application to all the parties and all the members of the arbitral tribunal: s. 21(5) of the AA 1996. Any appeal from a decision of the court under s. 21 of the AA 1996 requires the leave of the court: s. 21(6) of the AA 1996.

Section 20 of the AA 1996 deals with the appointment of a chairman. If the parties have agreed that two or more arbitrators are to be appointed and that there is to be a chairman, the parties are then free to agree the functions of the chairman regarding the making of decisions, orders and awards: s. 20(1) of the AA 1996. If the parties have not agreed the chairman's functions then decisions, orders and awards should be made by all or the majority of the arbitrators, which includes the chairman: s. 20(3) of the AA 1996. Section 22 of the AA 1996 deals with decision-making where no chairman or umpire has been appointed. If the parties have agreed that two or more arbitrators are to be appointed but that there is to be no chairman or umpire, the parties are free to agree how the arbitral tribunal is to make decisions, orders and awards: s. 22(1) of the AA 1996. Where there is no such agreement then the decisions, orders and awards shall be made by all or the majority of the arbitrators: s. 22(2) of the AA 1996.

The appointment of the chairman will usually be made by the members of the arbitral tribunal. In most arbitration rules the matter of the appointment of the chairman is specifically dealt with. Where the arbitral tribunal has the power to appoint the chairman then it need not seek permission from the parties for its choice. One of the parties may in fact be dissatisfied with the choice of chairman but unless both parties agree to revoke the authority of the chairman under s. 23 of the AA 1996 the fact that one party is dissatisfied will not affect the validity of the chairman's appointment: *Oliver* v *Collings* (1809) 11 East 367.

7.3   APPOINTMENT OF THE ARBITRAL TRIBUNAL

Every party to the arbitration must be notified of the appointment of an arbitrator. The person nominated or appointed should also be notified of the nomination or appointment and agree to act in order for the appointment to be valid: *Tradax Export SA* v *Volkswagenwerk AG* [1970] 1 QB 537.

The arbitral tribunal may be appointed by the agreement of the parties, an appointing authority or by the court. The arbitration agreement may provide for an appointing body to appoint the arbitral tribunal if the parties cannot agree. Examples of such bodies are the Chartered Institute of Arbitrators, the London Court of International Arbitration, the Royal Institute of British Architects and the Royal Institute of Chartered Surveyors.

7.3.1 Appointment by appointing authority

The appointing body's function is to appoint a suitable arbitral tribunal to hear the dispute. The type of arbitral tribunal required may be specified in the arbitration agreement. If the appointing body elects an arbitral tribunal which does not possess the qualifications specified within the arbitration agreement then, unless it is shown to have acted in bad faith, it will not be liable to the parties: s. 74(1) of the AA 1996. However, the arbitral tribunal may be removed under s. 24(1)(b) of the AA 1996.

7.3.2 Appointment by the court

The AA 1996 gives the parties the autonomy to choose the arbitral tribunal and the method of its appointment including the procedure to be adopted in the event that the parties' agreed method of appointment has failed (see 7.4). The AA 1996 limits the powers of the court to appoint the arbitral tribunal. The court will not intervene to make any appointment if the parties have agreed a procedure for appointing the arbitral tribunal. If there is no such agreement then the provisions for appointing an arbitral tribunal in s. 16 of the AA 1996 apply (see 7.4). Section 16 sets out the procedure to be adopted if the arbitral tribunal is to consist of one, two or three arbitrators or two arbitrators and an umpire. Section 16(7) provides that in any other case, particularly if there is a multi-party arbitration, the procedure stated in s. 18 applies. In such a case a party can apply to the court to exercise its powers under s. 18(3) to appoint an arbitral tribunal. Section 18 sets out the court's powers in the event that the procedure for appointing the arbitral tribunal has failed and the parties have not agreed what should happen in this circumstance. Under s. 18(2), any party can apply to the court to exercise its powers under s. 18(3), which gives the court wide powers regarding the appointment of an arbitrator (see 7.4).

In rare cases the parties may have made a specific provision in the arbitration agreement that the appointment of an arbitrator is to be made by the court, or they may have given their express consent to such a method of appointment. In such cases the court makes the appointment as an independent authority: *Medor Lines SpA* v *Traelandsfos A/S* [1969] 2 Lloyd's Rep 225.

Section 19 of the AA 1996 states that in deciding whether, and in considering how, to exercise its powers conferred by ss. 16 and 18: 'the court shall have due regard to any agreement of the parties as to the qualifications required of the arbitrators'. This follows the principle of party autonomy that is prevalent within the AA 1996.

7.4   PROCEDURE FOR APPOINTING THE ARBITRAL TRIBUNAL

Section 16(1) of the AA 1996 gives the parties the freedom to agree on the procedure for the appointment of the arbitral tribunal and the procedure for appointing any chairman or umpire. If there is no such agreement then, where the arbitral tribunal is to consist of a sole arbitrator, the parties shall jointly appoint the arbitrator not later than 28 days after service of a request in writing by either party to do so: s. 16(3) of the AA 1996. If the arbitral tribunal is to consist of two arbitrators then each party shall appoint one arbitrator not later than 14 days after service of a request in writing by either party to do so: s. 16(4) of the AA 1996. If the arbitral tribunal is to consist of three arbitrators then each party shall appoint one arbitrator not later than 14 days after service of a request in writing by either party to do so and the two appointed arbitrators shall then appoint a third arbitrator as the chairman of the arbitral tribunal: s. 16(5)(a) and (b) of the AA 1996. If the arbitral tribunal is to consist of two arbitrators and an umpire then each party shall appoint one arbitrator not later than 14 days after service of a request in writing by either party to do so: s. 16(6)(a) of the AA 1996. The two appointed arbitrators may appoint an umpire at any time after they themselves are appointed and shall do so before any substantive hearing or forthwith if they cannot agree on a matter relating to the arbitration: s. 16(6)(b) of the AA 1996. In any other case, particularly if there are more than two parties, the default procedure set out in s. 18 of the AA 1996 should be followed: s. 16(7) of the AA 1996.

7.5   DEFAULT IN THE APPOINTMENT OF A SOLE ARBITRATOR

Section 17 of the AA 1996 sets out the provisions to be applied if there has been a default in the appointment of a sole arbitrator. This is not a mandatory section of the AA 1996 and the parties are free to agree an alternative procedure. Unless the parties otherwise agree, where two parties to an arbitration agreement agree that each of them should appoint an arbitrator but one of the parties has refused or failed to do so within the time specified, then the other party, after having appointed its arbitrator, may give notice to the party in default that it proposes to appoint its arbitrator as a sole arbitrator: s. 17(1) of the AA 1996. If the party in default does not make the required appointment and notify the other party that it has done so within seven clear days of the other party's notice under s. 17(1) of the AA 1996 then the other party may appoint its arbitrator as the sole arbitrator: s. 17(2) of the AA 1996. That arbitrator's award will then be binding on both parties as if he had been appointed by the parties by agreement: s. 17(2) of the AA 1996. However, in cases where an appointment of an arbitrator has been made under s. 17(2) of the AA 1996, the party in default may, on notice to the appointing party, apply to the court, which may set aside the appointment: s. 17(3) of the AA 1996. The party making the application under s. 17(3) of the AA 1996 should do so immediately as any delay may result in the loss of the right to object under s. 73 of the AA 1996. Grounds on which the court has set aside the appointment of a sole arbitrator include: where the appointment was made prior to the seven days' notice expiring and where the notice had not been properly given: *Drummond* v *Hamer* [1942] 1 KB 352. Any appeal from a decision of the court under s. 17 requires the leave of the court: s. 17(4) of the AA 1996.

7.6 DEFAULT PROCEDURE GENERALLY

Section 18 of the AA 1996 provides rules where there is a default in the appointment process. The provisions of s. 18 of the AA 1996 are applicable where the parties have failed to agree a default procedure. Where there is an agreed procedure but a party has not followed it, s. 18 of the AA 1996 will not be activated as the agreed procedure will not be seen to have failed. Where the arbitral tribunal has been appointed under s. 17 of the AA 1996 then this will not be considered to be a failure of procedure unless the appointment is set aside. Section 18(3) of the AA 1996 sets out the default provisions where the parties have failed to agree in the appointment of the arbitral tribunal. The court's powers in default are:

(a) to give directions as to the making of any necessary appointments;
(b) to direct that the tribunal shall be constituted by such appointments (or any one or more of them) as have been made;
(c) to revoke any appointments already made;
(d) to make any necessary appointments itself.

The court has a discretion under s. 18(3) of the AA 1996 whether or not to exercise its powers: *Villa Denizcilik Sanayi Ve Ticaret AS* v *Longen SA* [1998] 1 Lloyd's Rep 195. Where the court makes an appointment under s. 18(3) of the AA 1996 then it is treated as having the same effect as if it had been made by the agreement of the parties: s. 18(4) of the AA 1996. Any appeal from the decision of the court under s. 18 of the AA 1996 requires the leave of the court: s. 18(5) of the AA 1996.

In *Villa Denizcilik Sanayi Ve Ticaret AS* v *Longen SA* [1998] 1 Lloyd's Rep 195 the applicants had applied to the court under s. 18(2) of the AA 1996 for the court to exercise its powers under s. 18(3) to appoint a sole arbitrator after the respondents had inadvertently allowed the 28-day period provided by s. 16(3) for a joint appointment of a sole arbitrator to be made to elapse. The applicants made the application because there was no agreement between the parties as to what procedure should be followed in the event that the procedure for appointing an arbitral tribunal should fail. The respondents desired more than one arbitrator to be appointed as this was customary in maritime arbitrations. The court held that it had no jurisdiction to appoint more than one arbitrator as s. 15(3) of the AA 1996 states that where, as in this case, the parties cannot agree the number of arbitrators the arbitral tribunal shall consist of a sole arbitrator.

7.7   CIRCUMSTANCES IN WHICH A MEMBER OF THE ARBITRAL TRIBUNAL CEASES TO HOLD OFFICE

A member of an arbitral tribunal ceases to hold office on the occurrence of the following: death, resignation, removal from office and revocation of its authority by the parties or the court.

7.7.1   Death of an arbitrator

Section 26(1) of the AA 1996, which is a mandatory section, provides that the authority of the arbitral tribunal is personal and ceases on the arbitrator's death. However under s. 26(2) of the AA 1996, unless otherwise agreed by the parties, the death of the person who appointed the arbitral tribunal does not revoke its authority.

7.7.2   Resignation of an arbitrator

Section 25 of the AA 1996 deals with the resignation of the arbitral tribunal. The parties are free to agree with an arbitrator as to the consequences of the resignation in respect of the arbitrator's entitlement (if any) to fees or expenses, and any liability for breach of the agreement to act which may ensue from the resignation: s. 25(1) of the AA 1996. Section 25(2) of the AA 1996 provides that if or to the extent that there is no such agreement then s. 25(3) of the AA 1996 applies. Under s. 25(3) of the AA 1996 an arbitrator who resigns may (upon notice) to the parties apply to the court:

(a)   to grant him relief from any liability thereby incurred by him, and
(b)   to make such orders as it thinks fit with respect to his entitlement (if any) to fees or expenses or the repayment of any fees or expenses already paid.

The court has the discretion under s. 25(4) of the AA 1996, if it is satisfied that in all the circumstances it was reasonable for the arbitral tribunal to resign, to grant the arbitral tribunal relief from any liability incurred by reason of its resignation on such terms as it thinks fit. There are no cases yet which indicate what reasons for resigning the court would consider to be reasonable in all the circumstances. The DAC at para. 115 of their February 1996 report envisage two situations in which it would be reasonable for the arbitral tribunal to resign. First, if there was a conflict between the arbitral tribunal's duty under s. 33 of the AA 1996 and the parties' agreement as to how the arbitration should proceed. Secondly, if the arbitration was proceeding for far longer than could have reasonably been expected when the arbitral tribunal accepted the appointment. The leave of the court is required for any appeal from a decision of the court under s. 25 of the AA 1996: s. 25(5) of the AA 1996.

7.7.3   Removal of an arbitrator

Section 24(1) of the AA 1996 states that a party to an arbitration may apply to the court to remove an arbitrator. The application under s. 24(1) of the AA 1996 must be on notice to the other parties, to the arbitrator concerned and to any other arbitrator: s. 24(1) of the AA 1996. The court shall not exercise its power to remove the arbitrator unless it is satisfied that the applicant has first exhausted any available recourse for removing the arbitrator: s. 24(2) of the AA 1996. This condition applies to circumstances where the parties have vested an arbitral or other institution or person with the power to remove an arbitrator. A party who objects to the conduct of the proceedings but who continues to take part in them must make the objection known as soon as it arises or that party may lose the right to object under s. 73(1)(b) of the AA 1996. Under s. 24(3) the arbitral tribunal may continue the arbitral proceedings and make an award while the application under s. 24(1) of the AA 1996 is pending. Where an arbitrator is removed by the court, the court may make such orders as it thinks fit regarding any entitlement he or she may have to fees and expenses including the repayment of fees and expenses to the appropriate party: s. 24(4) of the AA 1996. The arbitrator is permitted to appear and be heard by the court before it makes any order under s. 24 of the AA 1996: s. 24(5) of the AA 1996. The leave of the court is required for any appeal from a decision of the court under s. 24 of the AA 1996: s. 24(6) of the AA 1996. Section 24(1) of the AA 1996 provides that the application to remove an arbitral tribunal may be made on any of the following grounds:

  (a)   that circumstances exist that give rise to justifiable doubts as to his impartiality;
  (b)   that he does not possess the qualifications required by the arbitration agreement;
  (c)   that he is physically or mentally incapable of conducting the proceedings or there are justifiable doubts as to his capacity to do so;
  (d)   that he has refused or failed—
    (i)   properly to conduct the proceedings, or
    (ii)   to use all reasonable dispatch in conducting the proceedings or making an award,
and that substantial injustice has been or will be caused to the applicant.

7.7.3.1   Justifiable doubts as to the arbitral tribunal's impartiality   The requirement that an arbitral tribunal should be impartial is found at common law: *Re an Arbitration between SS Catalina (Owners) and MV Norma (Owners)* (1938) 61 Ll L Rep 360; *Damond Lock Grabowski and Partners* v *Laing Investments (Bracknell) Ltd* (1992) 60 BLR 112. In *Damond Lock Grabowski and Partners* v *Laing Investments (Bracknell) Ltd* the arbitrator was removed for refusing to hear representations from one party in respect of procedural matters. Gatehouse J summarised the arbitrator's conduct at p. 137:

The arbitrator has unquestionably pointed the finger at the applicants and repeatedly accused them, in my judgement unfairly, of deliberate delays. Above all, he has not paid proper heed to their objections and has insisted that the hearing must start on the date he ordered, when they cannot be in a position to conduct their case properly.

The arbitrator was removed on the grounds that a reasonable person would think that there was a real likelihood that the he could not or would not fairly determine the issues on the evidence and arguments to be adduced before him, following the test applied in *Ardahalian v Unifert International SA* [1984] 2 Lloyd's Rep 84. The requirement of impartiality is a principle of natural justice which has been embodied in the AA 1996. Section 1(a) of the AA 1996 states that 'the object of arbitration is to obtain the fair resolution of disputes by an impartial tribunal'. Under s. 33(1) of the AA 1996 it is the arbitral tribunal's mandatory duty to 'act fairly and impartially, between the parties, giving each party a reasonable opportunity of putting his case and dealing with that of the opponent'. If this duty is breached by the arbitral tribunal then its award can be challenged on the ground of serious irregularity under s. 68(1) of the AA 1996. The party making the application under s. 24(1)(a) of the AA 1996 does not have to prove actual impartiality on the part of the arbitral tribunal but merely 'justifiable doubts' as to its impartiality. The applicable test is whether in all the circumstances there is a real danger of bias in the sense that the arbitral tribunal may treat or has treated one party less favourably than the other: *R v Gough* [1993] AC 646; *Laker Airways Inc. v FLS Aerospace Ltd* (1999) *The Times*, 21 May.

An arbitral tribunal cannot be removed under s. 24 of the AA 1996 for lack of independence. Section 24 of the AA 1996 differs slightly from Article 12(2) of the UNCITRAL Model Law, under which the arbitral tribunal can be removed where it can be shown there is a lack of impartiality or independence. The DAC in para. 102 of their February 1996 report stated that they did not follow Article 12(2) of the UNCITRAL Model Law because: 'the inclusion of independence would give rise to endless arguments, as it has, for example, in Sweden and the United States, where almost any connection (however remote) has been put forward to challenge the "independence" of an arbitrator'. However, where the lack of independence raises justifiable doubts as to the impartiality of the arbitral tribunal then this will be a ground for removal of the arbitral tribunal under s. 24(1)(a) of the AA 1996.

7.7.3.2 Absence of required qualifications The arbitral tribunal may be removed under s. 24(1)(b) of the AA 1996 if it does not possess the qualifications required by the parties in their arbitration agreement. The parties are free to decide the qualifications of the arbitral tribunal. This right derives from the principle of party autonomy and is one of the perceived benefits of arbitration proceedings as opposed to court proceedings. For example, the parties may require that the arbitral tribunal consist of members of a certain trade or profession; or should be legally qualified or commercially experienced.

7.7.3.3 Incapacity A member of the arbitral tribunal may be removed under s. 24(1)(c) of the AA 1996 not only for actual physical or mental incapability in conducting the arbitration but also if there are any justifiable doubts as to that arbitrator's physical or mental capacity.

7.7.3.4 Refusing or failing to act as required The arbitral tribunal may be removed for refusing or failing to properly conduct the proceedings: s. 24(d)(i) of the AA 1996. The arbitral tribunal may also be removed for refusing or failing to use all reasonable dispatch in conducting the proceedings or in making the award: s. 24(d)(ii) of the AA 1996. In both cases it must be shown that this has caused or will cause substantial injustice to the party making the application. The DAC at para. 106 of their February 1996 report state that the court's power of removal was inserted as a measure to support the arbitral process and was not a power which should be used to subvert the proceedings:

> The provision is not intended to allow the court to substitute its own view as to how the arbitral proceedings should be conducted. Thus the choice by an arbitrator of a particular procedure, unless it breaches the duty laid on arbitrators by clause 33, should on no view justify the removal of an arbitrator, even if the court would not in itself have adopted that procedure. In short, this ground only exists to cover what we hope will be a very rare case where an arbitrator so conducts the proceedings that it can fairly be said that instead of carrying through with the object of arbitration as stated in the Bill, he is in effect frustrating that object.

The object of the Bill to which the DAC refer is now set out in s. 1(a) of the AA 1996 as being the attainment of 'the fair resolution of disputes by an impartial tribunal without unnecessary delay or expense'. It is clear that the DAC sought to have an arbitral tribunal removed only if it failed or refused to conduct the arbitration within the spirit of this objective and that this caused or would cause the applicant substantial injustice. In *Kelsey Association Ltd* v *Ruddy Developments Ltd* [1998] ADRLJ 6 an application made under s. 24 of the AA 1996 for the removal of the arbitral tribunal, on the basis of its incompetence, was refused. The court held that the arbitral tribunal was not so incompetent as to make a reasonable person lose confidence in it. In conducting the proceedings properly under s. 24(d) of the AA 1996 the arbitral tribunal should therefore adhere to its duty under s. 33(1) of the AA 1996.

7.7.4 Revocation of the arbitral tribunal's authority

The court has the power to revoke an appointment of the arbitral tribunal under s. 18(3)(c) of the AA 1996. The court can only exercise its power under this section on the basis that the parties have not agreed a default procedure in the event of the failure of the appointment procedure: s. 18(2) of the AA 1996. A party must make its application to the court on notice to the other parties: s. 18(2) of the AA 1996. The DAC at para. 88 of their February 1996 report stated that the power of the court under s. 18(3) of the AA 1996 is intended to be used:

Where unless the court took this step it might be suggested thereafter that the parties had not been fairly treated, since one had his own choice of arbitrator while the other had an arbitrator imposed on him by the court in circumstances that were no fault of his own.

This occurred in the French ICC case of *Siemens AG* v *Dutco Construction Co. (Pvt.) Ltd* (1992) 18 YB Com Arb 140.

The parties may agree in what circumstances the authority of an arbitral tribunal may be revoked under s. 23(1) of the AA 1996. If the parties have made no such agreement then the authority of the arbitral tribunal may not be revoked except by the parties acting jointly or by an arbitral or other institution having such powers: s. 23(3) of the AA 1996. Any revocation of the arbitral tribunal's authority must be agreed in writing: s. 23(4) of the AA 1996. The only exception to this exists if the parties agree to terminate the arbitration agreement: s. 23(4) of the AA 1996. Section 23(5) of the AA 1996 states that nothing within the provisions of s. 25 of the AA 1996 affects the power of the court to revoke an appointment under s. 18 of the AA 1996 or to remove an arbitrator under s. 24 of the AA 1996.

7.8 APPOINTMENT PROCEDURE WHERE THE ARBITRAL TRIBUNAL CEASES TO HOLD OFFICE

When the arbitral tribunal ceases to hold office the consequences for the parties will be extra costs and delay in the publishing of the award. The parties will seek to replace the arbitral tribunal as quickly as possible. Section 27(1) of the AA 1996 states that:

Where an arbitrator ceases to hold office, the parties are free to agree—
    (a)   whether and if so how the vacancy is to be filled,
    (b)   whether and if so to what extent the previous proceedings should stand, and
    (c)   what effect (if any) his ceasing to hold office has on any appointment made by him (alone or jointly).

If there is no such agreement then ss. 16 (procedure for appointment of arbitrators) and 18 (failure of appointment procedure) of the AA 1996 apply in relation to the filling of the vacancy as in relation to an original appointment: s. 27(3) of the AA 1996. The court has not retained the power it had under s. 25 of the AA 1950 to appoint an arbitrator to fill a vacancy. If the parties cannot agree the status of the previous proceedings, the newly reconstituted arbitral tribunal shall decide whether, and if so to what extent, the previous proceedings should stand: s. 27(4) of the AA 1996. This does not affect the right of any party to challenge the proceedings on any ground which had arisen before the arbitrator ceased to hold office: s. 27(4) of the AA 1996. The fact that a member of the arbitral tribunal has ceased to hold office does not affect any appointment which that arbitrator had made, whether alone or jointly with another arbitrator, particularly an appointment of a chairman or umpire: s. 27(5) of the AA 1996.

7.9 IMMUNITY OF THE ARBITRAL TRIBUNAL

Section 29 of the AA 1996 is a mandatory section which gives the arbitral tribunal immunity from suit for anything done or omitted to be done in the discharge or purported discharge of its function, unless the arbitral tribunal has shown to have acted in bad faith. The immunity extends to any employee or agent of the arbitral tribunal: s. 29(2) of the AA 1996. If the arbitral tribunal is removed by order of the court under s. 24 of the AA 1996 or its authority is revoked under s. 18(3)(c) of the AA 1996, the arbitral tribunal will still enjoy immunity from suit under s. 29(1) of the AA 1996. This immunity does not extend to any liability the arbitral tribunal may incur if it resigns: s. 29(3) of the AA 1996. However, the court may relieve the arbitral tribunal from any liability incurred, by reason of its resignation, where the arbitral tribunal has acted reasonably in resigning: s. 25(4) of the AA 1996.

Prior to the enactment of the AA 1996 the arbitral tribunal was generally thought to have immunity from prosecution but the position was not entirely clear. The DAC thought that the immunity of the arbitral tribunal should be the same as for a judge. In para. 132 of their February 1996 report the DAC stated their reasons as follows:

Arbitration and litigation share this in common, that both provide a means of dispute resolution, which depends upon a binding decision by an impartial third party. It is generally considered that immunity is necessary to enable that third party properly to perform an impartial decision-making function. Furthermore, we feel strongly that unless a degree of immunity is afforded, the finality of the arbitration process could well be undermined. The prospect of a losing party attempting to re-arbitrate the issues on the basis that a competent arbitrator would have decided them in favour of that party is one that we would view with dismay. The Bill provides in our view adequate safeguards to deal with cases where the arbitral process has gone wrong.

The arbitral tribunal will not be granted immunity from suit if it has acted in bad faith in the discharge or the purported discharge of its functions: s. 29(1) of the AA 1996. There is no definition of 'bad faith' in the AA 1996. The DAC in their February 1996 report directed that the test for 'bad faith' is to be found in the common law. 'Bad faith' was held to mean dishonesty in *Cannock Chase District Council* v *Kelly* [1978] 1 WLR 1. However, the DAC singled out the case of *Melton Medes Ltd* v *Securities and Investments Board* [1995] Ch 137 as an example of a case which defines 'bad faith'. In this case s. 187(3) of the Financial Services Act 1986 was considered. This section states that the SIB or any member, officer or servant of the SIB shall not be liable in damages for anything done or omitted in the discharge or purported discharge of its functions 'unless the act or omission is shown to have been in bad faith'. Lightman J said that 'bad faith' means different things depending on the context in which it is used and the type of person using it. He held that in the context of the tort of misfeasance in public office 'bad faith' had a restricted meaning and stated at p. 147 as follows:

> A moral element is an essential ingredient. Lack of good faith connotes either (a) malice in the sense of personal spite or a desire to injure for improper reasons or (b) knowledge of absence of power to make the decision in question.

He also held that the allegation of bad faith should only be made where there exists prima facie evidence to support it; and that if there was no reasonable evidence to support the allegation then a statement of claim making such an allegation would be struck out for abuse of process.

7.10   LIABILITY FOR ARBITRATOR'S FEES AND EXPENSES

7.10.1   Joint and several liability

Section 28 of the AA 1996 deals with the liability of the parties to the arbitral tribunal for its fees and expenses. The section is mandatory. It is a new provision but reflects in part the common law position prior to the AA 1996. At common law an arbitral tribunal was entitled to payment whether the amount of its fees was agreed or not: *Macintyre Brothers* v *Smith* (1912) 50 SLR 261. In *Crampton and Holt* v *Ridley and Co.* (1887) 20 QBD 48 and *Brown* v *Llandovery Terra Cotta etc. Co. Ltd* (1909) 25 TLR 625 it was held that the parties were jointly liable for the fees of the arbitral tribunal. It was unclear under the common law whether the parties were jointly and severally liable, although Mustill and Boyd, *Commercial Arbitration*, 2nd ed. (London: Butterworths, 1989), p. 235, n.13, considered that there was a joint and several liability. The position is now made absolutely clear by s. 28(1) of the AA 1996, which states that: 'The parties are jointly and severally liable to pay to the arbitrators such reasonable fees and expenses (if any) as are appropriate in the circumstances'.

Where the level of arbitral tribunal's fees and expenses have been agreed by the parties the parties are contractually obliged to pay all of the agreed fees and expenses whether they are reasonable or not. Section 28(5) of the AA 1996 makes it clear that the provision in s. 28(1) of the AA 1996 will not interfere with this obligation: 'Nothing in this section affects . . . any contractual right of an arbitrator to payment of his fees and expenses'.

Where one party has not been a party to the agreement with the arbitral tribunal in respect of the level of its fees and expenses then that party is not contractually obliged to pay those agreed fees and expenses. The joint and several liability of such a party is limited to the statutory obligation in s. 28(1) of the AA 1996 to pay only a reasonable sum. The reason for this is explained by the DAC in their February 1996 report at para. 123:

It seems to us that whilst arbitrators should be protected by this joint and several liability of the parties, a potentially unfair result must be avoided: a party who never agreed to the appointment by another party of an exceptionally expensive arbitrator should not be held jointly and severally liable for that arbitrator's exceptional fees.

The arbitral tribunal can recover its fees and expenses from any party under the principle of joint and several liability. These fees and expenses may be agreed or, where there is no agreement, may be whatever is reasonable in the circumstances: s. 28(1) of the AA 1996. However, s. 28(5) of the AA 1996 also states that nothing in s. 28 of the AA 1996 'affects any liability of a party to any other party to pay all or any of the costs of the arbitration'. If only one party pays the arbitral tribunal's fees and expenses, that party may have an entitlement to recover those fees and expenses from the other party to the arbitration. Such an entitlement may arise because of an agreement between the parties or where the arbitration award so orders. However, an agreement between the parties as to the payment of costs is only valid if it has been made after the dispute in question has arisen: s. 60 of the AA 1996.

7.10.2 Challenging the level of fees and expenses

Section 28(2) of the AA 1996 provides that:

> Any party may apply to the court (upon notice to the other parties and to the arbitrators) which may order that the amount of the arbitrators' fees and expenses shall be considered and adjusted by such means and upon such terms as it may direct.

This section should be considered with s. 56(2) of the AA 1996, which enables a party to the arbitration to apply to the court for a review of the arbitral tribunal's fees and expenses prior to an award being taken up. Section 28(2) of the AA 1996 allows a party to pay the fees and expenses of the arbitrator, so that it may obtain delivery of the award, and then make an application to the court to challenge the level of the fees and expenses. However, a party is not obliged to wait until the award has been issued before making such an application. A party can apply to the court at any time. Excessive interim fees of the arbitral tribunal may be challenged under this section. Under s. 28(2) 'any party' may make the application to the court. This wording has made a subtle change to the pre-existing law in that previously only the party taking up the award could so apply: *Rolimpex Centrala Handlu Zagranicznego* v *Haji E. Dossa and Sons Ltd* [1971] 1 Lloyd's Rep 380.

Section 28(3) of the AA 1996 provides that if an application under s. 28 is made after the fees and expenses have been paid by a party, the court can order 'the repayment of such amount (if any) as is shown to be excessive'. The court's power to order a repayment is, however, limited to cases where it is reasonable in the circumstances to order that repayment. Factors that the court will have in mind are not only the level of the fees and expenses claimed but also when the application was made. Where the level of the fees has been agreed by the parties so that the arbitral tribunal has a contractual right to them there will be no question as to what is reasonable. The court will not look behind the contractual agreement of the parties.

References to 'arbitrators' in s. 28 of the AA 1996 include an arbitrator who has ceased to act or an umpire who has not replaced the other arbitrators: s. 28(6) of the AA 1996. Section 28(1) to (3) of the AA 1996 applies subject to any order of the court under ss. 24(4) or 25(3)(b) of the AA 1996. These sections deal with the arbitral tribunal's entitlement to fees and expenses in cases where it has been removed or it has resigned. In such cases the court may make such order as it thinks fit in regard to the arbitral tribunal's entitlement to fees or expenses or may make an order requiring the repayment of fees and expenses which have already been paid by the parties.

8 *General Duty of the Arbitral Tribunal*

8.1 INTRODUCTION

The general duty of the arbitral tribunal is set out in s. 33(1) of the AA 1996 and is a mandatory duty. Before the AA 1996 came into force the duty of the arbitral tribunal was determined by principles of natural justice. The duty imposed by s. 33(1) of the AA 1996 is divided into two parts and is set out in s. 33(1)(a) and (b) of the AA 1996. Section 33(2) of the AA 1996 states that the arbitral tribunal must exercise this duty in making decisions not only on matters of procedure and evidence but also in respect of all the other powers that it has been given. Section 33(1) provides that the arbitral tribunal shall:

(a) act fairly and impartially as between the parties, giving each party a reasonable opportunity of putting his case and dealing with that of his opponent, and

(b) adopt procedures suitable to the circumstances of the particular case, avoiding unnecessary delay or expense, so as to provide a fair means for the resolution of the matters falling to be determined.

This provision reflects the principle in s. 1(a) of the Act that 'the object of arbitration is to obtain the fair resolution of disputes by an impartial tribunal without unnecessary delay or expense'. Section 1(a) sets out a main objective of the AA 1996. Section 33(1) imposes on the arbitral tribunal a mandatory duty to carry out that objective.

8.2 TRIBUNAL'S DUTY TO ACT FAIRLY AND IMPARTIALLY

The obligation to act fairly and impartially under s. 31(1)(a) of the AA 1996 is based on the common law duty to act in accordance with natural justice. For example, the arbitral tribunal must give each party an equal opportunity to present its case and reply to the opponent's case: *Montrose Canned Foods Ltd* v *Eric Wells (Merchants) Ltd* [1965] 1 Lloyd's Rep 597. If an arbitrator has been chosen for having expertise in the subject matter of the dispute then this knowledge must not be used by the arbitrator in secret. The arbitrator must reveal to the parties any use of this expertise in making any finding of facts. The parties must be given the opportunity to address the arbitrator on any such findings of fact: *Fox* v *P.G. Wellfair Ltd* [1981] 2 Lloyd's Rep 514. Any communication which the arbitral tribunal receives from one party should be immediately disclosed to the other party. Unless the parties agree to the contrary, the arbitral tribunal should not receive argument or evidence in the absence of one of the parties: *Ceylon* v *Chandris* [1963] 2 QB 327. The arbitral tribunal should not be biased towards any party: *Re an Arbitration between SS Catalina (Owners) and MV Norma (Owners)* (1938) 61 Ll L Rep 360. The arbitral tribunal should keep each party fully appraised of its intentions as to the conduct of the reference so that no party is taken by surprise: *Gbangbola* v *Smith and Sherriff Ltd* [1998] 3 All ER 730 at p. 740 and especially where one party is from another country: *Scrimaglio* v *Thornett and Fehr* (1923) 17 Ll L Rep 34.

The arbitral tribunal's duty to act fairly also includes the duty to avoid unnecessary delay and expense. One of the underlying principles of the AA 1996 is that arbitration proceedings should be a cheaper and quicker alternative to litigation. The AA 1996 stresses the importance of conducting the reference in this manner in both ss. 1(a) and 33(1). Saville LJ, 'An introduction to the 1996 Arbitration Act' (1996) 62 Journal of the Chartered Institute of Arbitrators 165 summed up the position as follows, at p. 166:

> Everyone accepts that the tribunal must strive to reach a just decision on the dispute. Equally important is that the decision must be reached by just means, i.e. by procedures which are fair and not unnecessarily expensive. Justice delayed or unnecessarily expensive justice is indeed justice denied. However 'correct' the final decision can be said to be, it will have produced injustice if it took too long or was too expensive.

The arbitral tribunal's power to decide procedural measures in s. 33(1)(b) of the AA 1996 is subject to the duty in s. 33(1)(a) to act fairly and impartially. It is not enough for an arbitral tribunal to claim that the procedure chosen is appropriate because it saves unnecessary costs. It must also be a fair means of resolving the dispute by complying with the rules of natural justice.

8.3   DUTY TO ADOPT SUITABLE PROCEDURES

8.3.1   Procedure agreed by the parties in writing

The arbitral tribunal must take account of the procedure the parties have expressly agreed in writing as the one to be adopted. Otherwise the arbitral tribunal will be guilty of a 'serious irregularity' under s. 68(1)(c) of the AA 1996 and its award may be challenged. The arbitral tribunal does not have the right to override the agreement of the parties as to the conduct of the reference. If there is no such agreement, the arbitral tribunal must decide what is appropriate in respect of the particular arbitration. As Saville LJ put it, commenting on the Bill which was enacted as the AA 1996, 'The Bill, in short, encourages a "horses for courses" approach even to the extent of giving the tribunal, in suitable cases, the right to act inquisitorially' ('An introduction to the 1996 Arbitration Act' (1996) 62 Journal of the Chartered Institute of Arbitrators 165).

The AA 1996 is silent as to what criteria the arbitral tribunal should consider in deciding the appropriate procedure other than stating, in s. 33(1)(b), that it should adopt a procedure which is 'suitable to the circumstances of the particular case, avoiding unnecessary delay or expense' so as to provide a fair means of resolving the dispute. The arbitral tribunal is therefore given a wide discretion. Whether a procedure is suitable and provides a fair means for resolving the dispute depends on the circumstances of each case at the time when the arbitral tribunal makes its decision. The court will be reluctant to interfere with the decision-making process of the arbitral tribunal unless the proceedings have been in breach of the AA 1996 Act.

A procedural decision of the arbitral tribunal can only be challenged in limited circumstances. A procedural decision on an interim matter cannot be challenged: *Three Valleys Water Committee* v *Binnie and Partners* (1990) 52 BLR 42. In *Three Valleys Water Committee* v *Binnie and Partners* the court held that it had no jurisdiction to correct procedural errors even if they could be categorised as misconduct. Further, the court concluded that s. 22 of the AA 1950 envisaged the reconsideration of a matter dealt with by an award and therefore there was no power for the court to order that an arbitral tribunal should reconsider a pre-award ruling (cf. *Fletamentos Maritimos SA* v *Effjohn International BV (No. 3)* [1997] 2 Lloyd's Rep 302). Similarly s. 68 of the AA 1996 (serious irregularity) envisages that reconsideration of a matter can only occur where there is an award (see 8.4.1). The effect of this is that where the arbitral tribunal fails to comply with its duty under s. 33 of the AA 1996 when dealing with an interlocutory matter, there is no right under the AA 1996 to challenge the tribunal's decision. Where, however, there is an award then a challenge may be made under s. 68(2)(a) of the AA 1996. However, the party challenging the award must not only show that the arbitral tribunal has failed to comply with its duty under s. 33 but that the party has also suffered substantial injustice. Furthermore, the arbitral tribunal can only be removed in the limited circumstances set out in s. 24(1)(a) to (d) (see 8.4.2).

8.3.2 Implied intentions of the parties

Where the parties have not expressly agreed the procedure to be followed in writing, or the parties' intentions are not clear in the written agreement, it is prudent for the arbitral tribunal to seek clarification directly from the parties. The arbitral tribunal may, however, have regard to the implied intentions of the parties. The implied intentions could be gleaned from the subject matter and nature of the dispute, the language of the arbitration agreement, the choice of the arbitral tribunal and the conduct of the parties before the arbitral tribunal had been appointed.

The subject matter and nature of the dispute are factors which, in any event, will help the arbitral tribunal determine what procedure is suitable to the circumstances of the particular case. For example, the arbitral tribunal should consider whether it is appropriate to adopt the usual procedure in respect of the trade or profession from which the dispute arises. This may indicate whether the arbitration should be conducted formally or informally. Shipping and commodity arbitrations are often conducted in an informal way: *Gunter Henck* v *Andre & Cie SA* [1970] 1 Lloyd's Rep 235; *Star International Hong Kong (UK) Ltd* v *Bergbau-Handel GmbH* [1966] 2 Lloyd's Rep 16; *The Myron* [1970] 1 QB 527. Complex construction and engineering arbitrations are commonly conducted in the same formal manner as High Court proceedings.

Where the arbitration agreement has been written in a legalistic style there is an implication that the parties intend to have a formal arbitration: *Ritchie* v *W. Jacks and Co.* (1922) 10 Ll L Rep 519 at p. 526. Stipulating for a legally qualified arbitrator, as opposed to a commercial arbitrator, has also been held to indicate the parties' desire for a formal arbitration: *Mediterranean and Eastern Export Co. Ltd* v *Fortress Fabrics (Manchester) Ltd* (1948) 81 Ll L Rep 401 at p. 403; *London Export Corporation* v *Jubilee Coffee Roasting Co. Ltd* [1958] 1 WLR 271. If the parties have commenced the arbitration in a particular manner, for example, by exchanging pleadings, such conduct was held to imply an intention between the parties as to how the arbitration should proceed: *Star International Hong Kong (UK) Ltd* v *Bergbau-Handel GmbH* [1966] 2 Lloyd's Rep 16 at p. 18.

The parties are likely to expect their reference to be conducted in the form usually adopted in their trade or profession, unless they have agreed otherwise. It would therefore be good practice for the arbitrator to consult the parties and obtain their agreement before departing from the usual procedure.

8.4   REMEDIES FOR BREACH OF THE ARBITRAL TRIBUNAL'S DUTY

It would be a breach of s. 33(1) of the AA 1996 for the arbitral tribunal to act unfairly or impartially and to adopt unsuitable measures. The AA 1996 provides for certain instances when the arbitral tribunal's decision may be challenged and the arbitral tribunal may be removed for breaching its general duty under s. 33(1) of the AA 1996.

8.4.1   Challenging the award

Section 68(1) of the AA 1996 provides that an arbitral tribunal's award may be challenged by any party on the ground that the arbitral tribunal has committed a 'serious irregularity' (see chapter 12). This specifically includes, according to s. 68(2)(a), 'failure by the tribunal to comply with section 33', if it has caused or will cause substantial injustice to the party challenging the award. Substantial injustice may be caused by a procedure that causes excessive delay and/or the incurring of excessive costs. The award may then be remitted back to the arbitral tribunal under s. 68(3)(a), set aside under s. 68(3)(b) or declared ineffective, in whole or in part, under s. 68(3)(c). The arbitral tribunal's fees may then be reduced by the court on the application of any party under s. 64(2).

8.4.2 Removal of the tribunal

Section 24(1) of the AA 1996 enables a party to apply to the court to have the arbitral tribunal removed and/or have its fees forfeited on certain grounds set out in s. 24(1)(a) to (d), if substantial injustice has been or will be caused to the applicant. The arbitral tribunal may be removed under s. 24(1)(a) if the proceedings have not been conducted impartially. Failing to act impartially is also a direct breach of s. 33(1)(a). The arbitral tribunal may be removed under s. 24(1)(d)(i) if it has refused or failed to conduct the proceedings properly; or under s. 24(1)(d)(ii) if it has failed to use all reasonable dispatch in conducting the proceedings or making an award. Such conduct would also be a breach of the arbitral tribunal's duty under s. 33(1) of the AA 1996. Additionally, the arbitral tribunal may be removed for not being qualified to conduct the arbitration as required by the arbitration agreement (s. 24(1)(b) of the AA 1996) or for being mentally or physically incapable of proceeding (s. 24(1)(c) of the AA 1996). (See also 7.7.3.)

8.5 TRIBUNAL'S DUTY AND PARTY AUTONOMY

8.5.1 Perceived inconsistencies between sections 33(1) and 34(1) of the AA 1996

A question arises as to whether the arbitral tribunal's mandatory duty under s. 33(1) of the AA 1996 is inconsistent with the parties' rights to decide the procedure for their reference under s. 34(1). In practice it is unlikely that the parties would make an agreement which conflicted with the arbitral tribunal's duty. The parties in their agreement would be seeking the same objectives, fairness and impartiality and the most appropriate procedure in the circumstances to avoid unnecessary delay and expense and to provide a fair means of resolving the dispute.

This question therefore anticipates a theoretical situation where the parties have agreed a procedure for their arbitration, which the arbitral tribunal believes is wholly unsuitable. There is then a potential conflict between the obligations of the arbitral tribunal under s. 33(1)(b) of the AA 1996, to decide the appropriate procedure for the reference, and the power given to the parties in s. 34(1) of the AA 1996 to agree their own arrangement in respect of any procedural or evidential matter. Section 34(1) stresses that 'It shall be for the tribunal to decide all procedural and evidential matters, subject to the right of the parties to agree any matter'.

The inconsistency, in theory at least, seems to become greater given the parties' mandatory duty under s. 40(1) and (2)(a) of the AA 1996 to comply with any order of the arbitral tribunal:

(1) The parties shall do all things necessary for the proper and expeditious conduct of the arbitral proceedings.

(2) This includes—

(a) complying without delay with any determination of the tribunal as to procedural or evidential matters, or with any order or directions of the tribunal.

It was a matter for debate, prior to the enactment of the AA 1996, whether it should be the parties or the arbitral tribunal who should decide how the proceedings should be conducted. The scenario illustrated above was considered at length in the DAC's report of February 1996 at para. 154–63. The DAC's recommendation was that party autonomy to decide the proceedings should ultimately prevail. This recommendation is reflected in the AA 1996. Section 34(1) of the AA 1996 provides the arbitral tribunal with non-mandatory powers, which are only exercisable if the parties have not agreed to the contrary. Section 34(1) states that the power of the arbitral tribunal to decide all procedural and evidential matters is 'subject to the right of the parties to agree any matter'. The parties are therefore free to make their own arrangements in respect of any procedural or evidential matters. However, in order for the parties' agreement to be enforceable it must be in writing, as required by s. 5(1) of the AA 1996.

Hence while the arbitral tribunal has a duty under s. 33(1)(b) of the AA 1996 to adopt procedures which best resolve the matter fairly without causing unnecessary expense and delay, the parties may agree any other procedure for the conduct of the arbitration proceedings. If these procedures are agreed in writing, the parties will not be in breach of s. 40 of the AA 1996. If the parties have not expressly agreed between themselves the procedure to be followed, the arbitral tribunal's decision will prevail and the parties will be bound to comply with it as provided by s. 40.

8.5.2 Conflicts between the arbitral tribunal and the parties

What would be the position of the arbitral tribunal if the parties agree a certain procedure to be followed which the arbitral tribunal believes will lead to a breach of its duty under s. 33(1) of the AA 1996? If the parties have agreed the procedure prior to the arbitral tribunal accepting its appointment then on accepting the appointment the arbitral tribunal will be bound to follow that agreed procedure. If, before being appointed, the arbitral tribunal objects to the agreed procedure then it should decline the appointment or accept it subject to writing to the parties to express any reservations about the procedure.

If the parties agree a procedural or evidential matter after the arbitral tribunal has been appointed and object to any procedural order which has been made, the arbitral tribunal may take the following course of action:

(a) The arbitral tribunal can resign. The parties can agree to pay any of the arbitral tribunal's entitlement to fees and expenses and to waive any liability that the arbitral tribunal has incurred by this action; or if there is no such agreement the arbitral tribunal can apply to the court in respect of fees and expenses and for relief from liability. The court must be satisfied that it was reasonable in all the circumstances for the arbitral tribunal to resign. See s. 25 of the AA 1996.

(b)   The arbitral tribunal can stand by the order. The parties may then seek to remove the arbitral tribunal or agree to abandon the arbitration.

(c)   The arbitral tribunal may yield to the parties' wishes, as it is their arbitration. It is unlikely that the parties will be able to claim later that the arbitral tribunal was in breach of s. 33 and thereby seek the arbitral tribunal's removal under s. 24(1), or challenge the arbitral tribunal's award under s. 68(2) or deny the arbitral tribunal's fees, as the breach would have been instigated by them.

Whatever decision the arbitral tribunal makes there will not be any personal liability attached to the decision unless there is evidence of bad faith. Under s. 29(1) of the AA 1996 the arbitral tribunal enjoys immunity from suit in the conduct of the arbitration.

9 Powers of the Arbitral Tribunal in Conducting the Reference

9.1 PROCEDURAL AND EVIDENTIAL POWERS

The powers of the arbitral tribunal to conduct the reference may be given to it by the parties specifically in the arbitration agreement, by reference to an administered scheme, by agreement in writing at a later stage, or by the adoption of a foreign law. In the absence of any such agreement, the AA 1996 provides the arbitral tribunal with specific powers to conduct the reference. These powers define the scope within which the arbitral tribunal can require a party to act. The main distinction between the arbitral tribunal's general duty under s. 33(1) of the AA 1996 and the arbitral tribunal's powers is that the arbitral tribunal must abide by its duty in conducting the arbitration proceedings, whereas it has a discretion whether or not to exercise any of its powers. The parties can exclude or vary the arbitral tribunal's powers contained in the AA 1996 by agreement in writing but they cannot exclude or vary the arbitral tribunal's duties under the AA 1996.

Although the AA 1996 promotes the parties' autonomy the intention of the Act was not to make the arbitral tribunal's role a passive one. Indeed it makes the arbitral tribunal's role in the proceedings a strongly proactive one. The AA 1996 provides the arbitral tribunal with a range of non-mandatory powers to conduct the reference, which can be used in the most appropriate way to obtain a just resolution in each particular dispute.

The arbitral tribunal's powers in conducting the reference are set out in the following sections of the AA 1996:

s. 34   Powers in relation to procedural and evidential matters.
s. 37(1)   Power to appoint experts, legal advisers or assessor.
s. 38   General powers of the arbitral tribunal including the power to order security for costs and powers in relation to property, examining witnesses and preserving evidence.
s. 39   Power to make provisional awards.
s. 41   Powers of the arbitral tribunal in the case of a party's default.

These powers are non-mandatory. The parties are therefore free to agree their own arrangements. However, s. 5(1) of the AA 1996 stipulates that in order for the parties' agreement to be subject to Part I of the Act it must be in writing.

Section 34(1) of the AA 1996 states that: 'It shall be for the tribunal to decide all procedural and evidential matters, subject to the right of the parties to agree any matter'. This section corresponds to s. 12 of the AA 1950 in so far as it sets out the arbitral tribunal's powers, subject to the parties' agreement. However, s. 34 of the AA 1996 is more clearly written than s. 12 of the AA 1950 and is more specific. Section 12(1) of the AA 1950 gave the arbitral tribunal a broad but vague discretion. For example, it included the power to examine the parties on oath or affirmation, to require the parties to produce all documents within their possession or power and to 'do all other things which during the proceedings on the reference the arbitrator or umpire may require'. Section 34 of the AA 1996 retains the arbitral tribunal's broadly based discretion to conduct the proceedings but clarifies the powers it has and the extent of its discretion in s. 34(2)(a) to (h).

The parties are free to agree to remove these powers from the arbitral tribunal or to vary them to suit their needs. For example, the parties can by a written agreement opt for a procedure laid down in an administered scheme, choose a documents-only arbitration and dispense with the rules of evidence.

The arbitral tribunal should therefore only exercise its powers under s. 34 of the AA 1996 if the arbitration agreement is silent as to evidential or procedural matters and there is no other contrary written agreement. Before exercising these powers it is prudent for the arbitral tribunal to enquire what the parties have expressly agreed regarding the conduct of the reference before or at the time they have submitted their dispute to arbitration.

The parties' agreement on how the arbitration should be conducted, whether it is contained in the underlying contract between the parties or is made at the time the dispute is referred to arbitration, may be written vaguely. For example, it may not contain a comprehensive code of procedure; it may simply state that the conduct of the arbitration shall proceed 'in the usual way'. The arbitral tribunal should ask the parties what they envisaged in the agreement before proceeding. In *Tritonia Shipping Inc.* v *South Nelson Forest Products Corporation* [1966] 1 Lloyd's Rep 114 the court interpreted the phrase 'in the usual way' to mean that the procedure should be followed in accordance with the practice in that trade or profession. The advantage of appointing an arbitral tribunal experienced in the trade or profession from which the subject matter of the reference arises is that it will be familiar with the usual practices of that trade or profession: *Laertis Shipping Corporation* v *Exportadora Espanola de Cementos Portland SA* [1982] 1 Lloyd's Rep 613.

If the parties have agreed that the arbitration should be conducted in accordance with the rules of a trade or profession or that it should follow an administered scheme then, as a general rule, it is the rules which are current which should be followed and not the rules which were in existence when the arbitration agreement was made: *Finzel, Berry and Co.* v *Eastcheap Dried Fruit Co.* [1962] 2 Lloyd's Rep 11. However, the rules that are to be applied may specifically deal with this matter and reference should be made to them. Under the ICC Arbitration Rules, Article 6.1, the parties are deemed to have submitted to the ICC Arbitration Rules in force at the date of the commencement of the arbitration unless the parties have agreed to be bound by the ICC Arbitration Rules in force at the date of the arbitration agreement.

Section 34(1) of the AA 1996 will be breached if the arbitral tribunal fails to comply with the procedure expressly agreed by the parties. The arbitral tribunal may be guilty of a serious irregularity under s. 68(2)(c) of the AA 1996. This section specifically defines serious irregularity as the 'failure by the arbitral tribunal to conduct the proceedings in accordance with the procedure agreed by the parties'. The award may be remitted back to the arbitral tribunal, or it may be set aside in whole or in part, or it may be declared to be of no effect, in whole or in part: s. 68(3)(a) to (c) of the AA 1996. However, the parties must make their objections clear to the arbitral tribunal in writing promptly, as otherwise they may be deemed to have accepted the procedure adopted by the arbitral tribunal and thereby waived their right to challenge the award under s. 73(1) of the AA 1996. The parties may then seek a reduction in the arbitral tribunal's fees. The court may on the application of any party determine what reasonable fees and expenses are appropriate in the circumstances under s. 64(2) of the AA 1996. Alternatively the parties can agree in writing to have the authority of the arbitral tribunal revoked under s. 23(3)(a) of the AA 1996. This may be the better option if the arbitration is at an early stage. The later the stage of the proceedings the more inconvenient it will be for the parties to terminate the arbitration and commence proceedings with a new arbitral tribunal. If the procedure of the arbitration is left to the discretion of the arbitral tribunal, the parties will have no recourse to challenge the arbitral tribunal's decision on matters of procedure under ss. 68 and 69 of the AA 1996. The court is reluctant to interfere with the arbitral tribunal's interim decisions: *Three Valleys Water Committee* v *Binnie and Partners* (1990) 52 BLR 42. See 11.13 for a further discussion on court intervention in procedural matters.

Section 34(2) of the AA 1996 lists procedural and evidential matters, which the arbitral tribunal may consider in conducting the reference. This is in effect a statutory checklist reminding the arbitral tribunal of the type of directions which should be considered at the early stages of the reference. Many of these directions are made by the arbitral tribunal at the preliminary hearing but they can be ordered at any stage of the proceedings. This is not an exhaustive list of the arbitral tribunal's powers.

Section 34(2) gives the arbitral tribunal broad powers to conduct the proceedings subject to its overriding duty under s. 33 of the AA 1996. Unlike a judge the arbitral tribunal is not bound by the Civil Procedure Rules 1998. The ethos of the AA 1996 was to create a genuine alternative to litigation proceedings and not 'litigation in suits'.

9.1.1 · Venue

Section 34(2)(a) of the AA 1996 empowers the arbitral tribunal to decide the most appropriate time and place for holding any part of the proceedings, if the parties cannot reach agreement in writing on this matter. Although there was no such express provision in s. 12 of the AA 1950 this power fell within the arbitral tribunal's general powers. The arbitral tribunal may order the reference to take place on board a ship in a maritime arbitration or on site in an engineering or construction dispute. The arbitration need not even take place in the country where the dispute arose. It may become appropriate for part of the reference to be held in one country and the remainder of the reference in another country.

The importance of the power to choose the place and time of the reference was recognised by the authors of the UNCITRAL Model Law. Section 34(2)(a) of the AA 1996 partly follows Article 20 of the Model Law, which provides the arbitral tribunal with a discretion to determine the place of the reference. However, s. 32(2)(a) of the AA 1996 gives the arbitral tribunal a wider discretion than is found in Article 20, as it enables the arbitral tribunal to make a direction as to the time of the reference as well. Article 20(1) of the UNCITRAL Model Law states that where the parties cannot agree, the discretion should be exercised by the arbitral tribunal 'having regard to the circumstances of the case, including the convenience of the parties'. Article 20(2) of the UNCITRAL Model Law adds that notwithstanding the provisions of Article 20(1) the arbitral tribunal is free to decide any meeting place it considers is appropriate for 'hearing witnesses, experts or the parties, or the inspection of goods, other property or documents'. Section 34(2)(a) of the AA 1996 does not restrict the arbitral tribunal by making such stipulations. It gives a broader discretion. The arbitral tribunal has the power to decide 'when and where any part of the proceedings is to be held'. Although s. 34(2)(a) of the AA 1996 does not specifically direct the arbitral tribunal to consider the convenience of the parties, the arbitral tribunal is bound to take account of this factor, in any event, in exercising its duty under s. 33(1) of the AA 1996.

The practical application of s. 34(2)(a) of the AA 1996 is that the arbitral tribunal is able to save the parties time and costs by considering their representations on the time and place of the reference and deciding what is the most suitable time and place in each case. For example, the arbitral tribunal may decide to hear interlocutory applications, examine witnesses and conduct site inspections away from the place of the final hearing if it considers it is appropriate to do so.

The arbitral tribunal should not be influenced by what is convenient to itself. The arbitral tribunal in deciding the appropriate venue may consider *inter alia*; where the subject matter of the dispute is located; where the parties' legal representatives are based, for example, where counsels' chambers are located; where the witnesses are based and the cost of travelling expenses and hotel bills. The building chosen for the hearing should have adequate facilities for holding the reference. The hiring of the venue should generally be left to the claimant.

9.1.2 Language of the proceedings

Court proceedings in England are always carried out in English with a court interpreter if required. In contrast s. 34(2)(b) of the AA 1996 enables the arbitral tribunal to decide, where the parties cannot reach agreement in writing, the language or languages to be used in the reference and whether any translations of any of the relevant documents are to be supplied. Section 34(2)(b) of the AA 1996 is another new practical provision preventing delays in commencing the proceedings in international arbitrations. There is a similar provision in Article 22 of the UNCITRAL Model Law.

In deciding the language of the reference and whether any translations are required the arbitral tribunal must exercise its duty under s. 33(1) of the AA 1996. It is essential, if the reference is to be carried out both appropriately and fairly, that all the parties are able to follow and understand the proceedings. However, the arbitral tribunal must also weigh up any extra costs or delay in the proceedings which may result from its decision.

9.1.3 Form of written statements of claim and defence

Section 34(2)(c) gives the arbitral tribunal the power to decide 'whether any and if so what form of written statements of claim and defence are to be used, when these should be supplied and the extent to which such statements can be later amended'. This power is discussed further at 15.6. Arbitral proceedings may take various forms. There may be an oral hearing without written statements, a documents-only hearing or a part oral and part written hearing, in which case the written statements may be either formal or informal. Alternatively a Scott schedule (see 15.6.4) may be used. The arbitral tribunal's decision will depend on what is appropriate in each reference, bearing in mind its duty under s. 33(1) of the AA 1996.

9.1.4 Disclosure and questions

Section 34(2)(d) of the AA 1996 gives the arbitral tribunal the power to decide 'whether and if so which documents or classes of documents should be disclosed between and produced by the parties and at what stage'. Disclosure is discussed further at 15.10. Section 34(2)(e) of the AA 1996 gives the arbitral tribunal the power to order that questions be put to and answered by a party to the arbitration. This power corresponds to the court's power to order requests for further information under CPR, r. 18.1. Section 34(2)(e) of the AA 1996 gives to the arbitral tribunal a wide discretion as to the type of question to be permitted. However, in order to comply with its duty under s. 33(1) of the AA 1996, the arbitral tribunal should also restrict the questions to those that are relevant to the matters in issue. Although in court proceedings the use of interrogatories is not common, in arbitration proceedings s. 34(2)(e) of the AA 1996 could prove to be a useful provision for parties to clarify at an early stage the issues between them, ultimately saving time and expense. Questions can be used not only to clarify the issues between the parties but also to obtain admissions relating to the facts in issues. In this respect the use of questions is currently an underutilised tactical weapon.

9.1.5 Acting inquisitorially

If the parties have not agreed to the contrary the arbitral tribunal has the power under s. 34(2)(g) of the AA 1996 to act inquisitorially to ascertain the facts and the law. Arbitration proceedings differ in this respect from court proceedings, which are run on a purely adversarial basis. Traditionally arbitration proceedings have been conducted in the adversarial manner and prior to the AA 1996 it was a point of debate whether an arbitral tribunal had the power to adopt an inquisitorial procedure. The AA 1996 not only settles this matter but also provides the arbitral tribunal with a discretion whether or not to act inquisitorially and to what extent it should do so. The arbitral tribunal, in exercising its discretion must comply with its duty under s. 33(1) of the AA 1996 to use whatever system it considers is suitable in the circumstances which will save time and costs and which will dispose of the dispute fairly.

The inquisitorial system may be distinguished from the adversarial system in so far as in an inquisitorial system the arbitral tribunal also investigates the factual and legal issues in the case and is responsible for taking any procedural steps. In an adversarial system it is the responsibility of the parties to initiate the procedure by taking whatever steps they deem to be necessary to get on with the arbitration. A party may take a procedural step forward by its own motion, such as by serving pleadings (statements of case) on its opponent, or seek an order from the arbitral tribunal to compel the other party to make a procedural step.

In the adversarial system the parties calling and examining witnesses submit evidence and argument in a hearing. The parties present their case by adducing evidence and submitting arguments. The arbitral tribunal will make its findings on the basis of what evidence and arguments the parties adduce. In an inquisitorial system the arbitral tribunal also examines the witnesses.

Many arbitrations, proceeding on a documents-only or part-oral/part-written basis, are conducted on the adversarial system with each party presenting its case. There is no reason why a documents-only or part-oral/part-written arbitration cannot be conducted inquisitorially. For example, the arbitral tribunal can write to each party with a list of questions and base its decisions on the replies.

In simple arbitrations where the parties are lay people representing themselves the inquisitorial approach may be a more suitable method of conducting the hearing. The arbitral tribunal can elicit the relevant facts and the evidence quickly by asking pertinent questions and thereby save time and costs to the parties, who will usually not be experienced advocates. Where the parties have chosen the arbitrator because of his or her expertise in a particular field it may be more efficient in the disposal of the matter for the arbitrator to proceed inquisitorially so as to identify the most important issues quickly. However, while the arbitrator may use any technical expertise to elicit facts this knowledge must not be used in secret: *Fox v P.G. Wellfair Ltd* [1981] 2 Lloyd's Rep 514. This would be a breach of duty under s. 33(1) of the AA 1996 and therefore a serious irregularity under s. 68(2)(a). The arbitral tribunal could be removed under s. 24(1)(a) for failing to be impartial and under s. 24(1)(d)(i) for failing to conduct the proceedings properly.

The AA 1996 has provided the arbitral tribunal with this alternative method of conducting the arbitration in order that it may have the choice to 'adopt procedures suitable to the circumstances of the particular case' as required by s. 33(1) of the AA 1996. However, the arbitral tribunal in complying with s. 33(1) should also ensure that the proceedings are carried out fairly. The arbitral tribunal in acting inquisitorially should not only be impartial but also appear to be so in order for the parties to consider the enquiries to be balanced and fair to both of them.

Prior to the AA 1996 it was thought by some practitioners that if an arbitral tribunal adopted an inquisitorial approach then it may no longer be immune from an action in negligence as the common law provided that an arbitral tribunal was only immune while acting in a judicial capacity: *Sutcliffe* v *Thackrah* [1974] AC 727. It was argued that investigating matters as opposed to deciding them was a non-judicial function. Section 29(1) of the AA 1996 now makes it clear that: 'An arbitrator is not liable for anything done or omitted to be done in the discharge or purported discharge of his functions as arbitrator'. As the AA 1996 provides for the arbitral tribunal to discharge its function in an inquisitorial capacity if it wishes to, it follows that the arbitral tribunal will be immune from any legal action as a result of so doing.

9.1.6 Oral or written evidence or submissions

The power given to the arbitral tribunal to decide whether there should be oral or written evidence or submissions, under s. 34(2)(h) of the AA 1996, further distinguishes arbitration proceedings from court proceedings. Court proceedings are run on an adversarial basis in which evidence and argument are usually submitted orally at a hearing or trial. Arbitration proceedings are more flexible. The arbitral tribunal may under s. 34(2)(h) of the AA 1996 decide whether and to what extent there should be oral or written evidence or submissions. The arbitral tribunal can decide that the entire reference shall be on a documents-only basis or on a part oral and part written basis.

The arbitral tribunal may decide that interim applications will be made and decided on the basis of written submissions but that the main issues of the dispute will be dealt with at an oral hearing. The arbitral tribunal may also decide that opening and closing speeches should be in writing so that the hearing is restricted to the examination of witnesses only. By curtailing the amount of time spent at the hearing, where the circumstances of the arbitration warrant it, the arbitral tribunal will be saving the parties unnecessary expense and time in compliance with the arbitral tribunal's duty under s. 33(1) of the AA 1996 (see the court's powers in support of the arbitral tribunal at 10.1.3.1).

9.1.7 Documents-only arbitrations

Before the AA 1996 came into force it was considered by most practitioners to be a breach of natural justice for the arbitral tribunal not to allow an oral hearing if one party requested it. It was held in *Henry Sotheran Ltd* v *Norwich Union Life Insurance Society* [1992] 2 EGLR 9 that an arbitral tribunal was guilty of misconduct for refusing a party's request for an oral hearing and publishing the award without first conducting the hearing. Section 34(2)(h) of the AA 1996 now makes it clear that unless the parties have agreed otherwise the arbitral tribunal can dispense with an oral hearing as it sees fit even if one party requests one. However, the arbitral tribunal is bound to make decisions bearing in mind the duty under s. 33(1) of the AA 1996, not only to save time and costs to the parties but also to act fairly.

In order to act fairly between the parties and to be seen to do so the arbitral tribunal would be wise to direct the parties to forward to it documents which adequately set out their respective cases with the issues clearly defined and the evidence in a comprehensible form, so that each party understands the case to be met. On receiving the documentation the arbitral tribunal must give equal attention to the arguments and evidence submitted by each party and keep the parties fully informed of any action to be taken.

In a documents-only arbitration the arbitral tribunal will determine the dispute by considering the written arguments and evidence submitted by each party. A documents-only arbitration may be informal in nature and could consist solely of a letter and supporting documents, or it may follow the procedure of an administered scheme provided by an independent body such as the Chartered Institute of Arbitrators, or a trade association.

Documents-only arbitrations are appropriate in simple disputes, or where the parties are situated far from one another and they consider a hearing inconvenient and unnecessary, or if the dispute revolves around a point of law, an interpretation of a document or a technical term. A documents-only arbitration may also be appropriate where written arguments can be submitted and there is no need to examine witnesses. Many trade associations provide documents-only administered arbitration schemes in conjunction with the Office of Fair Trading for the benefit of consumers who are seeking compensation for faulty goods or bad services.

The advantage of a documents-only reference is that not only is there a saving of costs and time to the parties but it is also less disruptive. The parties or their witnesses do not have to submit to cross-examination. It is not necessary to use lawyers or brief counsel. Each party can simply put its case in clear written terms. No time need be taken off by the parties or their witnesses to attend a hearing. There is no delay caused by arranging convenient dates for the hearing and the award is often made reasonably quickly after the documents have been sent to the arbitral tribunal.

The main disadvantage of this type of reference is that the parties do not have the opportunity to test the credibility of witnesses in cross-examination. The arbitral tribunal cannot see the demeanour of the witnesses and has no way of telling how genuine the evidence may be. Often the arbitral tribunal is faced with two versions of the same event and has to decide which version of facts is to be believed.

If there is little or no independent source of evidence other than the parties' own version of events, a documents-only reference is probably not the most appropriate method of resolving the dispute. An oral hearing will be a fairer way to decide the matter where the arbitral tribunal is able to observe the witnesses give evidence.

In some cases a party may not be able to put forward its best argument or evidence competently in writing. If the arbitral tribunal considers the case submitted is incomplete, because, for example, some relevant documents or letters have been referred to but not included, or are obviously missing, the arbitral tribunal may request further evidence or submissions as deemed necessary. However, in order to be fair to both parties any additional correspondence received from one party must be copied and sent to the other party to give that party an opportunity to comment on it.

Further discussion on documents-only arbitrations is provided in chapter 16 and in particular with regard to the ABTA scheme.

9.1.8   Time for compliance with directions

Section 34(3) of the AA 1996 gives the arbitral tribunal a discretion, subject to the parties' agreement to the contrary, to fix the time within which any directions given by it are to be complied with. In addition, the arbitral tribunal is given the discretionary power to extend the time given, whether or not it has expired. The parties are bound by s. 40(2) of the AA 1996 to comply with these time limits.

9.2   EXPERTS, LEGAL ADVISERS AND ASSESSORS

Section 37(1)(a) of the AA 1996 enables the arbitral tribunal, subject to the parties agreeing otherwise, to appoint experts or legal advisers to report to the arbitral tribunal or to the parties; or to appoint assessors to assist on technical matters. Unlike experts or legal advisers who may be called to give evidence, assessors will sit with the arbitral tribunal during the hearing and give specific advice on technical matters.

It is for the arbitral tribunal to decide whether the reference needs the appointment of persons of expertise. In making such a decision the arbitral tribunal should consider its duty under s. 33(1) of the AA 1996 to adopt suitable measures for the conduct of the reference. The arbitral tribunal may need to hear evidence from an expert witness on a specific issue to help it understand a technical matter where the parties have not called their own witnesses, or from a legal adviser on a point of law. It may be appropriate for the arbitral tribunal to appoint an expert, legal adviser or assessor where the proceedings are being conducted inquisitorially.

Section 37(1) of the AA 1996 is a new provision that derives from Article 26 of the UNCITRAL Model Law. The AA 1996 is, however, more restrictive than the UNCITRAL Model Law, which provides the arbitral tribunal with a discretion to require a party to give a tribunal-appointed expert information, or to produce or provide access to any relevant documents, goods or other property for inspection by such an expert. The AA 1996 does not make a similar provision. Instead it relies on the parties' duty under s. 40 of the AA 1996 to 'do all things necessary for the proper and expeditious conduct of the arbitral proceedings' to obtain the parties' cooperation in disclosing relevant evidence. The AA 1996 also provides the arbitral tribunal with specific powers under s. 34(d), (e) and (g) in relation to the disclosure and production of documents. In addition, under s. 38(4), the arbitral tribunal has a power to order the inspection of property in the possession of a party.

The arbitral tribunal may also, under s. 37(1)(a)(ii) of the AA 1996, allow any such expert, legal adviser or assessor to attend the proceedings and give evidence. Under s. 37(1)(b) the arbitral tribunal must give the parties a reasonable opportunity to comment on any information or advice which such a person may offer. Again the AA 1996 appears more restrictive than does the Model Law, which permits the parties specifically to question the expert and present their own witnesses to testify on the points in issue. Section 37(1)(a) of the AA 1996 gives the party only a 'reasonable opportunity to comment' on the matters raised by the expert, legal adviser and assessor. This accords with the arbitral tribunal's duty under s. 33(1) of the AA 1996 to conduct the proceedings fairly.

9.2.1 Fees and expenses of an expert, legal adviser or assessor

Section 37(2) of the AA 1996 is a mandatory section that cannot be excluded by the parties. It states that the fees and expenses of any expert, legal advisers or assessor appointed by the arbitral tribunal are expenses of the arbitral tribunal. This means that the parties are liable to pay them if they are reasonable, unless they have made a contrary agreement with the arbitral tribunal. Section 28(1) of the AA 1996 provides that the parties are jointly and severally liable to pay to the arbitral tribunal 'such reasonable fees and expenses (if any) as are appropriate in the circumstances'.

The arbitral tribunal is bound to consider whether it is appropriate in the circumstances to appoint experts, legal advisers or assessors and must avoid unnecessary expense in complying with its duty under s. 33(1) of the AA 1996. If the fees and expenses incurred are unreasonable in the circumstances then the arbitral tribunal may not only be in breach of s. 33(1) of the AA 1996 but may also be liable for them. It would therefore be prudent for the arbitral tribunal to obtain the parties' agreement in writing before appointing any expert, legal adviser or assessor.

9.3 GENERAL POWERS OF THE TRIBUNAL

Section 38(1) of the AA 1996 states that: 'The parties are free to agree on the powers exercisable by the arbitral tribunal for the purposes of and in relation to the proceedings'. This sets out what was the accepted position prior to the AA

1996. The section is illustrative of the second principle found in s. 1 of the AA 1996, that the parties are free to agree how their dispute is to be resolved subject to such necessary safeguards as are in the public interest. This section should be read with and is complementary to s. 34 of the AA 1996.

Section 38(2) of the AA 1996 provides that where there is no such agreement as to the powers to be exercised by the arbitral tribunal then the default provisions, within s. 38(3) to (6), apply. There can be no doubt that the parties are free to agree not to be bound by the default matters as set out in s. 38(3) to (6) of the AA 1996 if they so wish. It is also equally clear that the parties are entitled to apply such procedural rules as they think fit subject to the right of challenge for being contrary to public policy. What remains unclear, however, is the limitations on the arbitral tribunal where the parties elect to adopt institutional rules. An illustration of such a situation can be seen where the parties elect to adopt the ICC Arbitration Rules. The ICC Arbitration Rules make no provision for the taking of samples or experiments upon the property which is the subject of the proceedings. However s. 38(4)(c) of the AA 1996 gives the arbitral tribunal the power to order such things to be done. If the parties adopt the ICC Arbitration Rules, which make no reference to such power, it is unclear whether the arbitral tribunal is then entitled to order the examination of such property. Section 38(2) of the AA 1996 leaves the question unanswered. It merely states that: 'Unless otherwise agreed by the parties the arbitral tribunal has the following powers'. It is uncertain whether the adoption of an institutional set of rules which remains silent on a procedural matter means that the parties have 'otherwise agreed'. It is certainly arguable that the failure to make reference to a specific power is not an agreement by the parties for the arbitral tribunal not to exercise that power. However, this argument appears more difficult to sustain where the institutional rules are complex. There is further discussion on this issue in chapter 13 regarding orders for security for costs, for which provision is made in s. 38(3) of the AA 1996.

Section 38(4) of the AA 1996 provides the arbitral tribunal with powers to inspect and give directions relating to any property which is the subject of the proceedings, or associated with the proceedings, and which is owned by or in the possession of a party to the proceedings. The arbitral tribunal has the power to give directions:

(a)   for the inspection, photographing, preservation, custody or detention of the property by the tribunal, an expert or party, or
(b)   ordering that samples be taken from, or any observation be made of or experiment conducted upon, the property.

Any inspection by the arbitral tribunal must be carried out in accordance with its duty under s. 33 of the AA 1996. The court has wider powers of inspection under s. 44(2)(c) (see 10.1.3).

Section 38(5) of the AA 1996 provides that the arbitral tribunal may direct that a party or witness be examined on oath or affirmation. The arbitral tribunal has the power to administer any oath or affirmation. The administration of the oath is discussed in 15.10.3. The arbitral tribunal is unable to compel witnesses to attend a hearing or take evidence from a third party. A party to the arbitration must apply to the court under ss. 43 and 44(2)(a) of the AA 1996 for the court to do so. See 10.1.2 and 10.1.3.

Section 38(6) of the AA 1996 provides the arbitral tribunal with the power to give directions for the preservation of evidence in the custody of a party for the purposes of the proceedings. Such a direction can, however, only be given when the arbitral tribunal has been properly constituted. If such an order is required prior to the arbitral tribunal being constituted, an application must be made to the court. Applications to the court are discussed further at 10.1.3. It is also clear from the wording of s. 38(6) that any direction can only be made to a party to the arbitration. Again, recourse to the courts will be necessary where an order is required affecting a third party.

9.4 POWERS OF THE TRIBUNAL TO MAKE PROVISIONAL AWARDS

Although the marginal note to s. 39 of the AA 1996 states that it is concerned with a power to make a provisional award, the term 'award' does not feature in the text of s. 39. The term 'award' is misleading as the order made is provisional and therefore not final and binding on the parties and therefore does not comply with s. 58 of the AA 1996. The power under s. 39 of the AA 1996 is therefore hereafter termed a power to make provisional orders.

Section 39(1) of the AA 1996 states that the parties may agree to give the arbitral tribunal the power 'to order on a provisional basis any relief which it would have power to grant in a final award'. In s. 39(2) of the AA 1996 two examples of such provisional orders are given. The arbitral tribunal may make 'a provisional order for the payment of money or the disposition of property' or 'an order to make an interim payment on account of the costs of the arbitration'.

An arbitral tribunal which is given this power is bound to comply with s. 33(1) of the AA 1996 in exercising it. The AA 1996 provides no further guidance as to how this discretion should be exercised. It is likely to be used in cases of great hardship where a party is in need of immediate relief or where the defence to a claim appears shadowy. As the order is provisional a final award can overturn it so that money provisionally ordered to be paid may have to be returned.

It is further made clear in s. 39(3) of the AA 1996 that the arbitral tribunal's power under this section is a power to grant temporary relief only and that the order is subject to the arbitral tribunal's final adjudication. Section 39(3) of the AA 1996 states that the arbitral tribunal's final award in respect of the merits or costs of the arbitration will take account of any provisional order. It appears, therefore, that any hardship suffered by the successful party as a result of such an order having been made before the final adjudication will be redressed in the final award.

Section 39(4) of the AA 1996 states that the power to make provisional orders does not affect the tribunal's powers under s. 47 of the AA 1996. The power to make provisional orders is not to be confused with the arbitral tribunal's power under s. 47 to make interim awards. Unlike provisional orders, which are temporary in nature and not binding, any award made under s. 47 is final and binding.

It is doubted whether an appeal or challenge can be made to the courts from a provisional order under s. 39 of the AA 1996, by reason of s. 70(2) of the AA 1996. As the order is provisional it is subject to a process of appeal or review by the arbitral tribunal itself. Section 70(2) therefore effectively precludes such a provisional order being challenged in the courts.

9.5　POWERS IN THE CASE OF A PARTY'S DEFAULT

It is fundamental to the success of arbitration proceedings as a genuine alternative to litigation that the proceedings are run properly and expeditiously. The proper and expeditious conduct of the arbitral proceedings is that which enables the parties to obtain a fair resolution of disputes by an impartial arbitral tribunal without unnecessary delay or expense. This is one of the three general principles of the AA 1996 as set out in s. 1(a). The Act strives to achieve this purpose by providing certain mandatory and non-mandatory provisions to this effect.

For example, the requirement of expediency and proper conduct is reflected in the mandatory duty of the arbitral tribunal in s. 33(1)(b) of the AA 1996. The arbitral tribunal is required to 'adopt procedures suitable to the circumstances of the particular case, avoiding unnecessary delay or expense, so as to provide a fair means for the resolution of the matters falling to be determined'. If the arbitral tribunal fails to conduct the proceedings properly or to use all reasonable dispatch in so doing or in making the award, it may be removed under s. 24(1)(d)(i)and(ii) if substantial injustice has been caused to a party.

The importance of acting expeditiously is also reflected in s. 40 of the AA 1996, which is a mandatory provision requiring the parties to do all things 'necessary for the proper and expeditious conduct of the arbitral proceedings'. Section 41(1) of the AA 1996 also stresses the importance of being expedient, although it is not a mandatory provision. The parties are free to agree the powers of the arbitral tribunal in the case of a party's 'failure to do something necessary for the proper and expeditious conduct of the arbitration'.

Subject to the parties' contrary agreement, s. 41(1) of the AA 1996 gives the arbitral tribunal certain powers to deal with a party which fails to proceed properly and expeditiously with the arbitration, summarised as follows:

(a)　A claimant who pursues a claim with inordinate and inexcusable delay may have its action struck out under s. 41(3) of the AA 1996.

(b)　The arbitral tribunal may proceed in the absence of a party who fails to appear or be represented at a hearing of which due notice was given without showing sufficient cause under s. 41(4)(a) of the AA 1996.

(c)　The arbitral tribunal may proceed without written evidence or if a party fails to submit written evidence or make written submissions after due notice has been given in respect of a documents-only arbitration, without showing sufficient cause under s. 41(4)(b) of the AA 1996.

(d)   The arbitral tribunal may make a peremptory order against a party failing to comply with any order or direction of the arbitral tribunal without showing sufficient cause under s. 41(5) of the AA 1996.

(e)   The arbitral tribunal may dismiss the claim if a party fails to comply with any peremptory order of the arbitral tribunal to provide security for costs under s. 41(6) of the AA 1996.

(f)   The arbitral tribunal may make any other peremptory order as provided by s. 41(7) of the AA 1996.

The powers of the arbitral tribunal to proceed in the case of a party's default and in a party's absence are further discussed at 15.9.

9.6   WANT OF PROSECUTION

Section 41(3) of the AA 1996 provides that, unless otherwise agreed by the parties, an arbitral tribunal may make an award dismissing a claim if it is satisfied that there has been inordinate and inexcusable delay by a claimant in pursuing its claim which:

(a)   gives rise, or is likely to give rise, to a substantial risk that it is not possible to have a fair resolution of the issues in that claim, or

(b)   has caused, or is likely to cause, serious prejudice to the respondent.

The burden is on the respondent to satisfy the arbitral tribunal on the balance of probabilities that the criteria have been met. Under s. 82 of the AA 1996 the term 'claimant' includes 'counterclaimant', so an arbitral tribunal may dismiss a counterclaim for want of prosecution and leave the claim alive. An arbitral tribunal's powers to strike out a claim or counterclaim for inordinate delay are similar to those of the court: *Owen* v *Pugh* [1995] 3 All ER 345.

Arbitral tribunals were first given a discretionary power to strike out a claim under s. 102 of the Courts and Legal Services Act 1990, which added s. 13A to the AA 1950. Until then, unless the parties specifically provided the arbitral tribunal with the power to strike out a claim, the arbitral tribunal had no direct way of dealing with an inactive claimant. Section 41(3) of the AA 1996 preserves the powers contained in s. 13A of the AA 1950. There is a similar power in Article 25 of the UNCITRAL Model Law.

The principles for striking out a claim for want of prosecution in court and arbitration proceedings derive from the House of Lords decisions in *Birkett* v *James* [1978] AC 297 and in *Department of Transport* v *Chris Smaller (Transport) Ltd* [1989] AC 1197. Both s. 13A of the AA 1950 and its successor, s. 41(3) of the AA 1996, employ a similar language to that used by Lord Diplock in his judgment in *Birkett* v *James* [1978] AC 297.

9.6.1 Inordinate

'Inordinate' was defined by Cumming-Bruce LJ in *Tabata* v *Hetherington* (1983) *The Times*, 15 December 1983 as 'materially longer than the time, which was usually regarded by the courts and the profession as an acceptable period'.

9.6.2 Inexcusable

'Inexcusable' means that a claimant has no acceptable excuse for delaying the claim, such as being ill or obstacles caused by the respondent. It is not excusable if the respondent becomes insolvent: *Claremont Construction Ltd* v *GCT Construction Ltd* (1983) 127 SJ 461. Even if an action has been stayed by the order of the court, this will not be considered a good excuse if at any time the stay could have been lifted by the claimant: *Thomas Storey Engineers Ltd* v *Wailes Dove Bitumastic Ltd* (1988) *The Times*, 21 January 1988. Delay caused by the fault of a claimant's solicitor or counsel is also no excuse and whether or not there exists an alternative claim against a legal adviser is not relevant: *Birkett* v *James* [1978] AC 297.

9.6.3 Delay

Whether the delay is inordinate and inexcusable varies according to the facts of each case. Judge Bowsher held in *Secretary of State for Foreign and Commonwealth Affairs* v *Percy Thomas Partnership* (1998 unreported) that although the delay could be inordinate and inexcusable it had to be of sufficient duration for the claim to be dismissed under s. 41(3) of the AA 1996.

'Delay' has been held to include not only periods where no action was taken but also periods where only desultory steps were taken: *Lev* v *Fagan* (1988) *The Times*, 15 March 1988. In *L'Office Cherifien des Phosphates* v *Yamashita-Shinnihon Steamship Co. Ltd* [1994] 1 AC 486 the owners of the ship known as the *Boucraa* had referred their claim to arbitration in August 1985, which was before s. 13A of the AA 1950 was brought into force. Between December 1985 and November 1986 the claimants had served on the respondents points of claim and replies to points of claim. No further action was taken and in April 1991 the arbitral tribunal enquired whether the reference was still in progress. Although the claimants stated that the action was still live they did not begin to deal with the claim until December 1991. Section 13A of the AA 1950 came into force on 1 January 1992. In view of the new provision the respondents applied on 12 January 1993 to strike out the claim on the grounds of the claimant's inordinate and inexcusable delay, which they alleged had created a real risk of an unfair resolution of the dispute. The issue in this case was whether the arbitral tribunal was entitled to take account of any part of the delay which had preceded the coming into force of s. 13A of the AA 1950. The House of Lords held that, although s. 13A could not be held to have come into force with the original 1950 Act, as the arbitral tribunal in the case had found, the provision was partly retrospective. Their lordships found that the 'delay' in this section meant cumulative delay, which included delay both before and after the section came into force. The rationale behind this decision was that, although the authorities showed that there was a presumption against statutes working retrospectively, the basis of this rule was fairness and how this rule applied to individual statutes varied from case to case.

9.6.4   Delay within the limitation period

The House of Lords held in *Birkett* v *James* [1978] AC 297 that a court would have no power, in the absence of special circumstances, to dismiss a claim for want of prosecution because of inordinate and inexcusable delay before the limitation period had expired. This was because the claimant would, save in rare and exceptional cases, be entitled to issue a new claim for the same cause of action: *Spring Grove Services Ltd* v *Deane* (1972) 116 SJ 844. However, the later a claim is started, the greater the onus is on the claimant to prosecute it with due diligence: *Birkett* v *James* [1978] AC 297; *Tabata* v *Hetherington* (1983) *The Times*, 15 December 1983. The court can also take account of any delay in prosecuting the claim which occurred within the limitation period when considering an application to strike out the claim after the expiry of the limitation period: *Rath* v *C.S. Lawrence and Partners* [1991] 1 WLR 399; *Trill* v *Sacher* [1993] 1 WLR 1379. In *Rath* v *C.S. Lawrence and Partners* Farquharson LJ stated:

> Once a plaintiff has issued his writ and set the treadmill of litigation in motion, he is bound to observe the rules of the court. If he flouts them to the extent that the plaintiffs have in the present case, I can see no reason why the defendants should not rely upon it, after the limitation period has expired, to support an application to strike out.

Where there is an argument as to whether the limitation period has in fact expired the arbitral tribunal should dismiss the claim if the grounds in s. 41(3) of the AA 1996 have been made out: *Barclays Bank plc* v *Miller* [1990] 1 WLR 343. The Court of Appeal in *Barclays Bank plc* v *Miller* held, according to the headnote to the report at [1990] 1 All ER 1040, that in such a case the interests of justice are best served if the claim is dismissed and it is left 'to the plaintiff to bring a fresh action if he so chose, rather than allowing itself to become embroiled on such an application in complex arguments on whether some future action, if brought, would be time-barred'.

9.6.5   Delay before issuing a claim within the limitation period

Any delay before issuing a claim which is within the limitation period, save in exceptional cases, will not be considered to be 'inordinate' delay: *Trill* v *Sacher* [1993] 1 WLR 1379. Lord Diplock expressly stated in *Birkett* v *James* [1978] AC

297, at p. 320, that 'time elapsed before issue of the writ which does not extend beyond the limitation period cannot be treated as inordinate delay: the statute itself permits it'. It was further held in *Birkett* v *James* that if a claim has been issued within the limitation period but there has been a long delay between the time the action has accrued and issuing the claim, the claim could only be dismissed for want of prosecution on the following grounds:

(a)   if the delay following the issue of the claim exceeded the time limits prescribed by the rules of the court;
(b)   the delay before the issue of the claim was inordinate and inexcusable; and
(c)   the delay after the issue of the claim had increased by more than a minimal amount the prejudice that the defendant has already suffered because of the delay in bringing the claim. This point was upheld in *Department of Transport* v *Chris Smaller (Transport) Ltd* [1989] AC 1197.

9.6.6   Delay after expiry of the limitation period

It was held in *Department of Transport* v *Chris Smaller (Transport) Ltd* [1989] AC 1197 that inordinate and inexcusable delay after the expiry of the limitation period is not a ground for striking out unless the delay has caused prejudice to the defendant or rendered a fair trial impossible.

Whether the arbitral tribunal's power to strike out a claim is bound by these same principles was considered in *James Lazenby and Co.* v *McNicholas Construction Co. Ltd* [1995] 1 WLR 615. This case involved a dispute about the original pricing and ultimate costs of work undertaken by the claimants. In February 1988 Lazenby, the claimants, commenced proceedings in the county court in respect of their invoices which the respondent had not paid. The respondent relied on an arbitration clause in the contract and in May 1988 the county court proceedings were stayed by consent. There was then a period of 15 months' delay before the claimants commenced arbitration proceedings and an arbitrator was appointed. The arbitrator was appointed in May 1989. The defence was served later that year and a preliminary hearing took place in July 1991 followed by a directions hearing for the main hearing in October 1991. There was then a nine to 10 months' delay and the respondent applied to have the claim struck out in July 1992. In the meantime s. 13A of the AA 1950 had come into effect. The arbitrator held that he had no power to strike out the claim on the ground that s. 13A of the AA 1950 was not retrospective. In 1993 the House of Lords held in *L'Office Cherifien des Phosphates* v *Yamashita-Shinihon Steamship Co. Ltd* [1994] AC 486 that an arbitral tribunal could take account of any delay which occurred before the commencement of s. 13A of the AA 1950. Meanwhile the respondent had commenced a new reference to arbitration in order to protect its claim as the limitation period in respect of its original claim was to run out in 1993. The respondent also obtained leave to apply to the arbitrator to reconsider its application to strike out the claim. In 1994 the arbitrator struck out the claim on the ground that there had been inordinate and inexcusable delay on the claimants' part and that the delay had given rise to a substantial risk that it would not be possible to have a fair resolution of the issues in the claim. The arbitrator made this award notwithstanding that the statutory limitation period had not yet run out. The claimants appealed the decision on a question of law that, as their claim was not statute-barred, it was contrary to the principle in *Birkett* v *James* [1978] AC 297 to strike out their claim. The respondent's case was based in essence on the fact that arbitration proceedings were an alternative method of dispute resolution and that s. 13A of the AA 1950 should not therefore be considered as subject to the same principles as for court proceedings. The respondent also submitted, as an alternative argument, that if the principles in *Birkett* v *James* were applicable, the award should be upheld as there were exceptional facts in the case before the arbitrator which entitled him to strike out the claim even within the limitation period.

Rix J held that Parliament had not intended that the arbitral tribunal in exercising its power under s. 13A of the AA 1950 should go beyond the court's jurisdiction. He found that the wording of s. 13A indicated clearly that the powers to dismiss a claim in arbitration and the corresponding powers in litigation were to be exercised in the same way. It was also held that the arbitrator had a discretion to dismiss a claim within its limitation period if exceptional circumstances had arisen, such as where the other party had been misled. However in this case Rix J found that no exceptional circumstances existed.

9.6.7 Substantial risk that it is not possible to have a fair resolution of the issues

Under s. 41(3) of the AA 1996 the arbitral tribunal has to decide whether, on the evidence presented, there has been an inordinate and inexcusable delay. If there has been such a delay, it must go on to decide whether there is a 'substantial risk' that the issues cannot be resolved fairly because of the delay: s. 41(3)(a) of the AA 1996. In doing so the arbitral tribunal should consider how the reference would have proceeded but for the delay. If in the arbitral tribunal's view, based on the evidence presented, the delay has substantially prevented a fair resolution of the issues then it may grant the application. If there is no such evidence, the arbitral tribunal must not grant the application.

9.6.8 Serious prejudice

Prejudice is given its ordinary meaning of 'detriment'. Whether the respondent in an arbitration has been caused or is likely to be caused serious prejudice is a matter of fact and degree in every case: *Allen* v *Sir Alfred McAlpine and Sons Ltd* [1968] 2 QB 229. A respondent asserting that there has been prejudice has the onus of proving that its case has been seriously prejudiced overall because of the delay: *Slade* v *Adco* (1995) *The Times*, 7 December 1995. The prejudice suffered must be more than minimal: *Hornagold* v *Fairclough Building Ltd* [1993] PIQR P400. A mere inference of prejudice is not sufficient. In *Hornagold* v *Fairclough Building Ltd* Roch LJ said, at p. 409:

> There must, in my judgment, be more than the bald assertion that the delay has prejudiced the defendants, or that it has created a substantial risk that a fair trial will not be possible, or that it has to add to existing prejudice, or to the existing risk that a fair trial will not be possible.

Prejudice can be caused to the respondent where the lapse of time has affected the memory of witnesses or during that time a witness has died or disappeared. The loss of memory need not be proved but can be inferred because of the delay caused: *Shtun* v *Zalejska* [1996] 1 WLR 1270. Whether it is 'serious prejudice' depends on the circumstances of the case and the effect that this lack of evidence has on the respondent's case in relation to the issues and the other, available evidence. If the reference depends on oral evidence, the lack of independent witnesses through the lapse of time may seriously prejudice the respondent's case. In contrast, it was held in *National Insurance and Guarantee Corporation Ltd* v *Robert Bradford and Co. Ltd* (1970) 114 SJ 436 that it may be of much less importance in a well-documented commercial case. In exceptional cases a respondent may be prejudiced, not because of diminished evidence, but because of some other reason caused by protracted litigation. In *Biss* v *Lambeth, Southwark and Lewisham Area Health Authority (Teaching)* [1978] 1 WLR 382 the defendants, who were professional men, were held to have suffered prejudice to their reputations by having the matter prolonged for $11\frac{1}{2}$ years. Serious financial prejudice was a ground for striking out the proceedings where liability had been admitted but the issue of quantum remained to be tried in *Department of Transport* v *Chris Smaller (Transport) Ltd* [1989] AC 1197. Prejudice has also been held to include economic prejudice (*Gascoine* v *Haringey Health Authority* (1991) *The Times*, 21 January 1992), such as having to fund damages which have been caused by the delay: *Antcliffe* v *Gloucester Health Authority* [1992] 1 WLR 1044. However, it will rarely be the case that serious financial prejudice will occur by a mere postponement of the trial or arbitration: *Gahan* v *Szerelmey (UK) Ltd* [1996] 1 WLR 439. The arbitral tribunal should consider the prejudice to the respondent and ought not to refuse to strike out the reference because doing so would cause a greater prejudice to the claimant: *Pattison* v *Hobbs* (1985) *The Times*, 11 November 1985.

Prejudice which has been largely caused by the respondent may be disregarded: *Sterling* v *George Cohen and Sons and Co. Ltd* [1987] NI 409. Any conduct on the part of the respondent which induces the claimant to incur further expense following the claimant's inordinate and inexcusable delay should be taken into account by the arbitral tribunal in considering the striking-out application. Such conduct may not be an absolute bar to the respondent succeeding in the application. The arbitral tribunal should consider the weight to be attached to the respondent's conduct in all the circumstances of the case in exercising its discretion to strike out the claim: *Roebuck* v *Mungovin* [1994] 2 AC 224.

9.7   PROCEEDINGS IN THE ABSENCE OF A PARTY

Section 41(4) states as follows:

> If without showing sufficient cause a party—
> (a)   fails to attend or be represented at an oral hearing of which due notice was given, or
> (b)   where matters are to be dealt with in writing, fails after due notice to submit to written evidence or make written submissions,
> the tribunal may continue the proceedings in the absence of that party or, as the case may be, without any written evidence or submissions on his behalf, and may make an award on the basis of the evidence before it.

Section 41(4) of the AA 1996 empowers the arbitral tribunal to continue with the arbitration proceedings in the absence of a party in two circumstances: first, where a party fails to attend or be represented at a hearing and, secondly, in respect of a documents — only arbitration where a party has not submitted any written submissions on its behalf. The arbitral tribunal may simply make an award on the evidence before it. Section 41 of the AA 1996 is not a mandatory section and the parties can agree that this default power should not apply. There are two requirements before s. 41(4) can be applied. The absent party must not have a good reason for being absent or failing to participate, such as being ill, and must have had due notice of the requirement to attend a hearing or submit written evidence or submissions. There is a possible conflict between the arbitral tribunal duty under s.33(1)(a) of the AA 1996 to act fairly and give each party the opportunity to present its case and reply to its opponent's case, and the power given to it under s. 41(4) of the AA 1996 to proceed with the participation of only one party. The DAC addressed this issue in their February 1996 report at para. 208 by stating that the opportunity afforded to the parties should, for reasons of justice, be limited to a reasonable one. The DAC concluded that, 'If for no good reason such an opportunity is not taken up by a party then to our minds it is only fair to the other party that the tribunal should be able to proceed as we have set out in this Clause'.

In order to give the absent or non-participating party a reasonable opportunity, the arbitral tribunal should ensure that it has given that party sufficient notice that it intends to proceed with the arbitration despite that party's absence or non-participation, (see *Myron (Owners)* v *Tradax Export SA* [1969] 1 Lloyd's Rep 411). It would be fair for the arbitral tribunal to keep the absent or non-participating party abreast of the proceedings. However, this may not be required where such a party has challenged the arbitral tribunal's jurisdiction: *Maritime International Nominees Establishment* v *Kaplan Russin and Vecchi* [1994] ADRLJ 52. The case of *Fox* v *PG Wellfair Ltd* [1981] is still good authority for the proposition that the arbitral tribunal must not take up the case of the absent party and advocate on its behalf. The arbitral tribunal is bound to be impartial under its duty in s. 33(1)(a) of the AA 1996.

9.7.1   Peremptory orders

Section 41(5) of the AA 1996 states that:

> If without showing sufficient cause a party fails to comply with any order or directions of the tribunal, the tribunal may make a peremptory order to the same effect, prescribing such time for compliance with it as the tribunal considers appropriate.

Section 41 is not a mandatory section. The arbitral tribunal cannot make a peremptory order without having first made a direction or order with which a party has not complied. The DAC in their February 1996 report made this point at para. 209: 'It will be noted that a peremptory order must be 'to the same effect' as the preceding order which was disobeyed (subsection 5). It could be quite unfair for an arbitrator to be able to make any type of peremptory order, on any matter, regardless of its connection with the default in question.' If a peremptory order is not complied with, other than a peremptory order to provide security for costs, the arbitral tribunal has the discretionary power under s. 41(7) of the AA 1996 to do any of the following:

(a)   direct that the party in default shall not be entitled to rely upon any allegation or material which was the subject matter of the order;

(b)   draw such adverse inferences from the act of non-compliance as the circumstances justify;

(c)   proceed to an award on the basis of such materials as have been properly provided to it;

(d)   make such orders as it thinks fit as to the payment of costs of the arbitration incurred in consequence of the non-compliance.

The remedies provided by s. 41(7) of the AA 1996 are stated to be without prejudice to the power of the court to order the compliance of a peremptory order, unless the parties otherwise agree (s. 42 of the AA 1996). The powers of the court under s. 42 are discussed at 10.1.1. The remedies provided in s. 41(7) do not include the power to make an award against the party in default. The DAC in their February 1996 report at para. 211 stated that: 'The reason for this is that (unlike a failure to comply with a peremptory order to provide security) it seems to us that this is too draconian a remedy, and that the alternatives we have provided very much better fit the justice of the matter'.

If a claimant fails to comply with a peremptory order to provide security for costs, the arbitral tribunal may make an award dismissing the claim under s. 41(6) of the AA 1996.

10 Powers of the Court in the Course of Arbitral Proceedings

10.1 POWERS IN RESPECT OF PROCEDURAL STEPS

Section 1(c) of the AA 1996 provides: 'in matters governed by this Part the court should not intervene except as provided by this Part'. Section 1(c) sets out one of the principle tenets of the AA 1996, that the court's intervention in the arbitration should be minimal. The court cannot intervene where the arbitral tribunal has made an error which involves a question of fact. Since the AA 1996 came into force the court has no residual power to order discovery of documents (standard disclosure) or that a party provide security for costs (except for appeals and/or applications — CPR, PD 49G, para. 17.1). These powers have not been given to the court under s. 44 of the AA 1996. Such orders can only be made by the arbitral tribunal. Part 1 of the AA 1996 limits the role of the court to one of support. In this the AA 1996 follows the UNCITRAL Model Law.

10.1.1 Powers to enforce a peremptory order of the arbitral tribunal

Section 41 of the AA 1996 gives the arbitral tribunal, in the absence of a contrary agreement by the parties, certain powers to make peremptory orders. The arbitral tribunal is also given, by s. 41(6) and (7), the power to sanction a party in the event of non-compliance with a peremptory order. The arbitral tribunal is able under s. 41(6) to make an award dismissing the claim if a claimant fails to comply with a peremptory order to provide security for costs. In respect of all other peremptory orders the arbitral tribunal may, under s. 41(7) do any of the following:

(a) direct that the party in default shall not be entitled to rely upon any allegation or material which was the subject matter of the order;
(b) draw such adverse inferences from the act of non-compliance as the circumstances justify;
(c) proceed to an award on the basis of such materials as have been properly provided to it;

(d)   make such order as it thinks fit as to the payment of costs of the arbitration incurred in consequence of the non-compliance.

The powers that the arbitral tribunal possesses under s. 41(7) will usually be sufficient. In most cases the party will comply with the peremptory order rather than risk having one or more of the sanctions set out imposed upon it. However, the arbitral tribunal's powers are limited. It does not have an equivalent power to that of the court to order a party to be in contempt if an order is breached and liable to a fine or a term of imprisonment. An order from the court may be required where, for instance, a party does not disclose and allow inspection of documents which it is essential for the opposing party to have sight of in order to prove its case.

Section 42 of the AA 1996 enables the court to make an order requiring a party to comply with a peremptory order of the arbitral tribunal. Section 42 is not a mandatory section. The parties are free to exclude it by agreement. Section 42(2) of the AA 1996 states that:

An application for an order under this section may be made—
(a)   by the tribunal (upon notice to the parties),
(b)   by a party to the arbitral proceedings with the permission of the tribunal (and upon notice to the other parties), or
(c)   where the parties have agreed that the powers of the court under this section shall be available.

Where the arbitral tribunal's permission is required and there is more than one arbitrator it appears from ss. 20(3) and 22(2) of the AA 1996 that a majority decision will be sufficient. An application under s. 42 of the AA 1996 is made in the form prescribed under CPR, PD 49G (see 14.6.2. for further details). If the applicant has received the permission of the arbitral tribunal to make the application, this should be stated in the application.

The court's powers are only intended to be supportive of the arbitral tribunal's powers. The court's powers to enforce peremptory orders are only to be invoked if the party making the application has exhausted all available arbitral processes in respect of the other party's failure to comply with the order of the arbitral tribunal: s. 42(3) of the AA 1996. Section 42(4) of the AA 1996 states the court will not grant an application under s.42 unless it is satisfied that the party against whom the application has been directed has actually breached an order of the arbitral tribunal within the time given for compliance or, if no time was prescribed, within a reasonable time. Section 42(5) of the AA 1996 directs that any appeal from the decision of the court under s. 42 of the AA 1996 requires the leave of the court.

10.1.2   Power to secure the attendance of witnesses

The arbitral tribunal has no power to compel witnesses to attend a hearing. Section 43 of the AA 1996 is a mandatory section that derives from both s. 12(4) of the

AA 1950 and Article 27 of the UNCITRAL Model Law. Section 43(1) of the AA 1996 enables a party to an arbitration to use the same procedures as are available in court proceedings to secure the attendance before the arbitral tribunal of witnesses. A party to an arbitration may need to issue a witness summons to obtain the presence of a witness to give oral evidence or to produce documents or other material evidence stated in the witness summons.

The right of a party to use the same procedures as are available in legal proceedings to secure the attendance of a witness is subject to s. 43(2) of the AA 1996, which states that a party must first secure the permission of the arbitral tribunal or the agreement of the other parties. This condition did not appear in s. 12(4) of the AA 1950. If the arbitration is proceeding on a documents-only basis the other parties may not agree that a witness should attend to give oral testimony. The arbitral tribunal must consider whether in giving its permission it is acting within the remit of its duty under s. 33(1) of the AA 1996 which requires the arbitral tribunal to give each party a reasonable opportunity of putting its case.

Section 43(3)(a) and (b) of the AA 1996 restricts the use of a witness summons to secure the attendance of witnesses to cases where the witness is in the United Kingdom, and the arbitral proceedings are being conducted in England and Wales or Northern Ireland. However, s. 2(3) of the AA 1996 provides that the powers conferred in s.43 with respect to securing the attendance of witnesses apply even if the seat of the arbitration is outside England and Wales or Northern Ireland or if no seat has been designated or determined. In such cases the court may refuse to exercise its power to compel attendance if, in its opinion, the fact that the seat is, or is likely to be, outside these countries makes it inappropriate for it to do so.

The rules relating to the issue of a witness summons are dealt with in CPR, Part 34. A party to an arbitration which is conducted in England and Wales who wishes to rely on s. 43 of the AA 1996 to secure the attendance of a witness may apply for a witness summons in accordance with CPR, Part 34. The application is made to the Admiralty and Commercial Registry, or, if the attendance of the witness is required within the district of a district registry, at that registry at the option of that party: CPR, PD 49G, para. 16.1. A witness summons shall not be issued until the applicant files an affidavit or witness statement which shows that the application is made with the permission of the arbitral tribunal or with the agreement of the other parties: CPR, PD 49G, para. 16.2. The witness summons may be set aside if it has been issued without the proper permission of the arbitral tribunal or without the agreement of the other parties: *Sunderland Steamship P & I Association v Gatoil International Inc.* [1988] 1 Lloyd's Rep 180. A witness who does not comply with a witness summons which has been validly served will be in contempt of court.

Section 43(4) of the AA 1996 preserves the rule of privilege. The subsection states that a witness cannot be compelled to produce any document or other material evidence which would not be compellable in legal proceedings. This refers to evidence which is protected by the rule of privilege. The arbitral tribunal and the court have no power to order disclosure against a non-party to the arbitration. A party may issue a witness summons against a third party requiring that party to produce documents. However, the court is reluctant to allow witness summonses to be used as a way of obtaining a general disclosure or as a 'fishing expedition' against a third party: *Sunderland Steamship P & I Association* v *Gatoil International Inc.* [1988] 1 Lloyd's Rep 180.

10.1.3 General powers to support the arbitration process

Section 44 of the AA 1996 sets out the powers of the court which are intended to support the arbitration proceedings. Section 44(1) of the AA 1996 states, unless the parties otherwise agree, the court has the same powers for making orders in arbitration proceedings in respect of the matters listed in s. 44(2) of the AA 1996 as it does in civil proceedings in the High Court or county court. The powers of the court in s. 44 of the AA 1996 run in tandem with the corresponding powers of the arbitral tribunal in s. 38 of the AA 1996. Both sections are not mandatory. The arbitral tribunal's powers are the same as the court's powers save for a few exceptions. The arbitral tribunal is unable to sell any goods which are the subject of the proceedings, appoint a receiver or make interim injunctions. The AA 1996 seeks to discourage applications to the court in favour of applications to the arbitral tribunal. For this purpose the powers of the court are restricted in s. 44(3) to (5) of the AA 1996. If the case is one of urgency the court has the discretion to 'make such orders as it thinks necessary for the purpose of preserving evidence or assets': s. 44(3) of the AA 1996. In urgent cases an application under s. 44 of the AA 1996 is made in accordance with the rules in CPR, PD 49G, para. 18.1 (see Appendix 4). The application may be made without notice on affidavit or witness statement which shall state the following reasons:

(1)   why the application is made without notice; and

(2)   (where the application is made without the permission of the arbitral tribunal or the agreement of the other parties to the arbitral proceedings) why it was not practicable to obtain that permission or agreement; and

(3)   why the witness believes that the condition in s. 44(5) is satisfied.

The affidavit or witness statement must also deal with the matters required by CPR, PD 49G, para. 9.1 and 9.2 (see Appendix 4).

If the case is not one of urgency, a party or proposed party to the arbitration must make its application to the court on notice to all the parties to the arbitration and the arbitral tribunal. The court shall only then act if the application has been made either with the permission of the arbitral tribunal or with the agreement in writing of the other parties: s. 44(4) of the AA 1996. In a non-urgent case, the application under s. 44 of the AA 1996 is made in accordance with CPR, PD 49G, para. 18.2. The affidavit or witness statement must deal with the matters required by CPR, PD 49G, paras 9 and 18.1(3) and state that the application is made with the permission of the arbitral tribunal or with the written agreement of the parties to the arbitral proceedings (see Appendix 4).

In all cases the party making an application under s. 44 of the AA 1996 has to satisfy the court of the condition stated in s. 44(5), which provides that 'the court shall act only if or to the extent that the arbitral tribunal, and any arbitral or other institution or person vested by the parties with power in that regard, has no power or is unable for the time being to act effectively'. A party can only apply to the court for an order under s. 44 of the AA 1996 if the appointed tribunal has not been vested with the appropriate powers or the required order is one which only a court may order, such as an injunction, or the arbitral tribunal cannot act effectively because it has not yet been constituted. Once the arbitral tribunal is properly constituted, the court may return control of the proceedings. The arbitral tribunal may be granted the power to order that any court order made under s. 44(2)(a) of the AA 1996 shall cease to have effect in whole or in part: s. 44(6) of the AA 1996. Any appeal from a decision of the court under s. 44 requires the leave of the court: s. 44(7) of the AA 1996.

Section 2(3)(b) of the AA 1996 states that the court may exercise its powers conferred by s. 44 even if the seat of the arbitration is outside England and Wales or Northern Ireland or if no seat has been designated or determined. However, the court has a discretion whether to exercise its powers and may not do so if in its opinion the fact that the seat of the arbitration is outside England and Wales or Northern Ireland, or that when designated or determined the seat is likely to be outside England and Wales or Northern Ireland, makes it inappropriate to do so.

An application under s. 44 cannot be made by the court because the arbitral tribunal has refused to make a required order. The court's powers are only to be used where the arbitral tribunal is unable to act. Unless agreed by the parties, in relation to the matters listed in s. 44(2), the court has the same powers as it has in relation to legal proceedings. The matters listed in s. 44(2) are:

(a)   the taking of the evidence of witnesses;
(b)   the preservation of evidence;
(c)   making orders relating to property which is the subject of the proceedings or as to which any question arises in the proceedings—
    (i)   for the inspection, photographing, preservation, custody or detention of property, or
    (ii)   ordering that samples be taken from, or any observation be made of or experiment conducted upon, the property;
and for that purpose authorising any person to enter any premises in the possession or control of a party to the arbitration;
(d)   the sale of any goods the subject of the proceedings;
(e)   the granting of an interim injunction or the appointment of a receiver.

10.1.3.1   The taking of the evidence of witnesses   Where an arbitration is being conducted in England, Wales or Northern Ireland, it is common for witnesses who are abroad to give evidence by affidavit. However, where a party wishes to cross-examine a witness who is abroad the court has the power under s. 44(2)(a) of the AA 1996, on an application of a party, to order that a witness attend for examination before an officer of the court appointed for that purpose. A party to the arbitration may apply to the court under s. 44 when it is not possible to obtain an order under s. 43, because the arbitration is taking place in the United Kingdom and the witness is abroad or the arbitration is taking place abroad and the witness is in the United Kingdom. In such circumstances the arbitral tribunal has no power to order the attendance of a witness. An application under s. 44 of the AA 1996 can only be made if the seat of the arbitration is in England, Wales or Northern Ireland (s. 2(1) of the AA 1996). In rare cases a party may apply to the court under s. 44(2)(a) of the AA 1996 where the seat of the arbitration is in England and the witness is abroad, for an order to issue to a foreign court a request for the examination of a witness (see CPR r. 34.13).

10.1.3.2   The preservation of evidence   The arbitral tribunal's powers under s. 38(4) of the AA 1996 are restricted to the giving of directions to a party to the proceedings to preserve 'any evidence in his custody and control'. The arbitral tribunal has no power to order the preservation of evidence in the custody or control of a third party or to order the preservation of evidence for any reason other than the purposes of the proceedings. The court's powers to preserve evidence are wider than the arbitral tribunal's powers. Section 44(1) of the AA 1996 states that, unless the parties have agreed otherwise, the court has the same powers to make orders as it has in civil proceedings. Such orders are contained in CPR, r. 25.1(1) and associated Practice Directions. The court is therefore able to make an order to preserve evidence by making a freezing injunction under CPR, r. 25.1(1)(f) and, under s. 43(3) of the AA 1996, the court may make such an order before the arbitral tribunal has been appointed. Section 44(5) of the AA 1996 makes it clear that the court will only act if the arbitral tribunal has no power or is unable for the time being to act effectively.

10.1.3.3   Making orders relating to property   Section 44(2)(c) of the AA 1996 gives the court wider powers than those which the arbitral tribunal possesses under s. 38(4) of the AA 1996. Both sections are non-mandatory. Under s. 44(5) of the AA 1996 the court will not act where the arbitral tribunal has the same powers and is able to act effectively. Both the court and the arbitral tribunal are able to make orders relating to property which is the subject of the proceedings or as to which any question arises in the proceedings for the inspection, photographing, preservation, custody or detention of the property. In addition, both may make orders that samples be taken from, or any observation be made of or experiment conducted upon, the property. However, the arbitral tribunal under s. 38(4) of the AA 1996 has no power to give directions in respect of any property which is owned or in the possession of a third party. The arbitral tribunal under s. 38(4) of the AA 1996 is only able to order that inspection, photographing, preservation, custody or detention of the property be carried out by itself, an expert or a party. The court under s. 44(2)(c) of the AA 1996 has the power to authorise 'any person to enter any premises in the possession or control of a party to the arbitration'.

The term 'premises' is defined in s. 82(1) of the AA 1996 to include 'land, buildings, movable structures, vehicles, vessels, aircraft and hovercraft'. Property is an undefined term in the AA 1996. The court may make an order for disclosure of documents or inspection of property against a third party before proceedings have been commenced under CPR, r. 25.1(1)(i). In addition to ordering a freezing injunction, the court may also order a party to provide information about the location of relevant property or assets. Alternatively the court may order a party to provide information about relevant property or assets which are or may be the subject of a freezing injunction: CPR, r. 25.1(1)(g). Any party to the proceedings can also apply to the court for an application for a search order under CPR, r. 25.1(1)(h) requiring a party to admit another party to premises for the purpose of preserving evidence or property. Such an order will enable the person named in the order to enter premises in England and Wales and carry out a search for or inspection of anything described in the order.

As stated previously, the court has the same powers for making orders in arbitration proceedings in respect of the matters listed in s. 44(2) of the AA 1996 as it does in civil proceedings in the High Court or county court. There are therefore limits to the orders that a court can make in support of the arbitral process. In *Tsakos Shipping & Trading SA v Orizon Tanker Co. Ltd* [1998] CLC 1003 the parties entered into a contract for the sale of a vessel with a London arbitration clause. It was a condition of the agreement that the vessel remain in the same condition between the dates of inspection and delivery. The buyers suspected that the engines of the vessel had deteriorated since inspection and obtained an order without notice from the court for inspection. The sellers sought to discharge the order. It was held by Rix J that it was doubtful whether the court had the power to make such an order before a cause of action or circumstances giving rise to an injunction arose. Rix J held that to allow such an order would mean that the court was effectively rewriting the contract between the parties. Rix J concluded that such an order was not necessary to preserve evidence or protect the parties' contractual rights.

10.1.3.4 The sale of any goods the subject of the proceedings The arbitral tribunal has no corresponding power to order the sale of any goods which are the subject of the proceedings. The court has the power to sell such goods under s. 44(2)(d) of the AA 1996. The court can order the sale of goods which are of a perishable nature or which for any other good reason it is desirable to sell quickly. This power is also given to the court in CPR, r. 25.1(1)(c)(v). Once the court has ordered that goods be sold, it may also give directions regarding the application of the proceeds of sale, such as an order that the proceeds be paid into court until the conclusion of the arbitration. The AA 1996 provides no definition as to the meaning of 'goods'.

10.1.3.5 The granting of an interim injunction or the appointment of a re-ceiver Under s. 44(2)(e) of the AA 1996 the court is able to grant interim injunctions and appoint receivers unless the parties have agreed in writing to exclude the court's powers to do so. The agreement to exclude the court's powers in respect of granting ancillary relief in arbitral proceedings must be express: *Re: Q's Estate* [1999] 1 All ER (Comm) 499. In that case Rix J held that a clause giving the arbitral tribunal exclusive jurisdiction over any dispute deriving from or in connection with the agreement in question was not an agreement excluding the court's powers in respect of granting ancillary relief. The effect of such a clause was purely to emphasise that the substantive hearing had to be by way of arbitration. The court's powers to order interim injunctions and appoint receivers are found respectively in CPR, r. 25.1(1)(a) and RSC, ord. 30 in CPR, sch. 1.

The court's powers are restricted by s. 44(5) of the AA 1996 to where the arbitral tribunal does not have the corresponding power to make such an order or is unable to act effectively. The arbitral tribunal's powers may be considered ineffective where a party wishes to apply without notice for an immediate injunction and the process of enforcing an arbitral tribunal's peremptory order through the court would add undue delay. Equally, the arbitral tribunal's powers will be considered ineffective where an injunction is required before the arbitral tribunal has been properly constituted: *Channel Tunnel Group Ltd* v *Balfour Beatty Construction Ltd* [1993] AC 334; [1992] 2 Lloyd's Rep 7 at p. 13.

The freezing injunction (formerly *Mareva* injunction) is perhaps the most commonly used form of injunction in arbitral proceedings. A freezing injunction prevents a party from moving assets overseas or otherwise dealing with assets. A freezing injunction is defined in CPR, r. 25.1(1)(f) as an order restraining a party from removing from the jurisdiction assets located there; or as an order restraining a party from dealing with any assets whether located within the jurisdiction or not. There need not be a full hearing and the application can be made in the absence of the other party. If the application is made without notice, the party making the application must comply with CPR, PD 49G, paras 9 and 18(1) (see Appendix 4). The application is made on affidavit which must state the reasons why the application is being made without notice; why it was not practicable to obtain permission of the arbitral tribunal or the agreement of all the other parties to the proceedings; and why the deponent believes that the arbitral tribunal has no power or is unable for the time being to act effectively.

Under the AA 1950 a freezing injunction could only be applied for in connection with arbitral proceedings in England and Wales: *The Rena K* [1979] QB 337; *Siporex Trade SA* v *Comdel Commodities Ltd* [1986] 2 Lloyd's Rep 428. Recently, however, the courts have shown that they are willing in legal proceedings to issue worldwide freezing injunctions, affecting not only assets in England and Wales but also assets abroad. The jurisdictional rationale for the worldwide freezing order is discussed by A. Johnson, 'Interim measures of protection under the Arbitration Act 1996', [1997] Int ALR 13:

The jurisdiction to make such an order rests on the premise that an injunction operates personally against a defendant (and not *in rem* against his assets), and so if the defendant is subject to the jurisdiction of the English court, an order can be made against him in England controlling his dealing with assets abroad, and requiring him to disclose information or documents concerning his assets worldwide. The effect of such a worldwide *Mareva* injunction against third parties is limited by what is commonly referred to as the *Babanaft* proviso [*Babanaft International Co. SA* v *Bassatne* [1990] Ch 13], so that a third party who is resident wholly abroad will not be affected by the injunction unless it is made enforceable in the place where he is to be found. There would seem to be no reason in principle why a world *Mareva* injunction should not be granted in support of arbitration proceedings in England under the 1996 Act. The wording of s. 44 of the Act is wide enough to permit this.

10.2 COURT'S POWER TO PRESERVE ASSETS AND EVIDENCE

Section 44(3) of the AA 1996 states that in urgent cases the court has the discretionary power, on the application of a party or proposed party to the arbitration, to make 'such orders as it thinks necessary for the purpose of preserving evidence or assets'. The party making the application is not obliged under this section to obtain the permission of the arbitral tribunal or the written consent of the other parties. The powers under s. 44(3) of the AA 1996 include the power to make search orders and/or freezing injunctions.

A freezing injunction granted during the arbitration proceedings is particularly useful in cases where a party wishes to make sure that the respondent has enough assets to comply with the award or as a method of securing assets for the enforcement of an award: *Orwell Steel* v *Asphalt and Tarmac (UK)* [1984] 1 WLR 1097. It is also useful where there is concern that the assets or evidence may be disposed of before the arbitral tribunal has been appointed and the arbitration has commenced. In such cases the applicant has no option but to apply to the court. In cases where a party applies for a court order under s. 44 of the AA 1996, before the issue of an arbitration application, CPR, PD 49G, para. 18.3 states that any order which the court makes may be subject to terms providing for the issue of an arbitration claim form and other such terms, as the court thinks fit. Where an order has been made by the court before an arbitral tribunal has been properly constituted, s. 44(6) of the AA 1996 provides that the court may direct that the order shall cease to be effective in whole or in part on the order of the arbitral tribunal, once it has been properly constituted.

The court's powers to intervene and make orders under s. 44(3) of the AA 1996 are limited to orders for the purpose of preserving evidence or assets. Article 9 of the UNCITRAL Model Law is drafted in wider terms and does not restrict the type of interim measure a court may make. Article 9 of the UNCITRAL Model Law simply states as follows:

It is not incompatible with an arbitration agreement for a party to request, before or during arbitral proceedings, from a court an interim measure of protection and for a court to grant such measure.

It appears, however, that interim measures which have been granted under this Article have been restricted to the preservation of assets. The Hong Kong court granted a *Mareva* injunction in *Katran Shipping Vo. Ltd* v *Kenven Transportation Ltd* [1992] HKLD G9.

10.3   DETERMINATION OF A PRELIMINARY POINT OF LAW

Section 45 of the AA 1996 allows for an application to be made to the court for the determination of a preliminary point of law. The section therefore preserves what used to be known as the 'consultative case'. The drafters of the AA 1996 anticipated that a point of law could become a central issue in some arbitrations and that the early resolution of such points of law might therefore be required. They were also aware, as shown by para. 218 of the DAC report of February 1996, that an issue of law could be of general public interest and could be the subject of many arbitrations. There are restrictions on making applications under s. 45 of the AA 1996.

Section 2 of the AA 1979 provided for the court to intervene for the purpose of determining a preliminary point of law while the arbitration was in progress. The AA 1996 has retained this provision with some significant amendments. Section 45(1) of the AA 1996 gives the court the discretionary power, if a party makes an application under this section, to 'determine any question of law arising in the course of the proceedings which the court is satisfied substantially affects the rights of one or more of the parties' (this is also one of the requirements for the court to give leave to appeal on a point of law under s. 69(3)(a) of the AA 1996). The fact that a question of law has arisen in the arbitration is not in itself a sufficient ground for the court to decide to determine that question of law. The onus is on the party making the application to show that the question of law substantially affects a party's rights. This is a significant change from s. 1 of the AA 1979, which made no such provision. The drafters of the AA 1996 were keen to keep the interventionary powers of the court in an arbitration to a minimum. Section 45(1) of the AA 1996 is therefore not a mandatory section. The parties can exclude it by making a contrary agreement or by agreeing to dispense with reasons in the arbitral tribunal's award. Such an agreement would also disable a party from appealing an award on a point of law: s. 69(1) of the AA 1996.

The party making the application for the determination of a preliminary point of law has to satisfy the conditions in s. 45(1) and (2) of the AA 1996 for the court to even consider the application. Section 45(2) of the AA 1996 states that an application under s. 45 must not be considered unless:

(a)   it is made with the agreement of all the other parties to the proceedings, or

(b)   it is made with the permission of the tribunal and the court is satisfied —

(i)   that the determination of the question is likely to produce substantial savings in costs, and

(ii)   that the application was made without delay.

In respect of s. 45(2)(b), the court is able to exercise its discretion whether or not to grant the application. If the court decides to grant the application a separate hearing will be necessary on the question of law.

There are not as yet any cases on s. 45 of the AA 1996 which indicate what issues the court considers substantially affect the rights of the parties. However, these words were used in s. 1(4) of the AA 1979 which is re-enacted in s. 69(3) of the AA 1996. In *Secretary of State for the Environment* v *Reed International plc* [1994] 1 EGLR 22 and *Retla Steamship Co.* v *Gryphon Shipping Co. SA* [1982] 1 Lloyd's Rep 55 the court was satisfied that the rights of a party were substantially affected where a material amount of money was involved.

Section 45(5) of the AA 1996 states that unless the court gives leave, no appeal lies from the decision of the court whether the conditions specified in s. 45(2) have been met. Section 45 of the AA 1996 does not make any provision specifically in respect of an appeal on the basis that a court erred in deciding that the question of law does not substantially affect the rights of one or more of the parties under s. 45(1) of the AA 1996.

A party seeking an application for the determination of a preliminary point of law with the consent of all the other parties merely has to satisfy the condition in s. 45(1) of the AA 1996 before the court will entertain its application. In *Taylor Woodrow Civil Engineering Ltd* v *Hutchison IDH Development* [1998] CILL 1434 the court held that an agreement by the parties made prior to the arbitration proceedings beginning constituted an agreement for the purposes of the AA 1996.

The facts of *Taylor Woodrow Civil Engineering Ltd* v *Hutchison IDH Development* were that the parties entered into a JCT Intermediate Form of Contract, 1984. The base date for the contract was March 1996. Clause 9 of the contract stated: 'The parties hereby agree by consent pursuant to ss. 1(3)(a) and 2(1)(b) of the Arbitration Act 1979 that either party may appeal to the High Court on any question of law arising out of the award'. A dispute arose between the parties and arbitration was commenced after 31 January 1997. The question that the court was asked to consider was whether the agreement to refer questions of law to the High Court under the AA 1979 survived when the AA 1979 had been repealed by s. 107(2) of the AA 1996. Clarke J held that the agreement to refer questions of law to the High Court did survive the repeal of the AA 1979. Further, while the court accepted that there were more stringent rules under the AA 1996 than there were under the AA 1979 this did not in itself change the fact that the question of law to be referred remained the same. No point was raised by the parties as to whether consent prior to the dispute arising was sufficient for the purposes of s. 45(2)(a) of the AA 1996.

In *Vascroft (Contractors) Ltd* v *Seeboard plc* (1996) 78 BLR 132 Judge Lloyd QC held that parties can give consent in advance, at the agreement stage, before the dispute arises. In *Vascroft (Contractors) Ltd* v *Seeboard plc* the parties had entered into a DOM/2 standard form contract which contained a clause to the effect that the parties agreed and consented that either party could appeal to the court on any question of law arising out of an award and could apply to the court for a determination on a point of law pursuant to ss. 1(3) and 2(1)(b) of the AA 1979. These sections of the AA 1979 required the applications to be made with leave of the court in the absence of the parties' agreement. The arbitral tribunal made an interim award and Vascroft appealed against the decision. Seeboard argued that leave was required as they had not consented to the application. The judge held that the standard clause amounted to a valid consent within the meaning of s. 1(3) of the AA 1979 and therefore leave was not required. The decision was based on the fact that the parties had contracted on the basis of giving a blanket consent.

A party making an application without the consent of the other party has to satisfy the conditions in s. 45(2)(b) of the AA 1996 before the court will entertain the application. First, the applicant must obtain the permission of the arbitral tribunal to make the application. Where there is more than one arbitrator a majority decision is likely to be sufficient (see ss. 20(3) and 22(2) of the AA 1996). Secondly, the applicant must satisfy the court that the determination of the question of law is likely to produce substantial savings in costs as required by s. 45(2)(b)(i) of the AA 1996; and that the application was made without delay as required by s. 45(2)(b)(ii) of the AA 1996. A party which is guilty of delays will also fall foul of its general duty under s. 40(1) of the AA 1996 to 'do all things necessary for the proper and expeditious conduct of the arbitral proceedings'. Section 40(2)(b) specifically requires a party to take steps without delay to obtain a decision of the court on a preliminary question of law.

In considering whether to give its permission to a party to make an application under s. 45(2)(b) of the AA 1996 the arbitral tribunal is bound by its duty under s. 33(1)(a) to 'act fairly and impartially as between the parties, giving each party a reasonable opportunity of putting his case'. The arbitral tribunal will have to consider how far the unresolved question of law precludes the applicant from having a reasonable opportunity of putting its case. The arbitral tribunal will also have in mind its other duty under s. 33(1)(b) to avoid unnecessary delay or expense in the conduct of the arbitration. It is in order to deter a party from using delaying tactics for its own benefit that the AA 1996 makes these stringent provisions regarding delay.

The arbitral tribunal has no power to make an application on its own account under s. 45 of the AA 1996. If the arbitral tribunal wishes to have a question of law decided by the court, it must obtain the agreement of at least one of the parties who will then make the application. Under s. 21(1)(a) of the AA 1950 the arbitral tribunal had the power to apply to the court to seek a determination on a point of law arising in the course of the arbitration against the wishes of the parties. This provision was repealed by s. 8(3)(b) of the AA 1979.

A party making an application to the court for a determination of a preliminary point of law must give notice of the application to the other parties. Section 45(3) of the AA 1996 states that the application must identify the question of law to be determined by the court and, unless made with the agreement of all the other parties to the proceedings, must state the grounds upon which the question is to be decided by the court. CPR, PD 49G requires that an application to determine a preliminary point of law under s. 45 of the AA 1996, if made without the written agreement of the other parties, must be supported by an affidavit or witness statement setting out the evidence in support of the contention. Once the affidavits or witness statements have been lodged with the court the decision whether or not the court should consider the application is made. This decision is usually made on the basis of the evidence without a hearing unless the court orders otherwise.

Section 45(4) of the AA 1996 provides that, unless the parties otherwise agree, the arbitration may continue and an award may be published while an application under s. 45 is pending. This provision enables the parties to save time and costs by proceeding with the reference if this is what they want. If the parties request that the arbitration proceedings be stayed while the application is made to the court to determine a preliminary point of law, the arbitral tribunal would be wise to agree to this request. Where, however, the arbitral tribunal elects to proceed with the reference contrary to the request of the parties an application to the court under s. 45 of the AA 1996 may be coupled with an application for an injunction.

Section 45(6) of the AA 1996 deals with appeals against decisions on s. 45 applications. Section 45(6) states that a decision of the court on the question of law shall be treated as a judgment of the court for the purposes of the appeal. The court's decision will be final unless leave is given to appeal. Section 45(6) of the AA 1996 states that leave 'shall not be given unless the court considers that the question is one of general importance, or is one which for some special reason should be considered by the Court of Appeal'. These words are derived from ss. 1(7)(b) and 2(3)(b) of the AA 1979. They are also found in s. 69(8) of the AA 1996. In *Geogas SA* v *Trammo Gas Ltd* [1991] 2 QB 139 the Court of Appeal gave guidelines as to when a question of law will be of public importance and what other special reason should be considered. It stated that the test to be applied was whether 'the question of law is worthy of consideration by the Court of Appeal'. The majority of the Court of Appeal, Dillon LJ dissenting, stated that the test in *Pioneer Shipping Ltd* v *BTP Tioxide* [1982] AC 724 did not apply to whether the Court of Appeal should entertain an appeal from the High Court and that different tests were applicable to an appeal from an arbitral tribunal to the High Court than from the High Court to the Court of Appeal. Leggatt LJ stated, at p. 159:

In arbitration cases the important step to restrain is the transfer from the private to the public domain by way of appeal from arbitrators to a judge. It may be inconvenient to have conflicting decisions of arbitrators, but their decisions are not binding on each other. The decisions of courts, on the other hand, are of persuasive authority *inter se*, and at any rate in relation to commercial arbitrations are likely to be published. It is therefore of much greater importance that decisions of judges on appeal from arbitrators should be correct. That is best achieved by the application of a less strict test for allowing leave to appeal from judges than from arbitrators.

Leggatt LJ then proceeded to provide further reasons why an appeal from a decision of a judge should not be subject to the same rules as an appeal from an arbitrator. His lordship stated, at p. 160:

> There are obvious reasons of policy, such as moved the House of Lords in *Pioneer Shipping Ltd* v *BTP Tioxide Ltd* and *Antaios Compania Naviera SA* v *Salen Rederierna AB* to provide guidelines to inhibit appeals from arbitrators, why the parties should abide by decisions of the tribunal of their choice. But this principle is subject to three important qualifications. First, there may be a wider body of persons interested in the result than the parties themselves. Hence the provision for a certificate to be given that a question of law is of general public importance. Secondly, the principle itself provides a reason for allowing an unsuccessful party to appeal when a judge has overturned an arbitrators' award, since the effect of that is to deprive him of the benefit of the decision of his chosen tribunal. Thirdly, the parties are not to be presumed to have accepted the correctness of points of law that are wrong; no such result is necessitated by the desirability of avoiding delay or achieving finality of decision.

This appears to accept the definition of general public importance as provided for in *Pioneer Shipping Ltd* v *BTP Tioxide Ltd* [1982] AC 724 and *Antaios Compania Naviera SA* v *Salen Rederierna AB* [1985] AC 191. A 'one-off' contract will not therefore generally raise an issue of general public importance because there will not be a wider body of persons interested in the result. However, the phrase 'special other reasons' appears to have been interpreted broadly. The fact that the High Court and the arbitrator have reached inconsistent results appears to be a special reason. Equally, the fact that the point of law remains open to varying interpretations which could lead to uncertainty would also constitute a special reason.

10.4 POWER TO CHARGE PROPERTY RECOVERED IN THE PROCEEDINGS WITH THE PAYMENT OF SOLICITOR'S COSTS

Section 75 of the AA 1996 extends the power of the court under s. 73 of the Solicitors Act 1974 and Article 71H of the Solicitors (Northern Ireland) Order 1976 (SI 1976/582) to arbitration proceedings so as to permit a solicitor who has recovered or preserved property belonging to a client during an arbitration to place a charge over that property. If the court makes an order under this section, the solicitor is entitled to recover his or her costs out of the property. This section preserves the power of the court given in s. 18(5) of the AA 1950. It is a mandatory section and cannot be excluded by the parties' agreement.

11 The Award

11.1 RULES APPLICABLE TO SUBSTANCE OF DISPUTE

Section 46 of the AA 1996 is a mandatory section, which provides that the arbitral tribunal shall decide the dispute:

    (a) in accordance with the law chosen by the parties as applicable to the substance of the dispute, or
    (b) if the parties so agree, in accordance with such other considerations as are agreed by them or determined by the tribunal.

The choice of the laws of a country is stated in s. 46(2) to be the substantive law of a country and not its conflict of laws rules. This adopts the rule found in Article 28 of the UNCITRAL Model Law, which was included in the AA 1996 to avoid the problems of 'renvoi' (see 11.1.3).

11.1.1 Proper law of the contract

The law applicable to the substance of the dispute is referred to as the 'proper law of the contract'. This is the system of law of one country, by which the parties have agreed to be bound in the determination of the substantive dispute. Section 46(1)(a) of the AA 1996 makes it mandatory for the arbitral tribunal to decide the parties' dispute by applying the proper law of the contract even if the arbitration is held in a country other than the one whose law governs the arbitration agreement. Section 46 of the AA 1996 corresponds to Article 28(3) of the UNCITRAL Model Law. It also reflects the common law position as found in *Compagnie d'Armement Maritime SA* v *Compagnie Tunisienne de Navigation SA* [1971] AC 572, in which Lord Diplock stated, at p. 604:

It is not now open to question that if parties to a commercial contract have agreed expressly upon the system of law of one country as the proper law of their contract and have selected a different curial law by providing expressly that disputes under the contract shall be submitted to arbitration in another country, the arbitrators must apply as the proper law of the contract that system of law upon which the parties have expressly agreed.

11.1.2   Other considerations as are agreed

Section 46(1)(b) of the AA 1996 enables the parties to an arbitration to have their dispute decided on such other considerations, of fairness and justice, as they agree or are determined by the arbitral tribunal, rather than on an established system of law. This section reflects Article 28(3) of the UNCITRAL Model Law. An agreement between the parties to have their dispute determined by other considerations is normally contained in an 'equity clause'. The DAC at para. 223 of their February 1996 report recognised the existence of such clauses and found that there was no good reason for preventing the parties to an arbitration from agreeing to them. The parties have the autonomy not just to choose the arbitral tribunal but the rules upon which their dispute should be determined. A perceived disadvantage of an equity clause is that, as there is no proper system of law to be applied, there can be no appeal from the decision of the arbitral tribunal under s. 69 of the AA 1996. Nor can there be any application under s. 45 of the AA 1996 for the determination of a preliminary point of law. In *Channel Tunnel Group Ltd* v *Balfour Beatty Construction Ltd* [1993] AC 334 the House of Lords upheld the use of an equity clause but stated that there could be no appeal from the arbitral tribunal's decision.

11.1.3   No system of law adopted by the parties

Section 46(3) of the AA 1996 provides that: 'If or to the extent that there is no such choice or agreement, the tribunal shall apply the law determined by the conflict of laws rules which it considers applicable'. This subsection is applicable only where the parties have not made a positive choice of law for the determination of the substance of their dispute. The arbitral tribunal will then have to consider the characteristics of the dispute and apply the relevant conflict of laws rules. This in practice may cause difficulties for the parties where the arbitral tribunal, in applying the conflict of laws rules of one country, decides that the proper law of the contract is the law of another country and the conflict of laws rules of that other country would, if applied, mean that the proper law of the contract is that of a different country. This is a classic problem within the rules of conflict of laws known as 'renvoi'.

11.2   AWARDS ON DIFFERENT ISSUES

Section 47(1) of the AA 1996 is a non-mandatory section and provides that: 'Unless otherwise agreed by the parties, the tribunal may make more than one award at different times on different aspects of the matters to be determined'. This subsection is derived from s. 14 of the AA 1950, in which the phrase used was 'interim award'. The DAC, in their report in February 1996 at para. 233, considered that this was a misnomer as the award was not interim but in fact final and binding on the matters which had been decided. The DAC regarded the power of the arbitral tribunal to make partial awards as an aspect of the arbitral tribunal's general duty under s. 33(1)(a) of the AA 1996 to adopt procedures suitable to the circumstances of the particular case and thereby save time and costs. In particular the DAC envisaged that the arbitral tribunal would make partial awards in long and complex disputes.

There is no comparable provision to s. 47(1) of the AA 1996 within the UNCITRAL Model Law. At common law the rule was that the arbitral tribunal did not have power to make interim or partial awards. The arbitral tribunal's duty was to render a single award unless the parties had agreed otherwise. It was not until the AA 1889 that statute provided that the arbitral tribunal should be given the power to make partial awards. Some common law jurisdictions have chosen not to provide the arbitral tribunal with a statutory power to make partial awards: see the Gibraltar Arbitration Ordinance 1984.

Section 47(2) of the AA 1996 provides examples where the arbitral tribunal may make a partial award. These are 'an issue affecting the whole claim, or to a part only of the claims or cross-claims submitted to it for decision'. It is clear from the wording of this subsection that the examples provided are purely illustrative of the type of partial award which may be made. The arbitral tribunal would be entitled to make a partial award where the facts of the case showed that a defence of set-off to the claim was not made in good faith: *S.L. Sethia Liners Ltd* v *Naviagro Maritime Corporation* [1981] 1 Lloyd's Rep 18.

In deciding whether to make a partial award the arbitral tribunal must have in mind its obligations under s. 33 of the AA 1996. The arbitral tribunal is required to allow each party to have a reasonable opportunity of putting its case and dealing with the other party's case. In deciding whether a matter should proceed by way of partial award the tribunal must decide whether it will cause unnecessary delay and expense. If a timetable has been set out with a hearing date set in the not too distant future, any appeal from a partial award may affect the hearing of the remainder of the issues.

Where the arbitral tribunal decides that it can deal, by way of partial award, with only part of the claim or counterclaim, it should also have regard to the remainder of the claim. A claim or counterclaim, or a part of a claim or counterclaim, may be a discrete item easily and correctly dealt with by way of partial award. The arbitral tribunal, however, should be cautious before making an award of damages. The arbitral tribunal should consider whether the other party's claim or counterclaim will exceed in quantum the damages awarded. If this is the case, it would be appropriate only for an award on liability to be made and the question of quantum left to a later date. Alternatively the arbitral tribunal may make an award stating the sum found to be due but leaving any direction as to payment to a later date.

Section 47(3) of the AA 1996 requires that where the arbitral tribunal does proceed by way of partial award, '. . . it shall specify in its award the issue, or the claim or part of a claim, which is the subject matter of the award'. If the partial award does not specify this, a party to the arbitration may challenge the award under s. 68(2)(f) or (h) of the AA 1996. The parties must know what issues or claims the arbitral tribunal has considered so that they may decide whether to appeal the decision and what other matters they must address in the final award hearing.

There is a fundamental difference between a partial award made under s. 47 of the AA 1996 and a 'provisional order' under s. 39 of the AA 1996. A partial award is final and binding on the parties and any party claiming through or under them: s. 58 of the AA 1996. The award may be subject to appeal on a point of law unless the parties have agreed to the contrary. A 'provisional order', by contrast, is subject to the arbitral tribunal's final adjudication.

11.3 REMEDIES

Section 48 of the AA 1996 deals with the remedies that are available to the arbitral tribunal. The provision is new although it is based in part on s. 15 of the AA 1950. There is no comparable section within the UNCITRAL Model Law. The section is non-mandatory in that the parties are free to agree what remedies the arbitral tribunal shall possess: s. 48(1) of the AA 1996. If the parties to the arbitration have not agreed the powers exercisable by the arbitral tribunal as regards remedies then s. 48(2) of the AA 1996 provides that the powers contained in s. 48(3) to (5) of the AA 1996 apply.

11.3.1 Declaration

Section 48(3) of the AA 1996 provides that: 'The tribunal may make a declaration as to any matter to be determined in the proceedings'. The power to make a declaratory award is subject to any contrary agreement made by the parties: s. 48(1) of the AA 1996. Section 48(3) gives an arbitral tribunal the power to decide the precise meaning of the terms of a contract where they are contested or to state the meaning of a clause within a contract. It may be the case that a declaratory award will be sought as a partial award within the dispute as it may assist the parties to reach a settlement on the outstanding matters.

11.3.2 Orders

Section 48(4) of the AA 1996 gives the arbitral tribunal power to 'order the payment of a sum of money, in any currency'. This power to order payment 'in any currency' is relatively new to English arbitration law: *Jugoslavenska Oceanska Plovidba* v *Castle Investment Co. Inc.* [1973] 2 Lloyd's Rep 1. The party seeking to claim its losses in a foreign currency should, as a matter of practice, state in its points of claim that the claim is for a foreign currency, and unless the facts themselves clearly show this, state the facts relied on to support such a claim. This follows the High Court practice: see Practice Direction (Judgment: Foreign Currency) (No. 2) [1977] 1 WLR 197. The power to order that the claim be paid in a foreign currency should be exercised only in limited circumstances. In *Jugoslavenska Oceanska Plovidba* v *Castle Investment Co. Inc.* [1974] QB 292 the Court of Appeal held, according to the headnote in the report cited, 'that English arbitrators had jurisdiction to make awards in a foreign currency where that currency was the currency of the contract'. For circumstances where a claim for a foreign currency is based on a tort see *The Despina R* [1979] AC 685.

Section 48(5) of the AA 1996 provides the arbitral tribunal with the same powers as the court to make three types of order as follows:

(a) to order a party to do or refrain from doing anything;

(b) to order specific performance of a contract (other than a contract relating to land);

(c) to order the rectification, setting aside or cancellation of a deed or other document.

Section 48(5)(a) of the AA 1996 provides the arbitral tribunal with a power to order a party to do or refrain from doing anything. This power corresponds with the court's powers to order 'mandatory' or 'prohibitive' injunctions. However, the arbitral tribunal, unlike the court, cannot order an injunction against a person who is not a party to the arbitration. A mandatory injunction is one which requires a person to do an act. A prohibitive injunction is one which requires a person to refrain from doing an act. This is an important power for the arbitral tribunal and when exercising it the arbitral tribunal should have in mind the grounds upon which it will be exercised by the courts. The power is a discretionary power and is subject to the rules of equity.

The courts will generally only grant an injunction where the award of damages would not be an adequate remedy to a party. An injunction will generally not be granted where a party has been dilatory in its application: this is the equitable principle of laches. An injunction will not be granted unless the person applying has 'clean hands', that is, no blame can be attached to that party's actions. Any order made must also be clear in its intent and free from ambiguity: *Redland Bricks Ltd* v *Morris* [1970] AC 652.

Section 48(5)(b) of the AA 1996 entitles the arbitral tribunal to order specific performance of a contract. Specific performance is, like an injunction, a discretionary remedy and subject to equities. It would be unusual for an order for specific performance to be made in a building contract because of the nature of the form of order. Specific performance requires that an action be carried out. If the arbitral tribunal ordered that a contractor complete the building works which were the subject of the dispute then the arbitral tribunal, or an appointee of the arbitral tribunal, would have to oversee the works to make sure that they were completed. In effect, having made such an order, the arbitral tribunal would thereafter act as certifier in assessing whether the works were completed and to the standard and specification that was ordered. In such a case, whether the arbitral tribunal would thereafter be acting as 'arbitrator' or 'certifier' is then open to question.

Section 48(5)(c) of the AA 1996 provides that the arbitral tribunal has the power to rectify a contract. The power to rectify a contract is exercised by an arbitral tribunal when it decides that what was actually intended by the parties is not what is set out in the contract. It is a declaration of the true intent of the parties. The power to rectify a contract was possessed by arbitral tribunals at common law: *Ashville Investments Ltd* v *Elmer Contractors Ltd* [1989] QB 488. The parties should, however, be aware that this power may be abrogated by the wording of the arbitration agreement. An agreement to refer to arbitration disputes concerning 'these presents' has been held to exclude the power of the arbitral tribunal to rectify the contract (the 'presents') itself: *Printing Machinery Co. Ltd* v *Linotype and Machinery Ltd* [1912] 1 Ch 566. The power of the arbitral tribunal to set aside or cancel a deed or other document may be useful where the validity of the document is challenged.

11.4   INTEREST

Section 49 of the AA 1996 deals with the arbitral tribunal's power to grant interest. This section makes changes to the pre-existing law. It is a non-mandatory section. Section 49(1) of the AA 1996 provides that, 'The parties are free to agree on the powers of the tribunal as regards the award of interest'. Section 49(2) of the AA 1996 provides that, if the parties do not agree these powers, the provisions in s. 49(3) to (6) apply.

11.4.1.   Position before the AA 1996

Historically there was no power to award interest on general damages by either the court or an arbitral tribunal except for cases in the Admiralty Division of the High Court: *London, Chatham and Dover Railway Co.* v *South Eastern Railway Co.* [1893] AC 429. Interest claimed as special damages was, however, recoverable by reason of the special nature of the loss: *Hadley* v *Baxendale* (1854) 9 Ex 341. This type of claim for interest arose as part of the claim made. It was a loss which was in the reasonable contemplation of the parties at the time that the contract was entered into: *Wadsworth* v *Lydall* [1981] 1 WLR 598; *La Pintada Compania Navegacion SA* v *President of India* [1984] 2 Lloyd's Rep 9. In *Wadsworth* v *Lydall* the defendant failed to pay an agreed sum to the plaintiff who was forced to borrow money to pay for the purchase of another property that he had agreed to buy. The plaintiff incurred interest and legal charges by reason of the defendant's default. The Court of Appeal held that where the circumstances were such that there was a special loss, including the incurring of interest charges, as a consequence of non-payment of money under a contract, the loss was recoverable from the defaulting party. In construction contracts it is considered to be within the reasonable contemplation of the parties that if the employer fails to pay the contractor what is due to it, the contractor will have to borrow money to continue working. In such a case the contractor may be able to claim financing charges as part of its claim. These financing charges are a claim for interest on the money borrowed: *Rees and Kirby Ltd* v *Swansea City Council* (1985) 30 BLR 1; *F. G. Minter Ltd* v *Welsh Health Technical Services Organisation* (1980) 13 BLR 1.

The rule that the courts could not award interest by way of general damages was altered by the Law Reform (Miscellaneous Provisions) Act 1934. Although this Act did not refer to arbitration proceedings the Court of Appeal in *Chandris* v *Isbrandtsen-Moller Co. Inc.* [1951] 1 KB 240 held, by analogy with the Act, that an arbitral tribunal could award interest on the principal sum awarded. Interest could only, however, be awarded on a sum which was ordered to be paid as part of the award. In respect of sums claimed but paid prior to an award, interest could not be awarded. The Administration of Justice Act 1982 altered this position by inserting s. 19A into the AA 1950, which provided that interest could be paid on a sum claimed but paid prior to the award by the arbitral tribunal.

11.4.2 Position after the AA 1996

The parties are free to agree the powers of the arbitral tribunal in respect of awarding interest. Where the parties have not made any such agreement, s. 49(3)–(5) of the AA 1996 will apply. Section 49(3) of the AA 1996 now provides that:

> The tribunal may award simple or compound interest from such dates, at such rates and with such rests as it considers meets the justice of the case—
>
> (a)   on the whole or part of any amount awarded by the tribunal, in respect of any period up to the date of the award;
>
> (b)   on the whole or part of any amount claimed in the arbitration and outstanding at the commencement of the arbitral proceedings but paid before the award was made, in respect of any period up to the date of payment.

Section 49(3) of the AA 1996 deals with pre-award interest and s. 49(4) deals with post-award interest. Both subsections give the arbitral tribunal a wide discretion to decide whether or not to award interest and whether to award simple or compound interest and to determine the rests and the interest rate to be awarded as meets the justice of the case. The award of interest is discretionary under the AA 1996 and therefore the arbitral tribunal in dealing with interest must act judicially: *Metro-Cammell Hong Kong Ltd* v *FKI Engineering plc* (1996) 77 BLR 84; *Stotesbury* v *Turner* [1943] KB 371. Where interest is claimed the arbitral tribunal should award it unless there are justifiable reasons not to do so. It has been held that inordinate and unreasonable delay in prosecuting the claim is a justifiable reason for not awarding interest: *Panchaud Frères SA* v *R. Pagnan & Fratelli* [1974] 1 Lloyd's Rep 394. It was held in *Amec Building Ltd* v *Cadmus Investment Co. Ltd* [1997] 5 CL 33 that it was justifiable for the arbitral tribunal to make an award of interest even though the respondent had not been at fault, other than by having kept the claimant waiting for payment. The reason that the respondent made a late payment was because the times for payment had been varied by the arbitral tribunal. The court held that it could not interfere with the arbitral tribunal's use of its discretion in these circumstances despite the fact that it may have acted differently in the same set of circumstances.

A claim for interest cannot be made if it is the sole claim in the arbitration, except where the claim arises out of a claim for special damages: *President of India* v *Lips Maritime Corporation* [1988] AC 395. Where a party is late paying a debt but that debt is paid prior to the commencement of the arbitration proceedings no claim can be made solely for interest: *London, Chatham and Dover Railway Co.* v *South Eastern Railway Co.* [1893] AC 429. This rule has sometimes been criticised in that it may encourage late payment of debts without any sanction against the debtor.

11.4.3   Compound or simple interest

Section 49(3) of the AA 1996 makes a significant change to the pre-existing law. Interest may be awarded as either simple or compound interest. There was no power, in default of agreement to the contrary, to award compound interest under the AA 1950. The arbitral tribunal may award the compound interest with 'such rests as it considers meets the justice of the case'. The rests are the times at which the interest is compounded. The power of the arbitral tribunal to award compound interest as of right is a power beyond that possessed by the courts. In *Westdeutsche Landesbank Girozentrale* v *Islington London Borough Council* [1996] AC 669 the House of Lords restated the position that the courts do not have the power to order compound interest save in exceptional circumstances under their equitable jurisdiction. The power to award compound interest may be a factor in deciding to elect arbitration rather than litigation especially where a debt has been outstanding for a considerable period.

11.4.4   Rates of interest

Under s. 49(3) and (4) of the AA 1996 the arbitral tribunal has the discretion to decide the rate of interest to be applied. Under s. 20 of the AA 1950 (interest on awards) the arbitral tribunal could only award interest 'at the same rate as a judgment debt'. This in effect meant that interest on the award itself could only be at the prevailing judgment debt rate, which at 1 January 1999 was 8 per cent, or not at all. The arbitral tribunal's only discretion was whether it would award interest as a judgment debt or not: *London and Overseas Freighters Ltd* v *Timber Shipping Co. SA* [1972] AC 1. The arbitral tribunal is no longer so fettered under the AA 1996. It may award interest as either simple interest or compound interest from such date as is appropriate and meets the justice of the case. Under the AA 1950 interest was automatically payable from the award to the date of payment, 'unless the award otherwise directs'. Under the AA 1996 interest on an award will not automatically be payable and the arbitral tribunal should ensure that this matter is dealt with in the award. Whether a failure by the arbitral tribunal to award interest will amount to a serious irregularity under the AA 1996 is uncertain. There is no authority on this point.

11.4.5 Period of interest

Under s. 49(3) of the AA 1996 the arbitral tribunal must determine the starting date from which interest will be calculated. This will normally be the date when the sum owing fell due. However, the arbitral tribunal is entitled to look at the circumstances of the case when assessing this date. Equally the arbitral tribunal need not award interest for the whole of the period between the date when the sum fell due and the date of the award. The conduct of the party claiming interest may be such as to make it inequitable for the whole of the interest to be awarded: *Rees and Kirby Ltd* v *Swansea City Council* (1985) 30 BLR 1. It is likely, although there is no authority on this point, that the same principles will apply in respect to the award of interest as they do to the award of costs. Under s. 49(4) of the AA 1996 the period for which the arbitral tribunal can award interest runs from the date of the award or any later date which is appropriate until payment.

11.4.6 Declaration

Section 49(5) of the AA 1996 deals with the situation where the arbitral tribunal has made a declaration rather than an award of the payment of money. In such a case interest may be awarded on the amount that would be payable as a result of the declaration made.

Section 49(6) of the AA 1996 preserves the arbitral tribunal's powers to award interest otherwise than under s. 49. This subsection will be applicable where the contract under which the dispute arises provides within its conditions for the award of interest, or where interest is dealt with specifically in the institutional rules under which the arbitration is being conducted.

11.5 EXTENSION OF TIME FOR MAKING AN AWARD

Section 50 of the AA 1996 replaces and extends s. 13 of the AA 1950. It is a non-mandatory section and may be excluded with the agreement of the parties. The purpose of this section is to allow the parties or the arbitral tribunal to apply to the court for an extension of time for the making of the award. Under the arbitration agreement a time limit may be imposed on the arbitral tribunal for making the award after the close of the hearing. An extension of this time limit may be required where it is impossible for the arbitral tribunal to provide the award. Such circumstances may arise where the arbitral tribunal is ill or has other commitments. Section 50(1) of the AA 1996 provides that the court may extend the period of time for making the award in accordance with the provisions of s. 50(2) to (5).

Section 50(2) of the AA 1996 states:

An application for an order under this section may be made—
    (a) by the tribunal (upon notice to the parties), or
    (b) by any party to the proceedings (upon notice to the tribunal and the other parties),
but only after exhausting any available arbitral process for obtaining an extension of time.

An application under s. 50(2) can therefore only be made if the parties and the arbitral tribunal have exhausted all other processes available for extending the time period. Most institutional rules have rules dealing with extensions of time for the making of an award. The ICC Rules of Arbitration and the CIMAR Rules both make such provision. Article 24(1) of the ICC Rules requires that the arbitral tribunal produce a final award within six months. The date is calculated from the date of the last signature of the arbitral tribunal, or the parties on the terms of reference, or where approval has been sought from the International Court of Arbitration, the date of notification to the arbitral tribunal by the Secretariat of the approval. This time limit may be extended on receiving a written reasoned request by the arbitral tribunal or on the International Court of Arbitration's own initiative: Article 24(2) of the ICC Rules. A caveat to the court's power to extend the time for the making of the award is provided in s. 50(3) of the AA 1996. The court must not extend the time unless satisfied that 'a substantial injustice would otherwise be done'.

Section 50(4) of the AA 1996 provides that the court may extend the period on such terms as it thinks fit either prior to or after the time previously fixed has expired. An appeal from the decision of the court may only be made with the leave of the court: s. 50(5) of the AA 1996. Where, however, there is a judge-arbitrator then para. 5 of sch. 2 to the AA 1996 provides that the judge-arbitrator may exercise the powers to extend time personally and that an appeal from a decision of the judge-arbitrator lies to the Court of Appeal with the leave of that court. A judge-arbitrator is an arbitrator who is a judge of the Commercial Court or a judge of the Technology and Construction Court and is appointed under the provisions of s. 93 of the AA 1996. Section 50 of the AA 1996 is similar to s. 79 of the AA 1996, which provides general powers of the court to extend time limits relating to arbitral proceedings. Similar criteria apply in s. 79 of the AA 1996 as in s. 50 of the AA 1996.

11.6   SETTLEMENT

Section 51 of the AA 1996 is a new provision, which has been modelled on Article 30 of the UNCITRAL Model Law. This section formalises a common practice in arbitrations, namely, that a settlement of the dispute is recorded by the arbitral tribunal in an award. This was commonly termed a 'consent award'. The term 'consent award' has, however, not been used in the AA 1996 and the phrase 'agreed award' is used instead. The section is non-mandatory, although the corresponding provision in Article 30 of the UNCITRAL Model Law is.

Section 51(1) of the AA 1996 provides that where the parties settle their dispute then, if the parties have not agreed to the contrary, the provisions of s. 51(2) to (5) apply. Section 51(2) provides that: 'The tribunal shall terminate the substantive proceedings and, if so requested by the parties and not objected to by the tribunal, shall record the form of an agreed award'. It is clear, therefore, that the parties do not have an automatic right to insist that the arbitral tribunal record their settlement in the form of the award. In most cases the arbitral tribunal will have no objection to recording the agreement in an award unless it takes the view that it is contrary to public policy.

Recording a settlement in the form of an award makes it easier to enforce the settlement, particularly in an international arbitration where the settlement may have to be enforced in another country. A settlement recorded in the form of an award is also enforceable as a New York Convention award. Article 26 of the ICC Arbitration Rules provides that the arbitral tribunal may record the settlement in the form of an award if requested by the parties and if the arbitral tribunal agrees. The arbitral tribunal should only refuse if it has good reasons as it is under a duty to make sure that the award is enforceable in law: art. 35

Section 51(3) of the AA 1996 provides that an agreed award 'shall state that it is an award of the tribunal and shall have the same status and effect as any other award on the merits of the case'. Section 66(1) of the AA 1996 states that: 'An award made by the tribunal pursuant to an arbitration agreement may, by leave of the court, be enforced in the same manner as a judgment or order of the court to the same effect'. Section 51(4) confirms that, as an agreed award is treated as an award of the arbitral tribunal, it must comply with the formalities required by ss. 52 to 58. However, an agreed award does not contain reasons: s. 52(4). The date of the agreed award is relevant to any claim by the settling party for a contribution from a third party: s. 10(3)(b) of the Limitation Act 1980. The fact that the settlement has been recorded in an agreed award is not, however, evidence that the settlement is reasonable. The settling party, as against a third party, will need to show that it acted reasonably in agreeing to the settlement: *General Feeds Inc. Panama* v *Slobodna Providba Yugoslavia* [1999] 1 Lloyd's Rep 688.

Section 51(5) of the AA 1996 provides that unless the parties have reached settlement on the question of the costs of the arbitration, the provisions relating to costs in ss. 59 to 65 continue to apply. The question of costs should always be considered most seriously in any settlement agreement. Although a party may substantially succeed in the settlement agreement it does not always follow that that party will also succeed on costs if offers to compromise the dispute have been made. No mention is made of interest in s. 51 of the AA 1996. It appears that the settlement reached by the parties will therefore be considered to have included within it any interest that should have been payable.

11.7 FORM OF AWARD

Section 52(1) of the AA 1996 provides that the parties are free to agree the form of the award. Section 52(2) of the AA states that if the parties do not agree to the form of the award then the provisions in s. 52(3) to (5) apply. These sections set out rules regarding the form of the award. Parties who agree their own form of award should use these rules as a minimum standard or they may find it difficult to enforce the award in another jurisdiction. If, for example, the parties dispensed with the requirement that the award should be in writing, a party would be unable to have it recognised or enforced under the New York Convention as an original award or duly certified copy is required: see s. 102 of the AA 1996.

If the rules contained in s. 52(3) to (5) of the AA 1996 are adopted in the arbitration proceedings, any failure to comply with them is a serious irregularity under s. 68(h) of the AA 1996. For a challenge under s. 68(h) to be successful the court must be satisfied that the irregularity has caused or will cause a substantial injustice to the party challenging the award. It is doubted that a *de minimis* breach of the rules would cause a substantial injustice to a party.

Section 52(3) of the AA 1996 requires that: 'The award shall be in writing signed by all the arbitrators or all those assenting to the award'. Therefore an arbitrator who does not assent to the award does not have to sign it. This is provided that the arbitration agreement does not require the award to be signed by each member of the arbitral tribunal. If there is such a requirement in the arbitration agreement, all the members of the arbitral tribunal must sign the award, including any dissenting arbitrator. If a dissenting arbitrator refuses to do so, this will be construed as a breach of the arbitrator's duty under s. 33 of the AA 1996: *Cargill International SA* v *Sociedad Iberica de Molturacion SA* [1998] 1 Lloyd's Rep 489. These requirements are also found in Article 31 of the UNCITRAL Model Law. Prior to the AA 1996 there was no requirement that an award should be in writing and the fact that it was not in writing did not affect the enforceability of the award in England. As stated above there might be stricter requirements in other jurisdictions. It used to be the case that an award made by more than one arbitrator was required to be signed by each arbitrator in the presence of the others: *Wade* v *Dowling* (1854) 4 El & Bl 44. Whether this rule remains good law is doubtful: *Bank Mellat* v *GAA Development and Construction Co.* [1988] 2 Lloyd's Rep 44. Section 52(3) of the AA 1996 does not address this point. If the parties have not agreed what the date of the award should be taken to be and the arbitral tribunal has not decided this, then s. 54(2) of the AA applies. This section states that the date of the award shall be taken to be the date when it was signed by an arbitrator or, 'where more than one arbitrator signs the award, by the last of them'. These words suggest that the award can be signed at different times. In practice most arbitrators sign the award separately.

Section 52(4) of the AA 1996 requires that: 'The award shall contain reasons for the award unless it is an agreed award or the parties have agreed to dispense with reasons'. Prior to the AA 1996 reasons had to be requested and there was no duty on the arbitral tribunal to give a reasoned award in certain situations unless the arbitration agreement expressly required that reasons should be given. Under s. 69(1) of the AA 1996 an agreement between the parties to dispense with a reasoned award means that there can be no appeal on a question of law. An agreement to exclude a reasoned award can be made prior to or after the arbitration proceedings have commenced. The DAC decided to follow Article 31 of the UNCITRAL Model Law by requiring the arbitral tribunal to give reasons for its award. The DAC stated at para. 247 of their February 1996 report that: 'It is a basic rule of justice that those charged with making a binding decision affecting the rights and obligations of others should (unless those others agree) explain the reasons for making this decision'.

Section 52(5) of the AA 1996 states that: 'The award shall state the seat of the arbitration and the date when the award is made'. The requirement to state the seat of an arbitration is a new provision and is applicable to domestic arbitrations as well as to international arbitrations. As stated above it is unlikely that minor breaches in the form of the award could lead to a successful challenge under s. 68(h) of the AA 1996. The DAC gave an example of a minor breach at para. 250 of their February 1996 report as a failure to state the seat of the arbitration in a domestic arbitration, or a failure to state it correctly, and concluded that such a failure was unlikely to result in substantial injustice to the party challenging the award.

11.8 PLACE WHERE THE AWARD IS TREATED AS MADE

Section 53 of the AA 1996 states:

> Unless otherwise agreed by the parties, where the seat of the arbitration is in England and Wales or Northern Ireland, any award in the proceedings shall be treated as made there, regardless where it was signed, dispatched or delivered to any of the parties.

This section was introduced to reverse the common law position. In *Hiscox* v *Outhwaite* [1992] 1 AC 562 the House of Lords held that an award which had been signed in Paris, even though the whole of the arbitration had been conducted in England and the arbitration had no nexus with France, was an award 'made' in Paris. However, s. 53 of the AA 1996 only applies where the seat of the arbitration is in England and Wales or Northern Ireland. Where the seat of the arbitration is outside England and Wales or Northern Ireland but the award is signed within England and Wales or Northern Ireland, it will be treated by the courts of England and Wales or Northern Ireland as if it were 'made' where signed. Section 81 of the AA 1996 provides that nothing within Part I of the AA 1996 shall be construed as excluding the operation of any rule of law consistent with that Part. It therefore appears that the effect of s. 53 of the AA 1996 reverses only part of *Hiscox* v *Outhwaite*.

11.9 DATE OF AWARD

Section 54(1) of the AA 1996 provides the arbitral tribunal with a discretion to decide what is to be taken to be the date on which the award is made, unless this is otherwise agreed by the parties to the arbitration. Section 54(2) of the AA 1996 states that where neither the parties nor the arbitral tribunal make a decision then: 'the date of the award shall be taken to be the date on which it is signed by the arbitrator or, where more than one arbitrator signs the award, by the last of them'.

The date when the award is made is significant in relation to two matters. First, the date is relevant to the question of interest. Interest may be awarded by the arbitral tribunal in respect of any period up until the date when the award is made: s. 49(3)(a) of the AA 1996. After the award is made the arbitral tribunal may award interest on the outstanding amount of the award, interest and costs as from the date of the award: s. 49(4) of the AA 1996. Secondly, the date is relevant to any appeal to be made under the AA 1996. Appeals or challenges under ss. 67, 68 and 69 of the AA 1996 must be made within 28 days of the date of the award. Equally, applications for the correction of an award or a request for an additional award need to be made within 28 days: s. 57(4) of the AA 1996.

11.10   NOTIFICATION OF AWARD

Section 55(1) of the AA 1996 states that the parties to the arbitration are free to agree how the award should be notified to them. If there is no such agreement between the parties then s. 55(2) of the AA 1996 provides that: '. . . the award shall be notified to the parties by service on them of copies of the award, which shall be done without delay after the award is made'.

Both s. 55(1) and s. 55(2) of the AA 1996 refer to the award being notified to the 'parties' and not to 'a party'. The DAC purposely used the word 'parties'. The reason for this is stated at para. 255 of the February 1996 report. It is 'so as to prevent one party from obtaining the award and sitting on it without informing the other party until the expiry of time limits for appeal etc., which we are aware has happened in practice'. Under s. 70(3) of the AA 1996 an appeal must be lodged within 28 days of the date of the award, whether or not it has been served on the parties. Any application for the award to be corrected under s. 57(3)(a) or for an additional award to be made under s. 57(3)(b) of the AA 1996 must also be made within 28 days of the date of the award, unless the parties agree a longer period: s. 57(4) of the AA 1996. The arbitral tribunal can only justify a delay in serving the award if it has not been paid its fees and expenses: see ss. 55(3) and 56(1) of the AA 1996.

11.11   POWER TO WITHHOLD AWARD IN CASE OF NON-PAYMENT OF FEES AND EXPENSES

Section 56(1) of the AA 1996 is a mandatory section which gives statutory effect to the common law right of the arbitral tribunal to withhold the delivery of its award as a lien until its fees and expenses have been paid: *Scarfe* v *Morgan* (1838) 4 M & W 270; *Woodworth* v *Conroy* [1976] QB 884. Section 56(1) states: 'The tribunal may refuse to deliver an award to the parties except upon full payment of the fees and expenses of the arbitrators'.

The arbitral tribunal can also bring an action for breach of contract against the parties if its fees and expenses are not paid. Either party to the arbitration may pay the arbitral tribunal's fees and expenses and take delivery of the award. There is no longer a distinction between 'costs of the reference' and 'costs of the award' as there was in s. 18 of the AA 1950. Under s. 59(1) costs of the arbitration now include the fees and expenses of the arbitral tribunal and the fees and expenses of any arbitral institution as well as the legal or other costs of the parties.

There are two ways in which a challenge to the fees and expenses of the arbitral tribunal can be made. First, a party may pay the full fees and expenses and thereafter seek to challenge them under s. 28 of the AA 1996. Secondly, a party to an arbitration may apply to the court under s. 56(2) to (4) of the AA 1996 to order a release of the award and to assess and adjust the fees and expenses claimed. The court cannot assess and adjust the amount of the arbitral tribunal's fees and expenses if they have been contractually agreed by the parties and the arbitral tribunal: s. 28(5) of the AA 1996.

The application to the court may be made by a party to the arbitration proceedings. The application is made upon notice to the other parties in the arbitration proceedings and the arbitral tribunal: s. 56(2) of the AA 1996. The arbitral tribunal is obliged to deliver the award once the party making the application has paid into court the fees and expenses demanded by the arbitral tribunal or any lesser amount the court may specify. Under s. 19 of the AA 1950 the court did not have the discretion to order the payment of a lesser amount. Under s. 56(2)(b) of the AA 1996 the court is obliged to determine the amount of the fees and expenses by 'such means and upon such terms as the court may direct'. Section 56(2)(c) states that these fees and expenses shall be met out of the money which has been paid into court and any balance shall be paid back to the party that made the payment.

Section 56 of the AA 1996 does not refer to 'taxation' unlike s. 19 of the AA 1950, which it replaced. In civil procedure generally, the term 'taxation' has been replaced by 'detailed assessment'. In most cases it is envisaged that a review of the fees and expenses of an arbitral tribunal will be dealt with by the High Court costs judge. It is, however, also possible that the court may direct the arbitral tribunal to reconsider and re-assess its own costs or even direct a third party to do this. The amount payable will either be a reasonable sum, as determined by the costs judge or a third party, or the sum agreed to be paid under s. 28 of the AA 1996.

Section 56(4) of the AA 1996 provides that a party cannot make an application to the court under s. 56(2) where there is an arbitral process for review of the fees and expenses under the arbitration agreement. This envisages that a review may be made of the fees and expenses of the arbitral tribunal by an institutional body overseeing the conduct of the arbitration. The term 'arbitrators' as used in s. 56 of the AA 1996 includes arbitrators who have ceased to act, because they have been replaced, or resigned or there has been a revocation of their authority. The term also includes an umpire who has not replaced the other arbitrators: s. 56(5) of the

AA 1996. The term is also intended to cover arbitral institutions vested by the parties with powers in relation to the delivery of the arbitral award: s. 56(6) of the AA 1996. For example, the Chartered Institute of Arbitrators will in such circumstances take responsibility for the delivery of an award to the parties rather than leaving this to the arbitral tribunal.

Leave of the court is required for any appeal from a decision of the court under s. 56: s. 56(7) of the AA 1996. Section 56(8) of the AA 1996 states that: 'Nothing in this section shall be construed as excluding an application under section 28 where payment has been made to the arbitrators in order to obtain the award'.

11.12 CORRECTION OF AWARD OR ADDITIONAL AWARD

Section 57 of the AA 1996 deals with powers of the parties and the arbitral tribunal to correct the award or make additional awards. This section is non-mandatory and was included in the AA 1996 to enable the correction of an award, or an additional award to be made without a party having to apply to the court. Section 57 of the AA 1996 reflects Article 33 of the UNCITRAL Model Law and has extended the previous provisions in ss. 17 and 18(4) of the AA 1950. Section 57(1) of the AA 1996 provides that the parties are free to agree what powers the arbitral tribunal should possess in regard to the correcting of an award or the making of an additional award. Section 57(2) provides that in default of such an agreement between the parties the provisions s. 57(3) to (7) apply. An application to correct an award or request an additional award may be made by the arbitral tribunal on its own initiative or on the application of a party to the arbitral proceedings. Section 57(3)(a) of the AA 1996 provides that the arbitral tribunal may: 'correct an award so as to remove any clerical mistake or error arising from an accidental slip or omission or clarify or remove any ambiguity in the award'.

Clerical mistakes are distinct from errors 'arising from an accidental slip or omission'. A clerical mistake is a typographical or administrative mistake in the drawing up of the award. An error arising from an accidental slip or omission is broader in that it may encompass an error which has been made not only by the arbitrator but also by one of the parties or their representatives: *Mutual Shipping Corporation* v *Bayshore Shipping Co. Ltd* [1985] 1 WLR 625. Section 57(3)(a) of the AA 1996 does not permit the arbitral tribunal to give further thought to the award and review the decision made, nor to correct errors of judgment: *R* v *Cripps, ex parte Muldoon* [1984] QB 686; *Mutual Shipping Corporation* v *Bayshore Shipping Co. Ltd* [1985] 1 WLR 625. Section 57(3)(a) of the AA 1996 also enables the arbitral tribunal to 'clarify or remove any ambiguity in the award'. This power entitles the arbitral tribunal to explain or amend an aspect of the award where it is unclear or to change an inconsistency that creates an ambiguity. Section 57(3)(a) of the AA 1996 should be read alongside s. 68(2)(f) of the Act, which allows for a challenge to an award where there is ambiguity or uncertainty as to the effect of the award. In *Gbangbola* v *Smith and Sherriff Ltd* [1998] 3 All ER 730 Judge Lloyd QC held that where the uncertainty or ambiguity has affected or may affect that part of the award which is in question an application should be made under s. 57(3) before one is made under s. 68. The rationale for this is that s. 70(2)(b) prohibits a challenge under s. 68 being made unless the applicant has exhausted any available recourse under s. 57.

Section 57(3)(b) of the AA 1996 provides that the arbitral tribunal may: 'make an additional award in respect of any claim (including a claim for interest or costs) which was presented to the tribunal but was not dealt with in the award'. Section 57(3) reflects Article 33 of the UNCITRAL Model Law in that it now provides the arbitral tribunal with two separate powers — to correct an award and to make an additional award in respect of any claim. The power of the arbitral tribunal to make an additional award is no longer limited to the making of an additional award on costs as in s. 18(4) of the AA 1950. An additional award can only be made under s. 57(3)(b) of the AA 1996 on a matter which was presented to the arbitral tribunal.

The second paragraph of s. 57(3) of the AA 1996 stipulates that the powers of the arbitral tribunal in s. 57(3)(a) and (b) cannot be exercised without first offering the parties the opportunity to make representations. Section 57(3) clearly extends the powers of the arbitral tribunal to correct errors but does not give the arbitral tribunal the power to review and/or amend errors of judgment. Section 57(4) requires that an application for the exercise of the arbitral tribunal's powers to correct or make an additional award must be made within 28 days of the date of the award or such longer period as the parties may agree.

Section 57(5) of the AA 1996 states that the correction of the award shall be made within 28 days of the date when the application was received or, if the correction is to be made on the arbitral tribunal's own initiative, within 28 days of the date of the award. The parties are free to agree longer periods of time in writing. Any correction of the award forms part of the original award: s. 57(7) of the AA 1996. This does not cause problems where the correction itself gives a party a ground to challenge the award. Where the correction of the award takes place 28 days after the date when the award was made the time limits for challenging the award will only begin to run from the date when the applicant was notified of the result of the correction process: s. 70(3) of the AA 1996. Where an additional award is to be made this must be done within 56 days of the date of the original award or such longer period as the parties agree: s. 57(6) of the AA 1996.

11.13 EFFECT OF AWARD

Section 58(1) of the AA 1996 states that:

> Unless otherwise agreed by the parties, an award made by the tribunal pursuant to an arbitration agreement is final and binding both on the parties and on any persons claiming through or under them.

Section 58(1) is a non-mandatory section so that the parties are free to agree as to the status of the award. It would, however, be unlikely for the parties to agree that the award should have a status which was neither final nor binding. If the parties wish to have an independent person assess their dispute then there are forms of ADR, other than arbitration, which are quicker and less expensive that would achieve this result. The meaning of 'persons claiming through or under them' is discussed at 6.5. A final award cannot bind third parties. This is the case even if the parties have agreed that it should. See DAC report, February 1996, paras 263, 264.

Section 58(1) of the AA 1996 derives from the common law rule that an arbitration award is binding on the parties to the reference, and everyone who, by claiming through or under the parties to the reference, are privy to the reference: *Martin* v *Boulanger* (1883) 8 App Cas 296. In *Gbangbola* v *Smith and Sherriff Ltd* [1998] 3 All ER 730 this common law rule was restated and extended. Judge Lloyd QC held at p. 738: 'That finding is by virtue of s. 58(1) of the Arbitration Act final and binding on the parties if not challenged (and it has not been) and it is as binding on the arbitrator as much as the parties'.

Section 58(1) of the AA 1996 makes it clear that the arbitration award is final and binding on the parties to the reference and on the persons claiming through or under them. Section 58(2) of the AA 1996 states that: 'This does not affect the right of a person to challenge the award by any available arbitral process of appeal or review or in accordance with the provisions of this Part'.

A decision of an arbitral tribunal, where no application is made to appeal or review it, is therefore binding and final. However, where an appeal or review is initiated then the final and binding status of the award does not take place until that appeal or review is concluded. Where an award has become final and binding neither party to the reference nor the arbitral tribunal may reopen the issue that has been decided in any subsequent hearing. The rationale behind the rule that neither the parties nor the arbitral tribunal may reopen an award is that the matter has become 'res judicata or on the grounds of the extended principle known as issue estoppel': *Gbangbola* v *Smith and Sherriff Ltd* [1998] 3 All ER 730 at p. 739.

The final and binding status of the award is important, especially where enforcement of the award is sought. Until the award becomes final and binding, enforcement of the award, in the same way as a judgment of the court, will not usually be permitted: s. 66 of the AA 1996. Further, under Article V.1(e) of the New York Convention, a ground for refusing to recognise or enforce an award is that: 'The award has not yet become binding on the parties'.

A final award is one which deals with and resolves the issues which the parties have referred to the arbitral tribunal. If the arbitral tribunal dismisses the claim under s. 41(3) and (6) this is, in effect, a final award. However, it is not always clear whether the arbitral tribunal has made an award or a procedural ruling. The distinction is an important one. An award may be challenged under ss. 67 and 68 of the AA 1996. It is unlikely that the court will intervene in respect of a procedural decision made by the arbitral tribunal: *Saiko Place Investments Ltd* v *Wimpey Construction (UK) Ltd* (1980) 5 BLR 112, *Three Valleys Water Committee* v *Binnie and Partners* [1990] 52 BLR 42; see also *Exmar BV* v *National Iranian Tanker Co.* [1992] 1 Lloyd's Rep 169. The question of whether the arbitral tribunal had made an award arose in the recent case of *Ranko Group* v *Antartic Maritime SA* [1998] ADRLJ 35. In that case Toulson J held that the arbitral tribunal had made an award when it had made a ruling in respect of jurisdictional matters which were in dispute between the parties. Rix J in *Charles M Willie and Co. (Shipping) Ltd* v *Ocean Laser Shipping Ltd* [1999] 1 Lloyd's Rep 225 sought to clarify the position. Rix J held that a final award is made when the arbitral tribunal makes a ruling that finally disposes of the claim and all the issues. This follows the general test laid down in *The Vasso (Owners)* v *The Vasso (Cargo Owners)* [1983] 3 All ER 211, If the arbitral tribunal finally disposes of or determines any part of the issues, this is only a partial award. Rix J was of the view that the arbitral tribunal could, if they so desired, make any of their decisions in the form of an award, but that this was not to be encouraged, other than in appropriate circumstances. Rix J also doubted whether interlocutory decisions which were expressed as awards could be held to be awards (see also 20.2.1).

11.14 ENFORCEMENT OF THE AWARD

An award of an arbitral tribunal or an agreed award, where the seat of the arbitration is in England and Wales or Northern Ireland, is usually enforced by the court by way of summary procedure under s. 66(1) of the AA 1996. Where the seat of the arbitral tribunal is outside the jurisdiction of England and Wales or Northern Ireland then enforcement of the award may have to be based on other provisions of the AA 1996. A number of conventions regulate how an international award may be enforced. The most commonly invoked of these is the New York Convention. Enforcement under the New York Convention is dealt with in chapter 18. An award can also be enforced by bringing an action on the award and applying for a judgment from the court on the same terms as the award itself.

Section 66(1) of the AA 1996 states:

An award made by the tribunal pursuant to an arbitration agreement may, by leave of the court, be enforced in the same manner as a judgment or order of the court to the same effect.

Section 66 is a mandatory provision and reflects Article 35 of the UNCITRAL Model Law. The DAC at para. 273 of their February 1996 report commented that 'Enforcement through the court provides the classic case of using the court to support the arbitral process'. Section 66(3) of the AA provides the only mandatory ground for refusing leave to enforce an award under s. 66 of the AA 1996:

Leave to enforce an award shall not be given where, or to the extent that, the person against whom it is sought to be enforced shows that the tribunal lacked substantive jurisdiction to make the award.

Section 66(3) of the AA 1996 also states that the right to raise such an objection may be lost pursuant to s. 73 of the AA 1996. Under s. 73(1)(a) a party seeking to object that the tribunal lacked substantive jurisdiction must do so quickly. This will, however, often be difficult, especially where the arbitral tribunal has the power to rule on its own jurisdiction: see *Delta Civil Engineering Co. Ltd* v *London Docklands Development Corporation* (1996) 81 BLR 19 and the commentary therein. It is for the party opposing the application to enforce the award to demonstrate why leave to enforce should not be granted.

Where leave to enforce an award has been given by the court, a party may seek an order to enforce the award as if it were a judgment of the court under s. 66(1) of the AA 1996 or alternatively seek to have the award entered as a judgment in the terms of the award, under s. 66(2) of the AA 1996. The second alternative may be beneficial if the party wishes to register the judgment in a foreign court. A party may wish to do this where there are no arbitration conventions between the two countries but where there are reciprocal enforcement provisions for judgments. An example of such a case would be England and Malawi, where judgments of the High Court may be enforced pursuant to Part II of the Administration of Justice Act 1920. A judgment may also be a prerequisite for the bringing of other proceedings, for instance, the serving of a bankruptcy notice. A party can apply for enforcement of the award under this section even if the seat of the arbitration is outside England and Wales or Northern Ireland or no seat has been determined or designated: s. 2(2)(b) of the AA 1996.

Section 66(3) of the AA 1996 makes it clear that the court cannot grant leave to enforce an award where the arbitral tribunal lacked substantive jurisdiction to make the award. In all other cases the court only has a discretion to refuse leave to enforce an award. An example of where the court would not exercise its discretion to grant leave was given by the DAC in their February 1996 report at para. 273: 'where public policy would not recognise the validity of an award, for example awards purporting to decide matters which our law does not accept can be resolved by this means', see also s. 81(1)(c) of the AA 1996. If a party is successful in challenging the enforcement of the award, the court may set the award aside or direct that a court hearing should take place on the matter challenged. The court may refuse leave to enforce if:

(a)   a party to the arbitration agreement was under some incapacity;

(b)   a party was not given proper notice of the appointment of the arbitral tribunal or of the arbitration proceedings or was otherwise unable to present its case;

(c)   the award deals with a difference not contemplated by or not falling within the terms of the submission to arbitration or contains decisions on matters beyond the scope of the submission to arbitration;

(d)   the composition of the arbitral tribunal or the arbitral procedure was not in accordance with the agreement of the parties;

(e)   the award has not yet become binding on the parties;

(f)   enforcement of the award would be contrary to public policy;

(g)   the award is defective in form;

(h) the award seeks to determine matters not capable of resolution by arbitration or grants some relief which would improperly affect the rights of a third party.

The list is not exhaustive and it will be a question of fact in each case whether the court should refuse leave to enforce. These grounds are grounds which prevent a New York Convention award from being enforced.

Section 66(4) of the AA 1996 states that:

Nothing in this section affects the recognition or enforcement of an award under any other enactment or rule of law, in particular under Part II of the Arbitration Act 1950 (enforcement of awards under Geneva Convention) or the provisions of Part III of this Act relating to the recognition and enforcement of awards under the New York Convention or by an action on the award.

Recognition and enforcement under the Geneva Convention and under the New York Convention are dealt with in chapter 18.

The words in s. 66(4) of the AA 1996 'or by an action on the award' refer to the bringing of court proceedings founded on the award itself. This method of enforcement will generally only be used where the arbitration agreement falls outside the scope of the AA 1996. An action on the award is based on an implied promise to perform a valid award: *F.J. Bloemen Pty Ltd* v *Gold Coast City Council* [1973] AC 115. A party seeking to bring an action on the award must prove that there is a valid arbitration agreement, a valid award and a failure to perform the award.

12 Challenging the Award

12.1 SUBSTANTIVE JURISDICTION

Section 82 of the AA 1996 provides that the words 'substantive jurisdiction' refer to the matters specified in s. 30(1)(a) to (c) which are:

(a) whether there is a valid arbitration agreement,
(b) whether the tribunal is properly constituted, and
(c) what matters have been submitted to arbitration in accordance with the arbitration agreement.

Section 67(1)(a) of the AA 1996 provides a party with the power to challenge any award where the arbitral tribunal lacks substantive jurisdiction. The arbitral tribunal's jurisdiction can be challenged on questions of fact and law: see DAC report, February 1996 at para. 143. Under s. 67(1)(b) of the AA 1996 a party may, as an alternative to challenging an award under s. 67(1)(a) of the AA 1996, apply to the court for an order declaring 'that an award made by the tribunal on the merits to be of no effect, in whole or in part, because the tribunal did not have substantive jurisdiction'. However, an award, which deals with the substantive jurisdiction of the arbitral tribunal, cannot be challenged in part. Where an arbitral tribunal makes an award dealing with the issue of jurisdiction pursuant to s. 30 of the AA 1996, this may be challenged under s. 67 of the AA 1996. In such a case it may be appropriate for the court to re-hear witnesses who had previously given evidence and allow cross-examination upon that evidence. In *Azov Shipping Co.* v *Baltic Shipping Co.* [1999] 1 Lloyd's Rep 68 at p. 70, Rix J stated:

Where, however, there are substantial issues of fact as to whether a party has made the relevant agreement in the first place, then it seems to me that, even if there has already been a full hearing before the arbitrators the Court, upon a challenge under s. 67, should not be placed in a worse position than the arbitrator for the purpose of determining the challenge. . . . It is not as though the Court is required to review the challenge to the arbitrator's award on jurisdiction through the eyes of the arbitrator or on his findings of fact.

The provisions in s. 67 of the AA 1996 are distinct from the court's power in s. 32 to make a determination of a preliminary point of jurisdiction. An application under s. 32 is made in the course of the arbitration proceedings. The right to challenge under s. 67 is a right which exists only after an award has been made. Section 67 of the AA 1996 is a mandatory section and cannot be excluded by the parties.

An award must be challenged within 28 days of the date of the award or the date on which a party who sought an appeal or review of the award is notified of that appeal or review: s. 70(3) of the AA 1996. Where the arbitral tribunal has ruled upon matters of jurisdiction in a preliminary award, time runs from the date of that award: *Ranko Group* v *Antarctic Maritime SA* [1998] ADRLJ 35. However, a party may apply to the court under s. 79 of the AA 1996 to extend time. In *Ranko Group* v *Antarctic Maritime SA* [1998] ADRLJ 35 Toulson J did not grant the application to extend time for challenging the arbitral tribunal's jurisdiction. The reason for this was that the application centred on new evidence which the arbitral tribunal had not seen. An application under s. 67(1) of the AA 1996 is made pursuant to the requirements of CPR, PD 49G, upon notice to the other parties and to the arbitral tribunal. CPR, PD 49G, para. 14 sets out the rules relating to the directions for the hearing of evidence on an application to the court. The court is obliged to have in mind the just, expeditious and economic disposal of the case when it gives its directions. In *Azov Shipping Co.* v *Baltic Shipping Co.* [1999] 1 Lloyd's Rep 68, at p. 70, it was argued by the respondent that to allow a complete re-hearing of all the evidence would neither be just, expeditious or economical. The judge dealt with this argument by holding, at p. 71, that:

> Nevertheless, and although there may be some prejudice to the expeditious and economical disposal of the application by permitting oral evidence, it seems to me that the justice of the matter requires that I accede to Azov's application. Ultimately a question of justice, where it conflicts with a modest prejudice to expedition or increase in cost, must be given greater weight.

Section 67(2) of the AA 1996 provides that the arbitral tribunal may continue with the proceedings and make a further award while an application to the court under s. 67 is made. It is suggested that the parties should always be consulted as to whether the arbitral process should continue when an application has been made under s. 67. An application under s. 67 goes to the very heart of the arbitral process and a decision of the court which sets aside the award or varies it may have the effect of voiding any subsequent steps in the arbitral process.

12.1.1 Remedies

The court's powers in relation to an application under s. 67 of the AA 1996 are:

(a) to confirm the award,

(b)   to vary the award, or

(c)   to set aside the award in whole or in part.

In addition the court may order that security for costs should be given in respect of the appeal and that a failure to comply with such an order entitles the court to order that the appeal be dismissed: s. 70(6) of the AA 1996. The court may order that any money payable under the award shall be brought into court or secured pending the appeal and may dismiss the appeal if the order is not complied with: s. 70(7) of the AA 1996. In some cases the court may also consider it appropriate to order that the arbitral tribunal should give reasons for its award: s. 70(4) of the AA 1996 (see further 12.5).

12.1.2   Loss of right to object

The right of a party to make an application under s. 67(1) of the AA 1996 may be lost where that party continues the arbitral proceedings knowing that the arbitral tribunal lacks substantive jurisdiction to proceed or does not act timeously where it discovers the lack of substantive jurisdiction: s. 73(1) of the AA 1996. Where the arbitral tribunal rules on its own substantive jurisdiction the right to challenge that decision will be lost if the party does not appeal that decision within the permitted time: s. 73(2) of the AA 1996 (see 12.4).

If a party considers that the arbitral tribunal lacked substantive jurisdiction when the arbitration proceedings commenced, the time for raising an objection is before that party takes its first step in the proceeding to contest the merits of any matter: s. 31(1) of the AA 1996. During the course of the arbitration a party must object to the arbitral tribunal's lack of jurisdiction as soon as possible after the matter alleged to be beyond its jurisdiction is raised: s. 31(2) of the AA 1996. The arbitral tribunal has the power under s. 31(3) of the AA 1996 to admit an objection later than the time specified in s. 31(1) and (2) of the AA 1996 if it considers the delay is justified.

Section 70(2) of the AA 1996 is relevant to the question of whether a party has the right to challenge the award on the basis of a lack of substantive jurisdiction. Section 70(2)(a) provides that an application or appeal may not be brought if the applicant has not first exhausted any available arbitral process of appeal or review. Section 70(2)(b) provides that an application or appeal may not be brought if the applicant has not exhausted any available recourse under s. 57 to correct or make an additional award: see *Gbangbola* v *Smith and Sheriff* [1998] 3 All ER 730 and the further discussion at 12.2.6. However, s. 70(2) does not apply to a party who did not take part in the arbitration proceedings: s. 72(2). A person alleged to be a party to the arbitration but who does not take part in the proceedings has the same right to challenge the award under s. 67, on the ground of lack of substantial jurisdiction, as any participating party to the arbitration: s. 72(1) and (2) (see further 12.5).

12.2 SERIOUS IRREGULARITY

Section 68 of the AA 1996 derives from ss. 22(1) and 23 of the AA 1950 and Article 34 of the UNCITRAL Model Law. It is a mandatory section. Under s. 68(1) of the AA 1996 an application may be made to the court to challenge an award where there is a serious irregularity in respect of the arbitral tribunal's conduct in the proceedings or in the award. Any party to the arbitration may make the application under s. 68(1), including a party who did not participate in the proceedings: s. 72(2) of the AA 1996. The application is made pursuant to CPR, PD 49G, upon notice to the other parties and the tribunal. The phrase 'upon notice' is dealt with in s. 80 of the AA 1996. Where the serious irregularity goes to the substantive jurisdiction of the arbitral tribunal the challenge should properly be made under s. 67 of the AA 1996 and not under s. 68: see s. 68(2)(b). Where a party continues to take part in the arbitral proceedings knowing that the proceedings have been improperly conducted or that there has been any other irregularity affecting the arbitral tribunal or the proceedings then the right to object may be lost: s. 73(1)(b) and (d) (see further 12.4). Section 70(2) and (3) of the AA 1996 also applies to a party making an application under s. 68(1). Section 70(3) of the AA 1996 provides that the appeal must be brought within 28 days of the date of the award (see further 12.5).

Section 68(2) of the AA 1996 defines 'serious irregularity' as one or more of the nine irregularities which are set out in s. 68(2)(a) to (i) 'which the court considers has caused or will cause substantial injustice to the applicant'. Matters that do not fall within s. 68(2)(a) to (i) of the AA 1996 cannot be challenged under s. 68. In *Indian Oil Corporation* v *Coastal (Bermuda) Ltd* [1990] 2 Lloyd's Rep 407 an award was remitted back to the arbitral tribunal to deal with an argument which had not been submitted to it at the hearing. An award cannot now be remitted back to the arbitral tribunal for this reason under s. 68 of the AA 1996.

The grounds listed in s. 68(2) of the AA 1996 are as follows:

(a) failure by the tribunal to comply with section 33 (general duty of tribunal);

(b) the tribunal exceeding its powers (otherwise than by exceeding its substantive jurisdiction: see section 67);

(c) failure by the tribunal to conduct the proceedings in accordance with the procedure agreed by the parties;

(d) failure by the tribunal to deal with all the issues that were put to it;

(e) any arbitral or other institution or person vested by the parties with powers in relation to the proceedings or the award exceeding its powers;

(f) uncertainty or ambiguity as to the effect of the award;

(g) the award being obtained by fraud or the award or the way in which it was procured being contrary to public policy;

(h) failure to comply with the requirements as to the form of the award; or

(i) any irregularity in the conduct of the proceedings or in the award which is admitted by the tribunal or by any arbitral or other institution or person vested by the parties with powers in relation to the proceedings or the award.

12.2.1   Failure by the arbitral tribunal to comply with section 33 of the AA 1996

Section 33(1) of the AA 1996 imposes a mandatory duty on the arbitral tribunal to:

(a)   act fairly and impartially as between the parties, giving each party a reasonable opportunity of putting his case and dealing with that of his opponent, and

(b)   adopt procedures suitable to the circumstances of the particular case, avoiding any unnecessary delay or expense, so as to provide a fair means for the resolution of the matters falling to be determined.

Section 33(2) of the AA 1996 states that the arbitral tribunal must exercise this duty in making decisions not only on matters of procedure and evidence but also in respect of all the other powers that it has been given.

Section 33(1)(a) of the AA 1996 reflects the common law duty on the tribunal to act in accordance with natural justice. Natural justice requires that:

(a)   each party should have an equal opportunity to present its case and reply to the opponent's case: *Montrose Canned Foods Ltd* v *Eric Wells (Merchants) Ltd* [1965] 1 Lloyd's Rep 597;

(b)   each party should know the case that it has to meet: *Lovell Partnerships (Northern) Ltd* v *AW Construction plc* (1996) 81 BLR 83;

(c)   the arbitral tribunal should not act on secret knowledge: *Fox* v *P.G. Wellfair Ltd* [1981] 2 Lloyd's Rep 514;

(d)   the arbitral tribunal should not be biased towards any party: *Re an Arbitration between SS Catalina (Owners) and MV Norma (Owners)* (1938) 61 Ll L Rep 360;

(e)   the arbitral tribunal should keep each party fully appraised of its intentions as to the conduct of the reference so that no party is taken by surprise: *Scrimaglio* v *Thornett and Fehr* (1923) 17 Ll L Rep 34.

The arbitral tribunal's duty to act fairly is discussed in chapter 8. A failure by the arbitral tribunal to act in accordance with the principles of natural justice will amount to a serious irregularity. Whether there is substantial injustice will depend on each case. In *Gbangbola* v *Smith and Sherriff* [1998] 3 All ER 730 the arbitral tribunal failed to give a party the opportunity to address it on the award of costs. This was held to be a serious irregularity which justified the court's intervention. In *Ranko Group* v *Antarctic Maritime SA* [1998] ADRLJ 35 a failure by the arbitral tribunal to order the production of a document which the claimant alleged was relevant to its case did not justify judicial intervention. The court adopted a non-interventionist approach. In *Egmatra* v *Marco Trading Corp* [1998] CLC 1552 the arbitral tribunal refused to permit a party's expert witness to give evidence. Again the court took a non-interventionist approach and held that this had not caused that party a substantial injustice.

It may be difficult to show substantial injustice where there is a breach of s. 33(1)(b) of the AA 1996 which can be remedied. If an arbitral tribunal has adopted unsuitable procedures which have caused unnecessary costs, the appropriate remedy is an application to the court to adjust the arbitral tribunal's fees. In such circumstances it is unlikely that serious injustice has been caused or will be caused to the applicant.

12.2.2 The arbitral tribunal exceeding its powers

Under s. 68(2)(b) of the AA 1996 it is an irregularity for the arbitral tribunal to exceed its powers. The powers referred to here are those that the parties have conferred on the arbitral tribunal by their agreement, or in the absence of such an agreement the powers contained in the AA 1996. The general powers of the arbitral tribunal have been discussed in chapter 9. The arbitral tribunal's power to award costs is discussed in chapter 13 and its powers in relation to the conduct of the hearing in chapter 15. Section 68(2)(b) of the AA 1996 makes a distinction between the arbitral tribunal exceeding its powers and exceeding its substantive jurisdiction. An application to challenge the award on the ground of the arbitral tribunal's lack of substantive jurisdiction must be made under s. 67(1) of the AA 1996. There is a fundamental difference between jurisdiction and powers. An act in excess of jurisdiction goes to the root of the arbitral tribunal's authority whereas an act in excess of the arbitral tribunal's powers may not do so. The powers of the arbitral tribunal are the tools given to it in the parties' agreement, or in the absence of such an agreement by the AA 1996, to conduct the arbitration so that it may arrive at a decision. The arbitral tribunal's jurisdiction, however, is dependent on the parties' arbitration agreement. The arbitral tribunal has no substantive jurisdiction to act if the arbitration agreement is invalid and where it is valid the arbitral tribunal cannot act outside its remit.

12.2.3 Failure to conduct the proceedings as agreed by the parties

The arbitral tribunal must take account of the procedure the parties have expressly agreed in writing as the one to be adopted: ss. 1(b) and 34(1) of the AA 1996. The arbitral tribunal does not have the right to override the agreement of the parties as to the conduct of the reference. If the parties have elected that the arbitration should be run under a set of institutional rules, the arbitral tribunal cannot ignore those rules because, for instance, it is unfamiliar with them or they are not the norm for the type of dispute.

12.2.4 Failure by the arbitral tribunal to deal with all the issues

It is a principle of common law that a final award must deal with all the issues put to the arbitral tribunal: *Wakefield* v *Llanelly Railway and Dock Co.* (1865) 3 De G J & Sm 11. A final award that does not do so is imperfect. This does not mean that the arbitral tribunal must deal with each individual item separately, but each item must have been taken into consideration by it in arriving at its conclusion: *Sig. Bergesen DY & Co.* v *Mobil Shipping and Transportation Co.* [1992] 1 Lloyd's Rep 460. Only where the parties expressly or by inference intend that each item in dispute should be dealt with separately will the arbitral tribunal be obliged to deal with it in that way. Where the parties agree that their claims should be pleaded in the form of a Scott Schedule (see 15.6.4) such an inference may be founded and the arbitral tribunal will be obliged to address each aspect of the schedule: *Ledwood Construction* v *Kier Construction* (1996) 28 BLISS 5. Under the AA 1950 a failure to do so by the arbitral tribunal constituted misconduct and in *Ledwood Construction* v *Kier Construction* the court remitted the award back to the arbitral tribunal. Judge Hicks QC expressed the opinion: 'That there is really no room for doubt in my mind that both parties intended, expected and understood that the arbitrator would express his award by reference to the Scott Schedule'.

Section 68(2)(d) of the AA 1996 does not change the pre-existing law. The arbitral tribunal will not be obliged in every case to make a decision on every issue if those issues can be dealt with by a single decision. The arbitral tribunal may therefore award a lump sum for a series of claims: *Whitworth* v *Hulse* (1866) LR 1 Ex 251. Similarly the arbitral tribunal may give a single decision where there is a claim and cross-claim if the subject matter of both are the same: *Jewell* v *Christie* (1867) LR 2 CP 296. Where part of the dispute has been taken out of the reference that part need not be decided by the arbitral tribunal: *Rees* v *Waters* (1847) 16 M & W 263. There may be no irregularity on the part of the arbitral tribunal if it has not been presented with sufficient evidence to make a decision on a particular issue (*Montedipe SpA* v *JTP-RO Jugotanker* [1990] 2 Lloyd's Rep 11) or if it can be discerned from the circumstances that all the issues were actually considered in forming the award (*Sig. Bergesen DY & Co.* v *Mobil Shipping and Transportation Co.* [1992] 1 Lloyd's Rep 460).

12.2.5 Any arbitral or other institution exceeding its powers

Where institutional rules are adopted, such as the ICC Rules of Arbitration, the arbitration, or part of it, will be overseen by the relevant institution. That institution may have powers to review and revise the award of the arbitral tribunal or its role may be limited to the appointment of the arbitral tribunal. Each case will depend on the terms of the relevant rules. The institution, like the arbitral tribunal under s. 68(2)(b) of the AA 1996, cannot exceed the powers vested in it.

An example where an institution may exceed its powers can be shown in one of two ways. First, the institution may exceed the express powers that the parties have agreed. For example, the parties may agree, or the relevant rules provide, that the arbitral tribunal should be replaced in certain specified circumstances. If other circumstances arise which have not been specified in the agreement, the relevant institution will have no power to make a decision. Secondly, the *lex arbitri* (the law of the arbitration) may restrict the powers of the relevant institution, which will act in excess of its powers if it acts in breach of a mandatory provision of the law of the seat of the arbitration.

12.2.6 Uncertainty or ambiguity as to the effect of the award

The requirement that the award be certain and free from ambiguity derives from the common law. At common law an award which was uncertain was invalid: *Re an Arbitration between Marshall and Dresser* (1843) 3 QB 878; *Margulies Bros Ltd* v *Dafnis Thomaides and Co. (UK) Ltd* [1958] 1 Lloyd's Rep 250; *River Plate Products Netherlands BV* v *Etablissement Coargrain* [1982] 1 Lloyd's Rep 628. The test of whether an award is uncertain is whether the award is uncertain to the parties. The award may be uncertain to a third party but clear to the parties. In *Plummer* v *Lee* (1837) 2 M & W 495 an award which stated that interest should run from 'the date of the last settlement' was held to be valid as the parties were not in disagreement about that date. Equally, in *Wohlenberg* v *Lageman* (1815) 6 Taunt 251, an award that the parties should pay a debt in proportion to the percentage of shares that they held in a ship was held to be certain as there was no dispute about the percentages owned by the parties.

An award that is ambiguous renders the award uncertain: *Duke of Beaufort* v *Welch* (1839) 10 Ad & El 527. Where part only of the award is uncertain the courts may enforce part of the award and remit the remainder if this is possible: *Miller* v *De Burgh* (1850) 4 Ex 809; s. 68(3)(b) of the AA 1996. In addition to challenging the award under s. 68 of the AA 1996 a party may also seek to challenge the enforcement of any award under s. 66 of the AA 1996 for uncertainty and ambiguity.

In *Gbangbola* v *Smith and Sherriff Ltd* [1998] 3 All ER 730 an application, under s. 68 of the AA 1996, was made to the court to challenge an award *inter alia* on the basis that it contained ambiguities and uncertainties. It was argued by the respondent that before making any such challenge the applicant was obliged to go back to the arbitral tribunal under s. 57 of the AA 1996 to correct that ambiguity or uncertainty. The respondent argued that a failure to make such an application would be a bar, under s. 70(2)(b) of the AA 1996, to bringing a challenge under s. 68. This argument was not accepted by Judge Lloyd QC on the facts of the case. He considered at p. 736 'that there might be an award in which there is uncertainty or ambiguity as to its effect, without there being uncertainty and ambiguity requiring the possibility of correction, or clarification or removal under s. 57(3)'. The fact that there were ambiguities or uncertainties was therefore not necessarily a bar to bringing a challenge under s. 68 of the AA 1996 even if no application had been made under s. 57(3) of the AA 1996. The central issue was whether the uncertainty or ambiguity went to the part of the award that was in question. Judge Lloyd stated at pp. 736–7:

[Counsel for the respondent] says that the purpose of the Act is to ensure both that the arbitrator and the courts are not troubled by repeated applications, but also that the courts should have the totality of the arbitrator's views as clarified and with ambiguities removed in all respects before considering any appeal or process. He relies upon the words of subsections (2) and (3) in referring to *any* available process of appeal and any process of appeal or review.

I see the force of that argument. It certainly must apply where the uncertainty or ambiguity has affected or may affect that part of the result which is in question (and also perhaps in some cases the reasoning leading to that result). However, one must carefully consider what would be the point of delaying an appeal on a matter which as here would be completely unaffected by any possible outcome of going back to the arbitrator to clarify an ambiguity or uncertainty.

Following Judge Lloyd's reasoning in *Gbangbola* v *Smith and Sherriff Ltd* any party seeking to challenge an award under s. 68(2)(f) should examine whether the ambiguity or uncertainty affects the part of the award in question. If it is so affected, the applicant will be barred from bringing a challenge under s. 68(2)(f) if it has not first sought to have the ambiguity corrected under s. 57(3). If the uncertainty or ambiguity does not affect the part of the award in question, the applicant will be entitled to make an application under s. 68(2)(f) without first requesting that the arbitral tribunal correct the ambiguity or uncertainty.

12.2.7   The award being obtained by fraud or procured contrary to public policy

This ground covers both circumstances where a fraud has been perpetrated on the arbitral tribunal and circumstances where the award has been procured in a manner which is contrary to public policy, such as where the arbitral tribunal has been bribed or has acted fraudulently. A New York Convention award may not be recognised or enforced if this would be contrary to public policy: s. 103(3) of the AA 1996. In *Soleimany* v *Soleimany* [1998] 3 WLR 811 the court was asked to examine whether it should enforce an award admitted to be based on an illegal act. The facts of the case were that a dispute arose between a father and son relating to profits obtained from the sale of carpets which had been smuggled from Iran. The case was referred to arbitration before a beth din (a rabbinical court trying questions of Jewish law). There was no dispute that the carpets had been smuggled out of Iran. The award of the beth din recognised this illegality but found in favour of the son, holding that irrespective of the illegality he was entitled to half of the profits. The father appealed to the Court of Appeal, which held that it would not enforce the award. However, on similar facts a challenge could have been made under s. 68(2)(g) of the AA 1996. The award was procured in a way clearly contrary to public policy in that the contract had been founded on an intention to commit an illegal act and the beth din had found that there was illegality. By upholding the contract irrespective of that illegality the award was contrary to public policy. For further discussion on public policy and the enforcement of awards see 18.4 and 18.6.

12.2.8   Failure to comply with the requirements as to the form of the award

The requirements as to the form of the award are discussed in chapter 11. The form of the award may be agreed by the parties, but in default of agreement the provisions of s. 52(3) to (5) of the AA 1996 are applicable. These are:

(a) the award shall be in writing;

(b) the award shall be signed by all the arbitrators or those assenting to the award;

(c) the award shall contain reasons (unless agreed otherwise);

(d) the award shall state the seat of the arbitration; and

(e) the award shall state the date when it is made.

A breach of any of these grounds would therefore be a serious irregularity, but it will depend on the facts of the particular case whether such a breach causes substantial injustice. It is unlikely that in a domestic arbitration a breach of (d) above would ever cause substantial injustice.

12.2.9 Admitted irregularity in the conduct of the proceedings or in the award

Section 68(2)(i) is a catch-all provision whereby matters not falling within s. 68(2)(a) to (h) may provide a ground for an application under s. 68. It seeks to bring within the scope of s. 68 matters that were previously termed a 'technical misconduct' under the AA 1950. 'Technical misconduct' is a form of misconduct that does not go to the probity or impartiality of the arbitral tribunal. It may include the failure of the arbitral tribunal to read a letter received or to comprehend its content. As with the matters listed in s. 68(2)(a) to (h) an irregularity within s. 68(2)(i) is not a serious irregularity unless the court considers that it has caused, or will cause, substantial injustice to the applicant.

12.2.10 Substantial injustice

Although the AA 1996 does not give any definition of the meaning of substantial injustice the DAC report of February 1996 at para. 280 gives guidance on how it should be construed. The DAC makes it clear that the test of 'substantial injustice' was intended to be applied to support the arbitral process and not to interfere with that process. The DAC said that it expected the court to take action only where the arbitral tribunal has acted in a way that is far removed from what could reasonably be expected:

> The test is not what would have happened had the matter been litigated. To apply such a test would be to ignore the fact that the parties have agreed to arbitrate, not litigate. Having chosen arbitration, the parties cannot validly complain of substantial injustice unless what has happened simply cannot on any view be defended as an acceptable consequence of that choice. In short, clause 68 is really designed as a longstop, only available in extreme cases where the tribunal has gone so wrong in its conduct of the arbitration that justice calls out for it to be corrected.

The DAC also refers to a number of cases including *Indian Oil Corporation Ltd v Coastal (Bermuda) Ltd* [1990] 2 Lloyd's Rep 407, *King* v *Thomas McKenna Ltd*

[1991] 2 QB 480 and *Breakbulk Marine* v *Dateline* (19 March 1992 unreported). Under the AA 1950 these cases were remitted back to the arbitral tribunal because certain issues were not put to the arbitral tribunal during the arbitration. Under s. 68 of the AA 1996 it would not be possible for these cases to be challenged. First, such failures are unlikely to fall within any of the definitions in s. 68(2) of the AA 1996, unless they can be construed as an irregularity in the conduct of the proceedings. Secondly, it would not fall within the DAC's definition of substantial injustice.

The case of *Gbangbola* v *Smith and Sherriff Ltd* [1998] 3 All ER 730 suggests that the court will view the pecuniary loss to the applicant as material in deciding whether or not there has been substantial injustice. The merits of the application appear to be only one of a number of factors that the court will take into account. In *Gbangbola* v *Smith and Sherriff Ltd* an application was made under s. 68(2)(f) of the AA 1996 in respect of certain ambiguities and uncertainties arising from an arbitral tribunal's award. The monetary value of the items in dispute was relatively small. Judge Lloyd QC said, at p. 740:

> I am not satisfied that, and indeed I cannot see that, there has been, or will be, substantial injustice to the respondents as a result of these apparent uncertainties or ambiguities as to the effect of the award. This is particularly so in relation to the small item of window blinds and the other matters, the monetary value of which is not large. Accordingly it is perhaps strictly not necessary to decide whether the award is uncertain as to its effect although in my judgment it is not, although there may well be uncertainties or ambiguities in the arbitrator's reasoning. Unless substantial injustice can be established there is no serious irregularity for the purposes of s. 68(2).

In *Egmatra* v *Marco Trading Corp* [1998] CLC 1552 an application was made to the High Court that there had been a serious irregularity under s. 68 of the AA 1996 in that the arbitral tribunal had refused Egmatra to submit expert evidence on an issue in dispute. Tuckey J in the Commercial Court held that, although the decision of the arbitral tribunal could be criticised, it was not patently wrong and it was supported by evidence. The arbitral tribunals decision to refusal to allow Egmatra to call expert evidence was made after careful consideration and did not give rise to a substantial injustice.

12.2.11 Remedies

If a serious irregularity is shown to exist then under s. 68(3) of the AA 1996 the court may:

(a) remit the award to the tribunal, in whole or in part, for reconsideration;
(b) set the award aside in whole or in part, or
(c) declare the award to be of no effect, in whole or in part.

The court shall not exercise its power to set aside or declare the award to be of no effect, in whole or in part, unless it is satisfied that 'it would be inappropriate to remit the matters in question to the tribunal for reconsideration': s. 68(3) of the AA 1996.

Section 68(4) of the AA 1996 provides that the leave of the court is required for any appeal from a decision of the court under s. 68.

The supplementary provisions in s. 70 of the AA 1996 are relevant to any challenge to an award. The supplementary provisions provide that the court may order that further reasons be provided, security for costs be provided for the challenge and that money payable under the award be paid into court or otherwise secured (see 12.5).

12.3 APPEAL ON POINT OF LAW

Section 69 of the AA 1996 is derived from ss. 1 and 3 of the AA 1979 and the restrictions placed on s. 1 of the AA 1979 by the House of Lords in *Pioneer Shipping Ltd* v *BTP Tioxide Ltd* [1982] AC 724. Section 69 of the AA 1996 is non-mandatory. Section 69(1) provides that:

Unless otherwise agreed by the parties, a party to arbitral proceedings may (upon notice to the other parties and to the tribunal) appeal to the court on a question of law arising out of an award made in the proceedings.

Section 69 should be distinguished from s. 45, which deals with the power of the court to determine a question of law during the course of the arbitration. A 'question of law' is defined in s. 82(1) to mean a question of the law of England and Wales or Northern Ireland as appropriate.

12.3.1 Where the proper law of the contract is a foreign law

From the definition of a 'question of law' in s. 82(1) of the AA 1996, it is implicit that an appeal, under s. 69 of the AA 1996, cannot be made where the proper law of the contract is not that of England and Wales or Northern Ireland. There is, however, a rule of English procedure that the arbitral tribunal must assume that a foreign law, chosen by the parties as the proper law of the contract, is the same as English law unless the contrary is proved. Although English law may be applied, where no evidence is brought to prove that the foreign law is different to English law, this does not mean that the parties can appeal the decision. The law remains a foreign law. In any event, questions relating to the interpretation of a foreign law are questions of fact.

12.3.2 Where the parties have chosen a foreign law as the procedural law

Where the parties have chosen as the procedural law a foreign law then this will have the effect of ousting the non-mandatory provisions of the AA 1996 and no appeal can be made on a question of law under s. 69 of the AA 1996. Section 4(5) of the AA 1996 provides:

> The choice of a law other than the law of England and Wales or Northern Ireland as the applicable law in respect of a matter provided for by a non-mandatory provision of this Part is equivalent to an agreement making provision about that matter.

12.3.3   Where the parties have agreed to dispense with reasons in the award

An agreement to dispense with reasons in the arbitral tribunal's award is considered to be an agreement to exclude the court's jurisdiction under s. 69 of the AA 1996. The rationale for this is that it would not be possible for the court to find that there has been an error of law unless the arbitral tribunal gave reasons for its decision. Such an agreement also excludes the court's power to remit an award back to the arbitral tribunal for it to add reasons on an application by a party under s. 68(2)(h) of the AA 1996. Conversely, an agreement to dispense with an appeal does not mean that reasons should not be given. The arbitral tribunal is bound to give reasons for its award under s. 54(4) of the AA 1996 unless the parties have agreed otherwise. In such a case a party may apply to the court under s. 68(2)(h) for the award to be remitted back to the arbitral tribunal so that reasons can be added to the award. In order for Part I of AA 1996 to apply to an agreement to dispense with reasons in the arbitral tribunal's award, it must be made in writing: s. 5(1) of the AA 1996. It can be made either prior to or during the reference. There is now no distinction between domestic and non-domestic arbitrations in this respect, as the provisions of s. 87(1)(b) of the AA 1996 have not been brought into force.

12.3.4   An appeal can only be made where there is a question of law

An appeal under s. 68 of the AA 1996 is limited to questions of law. The arbitral tribunal's findings of fact are conclusive. This is in contrast to a challenge under s. 67 of the AA 1996 which can be made on a question of fact or law. This point was clearly made by Steyn LJ in *Geogas SA* v *Trammo Gas Ltd* [1993] 1 Lloyd's Rep 215 at pp. 227–8:

> This is an appeal under s. 1 of the AA 1979 on 'a question of law arising from an arbitration award'. For those concerned in this case that is a statement of the obvious. But it matters. It defines the limits of the jurisdiction of the court hearing an appeal under the 1979 Act. The arbitrators are the masters of the facts. On an appeal the court must decide any question of law arising from an award on the basis of a full and unqualified acceptance of the findings of fact of the arbitrators. It is irrelevant whether the court considers those findings of fact to be right or wrong. It also does not matter how obvious a mistake by the

arbitrators on issues of fact might be, or what the scale of the financial consequences of the mistake of fact might be.

Since this case it can no longer be argued that it is a question of law whether there is material to support a finding of fact. The question of law must arise from the award. In *Baytur SA* v *Finagro Holding SA* [1991] 4 All ER 129 one of the parties to an arbitration was a French company whose existence had been ended while the arbitration was in progress. At that point the arbitration proceedings were held to have terminated. Therefore the subsequent award was invalid and no appeal on a question of law could arise from it.

12.3.5 Requirements for an appeal

Section 69(2) of the AA 1996 provides that an appeal shall not be brought except:

(a) with the agreement of all the other parties to the proceedings, or
(b) with the leave of the court.

The right to appeal is subject to the restrictions set out in s. 70(2) and (3) of the AA 1996. Section 70(2)(a) provides that an application or appeal may not be brought if the applicant has not first exhausted any available arbitral process of appeal or review. Section 70(2)(b) provides that an application or appeal may not be brought if the applicant has not exhausted any recourse under s. 57. Section 70(3) provides that the appeal must be brought within 28 days of the date of the award (see 12.5).

An agreement by the parties to appeal to the court against an award may be made at the time the underlying contract is entered into or after a dispute has arisen. It may be a standard term within the underlying contract. In *Vascroft (Contractors) Ltd* v *Seeboard plc* (1996) 78 BLR 132 such an agreement formed part of the DOM/2 conditions of contract which the parties had entered into. The case involved an application under s. 1(3)(a) of the AA 1979 but the principles in the case are equally applicable under the AA 1996. Judge Lloyd QC said, at p. 149, that:

the parties are clearly to be taken to have contracted on the basis that the arbitrator may have to reach conclusions not only as to facts but also as to the parties' legal rights and obligations and that those latter conclusions may give rise to questions of law which one or other of the parties will be entitled to challenge free from the need to meet the requirements of s. 1(3)(b) and (4) of the [1979] Act [the requirements relating to leave].

The judge arrived at his decision following the 'concept of ''party autonomy'' as it is popularly called' (p. 149c). In many building contracts, therefore, especially those under the JCT forms of contract, leave will not be required as the standard terms of the contract will entitle the parties to appeal from a decision of the arbitrator without the requirement that the leave of the court be first obtained.

In *Taylor Woodrow Civil Engineering Ltd* v *Hutchison IDH Development* [1998] CILL 1434 the parties accepted the principle that an agreement by them to appeal to the court against an award may be made at the time the underlying contract is entered into. Their agreement was expressed to be subject to the AA 1979 even though the AA 1996 was then in force. Clarke J held that, even though the AA 1996 imposed different conditions in regard to appeals from the AA 1979, the agreement of the parties as to leave was not vitiated by the error.

12.3.6   Requirements for leave

Section 69(3) of the AA 1996 sets out the requirements on which leave to appeal a decision of the arbitral tribunal will be given. The court must be satisfied:

(a)   that the determination of the question will substantially affect the rights of one or more of the parties,
(b)   that the question is one which the tribunal was asked to determine,
(c)   that, on the basis of the finding of fact in the award—
   (i)   the decision of the tribunal on the question is obviously wrong, or
   (ii)   the question is one of general public importance and the decision of the tribunal is at least open to serious doubt, and
(d)   that, despite the agreement of the parties to resolve the matter by arbitration, it is just and proper in all the circumstances for the court to determine the question.

12.3.6.1   That the determination of the question will substantially affect the rights of one or more of the parties   Section 69(3)(a) of the AA 1996 is based on s. 1(4) of the AA 1979. There are, however, some differences between the two sections. First, the AA 1996 uses the words: 'the question will substantially affect the rights'. In the AA 1979 the wording used was: 'could substantially affect the rights'. This change means that an application under s. 69(3)(a) of the AA 1996 can now only be brought where the findings of fact of the arbitral tribunal are known. Previously an application could be brought before the arbitral tribunal had given its findings of fact.

The word 'substantially' means an effect on the parties of major importance. The size of the sum in dispute may make the effect of determining a question substantial: *International Sea Tankers Inc.* v *Hemisphere Shipping Co. Ltd* [1982] 1 Lloyd's Rep 128; *Secretary of State for the Environment* v *Reed International plc* [1994] 1 EGLR 22; *Gbangbola* v *Smith and Sherriff Ltd* [1998] 3 All ER 730.

It is possible to bring an appeal under s. 69 in relation to any aspect of an award which substantially affects parties' rights. In *President of India* v *Jadranska Slobodna Plovidba* [1992] 2 Lloyd's Rep 274 it was held that an appeal could arise from the arbitral tribunal's discretion as to costs. However, in every case it is necessary to show that the question substantially affects rights and that there is a question of law which needs to be resolved. In *Urban Small Space Ltd* v *Burford Investment Co. Ltd* [1990] 2 EGLR 120 the court held that there was no appeal from an interim award which ordered discovery (disclosure and inspection) as it was not certain that the issues would arise again at the substantive hearing and the court was not satisfied that the parties' rights would be substantially affected.

12.3.6.2 That the question is one which the tribunal was asked to determine Section 69(3)(b) of the AA 1996 is a new provision. The DAC in their report of February 1996 stated at para. 286(ii):

> The point of law must be one that was raised before the tribunal. The responses showed that in some cases applications for leave to appeal have been made and granted on the basis that an examination of the reasons for the award shows an error on a point of law that was not raised or debated in the arbitration. This method of proceeding has echoes of the old and long discarded common law rules relating to error on the face of the award, and is in our view a retrograde step. In our view the right to appeal should be limited as we suggest.

In *Gbangbola* v *Smith and Sherriff Ltd* [1998] 3 All ER 730 this issue was specifically raised. Judge Lloyd QC concluded that the issue of law need not have been specifically argued in front of the arbitral tribunal so long as the issue was integral to the resolution of the dispute which was argued before the arbitral tribunal. The judge took a common-sense approach to the wording of s. 69(3)(b) of the AA 1996, concluding that a more literal approach could cause unnecessary delay and expense. His reasoning, which is omitted from the report cited, was as follows:

> A point on the interpretation of s. 69(3) was raised, namely that the question of law for which leave is sought must have been raised specifically before the arbitrator and, if it were not, then the court had no jurisdiction to entertain the appeal. Mr Coster submitted that in this case none of the points that are listed in the grounds of appeal were actively argued as such before the arbitrator. I consider that the submissions of Miss Jackson are to be preferred, namely that the question of law has to arise out of the award (see s. 69(1)) and until the findings of fact are made it may not be possible to see why the decision is wrong (cf. s. 69(3)(c)) and how the question of law arises. Accordingly the question of law is admissible provided it was integral to the resolution of the dispute which was argued before the arbitrator.
> Any other construction would mean every possible question of law that might arise on the various permutations of the findings of fact open to the arbitrator would either have to be raised before the arbitrator or the arbitrator would be obliged to invite further argument if he came to the conclusion that on his likely findings of fact a point of law arose which was necessary to his decision but

which had not been debated. Either course seems to me to place an untoward burden on the parties and the arbitrator and to be inconsistent with the general principle of avoiding unnecessary delay and expense (see s. 1 of the Act). That burden would be heavy enough even if the parties were legally represented and even if the arbitrator were experienced, but it would be well nigh impossible to sustain in the form suggested if the parties were not legally represented or if the arbitrator were not sufficiently experienced. Even seemingly simple cases on investigation throw up questions of law and complex cases, such [as] those involving construction contracts, generate more. Section 36(1) permits a party to be represented by anyone and it would not be right to give the Act an interpretation which made parties feel obliged to retain a lawyer to protect their interests so that all alternatives were covered. Furthermore the construction contended for would increase the possibility that the court on an application for leave should have to investigate what took place before the arbitrator to see whether the question of law was precisely identified for decision. That again is inconsistent with s. 1 including the minimalist role there envisaged for the court. In my view s. 69(3)(b) is directed to excluding questions which on the cases presented the arbitrator did not have to decide in order to arrive at the decision or decisions made (or was not asked to decide) and it does not affect questions which the case of a party required the arbitrator to decide in order to arrive at the award.

This reasoning seems well founded as a more literal interpretation of this section (as suggested by the DAC) could possibly lead to unnecessary delay and expense.

12.3.6.3 That, on the basis of the finding of fact in the award, the decision of the tribunal on the question is obviously wrong, or the question is one of general public importance and the decision of the tribunal is at least open to serious doubt Section 69(3)(c) of the AA 1996 gives statutory effect to guidelines provided in *Pioneer Shipping Ltd* v *BTP Tioxide Ltd* [1982] AC 724, known as the *Nema* guidelines. *Pioneer Shipping Ltd* v *BTP Tioxide Ltd* concerned the chartering of a vessel called the *Nema* for the carrying of titanium slag from Canada to Europe. Strikes at the Canadian port meant that the ship was only able to make one voyage rather than the seven agreed. Two subsequent agreements were entered into by the parties. An arbitration was started to determine what the effect was on the contract. The arbitral tribunal held that there were three contracts and that the first contract had been frustrated. The matter was appealed to the House of Lords, which upheld the arbitral tribunal's decision. The House of Lords dealt with the question of leave to appeal under s. 1 of the AA 1979. Although strictly *obiter dicta* the House of Lords opinions on this point, and especially those of Lord Diplock, became recognised and accepted as guidelines for when an appeal would be allowed.

Lord Diplock stated at p. 742–3 that:

Where, as in the instant case, a question of law involved is the construction of a 'one-off' clause the application of which to the particular facts of the case is an issue in the arbitration, leave should not normally be given unless it is apparent to the judge upon a mere perusal of the reasoned award itself without the benefit of adversarial argument, that the meaning ascribed to the clause by the arbitrator is obviously wrong. But if on such perusal it appears to the judge that it is possible that argument might persuade him, despite first impression to the contrary, that the arbitrator might be right, he should not grant leave; the parties should be left to accept, for better or for worse, the decision of the tribunal that they had chosen to decide the matter in the first instance. The instant case was clearly one in which there was more than one possible view as to the meaning of the 'one-off' clause as it affected the issue of divisibility. It took two days' argument by counsel before the learned judge to satisfy him that the arbitrator was wrong on this and upon the interdependent question of frustration, four days' argument before the Court of Appeal to convince them that the judge was wrong and the arbitrator right and over three days' argument in trying to persuade this House to the contrary, even though it was not found necessary to call upon the respondent to address us on the merits. . . .

For reasons already sufficiently discussed, rather less strict criteria are in my view appropriate where questions of construction of contracts in standard terms are concerned. That there should be as high a degree of legal certainty as is practicable to obtain as to how such terms apply upon the occurrence of events of a kind that it is not unlikely may reproduce themselves in similar transactions between other parties engaged in the same trade, is a public interest that is recognised by the [AA 1979] particularly in s. 4. So, if the decision of the question of construction in the circumstances of the particular case would add significantly to the clarity and certainty of English commercial law it would be proper to give leave in a case sufficiently substantial to escape the ban imposed by the first part of s. 1(4) bearing in mind always that a superabundance if citable judicial decisions arising out of slightly different facts is calculated to hinder rather than to promote clarity in settled principles of commercial law. But leave should not be given even in such a case, unless the judge considered that a strong prima facie case had been made out that the arbitrator had been wrong in his construction; and when the events to which the standard clause fell to be applied in the particular arbitration were themselves 'one-off' events, stricter criteria should be applied on the same lines as those that I have suggested as appropriate to 'one-off' clauses.

In *Antaios Compania Naviera SA* v *Salen Rederierna AB* [1985] AC 191 the court affirmed Lord Diplock's distinction in *Pioneer Shipping Ltd* v *BTP Tioxide Ltd* [1982] AC 724 between 'one-off' contracts and 'standard-form' contracts. Lord Diplock's approach in *Antaios Compania Naviera SA* v *Salen Rederierna AB* was accepted and followed in *Aden Refinery Co. Ltd* v *Ugland Management Co. Ltd* [1987] 1 QB 650, in which Donaldson MR said, at p. 659:

Under the *Nema* guidelines, in the case of a 'one-off' contractual clause, judges are advised to refuse leave to appeal if they consider that the arbitrator might have been right. In the case of standard terms, of which the present is an example, they are advised to apply rather less strict criteria, taking account of whether or not a decision on the question or questions of law would add significantly to the clarity and certainty of English commercial law. But even then the advice is that leave to appeal should be refused, unless the judge considers that a strong prima facie case has been made out that the arbitrator has been wrong in his construction. If there was ever any doubt about the purely advisory, limited and mutable status of these guidelines, it was removed by Lord Diplock's speech in *Antaios Compania Naviera SA* v *Salen Rederierna AB* [1985] AC 191 at p. 200.

Section 69(3)(c) of the AA 1996 follows, to a great part, Lord Diplock's analysis in differentiating between 'one-off' contracts and 'standard-form' contracts. Where the contract is 'one-off', the court should not give leave to appeal under s. 69(2)(b) unless the decision is obviously wrong. Where there is a question of general public importance, it is sufficient if there is serious doubt that the decision is wrong. Contracts on standard forms are often considered by the court to be of general public importance if they are of a type that are commonly encountered in commercial transactions. The reason for this is that the general commercial community would benefit from an authoritative decision on its meaning or application: *Ipswich Borough Council* v *Fisons plc* [1990] 1 All ER 730. Lord Donaldson MR stated in that case at p. 734 that, in assessing the degree of serious doubt regard should be had to the type of arbitral tribunal in question:

> If the chosen arbitrator is a lawyer and the problem is purely one of construction, the parties must be assumed to have had good reason for relying on his expertise and the presumption in favour of finality, or to put it the other way round, the strength needed to rebut it, will be greater. So, too, if the dispute really centres on an issue calling for non-legal expertise, albeit with some underlying question of law, and the chosen arbitrator has that expertise. But if the chosen arbitrator is not a lawyer and the whole dispute centres on a difficult question of law, less strength may be required.

Even if the question of law is of general public importance, this does not mean that the court will exercise its discretion to grant leave to appeal. Lord Diplock also clarified in *Antaios Compania Navira SA* v *Salen Rederierna AB* [1985] AC 191 that the *Nema* guidelines were 'not intended to be all-embracing or immutable, but subject to adaption to match changes in practices when these occur or to refinement to meet problems of kinds that were not foreseen, and are not covered by, what was said by the House in *The Nema*'.

Mustill LJ, in *Aden Refinery Ltd* v *Ugland Management Co. Ltd* [1987] 1 QB 650, 668, continued the same theme that the *Nema* guidelines were only indicative of when leave to appeal should be granted:

... the guidelines are from time to time treated as if they constituted a complete and immutable code, converting the exercise of the discretion conferred on the judge by statute into a mechanical process yielding an answer which follows inexorably, once a dispute and the resulting award have been assigned to one of various categories. To employ the guidelines in this way would in my opinion be a mistake.

In *Anglian Water Authority* v *RDL Contracting Ltd* (1988) 43 BLR 98 leave to appeal was granted. Although the question of law to be determined arose because of the facts of the particular case, the events which had occurred were reasonably common in the construction industry. In that regard there was an important question to be determined which could recur and was therefore of general importance.

In *Anglian Water Authority* v *RDL Contracting Ltd* the court was asked to consider whether an engineer's decision under clause 66 of the ICE Conditions of Contract was valid. The arbitral tribunal, when first considering the case, had held that the engineer's decision was invalid on the basis that the project engineer and not the engineer himself had formulated it. Judge Fox-Andrews reviewed the *dicta* of the House of Lords in *Pioneer Shipping* Ltd v *BTP Tioxide Ltd* and *Antaios Compania Naviera* v *Salen Rederierna AB* and that of the Court of Appeal in *Aden Refinery Co. Ltd* v *Ugland Management Co. Ltd* relating to when leave should be granted. The judge held, at p. 108:

... the speeches of Lord Diplock in so far as they relate to the Parliamentary intentions are authoritative pronouncements as to the spirit in which the judge must approach the question of the manner in which he would exercise his discretion under section 1 [of the AA 1979]. Much of the rest of the speech in *Pioneer Shipping Ltd* v *BTP Tioxide Ltd* to which I have referred consists of valuable guidelines which where applicable must be followed. But they are guidelines, and each case must ultimately depend on its own facts.

In exercising its discretion whether or not to grant leave to appeal, the overriding factor which the court should have in mind is the presumption in the AA 1996 for finality. Both *Pioneer Shipping Ltd* v *BTP Tioxide Ltd* and *Antaios Compania Naviera* v *Salen Rederierna AB* address the question of finality within arbitral proceedings. As Lord Diplock stated in *Pioneer Shipping Ltd* v *BTP Tioxide Ltd* at p. 739: '... in weighing the rival merits of finality and meticulous legal accuracy there are . . . several indications in the Act itself of a Parliamentary intention to give effect to the turn of the tide in favour of finality in arbitral awards'. The Parliamentary intention is expressed even more clearly in the AA 1996. The general principles on which the AA 1996 is founded refer to a resolution of the arbitral proceedings without unnecessary delay and expense and that save as provided in the Act the court should not intervene in the arbitral process. As Lord Donaldson MR held, in attempting to define 'serious doubt' in *Ipswich Borough*

Council v *Fisons plc* [1990] 1 All ER 730, 'the bottom line must always, I think, be that the judge concludes that there is a more or less strong, but still "strong" *prima facie* case that the arbitrator has erred in law. To adopt any other approach would be to fly in the face of the legislature preference for finality'.

12.3.6.4   Despite the agreement of the parties to resolve the matter by arbitration, it is just and proper in all the circumstances for the court to determine the question   This requirement that it should be just and proper for the court to determine the question of law is new to the AA 1996. Its inclusion is explained in the DAC report of February 1996, at para. 290, as follows:

> We have been asked why we suggest this addition. The reason is that we think that it is desirable that this factor should be specifically addressed by the court when it is considering an application. It seems to us to be the basis on which the House of Lords acted as it did in *Pioneer Shipping Ltd* v *BTP Tioxide Ltd* [1982] AC 724. The court should be satisfied that justice dictates that there should be an appeal; and in considering what justice requires, the fact that the parties have agreed to arbitrate rather than litigate is an important and powerful factor.

12.3.7   Content and procedure for leave

Subsections (4), (5) and (6) of s. 69 of the AA 1996 deal with the content of an application and the procedure for obtaining leave from the court. An application for leave should identify the point of law which is sought to be determined and should state the grounds on which it is alleged that leave to appeal should be granted: s. 69(4) of the AA 1996. The application should be in sufficient detail to enable the court to exercise its discretion without the need to hear from the parties. The court shall determine the application without hearing from the parties unless it appears to the court that such a hearing is required: s. 69(5) of the AA 1996. The parties are not entitled to demand a hearing. This requirement follows on from the statement of Lord Diplock in *Pioneer Shipping Ltd* v *BTP Tioxide Ltd* [1982] AC 724 at p. 743 that there was regrettably a tendency for applications for leave to be turned into long and expensive court hearings. The DAC, in their report of February 1996, make the point that in cases where the appeal involves a point of law which is obviously wrong or open to serious doubt, the court should be able to decide whether to allow or reject the application on written material alone. If leave to appeal is refused, the court should not normally give reasons: *Antaios Compania Naviera* v *Salen Rederierna AB* [1985] AC 191.

The leave of the court is required for any appeal from a decision whether leave to appeal is granted or refused: s. 69(6) of the AA 1996.

12.3.8   Orders of the court

Section 69(7) of the AA 1996 sets out the variety of orders that the court may make. These include:

(a) confirming the award;

(b) varying the award;

(c) remitting the award back to the arbitral tribunal, in whole or in part, for reconsideration in light of the court's determination; and

(d) setting aside the award in whole or in part.

The power of the court to set aside the award should not be exercised unless it is inappropriate to remit the matters in question back to the arbitral tribunal: s. 69(7) of the AA 1996. Where an applicant is given leave to appeal then such leave may be on terms: s. 70(6) and (7) of the AA 1996. See 12.4.

Two possible means exist whereby an appeal can be made to the Court of Appeal. The first is in regard to the refusal to grant leave to appeal. The second is from a decision of the court that has heard the appeal. Leave is required in both cases. In the second case, where the court has heard the appeal and made a decision on the appeal, leave will only be granted if 'the court considers that the question is one of general importance or is one which for some other special reason should be considered by the Court of Appeal': s. 69(8) of the AA 1996.

12.4 LOSS OF RIGHT TO OBJECT

Section 73(1) of the AA 1996 provides that a party who takes part, or continues to take part, in an arbitration, despite having an objection to the proceedings, may lose the right to raise that objection before the arbitral tribunal or the court at a later stage. The right to object may be lost if that party failed to make its objection known as soon as it arose, or within the time limits provided either by the arbitration agreement, the arbitral tribunal or by any provision in Part I of the AA 1996. The exception to this rule is where a party 'shows that, at the time he took part or continued to take part in the proceedings, he did not know and could not with reasonable diligence have discovered the grounds for the objection'. The loss of the right to object only applies to the objections set out in s. 73(1)(a) to (d) of the AA 1996:

(a) that the tribunal lacks substantive jurisdiction,

(b) that the proceedings have been improperly conducted,

(c) that there has been a failure to comply with the arbitration agreement or with any provision of this Part, or

(d) that there has been any other irregularity affecting the tribunal or the proceedings.

If the arbitral tribunal rules that it has substantive jurisdiction, any party which objects to this ruling must question that ruling by using any available arbitral process or review or by challenging the award within the time limits specified in the arbitration agreement or any provision in Part I of the AA 1996. Otherwise the right to object to the arbitral tribunal's substantive jurisdiction may be lost at a later stage on any ground which was the subject of the arbitral tribunal's ruling: s. 73(2) of the AA 1996.

12.5 SUPPLEMENTARY PROVISIONS

Section 70 of the AA 1996 sets out a number of supplementary provisions applicable to ss. 67, 68 and 69 of the AA 1996. Section 70(2) states that an application or appeal may not be brought if the applicant has not first exhausted any available arbitral process of appeal or review, and any available recourse under s. 57. The question whether an application need be first made under s. 57 where the resolution of any ambiguity or uncertainty would not have an effect on the question of serious irregularity was addressed in *Gbangbola* v *Smith and Sherriff Ltd* [1998] 3 All ER 730 and has been discussed above.

Section 70(2) of the AA 1996 does not apply to a party who did not take part in the arbitration proceedings: s. 72(2). Section 70(3) requires that an application or appeal be brought within 28 days from the date of the award. The date of the award is defined by s. 54. The court has the power to extend this date under s. 80(5). Where there has been any arbitral process of appeal or review the 28-day time limit begins to run from the date when the applicant was notified of the result of that process.

Section 70(4) of the AA 1996 deals with no reasons or insufficient reasons given by the arbitral tribunal in the award. The court can order the arbitral tribunal to state its reasons in sufficient detail to enable the court to deal properly with the application or appeal. Under s. 52(4) the arbitral tribunal is obliged to give reasons in the award save where the award is agreed or where the parties have agreed to dispense with reasons. Where the parties have agreed to dispense with reasons s. 69(1) states that this is considered to be 'an agreement to exclude the court's jurisdiction under this section'. In such a case reasons cannot be ordered. Where the award is agreed then it unlikely that an appeal or application to challenge would be made. It would therefore appear that the purpose of s. 70(4) is to deal with the situation where the arbitral tribunal inadvertently omits to provide reasons. This is unlikely to occur frequently. It will be more usual for the court to order that further reasons be given where the award is deficient. In most cases, however, the parties should initially apply to the arbitral tribunal, under s. 57, to provide a further award which clarifies the original award. A party who fails to do this may find that his appeal is barred by reason of s. 70(2)(b). Where a court orders additional reasons it may also make a further order on additional costs resulting from the order. This could include, in extreme cases, a costs order against the arbitral tribunal.

Section 70(6) of the AA 1996 entitles the court to order the applicant to provide security for costs for the application or appeal. If the order is not complied with, the application or appeal may be dismissed. The court has a wide discretion to make such an order and the only express restriction is that security for costs should not be ordered only on the ground that the applicant or appellant is foreign.

However, it is implied that, like the arbitral tribunal, the court will exercise its discretion judicially. For analysis of the obligation to act judicially when ordering security for costs see chapter 13.

Section 70(7) of the AA 1996 provides that the court may order any money payable under an award be brought into court pending the application or appeal. Failure to comply with the order may result in the court dismissing the application or appeal.

Section 70(8) of the AA 1996 provides that the grant of leave to appeal may be made subject to the conditions set out in s. 70(6) and (7). The court may also impose such conditions as it may impose under its general discretion.

12.6   EFFECT OF ORDER OF THE COURT

Where an application or appeal is made to the court under ss. 67, 68 or 69 of the AA 1996 the provisions of s. 71(2) to (4) are applicable:

(2)   Where the award is varied, the variation has effect as part of the tribunal's award.

(3)   Where the award is remitted to the tribunal, in whole or in part, for reconsideration, the tribunal shall make a fresh award in respect of the matters remitted within three months of the date of the order for remission or such longer or shorter period as the court may direct.

(4)   Where the award is set aside or declared to be of no effect, in whole or in part, the court may also order that any provision that an award is a condition precedent to the bringing of legal proceedings in respect of a matter to which the arbitration agreement applies, is of no effect as regards the subject matter of the award or, as the case may be, the relevant part of the award.

Subsections (2) and (3) restate the position as it was prior to the AA 1996. Any new award must deal only with the matters remitted: *Huyton SA* v *Jakil SpA* [1998] CLC 937. In *D.F. Mooney* v *Henry Boot (Construction) Ltd* (11 April 1995 unreported) an arbitral tribunal's award was challenged. Judge Lloyd QC remitted part of the matters back to the arbitral tribunal. The arbitral tribunal in its new award failed to deal with all the issues remitted back to it and dealt with some issues which had not been remitted. On appeal the new award was set aside and the arbitral tribunal removed. Where not everything in the award is challenged the parts that have not been challenged will still stand and need not be the subject of a new award.

Section 70(4) of the AA 1996 deals with what are commonly known as *Scott* v *Avery* clauses, which have been discussed previously at 4.5.

13   Costs

13.1   COSTS OF THE ARBITRATION

Sections 59 to 65 of the AA 1996 set out a comprehensive code for awarding costs in arbitrations. Section 59 of the AA 1996 defines what is included in the costs of the reference. However, this section is non-mandatory: s. 4(1) of and sch. 1 to the AA 1996. The non-mandatory status of this section means that if the parties elected another law as the law of the arbitration, any rules in that law defining the costs of the arbitration would supersede this section.

Section 59(1) of the AA 1996 states that the costs of the arbitration include the following:

(a)   the arbitrators' fees and expenses,
(b)   the fees and expenses of any arbitral institution concerned, and
(c)   the legal or other costs of the parties.

The costs of the arbitration also include the costs of bringing any other proceedings to determine the amount of costs that are recoverable: s. 59(2) of the AA 1996.

13.1.1   Arbitral tribunal's fees and expenses

The arbitral tribunal's fees and expenses are recoverable costs under s. 59(1)(a) of the AA 1996. Included within these costs are any expenses which the arbitral tribunal has incurred in appointing experts, legal advisers or assessors pursuant to s. 37 of the AA 1996. The parties are jointly and severally liable for the arbitral tribunal's fees and expenses under s. 28(1) of the AA 1996. In many cases the arbitral tribunal will elect not to enter into a direct contract with the experts, legal advisers or assessors in instances where the financial stability of both parties is questionable. In such a case the experts, legal advisers or assessors will enter into a direct contract with the parties and any expenses which have been incurred will not be caught by s. 59(1)(a) of the AA 1996. However, these costs fall within the definition of costs in the arbitration under s. 59(1)(c) of the AA 1996 as the 'other costs of the parties'. In these circumstances the parties will not be jointly and severally liable for any of the fees incurred, unless this is provided for in the contract.

It is the usual practice for the arbitral tribunal to set out in the award its fees and expenses. The arbitral tribunal exercises a lien over the award until such fees and expenses are met. The award usually provides for one of the parties to meet these fees and expenses under the general principle that costs follow the event (see s. 61(2) of the AA 1996). However, the award should also state that if the party who takes up the award is not the party who has to bear the costs of the award, the opposing party shall forthwith reimburse the other party in that sum.

13.1.2 Fees and expenses of any arbitral institution concerned

Section 59(1)(b) of the AA 1996 gives the arbitral tribunal power to direct which party should pay the fees and expenses of any arbitral institution concerned. Almost invariably the institutional rules under which the arbitration is conducted will deal with this matter: see the LCIA Arbitration Rules 1998 and the ICC Rules of Arbitration 1998, Article 31(1).

13.1.3 Legal or other costs of the parties

Section 59(1)(c) of the AA 1996 gives the arbitral tribunal power to direct which party should pay the legal or other costs of the parties. The phrase 'other costs' enables any legitimate costs of the arbitration to be recoverable. Section 59(1)(c) therefore gives statutory effect to the common law rule that the costs of a non-legal representative who acts on a party's behalf are recoverable: *Piper Double Glazing Ltd* v *DC Contracts* [1994] 1 WLR 777. In this case the court held, according to the headnote to the report at [1994] 1 All ER 177, that:

> Where a party is represented in an arbitration by a person who is not qualified as a barrister or solicitor, but who provides similar services, and an award is made providing for payment of that party's costs by the other party or for such costs to be taxed in the High Court if not agreed, the court has power under RSC, ord. 62, r. 2(2), to allow the costs of the unqualified person in relation to the conduct of the arbitration. The prohibition in s. 25(1) of the Solicitors Act 1974 against the recovery of costs in respect of anything done by any unqualified person 'acting as a solicitor' does not apply to an unqualified person representing a party in an arbitration since an unqualified person does not 'act as a solicitor' within the meaning of s. 25(1) merely by doing acts of a kind commonly done by solicitors. . . . A person acting as an advocate for a party in arbitration proceedings who is not qualified as a barrister or solicitor and does not hold himself out as such is not acting as a barrister or solicitor and accordingly the party employing him is not precluded from entitlement to payment of his costs.

If the parties have not agreed what costs of the arbitration are recoverable, the arbitral tribunal or the court may determine this under the provisions of s. 63(3) and (4) of the AA 1996. The costs of the arbitration are restricted to a reasonable amount reasonably incurred, unless the arbitral tribunal or the court otherwise determines: s. 63(5) of the AA 1996. This principle is found in the common law: *Re an Arbitration between Autothreptic Steam Boiler Co. Ltd and Townsend Hook and Co.* (1888) 21 QBD 182. The common law gives some indication as to what would be the reasonable costs in respect of a claims consultant. In *William Tarr and Co. Ltd* v *Royal Insurance plc* (8 April 1989 unreported) Master Hurst suggested that the costs recoverable by a claims consultant in arbitration proceedings cannot, by virtue of RSC, ord. 62, r. 28(1), be more than the amount recoverable had the arbitration been conducted by solicitor and counsel. It was suggested that to allow more would be unreasonable. CPR, r. 44.1(1) applies the same test. In *Piper Double Glazing Ltd* v *DC Contracts* [1994] 1 WLR 777 Potter J did not think that there was any set rule of law which precluded a claims consultant charging more than a solicitor, although his lordship commented that it would be an anomalous position if in fact he could.

The legal or other costs of the parties also include the costs that a party incurred prior to the arbitration commencing, if those costs were incurred for the purpose of the arbitration. Although the terms 'costs of the reference' and 'costs of the award' are not used in the AA 1996 the costs of the arbitration include all such costs which were previously recoverable and included within these two legal terms. In *Re an Arbitration between Autothreptic Steam Boiler Co. Ltd and Townsend Hook and Co.* (1888) 21 QBD 182 at p. 183 Huddleston B stated that:

> I have no doubt whatever that my brother Denman was right; and that the master was wrong in not having allowed all the expenses incurred preliminary to the agreement to refer, but necessary for the purpose of putting the agreement of the parties into form.

The expenses preliminary to the agreement to arbitrate were in this case the costs of drafting the terms of the submission to arbitrate.

13.2   AGREEMENTS TO PAY COSTS AND THE AWARD OF COSTS

Section 60 of the AA 1996 is based on the old s. 18(3) of the AA 1950. Section 60 is mandatory and precludes the parties from agreeing, prior to a dispute having arisen between them, who will bear the costs of the arbitration: *Smeaton Hanscomb and Co. Ltd* v *Sassoon I. Setty, Son and Co. (No. 2)* [1953] 1 WLR 1481. The principle is said to have derived from public policy arguments that the courts should not give effect to any term that affected in advance the substantive content of an award: Mustill and Boyd, *Commercial Arbitration*, 2nd ed. (London: Butterworths, 1989), p. 284. Equally, such a term could be open to abuse with one party vexatiously pursuing a claim which it knows would have no chance of being successful if there was not the sanction of costs to act as a deterrent.

13.2.1   Award of costs

The parties may agree the allocation of the costs of the arbitration: s. 61(1) of the AA 1996. However, such an agreement must not contravene s. 60 of the AA 1996.

If the parties do not make such an agreement, s. 61(1) of the AA 1996 gives the arbitral tribunal a discretion as to how the costs should be awarded. The discretion is restricted by s. 61(2) of the AA 1996, which states that, unless otherwise agreed between the parties, 'the tribunal shall award costs on the general principle that costs should follow the event except where . . . in the circumstances this is not appropriate'.

The phrase 'costs follow the event' refers to a principle applied by the High Court that a successful party is generally entitled to receive its costs: *Donald Campbell and Co. Ltd* v *Pollak* [1927] AC 732. The 'event' element is sometimes difficult to define. A party seeking only a declaratory judgment will have an 'event' in its favour if that declaratory judgment is granted. A claimant that gets only nominal damages will not usually recover costs, as it cannot be said that there is an 'event' in its favour. Where there is a claim and counterclaim on which each party has succeeded the usual order is that the claimant receives the costs of the claim and the respondent receive the costs of the counterclaim. However, if the counterclaim is only in fact a defence to the claim, it is usual only to make an award that one of the parties receives its costs: *Tramountana Armadora SA* v *Atlantic Shipping Co. SA* [1978] 2 All ER 870. It may sometimes be extremely difficult to decide whether a party has in fact won. In *Perry* v *Stopher* [1959] 1 WLR 415 Willmer LJ illustrated the problem.

Who was the successful party in this case? . . . the plaintiff may be said to have been successful so far as £11 is concerned, but equally it may be said that the defendant has been successful as far as some £40 odd is concerned. One wonders what the plaintiff would have said if, just as he had finished reading the award of the arbitrator, some friends of his had come up to him and warmly congratulated him on the 'success' he had achieved in his case. I apprehend that the plaintiff would have regarded himself as having substantially failed in his claim. If so, the plaintiff having substantially failed in his claim, but the defendant not having wholly succeeded in defeating the claim, it was open to the arbitrator to take almost any course with regard to the costs in the exercise of his discretion.

13.2.2   Grounds for departing from the general rule that costs follow the event

The discretion of the arbitral tribunal, to make an award where the costs do not follow the event, can only be exercised where there are grounds for the use of such discretion. The phrase 'in the circumstances this is not appropriate', in s. 61(2) of the AA 1996, must be viewed objectively. The common law only permits the exercise of such a discretion where the case falls within certain limited situations.

The arbitral tribunal in exercising its power not to award costs which follow the event under s. 61(2) of the AA 1996 must act judicially: *Metro-Cammell Hong Kong Ltd* v *FKI Engineering plc* (1996) 77 BLR 84; *Stotesbury* v *Turner* [1943]

KB 370; *Everglade Maritime Inc.* v *Schiffahrtsgesellschaft Detlef Von Appen mbH* [1992] 2 Lloyd's Rep 167; *Gbangbola* v *Smith and Sherriff Ltd* [1998] 3 All ER 730. In *Gbangbola* v *Smith and Sherriff Ltd* Judge Lloyd QC said:

> In my judgment it is first necessary to go to the basic provisions of s. 61(2) of the Act, namely that the tribunal shall award costs on the general principle that costs should follow the event. When the section goes on to say 'except where it appears to the tribunal that in the circumstances this is not appropriate in relation to the whole or part of the costs', that is saying no more than in the ordinary way an order for costs has to be exercised in a judicial manner. . . . Accordingly, any departure from the general rule must be one which can be justified as the exercise of discretion in a judicial manner.

The arbitral tribunal does not have the freedom to depart from the general principle that costs follow the event unless there is a material basis for doing so: *Ratnam* v *Cumarasamy* [1965] 1 WLR 8; *Lewis* v *Haverfordwest Rural District Council* [1953] 1 WLR 1486; *Savill* v *Southend Health Authority* (1994) *The Times*, 28 December.

In *Lewis* v *Haverfordwest Rural District Council* Lord Goddard CJ held that in the absence of special circumstances costs should follow the event and that there is a need to show the grounds if this rule is to be departed from:

> It is a curious circumstance — and one experiences it time and time again — that lay arbitrators always seem to think that parties should pay their own costs. Perhaps the present case and *Smeaton Hanscomb and Co. Ltd* v *Sassoon I. Setty, Son and Co. (No. 2)* [1953] 1 WLR 1481 before Devlin J may be of some use as emphasising to lay arbitrators that it has been laid down by the House of Lords in *Donald Campbell and Co. Ltd* v *Pollak* [1927] AC 732, reaffirming the Court of Appeal in *Ritter* v *Godfrey* [1920] 2 KB 47, that there is a settled practice of the courts that in the absence of special circumstances a successful litigant should receive his costs and that it is necessary to show some grounds for exercising the discretion of refusing an order which would give them to him, and the discretion must be judicially exercised. Those words 'judicially exercised' are always somewhat difficult to apply, but they mean that the arbitrator must not act capriciously and must, if he is going to exercise his discretion, show a reason connected with the case and one which the court can see is a proper reason.

If there is no such reason, the arbitral tribunal would not be entitled to refuse the costs to the successful party: *Civil Service Co-operative Society Ltd* v *General Steam Navigation Co.* [1903] 2 KB 756. An arbitral tribunal which awarded an unsuccessful party its costs without reasons or made no award of costs to the successful party was, under the AA 1950, guilty of technical misconduct: *Smeaton Hanscomb and Co. Ltd* v *Sassoon I. Setty, Son and Co. (No. 2)* [1953] 1 WLR 1481. An arbitral tribunal which made an award of costs without hearing representations from the parties would also commit technical misconduct: *Harrison v Thompson* [1989] 1 WLR 1325. Under the AA 1996 such an action would now amount to a serious irregularity: *Gbangbola v Smith and Sherriff Ltd* [1998] 3 All ER 730.

One of the issues in *Gbangbola v Smith and Sherriff Ltd* was that both parties alleged that they had succeeded in the arbitration. The arbitral tribunal awarded costs to the claimant. The respondent challenged the award under s. 68 of the AA 1996 on the grounds that there had been a serious irregularity. The basis on which the arbitral tribunal awarded the costs was not one which had been argued before it. Judge Lloyd QC held that the general duty under s. 33(1)(a) of the AA 1996 obliged the arbitral tribunal to bring to the attention of the parties the matters it thought were influential in making its award on costs and allow the parties to deal with them. It was held that there was a breach of s. 33(1)(a) of the AA 1996 in that the arbitral tribunal did not act fairly and impartially. There was therefore a serious irregularity in dealing with the costs of the arbitration.

Mustill and Boyd, *Commercial Arbitration*, 2nd ed. (London: Butterworths, 1989), pp. 396–7, set out a number of factors which would justify not observing the normal principle that costs follow the event. These include:

(a)   Unsatisfactory conduct by a party in the course of the arbitration (*Unimarine SA v Canadian Transport Co. Ltd* [1982] 1 Lloyd's Rep 484), for example, where a party to the arbitration had not given proper disclosure or had not complied with the orders of the arbitral tribunal.

(b)   Failure on an issue which has taken up a large amount of time and expense in the arbitration: *Matheson and Co. Ltd v A. Tabah and Sons* [1963] 2 Lloyd's Rep 270; *Channel Island Ferries Ltd v Cenargo Navigation Ltd* [1994] 2 Lloyd's Rep 161.

(c)   Unreasonable refusal to accept an offer of settlement.

(d)   Extravagance in the conduct of the arbitration by one of the parties, for instance, by employing an excessive number of counsel.

(e)   Where the successful party has delayed in making its claim and the award is small: *Evmar Shipping Corporation v Japan Line Ltd* [1984] 2 Lloyd's Rep 581.

In *Tramountana Armadora SA v Atlantic Shipping Co. SA* [1978] 2 All ER 870 Donaldson J stated:

But I should like to stress that while the rule that costs follow the event and a determination of what that event is, is the usual rule, it may only be the starting point. It is subject to modification or even complete reversal if a party has conducted itself or the reference, unreasonably.

13.2.3   Giving reasons for departing from the general rule

Under the AA 1950 there was some debate whether an arbitral tribunal needed to give reasons in its award on the exercise of its discretion with regard to costs. In

L. Figueiredo Navegacas SA v *Reederei Richard Schroeder KG* [1974] 1 Lloyd's
Rep 192 Mocatta J said, at p. 193: '. . . there is no need for an umpire or arbitrator,
if he so exercises his discretion as to depart from the general rule [that costs follow
the event], to state the reason why he does so in his award'.

In *Tramountana Armadora SA* v *Atlantic Shipping Co. SA* [1978] 2 All ER 870
Donaldson J took a contrary view and held that there should always be a reason
for an award, and one which can be stated. A patent departure from the rule that
costs follow the event without giving sufficient reason for doing so gives rise to a
rebuttable presumption that the arbitrator has erred in law or not acted in a judicial
manner.

The position is now clear under s. 52 of the AA 1996. Unless the parties agree
otherwise the arbitral tribunal should give reasons for its award which includes its
findings on costs. Where the parties have agreed that reasons are not required the
arbitral tribunal need not give reasons either as to the substance of the dispute or
as to costs. In such a case it would not be a serious irregularity for the arbitral
tribunal to fail to supply reasons under s. 68 of the AA 1996 and no appeal would
lie under s. 69 of the AA 1996.

13.2.4 Challenging the arbitral tribunal for departing from the general rule

Where the award sets out the reasons why the arbitral tribunal did not make an
order that costs follow the event the award can only be challenged under s. 69 of
the AA 1996 on the basis that it is wrong in law. A party cannot simply challenge
the exercise of the arbitral tribunal's discretion: *Blexen Ltd* v *G. Percy Trentham
Ltd* [1990] 2 EGLR 9; *Donald Campbell and Co. Ltd* v *Pollak* [1927] AC 732;
President of India v *Jadranska Slobodna Plovidba* [1992] 2 Lloyd's Rep 274. If
the parties have agreed that the arbitral tribunal should not give reasons for its
award, they cannot appeal any award as to costs under s. 69(1) of the AA 1996.

13.2.5 Offers to settle and *Calderbank* letters

In *Tramountana Armadora SA* v *Atlantic Shipping Co. SA* [1978] 2 All ER 870
Donaldson J referred to three different types of offers of settlement: 'without
prejudice' offers, 'sealed' offers and 'open' offers. In arbitration proceedings there is
no mechanism whereby payments can be made into court. Written offers of
settlement therefore are made to stand in the place of a payment into court. A party
may, however, not wish to have these offers referred to and therefore such offers are
drafted in varying ways. Donaldson J, at p. 876, stated the basis for each type of offer:

> A 'without prejudice' offer can never be referred to by either party at any stage
> of the proceedings, because it is in the public interest that there should be a
> procedure whereby the parties can discuss their differences freely and frankly
> and make offers of settlement without fear of being embarrassed by these
> exchanges if, unhappily, they do not lead to a settlement.

A 'sealed offer' is the arbitral equivalent of making a payment into court in settlement of the litigation or of particular causes of action in that litigation. Neither the fact, nor the amount, of such a payment into court can be revealed to the judge trying the case until he has given his judgment on all matters other than costs. As it is customary for an award to deal at one and the same time both with the parties' claims and with the question of costs, the existence of a sealed offer has to be brought to the attention of the arbitrator before he has reached a decision. However, it should remain sealed at that stage and it would be wholly improper for the arbitrator to look at it before he has reached a final decision on the matters in dispute other than as to costs, or to revise that decision in the light of the terms of the sealed offer when he sees them.

I know that there are arbitrators and umpires who feel that this procedure is not as satisfactory as making a payment into court. They take the view that respondents will feel that their defence is weakened if the arbitrator knows that they have made a sealed offer, even if the figure is concealed. If this is so, respondents may be deterred from making a 'sealed offer'.

There may be something in this point of view, but the solution to the problem is not, I think, difficult. If an arbitrator or umpire thinks it appropriate, he can always invite, and possibly require, the respondents to give him at the end of the hearing a sealed envelope which is to contain either a statement that no sealed offer has been made or the sealed offer itself. If this procedure were adopted, the existence of a sealed offer would be hidden from the tribunal until the moment at which it had to consider that part of the award which related to costs, the delivery of a sealed envelope of itself being devoid of all significance.

An 'open offer', properly so called, is one to which either party can refer at any stage of the proceedings. In an appropriate case, it may influence the arbitrator both in his decision on the matters in dispute and on the order as to costs.

Where a sealed offer has been made the arbitral tribunal must enquire whether the claimant has achieved a greater or lesser sum than that offer. Where the claimant has achieved a greater sum the general principle, that costs follow the event, will apply and the claimant should get its costs. Where the claimant is awarded a lesser sum it should be awarded its costs to the date when the sealed offer was made. The respondent should be awarded the costs from the date the offer was made to the date of the award. The arbitral tribunal should have in mind whether the sealed offer includes interest or not. Where a large claim has been made dating back for many years the amount of interest may be substantial. Where the offer is of a lump sum the arbitral tribunal will be required to calculate the principal sum and the interest to the date of the sealed offer. The arbitral tribunal will then have to ascertain whether the sealed offer is in excess of the award or not. Even where there has been a sealed offer the question of costs remains discretionary. The fact that there has been an unbeaten sealed offer would not preclude the arbitral tribunal awarding the losing party the costs of the arbitration where the successful party had acted maliciously or unreasonably in the conduct of the arbitration.

A *Calderbank* offer is an offer that is written to a party and is expressed to be 'without prejudice save as to costs'. The use of *Calderbank* letters arose in a matrimonial dispute where a payment into court could not be made: *Calderbank* v *Calderbank* [1976] Fam 93. A *Calderbank* letter should contain:

(a)   An express statement that the letter will be referred to on the question of costs. Without such an express reservation the letter would be no more than a without prejudice offer and therefore could not be disclosed without the consent of both parties: *Stotesbury* v *Turner* [1943] KB 370.

(b)   Unambiguous terms of settlement.

(c)   A time limit within which the offer is to be accepted.

A *Calderbank* offer will usually include settlement of costs. For example, the party making the offer may propose to pay the other party's reasonable costs and those of the arbitral tribunal, or the offer may require that each party pays its own costs and that the costs of the arbitral tribunal should be shared. A *Calderbank* offer should also clearly state whether or not interest is included in the offer. Unlike a sealed offer a *Calderbank* offer remains open for a set time specified in the offer. After that time the offer lapses. A party relying on a successful *Calderbank* offer should only receive its costs after the date stated in the offer for its acceptance has elapsed.

13.2.6   Effect of agreement or award on costs

Section 62 of the AA 1996 provides that unless otherwise agreed by the parties, 'any obligation under an agreement between them as to how the costs of the arbitration are to be borne, or under an award allocating the costs of the arbitration, extends only to such costs as are recoverable'. If there is no contrary agreement between the parties, the award of costs is dealt with pursuant to ss. 63 and 64 of the AA 1996. The agreement, if made before the dispute has arisen, must not contravene the provisions of s. 60 of the AA 1996. The parties to an arbitration may wish to use s. 62 where they have arrived at a consent award or an award has been made by the arbitral tribunal but the question of costs has been reserved. In such a case the parties may be able to agree on the question of costs rather than let the arbitral tribunal determine the recoverable costs.

13.3   RECOVERABLE COSTS OF AN ARBITRATION

Section 63(1) of the AA 1996 provides that the parties are free to agree what costs of the arbitration are recoverable. The costs of the arbitration are defined by s. 59 of the AA 1996. Section 63(2) of the AA 1996 states that if there is no agreement about the recoverable costs, the provisions of s. 63(3) to (7) apply.

Section 63(3) of the AA 1996 deals with the determination by the arbitral tribunal of the costs. The recoverable costs may be dealt with by an award and the award should specify the basis on which the arbitral tribunal has acted, and the items of recoverable costs and the amount referable to each.

Section 63(4) of the AA 1996 provides that where the arbitral tribunal does not determine the recoverable costs any party may apply to the court for it to deal with the issue of recoverable costs. The court may determine the recoverable costs as it thinks fit or order that the recoverable costs be determined by such means or upon such terms as it may specify. 'Court' is defined in s. 105 of the AA 1996 and means either the High Court or a county court. The Lord Chancellor may allocate proceedings under the AA 1996 between the High Court and county courts. It would appear that the court is not bound to determine the issue of costs in the same way as if they were litigation costs. The phrase 'as it thinks fit' appears to give the court a wider discretion than it would usually have when dealing with litigation costs. The reference to 'such means and upon such terms as it may specify' indicates that the court can, if it is minded to do so, order that the costs be dealt with by a costs judge or by any other person.

Section 63(5) of the AA 1996 provides that unless the arbitral tribunal or court determines otherwise, the recoverable costs of the arbitration shall be determined on the basis of a reasonable amount in respect of all costs reasonably incurred. Any doubt whether costs were reasonably incurred or reasonable in amount will be resolved in favour of the paying party. Unlike the 'standard basis' for assessing court costs, recoverable arbitration costs are not limited to those which are proportionate to the matters in issue although they must be reasonably incurred. The alternate basis on which an arbitral tribunal or court may award costs is the 'indemnity basis', in which any doubts about whether costs are of an unreasonable amount or have been unreasonably incurred are resolved in favour of the receiving party.

The word 'doubt', which appears in s. 63(5) of the AA 1996, refers to the standard of proof to be applied. In arbitrations, as with any other civil matter, the test to be applied is whether on the balance of probabilities a party has proved its case. The word 'doubt' in relation to the question of costs indicates on which party the burden of passing this test rests. On the standard basis it is on the receiving party to show that the costs have been reasonably incurred while on the indemnity basis it is on the paying party to show that the costs have been unreasonably incurred.

Traditionally, costs have been awarded on an indemnity basis only in exceptional cases: *Johnson Matthey plc* v *Eros Casting Ltd* (1993) *The Times*, 7 December 1993. An exceptional case would include where the conduct of one of the parties has been unmeritorious. In *Singh* v *Observer Ltd* [1989] 2 All ER 751 an action was adjourned on three separate occasions where the plaintiff failed to attend at court and was supported throughout the litigation by a person having no interest in the litigation costs. Costs were awarded on an indemnity basis where there had been overt or deliberate dishonesty in the presentation of an arbitration: *Berkeley*

Administration Inc. v *McClelland* [1990] FSR 565. In *Hoffman-La Roche & Co. AG* v *Sieczko* [1968] RPC 460 the court ordered costs to be paid on an indemnity basis where a contempt had been committed. However, the Civil Procedure Rules now give the court a greater discretion in awarding indemnity costs. Indemnity costs may be awarded where a Part 36 offer by the claimant is not beaten by the defendant. There is no reason why an arbitral tribunal should not follow the court's lead. It is therefore likely that the award of indemnity costs will become more commonplace.

A court assessing recoverable costs would be unlikely ever to depart from the two usual bases for assessment, although s. 63(4) of the AA 1996 makes reference to 'such basis as [the court] thinks fit'. An arbitral tribunal should equally adhere to these two bases and if it does depart from the basis set out in s. 63(5), it should state clearly its reasons for doing so. A failure to state reasons may give grounds for challenge under s. 68. In any event an arbitral tribunal should never award costs greater than those that could be awarded on an indemnity basis: *Gundry* v *Sainsbury* [1910] 1 KB 99.

Section 63(6) of the AA 1996 makes the provisions of s. 63(1) to 63(5) subject to s. 64, which deals with the recoverable fees and expenses of the arbitral tribunal (see 13.4).

Section 63(7) of the AA 1996 states that nothing in s. 63 affects any of the rights of the arbitral tribunal, any expert, legal adviser or assessor appointed by the tribunal, or any arbitral institution, to payment of their fees and expenses. This means that if the paying party defaults in making payment to the arbitral tribunal or other person mentioned in s. 63(7) then the arbitral tribunal or other persons would be entitled to recover against the other party by reason of the joint and several liability of the parties to the arbitral tribunal for these fees and expenses created by s. 28 of the AA 1996.

13.4   RECOVERABLE FEES AND EXPENSES OF THE ARBITRAL TRIBUNAL

Section 64 of the AA 1996 deals with the recoverable costs of the arbitral tribunal. Section 64(1) applies: 'Unless otherwise agreed by the parties'. It is possible for the fees and expenses of the arbitral tribunal to be agreed at the outset as a lump sum. In such a case s. 64 of the AA 1996 will be inapplicable.

Section 64(1) of the AA 1996 states that the costs of the arbitral tribunal: 'shall include in respect of the fees and expenses of the arbitrators only such reasonable fees and expenses as are appropriate in the circumstances'. This must be read alongside s. 37, which provides that the fees for the appointment, by the arbitral tribunal, of experts, legal advisers and assessors are fees and expenses of the arbitral tribunal. Factors which will be relevant to the question of reasonableness are the seniority and experience of the arbitral tribunal, the complexity of the dispute and any other special circumstances of the case.

Section 64(2) of the AA 1996 provides for the resolution of any question arising in respect of the reasonable fees and expenses of the arbitral tribunal. Where a question is raised in relation to the fees and expenses either party to the arbitration may make an application to the court, which may determine the matter, or order that it be determined by such means and upon such terms as the court may specify. If the issue of assessment of the parties' costs is before the court when any question arises as to the arbitral tribunal's costs, no new application need be made. Where an application is made it is usual for the matter to be referred to a costs judge for his decision as to the reasonableness of fees and expenses.

Section 64(3) of the AA 1996 provides two qualifications to the general principle that the arbitral tribunal is entitled to recover its reasonable costs pursuant to s. 64(1). Where the arbitral tribunal is removed pursuant to s. 24 the court may make such order as it thinks fit in respect of the arbitral tribunal's fees and expenses. This may include an order that the arbitral tribunal repay fees and expenses already paid by one of the parties. Where an arbitral tribunal resigns under s. 25 of the AA 1996 the court may make such order as it thinks fit with respect to the entitlement of the arbitral tribunal to its fees and expenses. Again this may include an order that the arbitral tribunal repay fees and expenses already paid by the parties.

Section 64(4) of the AA 1996 states that: 'Nothing in this section affects any right of the arbitrator to payment of his fees and expenses'. This subsection needs to be read alongside s. 28 which provides for the joint and several liability of the parties for the arbitral tribunal's fees and expenses. Irrespective of whether the fees and expenses of the arbitral tribunal are reduced on assessment and irrespective of which party is ordered to pay the taxed fees and expenses, the liability of the other party remains in respect of those fees and expenses if they are not met. Where there is an agreement between the parties and the arbitral tribunal in respect of the tribunal's fees being at an hourly rate, it would be unusual for the court to change the hourly rate agreed. Assessment would deal with the question of the reasonableness of the amount of time spent by the arbitral tribunal.

13.5 POWER TO LIMIT RECOVERABLE COSTS

Section 65 of the AA 1996 provides a new power to the arbitral tribunal to cap recoverable costs. The section is one of the non-mandatory provisions but it is a power that the arbitral tribunal will possess unless agreed otherwise. There is no comparable provision within the UNCITRAL Model Law or the UNCITRAL Arbitration Rules. The section is radical and its purpose was described in the DAC report of February 1996, which stated that: '. . . this will have the added virtue of discouraging those who wish to use their financial muscle to intimidate their opponents into giving up through fear that by going on they might be subject to a costs order which they could not sustain'.

Section 65(1) of the AA 1996 provides that: '. . . the tribunal may direct that the recoverable costs of the arbitration, or of any part of the arbitral proceedings, shall be limited to a specified amount'. The costs of the arbitration are defined in s. 59 to include:

(a)   the arbitrators' fees and expenses,
(b)   the fees and expenses of the arbitral institution concerned, and
(c)   the legal or other costs of the parties.

It would appear that no application is needed from either of the parties before the arbitral tribunal exercises this power but that an arbitral tribunal may make an order capping the recoverable costs of its own volition. The capping of costs may apply to the arbitration as a whole or any part of the proceedings.

When making an order under s. 65 the arbitral tribunal should have in mind the mandatory obligations imposed by s. 33. The arbitral tribunal must act fairly and impartially between the parties and adopt suitable procedures thereby avoiding unnecessary delay and expense so as to provide a fair means for the resolution of the dispute.

Section 65(2) of the AA 1996 provides for the varying of any direction made relating to a cap on the recoverable costs of the arbitration so long as this is done sufficiently in advance of the costs being incurred. This section provides a safety valve whereby, if the proceedings become more complicated, because of developments in the perceived claims or otherwise, the cap on recoverable costs in the arbitration may be varied.

13.6   POWER TO ORDER SECURITY FOR COSTS

Section 38(3) of the AA 1996 provides that:

> The tribunal may order a claimant to provide security for costs of the arbitration. This power shall not be exercised on the ground that the claimant is—
> (a)   an individual ordinarily resident outside the United Kingdom, or
> (b)   a corporation or association incorporated or formed under the law of a country outside the United Kingdom, or whose central management and control is exercised outside the United Kingdom.

Section 38(3) of the AA 1996 is a non-mandatory provision and the parties may agree that the arbitral tribunal should not possess the power to order the claimant to provide security for costs. In default of such an agreement by the parties the power to make an order for security for costs vests with the arbitral tribunal. Prior to the AA 1996 the power to order that the claimant provide security for costs was one which the court inherently possessed. This power has now been removed from the court, in respect of arbitral proceedings, by s. 44 of the AA 1996. Therefore where the parties have agreed that the power to order security for costs should not be given to the arbitral tribunal there will be no authority from which an order for security for costs can be subsequently sought.

Prior to the AA 1996 the court's power to order a claimant to provide security for another's costs derived from a general principle of English law that a successful party is entitled to recover its costs. The general principle that 'costs follow the event' is now to be found in s. 61(2) of the AA 1996. Where the losing party has no funds an award ordering it to pay costs will be of little worth. It follows that in order to give protection to a party who defends a claim, that party may claim security for the costs of defending the matter during the arbitration. The claimant may therefore be ordered to provide security for part or all of the respondent's projected costs. A failure to comply with such an order would generally result in the claim being stayed.

The inclusion of the power in the AA 1996 for the arbitral tribunal to make an order for security for costs came about in no small part as a result of the House of Lords decision in *Coppée-Lavelin NV* v *Ken-Ren Chemicals and Fertilizers Ltd* [1995] 1 AC 38. The case involved a dispute under the ICC Rules of Arbitration regarding the construction of a chemical plant. The law of the contract was Belgian with London as the place of arbitration. Coppée-Lavelin applied to the court for security for costs on the basis that Ken-Ren was an insolvent company which was being supported in the arbitration by the Kenyan government, which was the majority shareholder in Ken-Ren. It was Coppée-Lavelin's case that if an order for costs was made against Ken-Ren the Government of Kenya would be under no liability to meet those costs.

Ken-Ren argued that the ICC Rules governed the whole conduct of the arbitration and that, following the Court of Appeal's reasoning in *Bank Mellat* v *Helliniki Techniki SA* [1984] QB 291, there was no scope to make such an order. Coppée-Lavelin responded that there was a residual power of the court to order security although they conceded that such a power should only be used in 'exceptional circumstances'. The House of Lords held by a majority that it did have this power and that there were the 'exceptional circumstances' that justified such an order being made.

Criticisms were levelled at the English courts by Continental commentators, who argued that the interventionist actions by the court sounded the death knell of London as a centre for international arbitration. As a result the power to award security for costs has now been given expressly to the arbitral tribunal under s. 38(3) of the AA 1996 and has been taken away from the courts.

13.6.1 Party residing outside the United Kingdom

Section 38(3) of the AA 1996 expressly prohibits security for costs being ordered simply because the claimant is resident outside the United Kingdom. The reason is to enhance London as a centre for international arbitration. Prior to the AA 1996 the power to award security for costs against a claimant who was ordinarily resident abroad was often removed by a provision in the agreement that deemed the claimant, for the purposes of the arbitration, to be resident in England. Although the arbitral tribunal cannot take into account the fact that the claimant is resident abroad the provision may be sidestepped by a party arguing that security should be ordered, not because the party is resident abroad, but because the claimant's assets are abroad. A party resident in England whose only assets are abroad may be ordered to provide security. This argument could equally apply to a foreign national who has no assets within the jurisdiction. Where, however, the foreign claimant is a member of an EC country then an order requiring security for costs may, unless it is based on other grounds, be contrary to Articles 59 and 60 of the EC Treaty: *Hubbard* v *Hamburger* (case C-20/92) [1993] ECR I-3777; cf. *Chequepoint SARL* v *McLelland* [1997] QB 51.

13.6.2 Potential injustices

It is significant that the power to order security for costs has been taken outside of the ambit of the court's powers (see s. 44 of the AA 1996). This has the potential to lead, in some cases, to an injustice. A 'Calderbank letter' is an offer which is made 'without prejudice save as to costs'. It therefore may be referred to in any application regarding costs but not otherwise. In arbitration proceedings its purpose is similar to a payment into court.

Where, in litigation proceedings, there is an application for security for costs and a payment into court has been made, it is usual for a judge other than the one who is to hear the case on liability to decide the issue. The rationale for this is that the payment into court may sway the judge when he or she resolves issues relating to liability. The payment into court is a material factor in the decision whether security for costs should be awarded. The same is true in regard to a 'Calderbank letter' in arbitral proceedings.

If an application for security for costs is made to the arbitral tribunal which is to decide liability and there is a 'Calderbank' offer, this fact should be brought to the arbitral tribunal's notice. The inevitable result, however, is that it may prejudice the decision of the arbitral tribunal when it later has to decide liability. In this regard there was some benefit in being able to apply to the court for security for costs. Now, the parties could agree that a person other than the arbitral tribunal hear the application or instruct the arbitral tribunal not to give weight to the Calderbank offer when deciding liability. In reality, however, a party who is asked to provide security for costs will not agree to either alternative. There is a danger in such a case that the party asked to provide the security will use the fact that a Calderbank offer has been made as a weapon forcing the other party not to proceed with the application.

13.6.3 Arbitral tribunal's discretion

The arbitral tribunal in exercising its discretion to make an order for the provision of security for costs is not bound by the strict rules of the court. By virtue of s. 33(1) of the AA 1996 the obligation on the arbitral tribunal is to act 'fairly and impartially'. If the agreement to award security for costs is drafted in wide enough terms there, is nothing wrong in principle why the arbitral tribunal should not award security in a situation where the courts would have no such power. The arbitral tribunal would be under no compunction to narrow the grounds upon which security could be granted to those cases where the High Court had power. Where the parties have not expressly agreed to expand the grounds upon which the arbitral tribunal can order security for costs the arbitral tribunal should only take into account the established grounds upon which security for costs would be ordered by the courts. If the arbitral tribunal does this, there can be no question that it has not acted in a judicial manner.

RSC, ord. 23 in CPR, sch. 1, sets out the governing principles when the court should grant an application for security for costs. In addition to these powers s. 726(1) of the Companies Act 1985 specifically provides another ground for ordering security for costs where the claimant is a limited company registered in Great Britain. The ground under this section is that 'it appears by credible testimony that there is reason to believe that the company will be unable to pay the defendant's costs if successful in his defence'. In *Bank Mellat* v *Helliniki Techniki SA* [1984] QB 291 the court held that an arbitral tribunal had a power analogous to s. 726(1) of the Companies Act 1985 in that it could order security for costs where there is reason to believe that the claimant company will be unable to pay the costs of the respondent if the respondent is successful in defending the claim.

The AA 1996 deliberately omitted any reference to the powers of the court in regard to ordering security for costs. In early drafts of the AA 1996 the arbitral tribunal's power to order security for costs was to be exercised on the same principles as are applicable to the High Court. However, in its final draft this provision was removed. Although the arbitral tribunal has a wide discretion as to how it may exercise the power to order security for costs there are limits to the use of the discretion.

When dealing with costs the arbitral tribunal must act judicially: *Metro-Cammell Hong Kong Ltd* v *FKI Engineering plc* (1996) 77 BLR 84; *Gbangbola* v *Smith & Sherriff Ltd* [1998] 3 All ER 730; *Stotesbury* v *Turner* [1943] KB 370. In *Stotesbury* v *Turner* the court held that the discretion of an arbitrator was the same as that of a judge and must be exercised judicially. It may therefore be inferred that the arbitral tribunal should only order security for costs in circumstances where the courts would so order (see M. O'Reilly, 'Orders for security for costs: from the arbitrator's perspective', *Arbitration* (November 1995), p. 248). The arbitral tribunal is clearly not bound by the Civil Procedure Rules 1998, but there are established principles that the arbitral tribunal should observe, and failure to follow them would be a breach of its obligation to act fairly: s. 33(1)(a) of the AA 1996.

The case of *Sir Lindsay Parkinson and Co. Ltd* v *Triplan Ltd* [1973] QB 609 provides guidance on the judicial principles that the courts follow when hearing an application for security for costs. The arbitral tribunal should examine:

(a) the bona fides of the claim, that is, whether the claim is put forward in good faith;

(b) admissions or offers which have been made which are not privileged;

(c) any oppressive features of the application.

One of the overriding factors that the arbitral tribunal should have in mind is whether there is a risk that ordering security for costs will stifle a genuine claim. The arbitral tribunal will have to weigh up the potential prejudice to the claimant if it is prohibited from pursuing a genuine claim against the potential prejudice to the respondent if the respondent, on winning the action, is unable to recover the costs of defending the claim.

In *Keary Developments Ltd* v *Tarmac Construction Ltd* [1995] 3 All ER 534 the Court of Appeal stated a number of factors that should be considered when deciding whether to make an order for security for costs:

(a)   whether the claimant was using its impecuniosity to put pressure on the respondent;

(b)   the claimant's prospects of success, without going into detail of the merits;

(c)   whether the claimant could raise the funds outside its own resources, the onus being on the claimant to show that no resources were available; and

(d)   the lateness of the application and whether this factor weighs against the claimant or respondent and who was to blame.

The arbitral tribunal, like the court, has no obligation to give security for the full amount of the claim. In *Roburn Construction Ltd* v *William Irwin (South) and Co. Ltd* [1991] BCC 726 it was held that a court need not order the full amount of security as long as what was ordered was more than nominal. This would be equally applicable in the case of an arbitration under the AA 1996.

Section 38(3) of the AA 1996 empowers an arbitral tribunal to order security to be provided by a 'claimant', which, by s. 82(1), includes a counterclaimant. There is therefore no change to the previously established position that security could not be sought against a respondent except where the respondent stood in the position of the claimant by way of counterclaim: *Sykes* v *Sacerdoti* (1885) 15 QBD 423; *Samuel J. Cohl Co.* v *Eastern Mediterranean Maritime Ltd* [1980] 1 Lloyd's Rep 371.

One of the more complex questions that the arbitral tribunal may have to decide is when to order security where the respondent has a counterclaim which overlaps with the claim or where the claimant seeks security from the respondent on the counterclaim. If the claim and counterclaim are distinct and do not arise from the same facts then generally the arbitral tribunal will not take the other party's claim into account. However, where the counterclaim arises out of the same facts as the claim this will be a relevant consideration for the arbitral tribunal in deciding whether to order security. A relevant consideration also will be whether the respondent intends to pursue the counterclaim. The arbitral tribunal should not generally order that security be given by the claimant where the counterclaim arises from substantially the same facts as the claim and the respondent intends to pursue the counterclaim: *B.J. Crabtree (Insulation) Ltd* v *GPT Communication Systems Ltd* (1990) 59 BLR 43; and *Flender Werft AG* v *Aegean Maritime Ltd* [1990] 2 Lloyd's Rep 27 at p. 31.

Where the claimant seeks security against the respondent on the counterclaim the arbitral tribunal must examine whether the case raised by the respondent is in fact a defence which gives rise to an independent counterclaim. Where it is in essence purely a defence then the arbitral tribunal should not order that the respondent provide security for the claimant's costs. Where there is some claim made by the respondent over and above the defence it will be a question of fact and degree in each case whether security should be given. Only where the claim made is independent of the defence should security be considered. In such cases the arbitral tribunal would be wise to address the question in the same terms as a court would do by considering whether in 'all the circumstances of the case, the court thinks it just to do so': RSC, ord. 23, r. 1 in CPR, sch. 1. There are no clear rules where the counterclaim is part independent and part defensive and there are conflicting authorities on whether the arbitral tribunal should order security when this is the case: *New Fenix Compagnie Anonyme d'Assurances de Madrid* v *General Accident, Fire and Life Assurance Corporation Ltd* [1911] 2 KB 619; *Cathery* v *Lithodomos Ltd* (1987) 41 BLR 76. Where there is a claim and an independent counterclaim and cross-applications are made the arbitral tribunal must consider whether to order security to be given from both the claimant and respondent.

13.6.4 No discretion

Perhaps the most notable difference between a security for costs application in the courts and under the AA 1996 is that the power conferred under the AA 1996 is expressed as a negative stipulation. The arbitral tribunal has no power to award security for costs under s. 38(3) of the AA 1996 on the sole basis that the claimant is either:

(a) an individual ordinarily resident outside the United Kingdom, or

(b) a corporation or association incorporated or formed under the law of a country outside the United Kingdom, or whose central management and control is exercised outside the United Kingdom.

An aim of the AA 1996 is therefore to encourage foreign disputants to arbitrate their differences in England. The Civil Procedure Rules 1998 do not share this aim. It is, however, clear that where there are other reasons why the arbitral tribunal should order security for costs from a foreign claimant s. 38(3) of the AA 1996 will not prohibit the arbitral tribunal from making that order.

13.6.5 Costs of the arbitration

Section 38(3) of the AA 1996 empowers the arbitral tribunal to order a claimant to provide security for the 'costs of the arbitration', which means, by s. 59(1):

(a) the arbitrators' fees and expenses,

(b)   the fees and expenses of any arbitral institution concerned, and

(c)   the legal or other costs of the parties.

The AA 1996 therefore makes a fundamental departure from the previous practice in ordering security for costs. Previously security for costs would only be given in respect of the legal fees of the respondent (or claimant on a counterclaim). Security for costs now may be ordered in respect of the arbitral tribunal's fees and expenses and the expenses and fees of the arbitral institution if applicable. Also, by s. 59(1)(c), security for costs may be ordered in respect of the fees (other than legal) of the parties.

The rules under which the arbitration is to be conducted may provide explicitly for the ordering of security for the arbitral tribunal's fees. More often, however, there will be no provision for such security. Under the AA 1950 there was no power for the tribunal to seek security for its own fees nor did the court possess such a power. One method was for the tribunal to agree, prior to being appointed, for the payment of its fees to be on account. In this way it would become part of the tribunal's terms of appointment. There is nothing within the AA 1996 that prohibits this practice from continuing.

The arbitral tribunal should, when thinking about using the power to order security for costs for its own fees, consider whether it would be appropriate to make such an order. First, the arbitral tribunal must decide who should provide the security. It is uncertain whether the arbitral tribunal will be bound by the same principles in ordering security for its own fees as it would be in ordering security to be given from one party or the other. Where, for instance, a respondent raises only a defence to the claim, is the arbitral tribunal entitled to seek security for its own fees from the respondent? The Practice Subcommittee of the Chartered Institute of Arbitrators has stated that: 'The factors to be borne in mind in relation to such an order are the same as those set out in relation to ordering security for the respondent's costs'. Professor Needham (*Arbitration* (February 1998), p. 77) has argued that the statement of the Practice Subcommittee is incorrect. He has suggested that the question that the arbitral tribunal must address is: 'Is what I am proposing to do absolutely fair to all parties under the particular circumstances of the case?' The obligation of fairness to the parties is placed on the arbitral tribunal by s. 33 of the AA 1996. This is a mandatory requirement that the arbitral tribunal must have in mind when addressing any issue.

The arbitral tribunal must also have in mind the fact that both parties are jointly and severally liable for the arbitral tribunal's fees under s. 28 of the AA 1996. If one or other of the parties can meet the arbitral tribunal's fees, the arbitral tribunal must seriously consider whether an order for the provision of security for the arbitral tribunal's costs should be made. The rationale for this is that if either of the parties could pay these fees, such fees are not in jeopardy. Conversely, to allow one party to continue the arbitration when that party would not be able to pay the arbitral tribunal's fees and expenses if that party loses, is to punish the winning party.

13.6.6 Form in which security is to be given

Generally in court proceedings the claimant will be obliged to pay the security into court. This, however, is not possible in an arbitration. The accepted procedure is for the respondent to request that security is provided by the claimant prior to making any application to the arbitral tribunal. If the claimant agrees to provide security through a personal undertaking or through a solicitor's undertaking which is acceptable to the respondent, no application need be made. Where such an undertaking is given this will last, unless agreed to the contrary, until the final award. It will be limited to the amount agreed in the undertaking.

An order that security for costs be provided must state the form in which the security shall be given. A bond or guarantee with sureties will usually be appropriate: *Societe Casa* v *Societe Cambior* (ICC Case No. 6697). As an alternative to ordering a bond to be issued the arbitral tribunal may order that the money is paid into a separate account. However, certain difficulties may arise if this approach is adopted. The status of such moneys paid into a separate account should be made clear. For example, if the claimant becomes insolvent, it is not clear whether the respondent would have better title to such moneys than any other unsecured creditor. If the respondent would not have better title, the order for security is in effect worthless to the respondent.

13.6.7 Sanctions

If the claimant fails to provide security for costs in accordance with an order of the arbitral tribunal, the respondent may apply for a peremptory order under s. 41(5) of the AA 1996. Section 41(6) of the AA 1996 gives a special sanction to the arbitral tribunal where a party fails to comply with a peremptory order that security for costs be provided. Under s. 41(6) the arbitral tribunal may make an award dismissing the claim.

14 Miscellaneous Provisions

14.1 DEFINITIONS

Section 82 of the AA 1996 sets out a number of minor definitions. These definitions are only applicable to Part I of the AA 1996. Included in this section are the definitions of 'arbitrator', 'claimant', 'peremptory order', 'premises' and 'substantive jurisdiction'. In addition s. 82(2) of the AA 1996 defines a 'party' as including 'any person claiming under or through a party to the agreement'. For a more detailed analysis of the word 'party' see chapter 6. Section 83 of the AA 1996 provides an index of defined expressions.

14.2 PERSONS TAKING NO PART IN THE PROCEEDINGS

Section 72 of the AA 1996 is a mandatory provision. It applies to a person who is alleged to be a party to an arbitration agreement but takes no part in the arbitral proceedings. Section 72(1) provides that a party who has not taken part in the proceedings may apply to the court for a declaration, injunction or other appropriate relief as to whether there is a valid arbitration agreement, or as to whether the arbitral tribunal was properly constituted, or as to whether the matters referred to arbitration are in accordance with the arbitration agreement.

Section 72 of the AA 1996 is less restrictive than s. 32. While s. 32 provides that a party to the arbitration may apply to the court to challenge the arbitral tribunal's jurisdiction, several conditions need to be met prior to the application being made. These include the consent of the parties to the arbitration agreement or, if consent is not provided, the permission of the arbitral tribunal. In addition the court must be satisfied that there will be a saving in costs, the application is made without delay and that there is good reason why the court should decide the matter. Section 72 has none of these preconditions. However, under s. 72 the party applying must have taken no part in the proceedings. Section 14 defines when the arbitral proceedings are deemed to be commenced. A notable difference, therefore, between s. 72 and s. 32 is that under s. 32 a party may participate in the appointment of the arbitral tribunal whereas if a party wishes to make an application under s. 72 of the AA 1996 it may not.

Section 72(1) of the AA 1996 may therefore provide benefits to a party if it considers that there is an initial invalidity in the arbitration agreement. If an application to the courts is made under s. 72(1) at the very outset of the arbitral proceedings, the arbitral tribunal should consider whether to stay the proceedings to await the decision of the court. Each case will depend on its own facts and the arbitral tribunal is not obliged to stay the arbitral proceedings while a court decides whether it has jurisdiction or not. However, the arbitral tribunal should have regard to the question of costs. As the person making the application under s. 72(1) has taken no part in the arbitral proceedings, and therefore is not a party in those proceedings, that person will have no joint and several liability for the arbitral tribunal's fees and expenses under s. 28(1) of the AA 1996 if its application is successful.

Section 72(2) of the AA 1996 deals with the challenging of an award where a party has taken no part in the proceedings. The award may be challenged on the basis that the arbitral tribunal lacked substantive jurisdiction or that there was a serious irregularity in the proceedings affecting that party. The obligation, under s. 70(2) of the AA 1996, to exhaust all arbitral procedures prior to making a challenge is specifically excluded. It is unlikely that this method of challenge will be used that frequently as a party risks a great deal in having an award made against it without either defending the claim or initially challenging the substantive jurisdiction of the arbitral tribunal. It is, however, foreseeable that where the claim against a party is indefensible, that party will not waste the time and costs of defending the arbitral proceedings. A better route would be to seek to challenge the award on the grounds of some technical failure relating to the substantive jurisdiction of the arbitral tribunal or the conduct of the proceedings. Any challenge under ss. 67 or 68 of the AA 1996 is, however, subject to the conditions applicable to those sections and in particular s. 70(3), which provides for a time limit under which any application shall be brought.

14.3 LOSS OF RIGHT TO OBJECT

Section 73 of the AA 1996 deals with the loss of a party's right to object to the conduct of the proceedings or jurisdiction of the arbitral tribunal. Section 73 is expressly referred to in ss. 32, 66, 67 and 68 of the AA 1996 and is discussed in chapters 5 and 12. The intent of this section is to prevent late challenges being made that the arbitral tribunal lacked substantive jurisdiction or that there was some serious irregularity in the conduct of the proceedings.

Section 73(1) provides that if a party is to raise an objection:

    (a)   that the tribunal lacks substantive jurisdiction,

    (b)   that the proceedings have been improperly conducted,

    (c)   that there has been a failure to comply with the arbitration agreement or with any provision of this Part, or

(d)   that there has been any other irregularity affecting the tribunal or the proceedings,

and this objection is not raised forthwith, or is raised outside the time limits imposed, then the party will have to show to the tribunal or to the court that it was unaware, or could not with reasonable diligence have discovered, the grounds for the objection. A party who therefore objects on any of the grounds mentioned above should write promptly to the arbitral tribunal and to the other parties noting its objection.

Section 73(2) of the AA 1996 deals specifically with the situation where .the arbitral tribunal has ruled on its own substantive jurisdiction. The right to object to the arbitral tribunal's award on the question of whether it has substantive jurisdiction will be lost if a party fails to make its objection within the time limit prescribed in s. 73(2).

14.4   RECKONING PERIODS OF TIME AND EXTENDING TIME LIMITS

Section 78 of the AA 1996 deals with the reckoning of time periods. The parties may agree on how to do this. Where no agreement is reached the default provisions apply. The default provisions have been included so that cross-references to other statutes or the Civil Procedure Rules 1998 to determine time periods need not occur.

The AA 1996 contains three different sections dealing with extension of time. Section 12 provides the court with power to extend time limits for beginning arbitral proceedings, where an arbitration agreement refers future disputes to arbitration. Section 50 provides that, unless otherwise agreed by the parties, the court may extend time for the making of an award. Section 79 provides that, unless otherwise agreed by the parties, the court may extend time limits relating to arbitral proceedings. It is specifically stated that s. 79 does not apply to a time limit to which s. 12 is applicable. Section 12 has been previously discussed in chapter 4. Section 50 has previously been discussed in chapter 11.

Section 79 of the AA 1996 is a non-mandatory section and may be excluded with the agreement of the parties. The purpose of this section is to allow the parties or the arbitral tribunal to apply to the court for an extension of time of 'any time limit agreed by them' or such time limits as are applicable by reason of the default provisions in Part I of the AA 1996. Section 79 does not however apply in regard for extending time for the beginning of the proceedings. The parties cannot apply under s. 79 for the court to extend any time limit that has not been agreed by them, such as statutory time limits. An extension of a time limit imposed under the arbitration agreement, or such institutional rules as may be applicable, may be required where it is impossible for a party or the arbitral tribunal to comply with these time limits. Section 79(1) of the AA 1996 provides that the court may extend any time limit in accordance with the provisions of s. 79(2) to (5).

Section 79(2) states:

An application for an order may be made—
(a) by any party to the arbitral proceedings (upon notice to the other parties and to the tribunal), or
(b) by the arbitral tribunal (upon notice to the parties).

Section 79(3)(a) of the AA 1996 provides that the court shall not exercise its power to extend a time limit unless all available recourse to the arbitral tribunal, or any available arbitral process for obtaining an extension of time has been exhausted. Most institutional rules will have rules dealing with extensions of time. The CIMAR, for instance, allow the arbitral tribunal to fix the time within which any order or direction is to be complied with and to extend or reduce that time limit at any stage: r. 5.6.

Section 79(3)(b) of the AA 1996 provides that the court's power to extend time limits is subject to the court being satisfied that 'a substantial injustice would otherwise be done'. The court is likely, although there is no authority on this point, to make a distinction between cases where the time limit is fixed within the arbitration agreement and where there has been no review, with cases where there has been a review by an arbitral institution or by the arbitral tribunal itself. In nearly every case a refusal to extend time will cause some injustice and probably a substantial injustice. However, where the matter has been the subject of review by an arbitral institution, and especially where the dispute is of an international character, it would be unlikely for a court to impose its own view and reverse a decision of an arbitral institution.

Section 79(5) of the AA 1996 provides that the court may extend the period on such terms as it thinks fit. An appeal from the decision of the court may only be made with the leave of the court: s. 79(6) of the AA 1996. Section 79 of the AA 1996 may be compared with s. 50, which provides the power for the court to extend time limits for making an award. The conditions in ss. 79 and 50 are identical.

14.5 SAVING FOR CERTAIN MATTERS GOVERNED BY COMMON LAW

Section 81 of the AA 1996 provides that nothing in Part I of the AA 1996 shall be construed as excluding any common law rule of law consistent with the provisions of the AA 1996. Section 81(1) of the AA 1996 provides a number of examples of common law rules which are preserved. The first example preserves the rule relating to matters which are not capable of settlement by arbitration. A minor, lacking contractual capacity, may not agree to settle a dispute by arbitration. There are two exceptions to this general rule. First, a minor may make a contract for necessities and secondly, a minor may make contracts of apprenticeship, education and service, though these are voidable at the minor's election. Where there is an arbitration agreement within a contract for necessities or for eduction, service or apprenticeship, the minor will be bound by that arbitration agreement where the contract is for the minor's benefit: *Slade* v *Metrodent Ltd* [1953] 2 QB 112.

The second example provided by s. 81(1) of the AA 1996 is that the rules relating to oral arbitration agreements are preserved. There is nothing wrong per se with an oral arbitration agreement. However, one of the many problems with arbitrating under an oral arbitration agreement is that the provisions of the AA 1996 are inapplicable. The AA 1996 only applies to agreements in writing. If a party arbitrates under an oral arbitration agreement, any award cannot therefore be enforced under s. 66 of the AA 1996. A party who obtains an award under an oral arbitration agreement is thereafter obliged to enforce it by way of action on the award. This is a separate action in the courts for breach of contract. The party's claim would be that it was an implied term of the oral arbitration agreement that the party would honour the award. Therefore it would be a breach of contract if that party did not honour the award.

The third example provided by s. 81(1) of the AA 1996 is that the rules relating to refusal to recognise or enforce an award by reason of public policy are preserved. This provision was originally included at s. 66 of the draft Bill. In *Soleimany* v *Soleimany* [1998] 3 WLR 811 the Court of Appeal refused to enforce an award on the ground that it was contrary to public policy. The facts of the case and the *ratio decidendi* of the Court of Appeal are more fully set out in chapter 18.

Section 81(2) of the AA 1996 provides that nothing in the Act 'shall be construed as reviving any jurisdiction of the courts to set aside or remit an award on the ground of errors of fact or law on the face of the award'. The common law rule relating to errors of fact and law on the face of an award can be found in a number of early cases including *Kent* v *Estob* (1802) 3 East 18. The court in this case admitted the practice of review on a point of law but held that this power only existed where the mistake of law was apparent on the face of the award or from a statement of reasons given in writing by the arbitrator at the time of giving the award. Section 1(1) of the AA 1979 expressly removed the jurisdiction of the High Court to set aside or remit an award for error of law or fact on the face of the award. As the AA 1979 was repealed by the AA 1996 it was thought that unless a provision was included in the AA 1996 which dealt with this common law power it could be revived.

14.6 PROCEDURE FOR APPLICATIONS TO THE COURT

Before, during and after the arbitration proceedings the parties may need to apply to the court to seek assistance. Such assistance may involve the appointment of the arbitral tribunal, the determination of preliminary points of law, the enforcement of peremptory orders, orders in support of the arbitral proceedings, the challenging or appealing of an award and the enforcement of an award. An arbitral tribunal has powers to conduct the arbitration but has fewer sanctions than the court. If a party to the arbitration fails to comply with the orders of the arbitral tribunal, the arbitral tribunal may make an award drawing such adverse inferences from the act of non-compliance as the circumstances justify: s. 41(7)(c) of the AA 1996. The arbitral tribunal may, in certain circumstances, proceed to a hearing without the attendance of one of the parties and may make an award on the evidence put before it. However, the court is needed to enforce any award. The arbitral tribunal cannot do this.

14.6.1 Allocation of arbitration proceedings

On 31 January 1997 the High Court and County Courts (Allocation of Arbitration Proceedings) Order 1996 (SI 1996/3215) came into force. Article 2 of the Order provides that proceedings under the AA 1996 shall be commenced and taken in the High Court subject to the exceptions set out in Articles 3 to 5 of the Order. An application to stay legal proceedings under s. 9 of the AA 1996 is to be made in the court where the legal proceedings are pending. Enforcement of an arbitration award, either under s. 66 or s. 101(2) of the AA 1996, may be done in any county court.

Article 5 of the Order provides that proceedings under the AA 1996 may also be commenced in the Central London County Court Business List. The jurisdiction of the Central London County Court is, however, limited to disputes not exceeding £200,000. Powers are also provided relating to the transfer of proceedings between the Central London County Court and the High Court. Factors that are relevant to the transfer of proceedings include: the financial substance of the dispute; the nature of the dispute (for example, whether it is a commercial matter or arises out of a building or engineering contract); whether the dispute raises questions of importance; and the convenience to the parties.

14.6.2 Civil Procedure Rules, Practice Direction 49G

The full text of CPR, PD 49G (Arbitrations) appears in Appendix 4. The Practice Direction was issued in March 1999 and replaced with modifications RSC, ord. 73. The overriding objective of the Practice Direction is founded on s. 1 of the AA 1996 and is to be construed accordingly. The Practice Direction is divided into three parts: Part I deals with applications to the court; Part II deals with applications to the courts under the pre-1996 regime; Part III deals with the enforcement of awards.

An application under CPR, PD 49G is required to be made in pratice form N8A. The application must include a concise statement of the relief or remedy claimed, and (where appropriate) the question which the court is asked to determined. The details of and grounds for any challenge to an award, and the name or names of the persons against whom costs are claimed must also be set out. An application CPR, PD 49G must also set out the section of the AA 1996 under which the application is brought, and a statement that the requirements of the AA 1996 have been met.

The requirements which are to be met for applications under CPR, PD 49G are as follows:

Application made	Statutory requirements
section 9 (stay of legal proceedings)	see section 9(3)
section 12 (extensions of time for beginning arbitral proceedings)	see section 12(2)
section 18 (failure of appointment procedure)	see section 18(2)
section 21 (umpires)	see section 21(5)
section 24 (removal of arbitrators)	see section 24(2)
section 32 (preliminary point of jurisdiction)	see section 32(3)
section 42 (enforcement of peremptory orders)	see section 42(3)
section 44 (powers in support of arbitral tribunal)	see section 44(3), (4), (5)
section 45 (preliminary point of law)	see section 45(3)
section 50 (extension of time for making an award)	see section 50(2)
section 56 (power to withhold an award)	see section 56(4)
section 67, 68 (challenge the award)	see section 70(2), (3)
section 69 (appeal on a point of law)	see sections 69(2), (4); 70(2), (3)
section 77 (service of documents)	see section 77(3)

The application must also state whether it is made with or without notice, whether it is made by a judge sitting in private or in public, and the date and time when the application is to be heard or whether no such date and time has yet been fixed. An application must be supported by an affidavit or witness statement which sets out the evidence on which the applicant seeks to rely.

CPR, PD 49G, para. 7 deals with the service of the arbitration application. Subject to certain specific paragraphs within the Practice Direction itself, the arbitration application must be served in accordance with CPR, Part 6. The requirements for service outside of jurisdiction are set out in CPR, PD 49G, para. 8. CPR, PD 49G, para. 11 deals with acknowledgement of service by the respondent and para. 12 deals with acknowledgment of service by the arbitral tribunal. There are automatic directions, which are applicable unless the court otherwise directs. These directions deal with the service of affidavits and witness statements, the bundles of documents in support of the application and the requirements for the applicant to provide a chronology of events, a list of persons involved and a skeleton argument. The respondent is also obliged to lodge with the court a skeleton argument in support of its case.

CPR, PD 49G, para. 22 deals with time limits for challenges to or appeals from awards. The applicant will not be taken to have complied with the time limit of 28 days referred to in s. 70(3) of the AA 1996 unless the application has been issued and all affidavits or witness statements have been filed by the expiry of that time limit. Where a challenge is to be made under ss. 67, 68 or 69 of the AA 1996, and the 28-day time limit has expired, the applicant must state in its application why the time limit should be extended and support such contention by affidavit or witness statement setting out the evidence on which it relies. The respondent may file an affidavit or witness statement within seven days opposing the application to extend time. The court decides whether to extend time without a hearing unless it considers one necessary.

The main modifications introduced by CPR, PD 49G are as follows:

(a) The requirement to serve affidavit evidence in support of applications under RSC, ord. 73 is now a requirement to file evidence. This evidence may be either by witness statement or affidavit.

(b) CPR, PD 49G adopts the new terminology used in civil litigation: 'chambers hearings' are now 'hearings in private'; 'ex parte' hearings are now hearings 'without notice'; 'leave' is now 'permission'. An application under s. 9 of the AA 1996 to 'stay proceedings' is now referred to as 'an application notice by which an application under section 9 of the Arbitration Act to stay proceedings is made'.

(c) Hearsay evidence is now expressly allowed to be given in witness statements and affidavits: CPR, PD 49G, para. 14.6. Although there was no express provision in RSC, ord. 73 the reality was that nearly all applications were made in private and that hearsay evidence was generally admissible under the Civil Evidence Act 1995.

Where the arbitration proceedings arise 'out of trade and commerce in general', regard should also be had to CPR, PD 49D. CPR, PD 49D relates to commercial court proceedings but para. 1.2(1) of the Practice Direction brings within its scope arbitral proceedings where they arise out of 'trade and commerce in general'.

14.7 JUDGE-ARBITRATORS

Section 93 of the AA 1996 deals with the appointment of judges as arbitrators. Section 93 is derived from s. 11 of the AA 1950 and s. 4 of the Administration of Justice Act 1970. Section 93 of the AA 1996 provides that a judge of the Commercial Court or an official referee (now a judge of the Technology and Construction Court) may, if in all the circumstances he thinks fit, accept appointment as a sole arbitrator or umpire under an arbitration agreement. This right to accept is qualified in that the Lord Chief Justice must have informed that judge, that having regard to the state of business of the court, he can be made available. Part I of the AA 1996 is applicable to an arbitration conducted by a judge-arbitrator save to the extent that it is amended by sch. 2.

Paragraph 2 of sch. 2 provides that references to the court in Part I shall be construed as references to the Court of Appeal and that references to the Court of Appeal in ss. 32(6), 45(6) and 69(8) shall be construed as references to the House of Lords. The court's powers in support of the arbitral process, under ss. 42 to 44, may be exercised either by the High Court or by the judge-arbitrator. In exercising powers under ss. 42 to 44 the judge-arbitrator is regarded as exercising such powers in his capacity as a High Court judge.

The judge-arbitrator possesses the power to extend the time for making an award under s. 50 of the AA 1996 and may extend the time limits relating to arbitral proceedings under s. 79. An appeal from the judge-arbitrator's decision, in either case, is made to the Court of Appeal. The judge-arbitrator possesses the power himself to withhold an award in the case of non-payment of fees and expenses: paras 6 and 7 of sch. 2 to the AA 1996. In addition the judge-arbitrator possesses the power to determine his own reasonable fees and expenses. However, the exercise of the judge-arbitrator's power is subject to the powers of the Court of Appeal under ss. 24(4) and 25(3)(b). The judge-arbitrator also possesses the power to give leave to enforce an award under s. 66.

A judge-arbitrator will generally not accept an appointment unless the matter in dispute is of a complex legal nature. Factors which will also have a bearing on whether a judge-arbitrator accepts an appointment will be the length of the hearing and whether the dispute raises a matter of general public importance. The use of judge-arbitrators for arbitration proceedings has not been that common although following the case of *Northern Regional Health Authority* v *Derek Crouch Construction Ltd* [1984] QB 644 more applications have been made. It is a misconception that when a judge-arbitrator is appointed the arbitration proceedings are more likely to be akin to litigation than if a technical arbitrator is appointed. The judge-arbitrator is obliged to comply with the requirements and obligations of the AA 1996. This includes adopting procedures suitable to the circumstances of the particular case.

14.8   SERVICE OF NOTICES AND DOCUMENTS

Section 76 of the AA 1996 deals with the service of notices or any other document required to be given or served under the arbitration agreement. The parties are free to agree the manner of service of any notice or document. Where no agreement is reached then the default provisions in s. 76(3) and (4) apply. Section 76 applies only to notices or documents to be given or served under the arbitration agreement and therefore does not apply to the service of documents for the purposes of legal proceedings.

Section 76(3) of the AA 1996 provides that a notice or document may be served on a person by any effective means. This gives the party serving the document almost unlimited scope in respect of how the document is to be served. However, where it is contested that service has not taken place it would be for the party who served the document to show that it has been effectively served. Section 76(4) of the AA 1996 provides that where a notice is addressed, prepaid and sent by post it will be treated as being effectively served if it is sent to the addressee's last known principal place of residence, last known principal business address or registered or principal office.

Section 77 of the AA 1996 deals with the situation where the parties have agreed on a method of service but that method turns out to be impractical. In such a case the court may make an order as to how service may be effected or dispense with the requirement for service altogether. A party may only apply to the court for such an order where all other available arbitral processes for resolving the matter have been exhausted.

15 Procedure for the Reference

15.1 CONDUCTING THE REFERENCE

The underlying jurisprudence which established the AA 1996 is to be found in s. 1 of the Act. This is that the object of arbitration is to obtain the fair resolution of disputes without unnecessary delay or expense, that party autonomy should prevail subject to such safeguards as are necessary in the public interest, and that court intervention should be kept to a minimum.

15.1.1 The arbitral tribunal

The AA 1996 provides the arbitral tribunal with certain duties and powers to give effect to the principles established in s. 1. The arbitral tribunal's duty in s. 33(1) is to conduct the arbitration fairly and impartially and to adopt suitable procedures which avoid unnecessary delay or expense but which still provide a fair means for the resolution of the parties' dispute. For example, the arbitral tribunal has to permit both parties to be heard on points of procedure as well as the substantive issues in the arbitration or it may be considered to be acting impartially: *Damond Lock Grabowski and Partners* v *Laing Investments (Bracknell) Ltd* (1992) 60 BLR 112. (The arbitral tribunal's duty under s. 33 of the AA 1996 is discussed in chapter 8.)

The arbitral tribunal's duty to be fair and impartial reflects the principles of natural justice and is fundamental to the concept of arbitration as a quasi-judicial process. The court may therefore remove the arbitral tribunal if circumstances exist which give rise to justifiable doubts as to its impartiality: s. 24(a) of the AA 1996 (see chapter 7). There is a wealth of case law which illustrates actual bias. In *Parker* v *Burroughs* (1702) Colles 257 the infamous Dr Titus Oates held a will to be invalid when he had not been invited to preach at the deceased's funeral. This decision was held to be invalid. In *Re an Arbitration between SS Catalina (Owners) and MV Norma (Owners)* (1938) 61 Ll L Rep 360 an arbitrator, during the hearing of the case, was heard to say:

> The Italians are all liars in these cases and will say anything to suit their book. The same thing applies to the Portuguese. But the other side here are Norwe-

gians, and in my experience the Norwegians are generally a truthful people. In this case I entirely accept the evidence of the master of the *Norma*.

The arbitrator was removed for misconduct under s. 11 of the AA 1889 as what he had said amounted to actual bias. In arriving at this decision the court referred to the much quoted dictum of Lord Hewart CJ in *R* v *Sussex Justices, ex parte McCarthy* [1924] 1 KB 256 that it is 'of fundamental importance that justice should not only be done, but should manifestly and undoubtedly be seen to be done'. The test to be applied is whether having regard to all the circumstances there is a real danger of bias on the part of the arbitral tribunal in that it may regard unfairly the case of one of the parties to the dispute: *R* v *Gough* [1993] AC 646 and *Laker Airways Inc.* v *FLS Aerospace Ltd* (1999) *The Times*, 21 May.

The arbitral tribunal's powers to conduct the proceedings are in the first place provided in the arbitration agreement. Where the parties have not agreed such powers the AA 1996 implies certain powers into the parties' agreement. The general powers of the arbitral tribunal on procedural and evidential matters are found in s. 34 of the AA 1996. In addition the arbitral tribunal has the power to appoint experts, legal advisers or assessors under s. 37; to order a claimant to provide security for costs of the arbitration under s. 38(3); to give directions in relation to any property which is the subject of the proceedings under s. 38(4); to direct that a party or witness may be examined on oath or affirmation under s. 38(5); to give directions to a party to preserve any evidence in its custody or control under s. 38(6); to make provisional awards under s. 39; and to penalise a party for failing to comply with a peremptory order. The arbitral tribunal's powers are wide in order for it to be able to deal effectively with most matters which may occur in the proceedings. The AA 1996 also provides, in the absence of a contrary agreement by the parties, that a party may apply to the court in respect of its ancillary powers in s. 44. The court's powers are only exercisable in support of the arbitral tribunal in keeping with the principle in s. 1(c) that the court's intervention should be kept to a minimum. To this end s. 44(5) states:

> In any case the court shall act only if or to the extent that the arbitral tribunal, and any arbitral or other institution or person vested by the parties with power in that regard, has no power or is unable for the time being to act effectively.

15.1.2 The parties

The AA 1996 is silent as to the procedure to be adopted by the arbitral tribunal in the conduct of the reference. The reason for this stems from the principle that the parties should be autonomous in the choice of the procedure to resolve their dispute. There is also a practical reason. Resolution of disputes by arbitration covers a broad spectrum of subject matters. The parties may elect that a complex building dispute be resolved by arbitration or the dispute may involve funeral arrangements, shipping matters, trade, rent review or disputes regarding a country's boundaries. It would not be possible for an Act to set out procedural rules which would be suitable for all or any of these disputes. The courts have similarly refused to set out rules under which the arbitration should be conducted. Arbitration is a creature of agreement of the parties to the dispute. It is for the parties to agree the procedure of the arbitration. The parties may do this on an ad hoc basis or they may refer to arbitration rules or institutional rules, which provide the procedural mechanism for the resolution of the dispute. In order to give effect to the principle of party autonomy the arbitral tribunal's wide powers to conduct the proceedings in the AA 1996 only apply where the parties have not agreed to the contrary. Similarly, the court's role is intended only to be supportive of the arbitral process and not interventionary. See for example ss. 18, 42(3) and 44(5) of the AA 1996 (see chapter 10).

The parties also have a mandatory duty in s. 40(1) of the AA 1996 to do 'all things necessary for the proper and expeditious conduct of the arbitral proceedings'. This includes complying without delay with any order made by the arbitral tribunal (s. 40(1)(a)) and taking without delay any necessary steps to obtain a decision of the court on a preliminary question of jurisdiction or law: s. 40(1)(b). If a party does not comply with a peremptory order of the arbitral tribunal then it may be penalised by the arbitral tribunal: s. 41. The court has further powers under s. 42 to enforce the arbitral tribunal's peremptory orders if a party defaults. However, ss. 41 and 42 are not mandatory. The parties are free to provide the arbitral tribunal with alternative powers in case of a party's default (s. 41(1)) and may exclude the enforcement powers of the court: s. 42(1).

The DAC committee throughout its February 1996 report stressed its desire that the parties should not use provisions of the AA 1996 to apply to the court so as to obstruct or delay the proper conduct of the arbitration. The AA 1996 therefore contains mandatory sections which the parties cannot exclude, such as s. 73, which was inserted into the Act as a 'put up or shut up' provision: see para. 105 of the DAC report of February 1996. Section 73 of the AA 1996 requires a party to object forthwith in the arbitration on any matter which it may later seek to raise before the arbitral tribunal or the court. Furthermore, s. 70 ensures that any challenge to the award under ss. 67 to 69 cannot be made unless the applicant or appellant has first exhausted any available arbitral process of appeal or review, or recourse under s. 57 to remit an award back to the arbitral tribunal or to seek an additional award (see chapter 12).

15.2 EXPRESS AGREEMENTS ON PROCEDURE

The parties may expressly agree in the arbitration agreement the procedure to be adopted in the arbitration or that the arbitration should be conducted under institutional rules or other arbitration rules. The parties may also choose to agree the procedural rules after the arbitration has been commenced.

Where the arbitration procedure is referred to or set out in the arbitration agreement, the arbitral tribunal is bound to follow that agreement. Where the agreement is made after the arbitral tribunal has been appointed, it may object to the procedure chosen if it considers that the procedure will prevent it fulfilling its mandatory duty under s. 33(1) of the AA 1996. The benefit of adopting arbitration rules for the conduct of the reference is that at the outset of the matter the parties are aware of a timetable for the submission of their respective claims and for other interlocutory procedures. This will usually save time and the expense of a preliminary hearing for the resolution of these matters. However, the arbitration rules adopted can at best be seen as a template for the conduct of the reference. It would be impossible to set out rules which would cover every eventuality and situation. The JCT Rules were often criticised for their inflexibility in imposing time constrictions on the parties which were wholly unrealistic in a complex building dispute. The JCT has now adopted the Construction Industry Model Arbitration Rules (CIMAR), which incorporate advisory procedures for use with its standard forms of contract. This is to be welcomed as the CIMAR allow for greater flexibility and are drafted to be applied with the AA 1996.

15.3   IMPLIED AGREEMENTS ON PROCEDURE

At common law the agreement of the parties to an arbitration need not be express but could be determined by their conduct. In *Star International Hong Kong (UK) Ltd* v *Bergbau-Handel GmbH* [1966] 2 Lloyd's Rep 16 it was held that the conduct of the parties indicated clearly that neither of them intended an oral hearing to take place and in light of such conduct there was created an implied agreement. If the arbitration agreement provided for the exchange of pleadings, it could be implied that a formal High Court procedure should be adopted: *London Export Corporation Ltd* v *Jubilee Coffee Roasting Co. Ltd* [1958] 1 WLR 271.

However, s. 34(1) of the AA 1996 states that: 'It shall be for the tribunal to decide all procedural and evidential matters, subject to the right of the parties to agree any matter'. The words 'agree any matter' refer to an agreement in writing within the provisions of s. 5. Where the parties have not expressly agreed procedural matters in writing, the arbitral tribunal should give both parties an opportunity to address it on matters of procedure which can be implied from the parties' agreement or from the parties' conduct, trade or business practices. In doing so the arbitral tribunal will be complying with its duty under s. 33(1) of the AA 1996.

15.4   COMMENCING THE ARBITRATION

Arbitration proceedings are normally commenced by one party serving on another party a notice of dispute requiring that party to appoint an arbitrator or to agree to the appointment of an arbitrator. However, there are alternative ways of commencing the arbitration under certain institutional rules. For example, Article 1 of the Rules of the London Court of International Arbitration requires a party who wishes to commence arbitration proceedings to 'send to the Registrar of the Court . . . a written request for arbitration'. Where the arbitration agreement stipulates a time limit for referring future disputes to arbitration a party who wishes to commence proceedings outside that time limit can apply to the court under s. 12(2) of the AA 1996 for an order to extend the time limit. This is further discussed in chapter 5. Appointing the arbitral tribunal is discussed in chapter 7.

15.5 PRELIMINARY MEETING

A preliminary meeting gives the first opportunity for the arbitral tribunal and the parties to meet and discuss the procedure for the reference. Where the parties have not agreed a procedural or evidential matter the arbitral tribunal has the power to decide these matters under s. 34 of the AA 1996. In many cases, particularly where the arbitral tribunal has been appointed by an institutional body such as the Chartered Institute of Arbitrators, the RICS or the ICC, the preliminary meeting will be the first opportunity for the arbitral tribunal to impose its authority on the reference and in some cases to confirm its fees.

It is customary practice for an arbitral tribunal to send to the parties an agenda for the conduct of the preliminary meeting. This will set out the matters that the arbitral tribunal wishes to be discussed, such as whether the strict rules of evidence are to be used (s. 34(2)(f) of the AA 1996) and whether and to what extent there should be oral or written submissions or evidence: s. 34(2)(h) of the AA 1996. If the arbitration is an international one, the arbitral tribunal may wish to discuss the language or languages to be used in the proceedings and whether any translations are necessary: s. 34(2)(b) of the AA 1996. If the parties to the arbitration are lay persons who are not being represented by lawyers, the arbitral tribunal may wish to discuss whether and to what extent it should proceed inquisitorially: s. 34(2)(g) of the AA 1996. The preliminary meeting is generally required only where the dispute is relatively complex. In a simple matter or in a documents-only claim a set of proposed directions may be sent to the parties for their comments. Upon receipt of the parties' comments a formal order for directions may be made.

Where there is a preliminary meeting a number of matters should be addressed. If the arbitral tribunal has not seen the arbitration agreement, this should be produced so that the tribunal may confirm that it has jurisdiction to act. In many cases, however, the arbitral tribunal may have already seen this document as a prerequisite to its appointment. At this point one or more of the parties may raise a preliminary issue which will need to be resolved by the arbitral tribunal. A party may object to the arbitral tribunal's substantive jurisdiction under s. 31 of the AA 1996. The preliminary meeting may have to be adjourned while the arbitral tribunal decides upon its jurisdiction under s. 30 of the AA 1996, unless the parties have excluded this right in their arbitration agreement. If this is the case, the party objecting will have to apply to the court to decide the matter under s. 32 of the AA 1996. The arbitral proceedings may continue if the parties agree: s. 32(4) of the AA 1996. Another issue which may have to be determined at this juncture is the seat of the arbitration.

The parties at the preliminary meeting may agree a statement of facts. Such a statement will save time and costs, as these facts will not have to be proved. The arbitral tribunal must take account of this statement in making its award: *Techno Ltd* v *Allied Dunbar Assurance plc* [1993] 1 EGLR 29. The arbitral tribunal has the discretion to hear submissions from the parties as to any of the facts in the statement if they are unclear or ambiguous. The arbitral tribunal should allow the parties to make full submissions on facts if they later agree to dispense with the agreement: s. 33 of the AA 1996; *Techno Ltd* v *Allied Dunbar Assurance plc.*

If the parties have not already decided whether they are to be represented by lawyers or other persons, this should be discussed. The parties have the right to legal representation under s. 36 of the AA 1996. There should also be a general discussion of the items in dispute to clarify the issues which the arbitral tribunal is to resolve. A programme for the conduct of the reference should also be determined. This will involve timetabling the service of the claim, defence and counterclaim, replies and other rejoinders, if this is appropriate: s. 34(2)(c) of the AA 1996. An agreement should be reached as to whether disclosure is to take place, whether it is to be limited to certain documents and the form for inspecting documents. If the parties can reach no agreement, the arbitral tribunal can exercise its discretion under s. 34(2)(d) of the AA 1996. An agreement as to the number of witnesses and experts and the time limits for obtaining statements from those witnesses and experts may also be made in the preliminary meeting. There may be a decision as to when the meeting of experts and the exchange of experts' statements should be undertaken: s. 34(2)(f) of the AA 1996. The arbitral tribunal and the parties should always be aware that setting a timetable which goes many months into the future leaves open the risk that further hearings will be needed to reformulate that timetable. Possible delays such as the illness of witnesses, experts and lawyers as well as other commitments that the parties have may jeopardise the timetable. The arbitral tribunal may wish to set the venue for the hearing: s. 34(2)(a) of the AA 1996.

Where a timetable is set down the arbitral tribunal should not slavishly adhere to it where a party has a reasonable excuse for not complying with some or all of the directions. In *Damond Lock Grabowski and Partners* v *Laing Investments (Bracknell) Ltd* (1992) 60 BLR 112 the arbitrator refused to adjourn the main hearing after one of the parties objected that it had not had sufficient time to prepare for the hearing because of the late disclosure of further documents by the other party. The arbitrator held that:

> The present situation is brought about by the lack of preparation in the early months by the respondent's unwillingness to comply with my orders for directions at the time a joinder was suggested . . . I cannot now assist and sufficient time must be found by the respondents and their agents for the necessary preparation.

The arbitrator's decision not to allow further time was overturned by the courts and he was removed. The court held that:

The latest and most serious complaint is the arbitrator's refusal to postpone the hearing date despite the fact that the applicant's solicitors and counsel are simply not ready for the hearing. Whether or not that is partly their fault (it cannot be wholly their fault in view of the late and enormous further discovery by the respondent) is not the question. The fact remains that their case is still unprepared for the hearing date insisted upon by the arbitrator. There was no suggestion of an adjournment in his letter to the court of 21 February, indeed quite the contrary. See paragraph 5 where he says 'I consider that any appeal should not be considered at this stage but deferred until I have heard the evidence and my award is made available'. . . . looking at the whole sorry history of the matter it seems to me clear that the arbitral tribunal has unquestionably pointed the finger at the applicants and repeatedly accused them, in my judgment unfairly, of deliberate delay. Above all, he has not paid proper heed to their objections and insisted that the hearing must start on the day he ordered when they cannot be in a position to conduct their case properly. In my judgment he must be removed.

15.6   A STATEMENT OF THE ISSUES

The arbitral tribunal has a discretion under s. 34(2)(c) of the AA 1996, unless the parties have agreed otherwise to consider 'whether any and if so what form of written statements of claim and defence are to be used'. The arbitral tribunal may dispense with written statements altogether. They are not necessary in every arbitration, such as in commodity arbitrations where the issue is one of deficiency in quality and the parties are aware of the issues in dispute. However, in most arbitrations there will be a requirement for some form of written statement detailing the case that each party alleges and the remedy each party seeks.

15.6.1   Pleadings

Statements of case (now referred to as 'pleadings' under the CPR 1999) should set out the facts in the dispute in a chronological form and the remedy that a party seeks.

In arbitrations the normal form which the pleadings take are:

    Points of claim.
    Points of defence and counterclaim (if any).
    Points of reply and defence to counterclaim (if any).
    Points of reply to defence to counterclaim (if any).

In addition to these standard forms of pleadings there may also be a rejoinder, which is a response to the points of reply to defence to counterclaim, and a surrejoinder, which is a response to the rejoinder. Rejoinders and surrejoinders are rare and would only be used if the points of reply to defence to counterclaim or the rejoinder raised new issues, such as fraud, which had not previously been raised.

Where a pleading is deficient, in that it fails to set out sufficiently the facts on which the claim is based, the arbitral tribunal may order, on request from a party to the arbitration, that other party to provide further information relating to that pleading. A request for further information will set out the part of the statement of case in which it is alleged that insufficient particulars were given and thereafter request the particulars required to remedy the defect. Alternatively the party which claims the pleading is deficient may seek further information to help clarify the pleading.

15.6.2 Statements of case in arbitration proceedings

Statements of case in arbitration proceedings should be distinguished from statements of case under the Civil Procedure Rules 1998. Statements of case in arbitration proceedings will provide more information than points of claim. A statement of case can include the law and evidence a party seeks to rely on as well as the material facts of the dispute. Under the JCT Arbitration Rules 1988 a statement of case was the form in which the issues to be determined had to be presented. The JCT Arbitration Rules 1988 provide in rules 3.4 and 3.5 that the statement of case shall be in writing, set out the factual and legal basis relied upon and specify the remedy sought and the monetary sum sought under each head of claim. Claims and defences made under the JCT Arbitration Rules 1988 must be supported with the principal documents on which reliance is placed. Reference to what should or should not be included in a statement of case can only be found within the arbitration rules that provide for the statement of case. Where there are no arbitration rules the arbitral tribunal should specify what it requires to be included within the statement of case.

15.6.3 Letters

The arbitral tribunal may order, or the parties may agree, that they set out their respective claims in informal letters rather than prepare and submit formal pleadings or a statement of case. This may occur when the matter in dispute is not complex, such as in a consumer arbitration where each party can submit to the arbitral tribunal its case in a simple letter with all the relevant evidence attached to it.

15.6.4 Scott Schedules

A Scott Schedule is a form of pleading which puts together in tabular form the parties' respective claim and defence. It also includes a column for the arbitral tribunal's comments. The concept behind the Scott Schedule is that there is a single document for the management of the parties' dispute. There is no set form of headings for a Scott Schedule and much will depend on whether it is being used in a case relating to defects or variations or work done by the contractor. For suggestions of which headings to use in any particular case see A. May, *Keating on Building Contracts*, 6th ed. (London: Sweet & Maxwell, 1995) pp. 480–7.

The purpose of the Scott Schedule is to inform the arbitral tribunal of the respective cases of the parties. To achieve this there are some basic requirements with which the Scott Schedule should comply. First, it should have a column for the numbering of each item in dispute between the parties. Secondly, it should have a full description of the claim made. There should be a column for liability and a column for quantum. Thirdly, there should be column for the respondent to address each of the claims made as to liability and to quantum. Fourthly, there should be a column for the arbitral tribunal to make its comments. In the *Supreme Court Practice 1997* (London: Sweet & Maxwell, 1996) the learned editors' note 18/12/15 says: 'The Scott Schedule is a useful procedural device which achieves a considerable saving in time and money'. The arbitral tribunal should therefore consider whether the use of a Scott Schedule would be of assistance when considering its obligations to the parties under s. 33 of the AA 1996. However, the preparation and completion of a Scott Schedule is a time-consuming and expensive process. Prior to ordering a Scott Schedule the arbitral tribunal should therefore hear representations from each party as to the suitability of pleading the matter in such a form.

Where the parties agree that their claims should be pleaded in the form of a Scott Schedule then the arbitral tribunal is obliged to address each aspect of the schedule: *Ledwood Construction* v *Kier Construction* (1996) 28 BLISS 5. Under the AA 1950 a failure to do so by the arbitral tribunal constituted misconduct and in *Ledwood Construction* v *Kier Construction* the court remitted the award back to the arbitral tribunal. Judge Hicks QC expressed the opinion: 'That there is really no room for doubt in my mind that both parties intended, expected and understood that the arbitral tribunal would express his award by reference to the Scott Schedule'. It follows that such a failure would constitute a serious irregularity under s. 68(2)(d) of the AA 1996.

15.6.5 Amendments

The parties are free to agree not to be restricted to written submissions produced at the beginning of the arbitration and that further matters may be disclosed at any time: *La Fontana Novela* v *Cornelius and Co. Ltd* [1996] ADRLN 9. Section 34(2)(c) of the AA 1996 enables the arbitral tribunal, unless the parties have agreed otherwise, to consider whether any amendments to the written statements of claim or defence should be permitted. If amendments are possible, the parties may amend their written statements at any time during the arbitration. Any amendment cannot go beyond the issues which the parties have agreed to submit to arbitration unless the parties agree to the amendment in writing and the arbitral tribunal agrees to have its jurisdiction extended: *Leif Hoegh & Co. A/S* v *Petrolsea Inc.* [1992]

1 Lloyd's Rep 45; *Ulysses Compania Naviera SA* v *Huntingdon Petroleum Services Ltd* [1990] 1 Lloyd's Rep 160. The discretion to permit amendments must be exercised by the arbitral tribunal in accordance with its duty under s. 33 of the AA 1996.

15.7 CROSS-CLAIMS

In English arbitration law a distinction needs to be made between two different forms of cross-claims: set-offs and counterclaims. The distinction is almost academic in litigation: *Hanak* v *Green* [1958] 2 QB 9. However, in arbitral proceedings the distinction is important. In litigation the English courts have for centuries had the jurisdiction to deal with both set-offs and counterclaims in the same action. In arbitration proceedings a set-off will always fall within the terms of the arbitration agreement. However, depending on the wording of the arbitration clause a counterclaim may not.

In *Re a Bankruptcy Notice* [1934] Ch 431 Lord Hanworth MR explained what was meant by a set-off:

> . . . 'set-off' . . . is a word well known and established in its meaning; it is something which provides a defence because the nature and quality of the sum so relied upon are such that it is a sum which is proper to be dealt with as diminishing the claim which is made, and against which the sum so demanded can be set off.

A set-off therefore can be raised in respect of goods sold where it can be shown that the quality of the goods were poor and therefore the seller should not be entitled to the whole or any of the sum claimed: *Mondel* v *Steel* (1841) 8 M & W 858. In contrast a counterclaim need not have any nexus with the claim raised. It need not be related to the claim. In the *Supreme Court Practice 1997* (London: Sweet & Maxwell, 1996) the learned editors' note 15/2/2 says:

> A set-off remains what it was — a defence to the plaintiff's claim or to a portion of it. . . . Every set-off can be pleaded as a counterclaim, if the defendant so desires; but every counterclaim cannot be pleaded as a set-off. A counterclaim is practically a cross-action. . . .
>
> The defendant's counterclaim need not be 'an action of the same nature as the original action' (per Fry J in *Beddall* v *Maitland* (1881) 17 ChD 174 at p. 181).

This distinction between set-offs and counterclaims is important as, in arbitral proceedings, a counterclaim can only be raised against a claim if it is a defence to the claim or the parties subsequently agree to allow the counterclaim to be raised in the same proceedings. A counterclaim that does not fulfil either of the above criteria will not be permitted to be pleaded in the arbitration. The parties may therefore be required to proceed by way of two separate and distinct proceedings.

In deciding whether a counterclaim can be pleaded in a subsisting matter reference must always be had to the wording of the arbitration agreement.

15.8 GLOBAL CLAIMS

A 'global claim' is a term which is used to describe a claim made which does not set out the causes of each breach and loss. The causal nexus between the wrongful act or omission of the respondent and the loss suffered by the claimant may have to be inferred: *Bernhard's Rugby Landscapes Ltd* v *Stockley Park Consortium Ltd* (1997) 82 BLR 39. A global claim only sets out the total loss. A global claim may be made in litigation, arbitration or during the course of the contract. It is for the claimant to decide whether to plead its case as a global claim unless it is a claim under the agreement of the parties: *Inserco Ltd* v *Honeywell Control Systems* (1998) CILL 1368. In *GMTC Tools and Equipment Ltd* v *Yuasa Warwick Machinery Ltd* (1994) 73 BLR 102 the Court of Appeal held that the plaintiffs should 'be permitted to formulate their claims for damages as they wish, and not be forced into a straitjacket of the judge's or their opponents' choosing' (per Leggatt LJ at p. 113). In *Crosby and Sons Ltd* v *Portland Urban District Council* (1967) 5 BLR 121 it was held that global claims are permissible subject to three conditions:

(a) The events which are the subject of the claim must be complex and interact so that it is difficult, if not impossible, to make an accurate apportionment. It is very tempting to take the easy course and to lump all the delaying events together in order to justify the total overrun or total financial shortfall. The argument is justifiable only if the alternative course is shown to be impractical.

(b) There must be no duplication. This point is self evident.

(c) Any financial claim must exclude profit, if profit is irrecoverable under one or more heads of the underlying claim.

In *Merton London Borough Council* v *Stanley Hugh Leach Ltd* (1985) 32 BLR 51 Vinelott J confirmed that where it is impractical to disentangle or disintegrate the part directly attributable to each head of claim, a global claim could be made. Vinelott J, however, also held that where the claimant had unreasonably delayed making the claim so that it had caused the complexity in the claim, this would prevent the claimant from making a global claim. The principles in *Crosby and Sons Ltd* v *Portland Urban District Council* and *Merton London Borough Council* v *Stanley Hugh Leach Ltd* were applied in *Bernhard's Rugby Landscapes Ltd* v *Stockley Park Consortium Ltd*, in which the court also added that in such cases causation could be implied rather than demonstrated. The court in *Bernhard's Rugby Landscapes Ltd* v *Stockley Park Consortium Ltd* also considered *British Airways Pension Trustees Ltd* v *Sir Robert McAlpine and Sons Ltd* (1994) 72 BLR 26 and whether global claims tended to embarrass, prejudice or delay a fair trial and held that this depended on the pleading itself. The plaintiff in *Wharf Properties Ltd* v *Eric Cumine Associates (No. 2)* (1991) 52 BLR 1 pleaded its case as a global claim which was struck out as being embarrassing to the respondent. The facts of the case were unusual, but one of the grounds on which the Judicial Committee of the Privy Council arrived at its decision was that the claim failed in a fundamental principle of natural justice, namely, that 'the purpose of the pleading is to indicate with clarity to the adverse party, and to the court, the case that the pleader is seeking to make'. A global claim cannot therefore be used to avoid setting out a proper claim. It should only be used where it is impractical or impossible to particularise the cause of each breach and loss such as in complex quantum disputes.

15.9   INTERIM HEARINGS AND APPLICATIONS

Where it is impractical to deal with all procedural matters at the outset of the arbitration further interim hearings will be required so that the case may proceed without delay. Where the parties cannot agree a procedural matter a decision will have to be made on the issue by the arbitral tribunal. It may be that the arbitral tribunal is able to deal with the issue by means of written submissions by the parties. Alternatively it may take the view that the matter should be resolved by oral representations. In either case both parties must be heard in respect of the matter: s. 33(1) of the AA 1996; *Damond Lock Grabowski and Partners* v *Laing Investments (Bracknell) Ltd* (1992) 60 BLR 112.

The parties are bound by s. 40(1) of the AA 1996 to do 'all things necessary for the proper and expeditious conduct of the arbitral proceedings' such as comply with any interim order made by the arbitral tribunal. Section 40(2)(a) specifically provides that the s. 40(1) duty includes a duty to comply 'without delay with any determination of the tribunal as to procedural or evidential matters, or with any order or directions of the tribunal'. If a claimant does not comply with an interim order, the arbitral tribunal may use its powers under s. 41(3) of the AA 1996 to sanction the non-compliant party (see 9.7.1).

If a party fails to attend or be represented at an oral hearing after notice of it has been served, the arbitral tribunal may continue the proceedings in the absence of that party: s. 41(4)(a) of the AA 1996. Similarly, where the arbitration is to be dealt with in writing, the arbitral tribunal may proceed to an award where a party fails to provide written evidence or make a written submission after the requisite notice has been served: s. 41(4)(b) of the AA 1996. The arbitral tribunal's powers under s. 41 of the AA 1996 are not mandatory. The parties are free to agree the powers of the arbitral tribunal in case a party fails to comply with its mandatory duty under s. 40 of the AA 1996: s. 41(1) of the AA 1996. If the parties have not made such an agreement, the provisions in s. 41(3) to (7) apply: s. 41(2) of the AA 1996.

The arbitral tribunal is under no obligation to state the reasons for an interim decision. The obligation to state reasons only applies to an award where the parties have not agreed otherwise: s. 52(4) of the AA 1996. Interim orders are not awards and cannot be challenged under the AA 1996. Interim orders are simply decisions on procedure. The case of *Three Valleys Water Committee* v *Binnie and Partners* (1990) 52 BLR 42 is as applicable to the AA 1996 as it was to the AA 1950. In it Steyn J held that even if the arbitrator had made an error there would have been no grounds for removing him since making errors is an occupational hazard for arbitrators. Where the arbitral tribunal has published an award that deals with procedural matters the court will not have the jurisdiction to overturn those procedural decisions: *Exmar BV* v *National Iranian Trader Co.* [1992] 1 Lloyd's Rep 169.

15.10 DISCLOSURE

Section 34(2)(d) of the AA 1996 gives the arbitral tribunal the power to make an order akin to an order for disclosure in court proceedings if the parties have not agreed otherwise. The arbitral tribunal has a discretion to decide: 'whether any and if so which documents or classes of documents should be disclosed between and produced by the parties and at what stage'.

Section 34(2)(d) of the AA 1996 does not place any restrictions on which documents should be disclosed. Unless the parties have agreed in writing to the contrary, the arbitral tribunal has a wide discretion to exercise its power subject only to its duty under s. 33(1) of the AA 1996. The arbitral tribunal may simply order that certain documents are to be attached to the claim or defence, or order that no documents need to be disclosed at all.

Disclosure is the new terminology in the courts for what was previously known as discovery. By CPR, r. 31.5(1) a court order for disclosure is an order for a party to give standard disclosure, unless the court directs otherwise. Under CPR, r. 31.6(1), standard disclosure requires a party to disclose only:

(a)   the documents on which he relies; and
(b)   the documents which:

   (i)   adversely affect his own case;
   (ii)   adversely affect another party's case; or
   (iii)   support another party's case; and

(c)   the documents which he is required to disclose by a relevant practice direction.

A party who is required to give standard disclosure is also required by CPR, r. 31.7 to make a reasonable search for the documents. The new rules regarding disclosure of documents only require a party to make an effort to disclose documents which is proportional to the type of case being litigated. The kind of search that will be necessary is determined by how many documents are involved and the cost and ease of retrieving them. The complexity of the issues and the significance of the documents will also be factors to consider. See generally CPR, r. 31 and PD 31 for the rules on disclosure.

If a party fails to comply with an order for disclosure, the arbitral tribunal may make a peremptory order to the same effect. The failure to comply with a peremptory order for disclosure of documents may lead to delays and the sanction of consequential costs penalties: s. 41(7)(d) of the AA 1996. The arbitral tribunal may also draw adverse inferences against such a party: s. 41(7)(b) of the AA 1996. However, the arbitral tribunal can only order disclosure of documents against the parties to the arbitration it is conducting: *Kirkawa Corporation* v *Gatoil Overseas Ltd, The Peter Kirk* [1990] 1 Lloyd's Rep 154. The arbitral tribunal does not have the power to order disclosure against a person who is not a party to the arbitration.

It would now be extremely unusual for the arbitral tribunal to order formal lists of documents for what was known as full English discovery. It may, in certain circumstances, be reasonable for the arbitral tribunal to dispense with disclosure altogether and/or proceed straight to the inspection of the documents stage or limit discovery to specific relevant documents. The effect of this may save time and costs to the parties and such action would therefore accord with the arbitral tribunal's duty under s. 33(1) of the AA 1996.

15.10.1 'Documents'

'Document' is defined in r. 31.4 of the CPR as 'anything in which information of any description is recorded'. This definition is identical to that found in s. 13 of the Civil Evidence Act 1995. In the old RSC, ord. 24 (discovery and inspection of documents), the term 'documents' was not defined but was held to include information recorded in a written form or in the form of a tape recording (*Grant* v *Southwestern and county Properties Ltd* [1975] Ch 185) or computer discs in so far as they contain information which is capable of being retrieved: *Derby and Co. Ltd* v *Weldon (No. 9)* [1991] 1 WLR 652.

It is unclear from the definition in CPR, r. 31.6(1) whether documents which contain information which may lead the opposing party into making inquiries to obtain evidence should now be disclosed. Previously, such documents were subject to the rules relating to discovery: *Compagnie Financiere et Commerciale du Pacifiqu* v *Peruvian Guano Co.* (1882) 11 QBD 5.

15.10.2 Privileged documents

The common law rules relating to privileged documents and without prejudice communications apply to arbitration proceedings: *K/S A/S Bill Biakh* v *Hyundai Corporation* [1988] 1 Lloyd's Rep 187. Certain documents, although relevant to the facts in issue, are privileged from production and inspection unless the party that is required to disclose has waived the privilege. Privileged documents can be divided into two categories. First, those documents which are privileged whether or not they were made in contemplation or pending legal proceedings, for example, any communications between a party and the party's legal adviser which are confidential and written to or by the party in a professional context for the purpose of obtaining legal advice and/or assistance: *Derby and Co. Ltd* v *Weldon (No. 7)* [1990] 1 WLR 1156. Secondly, documents which were made or came into existence when legal proceedings were contemplated or pending, for example, any communications between a party's legal adviser and a third party, such as witness statements and expert reports. The second category includes any communication between a party personally and a third party if the dominant purpose for preparing it was to submit it to the party's legal adviser in respect of contemplated or pending legal proceedings: *Waugh* v *British Railways Board* [1980] AC 521.

15.10.3 Without prejudice correspondence

The purpose of heading correspondence with the words 'without prejudice' is that the maker of the offer or statement is not prejudiced if the terms proposed are not accepted. Offers or statements which have been made in the course of negotiations on a without prejudice basis, including admissions, are inadmissible and therefore are not disclosed unless a party waives the right to privilege: *Walker* v *Wisher* (1889) 23 QBD 335 per Lindley LJ at p. 337; *Rush and Tompkins Ltd* v *Greater London Council* [1989] AC 1280. In arbitration proceedings the most common form of this type of without prejudice correspondence is the *Calderbank* letter. This is a letter which makes an offer of settlement and is headed 'without prejudice save as to costs'. It is used in arbitration proceedings because a party is unable to make a payment into court on condition that if the payment is not exceeded, in the hearing of the matter, the costs from the date when the payment in is made go to that party. *Calderbank* letters and their effect on the issue of costs have been dealt with in chapter 13.

An exception to this general rule exists where the without prejudice correspondence is not used in regard to an issue of liability but rather to show that a dispute exists between the parties. In *Secretary of State for Foreign and Commonwealth Affairs* v *Percy International & Kier International* (1998 Judgment — ORB No. 635) Judge Bowsher QC held that: 'such without prejudice communications may be admitted in evidence in proceedings such as the present to determine whether there was a dispute at the relevant time, but not when, if at all, there is a trial on liability'.

15.10.4 Documents in a party's control

A party's duty to disclose documents under CPR, r. 31.8(1) is limited to documents which are now or have been previously within a party's control. Under CPR, r. 31.8(2) a document is or was in a party's control if:

(a) it is or was in his physical possession;
(b) he has or has had a right to possession of it; or

(c) he has or had a right to inspect or take copies of it.

Under the old system of discovery, a party's duty to disclose documents was
limited to those documents which were in that party's possession, custody or
power. Section 34(2)(d) of the AA 1996 does not make any stipulation as to the
level of possession needed or the rights over the document before disclosure can
be ordered. Section 34(2)(d) of the AA 1996 merely states that '. . . documents or
classes of documents should be disclosed between and produced by the parties
. . .'. The arbitral tribunal's power is likely to be the same as it is in relation to
property which is the subject matter of the proceedings. Section 38(4) of the AA
1996 gives the arbitral tribunal the discretion to order the inspection, preservation,
custody or detention of any such property 'which is owned by or is in the possession
of a party to the proceedings . . .'. There is in practice a negligible difference between
having control over a document and having possession or power over it. Possession
of a document is distinguished from a mere holding of a document. The mere holding
of a document is 'custody'. A bailee or agent has possession of documents entrusted
to it but a servant or employee will merely have custody of them. Documents that are
in a person's power include those which, although not in the possession or custody of
that person, give that person a right to obtain them from a third party who has them,
for example, the owner of a document who has not parted with the right to
possession. It is a question of fact whether the documents of a subsidiary company
are within the power of its parent company: *Lonrho Ltd* v *Shell Petroleum Ltd* [1981]
2 All ER 456. However, as under the previous legislation, the arbitral tribunal has no
jurisdiction to make any order against a non-party to the reference and so cannot
order disclosure of a document in the possession of a third party.

15.11 THE HEARING

Prior to the AA 1996 the hearing of an arbitration had to be run on the basis of
an adversarial procedure rather than inquisitorially, unless the parties had agreed
otherwise. Section 34(2)(g) of the AA 1996 now provides that unless the parties
have agreed otherwise it is for the arbitral tribunal to decide 'whether and to what
extent the tribunal should itself take the initiative in ascertaining the facts and law'.
The right of the arbitral tribunal to act inquisitorially is subject, however, to the
mandatory obligations imposed on the arbitral tribunal. Section 33(1)(a) of the AA
1996 provides that the arbitral tribunal must 'act fairly and impartially as between
the parties, giving each party a reasonable opportunity of putting his case and
dealing with that of his opponent'. Although the arbitral tribunal can therefore act
in an inquisitorial manner the parties must be allowed to test whatever evidence is
disclosed. In *Drew* v *Drew and Lebrun* (1855) 2 Macq 1 Lord Cranworth said, at
p. 3, that:

The principles of universal justice require that the person who is to be prejudiced
by the evidence ought to be present to hear it taken, to suggest cross-examination

or himself to cross-examine, and to be able to find evidence, if he can, that shall meet and answer it; in short, to deal with it as in the ordinary course of legal proceedings.

This statement of principle is equally applicable to arbitrations under the AA 1996.

15.11.1   Hearings on documents or submissions

There had been a presumption, prior to the AA 1996, that if the parties had not expressly or impliedly agreed otherwise the arbitration was to proceed by full oral hearing: *Altco Ltd* v *Sutherland* [1971] 2 Lloyd's Rep 515 at p. 518. This presumption has now been displaced by s. 34(2)(h) of the AA 1996, which provides that unless the parties have agreed the matter the arbitral tribunal shall decide 'whether and to what extent there should be oral or written evidence or submissions'.

The election by the arbitral tribunal that the reference be conducted other than by oral evidence will often occur where the amount in dispute is small and where the issues between the parties are clear and well-documented. The decision by the arbitral tribunal that the resolution of the dispute be dealt with other than by oral hearing must be taken with due regard to the arbitral tribunal's obligations under s. 33 of the AA 1996. If one of the parties submits that only on the examination of the witnesses would the matter be fairly determined, the arbitral tribunal should err on the side of caution and order a full hearing. The question for the arbitral tribunal to address is whether ordering that the matter should be dealt with by documents only will deprive one of the parties of the reasonable opportunity of putting its case.

Where the arbitral tribunal orders that the hearing is to be conducted on a documents-only basis, s. 41(4)(b) of the AA 1996 provides a sanction if one of the parties does not make submissions or provide written evidence as required:

If without showing sufficient cause a party—
. . .
    (b)   where matters are to be dealt with in writing, fails after due notice to submit written evidence or make written submissions,
the tribunal may continue the proceedings in the absence of that party or, as the case may be, without any written evidence or submissions on his behalf, and may make an award on the basis of the evidence before it.

15.11.2   Minimum requirements for the hearing

Mustill and Boyd, *Commercial Arbitration*, 2nd ed. (London: Butterworths, 1989) p. 302, set out six minimum requirements where there is to be a full hearing:

Where there is to be a full oral hearing, the following conditions must be observed:

1.   Each party must have notice that the hearing is to take place.
2.   Each party must have a reasonable opportunity to be present at the hearing together with his advisers and witnesses.
3.   Each party must have the opportunity to be present throughout the hearing.
4.   Each party must have the reasonable opportunity to present evidence and argument in support of his own case.
5.   Each party must have a reasonable opportunity to test his opponent's case by cross-examining his witnesses, presenting rebutting evidence and addressing oral argument.
6.   The hearing must, unless the contrary is expressly agreed, be the occasion on which the parties present the whole of their evidence and argument.

15.11.2.1   Notice of the hearing   The requirement that there be notice of the hearing was a common law requirement founded on principles of natural justice: *The Warwick* (1890) 15 PD 189; *Oswald* v *Earl Grey* (1855) 24 LJ QB 69. The principle is not only that the parties will have notice of when and where the hearing is to take place but also of the type of hearing: *M. Golodetz* v *Schrier* (1947) 80 Ll L Rep 647; *Thorburn* v *Barnes* (1867) LR 2 CP 384.

Section 41(4) of the AA 1996 now gives statutory effect to the common law rule in that the arbitral tribunal may proceed with a hearing in the absence of a party only if the party in non-attendance has had due notice of the hearing. If an arbitral tribunal were to proceed without due notice having been given to one of the parties, it would be likely to amount to a serious irregularity, under s. 68(2) of the AA 1996. In addition to those grounds of challenge to an award for serious irregularity, a party may seek to challenge the enforcement of the award under s. 66 or s. 103 of the AA 1996, where the award is a New York Convention award, or s. 37 of the AA 1950, where the award is a 'foreign award'. Section 66 of the AA 1996 applies to all arbitrations irrespective of where the seat of the arbitration lies. Section 66 provides that an award may be enforced in the same manner as a judgment or order of the court where leave of the court is given. Section 66(3) provides that leave shall not be given where the arbitral tribunal lacked substantive jurisdiction to make the award. All other grounds for refusing leave are discretionary. In *M. Golodetz* v *Schrier* (1947) 80 Ll L Rep 647 it was suggested that the failure to notify a party of the hearing would be a ground which could form a defence to an action on the award.

15.11.2.2   Reasonable opportunity to be present   Each party must have a reasonable opportunity to be present at the hearing together with its advisers and witnesses. This requirement follows on from the requirement that a party is entitled to have notice of the hearing. The arbitral tribunal should take into account the availability of the parties to attend at hearings when giving directions although the question of fixing a date remains with it. The courts have only been willing to become involved where there has been a positive abuse by the arbitral tribunal that breaches principles of natural justice: *Fetherstone* v *Cooper* (1803)

9 Ves Jr 67; *Re Whitwham's Trustees etc. and Wrexham Mold and Connah's Quay Rly Co.* (1895) 39 SJ 692; *Nares v Drury* (1864) 10 LT 305.

Under the AA 1996 the right of the parties to attend at hearings is not expressly stated. It is suggested that the right is so embedded within English arbitration law that the drafter of the AA 1996 saw no point in expressing what appeared so very obvious. The right, however, can be inferred from the obligations imposed on the arbitral tribunal by s. 33 of the AA 1996. Section 41 of the AA 1996 also gives further inference that a party must be able to attend. Section 41(4)(a) of the AA 1996 prohibits an arbitral tribunal proceeding in the absence of a party who has not been given due notice of the hearing. Section 36 of the AA 1996 states that 'Unless otherwise agreed by the parties, a party to arbitral proceedings may be represented in the proceedings by a lawyer or other person chosen by him'. The right to attend therefore is possessed not only by the parties to the arbitration but also by their counsel whether legal or otherwise.

As a general rule it would be a serious irregularity affecting the proceedings if a party were excluded from part or all of the hearing. The right to be present derives from a common law principle of natural justice. Only in the most exceptional circumstances could an arbitral tribunal exclude a party where the conduct of that party was so insulting or so disruptive as to make the continuation of the arbitration impossible. In *Re Haigh, Haigh v Haigh* (1861) 3 De G F & J 157 Turner LJ said: 'I certainly do not mean to lay it down that an arbitrator is bound to submit to insults from those who attend him'. Where an arbitral tribunal does exclude a party on this basis it should take every care that the party excluded is not prejudiced by the exclusion. In such an exceptional case the arbitral tribunal should, and may be criticised if it did not, take the initiative in ascertaining the facts and law pursuant to its power under s. 34(2)(g) of the AA 1996, unless the parties have agreed otherwise.

15.11.2.3 Reasonable opportunity to present its case Each party must have a reasonable opportunity to present evidence and argument in support of its own case. This requirement stems from established common law principle: *Montrose Canned Foods Ltd v Eric Wells (Merchants) Ltd* [1965] 1 Lloyd's Rep 597. This requirement is to be found in s. 33 of the AA 1996. The arbitral tribunal must allow a party to address it on matters of fact and law: *Modern Engineering (Bristol) Ltd v C. Miskin and Sons Ltd* [1981] 1 Lloyd's Rep 135. Such submissions on fact or law will usually be made orally but may, if the parties or arbitral tribunal have elected otherwise, be made in writing.

15.11.2.4 Reasonable opportunity to test the opponent's case Each party must have a reasonable opportunity to test its opponent's case by cross-examining its witnesses, presenting rebutting evidence and addressing oral argument. This requirement is now found in s. 33(1)(a) of the AA 1996. It is a fundamental principle of arbitration law that a party should have the opportunity to address both the evidence and the arguments of the opposing party. In *W.H. Ireland and Co. v*

C.T. Bowring and Co. Ltd (1920) 2 Ll L Rep 220 Bailhache J described this as a 'sacred principle'. Although the arbitral tribunal has the right to adopt an inquisitorial approach such an approach must be tempered by the requirement that the party also has the right to test the evidence of the opposing party.

15.11.2.5   The occasion to present the whole of the evidence and argument   The hearing must, unless the contrary is expressly agreed, be the occasion on which the parties present the whole of their evidence and argument. This principle does not mean that the arbitral tribunal cannot order that the parties supply opening and closing submissions in writing but rather refers to the principle that the arbitral tribunal cannot take cognisance of matters referred to outside of the arbitration or of its own secret knowledge. The parties are entitled to assume that the arbitral tribunal bases its decision on the arguments and evidence that it has heard at the hearing. The arbitral tribunal may not decide the matter on arguments that it has invented for itself which have not been tested by the parties. Such reliance on secret knowledge would be ground for challenge by reason of a serious irregularity in the proceedings: *Fox* v *P.G. Wellfair Ltd* [1981] 2 Lloyd's Rep 514. Similarly the arbitral tribunal is not entitled to base its decision on matters that have been referred to outside of the hearing because either or both of the parties have not had the opportunity to test this evidence: *Eastcheap Dried Fruit Co. NV* v *Gebroeders Catz Handelsvereeniging* [1962] 1 Lloyd's Rep 283. For this reason any correspondence which one party sends to the arbitral tribunal must be disclosed to all the other parties and any inspection of property by the arbitral tribunal must be made with all the parties present, unless they have agreed otherwise.

15.12   PROCEDURE AT THE HEARING

Sections 34 to 39 and 41 of the AA 1996 set out the powers of the arbitral tribunal that may be employed in the conduct of the arbitration proceedings, subject to what the parties have agreed. The AA 1996 does not set out how the arbitration hearing is to be conducted. The reason for this is that the arbitration should be conducted in the manner the parties have agreed: s. 1(b) of the AA 1996. Where the parties have not agreed how the arbitration should proceed it should be tailored to fit the dispute in question: s. 33(1)(b) of the AA 1996. The arbitral tribunal may adopt inquisitorial procedures if it sees fit: s. 34(2)(g) of the AA 1996. However, it is common for arbitrations to be conducted on an adversarial basis.

The usual procedure in an oral hearing is for the claimant to begin by opening its case. An opening consists of informing the arbitral tribunal of the facts of the case and the claim made by the claimant against the respondent. This opening will be supported by legal submission. The claimant then calls its evidence in support. This may take the form of written statements or oral evidence. The evidence is then cross-examined by the respondent. The claimant then gives a closing speech. The respondent thereafter opens its case and calls its evidence. The respondent then closes its case. The claimant may thereafter make a speech in reply.

The evidence that is given at the arbitration may be administered on oath unless the parties have otherwise agreed. Section 38(5) of the AA 1996 states:

The tribunal may direct that a party or witness shall be examined on oath or affirmation, and may for that purpose administer any necessary oath or take any necessary affirmation.

Failure to administer an oath properly will prevent any prosecution being brought for perjury. An oath should be taken in the following way. The witness should take the New Testament or Old Testament, as appropriate, in uplifted hand and say:

I swear by Almighty God that the evidence I shall give shall be the truth, the whole truth, and nothing but the truth.

A witness who objects to this method may give an oath in a way that is appropriate to his or her religion. There is a list of accepted forms in Phipson, *Evidence*, 14th ed. paras 9–28 to 9–30. An affirmation is made by the witness repeating after the arbitrator:

I do solemnly, sincerely and truly declare and affirm that the evidence that I shall give shall be the truth, the whole truth, and nothing but the truth.

It is a misconception that the penalties for perjury do not apply to an affirmation. Historically, the common law excluded evidence from non-Christians because of the requirement that evidence must be given on oath. This rule was reversed in *Omychund v Barker* (1745) 1 Atk 21 and evidence was later permitted from atheists by the Evidence Further Amendment Act 1869. The present law relating to oaths and affirmations is to be found in the Oaths Act 1978, which provides for the same penalties for a breach under affirmation as under oath.

If, after the oath has been given, a party to the arbitration refuses to answer any question which has been properly asked, the arbitral tribunal cannot compel an answer. The refusal may, however, be taken into account when the arbitral tribunal considers the credibility of the witness. The examining party may elect to call on the assistance of the courts as allowed by s. 44(2) of the AA 1996, provided the permission of the arbitral tribunal or the agreement in writing of the other parties has been obtained: s. 44(4) of the AA 1996.

The power of the courts to compel a witness to give evidence will depend on whether that witness is both competent and compellable. A witness who is both competent and compellable commits contempt of court by refusing to testify and may face the penalty of imprisonment and/or a fine. In most arbitration proceedings nearly all categories of persons would be competent and compellable. However, there are exceptions to this rule. Children, diplomats, sovereigns and persons of unsound mind are subject to exceptions.

If a party wishes to adduce new evidence after the hearing but before the award is made, it is up to the arbitral tribunal to decide whether this evidence should be admitted. However, both parties must be given the opportunity to address the arbitral tribunal on the new evidence: s. 33(1)(a) of the AA 1996; *Sociedad Iberica de Molturacion SA* v *Nidera Handelscompagnie BV* [1990] 2 Lloyd's Rep 240.

15.13 EVIDENCE

In arbitration proceedings the parties may decide whether the strict rules of evidence or any other rules should apply to the arbitration, or whether no rules should apply and that all evidence is admissible regardless of whether it would be admissible in a court of law. In the absence of any such agreement the arbitral tribunal has the power to decide this matter under s. 34(2)(f) of the AA 1996. The main rules of evidence are discussed below:

15.13.1 Documents

For a general definition of 'documents' see 15.10.1. In court proceedings a party seeking to rely on a statement contained in a document is bound by s. 8(1)(a) of the Civil Evidence Act (CEA) 1995 to produce the original of that document if it is available. Alternatively that party is bound by s. 8(1)(b) of the CEA 1995 to produce a copy of that document or the material part of it, whether or not that document is still in existence, which should be authenticated in such manner as the court may approve, for example, by a witness identifying it as a true copy: *Kajala* v *Noble* (1982) 75 Cr App R 149. It is immaterial whether the copy of the document is a copy of the original: s. 8(2) of the CEA 1995.

It is now easier in civil proceedings to have business and public records admitted in evidence. By s. 9(1) of the CEA 1995 a document which is shown to form part of the records of a business or public authority may be received in evidence in civil proceedings without further proof. Section 9(2) of the CEA 1995 specifies that such a document shall be taken to form part of the records of a business or public authority if there is produced to the court a certificate to that effect signed by an officer of the business or public authority (a person in responsibility). Under s. 9(2)(a) of the CEA 1995 a certificate purporting to be signed by an officer of a business or public authority will be deemed to have been signed by such an officer and under s. 9(2)(b) the certificate will be treated as signed even if the certificate is in the form of a facsimile.

15.13.2 Secondary evidence

Secondary evidence of what a document contains is generally not admissible as evidence in court: *Augustien* v *Challis* (1847) 1 Ex 279. There are exceptions when the original is lost or impossible to produce; or a party or a stranger to the litigation fails or refuses to produce the original after having been given notice; or if it is part of a banker's book.

If the strict rules of evidence are to be applied to the arbitration, the arbitral tribunal should decide whether evidence contained in a document is authentic and, if secondary evidence is to be admitted, the weight to be attached to it. The arbitral tribunal should be satisfied that a letter has been signed by the person who wrote it and that a witness statement was in fact made by the witness in question. In a documents-only arbitration the authenticity of documents is more difficult to establish. The arbitral tribunal has to use its discretion in each case and keep in mind its duty under s. 33(1) of the AA 1996.

15.13.3 Hearsay evidence

Hearsay evidence is defined in s. 1(2) of the CEA 1995 as 'a statement made otherwise than by a person while giving oral evidence in the proceedings which is tendered as evidence of the matters stated'. Hearsay evidence is admissible in civil proceedings by virtue of s. 1(1) of the CEA 1995. The notice requirements under the CEA 1968 have been amended. Section 2 of the CEA 1995 provides that a party seeking to adduce hearsay evidence must give a notice of that fact to the other party and, if requested to do so, particulars of the evidence. The requirement to give notice only exists if it is reasonable and practicable in the circumstances to give notice for the purpose of enabling the other party to deal with any matters arising from the hearsay evidence. Under s. 2(3) of the CEA 1995 these provisions may be excluded by agreement of the parties or waived by the party to whom notice is required to be given. Section 2(4) of the CEA 1995 states that a failure to comply with the notice provisions does not render the evidence inadmissible but this may affect the weight to be given to the evidence and lead to costs penalties. A party may call a witness whose evidence has been tendered as hearsay by another party and cross-examine that witness on the statement under s. 3 of the CEA 1995.

Section 4 of the CEA 1995 contains guidelines which the court should consider in estimating the weight to be given to hearsay evidence. In particular the court should have regard to the factors listed in s. 4(2):

(a) whether it would have been reasonable and practicable for the party by whom the evidence was adduced to have produced the maker of the original statement as a witness;

(b) whether the original statement was made contemporaneously with the occurrence or existence of the matters stated;

(c) whether the evidence involves multiple hearsay;

(d) whether any person involved had any motive to conceal or misrepresent matters;

(e) whether the original statement was an edited account, or was made in collaboration with another or for a particular purpose;

(f) whether the circumstances in which the evidence is adduced as hearsay are such as to suggest an attempt to prevent proper evaluation of its weight.

Section 5 of the CEA 1995 provides that hearsay evidence may not be admitted if the maker of the statement was not competent as a witness when the statement was made. A 'not competent' witness is defined as a person suffering from a mental or physical infirmity, or lack of understanding. Section 5(2)(a) of the CEA 1995 allows for evidence to be admissible to impeach or support the credibility of a person whose statement has been adduced in evidence but has not been called as a witness. Evidence tending to show that such a person has made previous or later inconsistent statements, which are thereby contradictory to the statement which has been adduced as evidence, is also admissible under s. 5(2)(b) of the CEA 1995.

Section 6 of the CEA 1995 provides for previous consistent and inconsistent statements of a person who has been called as a witness to continue to be admissible. These statements will only be admissible as evidence of the matters stated with leave of the court or for the purpose of rebutting a suggestion that this witness's evidence has been fabricated.

In exercising its duty under s. 33(1) of the AA 1996 to act fairly and impartially the arbitral tribunal should weigh up the balance of prejudice to the parties of admitting or excluding hearsay evidence. The arbitral tribunal must exercise its discretion to admit or exclude hearsay evidence as is appropriate in the circumstances of the arbitration. For example, the arbitral tribunal should consider the reasons for the non-attendance of the maker of the statement and if the hearsay statement is admitted what weight should be attached to this evidence. The arbitral tribunal may be assisted by the guidelines to the court in considering the weight of hearsay evidence contained in s. 4 of the CEA 1995.

15.13.4   Expert evidence

Expert evidence will often be pivotal in proving a party's case. Lord Woolf found that the use of experts was one of the principle causes of excessive costs in civil litigation. Part 35 of the Civil Procedure Rules radically alters the previous position of the expert. Under CPR, r. 35.1, expert evidence shall be restricted to that which is reasonably required to resolve the proceedings. Under CPR, 35.3(1) and (2), it is the duty of an expert to help the court on matters within his expertise. This duty overrides any obligation to the person from whom he has received instructions or by whom he is paid. The parties to an arbitration may agree that an appointed expert should be bound by similar rules. In the absence of any contrary agreement, the arbitral tribunal's power in relation to making orders regarding expert witnesses and expert evidence is only subject to its duty under s. 33(1) of the AA 1996. The arbitral tribunal may decide the 'manner and form in which such material should be exchanged and presented'. This includes whether the strict rules of evidence should be applied: s. 34(2)(f) of the AA 1996.

Unless the parties have made a contrary agreement the arbitral tribunal is free to adopt the same strict procedures for disclosing expert evidence as practised by the court or to modify or exclude them as it sees fit: s. 34(2)(f) of the AA 1996. The advantage of prior disclosure of expert evidence by way of exchanging expert reports is that no party is taken by surprise at the hearing and that each party's expert has an opportunity to examine the other party's expert's evidence and consider which areas are agreed upon and which areas are disputed.

Conversely, the disadvantage of exchanging expert reports is that any weaknesses in the expert's evidence are also revealed. However, it is usual for expert reports to be exchanged in advance of the hearing in arbitration proceedings. It should be borne in mind that the narrowing down of the disputed areas will ultimately save time and costs and that it is fairer for both parties to know the substance of the expert evidence before the hearing.

15.14 CONFIDENTIALITY OF THE ARBITRATION PROCEEDINGS

The confidentiality of arbitration proceedings is an important feature to many parties. The privacy of an arbitration hearing is a benefit which litigating parties do not generally have. Colman J held in *Hassneh Insurance Co.* v *Mew* [1993] 2 Lloyd's Rep 243 that 'the informality attaching to a hearing held in private and the candour to which it may give rise is an essential ingredient of arbitration'. In *Ali Shipping Corporation* v *Shipyard Trogir* [1998] 2 All ER 136 the Court of Appeal held that the duty of confidentiality between parties to an arbitration did not come from the parties' intention but arose as a matter of law in every arbitration.

15.14.1 Confidentiality of the proceedings

A person who is not a party to the arbitration may be excluded from the arbitration hearing unless both parties agree that the non-party can attend: *Oxford Shipping Co. Ltd* v *Nippon Yusen Kaisha* [1984] 2 Lloyd's Rep 373. The arbitral tribunal is also under a duty of non-disclosure relating to the arbitral proceedings unless it is bound by law to give information. This is the case even if the arbitral tribunal is to hear concurrent arbitrations on similar facts and issues: *Oxford Shipping Co. Ltd* v *Nippon Yusen Kaisha* [1984] 2 Lloyd's Rep 373. See also *London and Leeds Estates Ltd* v *Paribas Ltd (No. 2)* [1995] 1 EGLR 102. In *Oxford Shipping Co. Ltd* v *Nippon Yusen Kaisha* Leggatt J said, at p. 379:

> The concept of private arbitrations derives simply from the fact that the parties have agreed to submit to arbitration particular disputes arising between them and only between them. It is implicit in this that strangers shall be excluded from the hearing and conduct of the arbitration and that neither the tribunal nor any of the parties can insist that the dispute shall be heard or determined concurrently with or even in consonance with another dispute, however convenient that course may be. . . The only powers which an arbitrator enjoys relate to the reference in which he has been appointed. They cannot be extended merely because a similar dispute exists which is capable of being and is referred separately to arbitration under a different agreement.

15.14.2   Confidentiality of the award

There are practical reasons why the arbitration award may not be subject to the duty of confidentiality. The parties' rights and obligations are ascertained from the award. The award, but not the other documents used in the proceedings, may therefore be disclosed if it was 'reasonably necessary' in order to protect a party's rights against a third party: *Hassneh Insurance Co.* v *Mew* [1993] 2 Lloyd's Rep 243; *Commonwealth of Australia* v *Cockatoo Dockyard Pty Ltd* (1995) 36 NSWLR 662. Equally, the award, and any reasons given by the arbitral tribunal in respect of the award, may be disclosed to the court where a party applies to the court to exercise any of its powers under the AA 1996 or to enforce the award: *Hassneh Insurance Co.* v *Mew* [1993] 2 Lloyd's Rep 243.

In *Hassneh Insurance Co.* v *Mew* arbitration proceedings began after a dispute arose between the parties. The plaintiff was an insurer and had entered a reinsurance contract through a broker with the defendant reinsurer. The dispute related to the reinsurance contract. An arbitration hearing was held and an interim award was made which largely found in favour of the defendant. The plaintiff then sued the broker for negligence. Before discovery the defendant sought to disclose the award and the reasons for the award to the broker. The defendant also sought to disclose at a later stage the transcript of the arbitration hearing and other documents from the proceedings. The plaintiff agreed that the award and some of the reasons could be disclosed but applied to the court for an injunction to prevent the defendant from making any more disclosures. The defendant asked the court to allow it to disclose any document which was reasonably necessary for the defendant to present its case.

Colman J found that there was a difference between the award and reasons for the award and other documents such as pleadings, witness statements, documents produced on disclosure and the transcript of the arbitration hearing. Colman J held that the duty of confidentiality in arbitration proceedings was subject to an exception which included the right to disclose the award for the purposes of enforcing it or appealing it. This also included the right to disclose the award and the reasons for the award if it was 'reasonably necessary' in order to protect or defend a right as against a third party.

Colman J in the later case of *Insurance Co.* v *Lloyd's Syndicate* [1995] 1 Lloyd's Rep 272 at p. 275 limited the scope of the test of 'reasonable necessity':

> The scope of the qualifications to the duty of confidence is implied as a matter of business efficacy. If one starts from the underlying assumption that the parties to an arbitration agreement impliedly agree that the award and reasons are to be kept as confidential as possible and only disclosed where that is unavoidably necessary for the protection of the rights of the parties, it follows that as a matter of business efficacy the scope of the qualification cannot possibly extend to purposes which are merely helpful, as distinct from necessary, for the protection of such rights.

In *Ali Shipping Corporation* v *Shipyard Trogir* [1998] 2 All ER 136 Potter LJ expanded upon the scope of 'reasonable necessity'. He held that the court should take a broad approach in requiring a party seeking disclosure to prove necessity. Potter LJ held that the court should take account of 'the nature and purposes of the proceedings for which the material is required, the powers and procedures of the tribunal in which the proceedings are being conducted, the issues to which the evidence or information sought is being directed and the practicality and expense of obtaining such evidence or information elsewhere'.

15.14.3 Confidentiality of material disclosed in the proceedings

Privileged documents are still subject to the rule of privilege when the arbitration has ended: *Calcraft* v *Guest* [1898] 1 QB 759. In *Dolling-Baker* v *Merrett* [1990] 1 WLR 1205 the court had to decide whether documents which were disclosed in an arbitration could be disclosed in later proceedings between the parties. In *Hassneh Insurance Co.* v *Mew* [1993] 2 Lloyd's Rep 243 the court had to decide whether documents disclosed in an arbitration could be disclosed in later proceedings between one party to the arbitration and a third party. In *Dolling-Baker* v *Merrett* Parker LJ held that there must be:

> . . . some implied obligation on both parties not to disclose or use for any other purpose any documents prepared for and used in the arbitration, of disclosed or produced in the arbitration, or transcripts or notes of evidence in the arbitration or the award — and indeed not to disclose in any other way what evidence had been given by any witness in the arbitration — save with the consent of the other party, or pursuant to an order or leave of the court.

Colman J reached a similar conclusion in *Hassneh Insurance Co.* v *Mew* [1993] 2 Lloyd's Rep 243. The extent of the parties' duty of confidentiality has now been clearly set out in *Ali Shipping Corporation* v *Shipyard Trogir* [1998] 2 All ER 136. The Court of Appeal held that there was, as matter of law, a duty of confidentiality between the parties to an arbitration. In deciding whether to override that duty, the appropriate test was whether disclosure was *reasonably* necessary either for disposing fairly of the action or for saving costs. Potter LJ listed the exceptions to the parties' duty of confidentiality:

1. where a party expressly or impliedly consents to the disclosure of documents or evidence which had been disclosed during the arbitration;
2. if a court makes an order or grants leave for disclosure of such documents or evidence;
3. when it was reasonably necessary to protect the legitimate interests of a party to the arbitration, applying Colman J's test in *Hassneh Insurance Co.* v *Mew* [1993] 2 Lloyd's Rep 243; and
4. where the interest of justice requires it, applying Mance J's test in *London and Leeds Estate Ltd* v *Paribas Ltd (No. 2)* [1995] 2 EG 1134.

In *Leeds Estate Ltd* v *Paribas Ltd (No. 2)* [1995] 2 EG 1134, Leeds Estate used an expert witness who had acted as an expert witness in previous arbitration proceedings between different parties. Paribas's expert witness was the arbitrator in that earlier arbitration. Paribas's expert witness told Paribas that Leeds Estate's expert witness was giving different evidence than he had given in the previous arbitration on very similar issues. Paribas applied for a subpoena under s. 12(4) of the AA 1950 against Leeds Estate's expert witness and for his proof of evidence in the previous arbitration. Mance J held that the proofs of evidence of Leeds Estate's expert witness were only admissible if they contained matters which were relevant to the issues in the present arbitration. The inconsistencies were relevant matters as they has a direct effect on the fair disposal of the present arbitration and Mance J held that it was in the general public interest in such circumstances for the duty of confidentiality to be overridden. Potter LJ later narrowed the exception to that of 'in the interest of justice' in *Ali Shipping Corporation* v *Shipyard Trogir*.

15.14.5 Australian decisions

The Australian courts have adopted a narrower approach to the English courts in respect of confidentiality of the arbitration proceedings. In *Esso Australia Resources Ltd* v *Plowman* (1995) 183 CLR 10 the High Court of Australia held that, although the arbitration hearing is private, this does not make the documents produced in the hearing confidential and that a party who has entered an arbitration agreement is not to be taken on that basis to have agreed to keep absolutely confidential all the documents produced and information disclosed to it by another party. The High Court of Australia further held that, where one party is bound to disclose documents or information to another party pursuant to an arbitration agreement, there should be an implied duty of non-disclosure except in the following cases. First, where a party in possession of a document or information is under a common law or statutory duty to disclose this material to a third party; secondly, where there is a duty, albeit not a legal one, to disclose the document or information to the public; thirdly, where the disclosure is necessary to protect the legitimate interests of a third party; and finally, where disclosure is made with the express or implied agreement of the party which produced the document or information.

The judgment of the High Court of Australia in *Esso Australia Resources Ltd* v *Plowman* was followed in *Commonwealth of Australia* v *Cockatoo Dockyard Pty Ltd* (1995) 36 NSWLR 662, which raised the issue whether the court could interfere with an interim direction made by the arbitral tribunal if it was in the public interest to do so. There is no English authority on this point. In *Commonwealth of Australia* v *Cockatoo Dockyard Pty Ltd* Cockatoo Dockyard asked the arbitrator to direct that various documents which related to the contamination of Cockatoo Island with toxic waste should be confidential. These documents were in the public interest. The court held that when an arbitration tribunal went beyond the established procedures necessary to conduct the arbitration and made orders which impinged on the public's interest, it was acting outside the boundaries of the arbitration and the court could therefore intervene.

16 Procedural Routes

16.1 AN OVERVIEW OF ADMINISTERED SCHEMES

Various organisations have adopted procedural schemes for the conduct of arbitrations. The rules of these various organisations can be referred to in the arbitration agreements or adopted after the dispute has arisen. In either case the rules will thereafter bind the parties. Section 4(3) of the AA 1996 provides that: 'The parties may make such arrangements [i.e., arrangements replacing the non-mandatory provisions of the Act] by agreeing to the application of institutional rules'.

It would be impossible to analyse each set of institutional rules. For international commercial disputes the International Chamber of Commerce (ICC) Rules of Conciliation and Arbitration are perhaps the best known and these and the UNCITRAL Arbitration Rules are discussed in chapters 19 and 20. In addition there are the Rules of the London Court of International Arbitration (LCIA Rules). In construction-related disputes the most commonly used rules are the JCT Rules and the Institution of Civil Engineers' Arbitration Procedure. The Construction Industry Model Arbitration Rules (CIMAR) have recently been published to be used with the AA 1996. The majority of marine arbitrations in London are conducted under the London Maritime Arbitrators' Association (LMAA) Terms. For commodity disputes there are the Grain and Feed Trade Association (GAFTA) Arbitration Rules. In insurance arbitrations there are the ARIAS Arbitration Rules which were developed to promote and assist in the development of arbitration for the insurance and reinsurance markets. There are also the Rules of the Chartered Institute of Arbitrators, which are designed for general use in domestic arbitrations.

The texts of many arbitration rules are collected in M.J. Chapman (ed.), *Commercial and Consumer Arbitration Statutes and Rules* (London: Blackstone Press, 1997).

The purpose of these rules is to provide a code for the conduct of an arbitration. The majority of the powers of the arbitral tribunal under the AA 1996 fall within the non-mandatory provisions of the AA 1996. The institutional rules can make express provision as to how and when the arbitral tribunal can exercise these powers. In addition the institutional rules may provide powers over and above those which are set out in the non-mandatory provisions. For example, the GAFTA

Arbitration Rules provide the arbitral tribunal with the power to join proceedings where disputes are substantially the same or connected.

The arbitration rules do not generally stand in isolation. The rules are often overseen by a relevant body whose function may be either a purely administrative or a supervisory one. Under the Rules of the Chartered Institute of Arbitrators if the parties fail to agree to the appointment of an arbitral tribunal, an appointing authority or the President or Vice-President may make the appointment: r. 3. Under Article 27 of the ICC Rules the Court of Arbitration of the ICC must approve the award.

The arbitral institution which the parties have requested or designated to appoint or nominate an arbitral tribunal is not liable for anything done or omitted in carrying out the appointment or nomination, unless bad faith is shown: s. 74(1) of the AA 1996. The arbitral institution is not liable, by reason of having appointed or nominated the arbitral tribunal, for anything it does or omits to do in the discharge or purported discharge of its functions: s. 74(2) of the AA 1996. Section 74 of the AA 1996 therefore complements s. 29 of the AA 1996, which provides immunity for the arbitral tribunal, save where there is bad faith. The section is mandatory so that the parties cannot agree between themselves to deprive the arbitral institution of the partial immunity that it possesses.

The term 'bad faith' has been used in respect of limiting judges' immunity at common law: *Sirros* v *Moore* [1975] QB 118. However, no definition was given as to its meaning. The phrase is used in the Financial Services Act 1986 and has been said to mean (a) malice in the sense of personal spite or desire to injure for improper reasons, or (b) knowledge of absence of power to make the decision in question: *Melton Medes Ltd* v *Securities and Investments Board* [1995] Ch 137; see also *Davis* v *Bromley Corporation* [1908] 1 KB 170.

There are also other authorities that suggest that the term bad faith, or mala fides, means anything which is not done in good faith, or bona fide. A person need not act maliciously to act in bad faith. Using one's powers for one's own ends rather than for the person whom one is obliged to help would be acting in bad faith: *Sydney Municipal Council* v *Campbell* [1925] AC 338.

16.2 CONSTRUCTION INDUSTRY MODEL ARBITRATION RULES

The CIMAR (the Rules) have been designed 'to provide for the fair, impartial, speedy, cost-effective and binding resolution of construction disputes': r. 1.2. The Rules are to be read in conjunction with the AA 1996 and the terms appearing within the Rules are to have the same meaning as those within the AA 1996: r. 1.1.

Rule 1.3 provides that once an arbitrator has been appointed the parties 'may not, without the agreement of the arbitrator, amend the Rules or impose procedures in conflict with them'. Rule 1.3 therefore appears to contradict the basic principle of party autonomy contained in s. 1(b) of the AA 1996, which states: 'the parties should be free to agree how their disputes are resolved'. The drafters of the Rules note this apparent contradiction, but say that 'the achievement of uniformity throughout the construction industry requires that general amendment of the Rules should be discouraged'.

Rule 2 provides for the commencing of arbitral proceedings and the appointment of the arbitral tribunal. Rule 2.1 states that the arbitral proceedings are begun 'when one party serves on the other party a written notice of arbitration identifying the dispute and requiring him to agree to the appointment of an arbitrator'. Rules 2.5 to 2.7 deal with the situation where there are related disputes. Duties are imposed on the persons who are to appoint arbitrators to give 'due consideration as to whether (i) the same arbitrator, or (ii) a different arbitrator should be appointed in respect of those arbitral proceedings'. The persons who are to appoint the arbitral tribunal should appoint the same arbitral tribunal unless sufficient grounds are shown for not doing so. If the above requirements are not complied with, the appointment of the arbitral tribunal may be challenged on the grounds that it was not in accordance with the Rules.

Rule 3 deals with the joinder of disputes and of parties in related disputes. Prior to the appointment of the arbitral tribunal, either party may raise new disputes in addition to the initial dispute. After the arbitral tribunal has been appointed a new dispute may only be added with the agreement of the arbitral tribunal. If the arbitral tribunal decides that the other dispute should not be referred to and consolidated with the initial dispute, it remains as a separate dispute. In such a case the parties may agree upon a new arbitral tribunal. In default of such agreement the provisions of rr. 2.3 and 2.4 apply.

Rule 3.5 provides that where any other dispute is referred to the arbitral tribunal dealing with the initial dispute the arbitral tribunal is empowered:

(i)   to decide any matter which may be a condition precedent to bringing the other dispute before the arbitrator;
(ii)   to abrogate any condition precedent to the bringing of arbitral proceedings in respect of the other dispute.

Rule 3.5 raises an interesting question as to the jurisdiction of the arbitral tribunal. Whilst the arbitral tribunal, under s. 30 of the AA 1996, has the power to rule on its own jurisdiction it cannot create its own jurisdiction. A condition precedent within the arbitration agreement may prevent the arbitration agreement from operating if that condition precedent has not been fulfilled. In *Smith* v *Martin* [1925] 1 KB 745 a building contract contained an arbitration clause and provided that the 'reference shall not be opened until after the completion of the works'. The Court of Appeal decided, with regret, that the arbitrator had no jurisdiction to determine whether the works had been completed, that in fact they had not been completed and therefore an award by the arbitrator was invalid.

By reason of s. 30 of the AA 1996 the arbitral tribunal can look into the matter to see if the condition precedent has been complied with. If it has not been complied with, the arbitral tribunal will not have jurisdiction to proceed. The arbitral tribunal 'abrogate any condition precedent to the bringing of arbitral proceedings'. The arbitral tribunal's jurisdiction is founded only if the condition precedent has been satisfied. The only way for the arbitral tribunal to abrogate any condition precedent to the bringing of arbitral proceedings is with the express consent of both parties to the arbitration proceedings.

Under r. 3.7 the arbitral tribunal may order concurrent proceedings where it is appointed in two or more related disputes which involve common issues. The concurrent proceedings may be of the whole claim or any issue. The parties need not be the same. The arbitral tribunal may only order consolidated proceedings if all the parties to those proceedings agree: r. 3.9. All other prerequisites for the ordering of consolidated proceedings are the same under r. 3.9 as they are under r. 3.7. Where there are concurrent proceedings separate awards are required unless the parties otherwise agree: r. 3.8. Where there are consolidated proceedings only one award is required unless the parties otherwise agree: r. 3.10. The award is final and binding on all the parties.

Rule 3.6 provides that: 'Arbitral proceedings in respect of any other dispute are begun when the notice of arbitration for that other dispute is served: see s. 13 [of the AA 1996] (application of Limitation Acts)'. Rule 3.6 is misleading because it does not distinguish between the joinder of parties and the joinder of disputes. In respect of the latter a further distinction needs to be made between new claims brought by the claimant and counterclaims brought by the respondent. Pursuant to s. 35(1)(b) of the Limitation Act 1980, set-offs and counterclaims are deemed to have been commenced on the same date as the original action. As s. 13 of the AA 1996 is a mandatory section within the AA 1996 this provision cannot be amended by the Rules.

Rule 4 provides the arbitral tribunal with its powers. These are the powers that are provided by ss. 30, 37 and 38 of the AA 1996. Rule 4.7 provides that: 'The arbitrator may give reasons for any decision under Rule 4.6 [power to order security for costs] if the parties so request and the arbitrator considers it appropriate'. An arbitral tribunal is not under an obligation to provide reasons for a pre-award ruling: *Three Valleys Water Committee* v *Binnie and Partners* (1990) 52 BLR 42. In the commentary to the judgment in the *Building Law Reports*, at p. 45, it is stated:

The case is nevertheless instructive because it makes clear — perhaps for the first time — that an arbitrator's interlocutory decision on a procedural point is not susceptible to challenge (unless of course it is a decision on a substantive issue and becomes an award). It follows that the court has no power to compel the arbitrator to give reasons for any such decision. Arbitrators would be well advised either not to give reasons for such interlocutory decisions or to provide the minimum necessary to assist the parties in the further preparation or conduct of the proceedings.

Rule 4.7 therefore provides a compromise position. It was adopted because of the wide range of views received by the Society of Construction Arbitrators on this point. If the decision of the arbitral tribunal in awarding, or not awarding, security for costs is obviously wrong or wrong in law, the fact that reasons have been provided will not assist either of the parties. Sections 68 and 69 of the AA 1996 apply only to awards. Only if the arbitral tribunal makes an award dismissing a claim or counterclaim, following a peremptory order by the arbitral tribunal requiring that security for costs should be provided, can an appeal or challenge be made under ss. 68 or 69 of the AA 1996.

Rule 5 deals with procedural and evidential matters. Rule 5.1 states that the arbitral tribunal shall decide all procedural and evidential matters including those set out in s. 34(2) of the AA 1996. However, this is subjɛ t to the right of the parties to agree any matter. Applications for security for costs, to strike out a claim or counterclaims for want of prosecution, or for provisional relief, and such other instances where the arbitral tribunal considers it appropriate, are to be supported by affidavit or some other formal record setting out the evidence: r. 5.7.

Rule 6 deals with the form of procedure and directions for the reference. As soon as the arbitral tribunal has been appointed, it must consider the form of procedure which is most appropriate to the dispute as required by s. 33 of the AA 1996: r. 6.1. As soon as it is practicable after the arbitral tribunal has been appointed the parties must provide to each other and to the arbitral tribunal notes setting out the nature of the dispute and an estimate of the amounts in issue. Included within this note should be an assessment of the need for and length of a hearing and proposals for the procedure which is considered to be appropriate to the dispute: r. 6.2.

Rule 6.3 requires the arbitral tribunal to convene a procedural meeting during which the procedure for the hearing is to be adopted and other procedures and time limits are to be imposed. The arbitral tribunal is also obliged to give directions as to the conduct of the reference: r. 6.4. Only where the parties agree, and the arbitral tribunal considers it appropriate, can the procedural matters be dealt with without a hearing: r. 6.6.

The CIMAR foresee that within the construction industry certain other bodies, representing classes or groups within that industry, may wish to issue supplementary rules. Rule 6.5 provides that the arbitral tribunal 'shall have regard to any advisory procedure and give effect to any supplementary procedure issued for use under any contract to which the dispute relates'. As at 31 December 1998 only the JCT had issued supplementary and advisory procedures.

Rules 7 to 9 of the CIMAR set out three different types of procedure for the hearing. Rule 7 provides for a short-form hearing, r. 8 for a documents-only hearing and r. 9 for a full procedure. The short-form hearing is designed for a 'touch-feel' type arbitration where the quality of work, materials or machinery are in question. Written statements of case, documents and witness statements are submitted. The hearing is limited to one day when the parties may address the matters in dispute with or without expert evidence. The arbitral tribunal must produce its award within one month, or such later time as it may require, following the last step in the hearing.

The documents-only procedure can be used where the sums in dispute are small or where no oral evidence will be required. Written statements of case are required which include an account of the relevant facts or opinions relied upon, witness statements and the remedy sought. Statements in reply may be served in response to the other parties' statement of case. The arbitral tribunal may thereafter put questions to the parties or request further written statements and/or direct that there should be a hearing of not more than one day so that questions may be put to any witness and comments may be made in additional evidence. The arbitral tribunal must produce its award within one month, or such later time as it may require, following the last step in the hearing.

The full procedure is adopted where neither the short-form hearing nor the documents-only hearing is appropriate. Rule 9 provides more detailed guidance on what should be included within the statement of claim or defence. Rule 9.3 allows for amendments to the statements of claim and defence. Directions should be given for the proceedings which include directions on further particulars or statements, disclosure, service of statements of fact, service of expert reports and the number of experts, meetings between experts and the arrangement for the hearing. Rule 9.6 provides that the arbitral tribunal may order the following to be provided in writing: any submission or speech by an advocate; questions intended to be put to witnesses; and answers by any witness to identified questions.

Rule 10 entitles the arbitral tribunal, on the application of a party or on its own motion, to make an order for provisional relief. This power corresponds to s. 39 of the AA 1996. Section 39 of the AA 1996 is, however, a non-mandatory provision and the power to order provisional relief is only given where 'the parties agree to confer such power on the tribunal'. Rule 10 therefore is an agreement to provide the arbitral tribunal with such a power. Section 39 of the AA 1996 describes this type of order as a provisional award. This is a misnomer as an order under this section is subject to the arbitral tribunal's final determination.

Where the arbitral tribunal considers it appropriate to do so it can order one party to pay to the other party a reasonable portion of the sum which is likely to be awarded against that party. Equally the arbitral tribunal can award that a party should pay a sum on account of any costs of the arbitration. This form of order will be appropriate where a defence is shadowy but is not wholly without substance.

Rule 11 provides for default powers and sanctions. Rule 11 should be read alongside s. 41 of the AA 1996. Rule 11.1 provides the arbitral tribunal with the power, as set out at s. 41(3) of the AA 1996, to dismiss a claim or counterclaim for inordinate or inexcusable delay. Rule 11.2 provides the arbitral tribunal with the power, as set out at s. 41(4) of the AA 1996, to proceed in the absence of a party. Rule 11.5 provides the arbitral tribunal with the power, as set out at s. 41(5), (6) and (7) of the AA 1996, to make peremptory orders. An application to the court requiring that a party comply with a peremptory order may be made only by or with the permission of the arbitral tribunal: r. 11.6. This requirement makes a slight change to s. 42(2) of the AA 1996 in that s. 42(2)(c) of the AA 1996 allows for an application to the court to be made by the parties with the consent of the arbitral tribunal, unless the parties have agreed to exclude the court's power under this section: s. 42(1) of the AA 1996. Rule 11.7 requires that there should be formal evidence on an application to strike out for inordinate or inexcusable delay or for failure to provide security for costs on a peremptory order.

Rule 11.3 provides for an additional power over and above the default powers provided under s. 41 of the AA 1996. Rule 11.3 states:

> The arbitrator may by any order direct that if a party fails to comply with that order he will:
>
> (a)   refuse to allow that party to rely on any allegation or material which was the subject of that order;
>
> (b)   draw such adverse inference from the act of non-compliance as the circumstances justify;
>
> and may, if that party fails to comply without showing sufficient cause, refuse to allow such reliance or draw such adverse inferences and may proceed to make an award on the basis of such materials as have been properly provided, and may make any order as to costs in consequence of such non-compliance.

Rule 11.3 allows for an arbitral tribunal to achieve the effect of a peremptory order in a single order. The use of such an order in not uncommon especially where a party has previously failed to comply with orders of the arbitral tribunal. The phrase 'peremptory order' is defined in s. 82(1) of the AA 1996 as meaning: 'an order made under section 41(5) or made in exercise of any corresponding power conferred by the parties'. Rule 11.3 is a corresponding power conferred by the parties and therefore an order made under it should be considered as a form of peremptory order. As such, a party may seek to enforce it under s. 42 of the AA 1996.

Rule 12 sets out the powers of the arbitral tribunal in respect of awards and remedies. The arbitral tribunal is given express powers in respect of making awards on different issues as set out in s. 47 of the AA 1996: r. 12.1. Where part of the dispute is dealt with separately it is for the arbitral tribunal to decide which issues or questions are to be determined: r. 12.2(a). The arbitral tribunal may make an award on the issues to be determined or may grant provisional relief: r. 12.2(b) and (c).

The arbitral tribunal is obliged to provide a target date for delivery of the award at the conclusion of a hearing: r. 12.3. The award must not deal with the allocation of costs or interest unless the parties have first been given the opportunity to be heard on the issue: *Harrison* v *Thompson* [1989] 1 WLR 1325. A failure to hear the parties on the question of costs would amount to a serious irregularity under s. 68 of the AA 1996: *Gbangbola* v *Smith and Sherriff Ltd* [1998] 3 All ER 730.

The award should be in writing, dated and signed and must comply with any other requirements of the contract: r. 4. The award should contain reasons unless the parties have otherwise agreed. The remedies that the arbitral tribunal may award are provided by s. 48 of the AA 1996. These include making a declaration, ordering the payment of money, ordering injunctions as between the parties, specific performance, or the rectification, setting aside or cancellation of any document. The award is final and binding pursuant to s. 58 of the AA 1996. Where the award requires that a party should carry out some specific act the arbitral tribunal may supervise the carrying out of that act or may delegate this responsibility to a suitably qualified person: r. 12.7.

The arbitral tribunal has the powers to award interest and to correct or provide additional awards: rr. 12.8 and 12.9. Rule 12.10 provides that the arbitral tribunal 'may notify an award or part of an award to the parties as a draft or proposal'. The parties may comment on the draft award but are not entitled to adduce further evidence unless the arbitrator otherwise directs. In arriving at a concluded award the arbitral tribunal shall consider only such comments as are notified to it within such time as it may specify: r. 12.10. Where an award on one issue is made and there remains an outstanding claim by the other party the arbitral tribunal may order that any sum payable under the award should be paid to a stakeholder on such terms as are appropriate: r. 12.11.

Rule 13 deals with costs. Rule 13.1 sets out the general principle that costs should be borne by the losing party, that is, costs should follow the event. However, r. 13.1 states that: 'Subject to any agreement between the parties, the arbitrator has the widest discretion in awarding which party should bear what proportion of the costs of the arbitration'. This reflects Article 40 of the UNCITRAL Arbitration Rules. The definition of costs of the arbitration is the same as provided for under s. 59 of the AA 1996. The basis on which costs are awarded, as set out in s. 63(3) to (7) of the AA 1996, is also expressly referred to: r. 13.10.

Rule 13.2 requires that the arbitral tribunal should have regard to all material circumstances in considering the question of costs. Rule 13.2 sets out a number of circumstances which may be considered relevant. These include:

(a) which of the claims has led to the incurring of substantial costs and whether they were successful;
(b) whether any claim which has succeeded was unreasonably exaggerated;
(c) the conduct of the party who succeeded on any claim and any concession made by the other party;
(d) the degree of success of each party.

These factors reflect the common law grounds for departing from the principle that costs should follow the event: *Unimarine SA* v *Canadian Transport Co. Ltd* [1982] 1 Lloyd's Rep 484; *Matheson and Co. Ltd* v *A. Tabah and Sons* [1963] 2 Lloyd's Rep 270; *Channel Island Ferries Ltd* v *Cenargo Navigation Ltd* [1994] 2 Lloyd's Rep 161; *Tramountana Armadora SA* v *Atlantic Shipping Co. SA* [1978] 2 All ER 870. In addition, r. 13.9 provides that the arbitral tribunal should have regard to offers of settlement or compromise.

Rule 13.3 provides that where there is both a claim and a counterclaim the costs in relation to each should be dealt with separately, unless the arbitral tribunal considers that the matters are so interconnected that they should be dealt with together. Rules 13.4 and 13.6 reflect s. 65 of the AA 1996 by empowering the arbitral tribunal to cap the costs, or any part of the costs, of the arbitration. Where the arbitral tribunal decides to cap the costs regard should be had to the amounts in dispute, or to the remedies claimed if the claim is not for money. Regard should also be had to any advisory or supplementary procedures applicable: r. 13.5. In allocating the costs, the arbitral tribunal must take account of any offer of settlement or compromise, whatever its description or form, made by either party. The arbitral tribunal should follow the general principle that a party who recovers less overall than was offered in settlement should only be able to recover its costs up to the date on which it was reasonable for that party to have accepted the offer: r. 13.9.

Rule 14 deals with a number of miscellaneous provisions. Rule 14.1 entitles the parties to be represented by one or more persons of their choice and by different persons at different times. Rule 14.2 requires that the arbitral tribunal should establish and record postal addresses and other means by which communications may be effected. Rule 14.3 adopts s. 78(3) to (5) of the AA 1996 for the purposes of reckoning periods of time. Rule 14.4 requires that the parties should promptly inform the arbitral tribunal of a settlement. Rule 14.5 requires that the parties should promptly inform the arbitral tribunal of any intended application to the court and should provide the arbitral tribunal with copies of such proceedings. The CIMAR conclude with an appendix, which sets out a number of definitions.

16.3 DOCUMENTS-ONLY ARBITRATIONS

Many disputes proceed to arbitration and are resolved on a documents-only basis. One of the best-known schemes is the ABTA Conciliation and Arbitration Scheme, which came into force on 1 April 1975. There are four steps to the Scheme. First, the tour operator tries to resolve the complaint. Second, a reference is made to ABTA, which appoints a conciliation officer who may ask that the tour operator reconsider. Thirdly, the conciliation officer will become actively involved. Fourthly, the holidaymaker will be invited to make a formal application to the Chartered Institute of Arbitrators to appoint an independent arbitrator to settle the dispute. There is no oral hearing and the dispute is resolved on documents only.

The main advantage of a documents-only arbitration is that there is no formal hearing. No one has to attend or wait around while the case is being heard. There are therefore no costs associated with the hire of rooms and with the attendance of counsel, experts or solicitors. The hearing can proceed much more swiftly and can be dealt with out of office hours if need be.

Documents-only arbitrations are, however, generally used only where the dispute is not complex. ABTA have stated that the arbitration scheme: 'is not designed to accommodate disputes in which issues are unusually complicated, the proper resolution of which would be likely to require a formal hearing and oral evidence'. Certain disputes involving allegations of fraud or fraudulent misrepresentations are also not suitable to proceed by documents only.

Where the matter is complex, proceeding by documents only may in fact make the matter more difficult to resolve than if there is an oral hearing. At an oral hearing ambiguities may be clarified and the credibility and reliability of the witnesses can be tested.

Where a documents-only arbitration is chosen in preference to an oral hearing the arbitral tribunal should tailor the procedure to the circumstances of the case. The complexity of each case will determine the formality of the proceedings. It may be appropriate that the matter should be resolved purely on written statements and correspondence. Alternatively full statements of case may be required, as well as further information, experts' reports, written submissions, statements and supplementary statements.

17 *International Arbitrations*

17.1 DIFFERING FORMS OF INTERNATIONAL ARBITRATION

International arbitrations take differing forms. They range from arbitrations between States, to highly technical and complex arbitrations involving construction, shipping or aviation, to fairly quick quality arbitrations. The parties may be governments, companies, joint ventures, individuals or a mixture of any of these. The arbitration may be run through a formal set of arbitration rules administered through an international body such as the ICC (International Chamber of Commerce) or may be an ad hoc arbitration with few if any rules set down.

17.1.1 State arbitrations

Arbitrations between differing States will usually involve matters which are non-commercial in nature. Where States are in dispute the matter is often referred to arbitration. Such matters are resolved under the provisions of a treaty, which may provide for a commission to deal with the dispute with a neutral umpire being appointed. It is usual for the arbitral tribunal to apply the existing law between the States, although it is not uncommon to find an equity clause allowing the arbitral tribunal to make decisions *ex aequo et bono*. The arbitral tribunal may also be empowered to lay down new law as between the parties to resolve the dispute as in *Free Zones* 1932 PCIJ (ser. A/B) No. 46. A State may also extend diplomatic protection to an individual so that the dispute in question is taken on by the State on its own behalf. Such a situation occurred in the case of the sinking of a Canadian ship: *I'm Alone*, Stuyt, *Survey of International Arbitrations 1794–1970*, 2nd ed., case No. 357.

As the number of international disputes between States increased, a Permanent Court of Arbitration was established in the Hague in 1899 to resolve these matters. It was, however, rarely used. Following the Second World War the International Court of Justice was established as the principal judicial organ of the United Nations. The International Court of Justice has dealt with a significant number of cases since its inception and continues to be the major institution for the resolution of disputes between States.

17.1.2   Commercial arbitrations between individuals

Commercial arbitrations between individuals, companies, joint ventures, corporations and such other legally defined individuals are the most common form of international arbitrations. These arbitrations will usually be conducted under institutional rules such as the ICC Rules, the UNCITRAL Arbitration Rules, the Rules of the London Court of International Arbitration or the London Maritime Arbitrators' Association Terms. It is usual for certain sets of rules to be adopted in certain categories of disputes. The rules provide a code under which the arbitration is to be conducted and provide the arbitral tribunal with certain powers it may not otherwise possess. Although the rules are of great assistance in the conduct of the reference their use is limited only to the reference itself and problems with the enforcement of any award may still exist.

Where there is a commercial dispute without reference to a set of institutional rules, problems regarding the powers of the arbitral tribunal and/or the law under which the arbitral tribunal is to function are more likely to arise. In such cases the first step is to establish where the arbitration is to have its 'seat'. The 'seat' is the place where the arbitration is to be decided. This can often be a complex question in itself and there is now established a substantial body of case law relating to the conflict of laws. Having established the seat of the arbitration the local law of that place will determine what powers the arbitral tribunal possesses and even whether arbitration is possible within that place. Once the award is made, questions of enforcement will have to be examined. The State where the arbitral award is to be enforced may refuse to recognise or enforce an arbitral award made in a particular place.

17.1.3   Where one party to the arbitration is a State

A dispute may arise which involves a company or an individual on the one hand and a State entity on the other. A number of such disputes arise out of loans to developing countries for construction and engineering works. These works are undertaken under standard bidding documents by companies which are often from countries different to that of the State where the work is carried out. Such disputes are further complicated if the major industrial and commercial enterprises for which the work is done are in State ownership.

Arbitrations arising from disputes between State and individual are often resolved under institutional rules such as the ICC Rules and the same principles as apply to arbitrations between individuals apply in these circumstances. As an alternative to the institutional rules an arbitration between an individual and State may be heard at the Peace Palace in the Hague under the 'Rules for arbitration and conciliation for settlement of international disputes between two parties of which one only is a State' or under the 'Convention on the settlement of investment disputes between States and nationals of other States' (the ICSID Convention).

17.2 DIFFERENCES BETWEEN DOMESTIC AND INTERNATIONAL ARBITRATIONS

The Arbitration Act 1996 (Commencement No. 1) Order 1996 (SI 1996/3146) was made on 16 December 1996 and brought into force the main provisions of the AA 1996 on 31 January 1996, though some formal provisions listed in sch. 1 to the Order were brought into force on 17 December 1995. Sections 85 to 87 of the AA 1996 were not and have not been brought into force. Those sections created a different regime for domestic arbitrations compared to non-domestic arbitrations and it was thought that, by discriminating between domestic and non-domestic arbitrations, they would cause a conflict between the AA 1996 and the United Kingdom's obligations under the Treaty of Rome and in particular Articles 6 and 59: *Philip Alexander Securities and Futures Ltd* v *Bamberger* (1996) 22 YB Com Arb 872. Domestic arbitration agreements are defined in s. 85(2) of the AA 1996 in terms almost identical to those of s. 1(4) of the AA 1975. Section 85(2) of the AA 1996 states:

For this purpose a 'domestic arbitration agreement' means an arbitration agreement to which none of the parties is—
(a) an individual who is a national of, or habitually resident in, a State other than the United Kingdom, or
(b) a body corporate which is incorporated in, or whose central control and management is exercised in, a State other than the United Kingdom,
and under which the seat of the arbitration (if the seat has been designated or determined) is in the United Kingdom.

Judge Jessup, *Transnational Law* (New Haven Conn: Yale University Press, 1956), defined a 'transnational' or 'international' agreement as an agreement that crossed national boundaries and therefore differed from a 'domestic' agreement. The distinction between 'international' arbitrations and 'domestic' arbitrations was, under the old English legislation, of importance in that the law affecting international agreements was generally not as strict as that affecting 'domestic' agreements. Under the old English legislation differences existed *inter alia* in the rights to stay court proceedings and the rights to exclude appeals between agreements which were 'domestic' in character rather than 'non-domestic'.

The question of whether a dispute is 'international' in character has usually been answered by reference to either one of two questions. First, the international nature of the agreement may be determined by reference to 'the nature of the dispute'; secondly, by reference to 'the identity of the parties', that is, whether one of the parties has some foreign element.

17.2.1 Nature of the dispute

Rather than examine who are the parties to the arbitration the ICC (International Chamber of Commerce) looks at the nature of the dispute to decide whether or not it has the power to decide the dispute in question. Article 1 of the Rules of Arbitration of the ICC provides that:

> The function of the Court is to provide for the settlement by arbitration of business disputes of an international character in accordance with the Rules of Arbitration of the International Chamber of Commerce (the 'Rules'). If so empowered by an arbitration agreement, the Court shall also provide for the settlement by arbitration in accordance with these Rules of business disputes not of an international character.

Certain countries, such as France, also look at the nature of the dispute to decide whether an agreement is international or not. Article 1492 of the French Code of Civil Procedure, Decree Law No. 81–500 of 12 May 1981 states that 'an arbitration is international when it involves the interests of international trade'. However, the courts of France have held that regard should also be had to other elements such as the nationality of the parties to determine whether or not the contract is of an international character.

17.2.2   Identity of the parties

The alternative approach to examining the nature of the dispute is to examine the identity of the parties. The approach of English legislation, as in s. 85(2) of the AA 1996, has been to set out a definition of a 'domestic arbitration agreement'. Anything that was not 'domestic' was therefore by implication international in character. This approach is to be found in some common law countries which have followed the English approach, for instance, Singapore.

The New York Convention, to which the United Kingdom is a signatory, does not help in clarifying what is a domestic arbitration agreement. Article I states:

> This Convention shall apply to the recognition and enforcement of arbitral awards made in the territory of a State other than the State where the recognition and enforcement of such awards are sought, and arising out of differences between persons, whether physical or legal. It shall also apply to arbitral awards not considered as domestic awards in the State where their recognition and enforcement are sought.

The AA 1996 has, however, reduced the importance of the previously accepted distinctions between domestic and international arbitration in England. In not bringing into force ss. 85–87 of the AA 1996 the differences between 'domestic' and 'non-domestic' arbitrations no longer exist except where enforcement outside the jurisdiction is sought. There are no extra controls or rules dependent on whether the arbitration is 'domestic' or 'non-domestic'. The important question that now decides what recourse the parties may have is: Where is the seat of the arbitration? If the seat of the arbitration is in England and Wales or Northern Ireland, Part I of the AA 1996 applies *in toto*. If the seat is outside, only certain provisions of the AA 1996 apply.

17.3 LAW OF THE ARBITRATION

17.3.1 Introduction

No arbitration is conducted in a 'legal vacuum' (Redfern and Hunter, *International Commercial Arbitration*, 2nd ed. (London: Sweet and Maxwell, 1991), p. 71). Although the issues in an arbitration may turn solely on questions of fact, without a system of law the arbitration award may not be worth the paper it is written on. International arbitrations can have a feature that is rarely found in domestic arbitrations, which is that the law governing the contract may often be different from the law governing the conduct of the arbitration. Two parties from separate countries may contract to build a bridge in Malawi under the laws of Malawi. However, neither party may want a dispute heard in the country where one of them is resident, perhaps fearing bias, or believing that the system of law governing the arbitration procedure is unsophisticated. The parties may therefore decide to have any dispute heard by an independent third party in an independent country. If they choose England as the seat of the arbitration, the laws governing the conduct of the arbitration will be English.

The law that governs the interpretation of the contract is hereafter described as 'the proper law of the contract'. The law governing the conduct of the arbitration is hereafter referred to as the *lex arbitri*. The *lex arbitri* is often referred to as the 'curial law' and the phrases are interchangeable. Further complication to the laws governing the arbitration may be introduced in an international arbitration when the award of the arbitrator is sought to be enforced. As the parties come from differing States the law applicable to the enforcement will be the law of the State where the award is to be enforced. This will often be the country of one of the parties but need not be. If one of the parties has assets in another country, it may be possible to enforce the award in that other country.

Questions relating to the proper law of the contract and the seat of the arbitration will therefore be of paramount importance at the outset of the contract. If the parties elect to have the arbitration conducted in a particular country, they must be sure that any award made in that country can be enforced in the countries where the parties are resident or where they have assets. An arbitration award is a pyrrhic victory if there is nothing to enforce it against.

The arbitration agreement and the contract, as a general proposition, will usually be governed by the same law. If the contract between the parties does not include an arbitration agreement, but, when a dispute arises the parties elect to have the matter arbitrated, they may enter into an ad hoc submission agreement. This submission agreement will therefore be distinct from the contract and governed by the law where it is made or such law as is expressly stated to govern it. The importance of correctly drafting the submission agreement cannot be overstated. If, for instance, the names of the parties differ in the main contract from those in the submission agreement, the award may be unenforceable: *Egypt* v *Southern Pacific Properties* (1984) 23 ILM 1048. The New York Convention, the UNCITRAL Model Law and the AA 1996 emphasise the need for a valid award before recognition and enforcement of the award will be given. In *Naviera Amazonica Peruana SA* v *Compania Internacional de Sugeros del Peru* [1988] 1 Lloyd's Rep 116 Kerr LJ examined how the relevant systems of law can have an effect on the arbitration and the award, including the law governing the arbitration agreement.

17.3.2 *Lex arbitri*

The *lex arbitri* not only governs the conduct of the arbitration but is also relevant to the enforcement of an award. The UNCITRAL Model Law was adopted by the United Nations Commission on International Trade Law on 21 June 1985 and since then has been adopted by a number of countries as diverse as Australia, Peru, Mexico and Scotland, bringing a greater degree of harmony in the *lex arbitri* of these countries. Where the UNCITRAL Model Law has been adopted and where that country is also a signatory to the New York Convention many of the problems regarding the enforceability of the arbitration award are diminished.

The fact that an arbitration is to be held in any particular country does not generally affect the proper law of the contract: *Compagnie d'Armement Maritime SA* v *Compagnie Tunisienne de Navigation SA* [1971] AC 572. Lord Diplock stated at p. 604:

> It is not now open to question that if parties to a commercial contract have agreed expressly upon the system of law of one country as the proper law of their contract and have selected a different curial law by providing expressly that disputes under the contract shall be submitted to arbitration in another country, the arbitrators must apply as the proper law of the contract that system of law upon which the parties have expressly agreed.

There can be no clear definition of what is included within the *lex arbitri*. Each country's law will determine whether a matter is within the *lex arbitri* or not. However, as a general rule matters affecting the jurisdiction of the arbitrator, the conduct of the reference and the form and finality of the award are likely to be covered by the *lex arbitri*.

17.3.2.1 The seat theory The seat theory holds that the place or the 'seat' where the arbitration is held is indicative of the *lex arbitri*. The seat theory is a concept widely accepted in international arbitrations and derives its origins from the idea of *siège d'arbitrage* developed by Professor Sausser-Hall in the late 1950s. The seat theory, although not the only theory to determine what is the *lex arbitri*, is the commonly accepted theory. Its acceptance is due, in no small part, to its being referred to in the Geneva Protocol, the New York Convention and the UNCITRAL Model Law. The AA 1996 also applies the seat theory.

In *India* v *McDonnell Douglas Corporation* [1993] 2 Lloyd's Rep 48 at p. 50 Saville J stated:

> If the parties do not make an express choice of procedural law to govern their arbitration, then the court will consider whether they have made an implicit choice. In this circumstance the fact that the parties have agreed to a place for the arbitration is a very strong pointer that implicitly they must have chosen the laws of that place to govern the procedures of the arbitration. The reason for this is essentially one of common sense. By choosing a country in which to arbitrate the parties have, *ex hypothesi*, created a close connection between the arbitration and that country and it is reasonable to assume from their choice that they attached some importance to the relevant laws of that country, i.e. those laws which would be relevant to an arbitration conducted in that country.

His Lordship then referred to, and accepted, a submission made by counsel for the defendants, stating that:

> In short, Mr Veeder suggested that the word 'seat' carried with it much more clearly the meaning conveyed by the French word '*siège*' than the English word 'place' though his submission was that this word too in an arbitration agreement would be primarily concerned with the legal rather than the physical place of the arbitration.

In *ABB Lummus Global Ltd* v *Keppel Fels Ltd* (1998) 12 CLN 1, Clarke J agreed with these observations. In considering what was the place of the arbitration of an arbitration conducted under the London Court of International Arbitration (LCIA) Rules, his lordship accepted the submissions of Andrew White QC that the 'place of the arbitration means legal place of the arbitration or seat of the arbitration'.

In contrast to the seat theory there is another theory referred to as 'transnational' arbitration or 'floating arbitration'. This theory stems from two cases: *Saudi Arabia* v *Arabian American Oil Co.* (1958) 27 ILR 117 and *Texaco Overseas Petroleum Co.* v *Libya* (1977) 17 ILM 3. These cases involved questions of sovereign immunity. The arbitral tribunals held that they could not subject one sovereign to the law of another State. The arbitral tribunal in the *Texaco* case found that a system of international law rather than any law of an individual State governed the arbitration. It is suggested that this theory may be right on the particular facts of these cases. It is relevant to consider that the theory if applied can only succeed if in fact the local courts where the arbitration is being heard do not apply the constraints of their own local law.

More importantly, however, the 'floating arbitration' theory may not produce an award which is capable of enforcement. In the *Aramco* and *Texaco* cases neither party required an enforceable award but rather an opinion from the arbitral tribunal. Enforcement under the New York Convention may be refused where the arbitration is not in accordance with the law of the country where the arbitration took place:

Article V.1(d). The DAC report of February 1996 made the following point in regard to 'floating' arbitrations: 'English law does not at present recognise the concept of an arbitration which has no seat, and we do not recommend that it should do so'. This remark was based on an *obiter dictum* of Kerr LJ in *Bank Mellat v Helliniki Techniki SA* [1984] QB 291 at 301: 'Despite suggestions to the contrary by some learned writers, our jurisprudence does not recognise the concept of arbitral procedures floating in the transnational firmament, unconnected with any municipal system of law'. Although the arbitral tribunal dealing with international arbitrations should be aware of the 'floating' arbitration theory it is unlikely that it is applicable to international arbitrations heard in England.

The seat theory allows for the local law of the country in which the arbitration has its seat to be applied to the arbitration. The laws of the country where the arbitration has its seat should be checked to ensure that they are suitable to the arbitration. In many cases the parties to an international arbitration will wish to be as free as they can from the control of the courts. It would therefore be unsuitable to elect the seat of the arbitration in a place where the laws relating to arbitration still allow for the case stated procedure to be applied. If the parties wish for a final and binding award, unchallengeable in a court of law, they will have to agree to have the seat in a country whose local laws permit such an exclusion agreement.

Although the seat of the arbitration is based in one country this does not mean that the arbitration cannot be conducted outside of that country, although such a course may not be free from problems. In international disputes it may be convenient to have many of the interim matters dealt with in a country other than the seat. Site visits may also be required and it may be convenient to have witnesses examined in their place of residence rather than in the country which is the seat of the arbitration. The fact that the arbitration proceedings can be conducted on a transnational basis does not affect the location of the seat of the arbitration and it is open to the arbitrator to conduct the hearings at any place convenient: per Kerr LJ in *Naviera Amazonica Peruana SA v Compania Internacional de Sugeros del Peru* [1988] 1 Lloyd's Rep 116 at p. 121.

Depending on the law applicable to the seat of the arbitration the award need not be made in the place where the arbitration is heard, though it is suggested that such a course is not advisable, because the New York Convention states that recognition or enforcement may be refused if the award is invalid under the law of the country where the award was made: Article V.1(a) and (e). In *Hiscox v Outhwaite* [1992] 1 AC 562 the House of Lords held that where an award had been signed in Paris, even though the whole of the arbitration had been conducted in England and the arbitration had no connection with France, it was an award 'made' in Paris. The AA 1996 has now attempted to reverse this position with a non-mandatory provision, which is applicable to arbitrations whose seat is in England, Wales or Northern Ireland. Section 53 of the AA 1996 states:

> Unless otherwise agreed by the parties, where the seat of the arbitration is in England and Wales or Northern Ireland, any award in the proceedings shall be

treated as made there, regardless of where it was signed, dispatched or delivered to any of the parties.

In English law there is also a requirement under s. 52(5) of the AA 1996 that: 'The award shall state the seat of the arbitration and the date when the award is made'. This requirement to state the seat of an arbitration is something new to English arbitrators and is applicable to domestic as well as international arbitrations. Although it is not thought that 'a failure to comply with s. 52 will "run the gauntlet" of ss. 68 and 73 and provide a satisfactory basis on which the award might be challenged, it might cause problems at the enforcement stage if it is a default award', J. Fry, *The Arbitration Act 1996: How your Award Might Be Challenged*, IBC Conference, 4 July 1996.

The *lex arbitri* may be indeterminable until the reference has begun. In *Star Shipping AS* v *China National Foreign Trade Transportation Corporation* [1993] 2 Lloyd's Rep 445 the arbitration clause stated that any disputes were to be referred to arbitration either in London or Beijing at the defendant's option. It was held by the Court of Appeal that this was a valid arbitration clause and the *lex arbitri* could therefore not be determined until the defendant had made the election.

17.3.2.2 The seat theory and the AA 1996 The AA 1996 gives a definition of 'the seat of the arbitration' in s. 3:

In this Part 'the seat of the arbitration' means the juridical seat of the arbitration designated—
(a) by the parties to the arbitration agreement, or
(b) by the arbitral or other institution or person vested by the parties with powers in that regard, or
(c) by the arbitral tribunal if so authorised by the parties,
or determined, in the absence of such designation, having regard to the parties' agreement and all the relevant circumstances.

The juridical seat can be different from the place where the hearing or other procedures relating to the arbitration are heard. It is clearly intended that this section does not affect the principle laid down by Kerr LJ in *Naviera Amazonica Peruana SA* v *Compania Internacional de Sugeros del Peru* [1988] 1 Lloyd's Rep 116 at p. 121 that the fact that the arbitration proceedings can be conducted on a transnational basis does not effect the location of the seat of the arbitration and it is open to the arbitral tribunal to conduct the hearings at any place convenient. Section 3 of the AA 1996 follows closely Article 20 of the UNCITRAL Model Law:

(1) The parties are free to agree on the place of the arbitration. Failing such agreement, the place of arbitration shall be determined by the arbitral tribunal having regard to the circumstances of the case, including the convenience of the parties.

(2)   Notwithstanding the provisions of paragraph (1) of this article, the arbitral tribunal may, unless otherwise agreed by the parties, meet at any place it considers appropriate for consultation among its members, for hearing witnesses, experts or the parties, or for the inspection of goods, other property or documents.

As stated previously the seat is an important concept as it will affect whether the arbitration can be enforced under Conventions applicable to where the seat is located. Even arbitrations which are governed by ICC Rules must therefore ultimately have a *lex arbitri* governed by the local law of the seat of the arbitration.

The seat of the arbitration is determined in one of three ways. First, the parties themselves may designate the seat of the arbitration. This will almost certainly be the most convenient method. However, secondly, the seat may be determined by an arbitral institution. This method will be common where the arbitration agreement provides for 'arbitration under ICC Rules' or similar reference to institutional rules. Here the ICC would designate the place of the arbitration. Article 14.1 of the ICC Rules states: 'The place of the arbitration shall be fixed by the Court unless agreed upon by the parties'. Where the parties have not designated the place of the arbitration or there is no overseeing arbitral institution the arbitral tribunal may designate the seat if authorised to do so. There is no express power in the AA 1996 for the arbitral tribunal to do so and therefore the power would have to come from the agreement of the parties or by reference to any applicable rules. Article 16(1) of the UNCITRAL Arbitration Rules provides that: 'Unless the parties have agreed upon the place where the arbitration is to be held, such place shall be determined by the arbitral tribunal, having regard to the circumstances of the arbitration'. If none of these three ways of determining the seat of the arbitration is applicable, the courts may determine where the arbitration has its seat having regard to the parties' agreement and all the relevant circumstances.

Section 2 of the AA 1996 deals with the scope of application of the provisions of the AA 1996. Since the whole of Part I of AA 1996 applies only where the seat of the arbitration is in England, Wales or Northern Ireland it is important to determine where the seat of the arbitration is at the outset. Section 2 of the AA 1996 states:

(1)   The provisions of this Part apply where the seat of the arbitration is in England and Wales or Northern Ireland.

(2)   The following sections apply even if the seat of the arbitration is outside England and Wales or Northern Ireland or no seat has been designated or determined—
      (a)   sections 9 to 11 (stay of legal proceedings, &c.), and
      (b)   section 66 (enforcement of arbitral awards).

(3)   The powers conferred by the following sections apply even if the seat of the arbitration is outside England and Wales or Northern Ireland or no seat has been designated or determined—

(a) section 43 (securing the attendance of witnesses), and

(b) section 44 (court powers exercisable in support of arbitral proceedings);

but the court may refuse to exercise any such power if, in the opinion of the court, the fact that the seat of the arbitration is outside England and Wales or Northern Ireland, or that when designated nor determined the seat is likely to be outside England and Wales or Northern Ireland, makes it inappropriate to do so.

(4) The court may exercise a power conferred by any provision of this Part not mentioned in subsection (2) or (3) for the purpose of supporting the arbitral process where—

(a) no seat of the arbitration has been designated or determined, and

(b) by reason of a connection with England and Wales or Northern Ireland the court is satisfied it is appropriate to do so.

(5) Section 7 (separability of arbitration agreement) and section 8 (death of a party) apply where the law applicable to the arbitration agreement is the law of England and Wales or Northern Ireland even if the seat of the arbitration is outside England and Wales or Northern Ireland or has not been designated or determined.

The basic rule stated by s. 2(1) is that if the seat of the arbitration is in England and Wales or Northern Ireland, Part I of the AA 1996 applies. This in effect follows the existing principle that the courts of England and Wales will exercise a supervisory role where the arbitration takes place in England or Wales: *Channel Tunnel Group Ltd* v *Balfour Beatty Construction Ltd* [1993] AC 334. However, even where the seat is not within England and Wales or Northern Ireland the courts will still exercise certain powers under the AA 1996; see s. 2(2) of the AA 1996. This provision was needed so that the United Kingdom would comply with its treaty obligations under the New York Convention. Section 2(2) of the AA 1996 therefore applies whether or not the seat of the arbitration is in England and Wales or Northern Ireland and where the seat has yet to be determined. Legal proceedings may be stayed in England and Wales or Northern Ireland under s. 9 of the AA 1996 where the contract provides for arbitration in a different country and an award in that arbitration will be enforceable in England and Wales or Northern Ireland pursuant to s. 66 of the AA 1996.

Section 2(3) of the AA 1996 supersedes s. 25 of the Civil Jurisdiction and Judgments Act 1982. The court has powers to order the attendance of witnesses or grant such interim relief as is set out in s. 44 of the AA 1996 where it is appropriate to do so in arbitration proceedings where the seat is outside England and Wales or Northern Ireland or no seat has been designated or determined. Section 2(4) of the AA 1996 entitles the court to exercise any of the powers in Part I of the AA 1996 where the seat of the arbitration has been neither designated nor determined, where it is appropriate to do so and where there is a connection between the dispute and England and Wales or Northern Ireland. This subsection will be used in cases where it is likely that the seat of the arbitration will be England and Wales or

Northern Ireland but where that determination or designation has yet to be made. A further use for s. 2(4) of the AA 1996 was stated by Harris, Planterose and Tecks, *The Arbitration Act 1996: A Commentary* (London: Blackwell Science, 1996), at p. 50:

> One of the most likely uses of this power will be where an appointment procedure has begun, but failed. Thus the powers likely to be relevant prior to designation or determination of the seat would appear to be those in s. 12 (power of court to extend time for beginning arbitral proceedings); s. 17(3) (power of the court to set aside appointment of sole arbitrator in default); s. 18 (failure of appointment procedure); s. 24 (power of the court to remove arbitrator); and s. 32 (power to determine preliminary point of jurisdiction).

The purpose of s. 2(5) of the AA 1996 was made clear by Saville LJ who steered the development of the AA 1996. In *The Arbitration Act 1996: Keynote Address*, IBC Conference, 4 July 1996 he said:

> Subsection (5) is necessary because of the way English law has developed. The problem arises in cases where there is no seat or the seat is abroad. Without this provision, if the parties had agreed that English law was the law applicable to their arbitration agreement, that law would be the English common law, not the law contained in this [Act] or it predecessors, for s. 2(1) would not apply and the other subsections have limited scope. Thus it could be argued that 'separability' of the arbitration agreement from its accompanying 'substantive' agreement, or the effect of the death of a party were different from the rules expressed in the [Act]. This would certainly be the case for the death of a party, since the common law is that an arbitration agreement is discharged by such a death. For many years this common law rule has been reversed by statute, but since we are repealing these statutes, the common law would revive unless we had put in this provision.

17.3.2.3 Where the law of the seat of the arbitration and the lex arbitri differ 'English law does admit of at least the theoretical possibility that the parties are free to choose to hold their arbitration in one country but subject to the procedural laws of another': *India* v *McDonnell Douglas Corporation* [1993] 2 Lloyd's Rep 48 per Saville J at p. 50. Such a decision 'is unusual but by no means unknown': Mustill and Boyd, *Commercial Arbitration*, 2nd ed. (London: Butterworths, 1989), p. 91. The effect of this would mean that the arbitration is subject to two sets of procedural law. In the country which is designated as the seat of the arbitration, the mandatory provisions of the applicable procedural law would apply. All other procedural law would be governed by the *lex arbitri* of the country which has been nominated as having the procedural law governing the arbitration. In *Black Clawson International Ltd* v *Papierwerke Waldhof-Aschaffenburg AG* [1981] 2 Lloyd's Rep 446 at p. 453 Lord Mustill described this as producing an absurd result; see also *India* v *McDonnell Douglas Corporation* [1993] 2 Lloyd's Rep 48 at p. 50. The problems inherent with an arbitration agreement being subject to differing sets of procedural law are illustrated by Redfern and Hunter, *International Commercial Arbitration*, 2nd ed. (London: Sweet & Maxwell, 1991) at p. 92, where analysis is undertaken of the problems of ordering a witness summons.

Under English law, prior to the AA 1996, the position was that the courts of England and Wales or Northern Ireland would not exercise jurisdiction over an arbitration whose seat was outside England and Wales or Northern Ireland. In *Naviera Amazonica Peruana SA* v *Compania Internacional de Sugeros del Peru* [1988] 1 Lloyd's Rep 116 at p. 120 Kerr LJ illustrated some of the practical difficulties:

> There is equally no reason in theory which precludes parties to agree that an arbitration shall be held at a place or in country X but subject to the procedural laws of Y. The limits and implications of any such agreement have been much discussed in the literature, but apart from the decision in the instant case there appears to be no reported case where this has happened. This is not surprising when one considers the complexities and inconveniences which such an agreement would involve. Thus, at any rate under the principles of English law, which rest upon the territorially limited jurisdiction of our courts, an agreement to arbitrate in X subject to English procedural law would not empower our courts to exercise jurisdiction over the arbitration in X.

This *obiter dictum* of Kerr LJ was applicable only to arbitrations as the courts of England had no power to exercise jurisdiction over foreign courts. Section 2(3) of the AA 1996 now gives the court powers under ss. 43 (securing the attendance of witnesses) and 44 (court's powers exercisable in support of arbitral proceedings) to make certain orders where the seat is outside the jurisdiction. The test to be applied under s. 2(3) of the AA 1996 is whether it is appropriate to make such orders. Where the parties have elected that the *lex arbitri* be English law, even though the seat is outside English jurisdiction, the question to be addressed is whether this would in itself be sufficient for the courts to exercise the powers given to them by ss. 43 and 44 of the AA 1996? The answer seems to be no. In commenting on these sections in his guide to the AA 1996, Professor Merkin, *Arbitration Act 1996: An Annotated Guide* (London: LLP, 1997) at pp. 16–17 stated:

> where the seat is abroad but the curial law is English law (by express choice — English law would almost certainly refuse to make such an implication), the procedures in s. 44 of the Act are available (so that, for example, interim relief can be granted in respect of a foreign arbitration) but the English courts can refuse to act by virtue of the proviso to s. 2(3) if the necessary link with the domestic jurisdiction is missing.

Clarke J in *ABB Lummus Global Ltd* v *Keppel Fels Ltd* (1998) 12 CLN 1 agreed with this analysis.

Section 2(4) of the AA 1996 requires, as a prerequisite to the court exercising any power under the AA 1996, that no seat has been designated or determined and that there be a connection with England and Wales or Northern Ireland. The mere fact that the parties have elected English law will not in itself be enough to establish that connection: *ABB Lummus Global Ltd* v *Keppel Fels Ltd.*

The situation where the seat of the arbitration was stated to be London and the arbitration procedure was to be conducted in accordance with the Indian Arbitration Act was addressed in *India* v *McDonnell Douglas Corporation* [1993] 2 Lloyd's Rep 48. It was held that the jurisdiction of the English courts under the Arbitration Acts over arbitration in England could not be excluded by an agreement between the parties to apply the laws of another country or indeed by any other means not sanctioned by the Acts. Therefore where the seat of the arbitration is England and Wales or Northern Ireland the mandatory provisions of the AA 1996 will apply irrespective of whether the parties have elected a foreign procedural law. Where the parties choose a system of procedural law that is different from the law of the seat of the arbitration it is clear that the non-mandatory provisions of the AA 1996 would not apply by reason of s. 4(5) of the AA 1996, which provides that:

> The choice of a law other than the law of England and Wales or Northern Ireland as the applicable law in respect of a matter provided for by a non-mandatory provision of this Part is equivalent to an agreement making provision about that matter.

The parties, therefore, in choosing a different procedural law to the law of the seat of the arbitration, have made an agreement making provision about that matter.

In *ABB Lummus Global Ltd* v *Keppel Fels Ltd* a contract for the provision of engineering, design and construction work on an offtake vessel had the following clauses:

> 37.1   This contract shall be governed by and interpreted in accordance with English law.
>
> 37.2   Disputes arising in connection with or as a result of the contract, and which are not resolved by mutual agreement, shall be referred to the London Court of International Arbitration. Disputes shall be settled in accordance with Singapore law.

Disputes arose regarding the valuation of varied work. ABB issued a notice of arbitration on Keppel and on the same day issued a writ in the High Court in England. The following day ABB issued a writ in the High Court of Singapore. An application was made to the High Court in England by ABB for a declaration that in serving the High Court proceedings in both England and Singapore ABB had not repudiated the arbitration agreement. Keppel's cross-application claimed that the High Court in England had no jurisdiction to entertain ABB's application. The question that Clarke J first had to address was whether the seat of the arbitration should be Singapore or London. Clarke J found that the parties had agreed that the arbitration be held in London. Having found that London was the seat of the arbitration Clarke J referred to Professor Merkin's commentary on the AA 1996, op. cit. at pp 16–17:

> where the seat is England, the Act applies irrespective of the chosen or applicable curial law, by virtue of s. 2(1), and the court must apply the mandatory parts of the Act listed in sch. 1 to the Act — as regards the non-mandatory aspects of the Act, under s. 4(5) any express or implied choice of another law operates to oust the Act in so far as that choice applies to those non-mandatory aspects — in the absence of such a choice, the fact that some other law is found to be applicable will not have the effect of disapplying the non-mandatory aspects of the Act.

Clarke J then analysed the possible alternatives. His lordship stated that:

> . . . it followed that London was to be the seat, so that the role of Singapore law could at best be that contemplated in . . . the extract from Professor Merkin's book quoted above. On that basis, it has the role identified in s. 4(5) of the Act, that is that Singapore is the applicable law in respect of the non-mandatory provisions in Part I of the Act.

However, Clarke J held that this alternative 'would not be a sensible agreement to make'. His lordship proceeded to conclude that clause 37.2 of the contract had been varied and that the parties had agreed that arbitration would be in London and by implication the *lex arbitri* would be English law.

17.4 PROPER LAW OF THE CONTRACT

It is often the case that the proper law of the contract will be evidenced in the contract between the parties by a 'choice of law' clause. FIDIC (Federation of International Civil Engineers) contracts contain a clause in the conditions whereby the parties state what law is to apply to the contract. Where the parties have chosen the proper law in almost every case that choice will be upheld. Dr Julian Lew stated in *Applicable Law in International Commercial Arbitration* (1978), p. 75:

> . . . despite their differences, common law, civil law and socialist countries have all equally been affected by the movement towards the rule allowing the parties to choose the law to govern their contractual relations. This development has come about independently in every country and without any concerted effort by the nations of the world; it is the result of separate, contemporaneous and pragmatic evolutions within the various national systems of conflict of laws.

This principle that the parties are free to choose the law to govern the dispute between them may apply not only when the contract is made but afterwards too.

Parties who are in dispute may at that time elect what law is to govern the contract between them and resolve the dispute in question. Lew, op. cit., p. 98, refers to a decision of Lagergren J from an ICC arbitration and states:

> The parties have agreed that Argentine law is the proper law of the commission agreement (or agreements), and should their choice of law, which was itself made during the course of the arbitration proceedings, not be itself binding on me, I have no doubts about the correctness of their conclusion in that respect.

Lagergren J concluded that the parties could elect the proper law even after arbitration proceedings had started. His alternative position was that the proper law of the contract was Argentine Law. In contrast, the decision in *Kuwait* v *American Independent Oil Co.* (1982) 21 ILM 976 suggests that this is not the case.

There are certain limited restrictions to the parties' right to choose the law that is to apply to their dispute. It seems that they must not choose a law whose provisions would be contrary to the public policy of the courts which the parties have chosen to apply those provisions. The choice of law is not restricted to a system of national law and the parties may elect as the law of the contract merchant law, public international law, equitable principles or the general principles of law. A detailed examination of the various types of law that can be chosen is given by Redfern and Hunter, *International Commercial Arbitration*, 2nd ed. (London: Sweet and Maxwell, 1991), pp. 101–22.

Having found the law to be applied the arbitral tribunal will then have to establish exactly what that law is. The law may have changed since the contract was made and the arbitral tribunal will be bound to apply the law applicable to the contract at the time the award is made rather than the law applicable at the time the contract was entered into. It is also possible that the contract will stipulate that the law to be applied to the contract is 'the law of X country as at [date]'. In such cases the arbitral tribunal will apply the law at the set date unless such a clause is contrary to the law of that country.

Unless it is made on a standard form it is not uncommon for a contract not to have a 'choice of law clause'. Where this is the situation the arbitral tribunal will have to decide what law is applicable to the contract. Complex battles of forms arising from instantaneous communications from one country to another may create a factual matrix which is hard to unravel. Further, the rules relating to the conflict of laws may add further and more complex questions into the decision that the arbitral tribunal will have to reach.

17.5 PROPER LAW OF THE CONTRACT AND THE AA 1996

Section 46 of the AA 1996 is one of the most significant new provisions in the Act. It provides:

(1) The arbitral tribunal shall decide the dispute—

(a)   in accordance with the law chosen by the parties as applicable to the substance of the dispute, or

(b)   if the parties so agree, in accordance with such other considerations as are agreed by them or determined by the tribunal.

(2)   For this purpose the choice of the laws of a country shall be understood to refer to the substantive laws of that country and not its conflict of laws rules.

(3)   If or to the event that there is no such choice or agreement, the tribunal shall apply the law determined by the conflict of laws rules which it considers applicable.

The effect of this section is that the parties are free to choose the law under which the dispute will be settled. Such a decision will usually mean the adoption of a system of national law, though the parties may agree to apply law merchant. Section 46(1)(b), however, provides for an alternative in that, if a system of law is not chosen, the parties are free to elect that the dispute be resolved taking into account such other considerations as they agree. This would mean that the parties could agree to have the dispute resolved *ex aequo et bono* or with the arbitral tribunal acting as an 'amiable compositeur'. Section 46(2) makes clear that the parties' choice of law refers to the substantive law and not the conflict of laws rules.

Section 46(3) of the AA 1996 requires that, failing a selection of the choice of law by the parties, the arbitral tribunal shall decide the law based on the relevant conflict of laws principles. Dr Julian Lew, *A Practical Guide to the New Arbitration Act 1996: Scope and purpose of the New Act,* IBC Conference, 4 July 1996, stated that s. 46(3) of the AA 1996 'would allow arbitrators to make a direct selection of the law which they think should apply and then look for a conflict rule to justify their selection'. Similarly, Harris, Planterose and Tecks, *The Arbitration Act 1996: A Commentary* (Blackwell Science Ltd, 1996), p. 187, state that: 'The tribunal must characterise the dispute or issues which it has to determine, apply the relevant conflict of law rules and thereby arrive at the substantive law that is to be applied'.

Where the parties have not chosen the proper law of the contract but the arbitral tribunal determines that the conflict of laws rules are those of England then it must proceed to apply those rules. These rules may be found in statutes or at common law. The Contracts (Applicable Law) Act 1990 gives effect to the Rome Convention on the Law Applicable to Contractual Obligations 1980. In England the Contracts (Applicable Law) Act 1990 applies to contractual disputes between nationals of States which are signatories to the Rome Convention. Where the Rome Convention does not apply, the accepted test in England is: 'the system of law with which the transaction has its closest and most real connection': ICC Case No. 7177 (1993) 7(1) ICC Bulletin 89.

Where the Contracts (Applicable Law) Act 1990 does not apply, because, for instance, one of the parties is not a national of a State which is a signatory to the Rome Convention, then the location of the seat of the arbitration may be a material consideration in deciding the proper law of the contract. In *Compagnie d'Armement Maritime SA* v *Compagnie Tunisienne de Navigation SA* [1971] AC 572 Lord Morris of Borth-y-Gest said, at p. 588:

> An agreement to refer disputes to arbitration in a particular country may carry with it, and is capable of carrying with it, an implication or inference that the parties have further agreed that the law governing the contract (as well as the law governing the arbitration procedure) is to be the law of that country. But I cannot agree that this is a necessary or irresistible inference or implication.

However, the reference to the seat of the arbitration as a factor for determining the choice of the proper law of the contract has not been generally applied in international cases. In ICC Case No. 7177 (1993) 7(1) ICC Bulletin 89 the seat of the arbitration was stated to be London. The proper law of the contract was not stated. On the facts of the case the arbitral tribunal found that the proper law of the contract was not English but Greek. Further complications arise when there is no proper law of the contract and no designated seat for the arbitration.

In ICC Case No. 6527 (1991) 7(1) ICC Bulletin 88 a dispute arose regarding the sale of goods between an Austrian buyer and a Turkish seller. The contract did not provide what was to be its proper law but included a provision that arbitration would be to the ICC (International Chamber of Commerce). Under the ICC rules applicable at the time, the arbitral tribunal was to decide the proper law in accordance with conflict of laws rules which it deemed appropriate. The arbitral tribunal considered whether it should apply the conflict of laws rules in force at the place of the arbitration: 'In accordance with the classical doctrine on conflicts of law'. The arbitral tribunal, however, noted that this doctrine had been criticised in respect of arbitral proceedings because the arbitral tribunal, unlike a judge, had no *lex fori* (law of the forum). The arbitral tribunal therefore applied general principles of private international law as stated in international conventions. The arbitral tribunal examined the Hague Convention, which provided that where the proper law of the contract was not specified it would be where the seller has his place of residence. The arbitral tribunal also considered the Rome Convention, which points to the State that has the most significant connection with the contract. The arbitral tribunal noted that although neither Convention had been ratified by Austria or Turkey it was entitled to take note of the Conventions as setting prevailing principles in private international law. On the facts of the case the arbitral tribunal found that the proper law of the contract was Turkish law.

18 Challenge, Recognition and Enforcement of International Awards

18.1 INTRODUCTION

The obtaining of an award by one party does not guarantee payment from the other party. A party which succeeds in obtaining an award in its favour may have to enforce that award. Where the arbitration has an international aspect, enforcement may have to take place in a country other than that where the arbitration had its seat. That other country will usually be the place where the other party resides, although the overriding question is whether that party has assets in the country where enforcement is sought.

Although there is no statistical proof, most arbitration awards appear to be carried out voluntarily by the parties. Where the award is not carried out, the party who succeeds must exert some pressure on the unsuccessful party so that it complies with the award. In such a situation the party who has received the award in its favour must seek the assistance of the courts in an attempt to seize assets to the value of the award.

Each jurisdiction has its own requirements that must be complied with before its courts will enforce an award and it would be impossible to list the requirements of each jurisdiction. However, there are certain prerequisites that are common to many jurisdictions. It is common in most jurisdictions that, before the courts will assist the successful party, there be an award that is final and binding. If the arbitration is conducted under institutional rules, these will often expressly refer to the final and binding nature of the award and the obligation of the parties to carry out the award without delay — see both the UNCITRAL and ICC Arbitration Rules. This in itself will not make the award final. Unless and until all appeals against the award have been heard the award cannot be construed as being final.

The position in many common law countries, and in a few civil law countries, is that a party may be permitted to make an appeal to the courts on any point of law arising from an award. The right to appeal may be almost unfettered or may exist subject to certain prerequisites being shown, for example, that the point of law involves a matter of general public importance. Over the past few decades a distinction has been made in many countries which are signatories of the New York Convention between domestic and non-domestic arbitrations. In a non-domestic arbitration the parties could exclude a right to appeal and make the award final and binding if this was the intent under the arbitration agreement. In England, s. 69 of the AA 1996 now allows for an exclusion agreement to be made in respect of both domestic and non-domestic arbitration agreements. However, the principle remains that when seeking to enforce an arbitration award the parties must ensure that the award is in fact final having regard to the *lex arbitri*.

18.2   CHALLENGING THE AWARD

Every country has its own system for the review of arbitral awards. A challenge to an award is a 'positive' attack on the award whereby a party seeks to overturn or remit the award back to the arbitral tribunal by reason of an error within the award or some injustice that has led to the award being made. The attack may take the form of a challenge on a point of law or to the substantive jurisdiction of the arbitral tribunal. It may also take the form of an allegation of some irregularity in the award or the conduct of the proceedings. The effect of a successful challenge is to render the part of the original decision which has been challenged a nullity. This has an effect not only in the country in which the award is made but may have an effect in the country in which the previously successful party intended to enforce the award. The New York Convention requires there to be an enforceable award in the country in which the award was made as a prerequisite for enforcement in another New York Convention country.

The challenge to the award is made in the courts where the seat of the arbitration is located. However, Redfern and Hunter, *International Commercial Arbitration* 2nd ed. (London: Sweet and Maxwell, 1991), p. 431, note an exception to this general principle in that where the procedural law and the seat of the arbitration are different the challenge is made in the courts of the procedural-law jurisdiction. The complexities of this situation are immense. In effect the courts of one country would be making orders effecting an arbitration held in a different country. As the powers of most courts are territorially limited, any orders made by a court regarding an arbitration which has its seat in another country may be unenforceable.

The grounds upon which an award can be challenged will vary from jurisdiction to jurisdiction. There are, however, some grounds which appear to be common to many jurisdictions. These are where there are defects in the award itself, issues of jurisdiction, procedural issues, reasons of State and issues of capacity.

In England, the AA 1996 creates a new regime whereby arbitral proceedings or an award may be challenged. Section 69 of the AA 1996 allows for appeals to be made on a point of law unless the parties otherwise agree. Sections 67 and 68 of the AA 1996 also allow for a challenge to be made to an award on the grounds that the arbitral tribunal did not have jurisdiction or that there was serious irregularity arising from the award affecting the arbitral tribunal, the proceedings or the award. Sections 67 and 68 are mandatory and may not be excluded by the agreement of the parties. These sections have been analysed in chapter 12. In addition to the rights of challenge given under statute there may also be rights of challenge at common law.

18.3 RECOGNITION AND ENFORCEMENT OF THE AWARD

Once an award has been given, the parties' interests become diametrically opposed. The successful party will wish to enforce the award and the unsuccessful party will wish to prevent enforcement. The unsuccessful party may seek an active challenge to the award or it may challenge the award passively. In challenging the award in a passive way the unsuccessful party does not make a positive case that the award should be overturned; rather it puts forward the case that the requirements needed for the enforcement of the award have not been met.

A distinction exists between the enforcement of an award in the jurisdiction which is the seat of the arbitration and enforcement elsewhere. The procedure for enforcing an award in the country where it was made is usually straightforward. The enforcement of an award in a country which has not been the seat of the arbitration is, however, a complex matter and much will turn on the relevant treaties and conventions to which that country is a signatory.

The words 'recognition' and 'enforcement' should be distinguished. An award may be recognised without being enforced. Recognition indicates that the award is accepted by one country as having been validly made. Enforcement is a positive action to recover or claim that which the award has ordered. The distinction between recognition and enforcement is important. A party may only wish that the award be recognised in one jurisdiction to prevent the losing party re-litigating the matters already decided in the arbitration. However, if the losing party has no assets in that jurisdiction, the winning party may not wish to enforce the award. It is a prerequisite in England, however, that where the enforcement of the award is sought there must also be recognition of the award. It is the recognition of the award that gives it its validity and which therefore permits it to be enforced.

The recognition and enforcement of the award are the final processes in the arbitration procedure but are not matters that the arbitral tribunal is involved with directly. After the award is made the arbitral tribunal is *functus officio*. It is the courts of the State where enforcement or recognition is sought that put the award into effect. The role of the arbitral tribunal or the arbitral institution is therefore secondary in any action to enforce. The ICC Arbitration Rules recognise this and also recognise that the prerequisites for enforcement in many countries will vary. A country may require, prior to the enforcement of an award, the production of the original or a certified copy of the award. Production of the arbitration agreement and sworn statements of the validity of the award by the arbitral tribunal may also be required. Where enforcement is sought in a country whose language is different to that of the award, a certified translation of the award and arbitration agreement may also be required. The formal requirements of most countries differ.

In England, s. 102 of the AA 1996 sets out the evidence to be produced by a party seeking recognition or enforcement of a New York Convention award. The ICC Arbitration Rules oblige the arbitral tribunal to take such steps as are reasonable to support the enforcement of an award (Article 35).

Enforcement by the winning party will inevitably be sought in a jurisdiction where the losing party has assets. It may be the case that the losing party has assets in many jurisdictions and the winning party will therefore have to decide in which of them it should enforce the award. Where this is the case the successful party must ascertain which jurisdictions will permit recognition and enforcement of the award. It follows that where the losing party has assets in two jurisdictions, but one will not recognise or enforce the award, the successful party is obliged to proceed in the jurisdiction which will permit recognition and enforcement of the award.

A successful party to an international arbitration must therefore first ascertain where the unsuccessful party's assets are located. Thereafter, the successful party must ascertain whether enforcement will be possible in the country or countries where the assets are located. It is the relationship between the country where enforcement is being sought and the seat of the arbitration that is all important in this regard. The successful party must therefore seek to discover whether there are reciprocal treaties between the two States, the views of the courts on the enforcement of foreign awards and, if the losing party is a State or government body, the laws of that country in relation to State immunity. Although the complexities of enforcing an international arbitration may be great it should be emphasised that it will often be easier to enforce an international arbitration award than a foreign judgment. The reason for this is that there are many more international treaties that permit enforcement of foreign awards than there are treaties which permit enforcement of foreign judgments.

When seeking to enforce an international award the successful party should be aware of any time limits that are imposed by any treaty or convention under which enforcement will be sought. The time limits under which enforcement may be commenced may vary from as little as three months to in excess of three years. Once a party applies to have an award recognised or enforced the opposing party will be under time limits to make a challenge to the application. In *Soinco SACI v Novokuznetsk Aluminium Plant (1997) The Times*, 29 December 1997, the claimant succeeded in an arbitration in Switzerland against the respondent. The claimant thereafter entered judgment against the respondent in England in January 1997. Entering judgment had the effect of recognising the award. The claimant then applied and was granted leave to enforce the award. The respondent applied for an extension of time in which to set aside the judgment. The extension of time was refused and the respondent appealed. On appeal an extension of time was again refused. The Court of Appeal held that once an arbitration award had been made, unless there was good reason not to, the court would assist the enforcement of an award by permitting it to be converted into a judgment. A failure to comply with the time limits for setting aside an award would not be treated lightly. The

Court of Appeal restated the principles governing applications for leave to appeal out of time as set out in *Norwich and Peterborough Building Society* v *Steed* [1991] 1 WLR 449. The factors that the court should be aware of include: the length of the delay; the reason for the delay; the applicant's prospects of success if leave is granted; and the risk of prejudice to the respondent.

18.4 THE NEW YORK CONVENTION

The New York Convention of 1958 is perhaps the most widely used convention in relation to international arbitrations. 82 countries are now signatories to the New York Convention, which encourages the enforcement of arbitral awards, and the English courts have interpreted it in this way: *Rosseel NV* v *Oriental Commercial Shipping Co. (UK) Ltd* [1991] 2 Lloyd's Rep 625. The method of enforcement of international arbitration awards provided by the New York Convention is simpler than those provided by its predecessors, the Geneva Protocol and Geneva Convention.

Article I(1) of the New York Convention states:

This Convention shall apply to the recognition and enforcement of arbitral awards made in the territory of a State other than the State where the recognition and enforcement of such awards are sought, and arising out of differences between persons, whether physical or legal. It shall also apply to arbitral awards not considered as domestic awards in the State where their recognition and enforcement are sought.

The New York Convention is not applicable to domestic arbitrations. Its applicability is to an arbitral award made in one country which will be enforced in another country. It is also applicable where enforcement is sought in the country where the award was made but the arbitration proceedings are considered to be non-domestic. Article I(2) defines what is meant by arbitral award. Not only is an award made by the arbitral tribunal included in this definition but also an award made by permanent arbitral bodies to which the parties have submitted.

The broad definition provided in Article I(1) as to what matters apply to the Convention is restricted in Article I(3), which allows signatories to the Convention to qualify the obligation to recognise and enforce an award. The first qualification is that a signatory to the Convention need not recognise or enforce an award made in a State that is not a contracting State. Of the 82 countries that are signatories to the New York Convention, 53 have signed it on the basis of reciprocity. The United Kingdom's acceptance of the New York Convention was based on reciprocity: see s. 100 of the AA 1996. It is of note that when drafting the AA 1996 it was decided not to follow ss. 35 and 36 of the UNCITRAL Model Law, which require that there be recognition and enforcement of an international award irrespective of where the award is made. The second reservation to the general principle in Article I(1) is that recognition and enforcement need only occur where the dispute is of a commercial nature in accordance with the law of the country applying this reservation. Thirty-one of the 82 states which are signatories to the Convention have made this reservation. Problems have arisen in regard to this reservation, as differing countries have given different interpretations to the word 'commercial'. In *Indian Organic Chemicals Ltd* v *Subsidiary 1 (US)* (1977) 4 YB Com Arb 271 and *India* v *Lief Hoegh & Co.* (1982) 9 YB Com Arb 405, the Indian courts reviewed the meaning of the word 'commercial'. The formalities required in obtaining recognition and enforcement of an award and the grounds upon which recognition and enforcement can be refused are discussed in 18.6 in examining English legislation.

Article II(1) of the Convention provides that the contracting States must recognise an agreement in writing under which the parties undertake to submit to arbitration the differences that arise between them. This requirement is fundamental to the New York Convention as it prohibits national courts from interfering in disputes that are the subject of an arbitration agreement. In England statutory effect was given to this principle in s. 1 of the AA 1975 and now in s. 9 of the AA 1996. This provision is, however, only applicable where the dispute or difference in question is capable of settlement by arbitration. This requirement that the matter be capable of settlement by arbitration is known as 'arbitrability'.

Article II(2) defines what is meant by an 'agreement in writing'. The term includes 'an arbitral clause in a contract or an arbitration agreement, signed by the parties or contained in an exchange of letters or telegrams'. The definition is non-exhaustive. Article II(3) requires that a court of a contracting State, when seised of a matter in respect of which there is an arbitration agreement shall, at the request of one of the parties, refer the matter to arbitration unless it finds that the arbitration agreement is null and void, inoperative or incapable of being performed. Section 9(4) of the AA 1996 mirrors this provision. The requirement to stay a matter to arbitration is not an obligation imposed on the contracting State per se. The obligation only arises where one of the parties makes an application for the matter to be stayed. Under English law a party loses the right to request that the matter be stayed when it has taken a step in those proceedings: s. 9(3) of the AA 1996. There is no similar requirement in the New York Convention. Article II(3) only requires that the request for a stay be made by one of the parties.

Article III requires each contracting State to recognise arbitral awards as binding and enforce them in accordance with the rules of procedure of that State, under the conditions laid down within the New York Convention. Fees and charges in regard to the recognition and enforcement of a New York Convention award are not permitted to be higher than those which would be imposed in respect of a domestic arbitration. This Article draws a distinction between the formalities that are required for a binding award and the enforcement of the award. The formalities that are required are set out in the New York Convention and the contracting States are obliged to comply with these conditions. The procedure for enforcement is not a matter dealt with in the New York Convention, which recognises that each State will have its own rules regarding enforcement. Some States may allow for the

attachment of earnings or the charging of property and impose specific requirements prior to the making of such orders; other States may have different methods
of enforcement or criteria. The New York Convention does not seek to create a
uniform method for the enforcement of an award but rather a uniform system
whereby the award is made enforceable.

Article IV sets out certain requirements for the recognition and enforcement of
an award. A party seeking recognition or enforcement of the award is obliged to
supply the duly authenticated original award or a duly certified copy and the
original agreement referred to in Article II of the Convention or a duly certified
copy. If the award or agreement are not in the official language of the State where
recognition is sought then translations, certified by an official or sworn translator
or diplomatic or consular agent, are required. This provision is mirrored in s. 102
of the AA 1996.

Article V deals with the situations where recognition or enforcement of the
award may be refused. Only the party against whom enforcement or recognition is
to be sought can make an application that the award should not be enforced. That
party has the burden of providing proof that the award should not be recognised
or enforced. There are five grounds under which the court may refuse recognition
or enforcement:

(a)   that under the law under which the arbitration was conducted the parties
were under some incapacity or the arbitration agreement was not valid;
(b)   that there had not been proper notice of the appointment of the arbitrator
or of the arbitration proceedings or the party was unable to present its case;
(c)   that the award deals with a matter outside the jurisdiction of the arbitral
tribunal;
(d)   that the composition of the arbitral tribunal or arbitral procedure was not
in accordance with the agreement of the parties or failing such agreement was not
in accordance with the law of the country where the arbitration took place.
(e)   that the award has not become binding or has been set aside in the country
in which it was made.

Article V does not require that the court must refuse to recognise or enforce an
award on these grounds but only that it may.

Recently, there has been a move away from automatically refusing to enforce
an award where the award has been set aside in the country in which it was made:
Re an Arbitration between Chromalloy Aeroservices and Egypt (1996) 939 F Supp
907; and see J. Paulsson, 'Enforcing arbitral awards notwithstanding a local
standard annulment' (1998) 9 (1) ICC Bulletin 14. For example, a court might
enforce an award, notwithstanding that it has been set aside by a court in the
country where it was made, if there are questions about the impartiality of the court
which set the award aside. Where there is an application in a court of the
country where the award was made to set aside the award, the enforcing court may
stay the proceedings within its jurisdiction until the result of the setting-aside

application is known. The question of when a court should exercise its discretion to stay proceedings was considered in *Soleh Boneh International Ltd* v *Uganda* [1993] 2 Lloyd's Rep 208.

Article V(2) sets out other grounds on which an award may be refused recognition or enforcement. These are where, by the law of the state where recognition or enforcement is sought, the subject matter of the arbitration is not capable of settlement by arbitration; and where recognition or enforcement would be contrary to public policy. The public policy ground is a matter that has been frequently commented upon, but under English law, no New York Convention award has ever been refused recognition or enforcement.

In the recent case of *Westacre Investments* v *Jugoimport-SDPR Holding Co. Ltd* [1999] 1 All ER (Comm) 865 the Court of Appeal had to consider whether it would enforce an award which was legal under the proper law of the contract and under the *lex arbitri* but illegal in the country of enforcement. The Court of Appeal were unanimous on this point that such an award should be enforced. In arriving at this decision, Waller LJ referred to the case of *Lemenda Trading Co. Ltd* v *African Middle East Petroleum Co. Ltd* [1988] 1 QB 448 and summarised Colman J's conclusions on that case at first instance [1998] 3 WLR 770):

1. He thought that it was difficult to see why, outside the field of such universally condemned activities such as terrorism, drug trafficking, prostitution, paedophilia, anything short of corruption or fraud in international commerce should invite the attention of English public policy in relation to contracts which are not performed within the jurisdiction of the English courts. It was, he thought, thus international comity (i.e., because performance in *Lemenda* was against public policy in the place of performance as well as England) that led the English court not to enforce the contract.

2. He thought that in this instance the fact that the court was concerned with enforcement of the award, valid by its curial law and by the proper law of the contract as opposed to the underlying contract, was material.

3. He thought that it was material that the illegality did not appear on the face of the award, and that it was necessary to have evidence relating to Kuwait.

4. He further thought that if one carried out a balancing exercise as between the public policy of enforcing awards and the public policy of not enforcing illegal contracts, since the offensiveness of the illegality alleged in this instance was not at the highest level, the balance was in favour of upholding the award.

Waller LJ further summarised what he considered had been decided in *Lemenda Trading Co. Ltd* v *African Middle East Petroleum Co. Ltd* his lordship stated at page 12 of the judgment:

(1) there are some rules of public policy which if infringed will lead to non-enforcement by the English court whatever their proper law and wherever

their place of performance but others are based on considerations which are purely domestic; (2) contracts for the purchase of influence are not of the former category; thus (3) contracts for the purchase of personal influence if to be performed in England would not be enforced as contrary to English domestic public policy; and (4) where such a contract is to be performed abroad, it is only if performance would be contrary to the domestic public policy of that country also that the English court would not enforce it.

In *Soleimany* v *Soleimany* [1998] 3 WLR 811 the Court of Appeal refused to enforce an award of the Beth Din on the grounds of public policy. The decision may be explained on the basis that the act complained of was not only illegal in the England where enforcement was sought but also in the place of performance.

Article VI of the New York Convention allows a competent authority in the State where recognition or enforcement is sought to order that the matter be adjourned and order that security be given by the party against whom enforcement is sought. Article VII states that multilateral or bilateral conventions concerning the recognition and enforcement of arbitral awards are not affected by the provisions of the New York Convention except the Geneva Protocol of 1923 and the Geneva Convention of 1927, which cease to apply between States bound by the New York Convention. The Geneva Protocol and Convention therefore do not cease to apply per se when a State becomes a contracting State of the New York Convention but they cease to apply between States who were signatories to them but are now signatories to the New York Convention. Articles VIII and IX of the New York Convention provide for who may become a signatory to the Convention. Article X deals with extending the Convention to territories which are dependencies of contracting States. Article XI sets out provisions relating to federal or non-unitary States. Article XII provides for when the Convention comes into force in respect of any contracting State.

Article XIII states that any contracting State may renounce the Convention by written notification to the Secretary-General of the United Nations. A contracting State which renounces its obligations under the Convention is, however, still obliged to comply with the rules relating to recognition and enforcement within the Convention for a period of one year from the date notification was received by the Secretary-General. This rule is equally applicable to dependencies of contracting States.

Article XIV states that a contracting State shall not be entitled to avail itself of the Convention against other contracting States except to the extent that it itself is bound to apply the Convention. Article XV sets out the requirement for the Secretary-General of the United Nations to notify all States contemplated in Article VIII of any signatures, ratifications, accessions, declarations, notifications, denunciations and dates when the Convention comes into force in respect of new signatories.

The States who are signatories to the New York Convention at 1 January 1999 are as follows:

Algeria
Antigua and Barbuda
Argentina
Australia (including external territories for whose international relations Australia
is responsible)
Austria
Bahrain
Belgium
Belize
Benin
Botswana
Bulgaria
Burkina Faso
Byelorussian Soviet Socialist Republic
Cambodia
Cameroon
Canada
Central African Republic
Chile
China
Colombia
Costa Rica
Cuba
Cyprus
Czechoslovakia (position unclear)
Denmark (including Greenland and the Faroe Islands)
Djibouti
Dominica
Ecuador
Egypt
Federal Republic of Germany
Finland
France (including all territories in the French Republic)
German Democratic Republic
Ghana
Greece
Guatemala
Haiti
Holy See
Hungary
India
Indonesia
Republic of Ireland
Israel

Italy
Japan
Jordan
Kenya
Korea
Kuwait
Luxembourg
Madagascar
Malaysia
Mexico
Monaco
Morocco
Netherlands (including Netherlands Antilles)
New Zealand
Niger
Nigeria
Norway
Panama
Peru
Philippines
Poland
Romania
San Marino
Singapore
South Africa
Spain
Sri Lanka
Sweden
Switzerland
Syria
Tanzania
Thailand
Trinidad and Tobago
Tunisia
Ukraine
Union of Soviet Socialist Republics (position unclear)
United Kingdom
United States of America (and territories)
Uruguay
Yugoslavia (position unclear).

18.5   THE GENEVA PROTOCOL AND CONVENTION

The Geneva Protocol of 1923 was one of the first treaties to recognise the importance of arbitrations in international commerce. The aim of the Protocol was twofold: first, to make all the signatories to the Protocol recognise an arbitration agreement between two parties subject to the jurisdiction of different signatory States, and secondly, to facilitate an easier method of enforcement of an award made under such an arbitration. However, it only provided a right to enforce an award in the State in which the seat of the arbitration was located. This meant that the Protocol had no application where, for example, the seat of the arbitration was in the United Kingdom but the successful party wished to enforce the award in Japan.

The Geneva Convention of 1927 sought to extend the power to enforce an award in any of the States which were signatories to the Convention, subject to certain conditions. Enforcement under the Geneva Convention of 1927 required the successful party to show that the arbitration agreement was one to which the Geneva Protocol of 1923 applied, that the award was made in one of the contracting States and that the parties to the award were subject to the jurisdiction of one of the contracting States to the Convention. The successful party also needed to show that the award was final in the country in which it was made and that recognition of the award was not contrary to public policy or the principles of law in the country in which it was to be enforced: Article 1(d) and (e) of the Geneva Convention of 1927.

The inclusion of the requirement that the award comply with the principles of the law of the country in which it was to be enforced is unclear. Awards made under differing laws in differing countries will invariably fail to comply with the law of the country where enforcement is sought. It is therefore not surprising that in Part II of the AA 1950, which gave effect to the Geneva Convention of 1927, this requirement was deliberately omitted.

18.6   ENFORCEMENT OF INTERNATIONAL AWARDS IN ENGLAND

18.6.1   Arbitration Act 1996, section 99

Section 99 of the AA 1996 states simply that Part II of the AA 1950 continues to apply in relation to foreign awards within the meaning of that Part of the AA 1950 which are not also New York Convention awards. Foreign awards are awards which are made and are subject to the United Kingdom's obligations under the Geneva Convention. Awards subject to the New York Convention are governed by ss. 100 to 104 of the AA 1996.

An award which is caught within s. 99 is to be treated as binding for all purposes on the persons between whom it was made. It may be relied upon by any of those persons by way of defence, set-off or otherwise in any legal proceedings in England: s. 36(2) of the AA 1950. The award is enforceable in the same manner as a domestic arbitration or by action (see s. 66 of the AA 1996). It is therefore the intent of Part II of the AA 1950 to put a foreign award on the same footing as a domestic award save that the conditions laid down in ss. 37 and 38 of the AA 1950 must be complied with: *Union Nationale des Co-opératives Agricoles de Céréales* v *Robert Catterall and Co. Ltd* [1959] 2 QB 44.

Under s. 37(1) of the AA 1950 for the award to be enforceable it must have:

(a)   been made in pursuance of an agreement for arbitration which was valid under the law by which it was governed;

(b)   been made by the tribunal provided for in the agreement or constituted in manner agreed upon by the parties;

(c)   been made in conformity with the law governing the arbitration procedure;

(d)   become final in the country in which it was made;

(e)   been in respect of a matter which may lawfully be referred to arbitration under the law of England;

and the enforcement thereof must not be contrary to the public policy or the law of England.

18.6.1.1   Public policy   The requirement that the award must not be contrary to public policy is a requirement that appears also within the UNCITRAL Model Law and the New York Convention. It is easy to see that no country would wish to enforce or recognise an award which offended certain minimum standards. In cases involving the New York Convention the phrase 'public policy' has been given a restrictive meaning. In *Parsons and Whittemore Overseas Co. Inc.* v *Société Générale de l'Industrie du Papier (RAKTA)* (1974) 508 F. 2d 969 the United States Court of Appeals, Second Circuit stated the Convention's public policy defence should be given a narrow interpretation and that such a defence should only exist 'where enforcement would violate the forum State's most basic notions of morality and justice'. Under English law the courts have also given a restrictive interpretation to the phrase 'public policy': *Dalmia Dairy Industries Ltd* v *National Bank of Pakistan* [1978] 2 Lloyd's Rep 223; *Deutsche Schachtbau- und Tiefbohr-Gesellschaft mbH* v *R'As al-Khaimah National Oil Co.* [1990] 1 AC 295.

In *Soleimany* v *Soleimany* [1998] 3 WLR 811 the Court of Appeal was asked to examine whether to enforce an award admitted to be based on an illegal act. The facts of the case were that a dispute arose between a father and son relating to profits obtained from the sale of carpets which had been smuggled from Iran. The case was referred to arbitration before a beth din which applied Jewish law. There was no dispute that the carpets had been smuggled out of Iran. The award of the beth din recognised this illegality but found in favour of the son, holding that irrespective of the illegality he was entitled to half of the profits. The son was granted leave under s. 26 of the AA 1950 to register the award as a judgment and the father applied to have the leave set aside. At first instance Judge Langan QC refused this application, but, on appeal, the Court of Appeal allowed it, holding that even if a foreign court found as a fact and recognised by its judgment that a contract had been entered into with the purpose of committing an illegal act in a foreign friendly State, an English court could not recognise the more relaxed attitude of that foreign jurisdiction because to do so would be contrary to English public policy. Therefore if the award was a judgment of a foreign court an English court would not enforce it. An award, whether domestic or foreign, would not be enforced by an English court if enforcement would be contrary to the public policy of this country, as it would be if it was based on an English contract which was illegal when made. The award in this case, which purported to enforce an illegal contract, was therefore not enforceable in England and Wales.

In *Westacre Investments* v *Jugoimport-SDPR Holding Co. Ltd* [1999] 1 All ER (Comm) 865 the Court of Appeal held that, where a foreign award was made that was both legal under the proper law of the contract and under the *lex arbitri* but illegal in the country of enforcement, the award would be enforced. The reasoning given by the Court of Appeal is set out at 18.4 above. The important difference in the facts between *Westacre Investments* v *Jugoimport-SDPR Holding Co. Ltd* and *Soleimany* v *Soleimany* [1998] 3 WLR 811 is that the acts complained of in *Westacre* were legal under the proper law of the contract and the *lex arbitri* whereas the acts complained of in *Soleimany* were illegal only under the proper law of the contract.

A majority of the Court of Appeal in *Westacre Investments* v *Jugoimport-SDPR Holding Co. Ltd* accepted Colman J's reasoning at first instance. Colman J had stated ([1998] 3 WLR 770) that 'it is entirely inappropriate in the context of the New York Convention that the enforcement Court should be invited to retry that very issue in the context of a public policy submission'. The contract was not illegal under the proper law and under the *lex arbitri*, Colman J stated:

> Given the weight to be attached to the public policy of sustaining the finality of international arbitration awards which I have already discussed, it is difficult to see how enforcement of such an award could be said to represent a lack of respect for the law of or administration of justice in Kuwait, so as to give that country, which is a party to the New York Convention, a just cause for complaint against the English Courts.

18.6.1.2 Other grounds for refusal Section 37(2) of the AA 1950 sets out further grounds which would entitle a court in England to refuse to enforce a foreign arbitration. These are that:

    (a)   the award has been annulled in the country in which it was made; or

    (b)   the party against whom it is sought to enforce the award was not given notice of the arbitration proceedings in sufficient time to enable him to present his case, or was under some legal incapacity and was not properly represented; or

    (c)   the award does not deal with all the questions referred to or contains decisions on matters beyond the scope of the agreement for arbitration.

Section 37(3) of the AA 1950, however, entitles a party to resist enforcement of a foreign award if there is any ground, other than the non-existence of the conditions specified in s. 37(1)(a) to (c) or the existence of the conditions specified in s. 37(2)(b) and (c), entitling the party to contest the validity of the award. It is therefore possible for a party to raise, by way of defence against enforcement, the requirement that the award comply with 'the principles of the law of the country in which it is sought to be relied upon': Article 1(e) of the Geneva Convention. The exclusion of this provision from ss. 35 to 42 of the AA 1950 shows that it was against the intent of the drafter of the AA 1950 that this defence should be raised to prevent enforcement. However, if accepted as a valid defence, a party would be able to re-litigate the matter in the place where the award is to be enforced to highlight differences between the proper law of the contract and the law of the place of enforcement.

18.6.1.3 Evidence Section 38 of the AA 1950 sets out the requirements of evidence needed before enforcement will be permitted. A party seeking to have an award enforced must provide the original award or a duly authenticated copy, evidence proving that the award has become final, evidence to show that the award is a 'foreign award' and that it was made under a valid arbitration agreement, was made by a valid arbitral tribunal and conforms to the law governing the arbitration procedure. If any document which is required to be produced is in a foreign language, the party must provide a certified translation certified as correct by a diplomatic or consular agent of the country to which the party belongs or in such other manner acceptable to the laws of England.

18.6.1.4 Final award Section 39 of the AA 1950 deals with the meaning of 'final award'. The section states that '. . . an award shall not be deemed final if any proceedings for the purpose of contesting the validity of the award are pending in the country in which it was made'. An award, however, is a 'final award' even though it may not be directly enforceable in the country in which it was made until a judgment has been entered in that country: *Union Nationale des Co-opératives Agricoles de Céréales* v *Robert Catterall and Co. Ltd* [1959] 2 QB 44.

18.6.2   Arbitration Act 1996, section 100

Section 100(1) of the AA 1996 defines a New York Convention award as being an award made, in pursuance of an arbitration agreement, in the territory of a State, other than the United Kingdom, which is a party to the New York Convention. Section 100 of the AA 1996 therefore replaces s. 7 of the AA 1975, which was repealed by the AA 1996. Section 100(2) of the AA 1996 provides that for the purposes of the definition in s. 100(1) an agreement in writing has the same meaning as in Part I of the AA 1996, where it is defined in s. 5(2) to (5).

Russell on Arbitration, 21st ed. (London: Sweet & Maxwell, 1996), at p. 44 states that a 'signature by the parties of a written agreement is required for an arbitration agreement to be valid under the New York Convention and the UNCITRAL Model Law. This is not part of English law.' This is supported by a reference to the case of *Zambia Steel and Building Supplies Ltd* v *James Clark and*

Eaton Ltd [1986] 2 Lloyd's Rep 225. If this were the case then s. 100 of the AA 1996 would be contrary to the United Kingdom's treaty obligations because it permits an award made under an unsigned arbitration agreement to be treated as a New York Convention award by reason of s. 5 of the AA 1996. When considering the Arbitration Bill the DAC commented in their report of February 1996 that the definition of 'in writing' given in s. 5 of the AA 1996 was consonant with Article II(2) of the New York Convention. The reasoning behind this conclusion was that Article II(2) states: 'The term "agreement in writing" *shall include* an arbitral clause in a contract or an arbitration agreement, signed by the parties or contained in an exchange of letters or telegrams' (emphasis added). The DAC concluded that the words 'shall include' indicated that Article II.2 gave a non-exhaustive definition and that the definition of 'agreement in writing' in the AA 1996 therefore was not in conflict with the New York Convention.

Section 100(2)(b) of the AA 1996 provides that the award is treated as being made at the seat of the arbitration irrespective of where it was signed, dispatched or delivered to any of the parties. The phrase 'seat of the arbitration' has the same meaning as in Part I of the AA 1996. Under s. 7 of the AA 1975 the requirement was that the award had to be made in the territory of a State which is a party to the New York Convention. In *Hiscox* v *Outhwaite* [1992] 1 AC 562 the House of Lords held that an award was made in the place where it was signed, irrespective of where the arbitration had been conducted. Section 100(2)(b) of the AA 1996 reverses this decision. A similar provision to s. 100(2)(b) is found in s. 53 of the AA 1996.

18.6.3   Arbitration Act 1996, section 101

Section 101 of the AA 1996 provides for the recognition and enforcement of a New York Convention award. Section 101(1) of the AA 1996 states that the 'award shall be recognised as binding on the persons as between whom it was made, and may accordingly be relied on by those persons by way of defence, set-off or otherwise in any legal proceedings in England and Wales or Northern Ireland'. Section 101(2) states that the 'award may, by leave of the court, be enforced in the same manner as a judgment or order of the court to the same effect'.

In *Minmetal Germagy GmbH* v *Ferco Steel Ltd* (1999) *The Times*, 1 March the Commercial Court considered when they would set aside leave granted under s. 101 of the AA 1996 to enforce two awards. The facts of the case were that a dispute arose between the claimant and defendant and an arbitration took place in China. Two awards were made in favour of Minmetal. Ferco, in its application to set aside leave to enforce the awards in England under s. 101 of the AA 1996, alleged that it had been denied a fair opportunity to present its case and that the procedure used in making the awards did not comply with the parties' agreement. Ferco alleged that there was substantial injustice in arriving at the award and therefore that it would be contrary to English public policy for the courts of England and Wales to enforce it.

The application of Ferco was dismissed. Colman J held that the criteria under Article 5 of the New York Convention, which applied in this case, meant that the enforcee had to show that it had been given a reasonable opportunity to present its case. In this regard the court, where enforcement is taking place, should examine the alleged injustice in the arbitral procedure and whether the enforcee had called upon the courts where the arbitration had taken place to exercise their supervisory jurisdiction, and if not, whether such failure by the enforcee was reasonable. The judge found that the arbitral tribunal had not acted in accordance with the agreement of the parties but that Ferco, the enforcee, had not sought to challenge the evidence even after the Beijing Court had ordered a resumed hearing. The judge concluded the Ferco had therefore waived its right to object and that a substantial injustice would not occur from the enforcement of the awards.

The accession provisions of the New York Convention are retroactive. An award made in a State prior to its accession to the New York Convention will be considered a New York Convention award so long as, at the date when recognition and enforcement of the award are sought, that State is a signatory to the New York Convention: *Minister of Public Works of the Government of the State of Kuwait* v *Sir Frederick Snow and Partners* [1984] AC 426. There is nothing within s. 101 of the AA 1996 to suggest that once judgment has been entered in the terms of the award it should be treated differently from any other judgment or order and therefore the court could entertain an application for a stay under RSC, ord. 45, r. 1; CPR, sch. 1: *Far Eastern Shipping Co.* v *AKP Sovcomflot* [1995] 1 Lloyd's Rep 520.

There appears not to be any substantial difference between the enforcement provisions of ss. 101 and 104 of the AA 1996 when compared to s. 36 of the AA 1950 for foreign awards. A party, where leave is given, may seek to enforce the award directly as if it were a judgment of the court or alternatively seek to have the award entered as a judgment in the terms of the award. The second alternative may be beneficial if the party wishes to register the judgment in a foreign court. In addition to the powers under s. 101(2) of the AA 1996 a party is given further powers to enforce an award under s. 104 of the AA 1996. The further powers provide that a party may seek to enforce the award by separate action on the award or use the powers conferred under s. 66 of the AA 1996. It would appear that the powers to enforce under s. 66 of the AA 1996 are substantially the same as those under s. 101 of the AA 1996. However, the grounds for refusal of recognition and enforcement of the award under Part I of the AA 1996 differ from those which apply under Part III of the Act and a party which elects to proceed under s. 66 to enforce may find greater difficulties than if it elects to proceed under s. 101.

18.6.4 Arbitration Act 1996, section 102

Section 102 of the AA 1996 states what evidence is required by a party seeking recognition or enforcement of a New York Convention award. The requirements under s. 102 are not as demanding as those to be found at s. 38 of the AA 1950 for recognition and enforcement of foreign awards. A party seeking enforcement of an award must provide the duly authenticated original award or a duly certified copy, and the original arbitration agreement or a duly certified copy. If the award or agreement is in a foreign language a translation of it certified by an official or sworn translator or by a diplomatic or consular agent must be provided. These requirements mirror those set out in Article IV of the Convention.

18.6.5   Arbitration Act 1996, section 103

Section 103 of the AA 1996 sets out the grounds for refusal of recognition or enforcement of a New York Convention award. It is for the person against whom the recognition or enforcement is sought to prove:

(a)   that a party to the arbitration agreement was (under the law applicable to him) under some incapacity;

(b)   that the arbitration agreement was not valid under the law to which the parties subjected it or, failing any indication thereon, under the law of the country where the award was made;

(c)   that he was not given proper notice of the appointment of the arbitrator or of the arbitration proceedings or was otherwise unable to present his case;

(d)   that the award deals with a difference not contemplated by or not falling within the terms of the submission to arbitration or contains decisions on matters beyond the scope of the submission to arbitration (but see subsection (4));

(e)   that the composition of the arbitral tribunal or the arbitral procedure was not in accordance with the agreement of the parties or, failing such agreement, with the law of the country in which the arbitration took place;

(f)   that the award has not yet become binding on the parties, or has been set aside or suspended by a competent authority of the country in which, or under the law of which, it was made.

Further, the enforcement or recognition of an award may be refused if it is in respect of something incapable of being arbitrated or contrary to public policy: s. 103(3) of the AA 1996; and see *Westacre Investments Inc.* v *Jugoimport-SPDR Holding Co. Ltd* [1997] 1 All ER (Comm) 865 (CA), and *Soleimany* v *Soleimany* [1998] 3 WLR 811. Where the award contains decisions on matters that have not been submitted to arbitration it may still be enforced in part if the matters that have been validly submitted and decided upon can be separated from those which have not been: s. 103(4) of the AA 1996. Where an application to set aside is made the enforcing court may adjourn its decision on whether to enforce the award: s. 103(5) of the AA 1996.

18.6.5.1   Incapacity   The incapacity is to be judged under the law applicable to the party to the arbitration agreement. The incapacity may relate to the age or competence of a party to enter into the arbitration agreement. Alternatively, it may relate to whether the party is prohibited from entering into an arbitration agreement. Under French law the State is prohibited from entering into arbitration agreement. In *Ministère Tunisien de l'Equipement* v *Soc. Bec. Frères* [1995] Rev Arb 275 the Paris Court of Appeal held that the State could not seek to rely on the prohibition to invalidate an international arbitration agreement.

18.6.5.2   The arbitration agreement not valid   The invalidity refers to a defect in the arbitration agreement rather than the incapacity of the parties or the fact that the matter is not capable of being dealt with by arbitration. An example of invalidity of an arbitration agreement would be where it has not been properly incorporated into the contract by reference. This has been discussed in chapter 5.

18.6.5.3   The absence of notice or unable to present case   Where a party shows that it did not have proper notice of the arbitration or the appointment of the arbitral tribunal this will be a ground for refusing to recognise or enforce an award. The word 'proper' refers to such requirements as exist under the contract. The phrase 'unable to present his case' has been held to refer to the standard of due process to be applied in the State where the arbitration took place. In *Parsons and Whittemore Overseas Co. Inc.* v *Société Générale du l'Industrie du Papier (RAKTA)* (1974) 508 F 2d 969 at p. 975 the court stated that the New York Convention 'essentially sanctions the application of the forum State's standards of due process'.

18.6.5.4   Excess of jurisdiction   This refers to the arbitral tribunal's obligation to deal only with the matters that are referred to it under the arbitration agreement. Where the arbitral tribunal deals with matters that do not fall within its jurisdiction partial enforcement of the award may be possible, but only where the courts are able to identify the areas of the award which are not in excess of jurisdiction.

18.6.5.5   Tribunal or procedure contrary to agreement   Where the parties have made an agreement for the appointment of the arbitral tribunal and the conduct of the arbitration, enforcement of any subsequent award may be refused if this agreement has not been complied with. In each case the court must examine the agreement and whether a party has waived the breach of the agreement. In some cases this may occur by the party not objecting at the outset or within a reasonable time after the breach took place.

18.6.5.6   Award not binding, set aside or suspended   Where the award has not yet become binding or has been set aside or is suspended by a competent authority enforcement may be refused. The reason an award has not become binding may be that it is subject to appeal or challenge at the seat of the arbitration. The enforcing court has a discretion whether to enforce the award: see 18.4.

18.6.5.7   Arbitrability   Section 103(3) of the AA 1996 refers to a matter not capable of settlement by arbitration. The enforcing court applies its own law in deciding whether a matter is capable of settlement by arbitration or not. Under English law, matters which would not be capable of settlement by arbitration would include:

(a)   decisions affecting the legal status of the parties;
(b)   decisions which affect the legal status or rights of non-parties; and
(c)   decisions reached which are not quasi-judicial (e.g., valuations, mediations and appraisements).

In the recent English case of *Halki Shipping Corporation* v *Sopex Oils Ltd* [1998] 1 WLR 726 it was held that indisputable and even undisputed claims are matters that are capable of settlement by arbitration in England, but indisputable or undisputed claims may not be matters capable of settlement by arbitration in other jurisdictions. It remains to be seen whether courts in other jurisdictions will refuse to enforce arbitral awards made on such claims where, under their law, they would be resolved by litigation.

18.6.5.8   Public policy   The same principles are applicable as are discussed in 18.6.1.1.

18.6.6   Arbitration Act 1996, section 104

Invariably a party will seek to enforce an award subject to the New York Convention under s. 101 of the AA 1996. Where, however, a party is unable to furnish the evidence which is required by s. 102 of the AA 1996 for enforcement to proceed, it will have to look at alternatives for enforcement. Section 104 of the AA 1996 provides that alternative by allowing a party to sue for breach of contract.

There is implied into every arbitration agreement a term that any future award will be carried out. This term is implied irrespective of whether the arbitration is domestic or foreign: *Norske Atlas Insurance Co. Ltd* v *London General Insurance Co. Ltd* (1927) 28 Ll L Rep 104. If a party fails to carry out an award, it will be in breach of contract. A party will then be able to sue for damages in the amount of the award on that breach of contract: *Bremer Oeltransport GmbH* v *Drewry* [1933] 1 KB 753. The party suing on the breach will have to show that there was a valid arbitration agreement, a valid award and a breach: *The Saint Anna* [1983] 1 WLR 895. A claim for breach of contract may be made while an application under s. 101 of the AA 1996 is pending. The limitation period for bringing a claim for breach of contract is six years from the date of the breach: *Agromet Motoimport* v *Maulden Engineering Co. (Beds) Ltd* [1985] 1 WLR 62.

18.7   CIVIL JURISDICTION AND JUDGMENTS ACT 1982

Sections 32 and 33 of the Civil Jurisdiction and Judgments Act 1982 are applicable to arbitration proceedings and the enforcement of a judgment of a foreign court.

Section 32 states that a judgment of a court of an overseas country will not be recognised or enforced where the proceedings were brought contrary to an agreement under which the dispute in question was to be resolved otherwise than by court proceedings, provided the party against whom the judgment was given did not bring the proceedings, or counterclaim in the proceedings or submit to the jurisdiction of the court.

Section 33 states that certain steps may not amount to a submission to jurisdiction of the overseas court. These steps include contesting the jurisdiction of the court, asking the court to dismiss or stay the proceedings on the ground that the question in dispute should be referred to arbitration and taking action to protect or obtain the release of seized property.

The rationale for these provisions is to stop claimants from bringing proceedings in foreign courts contrary to a valid agreement to arbitrate. If, however, the agreement to arbitrate is found to be illegal, void or unenforceable, or incapable of being performed for reasons not attributable to the party bringing the proceedings, the courts of the United Kingdom are not bound by the decision of the foreign court but must approach the dispute afresh applying English law.

19 UNCITRAL Model Law and Arbitration Rules

19.1 INTRODUCTION

Two of the most significant events in international arbitration law have been the adoption by the United Nations Commission on International Trade Law (UNCITRAL) of its Arbitration Rules and the Model Law on International Commercial Arbitration. The UNCITRAL Arbitration Rules and Model Law were adopted to help in the harmonious development of international trade. Resolution 31/98 of the UN Assembly stated:

> The General Assembly . . . Being convinced that the establishment of rules for . . . arbitration, that are acceptable in countries with different legal, social and economic systems, would significantly contribute to the development of harmonious international economic relations . . .

The UNCITRAL Arbitration Rules and Model Law continue the idea of a harmonious international system for arbitration. This concept first found significant international acceptance in the Geneva Protocol and Convention of 1923 and 1927 and the New York Convention in 1958. The Geneva Convention and Protocol were promoted by the International Chamber of Commerce and subsequently the idea of having internationally enforceable awards was taken up in the post-war era by the United Nations. The New York Convention is the most influential of the conventions that came into being in the post-war era, but there have been numerous other conventions such as the European Convention of 1961, the Washington Convention of 1965, the Moscow Convention of 1972 and the Panama Convention of 1975, which have all influenced the development of international arbitrations.

In 1966 UNCITRAL was established with the object of unifying and harmonising the law relating to international trade. Its aim was to coordinate, prepare and promote new conventions as well as to support and promote the New York Convention. Working groups were set up for the preparation of new conventions. The working drafts were sent out for consultation and comments subsequently referred back to UNCITRAL. The UNCITRAL Arbitration Rules were adopted on 15 December 1976, the UNCITRAL Conciliation Rules in 1980 and the UNCITRAL Model Law was adopted on 21 June 1985. In addition UNCITRAL have published guidelines for administering arbitrations under the UNCITRAL Arbitration Rules.

19.2   UNCITRAL ARBITRATION RULES

The UNCITRAL Arbitration Rules were adopted by the General Assembly by Resolution 31/98. The preface to the UNCITRAL Arbitration Rules states:

The General Assembly,
Recognising the value of arbitration as a method of settling disputes arising in the context of international commercial relations,
Being convinced that the establishment of rules for ad hoc arbitration that are acceptable in countries with different legal, social and economic systems would significantly contribute to the development of harmonious international economic relations,
Bearing in mind that the Arbitration Rules of the United Nations Commission on International Trade Law have been prepared after extensive consultation with arbitral institutions and centres of international commercial arbitration,
Noting that the Arbitration Rules were adopted by the United Nations Commission on International Trade Law at its ninth session after due deliberation,
1.   *Recommends* the use of the Arbitration Rules of the United Nations Commission on International Trade Law in the settlement of disputes arising in the context of international commercial relations, particularly by reference to the Arbitration Rules in commercial contracts;
2.   *Requests* the Secretary-General to arrange for the widest possible distribution of the Arbitration Rules.

19.2.1   Introductory rules

Article 1 of the UNCITRAL Arbitration Rules sets out the scope of application of the Rules. Article 1(1) states that the Rules are applicable where the parties to a contract have agreed in writing that disputes in relation to that contract should be settled in accordance with the Rules. It is therefore envisaged that the arbitration agreement will be written and apply to present or future disputes. A footnote to Article 1 gives a model arbitration clause, which states:

Any dispute, controversy or claim arising out of or relating to this contract, or the breach, termination or invalidity thereof, shall be settled by arbitration in accordance with the UNCITRAL Arbitration Rules as at present in force.

Parties drafting an arbitration clause are also informed that they should consider adding the name of the appointing authority, the number of arbitrators, the place where the arbitration is to be held and the language to be used in the arbitration proceedings. Under English law a reference to the UNCITRAL Arbitration Rules need not be written as s. 5(3) of the AA 1996 states that: 'Where parties agree otherwise than in writing by reference to terms which are in writing, they make an agreement in writing'. Therefore parties that verbally agree to apply the UNCIT-RAL Arbitration Rules to their dispute are deemed to have made an agreement in writing.

Article 1(2) states that the Rules are to govern an arbitration to which they have been applied under Article 1(1), but thereafter includes a proviso that where there is a conflict between the Rules and any rule of law applicable to the arbitration from which the parties are not entitled to derogate, that rule of law shall prevail. Article 1(2) therefore expresses the legal position in many countries that mandatory provisions within the law of the seat of the arbitration will prevail over terms agreed by the parties. In *India* v *McDonnell Douglas Corporation* [1993] 2 Lloyd's Rep 48 it was held that the jurisdiction of the English courts under the AAs 1950 to 1979 over arbitration in England could not be excluded by an agreement between the parties to apply the laws of another country or indeed by any other means, including the election of procedural rules, unless such were sanctioned by those Acts. This is equally the case under the AA 1996.

Article 2 of the UNCITRAL Arbitration Rules deals with notice and the calculation of periods of time under the Rules. Article 2(1) deems that notice has been received if it is physically delivered to the addressee or delivered at his habitual place of residence, place of business or mailing address. Where none of these can be found, after making reasonable enquiry, notice may be served at the addressee's last known place of residence. Notice will be deemed to have been received on the date it is delivered. Notification by post, fax and telegram are within this definition. A telephone conversation would, however, not be a physical delivery and therefore would not constitute notice. Whether email or any other similar electronic transmission can be said to have been physically delivered until the message has been downloaded is questionable. Unless and until the message has been downloaded no physical delivery of the message takes place. It is equally unclear whether a recorded message left on an answering machine would fall within the definition.

Article 2(2) states that time periods begin to run, for the purpose of calculating periods of time, on the day after the day when the notice, notification, communi-cation or proposal has been received. Where the last day of the time period is a public holiday or a non-business day the time period is extended to the first business day thereafter. Official holidays or non-business days occurring during the running of the period are included in calculating the period. This definition draws no distinction between short or long periods of time. Under English rules of court there are differing methods in calculating time periods. If the time period is seven days or less, a Saturday, Sunday, Christmas Day, Good Friday or bank holiday is not included within the reckoning period for that time: CPR, r. 2.8(4). It is suggested that this provides a common-sense approach if there have been short time periods imposed for certain acts or responses in the arbitration. However, the anomaly that does arise is that a party has less time to do an act if he is given eight days to do it rather than seven.

Article 3 of the UNCITRAL Arbitration Rules deals with notice of arbitration. The Rules provide that the terminology used in describing the parties to the dispute are claimant and respondent. Article 3(2) states that the arbitration proceedings are deemed to commence on the date when the notice of arbitration is received by the respondent. The notice of arbitration is relevant to any limitation period that may be applicable to the proceedings. Parties should be aware that there may be differing notices under the contract. A notice of intention to commence arbitration, for instance, under section 67 of FIDIC's Red Book has the effect of preventing an engineer's decision becoming final and binding. It is not, however, sufficient to stop the limitation period running and thereby creating a time bar to the claim. It is the notice under Article 3 of the UNCITRAL Arbitration Rules, or such other rules or law as is applicable, which has the effect of starting the arbitration proceedings and therefore determining the date relevant to limitation.

Article 3(3) sets out the requirements with which the arbitration notice must comply. The arbitration notice must: demand that the dispute be referred to arbitration; state the names and addresses of the parties; make reference to the arbitration clause of the contract or agreement; make reference to the contract out of which the dispute arises; state the general nature of the claim; indicate the amount involved; state the relief sought and state the number of arbitrators unless previously agreed. Article 3(4) sets out further matters that may be included in the notice of arbitration. The notice may contain: proposals for the appointment of an arbitrator or appointing authority; the notification of the appointment of an arbitral tribunal; and a statement of claim. Article 4 requires that a party notify the other party of the persons he has chosen to assist or represent him.

19.2.2   Composition of the arbitral tribunal

Article 5 of the UNCITRAL Arbitration rules deals with the number of arbitrators. It provides that if the parties have not previously agreed or cannot agree the number of the arbitrators within 15 days after the receipt of the notice of arbitration, the number shall be three. The election of a three-member arbitral tribunal is common in many civil law countries whereas in common law countries it is often provided that the default position is a single arbitrator. Under English law, s. 15(3) of the AA 1996 provides that the default position where the number of the arbitral tribunal cannot be agreed is a sole arbitrator. Section 15 of the AA 1996 is a non-mandatory provision and therefore, in an arbitration in England to be held under the UNCITRAL Arbitration Rules, Article 5 will apply.

Articles 6 to 8 deal with the appointment of an arbitral tribunal. Article 6 sets out how a sole arbitrator is to be appointed. Either party may propose the name of one or more persons who will serve and, if no appointing authority has been agreed upon by the parties, the name or names of such appointing authorities. If agreement is not reached within 30 days by the parties on the identity of the sole arbitrator, the arbitrator is to be appointed by the appointing authority. If no appointing authority has been agreed by the parties, or the appointing authority refuses to act within 60 days, either party may request the Secretary-General of the Permanent Court of Arbitration at the Hague to designate an appointing authority.

Where the appointing authority is to appoint a sole arbitrator it must do so as promptly as possible. There is a list procedure that the appointing authority is to use unless otherwise agreed by the parties or determined to be inappropriate by the appointing authority. The list procedure requires that the appointing authority communicate to both parties an identical list of at least three names. Thereafter the parties should respond within 15 days deleting names which they consider inappropriate. The sole arbitrator is then picked from one of the remaining names in accordance with the order of preference shown by the parties. If the appointment cannot be made in accordance with this procedure, the appointing authority must exercise its discretion in the appointment of the sole arbitrator. The appointing authority should have regard to the impartiality and independence of the sole arbitrator and, in exercising its discretion to appoint, should consider appointing an arbitrator of a neutral nationality where the parties are of differing nationalities.

Article 7 sets out the procedure for appointing a three-person arbitral tribunal. Article 7(1) states that each party should elect an arbitrator and the two arbitrators appointed should elect the third arbitrator who will act as the presiding arbitrator. There is a default clause included in this Article similar to that found in Article 6.

Where there is an appointing authority nominated the party requesting the appointing authority to act in default of agreement under Articles 7 and 8 should send to the appointing authority: a copy of the notice of arbitration, a copy of the contract out of which the dispute arises and a copy of the arbitration agreement if separate. The appointing authority thereafter may request additional information from either of the parties: Article 8(1). If a party encloses nominations for the proposed appointment as arbitrator, the names, addresses, nationality and qualifications of the nominees should be included: Article 8(2).

Articles 9 to 12 deal with challenging the appointment of the arbitral tribunal. Article 9 places on a prospective arbitrator the obligation to disclose, to the appointing authority and/or the parties, any matter likely to give rise to justifiable doubts about his impartiality or independence. Where circumstances exist that give doubts about that impartiality or independence of a member of the arbitral tribunal that member of the arbitral tribunal may be challenged: Article 10.

Article 11 deals with the procedure for challenge. A party which intends to challenge an arbitrator has 15 days to make that challenge from the date of notification of the appointment of the arbitrator or from the date when that party became aware of the grounds for challenge. The challenge is made in writing with reasons. Notification is given to the other party to the arbitration, to the challenged arbitrator and to other members of the arbitral tribunal. There is no requirement within this Article to notify the appointing authority. The other party to the arbitration may agree to the challenge or the arbitrator may unilaterally decide to withdraw. In such a case the procedure for replacement of the arbitrator is found in either Article 6 or 7. Article 12 deals with the situation where either the other party does not agree to the challenge or the arbitrator does not withdraw. A decision on whether the arbitrator should withdraw will be made by an appointing authority. If the appointing authority upholds the challenge, a substitute arbitrator will usually be appointed in accordance with the provisions of Articles 6 to 9.

Where an arbitrator either resigns or dies during the arbitral proceedings, Articles 6 to 9 may again be relied upon for the appointment of a substitute arbitrator: Article 13(1). Where an arbitrator fails to act, a new arbitrator will be appointed. Where the sole or presiding arbitrator is replaced, hearings previously held must be repeated. If any other member of the arbitral tribunal is replaced, whether the previous hearings should be repeated will be at the discretion of the arbitral tribunal: Article 14. Where an arbitrator appointed by one of the parties is replaced, the arbitral tribunal, prior to deciding whether to proceed or repeat previous hearings, should seek representations from both parties. Where the parties agree on how to proceed, the arbitral tribunal should generally follow that agreement unless in exercising their discretion they conclude that the basis for that agreement is clearly erroneous.

19.2.3 Arbitral proceedings

Articles 15 to 30 of the UNCITRAL Arbitration Rules deal with the arbitral proceedings. Article 15 provides that it is for the arbitral tribunal to conduct the reference as is appropriate, provided that the parties are treated with equality and that both sides are given a full opportunity of presenting their case. A similar provision relating to the treatment of the parties is to be found in Article 18 of the UNCITRAL Model Law. Section 33(1) of the AA 1996 has a similar provision save that the right of the parties to give a 'full' opportunity of presenting their case has been changed to allow only for a 'reasonable' opportunity. The rationale for this change under the AA 1996 is discussed at 19.5.2.

Either of the parties has the right to request an oral hearing and such request must be granted by the arbitral tribunal. Where no request is made the arbitral tribunal has a discretion to choose whether to proceed by documents only or by oral hearing. All documents sent to the arbitral tribunal by one of the parties must be copied to the other party.

Article 16 deals with the place of arbitration. 'Place' in this context is synonymous with 'seat' as defined under s. 3 of the AA 1996. Unless the parties have agreed the place where the arbitration is to take place, responsibility for this decision rests with the arbitral tribunal. If the place of the arbitration is agreed by the parties or determined by the arbitral tribunal, there is no obligation that all matters to be dealt with in the arbitration must be dealt with at the place of the arbitration. Examination of witnesses and the holding of meetings may take place at any location having due regard to the circumstances of the arbitration. Equally, the arbitral tribunal is not confined to the place of the arbitration if it needs to inspect goods, documents or property. It is, however, a requirement of the Rules that the award be made in the place of the arbitration.

Article 17 deals with the language of the arbitration. It is for the arbitral tribunal to decide the language of the arbitration promptly after its appointment subject to any agreement of the parties. Documents annexed to the pleadings may be required to be translated into the language of the arbitration.

Articles 18 to 20 deal with the pleadings. Article 18 requires that unless the statement of claim was annexed to the notice of arbitration a copy should be served within the time limit determined by the arbitral tribunal with a copy of the contract and arbitration agreement if separate. The statement of claim must include the names of the parties, a statement of the facts supporting the claim, the points in issue and the relief or remedy sought. The claimant may annexe to the statement of claim all relevant documents.

Article 19 provides for the service of a statement of defence. The statement of defence is to be served within a period to be determined by the arbitral tribunal and served on all members of the arbitral tribunal and the other party. The statement of defence must respond to the following matters within the statement of claim: the facts supporting the claim, the points in issue and the relief or remedy sought. A counterclaim can be served with the statement of defence or served at a later date if extra time is required and such extra time is considered justified by the arbitral tribunal. The counterclaim must, however, comply with the requirements of Article 18 of the Rules and must arise out of the same contract as the claim. This requirement that the counterclaim arise out of the same contract is peculiar to arbitrations. In court proceedings a counterclaim does not have to arise out of the same or similar facts as the claim but can relate to any matter where the defendant has a right of action against the claimant. The rationale behind this is that all matters in dispute between the parties can be dealt with in one set of proceedings. In arbitration proceedings this generally cannot occur as the jurisdiction of the arbitral tribunal arises out of the arbitration agreement, which is usually found within a contract. The arbitral tribunal's jurisdiction is therefore usually limited to disputes which arise out of that contract. Disputes or differences not connected with the contract cannot be consolidated into an existing arbitration unless the parties agree.

Article 20 provides that during the arbitral proceedings either party may amend or supplement the claim or defence. The arbitral tribunal has a discretion to refuse to allow an amendment. A claim may not, however, be amended where the amendment would fall outside the scope of the arbitration clause.

Article 21 states that the arbitral tribunal has power to rule on objections to its own jurisdiction and also the existence and validity of the arbitration agreement. The arbitral tribunal may also rule on the existence of the contract in which the arbitration forms part. The arbitration agreement is treated as a separate independent contract from the other terms of the agreement and therefore a ruling by the arbitral tribunal that the contract is void does not necessarily, as a matter of law, invalidate the arbitration clause. Any plea that the arbitral tribunal does not have jurisdiction should be raised no later than when the defence to the claim is served or when the defence to the counterclaim is served. A plea that the arbitral tribunal lacks jurisdiction should be treated as a preliminary issue by the arbitral tribunal. However, the arbitral tribunal may continue with the arbitration and rule on such a plea in its final award.

In addition to the statement of claim and statement of defence the arbitral tribunal may order that further written statements be provided. The arbitral tribunal has a discretion to decide how long may be given for the service of these statements, save that the time allowed should not exceed 45 days: Articles 22 and 23.

Articles 24 and 25 deal with evidence and hearings. Article 24 provides that each party has the burden of proving the facts that support its claim or defence. The arbitral tribunal may request that each of the parties provide a summary of the documents and other evidence on which it intends to rely. During the course of the hearing, the arbitral tribunal may require that the parties produce documents, exhibits or other evidence. The Rules do not provide for any limitation on the documents or other evidence that the arbitral tribunal may require. However, the right of the arbitral tribunal to require the disclosure of documents and other evidence will be subject to the general principles of law relating to disclosure. Therefore, the arbitral tribunal cannot under English law order that documents which contain privileged material be disclosed.

Article 25 states that if an oral hearing is to be held, the arbitral tribunal must give to the parties adequate notice of the time, date and place of the hearing. Where witnesses are to be heard the respective parties must, at least 15 days before the date of the hearing, give details to the arbitral tribunal of the names and addresses of the witnesses, language in which the testimony is to be given and the subject of the evidence. A written statement of the testimony of a witness is not a prerequisite for the giving of oral evidence. However, the arbitral tribunal may require that a statement is provided prior to the hearing pursuant to Article 24(2). The parties are free to present evidence in the form of written signed statements. The hearings are held privately unless the parties otherwise agree. Article 25(6) provides that the 'arbitral tribunal shall determine the admissibility, materiality and weight of evidence offered'.

Article 26 states that the arbitral tribunal may, at the request of one of the parties, take such interim measures as are necessary to protect the subject matter of the dispute. In addition a party may seek court intervention for the taking of such interim measures. Such a request to the court is deemed not to be incompatible or a waiver of the agreement to arbitrate. Article 27 deals with the arbitral tribunal's power to appoint experts. The report of an expert appointed by the arbitral tribunal is conveyed to the parties who may then express their opinions in regard to the content of the report in writing. The parties are entitled to examine any document on which the expert has relied. The parties may request that the expert attend at any oral hearing for cross-examination on the content of the report.

Article 28 deals with the default of the parties. Where the claimant, without sufficient cause, fails to serve its statement of claim within the required time, the arbitral tribunal may terminate the proceedings. Where the respondent, without sufficient cause, fails to serve its statement of defence within the required time, the arbitral tribunal may order that the proceedings continue. Where one of the parties fails to attend the hearing the arbitral tribunal may proceed with the arbitration. Where one of the parties fails to produce documentary evidence when so required the arbitral tribunal may proceed on the evidence before it.

Article 29 deals with the closure of the hearing. The arbitral tribunal is required to ask the parties if there is further evidence to be produced or submissions to be made and, if there are none, declare the hearings closed. The arbitral tribunal may however reopen the hearings prior to the award being made if there are exceptional circumstances. Article 30 states that a party which proceeds with the arbitration knowing that there has been failure to comply with these Rules and has not stated an objection shall be deemed to have waived the right to object.

19.2.4   Award

Article 31 states that where there are three arbitrators an award is made by majority decision. The Rules do not provide that the dissenting arbitrator is entitled to insist that his dissenting reasons are included in the award. Under English law the dissenting arbitrator would therefore have no right to insist that his dissenting reasons be included within the published award: *Cargill International SA v Sociedad Iberica de Molturacion SA* [1998] 1 Lloyd's Rep 489 (a case on the GAFTA arbitration rules). On matters of procedure the presiding arbitrator is required to make such decisions as are necessary where there is no majority or where the arbitral tribunal so authorises. A decision of the presiding arbitrator is subject to revision by the arbitral tribunal.

Article 32 provides for the form and the effect of an award. Awards may be final, interim, interlocutory or partial. The award is to be made in writing with reasons, unless otherwise agreed, and is final and binding on the parties. The parties are required to carry out the award without delay. The award is required to be signed and dated and to state the name of the place where the award was made. The award can be made public only with the consent of the parties.

Article 33 provides for the arbitral tribunal to apply the law designated by the parties in relation to the substance of the dispute. If no law has been designated, the arbitral tribunal must determine that law by the conflict of laws rules which it considers are applicable. Only where expressly requested may the arbitral tribunal act as amiable compositeur or apply principles of equity and only if allowed under the *lex arbitri*.

Article 34 deals with the settlement of the arbitration proceedings. Article 35 provides that within 30 days after receipt of an award a party may request that the arbitral tribunal give an interpretation of the award. This is a concept foreign to English law. The interpretation by the arbitral tribunal must be given within 45 days and forms part of the award. The interpretation must comply with the requirements of Article 32. Article 36 allows for the correction of clerical, computational and typographical errors. Article 37 allows for the parties to request that an additional award be made where it is considered that the award of the arbitral tribunal has failed to address a claim presented to it in the arbitral proceedings.

Articles 38 to 40 deal with the costs of the arbitration. Article 38 provides that the arbitral tribunal shall fix the costs of the arbitration in the award. Costs of the arbitration are limited to the reasonable fees of the arbitral tribunal; travel and other expenses of the arbitral tribunal; the costs of expert advice and other assistance; the travel and other expenses of witnesses; the reasonable costs of legal representation of the successful party if such were claimed; and any fees and expenses of an appointing authority. Article 41 provides that the arbitral tribunal may require each party to deposit an advance of costs to meet the costs referred to in Article 38.

19.3   UNCITRAL MODEL LAW

The origins of the UNCITRAL Model Law stem back to a request made in 1977 by the Asian-African Legal Consultative Committee to review the New York Convention in light of the apparent lack of uniformity in the enforcement of awards. The lack of uniformity in enforcement arises in part because of qualifications to the New York Convention. Signatories to the New York Convention may restrict their obligations imposed under the Convention in two ways. First, on the basis of reciprocity and secondly, on the basis that the dispute must be of a commercial nature. For further discussion in relation to these two qualifications see chapter 18.

Different countries have given differing interpretations to the word 'commercial': *Indian Organic Chemicals Ltd* v *Subsidiary 1 (US)* (1977) 4 YB Com Arb 271 and *India* v *Lief Hoegh & Co.* (1982) 9 YB Com Arb 405. Furthermore, different countries, when having to decide whether the award should be recognised and enforced within their jurisdiction, have interpreted the requirements of Article V of the New York Convention differently. One country, for instance, may decide that a matter is not capable of settlement by arbitration whereas another country may decide that it is, and similarly different countries may take different views on what is or is not a matter of public policy — Article V(2)(a) and (b).

In the report of the Secretary General of UNCITRAL entitled *Study on the Application and Interpretation of the Convention on the Recognition and Enforcement of Foreign Arbitral Awards* (UN Doc. A/CN/9/168) the conclusion reached was that harmonisation in respect of enforcement of foreign arbitral awards could be achieved more effectively if there was a model law that could be adopted by the States that were signatories to the New York Convention. A further report entitled *Possible Features of a Model Law on International Commercial Arbitrations* (UN Doc. A/CN/9/207) analysed what were to be the principles on which a model law should be based. The report advanced a number of specific policies including: autonomy of the parties, restriction of the role of national courts, the introduction of core clauses ensuring fairness and due process and clauses aiding in the recognition and enforcement of the award.

The UNCITRAL Model Law was adopted by the United Nations International Commission on Trade Law on 21 June 1985 and by the UN General Assembly on 11 December 1985. Lord Hacking, 'Arbitration law reform: the impact of the UNCITRAL Model Law on the English Arbitration Act 1996, *Arbitration*, November 1997, p. 292, states:

> The UNCITRAL Model Law in its presentation and content is indeed 'a model'. It commences by identifying an international arbitration and continues in a logical order through the whole process of arbitration down to enforcement of arbitration awards. Its language is simple and its text short.

19.4 PROVISIONS OF THE UNCITRAL MODEL LAW

19.4.1 General provisions

Article 1 states that the Model Law is applicable to international commercial arbitrations.

A footnote suggests that the word 'commercial' should be given a wide interpretation and gives a non-exhaustive list of dealings which are considered to be commercial in nature. These include: the supply or exchange of goods or services, distribution agreement, commercial representation or agency, factoring, leasing, construction of works, consulting, engineering, licensing, investment, financing, banking, insurance, exploitation agreement or concession, joint venture, carriage of goods or passengers by air, sea, rail or road.

The word 'international' is defined in Article 1(3). An arbitration is international if the parties to the arbitration agreement have, at the time when the arbitration agreement was concluded, their places of business in different States, or one of the parties has its place of business in a State other than that of the 'place' of arbitration, or a substantial part of the contract is to be performed in a State different to where one of the parties has its place of business.

Article 2 provides definitions of 'arbitration', 'arbitral tribunal' and 'court'. The Article then goes on to provide certain rules for interpretation. Article 3 deals with receipt of written communications. This Article deems *inter alia* that a written communication is received on the date that it is delivered unless otherwise agreed by the parties.

Article 4 deals with the waiver of the right to object where a party knows that any provision of the Model Law has not been complied with. The right to object will be lost if not made within any specified time period set down in the Model Law or made with undue delay if no time is specified within the Model Law. The wording used in the Model Law differs from that used in s. 73 of the AA 1996. Under s. 73 of the AA 1996 a party will lose its right to object unless it shows that it did not know or could not with reasonable diligence have discovered that there were grounds for the objection. The AA 1996 therefore uses both a subjective and objective test in deciding whether a party has waived its right to object. Under the UNCITRAL Model Law the test is purely subjective. It is suggested that this is an omission within the Model Law as it will be far more difficult to show that a person was unaware of the objection. Article 5 deals with the extent of intervention permissible by the court and is discussed subsequently.

19.4.2 Arbitration agreement

Article 7 of the UNCITRAL Model Law gives a definition of arbitration agreement. It is an agreement to submit disputes to arbitration 'which have arisen or which may arise' between the parties in respect of a defined legal relationship. A dispute between the parties may be contractual or otherwise. It would, however, appear that a dispute relating solely to the existence of a legal relationship would not be caught within the definition as that legal relationship has not been defined. The arbitration agreement may be part of a contract or in a separate form.

Article 7(2) requires an arbitration agreement to be in writing. An agreement is in writing if it is contained in a document signed by the parties or in an exchange of letters, telex or other means of telecommunication which provides a record of the agreement or in statements of claim and defence in which the existence of the agreement is alleged by one party and not denied by the other. A facsimile will therefore be caught within the definition. An arbitration agreement may also be in writing where it is referred to within a contract document.

Article 8 states that, where a claim is brought before a court which is subject to an arbitration agreement and a party so requests, the court shall refer the dispute to arbitration unless it finds the agreement null and void, inoperative or incapable of being performed. This provision mirrors Article II(3) of the New York Convention and is now found in similar terms in s. 9 of the AA 1996.

The definition of 'dispute' is of fundamental importance and the same problems may arise as with the differing interpretations of the word 'commercial'. The courts of one country may view a set of facts and hold that a dispute arises from them. On the same set of facts another court in a different country may hold there is no dispute. For instance, a court in England may hold that on a particular set of facts there is a dispute and the matter is capable of being referred to arbitration. An award is obtained by the claimant. The claimant seeks to enforce the award in India under the New York Convention. The respondent may then argue that Article V(2)(a) would provide a defence to the recognition and enforcement of the award because under the law of the country where enforcement is being sought the 'subject matter of the difference is not capable of settlement by arbitration', because there is no 'dispute' between the parties. In deciding whether there is a 'dispute' the court must look at the law of its own country and not the country where the arbitration took place.

Article 9 of the UNCITRAL Model Law provides that it is not incompatible with the arbitration agreement for a party to request before or during the proceedings that a court provide interim measures of protection.

19.4.3   Composition of arbitral tribunal

Articles 10 and 11 deal with the composition and setting up of the arbitral tribunal. Article 10 states that the parties are free to agree the number of arbitrators but in default of agreement the number shall be three. Article 11(1) provides that a person shall not be precluded from acting as an arbitrator by reason of his nationality unless agreed otherwise by the parties. Article 11(2) states that the parties are free to agree the procedure for appointing an arbitrator. Default provisions are provided in Article 11(4) and (5) where the appointment procedure is agreed by the parties.

Article 11(3) provides the default position where there is no agreement on the appointment procedure. Where there are three arbitrators each party shall nominate an arbitrator and the nominees must appoint the third arbitrator. Where one party fails to appoint an arbitrator or the two arbitrators fail to agree on a third arbitrator the appointment is made by the court or other authority specified in Article 6. Where arbitration is to be by sole arbitrator and no agreement can be reached between the parties the appointment is made by the court or other authority specified in Article 6.

Article 12 provides for grounds of challenge to the arbitrator. An arbitrator is obliged to disclose all circumstances giving rise to justifiable doubts about his impartiality or independence. This obligation continues throughout the arbitral process. The challenge procedure is set out in Article 13. Article 14 deals with the situation where the arbitrator becomes *de jure* or *de facto* unable to perform his functions or fails to act without undue delay. Article 15 deals with the replacement of an arbitrator who has ceased to act.

19.4.4   Jurisdiction of arbitral tribunal

Article 16 deals with the competence of an arbitral tribunal to rule on its jurisdiction. This power is divided into two distinct areas: the separability of the arbitration agreement and the arbitrability of the agreement. This is one of the cornerstones of the UNCITRAL Model Law. The rule that the arbitration agreement is separate to the main contract has been similarly included in s. 7 of the AA 1996. This means that even if the main contract is found to be null and void the arbitration agreement may still be binding on the parties. The question that the courts will have to examine is whether the act that rendered the underlying contract void or illegal also renders the arbitration agreement void: *Westacre Investments Inc.* v *Jugoimport-SPDR Holding Co. Ltd* [1999] 1 All ER (Comm) 865 (CA); [1998] 3 WLR 770 (Commercial Court). The arbitral tribunal may also rule on its own substantive jurisdiction. This deals with the situation where an objection is raised as to whether any matter has been referred to the arbitral tribunal for its decision. The decision of the arbitral tribunal may thereafter be challenged by the parties. There is a similar provision in ss. 30 to 32 of the AA 1996.

Article 17 deals with the power of the arbitral tribunal to make interim orders. This power is vested with the arbitral tribunal unless otherwise agreed by the parties. The power relates to protection of the subject matter of the dispute and the arbitral tribunal may require any party to provide appropriate security in connection with an interim measure.

19.4.5 Conduct of arbitral proceedings

Article 18 provides that the parties must be treated with 'equality and each party shall be given a full opportunity of presenting his case'. This is intended to reflect principles of natural justice.

Article 19(1) gives to the parties the right to agree on the procedure to be followed by the arbitral tribunal. In drafting the UNCITRAL Model Law it was realised that it would be used in both civil and common law countries. Article 19(1) therefore permits the parties to agree that the arbitral proceedings be conducted either inquisitorially or in an adversarial manner.

Article 19(2) deals with the procedure under which the arbitration is to be conducted failing any agreement under Article 19(1). It states that the arbitral tribunal may 'conduct the arbitration in such manner as it considers appropriate'. The powers conferred on the arbitral tribunal include, but are not limited to, the power to: 'determine the admissibility, relevance, materiality and weight of any evidence'.

Article 20(1) states that parties are free to agree on the place of the arbitration and that failing such an agreement the place of the arbitration shall be determined by the arbitral tribunal. Article 20(2) states that notwithstanding the provisions of Article 20(1) the arbitral tribunal may meet at any place it considers appropriate for hearing witnesses, experts or the parties, for consultation among its members, or for inspection of goods, other property or documents.

Article 21 provides that the date when the arbitration proceedings commence is the date when the respondent receives a request that the dispute is to be referred to arbitration. This Article is of importance in that the date on which the request is received by the respondent will be relevant to whether there is a limitation defence to the claim. In *Vosnoc Ltd* v *Trans Global Projects Ltd* [1998] 1 WLR 101 Judge Jack QC was required to consider when an arbitration had commenced under the AA 1996. He commented that there was a difference between the UNCITRAL Model Law and the AA 1996. Under the UNCITRAL Model Law the mere reference to arbitration was sufficient to commence proceedings. In contrast, under the AA 1996, in order to stop time running the notice must require a step to be taken which entails more than just the requirement that the arbitration commence. However, Judge Jack's analysis of s. 14 of the AA 1996 has recently received some criticism: *Allianz Versicherungs AG* v *Fortuna Co. Ltd* [1999] 2 All ER 625, see 4.8.

A request that the dispute be referred to arbitration at some future date is unlikely to satisfy the requirements of Article 21. In *Surrendra Overseas Ltd* v *Sri Lanka* [1977] 1 WLR 565 the following notice was held not to be sufficient to commence arbitration proceedings under the AA 1950: 'Owners will be putting the matter to arbitration. We will advise you concerning details of the arbitrator in due course.' Such a notice is not a request, in the present tense, that the dispute be referred to arbitration but a notice that at some future time the matter will be referred to arbitration.

Article 22 allows for the parties to choose the language for the proceedings. In default of agreement the arbitral tribunal may determine the language. Article 23 deals with the provision of statements of claim and defence. Documents which support the claim or defence may be annexed to the pleading or referred to in the pleadings. The parties, unless agreed otherwise, may amend their respective claims and defences during the course of the arbitration proceedings unless it is considered inappropriate by the arbitral tribunal having regard to the delay in making the amendment.

Article 24 provides that it is for the arbitral tribunal to decide whether there shall be oral hearings or documents-only hearings, subject to any contrary agreement by the parties. All statements, documents and other materials provided to the arbitral tribunal by one party shall be communicated to the other party: Article 24(3). If the claimant fails to communicate its claim in accordance with Article 23(1), the arbitral tribunal shall terminate the proceedings: Article 25(a). In contrast, failure by the respondent to communicate its defence will not be treated as an admission of the claim and the arbitral tribunal will continue with the proceedings: Article 25(b). If a party fails to attend a hearing or fails to produce documentary evidence in accordance with the provisions of the UNCITRAL Model Law, the arbitral tribunal shall continue on the evidence that is before it: Article 25(c).

Article 26 provides that unless otherwise agreed by the parties the arbitral tribunal may appoint one or more experts to report on specific issues to be determined by the arbitral tribunal. This Article is broad enough to allow the arbitral tribunal not only to appoint experts of fact but also legal assessors. Where an expert is appointed by the arbitral tribunal the parties are obliged, if required, to provide access to relevant documents, goods or their property for inspection. The expert may if so required also give oral evidence and be cross-examined at the hearing after the submission of his report. The second paragraph of Article 27(2) allows for the arbitral tribunal or a party with the approval of the arbitral tribunal to apply to the court for assistance in taking evidence.

19.4.6 Making of award and termination of proceedings

Article 28 provides that the arbitral tribunal shall decide the dispute in accordance with the law designated by the parties in relation to the substance of the dispute. Any designation of law or legal system is construed, unless otherwise expressed, as directly referring to the substantive law of the State and not to its conflict of laws rules. Only where there is no designation will the conflict of laws rules apply. Only where expressly requested by the parties may the arbitral tribunal act as amiable compositeur or apply principles of equity. This Article has been substantially reproduced in s. 46 of the AA 1996.

Article 29 provides that the decision-making of the arbitral tribunal shall be by majority or by the presiding arbitrator unless otherwise agreed. This reflects Article

31 of the UNCITRAL Arbitration Rules. Article 30 of the UNCITRAL Model Law provides for the settlement of the arbitration. Where settlement is reached the parties may request that it be embodied in an award.

Article 31 provides for the form and content of an award. The award is required to be made in writing and signed by the members of the arbitral tribunal or a majority of them. The award is required to be reasoned unless otherwise agreed. The award must state the date and the place where the arbitration was determined. The award is deemed to have been made at that place. A signed copy of the award is required to be delivered to the parties.

Article 32 provides for the termination of the arbitral proceedings. This may occur on the publication of the final award. It may also occur where the claim of the claimant is withdrawn unless the respondent objects; where the parties agree; or where continuation is either unnecessary or impossible.

Article 33 deals with residual powers of the arbitral tribunal after the issue of an award. The arbitral tribunal may on the request of a party or on its own initiative correct a clerical error in the award. If so agreed by the parties, a party may also request that the arbitral tribunal give an interpretation on a specific point or part of the award. A party may also request that the arbitral tribunal give an additional award where a claim presented to the arbitral tribunal has been omitted from the award. The arbitral tribunal is given a power to extend the time limit of 30 days in which the parties may make requests under this Article. An additional award or correction or interpretation of an award must comply with the requirements of Article 31.

19.4.7 Recourse against award

Article 34 provides that the award may only be set aside by a court in accordance with the provisions of this Article. The grounds on which the award may be set aside reflect those on which recognition and enforcement may be refused under the New York Convention. The grounds include:

(a) that a party to the arbitration was under some incapacity,

(b) that the agreement is not valid under the law applicable,

(c) that proper notice had not been given of the appointment of the arbitral tribunal or the proceedings,

(d) that a party was unable to present its case,

(e) that the award deals with matters outside the jurisdiction of the arbitral tribunal,

(f) that the composition of the arbitral tribunal was not in accordance with the agreement of the parties unless that agreement was contrary to the applicable law, and

(g) that the subject matter of the arbitration was not capable of settlement by arbitration under the law of the State in which the place of arbitration was located or the award is contrary to the public policy of that State.

In *Soleimany* v *Soleimany* [1998] 3 WLR 811 the award of the arbitral tribunal was held to be contrary to public policy. This case involved enforcement under s. 26 of the AA 1950 although the principles would be equally applicable to a matter falling within Article 34 of the UNCITRAL Model Law. However, see also the Court of Appeal's decision in *Westacre Investments Inc.* v *Jugoimport-SPDR Holding Co. Ltd* [1999] 1 All ER (Comm) 865 (CA). For further analysis of enforcement of international awards see chapter 18.

An application to set aside may not be made after a period of three months from the date of receipt of the award. The court when asked to set aside the award may, where appropriate, and so requested by a party, suspend the setting-aside proceedings to enable the arbitral tribunal to eliminate the grounds for setting aside.

19.4.8 Recognition and enforcement of awards

Article 35 deals with the enforcement of awards properly made. The award, irrespective of where it is made, shall be recognised and enforced. The UNCITRAL Model Law does not therefore require reciprocity in the recognition and enforcement. Article 35(2) deals with the conditions that are required before enforcement will be allowed.

Article 36 of the UNCITRAL Model Law deals with grounds for refusing recognition and enforcement. These grounds are identical to those in the New York Convention. An application that the award should not be enforced can only be made by the party against which enforcement or recognition is sought and that party has the burden of providing proof of the ground. The grounds include the following:

(a)   under the law under which the arbitration was conducted the parties were under some incapacity or the arbitration agreement was not valid;
(b)   there had not been proper notice of the appointment of the arbitrator or of the arbitration proceedings;
(c)   the party was unable to present its case;
(d)   the award deals with a matter outside the jurisdiction of the arbitral tribunal;
(e)   the composition of the arbitral tribunal or arbitral procedure was not in accordance with the agreement of the parties or failing such agreement was not in accordance with the law of the country where the arbitration took place;
(f)   the award has not become binding or has been set aside or suspended in the country in which it was made.

Article 36(1)(b) sets out other grounds on which the award may be refused recognition or enforcement. These are that the courts of the State where recognition or enforcement is sought find that under the law of that State the subject matter of the arbitration is not capable of settlement by arbitration or that the recognition or enforcement would be contrary to public policy.

19.5 COMPARISONS WITH THE ARBITRATION ACT 1996

It was expressed in clear terms in June 1989 by the Departmental Advisory Committee for Arbitration Law (the DAC), which was then chaired by Mustill LJ, that the UNCITRAL Model Law should not be adopted in England. The DAC made the recommendation at para. 108 of their February 1996 report that there was a need for a new and improved Arbitration Act. The new Arbitration Act 'should comprise a statement in statutory form of the more important principles of the English law of arbitration, statutory and (to the extent practicable) common law'. The UNCITRAL Model Law was not in any sense a statement of English arbitration law principles. However, much that was included in the UNCITRAL Model Law has been included in the AA 1996. The following are illustrations of some of the differences between the UNCITRAL Model Law and the AA 1996.

19.5.1 Court intervention

Article 5 of the UNCITRAL Model Law provides that 'no court shall intervene' in a matter governed by the Model Law except where so provided for in the Model Law. In the AA 1996 the word 'shall' is replaced with 'should'. In the Bill for the AA 1996 the word 'shall' was used. Whether the replacement of the word 'shall' by 'should' has any effect on the AA 1996 is unclear. In the AA 1996 it is a principle that the courts should not intervene and whether expressed in the permissive or not it remains a principle. The reason for the change was explained by T. Landau, *New Duties and Liabilities — Party Autonomy* v *Powers of the Tribunal*, IBC Conference, 4 July 1996:

> In earlier drafts [of the AA 1996], Article 5 of the Model Law had been reproduced verbatim, but this was then changed, given that it had the effect of sweeping aside the entirety of the court's inherent jurisdiction. This was considered undesirable. Apart from anything else, it is always dangerous to remove something without knowing the exact extent of the thing to be removed.
>
> It is not, however, envisaged that the court will have any real opportunity of exercising inherent powers, and certainly not in order to alter any of the areas covered by the Act where these powers are carefully delimited. Reference should be made in this respect to paras 20–2 of the DAC Report.

19.5.2 Presentation of a party's case

Article 18 of the UNCITRAL Model Law provides that the parties should be treated with 'equality and each party shall be given a full opportunity of presenting his case'. In s. 33(1) of the AA 1996 the obligation is imposed on the arbitral tribunal that it shall 'act fairly and impartially as between the parties, giving each party a reasonable opportunity of putting his case and dealing with that of his opponent'. T. Landau, *New Duties and Liabilities — Party Autonomy* v *Powers of the Tribunal*, IBC Conference, 4 July 1996, has explained the rationale behind the change from the word 'full' in the Model Law to 'reasonable' in the AA 1996:

> The word *'full'* was replaced by *'reasonable'*, given that a 'full' opportunity may not, in all the circumstances, be 'fair'. A party may argue, whatever the nature of the dispute, that he will need six months to present his case in 'full'.

19.5.3   Commencement of arbitration proceedings

Article 21 of the UNCITRAL Model Law states that: 'Unless otherwise agreed by the parties, the arbitral proceedings in respect of a particular dispute commence on the date on which a request for that dispute to be referred to arbitration is received by the respondent'. In comparison s. 14 of the AA 1996 requires that the claimant serve on the respondent a notice requiring the respondent to do a certain act. The requirements of s. 14 differ depending on whether the arbitral tribunal is named or is to be agreed, or is to be appointed by a third party.

In *Vosnoc Ltd* v *Trans Global Projects Ltd* [1998] 1 WLR 101 Jack QC was required to consider when an arbitration had commenced under the AA 1996. He held that:

> English law has taken the approach that something more must be done than to request that the matter be referred to arbitration. A step must be taken towards getting the arbitration under way, a step towards the appointment of the tribunal.

In *Nea Agrex SA* v *Baltic Shipping Co. Ltd* [1976] QB 933 Lord Denning MR took the view that the courts should not take an overly technical view when construing notices to commence. His Lordship stated:

> In such a case the arbitration is deemed to commence when the one party, expressly or by implication, requires the other party to appoint his arbitrator. If he simply says: 'I require the difference to be submitted to arbitration in accordance with our agreement' that is sufficient to commence the arbitration: because it is by implication a request to the other to appoint his arbitrator.

Vosnoc Ltd v *Trans Global Projects Ltd* therefore departs from the dictum of Lord Denning. The effect of this in relation to the UNCITRAL Model Law has been expressed by N. Shaw, 'Arbitration — timing the start', *Arbitration*, February 1998, p. 58, as follows:

> The decision has important policy implications in that it shows a disparity between English law and the UNCITRAL Model Law. Parties in jurisdictions where the Model Law applies to their own arbitration proceedings might feel aggrieved to fall foul of the English law position requiring them to do something more than merely refer the matter to arbitration.

Judge Jack QC in *Vosnoc Ltd* v *Trans Global Projects Ltd* also commented that there was a difference between the UNCITRAL Model Law and the AA 1996 in that, under the UNCITRAL Model Law, the mere reference to arbitration is sufficient to commence proceedings but, in contrast, under the AA 1996, in order to stop time running, the notice must require a step to be taken which is more than just a requirement that the arbitration commence. This distinction between the UNCITRAL Model Law and the AA 1996 has not been universally accepted. In *Allianz Versicherungs AG* v *Fortuna Co. Ltd* [1999] 2 All ER 625 Judge Jack's approach to the requirements needed to commence arbitral proceedings was criticised. See 4.10 for further discussion on this point.

19.5.4   Power to extend time limits

The power of the court to extend time limits for the commencement of arbitration proceedings is to be found in s. 12(1) and (3) of the AA 1996. The court is also provided with a power, unless the parties otherwise agree, to extend the time limits relating to the arbitral proceedings at any time during the course of the arbitration proceedings. There is no comparable provision within the UNCITRAL Model Law. The importance of these provisions were illustrated in the case of *Consolidated Investment and Contracting Co.* v *Saponaria Shipping Co. Ltd* [1978] 1 WLR 986. The case involved a dispute between cargo owners and shipowners. The contract provided that the shipowners would be free of all liability if arbitration proceedings were not commenced within one year of the delivery of the cargo. A dispute arose between the cargo owners and the shipowners, but the cargo owners did not commence arbitration proceedings because of comforting indications made by the shipowners' insurers. In these circumstances the Court of Appeal unanimously held that they would extend the time whereby the cargo owners could commence arbitration proceedings.

See also 4.8.

20   Rules of the International Chamber of Commerce

20.1   INTRODUCTION

The International Chamber of Commerce (the 'ICC') is only one of many bodies administering institutional rules. The ICC established an International Court of Arbitration (the 'Court of Arbitration') in 1923 and has now administered in excess of 10,000 arbitrations with parties and arbitrators from more than 100 countries. The success of the ICC has come about in no small part because of the quality of the service that it provides.

The past 30 years have seen an expansion in international trade. Trade and political barriers have been lowered and expertise in many areas of international commerce can be provided by video conferencing or over the Internet. Transportation is quicker, safer and cheaper. Industry no longer sees its markets as limited by national boundaries. As a result of many of these changes and developments within the law the ICC were obliged to revise their Rules of Arbitration (the 'Rules') to keep up with modern trends of business and to plug loopholes that had appeared within those Rules. This process was begun in 1995 with a proposal from the Court of Arbitration to modify the Rules in order to resolve a few problems that existed within them. A working group was established whose preliminary conclusion was that there was a need for a complete review of the Rules rather than any attempted modification of the existing Rules. This conclusion was adopted by the Commission on International Arbitration which directed that such a revision should seek to: reduce delays, reduce unpredictability, rationalise costs and improve defective rules while at the same time preserving the strengths and the fundamental characteristics of the ICC arbitration: R. Kriendler, 'Impending revision to the ICC Arbitration Rules — opportunities and hazards for experienced and inexperienced users alike' (1996) 13 (2) Journal of International Arbitration. The Commission on International Arbitration, however, noted many strengths of the ICC arbitration procedure. The 'universality' of the Rules to all legal systems was noted as a particular strength of the existing Rules. The use of the Terms of Reference, which set out the matters in dispute between the parties and define the jurisdiction of the arbitral tribunal and the role of the Court of Arbitration, was noted. The Court of Arbitration's role in scrutinising awards was also seen as a strength of the ICC arbitration procedure.

The Working Group set about drafting the new Rules and in particular dealing with the matters suggested by the Commission on International Arbitration. This involved the reviewing of the Rules generally, addressing the problem of administrative delays and setting out a new chronological structure that the Rules should follow. The Working Group submitted its draft to the Commission on International Arbitration in December 1996. This draft was reviewed and revised and was adopted in April 1997. On 1 January 1998 the ICC brought the new Rules into force. The new Rules represented the first substantial revision to the Rules in nearly 20 years.

Those coming to an arbitration under the ICC rules for the first time would note at the outset fundamental differences to almost any domestic arbitration that they had been involved with in England. The term 'Court of Arbitration' is a misnomer. It is not the Court of Arbitration that settles disputes but the 'arbitral tribunal' that the Court of Arbitration appoints. The arbitral tribunal publishes a draft arbitration award which is reviewed by the Court of Arbitration. The Court of Arbitration's function is to organise and supervise the arbitration and ensure compliance with the Rules. The Court of Arbitration, in addition to appointing the arbitral tribunal, fixes the seat of the arbitration, determines fees and costs as well as reviewing the draft award of the arbitral tribunal. In this respect the Court of Arbitration must be constantly aware of any changes in the law of any country in which the arbitration is being held or is subject to. The Court of Arbitration is supported by a secretariat which deals with the management of the cases.

The ICC recommend the use of their standard arbitration clause, which states:

All disputes arising out of or in connection with the present contract shall be finally settled under the Rules of Arbitration of the International Chamber of Commerce by one or more arbitrators appointed in accordance with the said Rules.

The ICC also recommend that the parties should consider whether they should stipulate within the arbitration clause the proper law of the contract, the seat of the arbitration and the language of the arbitration. The new Rules only apply to ICC arbitration proceedings where the Request for Arbitration has been made after 1 January 1998. The old Rules will therefore be applicable to arbitration proceedings in progress prior to 1 January 1998.

20.2 PROVISIONS OF THE RULES OF ARBITRATION OF THE ICC

The Rules are made up of 35 Articles with three appendices. In addition to the Rules of Arbitration there are ICC Rules of Optional Conciliation. Although conciliation is recommended prior to arbitration it is not a mandatory procedure. If the parties elect conciliation, this will not oblige them to proceed with arbitration if the conciliation procedure proves unsuccessful.

20.2.1 Introductory provisions

Article 1(1) of the ICC Rules sets out the function of the International Court of Arbitration. 'The function of the Court is to provide for the settlement by arbitration of business disputes of an international character'. One of the changes to the Rules is that Article 1 now goes on to provide that: 'If so empowered by an arbitration agreement, the Court shall also provide for the settlement by arbitration in accordance with these Rules of business disputes not of an international character'. This change to Article 1 was made to help clarify what may or may not be arbitrated under the ICC Rules. Under the old Rules, Article 1 of Appendix II stated that the Court of Arbitration 'may' accept jurisdiction over non-international business disputes, if it had jurisdiction by reason of an arbitration agreement. Many arbitration agreements in contracts did not make such an express provision and therefore, if the parties wished to have their dispute resolved by the ICC Rules, they would have to draft an ad hoc agreement so that the matter fell within that provision.

The remaining paragraphs of Article 1 set out the purpose of the Court of Arbitration and its powers to take urgent decisions, the seat of the Secretariat and the power to delegate. The power to delegate decision-making to Committees of the Court has become increasingly important as more and more cases are referred to ICC arbitration.

Article 2 provides definitions of 'arbitral tribunal', 'claimant' and 'respondent'. Although these terms are singular the definition provides that they also include the plural. 'Arbitral tribunal', for example, includes one or more arbitrators.

The term 'Award' is also defined in Article 2 as including an interim, partial or final award. However, no further indication of what is an award is given. While there will generally be no uncertainty about an arbitral tribunal's final award there may be some uncertainty when considering a prior ruling in the arbitral proceedings. In *Société Industrialexport-Import* v *Société GECI et GFC* 1993 Rev arb 303 the court was asked to determine whether three procedural orders were in fact awards. The arbitral tribunal had held that as it was competent to rule on its own jurisdiction, it could determine the applicable procedural rules and had rejected an application for suspension of the arbitral proceedings. The Paris Court of Appeal held that in each case the decisions of the arbitral tribunal were in fact awards because they 'constituted decisions of a jurisdictional nature'. In England the courts have held that they have no jurisdiction to correct procedural errors: *K/S A/S Bill Biakh* v *Hyundai Corporation* [1988] 1 Lloyd's Rep 187. It is implicit from *K/S A/S Bill Biakh* v *Hyundai Corporation* and from *Three Valleys Water Committee* v *Binnie and Partners* (1990) 52 BLR 42 that the English courts do not consider a pre-award ruling on a procedural matter as being an award.

Article 3(1) deals with the provision of pleadings and other written communications and requires that copies should be sent to each party, each arbitrator and one copy to the Secretariat. Paragraphs (2) to (4) of Article 3 deal with the sending of communications and the time limits applicable. Article 3(2) allows for most modern means of communication to be used for serving notifications and communications. The final sentence of Article 3(2) envisages developments in modern communications and provides for this by stating that notification or communication may be made by 'any other means of telecommunication that provides a record of the sending thereof'. Although this development is to be welcomed it would perhaps have been more logical and would have given more certainty if the Rules had stated that the other means of telecommunication provides a record of receipt rather than sending.

Article 3(3) provides that a communication will be deemed to have been made on the day it is received or would have been received if made in accordance with Article 3(2). This deeming provision may cause problems with the enforcement of an award where the document has never been received. A court in a country where enforcement is sought may refuse enforcement if an important document has not been received by a party to the arbitration agreement.

20.2.2 Commencing the arbitration

Article 4 sets out the procedure for the commencement of the arbitration. The first step in this procedure is to send a request for arbitration to the Secretariat. The details that are required to be included in the request are set out in Article 4(3). These are: the name, description and address of the parties; a description of the circumstances giving rise to the dispute; a statement of the relief or damages sought; the relevant agreements including the arbitration agreement; details of the number of arbitrators; comments as to the place of the arbitration, the proper law of the contract and *lex arbitri* and language of the arbitration. Copies of the request are required to be sent to the Secretariat, in accordance with Article 3(1), as well as the advance payment of the administrative expenses as detailed in Appendix III to the Rules.

The Secretariat notifies both claimant and respondent of the receipt of the request and the date of such receipt: Article 4(1). It is the date on which the request is received by the Secretariat that is deemed to be the date for the commencement of the arbitral proceedings: Article 4(2). A copy of the request and every document sent to the Secretariat is sent to the respondent once the Secretariat has received sufficient copies of the request and the required advance payment: Article 4(5). Article 4(6) deals with further claims which have been made and the joinder of these claims to other arbitration proceedings. Where the joinder of claims is requested by a party the Court of Arbitration must balance a party's right to choose its own members of the arbitral tribunal with the other party's right to have the dispute dealt with in one set of proceedings with the consequential savings in time and costs. An award may, however, be set aside where it is inequitable for the

Court of Arbitration to order consolidation: *OIAETI et Sofidif* v *Cogema* 1991 Rev arb 326.

A defence (the 'answer') must be supplied by the respondent in accordance with Article 5 of the Rules. The answer responds to each of the matters raised by the request: Article 5(1)(a) to (e). This answer should be supplied within 30 days, although the Secretariat may extend the time for the answer under Article 5(2). The respondent must submit the required number of copies of the answer to the Secretariat which then communicates the answer to the claimant. Article 5(5) sets out the requirements for any counterclaim that the respondent makes. These include a description of the nature and circumstances of the dispute giving rise to the counterclaim and a statement of the relief or damages sought. Article 5(6) deals with the submission of a reply to any counterclaim made.

The parties are deemed to have submitted to the ICC Rules in force at the date of the commencement of the arbitration unless they have agreed to be bound by the Rules in force at the date of the arbitration agreement: Article 6(1). Practitioners should ensure that they check the contract on this point as the costs have been increased under the new Rules and certain extra powers have also been given to the arbitral tribunal.

Article 6(2) deals with the jurisdiction of the arbitral tribunal and the Court of Arbitration to proceed where the respondent does not provide an answer. If the Court of Arbitration is not satisfied that there is an arbitration agreement under the Rules, the claimant may seek a declaration to that effect from any court of law having jurisdiction. Once the arbitral tribunal has become seised with any matter it may proceed with the arbitration irrespective of either party's failure to take part in the proceedings. Article 6(4) gives effect to the *Kompetenz-Kompetenz* principle that has previously been examined in chapter 5.

20.2.3 The arbitral tribunal

Articles 7 to 12 deal with the appointment, challenge and replacement of the arbitral tribunal. Article 7(1) sets out the basic requirement that: 'Every arbitrator must be and remain independent of the parties involved in the arbitration'. This requirement confirms in part the principle of natural justice that the arbitral tribunal should be free from any connection with the parties or the subject matter of the dispute. It is suggested that the meaning of 'independent' is determined by reference to whether there is a 'real danger' of bias rather than to the 'real likelihood' of bias: *R* v *Gough* [1993] AC 646. Each arbitrator is required to sign a statement of independence and disclose to the Secretariat all such matters as may call into question his or her independence. The obligation of disclosure of matters affecting the independence of an arbitrator continues throughout the course of the reference. The Secretariat gives the parties a copy of the arbitrator's statement of independence and there is a time frame set for the parties to comment. The appointment of an arbitrator is thereafter made by a decision of the Court of Arbitration.

The Arbitral Tribunal is constituted in accordance with Articles 8, 9 and 10 unless the parties have otherwise provided. Article 8(1) states that the dispute will be resolved either by a sole arbitrator or by three arbitrators. The general rule is that the Court of Arbitration will appoint a sole arbitrator unless it appears to them that the complexity of the dispute warrants the appointment of three arbitrators. Time limits are set down in Article 8(2), (3) and (4) for the parties to nominate arbitrators. A sole arbitrator will usually be of a different nationality from the parties although in suitable circumstances, where neither party objects, the Court of Arbitration may appoint a sole arbitrator from the country of one of the parties. In default of a party failing to nominate an arbitrator the Court of Arbitration will make the appointment upon the recommendation of the National Committee of the country of which the defaulting party is a national. The Court of Arbitration, however, retains an overriding power to reject any proposal made by a National Committee and appoint anyone whom it considers suitable.

Where the dispute has multiple parties the claimants appoint one arbitrator jointly and the respondents appoint one arbitrator jointly. Where there is a failure by the claimants or respondents to agree, the Court of Arbitration may appoint each member of the arbitral tribunal. Article 10(2) permits the Court of Arbitration to appoint the whole arbitral tribunal. Article 10(2) was a response to the case of *Siemens AG* v *Dutco Construction Co.* (1992) 18 YB Com Arb 140. In the *Dutco* case the French Cour de Cassation held that it was a matter of public policy to allow the parties equality in appointing the arbitral tribunal. The facts of *Dutco* were that there were multiple respondents. The claimant nominated a member of the arbitral tribunal, but the respondents could not agree on a member and the Court of Arbitration therefore nominated a person as the respondents' member of the tribunal. The Cour de Cassation held that it was inequitable to allow one party to nominate a member of the arbitral tribunal but to impose a person on the other party. The *Dutco* case is applicable to arbitration proceedings in France but not necessarily to proceedings in other jurisdictions. Where there are to be arbitration proceedings in a country other than France, the Court of Arbitration may still exercise its power to nominate a person as the defaulting parties' member of the arbitral tribunal while permitting the other party to nominate its member of the arbitral tribunal.

Article 11 provides a procedure for challenging the appointment of an arbitrator. A challenge can be made for 'lack of independence or otherwise'. The challenge is made in a written letter to the Secretariat, setting out the facts and circumstances on which the challenge is based. A time limit of 30 days is imposed, from the date of receipt of the notification of the appointment of an arbitrator, for a party to make a challenge or 30 days from the date when the party was informed of the facts giving rise to the challenge. The arbitrator, the other party or parties and other members of the arbitral tribunal may comment on the grounds of challenge. The Court of Arbitration will then decide on the merits of the challenge.

Article 12 provides that an arbitrator will be replaced upon his or her death or resignation, upon acceptance by the Court of Arbitration of a challenge to the arbitrators appointment or upon request of all of the parties. The Court of Arbitration also has the power to replace an arbitrator where that person is prevented *de jure* or *de facto* from fulfilling his or her duties. If the arbitrator dies or is removed pursuant to Article 12(1) or (2) of the Rules, the Court of Arbitration has a discretion whether to replace that arbitrator or allow the remaining arbitrator to decide the dispute in question. However, this discretion may only be exercised where the proceedings have been closed. If the death or removal of the arbitrator takes place before the proceedings have closed, the deceased arbitrator should be replaced.

20.2.4 Arbitral proceedings

Articles 13 to 23 deal with the general procedure to be adopted and the powers of the arbitral tribunal. Once the arbitral tribunal has been constituted, and the advance costs have been paid, the Secretariat will pass the file to the arbitral tribunal: Article 13. The seat of the arbitration is fixed by the Court of Arbitration unless previously agreed by the parties: Article 14(1). The hearings and meetings relating to the arbitration may be held at any location the arbitral tribunal considers appropriate after consultation with the parties: Article 14(2). The arbitral tribunal may, however, deliberate at any location it considers appropriate: Article 14(3).

The proceedings before the arbitral tribunal are governed by the Rules, but where the Rules are silent the parties are free to adopt any rules agreed by them or, failing such agreement, chosen by the arbitral tribunal. There is a general principle to be applied in all cases that 'the arbitral tribunal shall act fairly and impartially and ensure that each party has a reasonable opportunity to present its case': Article 15(2). Where no language has been chosen by the parties for the conduct of the reference the arbitral tribunal chooses the language having regard to all the circumstances and the language of the contract: Article 16.

Article 17 deals with the choice of law for the merits of the dispute. The parties are free to agree the law to be used. Failing agreement the arbitral tribunal shall apply the law which it determines to be appropriate. Regard, however, must be had to the terms of the contract and any relevant trade customs. The law need not be a national law but may be law merchant or public international law. Article 17(3) however, restricts the arbitral tribunal from acting as an amiable compositeur or deciding *ex aequo et bono* without the consent of the parties.

Article 18(1) deals with the arbitral tribunal's obligations in regard to drafting the terms of reference. The document setting out the terms of reference summarises the dispute between the parties and evidences the jurisdiction that the arbitral tribunal possesses. Included within the terms of reference are:

(a)   the full names and description of the parties;
(b)   the addresses of the parties to which notifications and communications arising in the course of the arbitration may be made;
(c)   a summary of the parties' respective claims and the relief sought by each party, with an indication to the extent possible of the amounts claimed or counterclaimed;

(d) unless the arbitral tribunal considers it inappropriate, a list of the issues to be determined;

(e) the full names, descriptions and addresses of the arbitrators;

(f) the place of the arbitration; and

(g) particulars of the applicable procedural rules and, if such is the case, reference to the power conferred upon the arbitral tribunal to act as amiable compositeur or to decide *ex aequo et bono*.

The parties should sign the terms of reference but where they fail to do so the terms of reference will be submitted to the Court of Arbitration for its approval. It is not until the terms of reference are either signed or approved that the arbitration process begins.

Having signed or had the terms of reference approved the first step in the proceedings is to establish a timetable for the conduct of the reference. After the terms of reference have been signed or approved no new claims which are outside the limits of the terms of reference may be made by either party unless authorised to do so by the arbitral tribunal: Article 19. It would appear that either party may bring new claims at any time before the end of the proceedings which fall within the limits of the terms of reference. The terms of reference should therefore be considered carefully by each party. Drafting the limits in a very precise manner may prevent any new claim being brought unless the authority of the arbitral tribunal is given. Conversely, if the limits are too wide there may be little to prevent a party from bringing new claims throughout the course of the reference.

Article 20 imposes an obligation on the arbitral tribunal to establish the facts of the case within as short a time as possible. Having studied the written submissions of the parties the arbitral tribunal shall hear the parties if the parties so request or, failing such a request by either party, on its own motion. Unless otherwise required by the parties, the arbitral tribunal may proceed by documents only and this is expressly set out in Article 20(6).

The arbitral tribunal has the discretion to hear witnesses and experts and may proceed to hear the witnesses in a party's absence if that party has been duly summoned: Article 20(3). It is implicit from this that the arbitral tribunal may act inquisitorially. In *Dalmia Dairy Industries Ltd* v *National Bank of Pakistan* [1978] 2 Lloyd's Rep 223 a sole arbitrator refused to hear oral evidence from witnesses called by the defendant. The arbitrator had reviewed some eight volumes of documents containing in excess of 1,000 pages. The arbitrator stated that the calling of witnesses to give oral evidence was 'completely unnecessary . . . the facts are simple and to a large extent undisputed'. The decision of the arbitrator was upheld by the English Court of Appeal. An ICC arbitral tribunal also has the power to appoint its own expert after having consulted with the parties: Article 20(4). The arbitral tribunal may also summon any party to provide additional evidence: Article 20(5). This power is another indication that the arbitral tribunal may act in an inquisitorial role.

The hearing is to be held with reasonable notice given to the parties: Article 21(1). If either party fails to appear, the arbitral tribunal may proceed in its absence: Article 21(2). The arbitral tribunal has full control over the conduct of the hearing, which is open only to persons involved in the proceedings, save where the parties and the arbitral tribunal agree otherwise: Article 21(3). At the end of the hearing the arbitral tribunal will declare the proceedings closed and no further submissions or evidence are allowed except with the consent of the arbitral tribunal: Article 22(1). After the hearing is closed the arbitral tribunal is obliged to notify the Secretariat when the draft award is likely to be ready: Article 22(2).

Article 23 deals with the powers of the arbitral tribunal to order interim or conservatory measures which it deems appropriate. This power is wide enough not only to protect the property in dispute but also to allow the arbitral tribunal to order that appropriate security be given. An interim or conservatory measure must be made either as an order with reasons or as an award, whichever is appropriate. Before the file has been given to the arbitral tribunal the parties may apply to any competent judicial authority for an interim or conservatory measure. Such an application is not deemed to be a waiver or infringement of the arbitration agreement.

20.2.5 Awards

Article 24(1) requires that the arbitral tribunal produces a final award within six months from the date of the last signature of the arbitral tribunal or the parties on the terms of reference or, where approval has been sought from the Court of Arbitration, the date of notification to the arbitral tribunal by the Secretariat of the approval. This time limit may be extended on receiving a written reasoned request by the arbitral tribunal or on the Court of Arbitration's own initiative: Article 24(2).

Where the arbitral tribunal is composed of three persons a decision is reached by majority verdict. If there is no majority the decision is reached by the chairman of the arbitral tribunal alone. The arbitral tribunal is obliged to provide a reasoned award. The award is deemed to be made at the place of the arbitration on the date stated therein: Article 25(3). This deeming provision resolves any problem that could have arisen where the award is signed at a place other than the seat of the arbitration. In *Hiscox* v *Outhwaite* [1992] 1 AC 562 the House of Lords held that an award signed in Paris had been 'made' in Paris, even though the whole of the arbitration had been conducted in England the arbitration had no connection with France.

Article 26 provides that where a settlement is reached between the parties after the arbitral tribunal has received the file, the settlement shall be recorded in the form of an award made by consent if requested by the parties and if the arbitral tribunal agrees. The arbitral tribunal therefore retains a discretion whether to record the settlement or not. It would be rare for the arbitral tribunal to refuse its consent to record the settlement in the form of an award, but where the agreement would be contrary to public policy it would be appropriate for the arbitral tribunal to refuse.

Prior to the arbitral tribunal signing the award a draft award is submitted to the Court of Arbitration for its approval. Matters of form and substance may be referred back to the arbitral tribunal by the Court of Arbitration. No award can be given until the Court of Arbitration has approved the form of the award: Article 27.

The Secretariat supplies to the parties the signed text of the award, provided the ICC costs have been paid. Certified additional copies can be obtained and the Secretariat and the arbitral tribunal are also required to assist in any other formalities that may be necessary. These formalities will usually be with reference to the enforcement of the award and the requirements of each particular jurisdiction to register the award. The award is stated to be binding on the parties and the parties undertake to carry out the award without delay and are deemed to waive any further recourse in so far as such waiver is validly made: Article 28. The final and binding nature of the award is therefore deemed to be unchallengeable so far as the jurisdiction in which the award was made permits this. There are many countries which do not permit the jurisdiction of the courts to be totally ousted by an arbitration, whether the arbitration is an international one or not. Some countries allow for rights of appeal to be excluded only where the arbitration is non-domestic. Under the AA 1996 the parties to an arbitration may effectively exclude any appeal on a point of law, whether in a partial or a final award, making an award under the ICC Rules final and binding.

Article 29 provides a slip rule for the correction of clerical, computational or typographical errors or errors of a similar nature in the award. The decision to correct an error is made in the form of an addendum to the award and constitutes part of the award. There is, however, a time limit in which an application under Article 29 can be made.

20.2.6 Costs

Once a request for arbitration has been received the Secretary General may request the claimant to pay a provisional advance in respect of costs to cover the fees incurred up until the terms of reference are drawn up: Article 30(1). The Court of Arbitration estimates the likely costs to be incurred in respect of the claims made and may fix separate advances for claims and counterclaims: Article 30(2). The claimant and respondent are required to pay the advance on costs in equal shares: Article 30(3). If either party defaults, the other may pay the whole of the advance. If the advance costs are not met, the arbitration proceedings may be suspended, and if the costs of the claim or counterclaim are not met within the time limit imposed, the claim or counterclaim shall be considered as withdrawn: Article 30(4).

The costs include all fees and expenses of the arbitral tribunal and the ICC: Article 31. There are scales of costs that determine the fees of the arbitral tribunal although the Court of Arbitration may fix fees higher or lower than those set out, depending on the complexity of the case. The final award fixes the costs of the arbitration and decides which of the parties shall bear them. In most common law countries costs will follow the event. However, in arbitration proceedings held in civil law jurisdictions the usual rule is that each party bears its own costs in the arbitration.

20.2.7   Miscellaneous

Article 32 allows for the parties to shorten the time limits set out in the Rules. Where the arbitral tribunal has already been constituted its approval will be required in order to vary time limits. The Court of Arbitration may extend any of the shortened time limits if it feels it is appropriate to do so in order for the arbitral tribunal or the Court of Arbitration to fulfil their functions under the Rules.

Article 33 deals with a party's deemed waiver of objection to a failure to comply with the Rules or other irregularities. A party which proceeds with the arbitration without objection after an irregularity has occurred is deemed to waive the irregularity. On a strict reading of this Article it would appear not to matter whether the party has knowledge of the irregularity or in fact whether that party could have known about the irregularity. The test to be applied would appear to be whether the party has proceeded after the irregularity. However, this is not the intent. Many of the Rules are drafted in broad terms. Article 33 does not provide for any time limits within which an objection is to be made or any form for the objection. Matters such as the form of the objection and the time for it to be made are within the arbitral tribunal's discretion in considering whether a waiver of the irregularity has in fact occurred.

Article 34 is an exclusion of liability clause for the arbitral tribunal, the Court of Arbitration and the ICC. The exclusion states that there shall be no liability 'to any person for any act or omission in connection with the arbitration'. This Article will be subject to the law relating to arbitrators' immunity and the immunity of institutional bodies of the country where the seat of the arbitration is located. Under s. 74 of the AA 1996 arbitral institutions are immune from suit unless bad faith is shown. There is a similar provision in s. 29 of the AA 1996 in respect of the arbitral tribunal. These sections of the AA 1996 are mandatory. Therefore, under English law, if bad faith is shown on the part of the ICC or the arbitral tribunal neither could hide behind Article 34. Article 35 provides for a general duty on the Court of Arbitration and the arbitral tribunal to attempt to make every effort to make sure that the Award is enforceable in law.

20.2.8   Statutes of the International Court of Arbitration of the ICC

The constitutional document of the Court of Arbitration is called the 'Statutes' of the Court and is reproduced in appendix I to the ICC Rules. The Statutes have seven Articles dealing with the Court's function, composition, appointment, plenary sessions and committees, confidentiality and the procedure for modifying the Arbitration Rules.

Article 1 states that the function of the Court of Arbitration is to ensure the application of the Rules of Arbitration and the Rules of Conciliation. The Court of Arbitration is an autonomous body independent of the ICC and the ICC National Committees. The Court of Arbitration consists of a Chairman, Vice-Chairman and members assisted by the Secretariat: Article 2. The Chairman is elected by the ICC Council on the recommendation of the Executive Board of the ICC. The Vice-Chairman is an appointee of the ICC Council. Members are appointed by the ICC Council on the proposal of the National Committee, one member from each National Committee. Alternate members may be appointed by the Chairman. Members are appointed for a term of three years: Article 3.

Article 4 deals with the plenary sessions of the Court of Arbitration. These sessions are made up of at least six members and are presided over by the Chairman or Vice-Chairman. Decisions are taken by majority vote with the Chairman or Vice-Chairman having the casting vote. Article 5 deals with the powers of the Court of Arbitration to set up committees. Article 6 emphasises the confidential nature of the work of the Court of Arbitration. Article 7 sets out the procedure by which amendments to the Rules are made.

20.2.9 Internal rules of the International Court of Arbitration of the ICC

There are six Articles in Appendix II to the ICC Arbitration Rules dealing with the rules governing the Court of Arbitration. Article 1 deals with the confidential nature of the work of the Court of Arbitration. The Court of Arbitration keeps copies of all awards, terms of reference and other pertinent documents. Other documents may be returned on request to the parties or arbitrator on payment of reasonable costs. If no such request is made, these other documents will be destroyed.

Article 2 prohibits the Chairman or members of the Secretariat from acting as members of an arbitral tribunal. The Vice-Chairman and members of the Court of Arbitration may not be appointed as members of an arbitral tribunal by the Court of Arbitration but may accept the appointment if chosen by the parties. In such a case this must be disclosed to the Secretary General of the Court of Arbitration. Where the Vice-Chairman or members of the Court of Arbitration are chosen by the parties or act in ICC arbitrations they must refrain from being involved in any discussion or proceeding involving that matter which is before the Court of Arbitration.

Article 3 deals with the relationship between members of the Court of Arbitration and National Committees who propose them. Article 4 deals with the Committee of the Court of Arbitration and its composition. Article 5 sets out the duties of the Court Secretariat. Article 6 deals with the scrutiny of draft awards. The Court of Arbitration is obliged under this Article to consider the requirements of mandatory law at the place of the arbitration. This Article reinforces Article 35 of the Rules, which provides that the Court of Arbitration will make every effort to make sure that an award is enforceable in law, which may be difficult if it fails to comply with the mandatory law of the place of the arbitration.

20.2.10 Arbitration costs and fees

Appendix III to the ICC Arbitration Rules sets out the principles and scales upon which costs and fees are payable under ICC arbitration. An advance fee is payable by the claimant in respect of each request for arbitration of $2,500 which is non-refundable and is credited to the claimant's portion of the advance costs. Administrative costs and fees of the arbitral tribunal are worked out on a sliding scale whereby a percentage of the sum in dispute is claimed. The higher the figures in dispute the lower the percentage figure which may be claimed for administrative expenses and fees.

20.3 MAIN CHANGES INTRODUCED BY THE 1998 RULES

The main changes to the Rules which the working group recommended were to reduce delays, reduce unpredictability, rationalise costs and improve defective rules. H. Lesguillons, *International Business Law Journal* (1997), No. 8, p. 994, states how the reduction in delays is to be achieved: 'The new Rules intend to accelerate the constitution process of the arbitral tribunal and the transmission of the file, on the basis of which the terms of reference shall be established.' The ICC have sought to include new and clearer provisions dealing with the conduct of the arbitration process and have made changes where perceived lacunae existed.

20.3.1 Reduction in delays

The procedure to begin the arbitration has been amended so that under Article 4(1) of the Rules the filing of a request for arbitration is now made to the Secretariat and not through a National Committee. The rules relating to the formation of the arbitral tribunal have also been amended. Responsibility for the appointment of the arbitral tribunal can be exercised by the Secretary General of the Court rather than awaiting a session of the Court of Arbitration, provided the parties do not question the independence of the arbitral tribunal: Article 9(2).

Amendments have been made to the request for arbitration and answer to the request. The requirement under the old Rules that the request include: 'a statement of the claimant's case' has been replaced in Article 4(3) with the requirement that the request contain 'a description of the nature and circumstances giving rise to the claims' and the nature of the relief sought. This is hoped to reduce delays by making it possible for the claimant to submit a claim which is not a substantial submission. The respondent is not obliged under the new Rules 'to set out his defence and supply relevant documents' as under Article 4(1) of the old Rules. Article 5(1) states that the obligation on the respondent is to comment on 'the nature and circumstances of the dispute giving rise to the claim(s)'. Where the Court of Arbitration have before them an indication of the type of claim and response then it is hoped that the procedural matters such as the number of arbitrators, the constitution of the arbitral tribunal, the place of the arbitration and the law and language of the arbitration may be decided upon without substantial delay.

The new Rules have made amendments to the advance on costs: Article 30(1). Under the old Rules the advance on costs was to be met by both parties in equal shares. If the respondent failed to pay this sum, there could be delay. Under the new Rules the advance on costs, up until the terms of reference have been drawn up, is to be met by the claimant. Article 1(2) of Appendix III gives guidance on the amount of costs that the claimant may be expected to incur. Again the rationale behind this Rule is that the claimant will not be prejudiced by the dilatory actions of the respondent and that the composition of the arbitral tribunal can proceed without unnecessary delay by a recalcitrant respondent.

Article 18 of the new Rules provides for the arbitral tribunal to draw up terms of reference. Article 18.1(d) provides that the terms of reference shall include: 'unless the arbitral tribunal considers it inappropriate, a list of issues to be determined'. Although the wording is indicative that a list of issues should be drawn up the arbitral tribunal has some discretion on this matter. Some criticism has been made of the use of the terms of reference, but the ICC took the view that overall the benefits of having them outweigh the negative effect. H. Lesguillons, *International Business Law Journal* (1997) No. 8, pp. 997–8, states:

> The Working Group examined, i.a. the question of whether or not terms of reference should be preserved. It considered that the advantages of such a document overweigh the negative effect which they may have on the speed of the procedure. It held that, by setting forth the particulars of the dispute and, above all, the claims of the parties within one document, the terms of reference are extremely helpful in *ultra petita* control, not only for the arbitral tribunal when it drafts its award but also for the ICC Court when scrutinising the draft arbitral award before it is rendered.

Article 18(4) now requires that the arbitral tribunal produce a procedural timetable when drawing up the terms of reference or as soon as possible thereafter. This requirement is also designed to reduce delay.

Article 22 provides that where the arbitral tribunal 'is satisfied that the parties have had a reasonable opportunity to present their cases' it may then declare the proceedings closed. Once the arbitral tribunal has declared the proceedings closed it must indicate to the Secretariat when the draft award will be submitted to the Court of Arbitration. No further submissions can be made by the parties unless authorised by the arbitral tribunal. The rationale behind this provision is that it will prevent delays in a party completing its case.

Article 32(1) provides for the parties to agree a fast track arbitration. Once the arbitral tribunal has been constituted there is a requirement for its consent to the reduction in time limits. Article 32(2) provides a safeguard that allows for the Court of Arbitration to extend any time which has been modified pursuant to Article 32(1).

20.3.2 Reduction in uncertainties of procedure

Article 6(2) has made a major amendment to the old Rules in that it has sought to clarify the position where there is disagreement between the parties about whether there is or is not an arbitration agreement. Article 6(2) now permits the Court of Arbitration to decide whether it is prima facie satisfied that an arbitration agreement exists and if it concludes that it is so satisfied, the matter proceeds by referral to the arbitral tribunal. If the Court of Arbitration is not so satisfied, the parties are notified that the matter cannot proceed. Once the arbitral tribunal is seised of the matter it then decides the question whether or not there is a valid arbitration agreement. This amendment was made so that it would be more difficult for the Court of Arbitration not to start the arbitration process.

Article 17 allows the arbitral tribunal to apply the rules of law which it determines are appropriate where the parties have not agreed a choice of law. This marks a change from Article 13(3) of the old Rules, under which the arbitral tribunal was obliged to determine the rules of law 'by the rule of conflict' which was deemed to be appropriate. This change in the new Rules follows Article 28(1) of the UNCITRAL Model Law and puts 'the ICC Rules in tune with a practice, which has shown that arbitrators more and more often decide to determine the applicable law by the *"voie directe"*, without reference to any national law systems or conflict of law rules': H. Lesguillons, *International Business Law Journal* (1997) No. 8, p. 1009.

Article 23(1) gives the arbitral tribunal power to order any interim or conservatory measures it deems appropriate, subject to appropriate security being furnished. Under the old Rules there was no explicit power to make an order such as giving security for the other party's legal costs. It was, in part, this lack of express power that led to the House of Lords decision in *Coppée-Lavalin NV v Ken-Ren Chemicals and Fertilizers Ltd* [1995] 1 AC 38. The case involved a dispute under the old Rules. The law of the contract was Belgian with London as the place of arbitration. Coppée-Lavalin applied to the English High Court for security for their costs on the basis that Ken-Ren was an insolvent company which was being supported in the arbitration by the Kenyan government, which was the majority shareholder in Ken-Ren. It was Coppée-Lavalin's case that if an order for costs was made against Ken-Ren, the government of Kenya would be under no liability to meet those costs. Ken-Ren argued that the ICC Rules governed the whole conduct of the arbitration and that following the Court of Appeal's reasoning in *Bank Mellat v Helliniki Techniki SA* [1984] QB 291 there was no scope to make such an order. Coppée-Lavalin responded that there was a residual power of the court to order security although they conceded that such a power should only be used in 'exceptional circumstances'. The House of Lords held by a majority that the court did have the power and that there were the 'exceptional circumstances' that justified such an order being made. The amendment by the ICC to Article 23 was made specifically to avoid situations such as that in the Ken-Ren case.

The AA 1996 has now altered the position in England in that the courts no longer have any power to make an order for security for costs in an arbitration, whether domestic or international. Whether Article 23(1) of the new Rules has the effect of preventing a court from exercising such discretionary power to make an order for security for costs as it possesses remains to be seen.

Article 19 allows the arbitral tribunal in its discretion to admit new claims and counterclaims after the signing of the terms of reference. The old Rules only allowed new claims to be brought if within the terms of reference or included within a rider to the terms of reference. This rule had often been criticised in that it prevented the efficient administration of the arbitration. New disputes in complex cases sometimes arose between the same parties and from the same contract as an existing arbitration and it was not efficient in time or money if these matters had to be the subject of fresh arbitration proceedings because they fell outside the limits of the terms of reference. Article 19 was therefore drafted to give more flexibility to the arbitration procedure.

Article 10 provides a new procedure for the appointment of an arbitral tribunal in multiparty arbitrations. This new procedure was brought about by the case of *Siemens AG* v *Dutco Construction Co.* (1992) 18 YB Com Arb 140, which has been discussed at 20.2.3.

20.3.3 Elimination of perceived lacunae

Article 20(7) provides that: 'The Arbitral Tribunal may take measures for protecting trade secrets and confidential information'. A frequently cited benefit of the arbitration process over litigation has been the assumption that arbitration is a confidential process (see 15.14).

Article 20(7) does not create an express positive duty of confidentiality on the part of the parties to the arbitration process. However, it does provide some security for the parties. If it is suspected that confidential information is being disclosed, a party may now apply to the arbitral tribunal for an order restraining the disclosure of the confidential information.

Other perceived lacunae that the new Rules have addressed include: proceeding by a truncated arbitral tribunal (Article 12(5)) waiver of irregularities (Article 33) and the exclusion of liability (Article 34). These Articles have all been discussed at 20.2.

21 Precedents

21.1 ARBITRATION AGREEMENT

In drafting an arbitration agreement clause a party should always have regard to the specific circumstances of the case. Precedents are a useful tool but they should not be followed blindly. Prior to using a precedent a party should always set out the matters essential to it. If these matters are not included in the precedent, it should be rejected or amended accordingly.

An arbitration agreement can be as simple as:

> It is agreed that all disputes and differences between us shall be referred to arbitration.
> Dated
> Signed

An arbitration agreement may be more specific:

> It is agreed that all disputes and differences between us shall be referred to arbitration to be determined by a sole arbitrator appointed in accordance with s. 16(3) of the Arbitration Act 1996. In the event that we fail to agree the appointment of the sole arbitrator the appointment shall be made by the President of the Chartered Institute of Arbitrators. The designated seat of the arbitration is London.
> Dated
> Signed

Where it is intended that the arbitration will be conducted under institutional rules the parties may check to see whether those rules contain recommended arbitration clauses. The London Court of International Arbitration provides two recommended clauses. One for future disputes and one for existing disputes.

Future disputes
Any dispute arising out of or in connection with this contract, including any question regarding its existence, validity or termination, shall be referred to and finally resolved by arbitration under the LCIA Rules, which rules are deemed to be incorporated by reference into this clause.

The number of arbitrators shall be [*one/three*].
The place of the arbitration shall be [*city and/or country*].
The language to be used in the arbitral proceedings shall be [ ].
The governing law of the contract shall be the substantive law of [ ].

Existing disputes
A dispute having arisen between the parties concerning [ ], the parties
hereby agree that the dispute shall be referred to and finally resolved by
arbitration under the LCIA Rules.
The number of arbitrators shall be [*one/three*].
The place of the arbitration shall be [*city and/or country*].
The language to be used in the arbitral proceedings shall be [ ].
The governing law of the contract shall be the substantive law of [ ].

The International Chamber of Commerce recommend the use of their standard
arbitration clause where the parties propose an ICC arbitration. The parties are
reminded that they are at liberty to stipulate the number of arbitrators, the place
and language of the arbitration and the governing law of the contract:

All disputes arising out of or in connection with the present contract shall be
finally settled under the Rules of Arbitration of the International Chamber of
Commerce by one or more arbitrators appointed in accordance with the said Rules.

21.2 NOTICE OF APPOINTMENT

The notice of appointment will often be the tool under which the arbitration
proceedings are commenced. The notice is therefore important for a number of
reasons and not least because it has the effect of stopping time running for
limitation purposes. Under s. 14 of the AA 1996 the parties are free to agree when
arbitral proceedings are commenced. If institutional rules are adopted, the rules
may deal with this matter. If no agreement exists between the parties as to when
arbitral proceedings are to be regarded as being commenced, a party should take
careful note of the requirements of s. 14 of the AA 1996.

The following precedent is drafted on the basis that the parties are to agree on
the appointment of the arbitral tribunal:

IN THE MATTER OF THE ARBITRATION ACT 1996
AND
IN THE MATTER OF AN ARBITRATION
BETWEEN

A.B. LTD   Claimant

and

C.D. LTD   Respondent

NOTICE TO CONCUR

WHEREAS by a contract entered into on [date] the Respondent agreed to manufacture and supply 1,000 widgets.

AND WHEREAS the said contract contained at clause 27 an agreement to refer disputes to arbitration.

AND WHEREAS disputes and differences within the meaning of the said agreement to arbitrate have arisen, *inter alia*, in relation to defects in the materials supplied by the Respondent.

AND WHEREAS the said disputes and differences will be fully particularised in the Claimant's pleading in due course.

AND WHEREAS the Claimant wishes to refer and hereby refers the said disputes to arbitration.

TAKE NOTICE that the Claimant hereby refers the disputes or differences to arbitration and requires the Respondent to concur in the appointment of JOHN DOE of [address] as arbitrator;

AND TAKE NOTICE that in the event of the Respondent failing to agree on the appointment of the person named above as arbitrator within 14 days of the date of service of this notice the Claimant will apply for the nomination of an arbitrator by the President for the time being of the Royal Institution of Chartered Surveyors.

Dated
Solicitors for the Claimant
[address]   Ref KDT/AGT
For and on behalf of A.B. Ltd, the Claimants, whose registered office is situated at [address]

21.3   ACCEPTANCE OF APPOINTMENT

Dear Sirs,

Re: A.B. Ltd v C.D. Ltd

I write further to yesterday's meeting between the parties and myself.

I confirm that I accept the appointment of Arbitrator in the dispute between yourselves and C.D. Ltd on the following terms and conditions:

1.   A minimum fee of £500 to be paid to me by the Claimant, which amount will be security for the eventual fees and expenses payable in accordance with the terms set out hereafter.

2.   My fees are calculated as follows:

(a)   At the rate of £75.00 per hour spent upon the conduct of the arbitration whether the matter proceeds to a hearing, award or otherwise.

(b)   At the rate of £500.00 for each day or part of a day spent on any hearing of the substantive matters in dispute. Attendance at preliminary meetings and interlocutory hearings are charged at my hourly rate.

(c)   Travelling time by car will be charged at half my hourly rate. I do not charge for travelling time by train unless I am unable to do other work.

3.   Expenses are charged at net cost.

4.   Once hearing dates are fixed a fee shall be charged for such time set aside and not spent calculated as a percentage of the daily fee rate stated in item 2 above. Such percentage is calculated on the notice of cancellation given by either party before the first day fixed for the hearing.

More than 6 months	0%
Between 3 months and 6 months	15%
Between 1 month and 3 months	50%
Between 1 week and 1 month	75%
Less than 1 week or after the hearing has commenced	100%

5.   The parties shall lodge such security in such proportions as I deem fit. Payment shall be made within 21 days of notification to my address stated above.

6.   The parties shall be jointly and severally liable for the payment of my fees and expenses in any event.

7.   Any fees and expenses not paid within the time limit stated above shall be subject to an addition of simple interest at 2% above National Westminster Bank Base Rate from the expiry of the time limit to payment.

I shall be pleased to be notified that such security as stated above has been supplied by the claimant. I trust that these terms and conditions meet with your approval.

A similar letter has been sent to the Respondent, C.D. Ltd.

Yours faithfully,

Signed

21.4   ORDER FOR DIRECTIONS

Directions inevitably vary from case to case. The precedent that follows is illustrative of the most commonly found types of direction. Matters that the parties might wish to include in the order for directions are: the consolidation of other arbitral proceedings, the choice of law, the language of the arbitration, amendments to existing pleadings, partial awards, provisional orders, the selection of a hearing date, matters relating to evidence, whether the arbitral tribunal will act inquisitorially and whether there should be reasons given in the award. In addition other specific applications may be applied for. These could include security for costs, interim payments and the preservation and protection of the subject matter of the dispute.

IN THE MATTER OF THE ARBITRATION ACT 1996
AND
IN THE MATTER OF AN ARBITRATION
BETWEEN

A.B. LTD   Claimant

and

C.D. LTD   Respondent

ORDER FOR DIRECTIONS

Upon hearing Counsel for the Claimant and Respondent and upon consideration of the written and oral evidence I JOHN DOE hereby order and direct that:

1. The Claimant shall serve a Statement of Case within 56 days of the date hereof.
2. The Respondent shall serve a Defence or Defence and Counterclaim to the Statement of Case within 56 days thereafter.
3. The Claimant shall serve a Reply to the Defence or a Reply and Defence to Counterclaim within 42 days thereafter.
4. The Respondent be at liberty to serve a Reply to Defence to Counterclaim if so advised within 14 days thereafter.
5. Copies of all pleadings to be sent to myself.
6. The parties be at liberty to request of each other production of specific documents or classes of documents to be incorporated into the list of documents by [date].
7. The parties to exchange lists of documents upon which they respectively intend to rely at any hearing incorporating such documents as have been requested by the other party by [date].
8. Inspection on 7 days' notice.
9. Each party shall serve and copy to myself the signed statements of every witness of fact on which they intend to rely at the hearing by [date]. All such statements shall stand as evidence in chief.
10. Leave to each party to call [No.] experts and experts' reports shall be served and copied to myself by [date].
11. Experts shall meet as and when necessary, on a without prejudice basis, prior to the exchange of reports in order to agree technical issues and narrow the facts.

12. Experts shall prepare and sign statements setting out the facts, matters and opinions which are those not agreed between them by [date]. The statement shall be copied to myself.

13. A pre-trial review shall take place on [date and time].

Ordered this [date] at [place]
Signed

21.5 LIST OF DOCUMENTS

IN THE MATTER OF THE ARBITRATION ACT 1996
AND
IN THE MATTER OF AN ARBITRATION
BETWEEN:

A.B. LTD <u>Claimant</u>

and

C.D. LTD <u>Respondent</u>

LIST OF DOCUMENTS

Disclosure Statement

I state that I have carried out a reasonable and proportionate search to locate all the documents which I am required to disclose under the order made by the Arbitrator on   1999

(I did not search for documents—
1. Pre-dating ....
2. Located elsewhere than ....
....
3. In categories other than ....
....)

I certify that I understand the duty of disclosure and to the best of my knowledge I have carried out that duty. I further certify that the list of documents set out in or attached to this form, is a complete list of all documents which are or have been in my control and which I am obliged under the order to disclose.

I understand that I must inform the Arbitrator and the other parties immediately if any further document required to be disclosed comes into my control at any time before the conclusion of the case.

(I have not permitted inspection of documents within the category or class of documents (as set out below) on the grounds that to do so would be disproportionate to the issues in the case.)

Signed

Claimant/Respondent

Date

Position or office held

(If signing on behalf of a company or firm) Please state why you are the appropriate person to make this disclosure statement

I have control of the documents numbered and listed here. I do not object to you inspecting them/producing copies:

No	Date	From	To	Description
1	27/10/88	CD	AB	Receipt of tender confirmation
2	08/02/89	CD	AB	Revised tender
3	18/02/89	AB	CD	Tender acceptance
Etc	Etc	Etc	Etc	Etc

I have control of the following documents numbered and listed here, but I object to you inspecting them:

No	Date	From	To	Description
1	01/10/90	CD	Lawyer	Advice
2	08/02/90	CD	Lawyer	Advice
Etc	Etc	Etc	Etc	Etc

I have had the documents numbered and listed below, but they are no longer in my control:

No	Date	From	To	Description
1	Etc	Etc	Etc	Etc

21.6 ARBITRATOR'S FINAL AWARD

IN THE MATTER OF THE ARBITRATION ACT 1996
AND
IN THE MATTER OF AN ARBITRATION
BETWEEN

A.B. LTD Claimant

and

C.D. LTD Respondent

ARBITRATOR'S FINAL AWARD

WHEREAS by a contract entered into on [date] the Respondent agreed to manufacture and supply 1,000 widgets.
AND WHEREAS the said contract contained at clause 27 an agreement to refer disputes to arbitration.
AND WHEREAS disputes and differences within the meaning of the said agreement to arbitrate have arisen, *inter alia*, in relation to defects in the materials supplied by the Respondent.
AND WHEREAS at the request of the Claimant, the President of the Chartered Institute of Arbitrators appointed me, JOHN DOE, to be the Arbitrator on [date].
AND WHEREAS I the said John Doe accepted the said appointment at a preliminary meeting on [date].

[Detail any interlocutory applications if appropriate]

AND WHEREAS a hearing took place on [date] at which the parties were represented by Mr Laurel for the Claimant and Mr Hardy for the Respondent.

NOW I, John Doe, do hereby make, issue and publish my award.

[Set out the facts of the matter giving rise to the dispute]
[Set out the matters in dispute]
[Set out a reasoned decision on each of the matters in dispute applying the facts and law as found]

I ACCORDINGLY HEREBY AWARD AND DIRECT AS FOLLOWS:

[Set out details of award e.g., C.D. Ltd to pay A.B. Ltd the sum of £ . . . .]
[Set out interest payable]
[Set out costs unless this is to be dealt with by way of further award]

Signed
This Award was made in London this [date].

21.7 AGREED AWARDS

IN THE MATTER OF THE ARBITRATION ACT 1996
AND
IN THE MATTER OF AN ARBITRATION
BETWEEN

A.B. LTD   <u>Claimant</u>

and

C.D. LTD   <u>Respondent</u>

<u>AGREED AWARD</u>

WHEREAS by a contract entered into on [date] the Respondent agreed to manufacture and supply 1,000 widgets.

AND WHEREAS the said contract contained at clause 27 an agreement to refer disputes to arbitration.

AND WHEREAS disputes and differences within the meaning of the said agreement to arbitrate have arisen, *nter alia* in relation to defects in the materials supplied by the Respondent.

AND WHEREAS at the request of the Claimant, the President of the Chartered Institute of Arbitrators appointed me, JOHN DOE, to be the Arbitrator on [date].

AND WHEREAS I the said John Doe accepted the said appointment at a preliminary meeting on [date].

AND WHEREAS at the said preliminary meeting it was indicated to me that the parties were likely to reach a settlement on this matter and I subsequently received on [date] a letter signed by both Claimant and Respondent notifying me of consent terms of a settlement between them.

AND WHEREAS it was requested by the parties that I should record the settlement in an 'agreed award'.

AND WHEREAS as a result of agreement having been reached between the parties I sent a notice to the parties dated [date] whereby I terminated the substantive proceedings.

NOW I, John Doe, having been notified of the terms of the agreed settlement incorporate those terms in this agreed award and publish this agreed award which shall have the same effect and status as any other award on the merits of the case.

[Set out the terms of the settlement]

Signed
This Award was made in London this [date].

21.8 *CALDERBANK* OFFER

Calderbank letters have been discussed in 13.2.3. *Calderbank* letters are expressed to be 'without prejudice save as to costs'. They are used in arbitration proceedings because there is no mechanism in arbitration proceedings similar to a payment into court in litigation. A party which accepts that it has some liability to the other party in the arbitration may protect itself on the question of costs by offering the other party a sum in final settlement of its claim. As the offer is made without prejudice save as to costs the fact that the offer has been made cannot be brought to the attention of the arbitral tribunal until after an award on the merits has been made.

Without Prejudice Save As To Costs

Dear Sirs,

Re: an Arbitration Between A.B. Ltd and C.D. Ltd

Our clients, C.D. Ltd, have decided to make an unconditional offer, in full and final settlement of all claims your clients have against them, including any claims for interest. Costs and fees are to be taxed if not agreed and will be met by our client.
    The offer will remain open for 21 days from today's date.

Yours faithfully

Appendix 1

ARBITRATION ACT 1996
(1996 c. 23)

ARRANGEMENT OF SECTIONS

PART I
ARBITRATION PURSUANT TO AN ARBITRATION AGREEMENT

Introductory

The arbitration agreement

Stay of legal proceedings

Commencement of arbitral proceedings

The arbitral tribunal

An Act to restate and improve the law relating to arbitration pursuant to an arbitration agreement; to make other provision relating to arbitration and arbitration awards; and for connected purposes.   [17th June 1996]

Be it enacted by the Queen's most Excellent Majesty, by and with the advice and consent of the Lords Spiritual and Temporal, and Commons, in this present Parliament assembled, and by the authority of the same as follows:—

PART I
ARBITRATION PURSUANT TO AN ARBITRATION AGREEMENT
Introductory

1.   General principles
The provisions of this Part are founded on the following principles, and shall be construed accordingly—
   (a)   the object of arbitration is to obtain the fair resolution of disputes by an impartial tribunal without unnecessary delay or expense;
   (b)   the parties should be free to agree how their disputes are resolved, subject only to such safeguards as are necessary in the public interest;
   (c)   in matters governed by this Part the court should not intervene except as provided by this Part.

2.   Scope of application of provisions
   (1)   The provisions of this Part apply where the seat of the arbitration is in England and Wales or Northern Ireland.
   (2)   The following sections apply even if the seat of the arbitration is outside England and Wales or Northern Ireland or no seat has been designated or determined—

(a)   sections 9 to 11 (stay of legal proceedings, &c.), and

(b)   section 66 (enforcement of arbitral awards).

(3)   The powers conferred by the following sections apply even if the seat of the arbitration is outside England and Wales or Northern Ireland or no seat has been designated or determined—

(a)   section 43 (securing the attendance of witnesses), and

(b)   section 44 (court powers exercisable in support of arbitral proceedings);

but the court may refuse to exercise any such power if, in the opinion of the court, the fact that the seat of the arbitration is outside England and Wales or Northern Ireland, or that when designated or determined the seat is likely to be outside England and Wales or Northern Ireland, makes it inappropriate to do so.

(4)   The court may exercise a power conferred by any provision of this Part not mentioned in subsection (2) or (3) for the purpose of supporting the arbitral process where—

(a)   no seat of the arbitration has been designated or determined, and

(b)   by reason of a connection with England and Wales or Northern Ireland the court is satisfied that it is appropriate to do so.

(5)   Section 7 (separability of arbitration agreement) and section 8 (death of a party) apply where the law applicable to the arbitration agreement is the law of England and Wales or Northern Ireland even if the seat of the arbitration is outside England and Wales or Northern Ireland or has not been designated or determined.

3.   The seat of the arbitration

In this Part 'the seat of the arbitration' means the juridical seat of the arbitration designated—

(a)   by the parties to the arbitration agreement, or

(b)   by any arbitral or other institution or person vested by the parties with powers in that regard, or

(c)   by the arbitral tribunal if so authorised by the parties,

or determined, in the absence of any such designation, having regard to the parties' agreement and all the relevant circumstances.

4.   Mandatory and non-mandatory provisions

(1)   The mandatory provisions of this Part are listed in Schedule 1 and have effect notwithstanding any agreement to the contrary.

(2)   The other provisions of this Part (the 'non-mandatory provisions') allow the parties to make their own arrangements by agreement but provide rules which apply in the absence of such agreement.

(3)   The parties may make such arrangements by agreeing to the application of institutional rules or providing any other means by which a matter may be decided.

(4)   It is immaterial whether or not the law applicable to the parties' agreement is the law of England and Wales or, as the case may be, Northern Ireland.

(5)   The choice of a law other than the law of England and Wales or Northern Ireland as the applicable law in respect of a matter provided for by a non-mandatory provision of this Part is equivalent to an agreement making provision about that matter.

For this purpose an applicable law determined in accordance with the parties' agreement, or which is objectively determined in the absence of any express or implied choice, shall be treated as chosen by the parties.

5.   Agreements to be in writing

(1)   The provisions of this Part apply only where the arbitration agreement is in writing, and any other agreement between the parties as to any matter is effective for the purposes of this Part only if in writing.

The expressions 'agreement', 'agree' and 'agreed' shall be construed accordingly.

(2)   There is an agreement in writing—

(a)   if the agreement is made in writing (whether or not it is signed by the parties),

(b)   if the agreement is made by exchange of communications in writing, or

(c) if the agreement is evidenced in writing.

(3) Where parties agree otherwise than in writing by reference to terms which are in writing, they make an agreement in writing.

(4) An agreement is evidenced in writing if an agreement made otherwise than in writing is recorded by one of the parties, or by a third party, with the authority of the parties to the agreement.

(5) An exchange of written submissions in arbitral or legal proceedings in which the existence of an agreement otherwise than in writing is alleged by one party against another party and not denied by the other party in his response constitutes as between those parties an agreement in writing to the effect alleged.

(6) References in this Part to anything being written or in writing include its being recorded by any means.

The arbitration agreement

6. Definition of arbitration agreement

(1) In this Part an 'arbitration agreement' means an agreement to submit to arbitration present or future disputes (whether they are contractual or not).

(2) The reference in an agreement to a written form of arbitration clause or to a document containing an arbitration clause constitutes an arbitration agreement if the reference is such as to make that clause part of the agreement.

7. Separability of arbitration agreement

Unless otherwise agreed by the parties, an arbitration agreement which forms or was intended to form part of another agreement (whether or not in writing) shall not be regarded as invalid, non-existent or ineffective because that other agreement is invalid, or did not come into existence or has become ineffective, and it shall for that purpose be treated as a distinct agreement.

8. Whether agreement discharged by death of a party

(1) Unless otherwise agreed by the parties, an arbitration agreement is not discharged by the death of a party and may be enforced by or against the personal representatives of that party.

(2) Subsection (1) does not affect the operation of any enactment or rule of law by virtue of which a substantive right or obligation is extinguished by death.

Stay of legal proceedings

9. Stay of legal proceedings

(1) A party to an arbitration agreement against whom legal proceedings are brought (whether by way of claim or counterclaim) in respect of a matter which under the agreement is to be referred to arbitration may (upon notice to the other parties to the proceedings) apply to the court in which the proceedings have been brought to stay the proceedings so far as they concern that matter.

(2) An application may be made notwithstanding that the matter is to be referred to arbitration only after the exhaustion of other dispute resolution procedures.

(3) An application may not be made by a person before taking the appropriate procedural step (if any) to acknowledge the legal proceedings against him or after he has taken any step in those proceedings to answer the substantive claim.

(4) On an application under this section the court shall grant a stay unless satisfied that the arbitration agreement is null and void, inoperative, or incapable of being performed.

(5) If the court refuses to stay the legal proceedings, any provision that an award is a condition precedent to the bringing of legal proceedings in respect of any matter is of no effect in relation to those proceedings.

10. Reference of interpleader issue to arbitration.

(1) Where in legal proceedings relief by way of interpleader is granted and any issue between the claimants is one in respect of which there is an arbitration agreement between

them, the court granting the relief shall direct that the issue be determined in accordance
with the agreement unless the circumstances are such that proceedings brought by a claimant
in respect of the matter would not be stayed.

(2) Where subsection (1) applies but the court does not direct that the issue be
determined in accordance with the arbitration agreement, any provision that an award is a
condition precedent to the bringing of legal proceedings in respect of any matter shall not
affect the determination of that issue by the court.

11. Retention of security where Admiralty proceedings stayed.

(1) Where Admiralty proceedings are stayed on the ground that the dispute in question
should be submitted to arbitration, the court granting the stay may, if in those proceedings
property has been arrested or bail or other security has been given to prevent or obtain
release from arrest—

(a) order that the property arrested be retained as security for the satisfaction of any
award given in the arbitration in respect of that dispute, or

(b) order that the stay of those proceedings be conditional on the provision of
equivalent security for the satisfaction of any such award.

(2) Subject to any provision made by rules of court and to any necessary modifications,
the same law and practice shall apply in relation to property retained in pursuance of an
order as would apply if it were held for the purposes of proceedings in the court making
the order.

Commencement of arbitral proceedings

12. Power of court to extend time for beginning arbitral proceedings, &c.

(1) Where an arbitration agreement to refer future disputes to arbitration provides that
a claim shall be barred, or the claimant's right extinguished, unless the claimant takes within
a time fixed by the agreement some step–

(a) to begin arbitral proceedings, or

(b) to begin other dispute resolution procedures which must be exhausted before
arbitral proceedings can be begun,

the court may by order extend the time for taking that step.

(2) Any party to the arbitration agreement may apply for such an order (upon notice to
the other parties), but only after a claim has arisen and after exhausting any available arbitral
process for obtaining an extension of time.

(3) The court shall make an order only if satisfied—

(a) that the circumstances are such as were outside the reasonable contemplation
of the parties when they agreed the provision in question, and that it would be just to extend
the time, or

(b) that the conduct of one party makes it unjust to hold the other party to the strict
terms of the provision in question.

(4) The court may extend the time for such period and on such terms as it thinks fit,
and may do so whether or not the time previously fixed (by agreement or by a previous
order) has expired.

(5) An order under this section does not affect the operation of the Limitation Acts (see
section 13).

(6) The leave of the court is required for any appeal from a decision of the court under
this section.

13. Application of Limitation Acts

(1) The Limitation Acts apply to arbitral proceedings as they apply to legal proceedings.

(2) The court may order that in computing the time prescribed by the Limitation Acts
for the commencement of proceedings (including arbitral proceedings) in respect of a
dispute which was the subject matter—

(a) of an award which the court orders to be set aside or declares to be of no effect, or

(b) of the affected part of an award which the court orders to be set aside in part, or declares to be in part of no effect,
the period between the commencement of the arbitration and the date of the order referred to in paragraph (a) or (b) shall be excluded.

(3) In determining for the purposes of the Limitation Acts when a cause of action accrued, any provision that an award is a condition precedent to the bringing of legal proceedings in respect of a matter to which an arbitration agreement applies shall be disregarded.

(4) In this Part 'the Limitation Acts' means—

(a) in England and Wales, the Limitation Act 1980, the Foreign Limitation Periods Act 1984 and any other enactment (whenever passed) relating to the limitation of actions;

(b) in Northern Ireland, the Limitation (Northern Ireland) Order 1989, the Foreign Limitation Periods (Northern Ireland) Order 1985 and any other enactment (whenever passed) relating to the limitation of actions.

14. Commencement of arbitral proceedings

(1) The parties are free to agree when arbitral proceedings are to be regarded as commenced for the purposes of this Part and for the purposes of the Limitation Acts.

(2) If there is no such agreement the following provisions apply.

(3) Where the arbitrator is named or designated in the arbitration agreement, arbitral proceedings are commenced in respect of a matter when one party serves on the other party or parties a notice in writing requiring him or them to submit that matter to the person so named or designated.

(4) Where the arbitrator or arbitrators are to be appointed by the parties, arbitral proceedings are commenced in respect of a matter when one party serves on the other party or parties notice in writing requiring him or them to appoint an arbitrator or to agree to the appointment of an arbitrator in respect of that matter.

(5) Where the arbitrator or arbitrators are to be appointed by a person other than a party to the proceedings, arbitral proceedings are commenced in respect of a matter when one party gives notice in writing to that person requesting him to make the appointment in respect of that matter.

The arbitral tribunal

15. The arbitral tribunal

(1) The parties are free to agree on the number of arbitrators to form the tribunal and whether there is to be a chairman or umpire.

(2) Unless otherwise agreed by the parties, an agreement that the number of arbitrators shall be two or any other even number shall be understood as requiring the appointment of an additional arbitrator as chairman of the tribunal.

(3) If there is no agreement as to the number of arbitrators, the tribunal shall consist of a sole arbitrator.

16. Procedure for appointment of arbitrators

(1) The parties are free to agree on the procedure for appointing the arbitrator or arbitrators, including the procedure for appointing any chairman or umpire.

(2) If or to the extent that there is no such agreement, the following provisions apply.

(3) If the tribunal is to consist of a sole arbitrator, the parties shall jointly appoint the arbitrator not later than 28 days after service of a request in writing by either party to do so.

(4) If the tribunal is to consist of two arbitrators, each party shall appoint one arbitrator not later than 14 days after service of a request in writing by either party to do so.

(5) If the tribunal is to consist of three arbitrators—

(a) each party shall appoint one arbitrator not later than 14 days after service of a request in writing by either party to do so, and

(b) the two so appointed shall forthwith appoint a third arbitrator as the chairman of the tribunal.

(6)   If the tribunal is to consist of two arbitrators and an umpire—

(a)   each party shall appoint one arbitrator not later than 14 days after service of a request in writing by either party to do so, and

(b)   the two so appointed may appoint an umpire at any time after they themselves are appointed and shall do so before any substantive hearing or forthwith if they cannot agree on a matter relating to the arbitration.

(7)   In any other case (in particular, if there are more than two parties) section 18 applies as in the case of a failure of the agreed appointment procedure.

17.   Power in case of default to appoint sole arbitrator

(1)   Unless the parties otherwise agree, where each of two parties to an arbitration agreement is to appoint an arbitrator and one party ('the party in default') refuses to do so, or fails to do so within the time specified, the other party, having duly appointed his arbitrator, may give notice in writing to the party in default that he proposes to appoint his arbitrator to act as sole arbitrator.

(2)   If the party in default does not within 7 clear days of that notice being given—

(a)   make the required appointment, and

(b)   notify the other party that he has done so,

the other party may appoint his arbitrator as sole arbitrator whose award shall be binding on both parties as if he had been so appointed by agreement.

(3)   Where a sole arbitrator has been appointed under subsection (2), the party in default may (upon notice to the appointing party) apply to the court which may set aside the appointment.

(4)   The leave of the court is required for any appeal from a decision of the court under this section.

18.   Failure of appointment procedure

(1)   The parties are free to agree what is to happen in the event of a failure of the procedure for the appointment of the arbitral tribunal.

There is no failure if an appointment is duly made under section 17 (power in case of default to appoint sole arbitrator), unless that appointment is set aside.

(2)   If or to the extent that there is no such agreement any party to the arbitration agreement may (upon notice to the other parties) apply to the court to exercise its powers under this section.

(3)   Those powers are—

(a)   to give directions as to the making of any necessary appointments;

(b)   to direct that the tribunal shall be constituted by such appointments (or any one or more of them) as have been made;

(c)   to revoke any appointments already made;

(d)   to make any necessary appointments itself.

(4)   An appointment made by the court under this section has effect as if made with the agreement of the parties.

(5)   The leave of the court is required for any appeal from a decision of the court under this section.

19.   Court to have regard to agreed qualifications

In deciding whether to exercise, and in considering how to exercise, any of its powers under section 16 (procedure for appointment of arbitrators) or section 18 (failure of appointment procedure), the court shall have due regard to any agreement of the parties as to the qualifications required of the arbitrators.

20.   Chairman

(1)   Where the parties have agreed that there is to be a chairman, they are free to agree what the functions of the chairman are to be in relation to the making of decisions, orders and awards.

(2)   If or to the extent that there is no such agreement, the following provisions apply.

(3)   Decisions, orders and awards shall be made by all or a majority of the arbitrators (including the chairman).

(4)   The view of the chairman shall prevail in relation to a decision, order or award in respect of which there is neither unanimity nor a majority under subsection (3).

21.   Umpire

(1)   Where the parties have agreed that there is to be an umpire, they are free to agree what the functions of the umpire are to be, and in particular—

(a)   whether he is to attend the proceedings, and

(b)   when he is to replace the other arbitrators as the tribunal with power to make decisions, orders and awards.

(2)   If or to the extent that there is no such agreement, the following provisions apply.

(3)   The umpire shall attend the proceedings and be supplied with the same documents and other materials as are supplied to the other arbitrators.

(4)   Decisions, orders and awards shall be made by the other arbitrators unless and until they cannot agree on a matter relating to the arbitration.

In that event they shall forthwith give notice in writing to the parties and the umpire, whereupon the umpire shall replace them as the tribunal with power to make decisions, orders and awards as if he were sole arbitrator.

(5)   If the arbitrators cannot agree but fail to give notice of that fact, or if any of them fails to join in the giving of notice, any party to the arbitral proceedings may (upon notice to the other parties and to the tribunal) apply to the court which may order that the umpire shall replace the other arbitrators as the tribunal with power to make decisions, orders and awards as if he were sole arbitrator.

(6)   The leave of the court is required for any appeal from a decision of the court under this section.

22.   Decision-making where no chairman or umpire

(1)   Where the parties agree that there shall be two or more arbitrators with no chairman or umpire, the parties are free to agree how the tribunal is to make decisions, orders and awards.

(2)   If there is no such agreement, decisions, orders and awards shall be made by all or a majority of the arbitrators.

23.   Revocation of arbitrator's authority

(1)   The parties are free to agree in what circumstances the authority of an arbitrator may be revoked.

(2)   If or to the extent that there is no such agreement the following provisions apply.

(3)   The authority of an arbitrator may not be revoked except—

(a)   by the parties acting jointly, or

(b)   by an arbitral or other institution or person vested by the parties with powers in that regard.

(4)   Revocation of the authority of an arbitrator by the parties acting jointly must be agreed in writing unless the parties also agree (whether or not in writing) to terminate the arbitration agreement.

(5)   Nothing in this section affects the power of the court—

(a)   to revoke an appointment under section 18 (powers exercisable in case of failure of appointment procedure), or

(b)   to remove an arbitrator on the grounds specified in section 24.

24.   Power of court to remove arbitrator

(1)   A party to arbitral proceedings may (upon notice to the other parties, to the arbitrator concerned and to any other arbitrator) apply to the court to remove an arbitrator on any of the following grounds—

(a)   that circumstances exist that give rise to justifiable doubts as to his impartiality;

(b)   that he does not possess the qualifications required by the arbitration agreement;

(c)   that he is physically or mentally incapable of conducting the proceedings or there are justifiable doubts as to his capacity to do so;

(d)   that he has refused or failed—

    (i)   properly to conduct the proceedings, or

    (ii)   to use all reasonable despatch in conducting the proceedings or making an award, and that substantial injustice has been or will be caused to the applicant.

(2)   If there is an arbitral or other institution or person vested by the parties with power to remove an arbitrator, the court shall not exercise its power of removal unless satisfied that the applicant has first exhausted any available recourse to that institution or person.

(3)   The arbitral tribunal may continue the arbitral proceedings and make an award while an application to the court under this section is pending.

(4)   Where the court removes an arbitrator, it may make such order as it thinks fit with respect to his entitlement (if any) to fees or expenses, or the repayment of any fees or expenses already paid.

(5)   The arbitrator concerned is entitled to appear and be heard by the court before it makes any order under this section.

(6)   The leave of the court is required for any appeal from a decision of the court under this section.

25. Resignation of arbitrator

(1)   The parties are free to agree with an arbitrator as to the consequences of his resignation as regards—

(a)   his entitlement (if any) to fees or expenses, and

(b)   any liability thereby incurred by him.

(2)   If or to the extent that there is no such agreement the following provisions apply.

(3)   An arbitrator who resigns his appointment may (upon notice to the parties) apply to the court—

(a)   to grant him relief from any liability thereby incurred by him, and

(b)   to make such order as it thinks fit with respect to his entitlement (if any) to fees or expenses or the repayment of any fees or expenses already paid.

(4)   If the court is satisfied that in all the circumstances it was reasonable for the arbitrator to resign, it may grant such relief as is mentioned in subsection (3)(a) on such terms as it thinks fit.

(5)   The leave of the court is required for any appeal from a decision of the court under this section.

26. Death of arbitrator or person appointing him

(1)   The authority of an arbitrator is personal and ceases on his death.

(2)   Unless otherwise agreed by the parties, the death of the person by whom an arbitrator was appointed does not revoke the arbitrator's authority.

27. Filling of vacancy, &c.

(1)   Where an arbitrator ceases to hold office, the parties are free to agree—

(a)   whether and if so how the vacancy is to be filled,

(b)   whether and if so to what extent the previous proceedings should stand, and

(c)   what effect (if any) his ceasing to hold office has on any appointment made by him (alone or jointly).

(2)   If or to the extent that there is no such agreement, the following provisions apply.

(3)   The provisions of sections 16 (procedure for appointment of arbitrators) and 18 (failure of appointment procedure) apply in relation to the filling of the vacancy as in relation to an original appointment.

(4)   The tribunal (when reconstituted) shall determine whether and if so to what extent the previous proceedings should stand.

This does not affect any right of a party to challenge those proceedings on any ground which had arisen before the arbitrator ceased to hold office.

(5)   His ceasing to hold office does not affect any appointment by him (alone or jointly) of another arbitrator, in particular any appointment of a chairman or umpire.

28.   Joint and several liability of parties to arbitrators for fees and expenses

(1)   The parties are jointly and severally liable to pay to the arbitrators such reasonable fees and expenses (if any) as are appropriate in the circumstances.

(2)   Any party may apply to the court (upon notice to the other parties and to the arbitrators) which may order that the amount of the arbitrators' fees and expenses shall be considered and adjusted by such means and upon such terms as it may direct.

(3)   If the application is made after any amount has been paid to the arbitrators by way of fees or expenses, the court may order the repayment of such amount (if any) as is shown to be excessive, but shall not do so unless it is shown that it is reasonable in the circumstances to order repayment.

(4)   The above provisions have effect subject to any order of the court under section 24(4) or 25(3)(b) (order as to entitlement to fees or expenses in case of removal or resignation of arbitrator).

(5)   Nothing in this section affects any liability of a party to any other party to pay all or any of the costs of the arbitration (see sections 59 to 65) or any contractual right of an arbitrator to payment of his fees and expenses.

(6)   In this section references to arbitrators include an arbitrator who has ceased to act and an umpire who has not replaced the other arbitrators.

29.   Immunity of arbitrator

(1)   An arbitrator is not liable for anything done or omitted in the discharge or purported discharge of his functions as arbitrator unless the act or omission is shown to have been in bad faith.

(2)   Subsection (1) applies to an employee or agent of an arbitrator as it applies to the arbitrator himself.

(3)   This section does not affect any liability incurred by an arbitrator by reason of his resigning (but see section 25).

Jurisdiction of the arbitral tribunal

30.   Competence of tribunal to rule on its own jurisdiction

(1)   Unless otherwise agreed by the parties, the arbitral tribunal may rule on its own substantive jurisdiction, that is, as to—
   (a)   whether there is a valid arbitration agreement,
   (b)   whether the tribunal is properly constituted, and
   (c)   what matters have been submitted to arbitration in accordance with the arbitration agreement.

(2)   Any such ruling may be challenged by any available arbitral process of appeal or review or in accordance with the provisions of this Part.

31.   Objection to substantive jurisdiction of tribunal

(1)   An objection that the arbitral tribunal lacks substantive jurisdiction at the outset of the proceedings must be raised by a party not later than the time he takes the first step in the proceedings to contest the merits of any matter in relation to which he challenges the tribunal's jurisdiction.
A party is not precluded from raising such an objection by the fact that he has appointed or participated in the appointment of an arbitrator.

(2)   Any objection during the course of the arbitral proceedings that the arbitral tribunal is exceeding its substantive jurisdiction must be made as soon as possible after the matter alleged to be beyond its jurisdiction is raised.

(3)   The arbitral tribunal may admit an objection later than the time specified in subsection (1) or (2) if it considers the delay justified.

(4)   Where an objection is duly taken to the tribunal's substantive jurisdiction and the tribunal has power to rule on its own jurisdiction, it may—

(a)   rule on the matter in an award as to jurisdiction, or

(b)   deal with the objection in its award on the merits.

If the parties agree which of these courses the tribunal should take, the tribunal shall proceed accordingly.

(5)   The tribunal may in any case, and shall if the parties so agree, stay proceedings whilst an application is made to the court under section 32 (determination of preliminary point of jurisdiction).

32.   Determination of preliminary point of jurisdiction

(1)   The court may, on the application of a party to arbitral proceedings (upon notice to the other parties), determine any question as to the substantive jurisdiction of the tribunal.

A party may lose the right to object (see section 73).

(2)   An application under this section shall not be considered unless—

(a)   it is made with the agreement in writing of all the other parties to the proceedings, or

(b)   it is made with the permission of the tribunal and the court is satisfied—

(i)   that the determination of the question is likely to produce substantial savings in costs,

(ii)   that the application was made without delay, and

(iii)   that there is good reason why the matter should be decided by the court.

(3)   An application under this section, unless made with the agreement of all the other parties to the proceedings, shall state the grounds on which it is said that the matter should be decided by the court.

(4)   Unless otherwise agreed by the parties, the arbitral tribunal may continue the arbitral proceedings and make an award while an application to the court under this section is pending.

(5)   Unless the court gives leave, no appeal lies from a decision of the court whether the conditions specified in subsection (2) are met.

(6)   The decision of the court on the question of jurisdiction shall be treated as a judgment of the court for the purposes of an appeal.

But no appeal lies without the leave of the court which shall not be given unless the court considers that the question involves a point of law which is one of general importance or is one which for some other special reason should be considered by the Court of Appeal.

The arbitral proceedings

33.   General duty of the tribunal

(1)   The tribunal shall—

(a)   act fairly and impartially as between the parties, giving each party a reasonable opportunity of putting his case and dealing with that of his opponent, and

(b)   adopt procedures suitable to the circumstances of the particular case, avoiding unnecessary delay or expense, so as to provide a fair means for the resolution of the matters falling to be determined.

(2)   The tribunal shall comply with that general duty in conducting the arbitral proceedings, in its decisions on matters of procedure and evidence and in the exercise of all other powers conferred on it.

34.   Procedural and evidential matters

(1)   It shall be for the tribunal to decide all procedural and evidential matters, subject to the right of the parties to agree any matter.

(2)   Procedural and evidential matters include—

(a)   when and where any part of the proceedings is to be held;

(b)   the language or languages to be used in the proceedings and whether translations of any relevant documents are to be supplied;

(c)   whether any and if so what form of written statements of claim and defence are to be used, when these should be supplied and the extent to which such statements can be later amended;

(d)   whether any and if so which documents or classes of documents should be disclosed between and produced by the parties and at what stage;

(e)   whether any and if so what questions should be put to and answered by the respective parties and when and in what form this should be done;

(f)   whether to apply strict rules of evidence (or any other rules) as to the admissibility, relevance or weight of any material (oral, written or other) sought to be tendered on any matters of fact or opinion, and the time, manner and form in which such material should be exchanged and presented;

(g)   whether and to what extent the tribunal should itself take the initiative in ascertaining the facts and the law;

(h)   whether and to what extent there should be oral or written evidence or submissions.

(3)   The tribunal may fix the time within which any directions given by it are to be complied with, and may if it thinks fit extend the time so fixed (whether or not it has expired).

35.   Consolidation of proceedings and concurrent hearings

(1)   The parties are free to agree—

(a)   that the arbitral proceedings shall be consolidated with other arbitral proceedings, or

(b)   that concurrent hearings shall be held,

on such terms as may be agreed.

(2)   Unless the parties agree to confer such power on the tribunal, the tribunal has no power to order consolidation of proceedings or concurrent hearings.

36.   Legal or other representation

Unless otherwise agreed by the parties, a party to arbitral proceedings may be represented in the proceedings by a lawyer or other person chosen by him.

37.   Power to appoint experts, legal advisers or assessors

(1)   Unless otherwise agreed by the parties—

(a)   the tribunal may—

(i)   appoint experts or legal advisers to report to it and the parties, or

(ii)   appoint assessors to assist it on technical matters,

and may allow any such expert, legal adviser or assessor to attend the proceedings; and

(b)   the parties shall be given a reasonable opportunity to comment on any information, opinion or advice offered by any such person.

(2)   The fees and expenses of an expert, legal adviser or assessor appointed by the tribunal for which the arbitrators are liable are expenses of the arbitrators for the purposes of this Part.

38.   General powers exercisable by the tribunal

(1)   The parties are free to agree on the powers exercisable by the arbitral tribunal for the purposes of and in relation to the proceedings.

(2)   Unless otherwise agreed by the parties the tribunal has the following powers.

(3)   The tribunal may order a claimant to provide security for the costs of the arbitration. This power shall not be exercised on the ground that the claimant is—

(a)   an individual ordinarily resident outside the United Kingdom, or

(b)   a corporation or association incorporated or formed under the law of a country outside the United Kingdom, or whose central management and control is exercised outside the United Kingdom.

(4)   The tribunal may give directions in relation to any property which is the subject of the proceedings or as to which any question arises in the proceedings, and which is owned by or is in the possession of a party to the proceedings—

(a)   for the inspection, photographing, preservation, custody or detention of the property by the tribunal, an expert or a party, or

(b)   ordering that samples be taken from, or any observation be made of or experiment conducted upon, the property.

(5)   The tribunal may direct that a party or witness shall be examined on oath or affirmation, and may for that purpose administer any necessary oath or take any necessary affirmation.

(6)   The tribunal may give directions to a party for the preservation for the purposes of the proceedings of any evidence in his custody or control.

39.   Power to make provisional awards

(1)   The parties are free to agree that the tribunal shall have power to order on a provisional basis any relief which it would have power to grant in a final award.

(2)   This includes, for instance, making—

(a)   a provisional order for the payment of money or the disposition of property as between the parties, or

(b)   an order to make an interim payment on account of the costs of the arbitration.

(3)   Any such order shall be subject to the tribunal's final adjudication; and the tribunal's final award, on the merits or as to costs, shall take account of any such order.

(4)   Unless the parties agree to confer such power on the tribunal, the tribunal has no such power.

This does not affect its powers under section 47 (awards on different issues, &c.).

40.   General duty of parties

(1)   The parties shall do all things necessary for the proper and expeditious conduct of the arbitral proceedings.

(2)   This includes—

(a)   complying without delay with any determination of the tribunal as to procedural or evidential matters, or with any order or directions of the tribunal, and

(b)   where appropriate, taking without delay any necessary steps to obtain a decision of the court on a preliminary question of jurisdiction or law (see sections 32 and 45).

41.   Powers of tribunal in case of party's default

(1)   The parties are free to agree on the powers of the tribunal in case of a party's failure to do something necessary for the proper and expeditious conduct of the arbitration.

(2)   Unless otherwise agreed by the parties, the following provisions apply.

(3)   If the tribunal is satisfied that there has been inordinate and inexcusable delay on the part of the claimant in pursuing his claim and that the delay—

(a)   gives rise, or is likely to give rise, to a substantial risk that it is not possible to have a fair resolution of the issues in that claim, or

(b)   has caused, or is likely to cause, serious prejudice to the respondent,

the tribunal may make an award dismissing the claim.

(4)   If without showing sufficient cause a party—

(a)   fails to attend or be represented at an oral hearing of which due notice was given, or

(b)   where matters are to be dealt with in writing, fails after due notice to submit written evidence or make written submissions,

the tribunal may continue the proceedings in the absence of that party or, as the case may be, without any written evidence or submissions on his behalf, and may make an award on the basis of the evidence before it.

(5)   If without showing sufficient cause a party fails to comply with any order or directions of the tribunal, the tribunal may make a peremptory order to the same effect, prescribing such time for compliance with it as the tribunal considers appropriate.

(6) If a claimant fails to comply with a peremptory order of the tribunal to provide security for costs, the tribunal may make an award dismissing his claim.

(7) If a party fails to comply with any other kind of peremptory order, then, without prejudice to section 42 (enforcement by court of tribunal's peremptory orders), the tribunal may do any of the following—

(a) direct that the party in default shall not be entitled to rely upon any allegation or material which was the subject matter of the order;

(b) draw such adverse inferences from the act of non-compliance as the circumstances justify;

(c) proceed to an award on the basis of such materials as have been properly provided to it;

(d) make such order as it thinks fit as to the payment of costs of the arbitration incurred in consequence of the non-compliance.

Powers of court in relation to arbitral proceedings

42. Enforcement of peremptory orders of tribunal

(1) Unless otherwise agreed by the parties, the court may make an order requiring a party to comply with a peremptory order made by the tribunal.

(2) An application for an order under this section may be made—

(a) by the tribunal (upon notice to the parties),

(b) by a party to the arbitral proceedings with the permission of the tribunal (and upon notice to the other parties), or

(c) where the parties have agreed that the powers of the court under this section shall be available.

(3) The court shall not act unless it is satisfied that the applicant has exhausted any available arbitral process in respect of failure to comply with the tribunal's order.

(4) No order shall be made under this section unless the court is satisfied that the person to whom the tribunal's order was directed has failed to comply with it within the time prescribed in the order or, if no time was prescribed, within a reasonable time.

(5) The leave of the court is required for any appeal from a decision of the court under this section.

43. Securing the attendance of witnesses

(1) A party to arbitral proceedings may use the same court procedures as are available in relation to legal proceedings to secure the attendance before the tribunal of a witness in order to give oral testimony or to produce documents or other material evidence.

(2) This may only be done with the permission of the tribunal or the agreement of the other parties.

(3) The court procedures may only be used if—

(a) the witness is in the United Kingdom, and

(b) the arbitral proceedings are being conducted in England and Wales or, as the case may be, Northern Ireland.

(4) A person shall not be compelled by virtue of this section to produce any document or other material evidence which he could not be compelled to produce in legal proceedings.

44. Court powers exercisable in support of arbitral proceedings

(1) Unless otherwise agreed by the parties, the court has for the purposes of and in relation to arbitral proceedings the same power of making orders about the matters listed below as it has for the purposes of and in relation to legal proceedings.

(2) Those matters are—

(a) the taking of the evidence of witnesses;

(b) the preservation of evidence;

(c) making orders relating to property which is the subject of the proceedings or as to which any question arises in the proceedings—

    (i)   for the inspection, photographing, preservation, custody or detention of the property, or
    (ii)   ordering that samples be taken from, or any observation be made of or experiment conducted upon, the property;
and for that purpose authorising any person to enter any premises in the possession or control of a party to the arbitration;
    (d)   the sale of any goods the subject of the proceedings;
    (e)   the granting of an interim injunction or the appointment of a receiver.

    (3)   If the case is one of urgency, the court may, on the application of a party or proposed party to the arbitral proceedings, make such orders as it thinks necessary for the purpose of preserving evidence or assets.

    (4)   If the case is not one of urgency, the court shall act only on the application of a party to the arbitral proceedings (upon notice to the other parties and to the tribunal) made with the permission of the tribunal or the agreement in writing of the other parties.

    (5)   In any case the court shall act only if or to the extent that the arbitral tribunal, and any arbitral or other institution or person vested by the parties with power in that regard, has no power or is unable for the time being to act effectively.

    (6)   If the court so orders, an order made by it under this section shall cease to have effect in whole or in part on the order of the tribunal or of any such arbitral or other institution or person having power to act in relation to the subject-matter of the order.

    (7)   The leave of the court is required for any appeal from a decision of the court under this section.

45. Determination of preliminary point of law

    (1)   Unless otherwise agreed by the parties, the court may on the application of a party to arbitral proceedings (upon notice to the other parties) determine any question of law arising in the course of the proceedings which the court is satisfied substantially affects the rights of one or more of the parties.
An agreement to dispense with reasons for the tribunal's award shall be considered an agreement to exclude the court's jurisdiction under this section.

    (2)   An application under this section shall not be considered unless—
    (a)   it is made with the agreement of all the other parties to the proceedings, or
    (b)   it is made with the permission of the tribunal and the court is satisfied—
       (i)   that the determination of the question is likely to produce substantial savings in costs, and
       (ii)   that the application was made without delay.

    (3)   The application shall identify the question of law to be determined and, unless made with the agreement of all the other parties to the proceedings, shall state the grounds on which it is said that the question should be decided by the court.

    (4)   Unless otherwise agreed by the parties, the arbitral tribunal may continue the arbitral proceedings and make an award while an application to the court under this section is pending.

    (5)   Unless the court gives leave, no appeal lies from a decision of the court whether the conditions specified in subsection (2) are met.

    (6)   The decision of the court on the question of law shall be treated as a judgment of the court for the purposes of an appeal.
But no appeal lies without the leave of the court which shall not be given unless the court considers that the question is one of general importance, or is one which for some other special reason should be considered by the Court of Appeal.

The award

46. Rules applicable to substance of dispute

    (1)   The arbitral tribunal shall decide the dispute—

(a) in accordance with the law chosen by the parties as applicable to the substance of the dispute, or

(b) if the parties so agree, in accordance with such other considerations as are agreed by them or determined by the tribunal.

(2) For this purpose the choice of the laws of a country shall be understood to refer to the substantive laws of that country and not its conflict of laws rules.

(3) If or to the extent that there is no such choice or agreement, the tribunal shall apply the law determined by the conflict of laws rules which it considers applicable.

47. Awards on different issues, &c.

(1) Unless otherwise agreed by the parties, the tribunal may make more than one award at different times on different aspects of the matters to be determined.

(2) The tribunal may, in particular, make an award relating—

(a) to an issue affecting the whole claim, or

(b) to a part only of the claims or cross-claims submitted to it for decision.

(3) If the tribunal does so, it shall specify in its award the issue, or the claim or part of a claim, which is the subject matter of the award.

48. Remedies

(1) The parties are free to agree on the powers exercisable by the arbitral tribunal as regards remedies.

(2) Unless otherwise agreed by the parties, the tribunal has the following powers.

(3) The tribunal may make a declaration as to any matter to be determined in the proceedings.

(4) The tribunal may order the payment of a sum of money, in any currency.

(5) The tribunal has the same powers as the court—

(a) to order a party to do or refrain from doing anything;

(b) to order specific performance of a contract (other than a contract relating to land);

(c) to order the rectification, setting aside or cancellation of a deed or other document.

49. Interest

(1) The parties are free to agree on the powers of the tribunal as regards the award of interest.

(2) Unless otherwise agreed by the parties the following provisions apply.

(3) The tribunal may award simple or compound interest from such dates, at such rates and with such rests as it considers meets the justice of the case—

(a) on the whole or part of any amount awarded by the tribunal, in respect of any period up to the date of the award;

(b) on the whole or part of any amount claimed in the arbitration and outstanding at the commencement of the arbitral proceedings but paid before the award was made, in respect of any period up to the date of payment.

(4) The tribunal may award simple or compound interest from the date of the award (or any later date) until payment, at such rates and with such rests as it considers meets the justice of the case, on the outstanding amount of any award (including any award of interest under subsection (3) and any award as to costs).

(5) References in this section to an amount awarded by the tribunal include an amount payable in consequence of a declaratory award by the tribunal.

(6) The above provisions do not affect any other power of the tribunal to award interest.

50. Extension of time for making award

(1) Where the time for making an award is limited by or in pursuance of the arbitration agreement, then, unless otherwise agreed by the parties, the court may in accordance with the following provisions by order extend that time.

(2) An application for an order under this section may be made—

(a) by the tribunal (upon notice to the parties), or

(b)   by any party to the proceedings (upon notice to the tribunal and the other parties), but only after exhausting any available arbitral process for obtaining an extension of time.

(3)   The court shall only make an order if satisfied that a substantial injustice would otherwise be done.

(4)   The court may extend the time for such period and on such terms as it thinks fit, and may do so whether or not the time previously fixed (by or under the agreement or by a previous order) has expired.

(5)   The leave of the court is required for any appeal from a decision of the court under this section.

51.   Settlement

(1)   If during arbitral proceedings the parties settle the dispute, the following provisions apply unless otherwise agreed by the parties.

(2)   The tribunal shall terminate the substantive proceedings and, if so requested by the parties and not objected to by the tribunal, shall record the settlement in the form of an agreed award.

(3)   An agreed award shall state that it is an award of the tribunal and shall have the same status and effect as any other award on the merits of the case.

(4)   The following provisions of this Part relating to awards (sections 52 to 58) apply to an agreed award.

(5)   Unless the parties have also settled the matter of the payment of the costs of the arbitration, the provisions of this Part relating to costs (sections 59 to 65) continue to apply.

52.   Form of award

(1)   The parties are free to agree on the form of an award.

(2)   If or to the extent that there is no such agreement, the following provisions apply.

(3)   The award shall be in writing signed by all the arbitrators or all those assenting to the award.

(4)   The award shall contain the reasons for the award unless it is an agreed award or the parties have agreed to dispense with reasons.

(5)   The award shall state the seat of the arbitration and the date when the award is made.

53.   Place where award treated as made

Unless otherwise agreed by the parties, where the seat of the arbitration is in England and Wales or Northern Ireland, any award in the proceedings shall be treated as made there, regardless of where it was signed, despatched or delivered to any of the parties.

54.   Date of award

(1)   Unless otherwise agreed by the parties, the tribunal may decide what is to be taken to be the date on which the award was made.

(2)   In the absence of any such decision, the date of the award shall be taken to be the date on which it is signed by the arbitrator or, where more than one arbitrator signs the award, by the last of them.

55.   Notification of award

(1)   The parties are free to agree on the requirements as to notification of the award to the parties.

(2)   If there is no such agreement, the award shall be notified to the parties by service on them of copies of the award, which shall be done without delay after the award is made.

(3)   Nothing in this section affects section 56 (power to withhold award in case of non-payment).

56.   Power to withhold award in case of non-payment

(1)   The tribunal may refuse to deliver an award to the parties except upon full payment of the fees and expenses of the arbitrators.

(2)   If the tribunal refuses on that ground to deliver an award, a party to the arbitral proceedings may (upon notice to the other parties and the tribunal) apply to the court, which may order that—

(a)   the tribunal shall deliver the award on the payment into court by the applicant of the fees and expenses demanded, or such lesser amount as the court may specify,

(b)   the amount of the fees and expenses properly payable shall be determined by such means and upon such terms as the court may direct, and

(c)   out of the money paid into court there shall be paid out such fees and expenses as may be found to be properly payable and the balance of the money (if any) shall be paid out to the applicant.

(3)   For this purpose the amount of fees and expenses properly payable is the amount the applicant is liable to pay under section 28 or any agreement relating to the payment of the arbitrators.

(4)   No application to the court may be made where there is any available arbitral process for appeal or review of the amount of the fees or expenses demanded.

(5)   References in this section to arbitrators include an arbitrator who has ceased to act and an umpire who has not replaced the other arbitrators.

(6)   The above provisions of this section also apply in relation to any arbitral or other institution or person vested by the parties with powers in relation to the delivery of the tribunal's award.

As they so apply, the references to the fees and expenses of the arbitrators shall be construed as including the fees and expenses of that institution or person.

(7)   The leave of the court is required for any appeal from a decision of the court under this section.

(8)   Nothing in this section shall be construed as excluding an application under section 28 where payment has been made to the arbitrators in order to obtain the award.

57.   Correction of award or additional award

(1)   The parties are free to agree on the powers of the tribunal to correct an award or make an additional award.

(2)   If or to the extent there is no such agreement, the following provisions apply.

(3)   The tribunal may on its own initiative or on the application of a party—

(a)   correct an award so as to remove any clerical mistake or error arising from an accidental slip or omission or clarify or remove any ambiguity in the award, or

(b)   make an additional award in respect of any claim (including a claim for interest or costs) which was presented to the tribunal but was not dealt with in the award.

These powers shall not be exercised without first affording the other parties a reasonable opportunity to make representations to the tribunal.

(4)   Any application for the exercise of those powers must be made within 28 days of the date of the award or such longer period as the parties may agree.

(5)   Any correction of an award shall be made within 28 days of the date the application was received by the tribunal or, where the correction is made by the tribunal on its own initiative, within 28 days of the date of the award or, in either case, such longer period as the parties may agree.

(6)   Any additional award shall be made within 56 days of the date of the original award or such longer period as the parties may agree.

(7)   Any correction of an award shall form part of the award.

58.   Effect of award

(1)   Unless otherwise agreed by the parties, an award made by the tribunal pursuant to an arbitration agreement is final and binding both on the parties and on any persons claiming through or under them.

(2)   This does not affect the right of a person to challenge the award by any available arbitral process of appeal or review or in accordance with the provisions of this Part.

Costs of the arbitration

59. Costs of the arbitration
(1)   References in this Part to the costs of the arbitration are to—
  (a)   the arbitrators' fees and expenses,
  (b)   the fees and expenses of any arbitral institution concerned, and
  (c)   the legal or other costs of the parties.
(2)   Any such reference includes the costs of or incidental to any proceedings to determine the amount of the recoverable costs of the arbitration (see section 63).

60. Agreement to pay costs in any event
An agreement which has the effect that a party is to pay the whole or part of the costs of the arbitration in any event is only valid if made after the dispute in question has arisen.

61. Award of costs
(1)   The tribunal may make an award allocating the costs of the arbitration as between the parties, subject to any agreement of the parties.
(2)   Unless the parties otherwise agree, the tribunal shall award costs on the general principle that costs should follow the event except where it appears to the tribunal that in the circumstances this is not appropriate in relation to the whole or part of the costs.

62. Effect of agreement or award about costs
Unless the parties otherwise agree, any obligation under an agreement between them as to how the costs of the arbitration are to be borne, or under an award allocating the costs of the arbitration, extends only to such costs as are recoverable.

63. The recoverable costs of the arbitration
(1)   The parties are free to agree what costs of the arbitration are recoverable.
(2)   If or to the extent there is no such agreement, the following provisions apply.
(3)   The tribunal may determine by award the recoverable costs of the arbitration on such basis as it thinks fit.
  If it does so, it shall specify—
  (a)   the basis on which it has acted, and
  (b)   the items of recoverable costs and the amount referable to each.
(4)   If the tribunal does not determine the recoverable costs of the arbitration, any party to the arbitral proceedings may apply to the court (upon notice to the other parties) which may—
  (a)   determine the recoverable costs of the arbitration on such basis as it thinks fit, or
  (b)   order that they shall be determined by such means and upon such terms as it may specify.
(5)   Unless the tribunal or the court determines otherwise—
  (a)   the recoverable costs of the arbitration shall be determined on the basis that there shall be allowed a reasonable amount in respect of all costs reasonably incurred, and
  (b)   any doubt as to whether costs were reasonably incurred or were reasonable in amount shall be resolved in favour of the paying party.
(6)   The above provisions have effect subject to section 64 (recoverable fees and expenses of arbitrators).
(7)   Nothing in this section affects any right of the arbitrators, any expert, legal adviser or assessor appointed by the tribunal, or any arbitral institution, to payment of their fees and expenses.

64. Recoverable fees and expenses of arbitrators
(1)   Unless otherwise agreed by the parties, the recoverable costs of the arbitration shall include in respect of the fees and expenses of the arbitrators only such reasonable fees and expenses as are appropriate in the circumstances.

(2)   If there is any question as to what reasonable fees and expenses are appropriate in the circumstances, and the matter is not already before the court on an application under section 63(4), the court may on the application of any party (upon notice to the other parties)—

(a)   determine the matter, or

(b)   order that it be determined by such means and upon such terms as the court may specify.

(3)   Subsection (1) has effect subject to any order of the court under section 24(4) or 25(3)(b) (order as to entitlement to fees or expenses in case of removal or resignation of arbitrator).

(4)   Nothing in this section affects any right of the arbitrator to payment of his fees and expenses.

65.   Power to limit recoverable costs

(1)   Unless otherwise agreed by the parties, the tribunal may direct that the recoverable costs of the arbitration, or of any part of the arbitral proceedings, shall be limited to a specified amount.

(2)   Any direction may be made or varied at any stage, but this must be done sufficiently in advance of the incurring of costs to which it relates, or the taking of any steps in the proceedings which may be affected by it, for the limit to be taken into account.

Powers of the court in relation to award

66.   Enforcement of the award

(1)   An award made by the tribunal pursuant to an arbitration agreement may, by leave of the court, be enforced in the same manner as a judgment or order of the court to the same effect.

(2)   Where leave is so given, judgment may be entered in terms of the award.

(3)   Leave to enforce an award shall not be given where, or to the extent that, the person against whom it is sought to be enforced shows that the tribunal lacked substantive jurisdiction to make the award.

The right to raise such an objection may have been lost (see section 73).

(4)   Nothing in this section affects the recognition or enforcement of an award under any other enactment or rule of law, in particular under Part II of the Arbitration Act 1950 (enforcement of awards under Geneva Convention) or the provisions of Part III of this Act relating to the recognition and enforcement of awards under the New York Convention or by an action on the award.

67.   Challenging the award: substantive jurisdiction

(1)   A party to arbitral proceedings may (upon notice to the other parties and to the tribunal) apply to the court—

(a)   challenging any award of the arbitral tribunal as to its substantive jurisdiction; or

(b)   for an order declaring an award made by the tribunal on the merits to be of no effect, in whole or in part, because the tribunal did not have substantive jurisdiction.

A party may lose the right to object (see section 73) and the right to apply is subject to the restrictions in section 70(2) and (3).

(2)   The arbitral tribunal may continue the arbitral proceedings and make a further award while an application to the court under this section is pending in relation to an award as to jurisdiction.

(3)   On an application under this section challenging an award of the arbitral tribunal as to its substantive jurisdiction, the court may by order—

(a)   confirm the award,

(b)   vary the award, or

(c)   set aside the award in whole or in part.

(4)   The leave of the court is required for any appeal from a decision of the court under this section.

68. Challenging the award: serious irregularity

(1)   A party to arbitral proceedings may (upon notice to the other parties and to the tribunal) apply to the court challenging an award in the proceedings on the ground of serious irregularity affecting the tribunal, the proceedings or the award.

A party may lose the right to object (see section 73) and the right to apply is subject to the restrictions in section 70(2) and (3).

(2)   Serious irregularity means an irregularity of one or more of the following kinds which the court considers has caused or will cause substantial injustice to the applicant—

(a)   failure by the tribunal to comply with section 33 (general duty of tribunal);

(b)   the tribunal exceeding its powers (otherwise than by exceeding its substantive jurisdiction: see section 67);

(c)   failure by the tribunal to conduct the proceedings in accordance with the procedure agreed by the parties;

(d)   failure by the tribunal to deal with all the issues that were put to it;

(e)   any arbitral or other institution or person vested by the parties with powers in relation to the proceedings or the award exceeding its powers;

(f)   uncertainty or ambiguity as to the effect of the award;

(g)   the award being obtained by fraud or the award or the way in which it was procured being contrary to public policy;

(h)   failure to comply with the requirements as to the form of the award; or

(i)   any irregularity in the conduct of the proceedings or in the award which is admitted by the tribunal or by any arbitral or other institution or person vested by the parties with powers in relation to the proceedings or the award.

(3)   If there is shown to be serious irregularity affecting the tribunal, the proceedings or the award, the court may—

(a)   remit the award to the tribunal, in whole or in part, for reconsideration,

(b)   set the award aside in whole or in part, or

(c)   declare the award to be of no effect, in whole or in part.

The court shall not exercise its power to set aside or to declare an award to be of no effect, in whole or in part, unless it is satisfied that it would be inappropriate to remit the matters in question to the tribunal for reconsideration.

(4)   The leave of the court is required for any appeal from a decision of the court under this section.

69. Appeal on point of law

(1)   Unless otherwise agreed by the parties, a party to arbitral proceedings may (upon notice to the other parties and to the tribunal) appeal to the court on a question of law arising out of an award made in the proceedings.

An agreement to dispense with reasons for the tribunal's award shall be considered an agreement to exclude the court's jurisdiction under this section.

(2)   An appeal shall not be brought under this section except—

(a)   with the agreement of all the other parties to the proceedings, or

(b)   with the leave of the court.

The right to appeal is also subject to the restrictions in section 70(2) and (3).

(3)   Leave to appeal shall be given only if the court is satisfied—

(a)   that the determination of the question will substantially affect the rights of one or more of the parties,

(b)   that the question is one which the tribunal was asked to determine,

(c)   that, on the basis of the findings of fact in the award—

(i)   the decision of the tribunal on the question is obviously wrong, or

(ii)   the question is one of general public importance and the decision of the tribunal is at least open to serious doubt, and

(d) that, despite the agreement of the parties to resolve the matter by arbitration, it is just and proper in all the circumstances for the court to determine the question.

(4) An application for leave to appeal under this section shall identify the question of law to be determined and state the grounds on which it is alleged that leave to appeal should be granted.

(5) The court shall determine an application for leave to appeal under this section without a hearing unless it appears to the court that a hearing is required.

(6) The leave of the court is required for any appeal from a decision of the court under this section to grant or refuse leave to appeal.

(7) On an appeal under this section the court may by order—
(a) confirm the award,
(b) vary the award,
(c) remit the award to the tribunal, in whole or in part, for reconsideration in the light of the court's determination, or
(d) set aside the award in whole or in part.
The court shall not exercise its power to set aside an award, in whole or in part, unless it is satisfied that it would be inappropriate to remit the matters in question to the tribunal for reconsideration.

(8) The decision of the court on an appeal under this section shall be treated as a judgment of the court for the purposes of a further appeal.
But no such appeal lies without the leave of the court which shall not be given unless the court considers that the question is one of general importance or is one which for some other special reason should be considered by the Court of Appeal.

70. Challenge or appeal: supplementary provisions

(1) The following provisions apply to an application or appeal under section 67, 68 or 69.

(2) An application or appeal may not be brought if the applicant or appellant has not first exhausted—
(a) any available arbitral process of appeal or review, and
(b) any available recourse under section 57 (correction of award or additional award).

(3) Any application or appeal must be brought within 28 days of the date of the award or, if there has been any arbitral process of appeal or review, of the date when the applicant or appellant was notified of the result of that process.

(4) If on an application or appeal it appears to the court that the award—
(a) does not contain the tribunal's reasons, or
(b) does not set out the tribunal's reasons in sufficient detail to enable the court properly to consider the application or appeal,
the court may order the tribunal to state the reasons for its award in sufficient detail for that purpose.

(5) Where the court makes an order under subsection (4), it may make such further order as it thinks fit with respect to any additional costs of the arbitration resulting from its order.

(6) The court may order the applicant or appellant to provide security for the costs of the application or appeal, and may direct that the application or appeal be dismissed if the order is not complied with.
The power to order security for costs shall not be exercised on the ground that the applicant or appellant is—
(a) an individual ordinarily resident outside the United Kingdom, or
(b) a corporation or association incorporated or formed under the law of a country outside the United Kingdom, or whose central management and control is exercised outside the United Kingdom.

(7) The court may order that any money payable under the award shall be brought into court or otherwise secured pending the determination of the application or appeal, and may direct that the application or appeal be dismissed if the order is not complied with.

(8)   The court may grant leave to appeal subject to conditions to the same or similar effect as an order under subsection (6) or (7).

This does not affect the general discretion of the court to grant leave subject to conditions.

71.   Challenge or appeal: effect of order of court

(1)   The following provisions have effect where the court makes an order under section 67, 68 or 69 with respect to an award.

(2)   Where the award is varied, the variation has effect as part of the tribunal's award.

(3)   Where the award is remitted to the tribunal, in whole or in part, for reconsideration, the tribunal shall make a fresh award in respect of the matters remitted within three months of the date of the order for remission or such longer or shorter period as the court may direct.

(4)   Where the award is set aside or declared to be of no effect, in whole or in part, the court may also order that any provision that an award is a condition precedent to the bringing of legal proceedings in respect of a matter to which the arbitration agreement applies, is of no effect as regards the subject matter of the award or, as the case may be, the relevant part of the award.

Miscellaneous

72.   Saving for rights of person who takes no part in proceedings

(1)   A person alleged to be a party to arbitral proceedings but who takes no part in the proceedings may question—

(a)   whether there is a valid arbitration agreement,

(b)   whether the tribunal is properly constituted, or

(c)   what matters have been submitted to arbitration in accordance with the arbitration agreement,

by proceedings in the court for a declaration or injunction or other appropriate relief.

(2)   He also has the same right as a party to the arbitral proceedings to challenge an award—

(a)   by an application under section 67 on the ground of lack of substantive jurisdiction in relation to him, or

(b)   by an application under section 68 on the ground of serious irregularity (within the meaning of that section) affecting him;

and section 70(2) (duty to exhaust arbitral procedures) does not apply in his case.

73.   Loss of right to object

(1)   If a party to arbitral proceedings takes part, or continues to take part, in the proceedings without making, either forthwith or within such time as is allowed by the arbitration agreement or the tribunal or by any provision of this Part, any objection—

(a)   that the tribunal lacks substantive jurisdiction,

(b)   that the proceedings have been improperly conducted,

(c)   that there has been a failure to comply with the arbitration agreement or with any provision of this Part, or

(d)   that there has been any other irregularity affecting the tribunal or the proceedings,

he may not raise that objection later, before the tribunal or the court, unless he shows that, at the time he took part or continued to take part in the proceedings, he did not know and could not with reasonable diligence have discovered the grounds for the objection.

(2)   Where the arbitral tribunal rules that it has substantive jurisdiction and a party to arbitral proceedings who could have questioned that ruling—

(a)   by any available arbitral process of appeal or review, or

(b)   by challenging the award,

does not do so, or does not do so within the time allowed by the arbitration agreement or any provision of this Part, he may not object later to the tribunal's substantive jurisdiction on any ground which was the subject of that ruling.

74. Immunity of arbitral institutions, &c.

(1)   An arbitral or other institution or person designated or requested by the parties to appoint or nominate an arbitrator is not liable for anything done or omitted in the discharge or purported discharge of that function unless the act or omission is shown to have been in bad faith.

(2)   An arbitral or other institution or person by whom an arbitrator is appointed or nominated is not liable, by reason of having appointed or nominated him, for anything done or omitted by the arbitrator (or his employees or agents) in the discharge or purported discharge of his functions as arbitrator.

(3)   The above provisions apply to an employee or agent of an arbitral or other institution or person as they apply to the institution or person himself.

75.   Charge to secure payment of solicitors' costs
The powers of the court to make declarations and orders under section 73 of the Solicitors Act 1974 or Article 71H of the Solicitors (Northern Ireland) Order 1976 (power to charge property recovered in the proceedings with the payment of solicitors' costs) may be exercised in relation to arbitral proceedings as if those proceedings were proceedings in the court.

Supplementary

76.   Service of notices, &c.

(1)   The parties are free to agree on the manner of service of any notice or other document required or authorised to be given or served in pursuance of the arbitration agreement or for the purposes of the arbitral proceedings.

(2)   If or to the extent that there is no such agreement the following provisions apply.

(3)   A notice or other document may be served on a person by any effective means.

(4)   If a notice or other document is addressed, pre-paid and delivered by post—

(a)   to the addressee's last known principal residence or, if he is or has been carrying on a trade, profession or business, his last known principal business address, or

(b)   where the addressee is a body corporate, to the body's registered or principal office,

it shall be treated as effectively served.

(5)   This section does not apply to the service of documents for the purposes of legal proceedings, for which provision is made by rules of court.

(6)   References in this Part to a notice or other document include any form of communication in writing and references to giving or serving a notice or other document shall be construed accordingly.

77.   Powers of court in relation to service of documents

(1)   This section applies where service of a document on a person in the manner agreed by the parties, or in accordance with provisions of section 76 having effect in default of agreement, is not reasonably practicable.

(2)   Unless otherwise agreed by the parties, the court may make such order as it thinks fit—

(a)   for service in such manner as the court may direct, or

(b)   dispensing with service of the document.

(3)   Any party to the arbitration agreement may apply for an order, but only after exhausting any available arbitral process for resolving the matter.

(4)   The leave of the court is required for any appeal from a decision of the court under this section.

78.   Reckoning periods of time

(1)   The parties are free to agree on the method of reckoning periods of time for the purposes of any provision agreed by them or any provision of this Part having effect in default of such agreement.

(2)   If or to the extent there is no such agreement, periods of time shall be reckoned in accordance with the following provisions.

(3)   Where the act is required to be done within a specified period after or from a specified date, the period begins immediately after that date.

(4)   Where the act is required to be done a specified number of clear days after a specified date, at least that number of days must intervene between the day on which the act is done and that date.

(5)   Where the period is a period of seven days or less which would include a Saturday, Sunday or a public holiday in the place where anything which has to be done within the period falls to be done, that day shall be excluded.

In relation to England and Wales or Northern Ireland, a 'public holiday' means Christmas Day, Good Friday or a day which under the Banking and Financial Dealings Act 1971 is a bank holiday.

79.   Power of court to extend time limits relating to arbitral proceedings

(1)   Unless the parties otherwise agree, the court may by order extend any time limit agreed by them in relation to any matter relating to the arbitral proceedings or specified in any provision of this Part having effect in default of such agreement.

This section does not apply to a time limit to which section 12 applies (power of court to extend time for beginning arbitral proceedings, &c.).

(2)   An application for an order may be made—

(a)   by any party to the arbitral proceedings (upon notice to the other parties and to the tribunal), or

(b)   by the arbitral tribunal (upon notice to the parties).

(3)   The court shall not exercise its power to extend a time limit unless it is satisfied—

(a)   that any available recourse to the tribunal, or to any arbitral or other institution or person vested by the parties with power in that regard, has first been exhausted, and

(b)   that a substantial injustice would otherwise be done.

(4)   The court's power under this section may be exercised whether or not the time has already expired.

(5)   An order under this section may be made on such terms as the court thinks fit.

(6)   The leave of the court is required for any appeal from a decision of the court under this section.

80.   Notice and other requirements in connection with legal proceedings

(1)   References in this Part to an application, appeal or other step in relation to legal proceedings being taken 'upon notice' to the other parties to the arbitral proceedings, or to the tribunal, are to such notice of the originating process as is required by rules of court and do not impose any separate requirement.

(2)   Rules of court shall be made—

(a)   requiring such notice to be given as indicated by any provision of this Part, and

(b)   as to the manner, form and content of any such notice.

(3)   Subject to any provision made by rules of court, a requirement to give notice to the tribunal of legal proceedings shall be construed—

(a)   if there is more than one arbitrator, as a requirement to give notice to each of them; and

(b)   if the tribunal is not fully constituted, as a requirement to give notice to any arbitrator who has been appointed.

(4)   References in this Part to making an application or appeal to the court within a specified period are to the issue within that period of the appropriate originating process in accordance with rules of court.

(5)   Where any provision of this Part requires an application or appeal to be made to the court within a specified time, the rules of court relating to the reckoning of periods, the extending or abridging of periods, and the consequences of not taking a step within the period prescribed by the rules, apply in relation to that requirement.

(6)   Provision may be made by rules of court amending the provisions of this Part—

(a)   with respect to the time within which any application or appeal to the court must be made,

(b)   so as to keep any provision made by this Part in relation to arbitral proceedings in step with the corresponding provision of rules of court applying in relation to proceedings in the court, or

(c)   so as to keep any provision made by this Part in relation to legal proceedings in step with the corresponding provision of rules of court applying generally in relation to proceedings in the court.

(7)   Nothing in this section affects the generality of the power to make rules of court.

81.   Saving for certain matters governed by common law

(1)   Nothing in this Part shall be construed as excluding the operation of any rule of law consistent with the provisions of this Part, in particular, any rule of law as to—

(a)   matters which are not capable of settlement by arbitration;

(b)   the effect of an oral arbitration agreement; or

(c)   the refusal of recognition or enforcement of an arbitral award on grounds of public policy.

(2)   Nothing in this Act shall be construed as reviving any jurisdiction of the court to set aside or remit an award on the ground of errors of fact or law on the face of the award.

82.   Minor definitions

(1)   In this Part—

'arbitrator', unless the context otherwise requires, includes an umpire;

'available arbitral process', in relation to any matter, includes any process of appeal to or review by an arbitral or other institution or person vested by the parties with powers in relation to that matter;

'claimant', unless the context otherwise requires, includes a counterclaimant, and related expressions shall be construed accordingly;

'dispute' includes any difference;

'enactment' includes an enactment contained in Northern Ireland legislation;

'legal proceedings' means civil proceedings in the High Court or a county court;

'peremptory order' means an order made under section 41(5) or made in exercise of any corresponding power conferred by the parties;

'premises' includes land, buildings, moveable structures, vehicles, vessels, aircraft and hovercraft;

'question of law' means—

(a)   for a court in England and Wales, a question of the law of England and Wales, and

(b)   for a court in Northern Ireland, a question of the law of Northern Ireland;

'substantive jurisdiction', in relation to an arbitral tribunal, refers to the matters specified in section 30(1)(a) to (c), and references to the tribunal exceeding its substantive jurisdiction shall be construed accordingly.

(2)   References in this Part to a party to an arbitration agreement include any person claiming under or through a party to the agreement.

83.   Index of defined expressions: Part I

In this Part the expressions listed below are defined or otherwise explained by the provisions indicated—

agreement, agree and agreed	section 5(1)
agreement in writing	section 5(2) to (5)
arbitration agreement	sections 6 and 5(1)
arbitrator	section 82(1)
available arbitral process	section 82(1)

claimant	section 82(1)
commencement (in relation to arbitral proceedings)	section 14
costs of the arbitration	section 59
the court	section 105
dispute	section 82(1)
enactment	section 82(1)
legal proceedings	section 82(1)
Limitation Acts	section 13(4)
notice (or other document)	section 76(6)
party—	
—in relation to an arbitration agreement	section 82(2)
—where section 106(2) or (3) applies	section 106(4)
peremptory order	section 82(1) (and see section 41(5))
premises	section 82(1)
question of law	section 82(1)
recoverable costs	sections 63 and 64
seat of the arbitration	section 3
serve and service (of notice or other document)	section 76(6)
substantive jurisdiction (in relation to an arbitral tribunal)	section 82(1) (and see section 30(1)(a) to (c))
upon notice (to the parties or the tribunal)	section 80
written and in writing	section 5(6)

84. Transitional provisions

(1)   The provisions of this Part do not apply to arbitral proceedings commenced before the date on which this Part comes into force.

(2)   They apply to arbitral proceedings commenced on or after that date under an arbitration agreement whenever made.

(3)   The above provisions have effect subject to any transitional provision made by an order under section 109(2) (power to include transitional provisions in commencement order).

PART II

OTHER PROVISIONS RELATING TO ARBITRATION

Domestic arbitration agreements

85. Modification of Part I in relation to domestic arbitration agreement

(1)   In the case of a domestic arbitration agreement the provisions of Part I are modified in accordance with the following sections.

(2)   For this purpose a 'domestic arbitration agreement' means an arbitration agreement to which none of the parties is—

(a)   an individual who is a national of, or habitually resident in, a state other than the United Kingdom, or

(b)   a body corporate which is incorporated in, or whose central control and management is exercised in, a state other than the United Kingdom,

and under which the seat of the arbitration (if the seat has been designated or determined) is in the United Kingdom.

(3)   In subsection (2) 'arbitration agreement' and 'seat of the arbitration' have the same meaning as in Part I (see sections 3, 5(1) and 6).

86. Staying of legal proceedings

(1)   In section 9 (stay of legal proceedings), subsection (4) (stay unless the arbitration agreement is null and void, inoperative, or incapable of being performed) does not apply to a domestic arbitration agreement.

(2)   On an application under that section in relation to a domestic arbitration agreement the court shall grant a stay unless satisfied—

(a)   that the arbitration agreement is null and void, inoperative, or incapable of being performed, or

(b)   that there are other sufficient grounds for not requiring the parties to abide by the arbitration agreement.

(3)   The court may treat as a sufficient ground under subsection (2)(b) the fact that the applicant is or was at any material time not ready and willing to do all things necessary for the proper conduct of the arbitration or of any other dispute resolution procedures required to be exhausted before resorting to arbitration.

(4)   For the purposes of this section the question whether an arbitration agreement is a domestic arbitration agreement shall be determined by reference to the facts at the time the legal proceedings are commenced.

87. Effectiveness of agreement to exclude court's jurisdiction

(1)   In the case of a domestic arbitration agreement any agreement to exclude the jurisdiction of the court under—

(a)   section 45 (determination of preliminary point of law), or

(b)   section 69 (challenging the award: appeal on point of law),

is not effective unless entered into after the commencement of the arbitral proceedings in which the question arises or the award is made.

(2)   For this purpose the commencement of the arbitral proceedings has the same meaning as in Part I (see section 14).

(3)   For the purposes of this section the question whether an arbitration agreement is a domestic arbitration agreement shall be determined by reference to the facts at the time the agreement is entered into.

88. Power to repeal or amend sections 85 to 87

(1)   The Secretary of State may by order repeal or amend the provisions of sections 85 to 87.

(2)   An order under this section may contain such supplementary, incidental and transitional provisions as appear to the Secretary of State to be appropriate.

(3)   An order under this section shall be made by statutory instrument and no such order shall be made unless a draft of it has been laid before and approved by a resolution of each House of Parliament.

Consumer arbitration agreements

89. Application of unfair terms regulations to consumer arbitration agreements

(1)   The following sections extend the application of the Unfair Terms in Consumer Contracts Regulations 1994 in relation to a term which constitutes an arbitration agreement.

For this purpose 'arbitration agreement' means an agreement to submit to arbitration present or future disputes or differences (whether or not contractual).

(2)   In those sections 'the Regulations' means those regulations and includes any regulations amending or replacing those regulations.

(3)   Those sections apply whatever the law applicable to the arbitration agreement.

90. Regulations apply where consumer is a legal person

The Regulations apply where the consumer is a legal person as they apply where the consumer is a natural person.

91.   Arbitration agreement unfair where modest amount sought
(1)   A term which constitutes an arbitration agreement is unfair for the purposes of the Regulations so far as it relates to a claim for a pecuniary remedy which does not exceed the amount specified by order for the purposes of this section.
(2)   Orders under this section may make different provision for different cases and for different purposes.
(3)   The power to make orders under this section is exercisable—
   (a)   for England and Wales, by the Secretary of State with the concurrence of the Lord Chancellor,
   (b)   for Scotland, by the Secretary of State with the concurrence of the Lord Advocate, and
   (c)   for Northern Ireland, by the Department of Economic Development for Northern Ireland with the concurrence of the Lord Chancellor.
(4)   Any such order for England and Wales or Scotland shall be made by statutory instrument which shall be subject to annulment in pursuance of a resolution of either House of Parliament.
(5)   Any such order for Northern Ireland shall be a statutory rule for the purposes of the Statutory Rules (Northern Ireland) Order 1979 and shall be subject to negative resolution, within the meaning of section 41(6) of the Interpretation Act (Northern Ireland) 1954.

Small claims arbitration in the county court

92.   Exclusion of Part I in relation to small claims arbitration in the county court
Nothing in Part I of this Act applies to arbitration under section 64 of the County Courts Act 1984.

Appointment of judges as arbitrators

93.   Appointment of judges as arbitrators
(1)   A judge of the Commercial Court or an official referee may, if in all the circumstances he thinks fit, accept appointment as a sole arbitrator or as umpire by or by virtue of an arbitration agreement.
(2)   A judge of the Commercial Court shall not do so unless the Lord Chief Justice has informed him that, having regard to the state of business in the High Court and the Crown Court, he can be made available.
(3)   An official referee shall not do so unless the Lord Chief Justice has informed him that, having regard to the state of official referees' business, he can be made available.
(4)   The fees payable for the services of a judge of the Commercial Court or official referee as arbitrator or umpire shall be taken in the High Court.
(5)   In this section—
'arbitration agreement' has the same meaning as in Part I; and
'official referee' means a person nominated under section 68(1)(a) of the Supreme Court Act 1981 to deal with official referees' business.
(6)   The provisions of Part I of this Act apply to arbitration before a person appointed under this section with the modifications specified in Schedule 2.

Statutory arbitrations

94.   Application of Part I to statutory arbitrations
(1)   The provisions of Part I apply to every arbitration under an enactment (a 'statutory arbitration'), whether the enactment was passed or made before or after the commencement of this Act, subject to the adaptations and exclusions specified in sections 95 to 98.
(2)   The provisions of Part I do not apply to a statutory arbitration if or to the extent that their application—
   (a)   is inconsistent with the provisions of the enactment concerned, with any rules or procedure authorised or recognised by it, or
   (b)   is excluded by any other enactment.
(3)   In this section and the following provisions of this Part 'enactment'—

    (a)   in England and Wales, includes an enactment contained in subordinate legislation within the meaning of the Interpretation Act 1978;

    (b)   in Northern Ireland, means a statutory provision within the meaning of section 1(f) of the Interpretation Act (Northern Ireland) 1954.

95. General adaptation of provisions in relation to statutory arbitrations

    (1)   The provisions of Part I apply to a statutory arbitration—

    (a)   as if the arbitration were pursuant to an arbitration agreement and as if the enactment were that agreement, and

    (b)   as if the persons by and against whom a claim subject to arbitration in pursuance of the enactment may be or has been made were parties to that agreement.

    (2)   Every statutory arbitration shall be taken to have its seat in England and Wales or, as the case may be, in Northern Ireland.

96. Specific adaptations of provisions in relation to statutory arbitrations

    (1)   The following provisions of Part I apply to a statutory arbitration with the following adaptations.

    (2)   In section 30(1) (competence of tribunal to rule on its own jurisdiction), the reference in paragraph (a) to whether there is a valid arbitration agreement shall be construed as a reference to whether the enactment applies to the dispute or difference in question.

    (3)   Section 35 (consolidation of proceedings and concurrent hearings) applies only so as to authorise the consolidation of proceedings, or concurrent hearings in proceedings, under the same enactment.

    (4)   Section 46 (rules applicable to substance of dispute) applies with the omission of subsection (1)(b) (determination in accordance with considerations agreed by parties).

97. Provisions excluded from applying to statutory arbitrations

The following provisions of Part I do not apply in relation to a statutory arbitration—

    (a)   section 8 (whether agreement discharged by death of a party);

    (b)   section 12 (power of court to extend agreed time limits);

    (c)   sections 9(5), 10(2) and 71(4) (restrictions on effect of provision that award condition precedent to right to bring legal proceedings).

98. Power to make further provision by regulations

    (1)   The Secretary of State may make provision by regulations for adapting or excluding any provision of Part I in relation to statutory arbitrations in general or statutory arbitrations of any particular description.

    (2)   The power is exercisable whether the enactment concerned is passed or made before or after the commencement of this Act.

    (3)   Regulations under this section shall be made by statutory instrument which shall be subject to annulment in pursuance of a resolution of either House of Parliament.

PART III

RECOGNITION AND ENFORCEMENT OF CERTAIN FOREIGN AWARDS

Enforcement of Geneva Convention awards

99. Continuation of Part II of the Arbitration Act 1950

Part II of the Arbitration Act 1950 (enforcement of certain foreign awards) continues to apply in relation to foreign awards within the meaning of that Part which are not also New York Convention awards.

Recognition and enforcement of New York Convention awards

100. New York Convention awards

    (1)   In this Part a 'New York Convention award' means an award made, in pursuance of an arbitration agreement, in the territory of a state (other than the United Kingdom) which is a party to the New York Convention.

(2)   For the purposes of subsection (1) and of the provisions of this Part relating to such awards—

    (a)   'arbitration agreement' means an arbitration agreement in writing, and

    (b)   an award shall be treated as made at the seat of the arbitration, regardless of where it was signed, despatched or delivered to any of the parties.

In this subsection 'agreement in writing' and 'seat of the arbitration' have the same meaning as in Part I.

(3)   If Her Majesty by Order in Council declares that a state specified in the Order is a party to the New York Convention, or is a party in respect of any territory so specified, the Order shall, while in force, be conclusive evidence of that fact.

(4)   In this section 'the New York Convention' means the Convention on the Recognition and Enforcement of Foreign Arbitral Awards adopted by the United Nations Conference on International Commercial Arbitration on 10th June 1958.

101.   Recognition and enforcement of awards

(1)   A New York Convention award shall be recognised as binding on the persons as between whom it was made, and may accordingly be relied on by those persons by way of defence, set-off or otherwise in any legal proceedings in England and Wales or Northern Ireland.

(2)   A New York Convention award may, by leave of the court, be enforced in the same manner as a judgment or order of the court to the same effect.

As to the meaning of 'the court' see section 105.

(3)   Where leave is so given, judgment may be entered in terms of the award.

102.   Evidence to be produced by party seeking recognition or enforcement

(1)   A party seeking the recognition or enforcement of a New York Convention award must produce—

    (a)   the duly authenticated original award or a duly certified copy of it, and

    (b)   the original arbitration agreement or a duly certified copy of it.

(2)   If the award or agreement is in a foreign language, the party must also produce a translation of it certified by an official or sworn translator or by a diplomatic or consular agent.

103.   Refusal of recognition or enforcement

(1)   Recognition or enforcement of a New York Convention award shall not be refused except in the following cases.

(2)   Recognition or enforcement of the award may be refused if the person against whom it is invoked proves—

    (a)   that a party to the arbitration agreement was (under the law applicable to him) under some incapacity;

    (b)   that the arbitration agreement was not valid under the law to which the parties subjected it or, failing any indication thereon, under the law of the country where the award was made;

    (c)   that he was not given proper notice of the appointment of the arbitrator or of the arbitration proceedings or was otherwise unable to present his case;

    (d)   that the award deals with a difference not contemplated by or not falling within the terms of the submission to arbitration or contains decisions on matters beyond the scope of the submission to arbitration (but see subsection (4));

    (e)   that the composition of the arbitral tribunal or the arbitral procedure was not in accordance with the agreement of the parties or, failing such agreement, with the law of the country in which the arbitration took place;

    (f)   that the award has not yet become binding on the parties, or has been set aside or suspended by a competent authority of the country in which, or under the law of which, it was made.

(3)   Recognition or enforcement of the award may also be refused if the award is in respect of a matter which is not capable of settlement by arbitration, or if it would be contrary to public policy to recognise or enforce the award.

(4)   An award which contains decisions on matters not submitted to arbitration may be recognised or enforced to the extent that it contains decisions on matters submitted to arbitration which can be separated from those on matters not so submitted.

(5)   Where an application for the setting aside or suspension of the award has been made to such a competent authority as is mentioned in subsection (2)(f), the court before which the award is sought to be relied upon may, if it considers it proper, adjourn the decision on the recognition or enforcement of the award.

It may also on the application of the party claiming recognition or enforcement of the award order the other party to give suitable security.

104.   Saving for other bases of recognition or enforcement
Nothing in the preceding provisions of this Part affects any right to rely upon or enforce a New York Convention award at common law or under section 66.

PART IV
GENERAL PROVISIONS

105.   Meaning of 'the court': jurisdiction of High Court and county court
(1)   In this Act 'the court' means the High Court or a county court, subject to the following provisions.

(2)   The Lord Chancellor may by order make provision—
    (a)   allocating proceedings under this Act to the High Court or to county courts; or
    (b)   specifying proceedings under this Act which may be commenced or taken only in the High Court or in a county court.

(3)   The Lord Chancellor may by order make provision requiring proceedings of any specified description under this Act in relation to which a county court has jurisdiction to be commenced or taken in one or more specified county courts.

Any jurisdiction so exercisable by a specified county court is exercisable throughout England and Wales or, as the case may be, Northern Ireland.

(4)   An order under this section—
    (a)   may differentiate between categories of proceedings by reference to such criteria as the Lord Chancellor sees fit to specify, and
    (b)   may make such incidental or transitional provision as the Lord Chancellor considers necessary or expedient.

(5)   An order under this section for England and Wales shall be made by statutory instrument which shall be subject to annulment in pursuance of a resolution of either House of Parliament.

(6)   An order under this section for Northern Ireland shall be a statutory rule for the purposes of the Statutory Rules (Northern Ireland) Order 1979 which shall be subject to annulment in pursuance of a resolution of either House of Parliament in like manner as a statutory instrument and section 5 of the Statutory Instruments Act 1946 shall apply accordingly.

106.   Crown application
(1)   Part I of this Act applies to any arbitration agreement to which Her Majesty, either in right of the Crown or of the Duchy of Lancaster or otherwise, or the Duke of Cornwall, is a party.

(2)   Where Her Majesty is party to an arbitration agreement otherwise than in right of the Crown, Her Majesty shall be represented for the purposes of any arbitral proceedings—
    (a)   where the agreement was entered into by Her Majesty in right of the Duchy of Lancaster, by the Chancellor of the Duchy or such person as he may appoint, and
    (b)   in any other case, by such person as Her Majesty may appoint in writing under the Royal Sign Manual.

(3)   Where the Duke of Cornwall is party to an arbitration agreement, he shall be represented for the purposes of any arbitral proceedings by such person as he may appoint.

(4)   References in Part I to a party or the parties to the arbitration agreement or to arbitral proceedings shall be construed, where subsection (2) or (3) applies, as references to the person representing Her Majesty or the Duke of Cornwall.

107.   Consequential amendments and repeals
(1)   The enactments specified in Schedule 3 are amended in accordance with that Schedule, the amendments being consequential on the provisions of this Act.
(2)   The enactments specified in Schedule 4 are repealed to the extent specified.

108.   Extent
(1)   The provisions of this Act extend to England and Wales and, except as mentioned below, to Northern Ireland.
(2)   The following provisions of Part II do not extend to Northern Ireland—
    section 92 (exclusion of Part I in relation to small claims arbitration in the county court), and
    section 93 and Schedule 2 (appointment of judges as arbitrators).
(3)   Sections 89, 90 and 91 (consumer arbitration agreements) extend to Scotland and the provisions of Schedules 3 and 4 (consequential amendments and repeals) extend to Scotland so far as they relate to enactments which so extend, subject as follows.
(4)   The repeal of the Arbitration Act 1975 extends only to England and Wales and Northern Ireland.

109.   Commencement
(1)   The provisions of this Act come into force on such day as the Secretary of State may appoint by order made by statutory instrument, and different days may be appointed for different purposes.
(2)   An order under subsection (1) may contain such transitional provisions as appear to the Secretary of State to be appropriate.

110.   Short title
This Act may be cited as the Arbitration Act 1996.

SCHEDULES

Section 4(1)   SCHEDULE 1
                                    MANDATORY PROVISIONS OF PART I

sections 9 to 11	(stay of legal proceedings);
section 12	(power of court to extend agreed time limits);
section 13	(application of Limitation Acts);
section 24	(power of court to remove arbitrator);
section 26(1)	(effect of death of arbitrator);
section 28	(liability of parties for fees and expenses of arbitrators);
section 29	(immunity of arbitrator);
section 31	(objection to substantive jurisdiction of tribunal);
section 32	(determination of preliminary point of jurisdiction);
section 33	(general duty of tribunal);
section 37(2)	(items to be treated as expenses of arbitrators);
section 40	(general duty of parties);
section 43	(securing the attendance of witnesses);
section 56	(power to withhold award in case of non-payment);
section 60	(effectiveness of agreement for payment of costs in any event);
section 66	(enforcement of award);
sections 67 and 68	(challenging the award: substantive jurisdiction and serious irregularity), and sections 70 and 71 (supplementary provisions; effect of order of court) so far as relating to those sections;

section 72	(saving for rights of person who takes no part in proceedings);
section 73	(loss of right to object);
section 74	(immunity of arbitral institutions, &c.);
section 75	(charge to secure payment of solicitors' costs).

Section 93(6)   SCHEDULE 2
MODIFICATIONS OF PART I IN RELATION
TO JUDGE-ARBITRATORS

Introductory

1. In this Schedule 'judge-arbitrator' means a judge of the Commercial Court or official referee appointed as arbitrator or umpire under section 93.

General

2.—(1) Subject to the following provisions of this Schedule, references in Part I to the court shall be construed in relation to a judge-arbitrator, or in relation to the appointment of a judge-arbitrator, as references to the Court of Appeal.

(2) The references in sections 32(6), 45(6) and 69(8) to the Court of Appeal shall in such a case be construed as references to the House of Lords.

Arbitrator's fees

3.—(1) The power of the court in section 28(2) to order consideration and adjustment of the liability of a party for the fees of an arbitrator may be exercised by a judge-arbitrator.

(2) Any such exercise of the power is subject to the powers of the Court of Appeal under sections 24(4) and 25(3)(b) (directions as to entitlement to fees or expenses in case of removal or resignation).

Exercise of court powers in support of arbitration

4.—(1) Where the arbitral tribunal consists of or includes a judge-arbitrator the powers of the court under sections 42 to 44 (enforcement of peremptory orders, summoning witnesses, and other court powers) are exercisable by the High Court and also by the judge-arbitrator himself.

(2) Anything done by a judge-arbitrator in the exercise of those powers shall be regarded as done by him in his capacity as judge of the High Court and have effect as if done by that court.

Nothing in this sub-paragraph prejudices any power vested in him as arbitrator or umpire.

Extension of time for making award

5.—(1) The power conferred by section 50 (extension of time for making award) is exercisable by the judge-arbitrator himself.

(2) Any appeal from a decision of a judge-arbitrator under that section lies to the Court of Appeal with the leave of that court.

Withholding award in case of non-payment

6.—(1) The provisions of paragraph 7 apply in place of the provisions of section 56 (power to withhold award in the case of non-payment) in relation to the withholding of an award for non-payment of the fees and expenses of a judge-arbitrator.

(2) This does not affect the application of section 56 in relation to the delivery of such an award by an arbitral or other institution or person vested by the parties with powers in relation to the delivery of the award.

7.—(1) A judge-arbitrator may refuse to deliver an award except upon payment of the fees and expenses mentioned in section 56(1).

(2)   The judge-arbitrator may, on an application by a party to the arbitral proceedings, order that if he pays into the High Court the fees and expenses demanded, or such lesser amount as the judge-arbitrator may specify—

(a)   the award shall be delivered,

(b)   the amount of the fees and expenses properly payable shall be determined by such means and upon such terms as he may direct, and

(c)   out of the money paid into court there shall be paid out such fees and expenses as may be found to be properly payable and the balance of the money (if any) shall be paid out to the applicant.

(3)   For this purpose the amount of fees and expenses properly payable is the amount the applicant is liable to pay under section 28 or any agreement relating to the payment of the arbitrator.

(4)   No application to the judge-arbitrator under this paragraph may be made where there is any available arbitral process for appeal or review of the amount of the fees or expenses demanded.

(5)   Any appeal from a decision of a judge-arbitrator under this paragraph lies to the Court of Appeal with the leave of that court.

(6)   Where a party to arbitral proceedings appeals under sub-paragraph (5), an arbitrator is entitled to appear and be heard.

Correction of award or additional award

8.   Subsections (4) to (6) of section 57 (correction of award or additional award: time limit for application or exercise of power) do not apply to a judge-arbitrator.

Costs

9.   Where the arbitral tribunal consists of or includes a judge-arbitrator the powers of the court under section 63(4) (determination of recoverable costs) shall be exercised by the High Court.

10.—(1)   The power of the court under section 64 to determine an arbitrator's reasonable fees and expenses may be exercised by a judge-arbitrator.

(2)   Any such exercise of the power is subject to the powers of the Court of Appeal under sections 24(4) and 25(3)(b) (directions as to entitlement to fees or expenses in case of removal or resignation).

Enforcement of award

11.   The leave of the court required by section 66 (enforcement of award) may in the case of an award of a judge-arbitrator be given by the judge-arbitrator himself.

Solicitors' costs

12.   The powers of the court to make declarations and orders under the provisions applied by section 75 (power to charge property recovered in arbitral proceedings with the payment of solicitors' costs) may be exercised by the judge-arbitrator.

Powers of court in relation to service of documents

13.—(1)   The power of the court under section 77(2) (powers of court in relation to service of documents) is exercisable by the judge-arbitrator.

(2)   Any appeal from a decision of a judge-arbitrator under that section lies to the Court of Appeal with the leave of that court.

Powers of court to extend time limits relating to arbitral proceedings

14.—(1)   The power conferred by section 79 (power of court to extend time limits relating to arbitral proceedings) is exercisable by the judge-arbitrator himself.

(2)   Any appeal from a decision of a judge-arbitrator under that section lies to the Court of Appeal with the leave of that court.

Section 107(1) SCHEDULE 3
CONSEQUENTIAL AMENDMENTS

MERCHANT SHIPPING ACT 1894
(c. 60)

1. In section 496 of the Merchant Shipping Act 1894 (provisions as to deposits by owners of goods), after subsection (4) insert—
    '(5) In subsection (3) the expression "legal proceedings" includes arbitral proceedings and as respects England and Wales and Northern Ireland the provisions of section 14 of the Arbitration Act 1996 apply to determine when such proceedings are commenced.'.

STANNARIES COURT (ABOLITION) ACT 1896
(c. 45)

2. In section 4(1) of the Stannaries Court (Abolition) Act 1896 (references of certain disputes to arbitration), for the words from 'tried before' to 'any such reference' substitute 'referred to arbitration before himself or before an arbitrator agreed on by the parties or an officer of the court'.

TITHE ACT 1936
(c. 43)

3. In section 39(1) of the Tithe Act 1936 (proceedings of Tithe Redemption Commission)—
    (a) for 'the Arbitration Acts 1889 to 1934' substitute 'Part I of the Arbitration Act 1996';
    (b) for paragraph (e) substitute—
        '(e) the making of an application to the court to determine a preliminary point of law and the bringing of an appeal to the court on a point of law;';
    (c) for 'the said Acts' substitute 'Part I of the Arbitration Act 1996'.

EDUCATION ACT 1944
(c. 31)

4. In section 75(2) of the Education Act 1944 (proceedings of Independent School Tribunals) for 'the Arbitration Acts 1889 to 1934' substitute 'Part I of the Arbitration Act 1996'.

COMMONWEALTH TELEGRAPHS ACT 1949
(c. 39)

5. In section 8(2) of the Commonwealth Telegraphs Act 1949 (proceedings of referees under the Act) for 'the Arbitration Acts 1889 to 1934, or the Arbitration Act (Northern Ireland) 1937,' substitute 'Part I of the Arbitration Act 1996'.

LANDS TRIBUNAL ACT 1949
(c. 42)

6. In section 3 of the Lands Tribunal Act 1949 (proceedings before the Lands Tribunal)—
    (a) in subsection (6)(c) (procedural rules: power to apply Arbitration Acts), and
    (b) in subsection (8) (exclusion of Arbitration Acts except as applied by rules),
for 'the Arbitration Acts 1889 to 1934' substitute 'Part I of the Arbitration Act 1996'.

WIRELESS TELEGRAPHY ACT 1949
(c. 54)

7.   In the Wireless Telegraphy Act 1949, Schedule 2 (procedure of appeals tribunal), in paragraph 3(1)—
(a)   for the words 'the Arbitration Acts 1889 to 1934' substitute 'Part I of the Arbitration Act 1996';
(b)   after the word 'Wales' insert 'or Northern Ireland'; and
(c)   for 'the said Acts' substitute 'Part I of that Act'.

PATENTS ACT 1949
(c. 87)

8.   In section 67 of the Patents Act 1949 (proceedings as to infringement of pre-1978 patents referred to comptroller), for 'The Arbitration Acts 1889 to 1934' substitute 'Part I of the Arbitration Act 1996'.

NATIONAL HEALTH SERVICE (AMENDMENT) ACT 1949
(c. 93)

9.   In section 7(8) of the National Health Service (Amendment) Act 1949 (arbitration in relation to hardship arising from the National Health Service Act 1946 or the Act), for 'the Arbitration Acts 1889 to 1934' substitute 'Part I of the Arbitration Act 1996' and for 'the said Acts' substitute 'Part I of that Act'.

ARBITRATION ACT 1950
(c. 27)

10.   In section 36(1) of the Arbitration Act 1950 (effect of foreign awards enforceable under Part II of that Act) for 'section 26 of this Act' substitute 'section 66 of the Arbitration Act 1996'.

INTERPRETATION ACT (NORTHERN IRELAND) 1954
(c. 33 (N.I.))

11.   In section 46(2) of the Interpretation Act (Northern Ireland) 1954 (miscellaneous definitions), for the definition of 'arbitrator' substitute—
'"arbitrator" has the same meaning as in Part I of the Arbitration Act 1996;'.

AGRICULTURAL MARKETING ACT 1958
(c. 47)

12.   In section 12(1) of the Agricultural Marketing Act 1958 (application of provisions of Arbitration Act 1950)—
(a)   for the words from the beginning to 'shall apply' substitute 'Sections 45 and 69 of the Arbitration Act 1996 (which relate to the determination by the court of questions of law) and section 66 of that Act (enforcement of awards) apply'; and
(b)   for 'an arbitration' substitute 'arbitral proceedings'.

CARRIAGE BY AIR ACT 1961
(c. 27)

13.—(1)   The Carriage by Air Act 1961 is amended as follows.
(2)   In section 5(3) (time for bringing proceedings)—
(a)   for 'an arbitration' in the first place where it occurs substitute 'arbitral proceedings'; and

(b)   for the words from 'and subsections (3) and (4)' to the end substitute 'and the provisions of section 14 of the Arbitration Act 1996 apply to determine when such proceedings are commenced.'.

(3)   In section 11(c) (application of section 5 to Scotland)—

(a)   for 'subsections (3) and (4)' substitute 'the provisions of section 14 of the Arbitration Act 1996'; and

(b)   for 'an arbitration' substitute 'arbitral proceedings'.

FACTORIES ACT 1961
(c. 34)

14.   In the Factories Act 1961, for section 171 (application of Arbitration Act 1950), substitute—

'171.   Application of the Arbitration Act 1996
Part I of the Arbitration Act 1996 does not apply to proceedings under this Act except in so far as it may be applied by regulations made under this Act.'.

CLERGY PENSIONS MEASURE 1961
(No. 3)

15.   In the Clergy Pensions Measure 1961, section 38(4) (determination of questions), for the words 'The Arbitration Act 1950' substitute 'Part I of the Arbitration Act 1996'.

TRANSPORT ACT 1962
(c. 46)

16.—(1)   The Transport Act 1962 is amended as follows.

(2)   In section 74(6)(f) (proceedings before referees in pension disputes), for the words 'the Arbitration Act 1950' substitute 'Part I of the Arbitration Act 1996'.

(3)   In section 81(7) (proceedings before referees in compensation disputes), for the words 'the Arbitration Act 1950' substitute 'Part I of the Arbitration Act 1996'.

(4)   In Schedule 7, Part IV (pensions), in paragraph 17(5) for the words 'the Arbitration Act 1950' substitute 'Part I of the Arbitration Act 1996'.

CORN RENTS ACT 1963
(c. 14)

17.   In the Corn Rents Act 1963, section 1(5) (schemes for apportioning corn rents, &c.), for the words 'the Arbitration Act 1950' substitute 'Part I of the Arbitration Act 1996'.

PLANT VARIETIES AND SEEDS ACT 1964
(c. 14)

18.   In section 10(6) of the Plant Varieties and Seeds Act 1964 (meaning of 'arbitration agreement'), for 'the meaning given by section 32 of the Arbitration Act 1950' substitute 'the same meaning as in Part I of the Arbitration Act 1996'.

LANDS TRIBUNAL AND COMPENSATION ACT (NORTHERN IRELAND) 1964
(c. 29 (N.I.))

19.   In section 9 of the Lands Tribunal and Compensation Act (Northern Ireland) 1964 (proceedings of Lands Tribunal), in subsection (3) (where Tribunal acts as arbitrator) for 'the Arbitration Act (Northern Ireland) 1937' substitute 'Part I of the Arbitration Act 1996'.

INDUSTRIAL AND PROVIDENT SOCIETIES ACT 1965
(c. 12)

20.—(1)   Section 60 of the Industrial and Provident Societies Act 1965 is amended as follows.

(2)   In subsection (8) (procedure for hearing disputes between society and member, &c.)—

(a)   in paragraph (a) for 'the Arbitration Act 1950' substitute 'Part I of the Arbitration Act 1996'; and

(b)   in paragraph (b) omit 'by virtue of section 12 of the said Act of 1950'.

(3)   For subsection (9) substitute—

'(9)   The court or registrar to whom any dispute is referred under subsections (2) to (7) may at the request of either party state a case on any question of law arising in the dispute for the opinion of the High Court or, as the case may be, the Court of Session.'.

CARRIAGE OF GOODS BY ROAD ACT 1965
(c. 37)

21.   In section 7(2) of the Carriage of Goods by Road Act 1965 (arbitrations: time at which deemed to commence), for paragraphs (a) and (b) substitute—

'(a)   as respects England and Wales and Northern Ireland, the provisions of section 14(3) to (5) of the Arbitration Act 1996 (which determine the time at which an arbitration is commenced) apply;'.

FACTORIES ACT (NORTHERN IRELAND) 1965
(c. 20 (N.I.))

22.   In section 171 of the Factories Act (Northern Ireland) 1965 (application of Arbitration Act), for 'The Arbitration Act (Northern Ireland) 1937' substitute 'Part I of the Arbitration Act 1996'.

COMMONWEALTH SECRETARIAT ACT 1966
(c. 10)

23.   In section 1(3) of the Commonwealth Secretariat Act 1966 (contracts with Commonwealth Secretariat to be deemed to contain provision for arbitration), for 'the Arbitration Act 1950 and the Arbitration Act (Northern Ireland) 1937' substitute 'Part I of the Arbitration Act 1996'.

ARBITRATION (INTERNATIONAL INVESTMENT DISPUTES) ACT 1966
(c. 41)

24.   In the Arbitration (International Investment Disputes) Act 1966, for section 3 (application of Arbitration Act 1950 and other enactments) substitute—

'3.   **Application of provisions of Arbitration Act 1996**

(1)   The Lord Chancellor may by order direct that any of the provisions contained in sections 36 and 38 to 44 of the Arbitration Act 1996 (provisions concerning the conduct of arbitral proceedings, &c.) shall apply to such proceedings pursuant to the Convention as are specified in the order with or without any modifications or exceptions specified in the order.

(2)   Subject to subsection (1), the Arbitration Act 1996 shall not apply to proceedings pursuant to the Convention, but this subsection shall not be taken as affecting section 9 of that Act (stay of legal proceedings in respect of matter subject to arbitration).

(3)   An order made under this section—

(a)   may be varied or revoked by a subsequent order so made, and

(b)   shall be contained in a statutory instrument.'.

POULTRY IMPROVEMENT ACT (NORTHERN IRELAND) 1968
(c. 12) (N.I.))

25. In paragraph 10(4) of the Schedule to the Poultry Improvement Act (Northern Ireland) 1968 (reference of disputes), for 'The Arbitration Act (Northern Ireland) 1937' substitute 'Part I of the Arbitration Act 1996'.

INDUSTRIAL AND PROVIDENT SOCIETIES ACT (NORTHERN IRELAND) 1969
(c. 24 (N.I.))

26.—(1) Section 69 of the Industrial and Provident Societies Act (Northern Ireland) 1969 (decision of disputes) is amended as follows.

(2) In subsection (7) (decision of disputes)—

(a) in the opening words, omit the words from 'and without prejudice' to '1937';

(b) at the beginning of paragraph (a) insert 'without prejudice to any powers exercisable by virtue of Part I of the Arbitration Act 1996,'; and

(c) in paragraph (b) omit 'the registrar or' and 'registrar or' and for the words from 'as might have been granted by the High Court' to the end substitute 'as might be granted by the registrar'.

(3) For subsection (8) substitute—

'(8) The court or registrar to whom any dispute is referred under subsections (2) to (6) may at the request of either party state a case on any question of law arising in the dispute for the opinion of the High Court.'.

HEALTH AND PERSONAL SOCIAL SERVICES (NORTHERN IRELAND)
ORDER 1972
(N.I.14)

27. In Article 105(6) of the Health and Personal Social Services (Northern Ireland) Order 1972 (arbitrations under the Order), for 'the Arbitration Act (Northern Ireland) 1937' substitute 'Part I of the Arbitration Act 1996'.

CONSUMER CREDIT ACT 1974
(c. 39)

28.—(1) Section 146 of the Consumer Credit Act 1974 is amended as follows.

(2) In subsection (2) (solicitor engaged in contentious business), for 'section 86(1) of the Solicitors Act 1957' substitute 'section 87(1) of the Solicitors Act 1974'.

(3) In subsection (4) (solicitor in Northern Ireland engaged in contentious business), for the words from 'business done' to 'Administration of Estates (Northern Ireland) Order 1979' substitute 'contentious business (as defined in Article 3(2) of the Solicitors (Northern Ireland) Order 1976.'.

FRIENDLY SOCIETIES ACT 1974
(c. 46)

29.—(1) The Friendly Societies Act 1974 is amended as follows.

(2) For section 78(1) (statement of case) substitute—

'(1) Any arbitrator, arbiter or umpire to whom a dispute falling within section 76 above is referred under the rules of a registered society or branch may at the request of either party state a case on any question of law arising in the dispute for the opinion of the High Court or, as the case may be, the Court of Session.'.

(3) In section 83(3) (procedure on objections to amalgamations &c. of friendly societies), for 'the Arbitration Act 1950 or, in Northern Ireland, the Arbitration Act (Northern Ireland) 1937' substitute 'Part I of the Arbitration Act 1996'.

INDUSTRY ACT 1975
(c. 68)

30. In Schedule 3 to the Industry Act (arbitration of disputes relating to vesting and compensation orders), in paragraph 14 (application of certain provisions of Arbitration Acts)—
  (a) for 'the Arbitration Act 1950 or, in Northern Ireland, the Arbitration Act (Northern Ireland) 1937' substitute 'Part I of the Arbitration Act 1996', and
  (b) for 'that Act' substitute 'that Part'.

INDUSTRIAL RELATIONS (NORTHERN IRELAND) ORDER 1976
(N.I.16)

31. In Article 59(9) of the Industrial Relations (Northern Ireland) Order 1976 (proceedings of industrial tribunal), for 'The Arbitration Act (Northern Ireland) 1937' substitute 'Part I of the Arbitration Act 1996'.

AIRCRAFT AND SHIPBUILDING INDUSTRIES ACT 1977
(c. 3)

32. In Schedule 7 to the Aircraft and Shipbuilding Industries Act 1977 (procedure of Arbitration Tribunal), in paragraph 2—
  (a) for 'the Arbitration Act 1950 or, in Northern Ireland, the Arbitration Act (Northern Ireland) 1937' substitute 'Part I of the Arbitration Act 1996', and
  (b) for 'that Act' substitute 'that Part'.

PATENTS ACT 1977
(c. 37)

33. In section 130 of the Patents Act 1977 (interpretation), in subsection (8) (exclusion of Arbitration Act) for 'The Arbitration Act 1950' substitute 'Part I of the Arbitration Act 1996'.

JUDICATURE (NORTHERN IRELAND) ACT 1978
(c. 23)

34.—(1) The Judicature (Northern Ireland) Act 1978 is amended as follows.
  (2) In section 35(2) (restrictions on appeals to the Court of Appeal), after paragraph (f) insert—
    '(fa) except as provided by Part I of the Arbitration Act 1996, from any decision of the High Court under that Part;'.
  (3) In section 55(2) (rules of court) after paragraph (c) insert—
    '(cc) providing for any prescribed part of the jurisdiction of the High Court in relation to the trial of any action involving matters of account to be exercised in the prescribed manner by a person agreed by the parties and for the remuneration of any such person;'.

HEALTH AND SAFETY AT WORK (NORTHERN IRELAND) ORDER 1978
(N.I.9)

35. In Schedule 4 to the Health and Safety at Work (Northern Ireland) Order 1978 (licensing provisions), in paragraph 3, for 'The Arbitration Act (Northern Ireland) 1937' substitute 'Part I of the Arbitration Act 1996'.

COUNTY COURTS (NORTHERN IRELAND) ORDER 1980
(N.I.3)

36.—(1)   The County Courts (Northern Ireland) Order 1980 is amended as follows.

(2)   In Article 30 (civil jurisdiction exercisable by district judge)—

(a)   for paragraph (2) substitute—

'(2)   Any order, decision or determination made by a district judge under this Article (other than one made in dealing with a claim by way of arbitration under paragraph (3)) shall be embodied in a decree which for all purposes (including the right of appeal under Part VI) shall have the like effect as a decree pronounced by a county court judge.';

(b)   for paragraphs (4) and (5) substitute—

'(4)   Where in any action to which paragraph (1) applies the claim is dealt with by way of arbitration under paragraph (3)—

(a)   any award made by the district judge in dealing with the claim shall be embodied in a decree which for all purposes (except the right of appeal under Part VI) shall have the like effect as a decree pronounced by a county court judge;

(b)   the district judge may, and shall if so required by the High Court, state for the determination of the High Court any question of law arising out of an award so made;

(c)   except as provided by sub-paragraph (b), any award so made shall be final; and

(d)   except as otherwise provided by county court rules, no costs shall be awarded in connection with the action.

(5)   Subject to paragraph (4), county court rules may—

(a)   apply any of the provisions of Part I of the Arbitration Act 1996 to arbitrations under paragraph (3) with such modifications as may be prescribed;

(b)   prescribe the rules of evidence to be followed on any arbitration under paragraph (3) and, in particular, make provision with respect to the manner of taking and questioning evidence.

(5A)   Except as provided by virtue of paragraph (5)(a), Part I of the Arbitration Act 1996 shall not apply to an arbitration under paragraph (3).'.

(3)   After Article 61 insert—

'61A.   Appeals from decisions under Part I of the Arbitration Act 1996

(1)   Article 61 does not apply to a decision of a county court judge made in the exercise of the jurisdiction conferred by Part I of the Arbitration Act 1996.

(2)   Any party dissatisfied with a decision of the county court made in the exercise of the jurisdiction conferred by any of the following provisions of Part I of the Arbitration Act 1996, namely—

(a)   section 32 (question as to substantive jurisdiction of arbitral tribunal);

(b)   section 45 (question of law arising in course of arbitral proceedings);

(c)   section 67 (challenging award of arbitral tribunal: substantive jurisdiction);

(d)   section 68 (challenging award of arbitral tribunal: serious irregularity);

(e)   section 69 (appeal on point of law),

may, subject to the provisions of that Part, appeal from that decision to the Court of Appeal.

(3)   Any party dissatisfied with any decision of a county court made in the exercise of the jurisdiction conferred by any other provision of Part I of the Arbitration Act 1996 may, subject to the provisions of that Part, appeal from that decision to the High Court.

(4)   The decision of the Court of Appeal on an appeal under paragraph (2) shall be final.'.

SUPREME COURT ACT 1981
(c. 54)

37.—(1)   The Supreme Court Act 1981 is amended as follows.
(2)   In section 18(1) (restrictions on appeals to the Court of Appeal), for paragraph (g) substitute—
'(g)   except as provided by Part I of the Arbitration Act 1996, from any decision of the High Court under that Part;'.
(3)   In section 151 (interpretation, &c.), in the definition of 'arbitration agreement', for 'the Arbitration Act 1950 by virtue of section 32 of that Act;' substitute 'Part I of the Arbitration Act 1996;'.

MERCHANT SHIPPING (LINER CONFERENCES) ACT 1982
(c. 37)

38.   In section 7(5) of the Merchant Shipping (Liner Conferences) Act 1982 (stay of legal proceedings), for the words from 'section 4(1)' to the end substitute 'section 9 of the Arbitration Act 1996 (which also provides for the staying of legal proceedings).'.

AGRICULTURAL MARKETING (NORTHERN IRELAND) ORDER 1982
(N.I.12)

39.   In Article 14 of the Agricultural Marketing (Northern Ireland) Order 1982 (application of provisions of Arbitration Act (Northern Ireland) 1937)—
(a)   for the words from the beginning to 'shall apply' substitute 'Section 45 and 69 of the Arbitration Act 1996 (which relate to the determination by the court of questions of law) and section 66 of that Act (enforcement of awards)' apply; and
(b)   for 'an arbitration' substitute 'arbitral proceedings'.

MENTAL HEALTH ACT 1983
(c. 20)

40.   In section 78 of the Mental Health Act 1983 (procedure of Mental Health Review Tribunals), in subsection (9) for 'The Arbitration Act 1950' substitute 'Part I of the Arbitration Act 1996'.

REGISTERED HOMES ACT 1984
(c. 23)

41.   In section 43 of the Registered Homes Act 1984 (procedure of Registered Homes Tribunals), in subsection (3) for 'The Arbitration Act 1950' substitute 'Part I of the Arbitration Act 1996'.

HOUSING ACT 1985
(c. 68)

42.   In section 47(3) of the Housing Act 1985 (agreement as to determination of matters relating to service charges) for 'section 32 of the Arbitration Act 1950' substitute 'Part I of the Arbitration Act 1996'.

LANDLORD AND TENANT ACT 1985
(c. 70)

43.   In section 19(3) of the Landlord and Tenant Act 1985 (agreement as to determination of matters relating to service charges), for 'section 32 of the Arbitration Act 1950' substitute 'Part I of the Arbitration Act 1996'.

CREDIT UNIONS (NORTHERN IRELAND) ORDER 1985
(N.I.12)

44.—(1) Article 72 of the Credit Unions (Northern Ireland) Order 1985 (decision of disputes) is amended as follows.

(2) In paragraph (7)—

(a) in the opening words, omit the words from 'and without prejudice' to '1937';

(b) at the beginning of sub-paragraph (a) insert 'without prejudice to any powers exercisable by virtue of Part I of the Arbitration Act 1996,'; and

(c) in sub-paragraph (b) omit 'the registrar or' and 'registrar or' and for the words from 'as might have been granted by the High Court' to the end substitute 'as might be granted by the registrar'.

(3) For paragraph (8) substitute—

'(8) The court or registrar to whom any dispute is referred under paragraphs (2) to (6) may at the request of either party state a case on any question of law arising in the dispute for the opinion of the High Court.'.

AGRICULTURAL HOLDINGS ACT 1986
(c. 5)

45. In section 84(1) of the Agricultural Holdings Act 1986 (provisions relating to arbitration), for 'the Arbitration Act 1950' substitute 'Part I of the Arbitration Act 1996'.

INSOLVENCY ACT 1986
(c. 45)

46. In the Insolvency Act 1986, after section 349 insert—

'349A. Arbitration agreements to which bankrupt is party

(1) This section applies where a bankrupt had become party to a contract containing an arbitration agreement before the commencement of his bankruptcy.

(2) If the trustee in bankruptcy adopts the contract, the arbitration agreement is enforceable by or against the trustee in relation to matters arising from or connected with the contract.

(3) If the trustee in bankruptcy does not adopt the contract and a matter to which the arbitration agreement applies requires to be determined in connection with or for the purposes of the bankruptcy proceedings—

(a) the trustee with the consent of the creditors' committee, or

(b) any other party to the agreement,

may apply to the court which may, if it thinks fit in all the circumstances of the case, order that the matter be referred to arbitration in accordance with the arbitration agreement.

(4) In this section—

"arbitration agreement" has the same meaning as in Part I of the Arbitration Act 1996; and

"the court" means the court which has jurisdiction in the bankruptcy proceedings.'.

BUILDING SOCIETIES ACT 1986
(c. 53)

47. In Part II of Schedule 14 to the Building Societies Act 1986 (settlement of disputes: arbitration), in paragraph 5(6) for 'the Arbitration Act 1950 and the Arbitration Act 1979

or, in Northern Ireland, the Arbitration Act (Northern Ireland) 1937' substitute 'Part I of the Arbitration Act 1996'.

MENTAL HEALTH (NORTHERN IRELAND) ORDER 1986
(N.I.4)

48.   In Article 83 of the Mental Health (Northern Ireland) Order 1986 (procedure of Mental Health Review Tribunal), in paragraph (8) for 'The Arbitration Act (Northern Ireland) 1937' substitute 'Part I of the Arbitration Act 1996'.

MULTILATERAL INVESTMENT GUARANTEE AGENCY ACT 1988
(c. 8)

49.   For section 6 of the Multilateral Investment Guarantee Agency Act 1988 (application of Arbitration Act) substitute—

   '6.   Application of Arbitration Act
   (1)   The Lord Chancellor may by order made by statutory instrument direct that any of the provisions of sections 36 and 38 to 44 of the Arbitration Act 1996 (provisions in relation to the conduct of the arbitral proceedings, &c.) apply, with such modifications or exceptions as are specified in the order, to such arbitration proceedings pursuant to Annex II to the Convention as are specified in the order.
   (2)   Except as provided by an order under subsection (1) above, no provision of Part I of the Arbitration Act 1996 other than section 9 (stay of legal proceedings) applies to any such proceedings.'.

COPYRIGHT, DESIGNS AND PATENTS ACT 1988
(c. 48)

50.   In section 150 of the Copyright, Designs and Patents Act 1988 (Lord Chancellor's power to make rules for Copyright Tribunal), for subsection (2) substitute—
   '(2)   The rules may apply in relation to the Tribunal, as respects proceedings in England and Wales or Northern Ireland, any of the provisions of Part I of the Arbitration Act 1996.'.

FAIR EMPLOYMENT (NORTHERN IRELAND) ACT 1989
(c. 32)

51.   In the Fair Employment (Northern Ireland) Act 1989, section 5(7) (procedure of Fair Employment Tribunal), for 'The Arbitration Act (Northern Ireland) 1937' substitute 'Part I of the Arbitration Act 1996'.

LIMITATION (NORTHERN IRELAND) ORDER 1989
(N.I.11)

52.   In Article 2(2) of the Limitation (Northern Ireland) Order 1989 (interpretation), in the definition of 'arbitration agreement', for 'the Arbitration Act (Northern Ireland) 1937' substitute 'Part I of the Arbitration Act 1996'.

INSOLVENCY (NORTHERN IRELAND) ORDER 1989
(N.I.19)

53.   In the Insolvency (Northern Ireland) Order 1989, after Article 320 insert—

'320A. Arbitration agreements to which bankrupt is party

(1) This Article applies where a bankrupt had become party to a contract containing an arbitration agreement before the commencement of his bankruptcy.

(2) If the trustee in bankruptcy adopts the contract, the arbitration agreement is enforceable by or against the trustee in relation to matters arising from or connected with the contract.

(3) If the trustee in bankruptcy does not adopt the contract and a matter to which the arbitration agreement applies requires to be determined in connection with or for the purposes of the bankruptcy proceedings—

    (a) the trustee with the consent of the creditors' committee, or

    (b) any other party to the agreement,

may apply to the court which may, if it thinks fit in all the circumstances of the case, order that the matter be referred to arbitration in accordance with the arbitration agreement.

(4) In this Article—

"arbitration agreement" has the same meaning as in Part I of the Arbitration Act 1996; and

"the court" means the court which has jurisdiction in the bankruptcy proceedings.'.

SOCIAL SECURITY ADMINISTRATION ACT 1992
(c. 5)

54. In section 59 of the Social Security Administration Act 1992 (procedure for inquiries, &c.), in subsection (7), for 'The Arbitration Act 1950' substitute 'Part I of the Arbitration Act 1996'.

SOCIAL SECURITY ADMINISTRATION (NORTHERN IRELAND) ACT 1992
(c. 8)

55. In section 57 of the Social Security Administration (Northern Ireland) Act 1992 (procedure for inquiries, &c.), in subsection (6) for 'the Arbitration Act (Northern Ireland) 1937' substitute 'Part I of the Arbitration Act 1996'.

TRADE UNION AND LABOUR RELATIONS (CONSOLIDATION) ACT 1992
(c. 52)

56. In sections 212(5) and 263(6) of the Trade Union and Labour Relations (Consolidation) Act 1992 (application of Arbitration Act) for 'the Arbitration Act 1950' substitute 'Part I of the Arbitration Act 1996'.

INDUSTRIAL RELATIONS (NORTHERN IRELAND) ORDER 1992
(N.I.5)

57. In Articles 84(9) and 92(5) of the Industrial Relations (Northern Ireland) Order 1992 (application of Arbitration Act) for 'The Arbitration Act (Northern Ireland) 1937' substitute 'Part I of the Arbitration Act 1996'.

REGISTERED HOMES (NORTHERN IRELAND) ORDER 1992
(N.I.20)

58. In Article 33(3) of the Registered Homes (Northern Ireland) Order 1992 (procedure of Registered Homes Tribunal) for 'The Arbitration Act (Northern Ireland) 1937' substitute 'Part I of the Arbitration Act 1996'.

EDUCATION ACT 1993
(c. 35)

59.   In section 180(4) of the Education Act 1993 (procedure of Special Educational Needs Tribunal), for 'The Arbitration Act 1950' substitute 'Part I of the Arbitration Act 1996'.

Roads (Northern Ireland) Order 1993
(N.I.15)

60.—(1)   The Roads (Northern Ireland) Order 1993 is amended as follows.

(2)   In Article 131 (application of Arbitration Act) for 'the Arbitration Act (Northern Ireland) 1937' substitute 'Part I of the Arbitration Act 1996'.

(3)   In Schedule 4 (disputes), in paragraph 3(2) for 'the Arbitration Act (Northern Ireland) 1937' substitute 'Part I of the Arbitration Act 1996'.

MERCHANT SHIPPING ACT 1995
(c. 21)

61.   In Part II of Schedule 6 to the Merchant Shipping Act 1995 (provisions having effect in connection with Convention Relating to the Carriage of Passengers and Their Luggage by Sea), for paragraph 7 substitute—

'7.   Article 16 shall apply to arbitral proceedings as it applies to an action; and, as respects England and Wales and Northern Ireland, the provisions of section 14 of the Arbitration Act 1996 apply to determine for the purposes of that Article when an arbitration is commenced.'.

INDUSTRIAL TRIBUNALS ACT 1996
(c. 17)

62.   In section 6(2) of the Industrial Tribunals Act 1996 (procedure of industrial tribunals), for 'The Arbitration Act 1950' substitute 'Part I of the Arbitration Act 1996'.

Section 107(2)   SCHEDULE 4
                                REPEALS

Chapter	Short title	Extent of repeal
1892 c. 43.	Military Land Act 1892.	In section 21(b), the words 'under the Arbitration Act 1889'.
1922 c. 51.	Allotments Act 1922.	In section 21(3), the words 'under the Arbitration Act 1889'.
1937 c. 8 (N.I.).	Arbitration Act (Northern Ireland) 1937.	The whole Act.
1949 c. 54	Wireless Telegraphy Act 1949.	In Schedule 2, paragraph 3(3).
1949 c. 97	National Parks and Access to the Countryside Act 1949.	In section 18(4), the words from 'Without prejudice' to 'England or Wales'.
1950 c. 27.	Arbitration Act 1950.	Part I. Section 42(3).
1958 c. 47.	Agricultural Marketing Act 1958.	Section 53(8).
1962 c. 46.	Transport Act 1962.	In Schedule 11, Part II, paragraph 7.
1964 c. 14.	Plant Varieties and Seeds Act 1964.	In section 10(4) the words from 'or in section 9' to 'three arbitrators)'. Section 39(3)(b)(i).

Chapter	Short title	Extent of repeal
1964 c. 29 (N.I.)	Land Tribunal and Compensation Act (Northern Ireland) 1964.	In section 9(3) the words from 'so, however, that' to the end.
1965 c. 12.	Industrial and Provident Societies Act 1965.	In section 60(8)(b), the words 'by virtue of section 12 of the said Act of 1950'.
1965 c. 37	Carriage of Goods by Road Act 1965.	Section 7(2)(b).
1965 c. 13 (N.I.).	New Towns Act (Northern Ireland) 1965	In section 27(2), the words from 'under and in accordance with' to the end.
1969 c. 24 (N.I).	Industrial and Provident Societies Act (Northern Ireland) 1969.	In section 69(7)— (a) in the opening words, the words from 'and without prejudice' to '1937'; (b) in paragraph (b), the words 'the registrar or' and 'registrar or'.
1970 c. 31.	Administration of Justice Act 1970.	Section 4. Schedule 3.
1973 c. 41.	Fair Trading Act 1973.	Section 33(2)(d).
1973 N.I. 1.	Drainage (Northern Ireland) Order 1973.	In Article 15(4), the words from 'under and in accordance' to the end. Article 40(4). In Schedule 7, in paragraph 9(2), the words from 'under and in accordance' to the end.
1974 c. 47.	Solicitors Act 1974.	In section 87(1), in the definition of 'contentious business', the words 'appointed under the Arbitration Act 1950'.
1975 c. 3	Arbitration Act 1975.	The whole Act.
1975 c. 74.	Petroleum and Submarine Pipe-Lines Act 1975.	In Part II of Schedule 2— (a) in model clause 40(2), the words 'in accordance with the Arbitration Act 1950'; (b) in model clause 40(2B), the words 'in accordance with the Arbitration Act (Northern Ireland) 1937'.

Chapter	Short title	Extent of repeal
1976 N.I. 12.	Solicitors (Northern Ireland) Order 1976.	In Part II of Schedule 3, in model clause 38(2), the words 'in accordance with the Arbitration Act 1950'. In Article 3(2), in the entry 'contentious business' the words 'appointed under the Arbitration Act (Northern Ireland) 1937'. Article 71H(3).
1977 c. 37.	Patents Act 1977.	In section 52(4) the words 'section 21 of the Arbitration Act 1950 or, as the case may be, section 22 of the Arbitration Act (Northern Ireland) 1937 (statement of cases by arbitrators); but'. Section 131(e).
1977 c. 38.	Administration of Justice Act 1977.	Section 17(2).
1978 c. 23.	Judicature (Northern Ireland) Act 1978.	In section 35(2), paragraph (g)(v). In Schedule 5, the amendment to the Arbitration Act 1950.
1979 c. 42.	Arbitration Act 1979.	The whole Act.
1980 c. 58.	Limitation Act 1980.	Section 34.
1980 N.I. 3.	County Courts (Northern Ireland) Order 1980.	Article 31(3).
1981 c. 54.	Supreme Court Act 1981.	Section 148.
1982 c. 27.	Civil Jurisdiction and Judgments Act 1982.	Section 25(3)(c) and (5). In section 26— (a) in subsection (1), the words 'to arbitration or'; (b) in subsection (1)(a)(i), the words 'arbitration or'; (c) in subsection (2), the words 'arbitration or'.
1982 c. 53.	Administration of Justice Act 1982.	Section 15(6). In Schedule 1, Part IV.
1984 c. 5.	Merchant Shipping Act 1984.	Section 4(8).
1984 c. 12.	Telecommunications Act 1984.	Schedule 2, paragraph 13(8).

Chapter	Short title	Extent of repeal
1984 c. 16.	Foreign Limitation Periods Act 1984.	Section 5.
1984 c. 28.	County Courts Act 1984.	In Schedule 2, paragraph 70.
1985 c. 61	Administration of Justice Act 1985.	Section 58. In Schedule 9, paragraph 15.
1985 c. 68.	Housing Act 1985.	In Schedule 18, in paragraph 6(2) the words from 'and the Arbitration Act 1950' to the end.
1985 N.I. 12.	Credit Unions (Northern Ireland) Order 1985.	In Article 72(7)— (a) in the opening words, the words from 'and without prejudice' to '1937'; (b) in sub-paragraph (b), the words 'the registrar or' and 'registrar or'.
1986 c. 45.	Insolvency Act 1986.	In Schedule 14, the entry relating to the Arbitration Act 1950.
1988 c. 8.	Multilateral Investment Guarantee Agency Act 1988.	Section 8(3).
1988 c. 21.	Consumer Arbitration Agreements Act 1988.	The whole Act.
1989 N.I. 11.	Limitation (Northern Ireland) Order 1989.	Article 72. In Schedule 3, paragraph 1.
1989 N.I. 19.	Insolvency (Northern Ireland) Order 1989.	In Part II of Schedule 9, paragraph 66.
1990 c. 41.	Courts and Legal Services Act 1990.	Sections 99 and 101 to 103.
1991 N.I. 7.	Food Safety (Northern Ireland) Order 1991.	In Articles 8(8) and 11(10), the words from 'and the provisions' to the end.
1992 c. 40.	Friendly Societies Act 1992.	In Schedule 16, paragraph 30(1).
1995 c. 8.	Agricultural Tenancies Act 1995.	Section 28(4).
1995 c. 21.	Merchant Shipping Act 1995.	Section 96(10). Section 264(9).
1995 c. 42.	Private International Law (Miscellaneous Provisions) Act 1995.	Section 3.

Appendix 2

ARBITRATION ACT 1950
(1950 c. 27)

PART II
ENFORCEMENT OF CERTAIN FOREIGN AWARDS

35. Awards to which Part II applies

(1) This Part of this Act applies to any award made after the twenty-eighth day of July, nineteen hundred and twenty-four—

(a) in pursuance of an agreement for arbitration to which the protocol set out in the First Schedule to this Act applies; and

(b) between persons of whom one is subject to the jurisdiction of some one of such Powers as His Majesty, being satisfied that reciprocal provisions have been made, may by Order in Council declare to be parties to the convention set out in the Second Schedule to this Act, and of whom the other is subject to the jurisdiction of some other of the Powers aforesaid; and

(c) in one of such territories as His Majesty, being satisfied that reciprocal provisions have been made, may by Order in Council declare to be territories to which the said convention applies;

and an award to which this Part of this Act applies is in this Part of this Act referred to as 'a foreign award'.

(2) His Majesty may by a subsequent Order in Council vary or revoke any Order previously made under this section.

(3) Any Order in Council under section one of the Arbitration (Foreign Awards) Act 1930, which is in force at the commencement of this Act shall have effect as if it had been made under this section.

36. Effect of foreign award

(1) A foreign award shall, subject to the provisions of this Part of this Act, be enforceable in England either by action or in the same manner as the award of an arbitrator is enforceable by virtue of section twenty-six of this Act.

(2) Any foreign award which would be enforceable under this Part of this Act shall be treated as binding for all purposes on the persons as between whom it was made, and may accordingly be relied on by any of those persons by way of defence, set off or otherwise in any legal proceedings in England, and any references in this Part of this Act to enforcing a foreign award shall be construed as including references to relying on an award.

37. Conditions for enforcement of foreign awards

(1) In order that a foreign award may be enforceable under this Part of this Act it must have—

(a) been made in pursuance of an agreement for arbitration which was valid under the law by which it was governed;

(b) been made by the tribunal provided for in the agreement or constituted in manner agreed upon by the parties;

(c)   been made in conformity with the law governing the arbitration procedure;

(d)   become final in the country in which it was made;

(c)   been in respect of a matter which may lawfully be referred to arbitration under the law of England;

and the enforcement thereof must not be contrary to the public policy or the law of England.

(2)   Subject to the provisions of this subsection, a foreign award shall not be enforceable under this Part of this Act if the court dealing with the case is satisfied that—

(a)   the award has been annulled in the country in which it was made; or

(b)   the party against whom it is sought to enforce the award was not given notice of the arbitration proceedings in sufficient time to enable him to present his case, or was under some legal incapacity and was not properly represented; or

(c)   the award does not deal with all the questions referred or contains decisions on matters beyond the scope of the agreement for arbitration.

Provided that, if the award does not deal with all the questions referred, the court may, if it thinks fit, either postpone the enforcement of the award or order its enforcement subject to the giving of such security by the person seeking to enforce it as the court may think fit.

(3)   If a party seeking to resist the enforcement of a foreign award proves that there is any ground other than the non-existence of the conditions specified in paragraphs (a), (b) and (c) of subsection (1) of this section, or the existence of the conditions specified in paragraphs (b) and (c) of subsection (2) of this section, entitling him to contest the validity of the award, the court may, if it thinks fit, either refuse to enforce the award or adjourn the hearing until after the expiration of such period as appears to the court to be reasonably sufficient to enable that party to take the necessary steps to have the award annulled by the competent tribunal.

38.   Evidence

(1)   The party seeking to enforce a foreign award must produce—

(a)   the original award or a copy thereof duly authenticated in manner required by the law of the country in which it was made; and

(b)   evidence proving that the award has become final; and

(c)   such evidence as may be necessary to prove that the award is a foreign award and that the conditions mentioned in paragraphs (a), (b) and (c) of subsection (1) of the last foregoing section are satisfied.

(2)   In any case where any document required to be produced under subsection (1) of this section is in a foreign language, it shall be the duty of the party seeking to enforce the award to produce a translation certified as correct by a diplomatic or consular agent of the country to which that party belongs, or certified as correct in such other manner as may be sufficient according to the law of England.

(3)   Subject to the provisions of this section, rules of court may be made under section 84 of the Supreme Court Act 1981, with respect to the evidence which must be furnished by a party seeking to enforce an award under this Part of this Act.

39.   Meaning of 'final award'

For the purposes of this Part of this Act, an award shall not be deemed final if any proceedings for the purpose of contesting the validity of the award are pending in the country in which it was made.

40.   Saving for other rights, &c.

Nothing in this Part of this Act shall—

(a)   prejudice any rights which any person would have had of enforcing in England any award or of availing himself in England of any award if neither this Part of this Act nor Part I of the Arbitration (Foreign Awards) Act 1930, had been enacted; or

(b)   apply to any award made on an arbitration agreement governed by the law of England.

41.   Application of Part II to Scotland

(1)   The following provisions of this section shall have effect for the purpose of the application of this Part of this Act to Scotland.

(2)   For the references to England there shall be substituted references to Scotland.

(3)   For subsection (1) of section thirty-six there shall be substituted the following subsection:

'(1)   A foreign award shall, subject to the provisions of this Part of this Act, be enforceable by action, or, if the agreement for arbitration contains consent to the registration of the award in the Books of Council and Session for execution and the award is so registered, it shall, subject as aforesaid, be enforceable by summary diligence'.

(4)   For subsection (3) of section thirty-eight there shall be substituted the following subsection:

'(3)   The Court of Session shall, subject to the provision of this section, have power, exercisable by statutory instrument, to make provision by Act of Sederunt with respect to the evidence which must be furnished by a party seeking to enforce in Scotland an award under this Part of this Act'.

Note: This section is printed as amended by the Statutory Instruments Act 1946 and the Law Reform Miscellaneous Provisions (Scotland) Act 1966.

42.   Application of Part II to Northern Ireland

(1)   The following provisions of this section shall have effect for the purpose of the application of this Part of this Act to Northern Ireland.

(2)   For the references to England there shall be substituted references to Northern Ireland.

(3)   For subsection (1) of section thirty-six there shall be substituted the following subsection:

'(1)   A foreign award shall, subject to the provisions of this Part of this Act, be enforceable either by action or in the same manner as the award of an arbitrator under the provisions of the Common Law Procedure Amendment Act (Ireland) 1856 was enforceable at the date of the passing of the Arbitration (Foreign Awards) Act 1930'.

PART III

GENERAL

44.   Short title, commencement and repeal

(1)   This Act may be cited as the Arbitration Act 1950.

(2)   This Act shall come into operation on the first day of September, nineteen hundred and fifty.

(3)   The Arbitration Act 1889, the Arbitration Clauses (Protocol) Act 1924, and the Arbitration Act 1934 are hereby repealed except in relation to arbitrations commenced (within the meaning of subsection (2) of section twenty-nine of this Act) before the commencement of this Act, and the Arbitration (Foreign Awards) Act 1930 is hereby repealed; and any reference in any Act or other document to any enactment hereby repealed shall be construed as including a reference to the corresponding provision of this Act.

SCHEDULES

Section 35   FIRST SCHEDULE

Protocol on Arbitration Clauses signed on behalf of His Majesty at a Meeting of the Assembly of the League of Nations held on the twenty-fourth day of September, nineteen hundred and twenty-three

The undersigned, being duly authorised, declare that they accept, on behalf of the countries which they represent, the following provisions:

1.   Each of the Contracting States recognises the validity of an agreement whether relating to existing or future differences between parties, subject respectively to the

jurisdiction of different Contracting States by which the parties to a contract agree to submit to arbitration all or any differences that may arise in connection with such contract relating to commercial matters or to any other matter capable of settlement by arbitration, whether or not the arbitration is to take place in a country to whose jurisdiction none of the parties is subject.

Each Contracting State reserves the right to limit the obligation mentioned above to contracts which are considered as commercial under its national law. Any Contracting State which avails itself of this right will notify the Secretary-General of the League of Nations, in order that the other Contracting States may be so informed.

2. The arbitral procedure, including the constitution of the arbitral tribunal, shall be governed by the will of the parties and by the law of the country in whose territory the arbitration takes place.

The Contracting States agree to facilitate all steps in the procedure which require to be taken in their own territories, in accordance with the provisions of their law governing arbitral procedure applicable to existing differences.

3. Each Contracting State undertakes to ensure the execution by its authorities and in accordance with the provisions of its national laws of arbitral awards made in its own territory under the preceding articles.

4. The tribunals of the Contracting Parties, on being seized of a dispute regarding a contract made between persons to whom Article 1 applies and including an arbitration agreement whether referring to present or future differences which is valid in virtue of the said article and capable of being carried into effect, shall refer the parties on the application of either of them to the decision of the arbitrators.

Such reference shall not prejudice the competence of the judicial tribunals in case the agreement or the arbitration cannot proceed or becomes inoperative.

5. The present Protocol, which shall remain open for signature by all States, shall be ratified. The ratifications shall be deposited as soon as possible with the Secretary-General of the League of Nations, who shall notify such deposit to all the signatory States.

6. The present Protocol shall come into force as soon as two ratifications have been deposited. Thereafter it will take effect, in the case of each Contracting State, one month after the notification by the Secretary-General of the deposit of its ratification.

7. The present Protocol may be denounced by any Contracting State on giving one year's notice. Denunciation shall be effected by a notification addressed to the Secretary-General of the League, who will immediately transmit copies of such notification to all the other signatory States and inform them of the date of which it was received. The denunciation shall take effect one year after the date on which it was notified to the Secretary-General, and shall operate only in respect of the notifying State.

8. The Contracting States may declare that their acceptance of the present Protocol does not include any or all of the under-mentioned territories: that is to say, their colonies, overseas possessions or territories, protectorates or the territories over which they exercise a mandate.

The said States may subsequently adhere separately on behalf of any territory thus excluded. The Secretary-General of the League of Nations shall be informed as soon as possible of such adhesions. He shall notify such adhesions to all signatory States. They will take effect one month after the notification by the Secretary-General to all signatory States.

The Contracting States may also denounce the Protocol separately on behalf of any of the territories referred to above. Article 7 applies to such denunciation.

Section 35　　　　SECOND SCHEDULE

Convention on the Execution of Foreign Arbitral Awards signed at Geneva on behalf of His Majesty on the twenty-sixth day of September, nineteen hundred and twenty-seven

Article 1

In the territories of any High Contracting Party to which the present Convention applies, an arbitral award made in pursuance of an agreement, whether relating to existing or future differences (herein-after called 'a submission to arbitration') covered by the Protocol on Arbitration Clauses, opened at Geneva on September 24th 1923, shall be recognised as binding and shall be enforced in accordance with the rules of the procedure of the territory where the award is relied upon, provided that the said award has been made in a territory of one of the High Contracting Parties to which the present Convention applies and between persons who are subject to the jurisdiction of one of the High Contracting Parties.

To obtain such recognition or enforcement, it shall, further, be necessary:

(a)   That the award has been made in pursuance of a submission to arbitration which is valid under the law applicable thereto;

(b)   That the subject-matter of the award is capable of settlement by arbitration under the law of the country in which the award is sought to be relied upon;

(c)   That the award has been made by the Arbitral Tribunal provided for in the submission to arbitration or constituted in the manner agreed upon by the parties and in conformity with the law governing the arbitration procedure;

(d)   That the award has become final in the country in which it has been made, in the sense that it will not be considered as such if it is open to *opposition, appel or pourvoi en cassation* (in the countries where such forms of procedure exist) or if it is proved that any proceedings for the purpose of contesting the validity of the award are pending;

(e)   That the recognition or enforcement of the award is not contrary to the public policy or to the principles of the law of the country in which it is sought to be relied upon.

Article 2

Even if the conditions laid down in Article 1 hereof are fulfilled, recognition and enforcement of the award shall be refused if the Court is satisfied:

(a)   That the award has been annulled in the country in which it was made;

(b)   That the party against whom it is sought to use the award was not given notice of the arbitration proceedings in sufficient time to enable him to present his case; or that being under a legal incapacity, he was not properly represented;

(c)   That the award does not deal with differences contemplated by or falling within the terms of the submission to arbitration or that it contains decisions on matters beyond the scope of the submission to arbitration.

If the award has not covered all the questions submitted to the arbitral tribunal, the competent authority of the country where recognition or enforcement of the award is sought can, if it think fit, postpone such recognition or enforcement or grant it subject to such guarantee as that authority may decide.

Article 3

If the party against whom the award has been made proves that under the law governing the arbitration procedure, there is a ground, other than the grounds referred to in Article 1(a) and (c), and Article 2(b) and (c), entitling him to contest the validity of the award in a Court of Law, the Court may, if it thinks fit, either refuse recognition or enforcement of the award or adjourn the consideration thereof, giving such party a reasonable time within which to have the award annulled by the competent tribunal.

Article 4

The party relying upon an award or claiming its enforcement must supply, in particular:

(1)   The original award or a copy thereof duly authenticated, according to the requirements of the law of the country in which it was made;

(2)   Documentary or other evidence to prove that the award has become final, in the sense defined in Article 1(d), in the country in which it was made;

(3)   When necessary, documentary or other evidence to prove that the conditions laid down in Article 1, paragraph 1 and paragraph 2(a) and (c), have been fulfilled.

A translation of the award and of the other documents mentioned in this Article into the official language of the country where the award is sought to be relied upon may be demanded. Such translation must be certified correct by a diplomatic or consular agent of the country to which the party who seeks to rely upon the award belongs or by a sworn translator of the country where the award is sought to be relied upon.

Article 5

The provisions of the above Articles shall not deprive any interested party of the right of availing himself of an arbitral award in the manner and to the extent allowed by the law or the treaties of the country where such award is sought to be relied upon.

Article 6

The present Convention applies only to arbitral awards made after the coming into force of the Protocol on Arbitration Clauses, opened at Geneva on September 24th 1923.

Article 7

The present Convention, which will remain open to the signature of all the signatories of the Protocol of 1923 on Arbitration Clauses, shall be ratified.

It may be ratified only on behalf of those Members of the League of Nations and non-Member States on whose behalf the Protocol of 1923 shall have been ratified.

Ratifications shall be deposited as soon as possible with the Secretary-General of the League of Nations, who will notify such deposit to all the signatories.

Article 8

The present Convention shall come into force three months after it shall have been ratified on behalf of two High Contracting Parties. Thereafter, it shall take effect, in the case of each High Contracting Party, three months after the deposit of the ratification on its behalf with the Secretary-General of the League of Nations.

Article 9

The present Convention may be denounced on behalf of any Member of the League or non-Member State. Denunciation shall be notified in writing to the Secretary-General of the League of Nations, who will immediately send a copy thereof, certified to be in conformity with the notification, to all the other Contracting Parties, at the same time informing them of the date on which he received it.

The denunciation shall come into force only in respect of the High Contracting Party which shall have notified it and one year after such notification shall have reached the Secretary-General of the League of Nations.

The denunciation of the Protocol on Arbitration Clause shall entail, ipso facto, the denunciation of the present Convention.

Article 10

The present Convention does not apply to the Colonies, Protectorates or territories under suzerainty or mandate of any High Contracting Party unless they are specially mentioned.

The application of this Convention to one or more of such Colonies, Protectorates or territories to which the Protocol on Arbitration Clauses, opened at Geneva at September 24th 1923, applies, can be effected at any time by means of a declaration addressed to the Secretary-General of the League of Nations by one of the High Contracting Parties.

Such declaration shall take effect three months after the deposit thereof.

The High Contracting Parties can at any time denounce the Convention for all or any of the Colonies, Protectorates or territories referred to above. Article 9 hereof applies to such denunciation.

Article 11

A certified copy of the present Convention shall be transmitted by the Secretary-General of the League of Nations to every Member of the League of Nations and to every non-Member State which signs the same.

Appendix 3

CIVIL JURISDICTION AND JUDGMENTS ACT 1982
(1982 c. 27)

32. Overseas judgments given in proceedings brought in breach of agreement for settlement of disputes

(1)   Subject to the following provisions of this section, a judgment given by a court of an overseas country in any proceedings shall not be recognised or enforced in the United Kingdom if—

(a)   the bringing of those proceedings in that court was contrary to an agreement under which the dispute in question was to be settled otherwise than by proceedings in the courts of that country; and

(b)   those proceedings were not brought in that court by, or with the agreement of, the person against whom the judgment was given; and

(c)   that person did not counterclaim in the proceedings or otherwise submit to the jurisdiction of that court.

(2)   Subsection (1) does not apply where the agreement referred to in paragraph (a) of that subsection was illegal, void or unenforceable or was incapable of being performed for reasons not attributable to the fault of the party bringing the proceedings in which the judgment was given.

(3)   In determining whether a judgment given by a court of an overseas country should be recognised or enforced in the United Kingdom, a court in the United Kingdom shall not be bound by any decision of the overseas court relating to any of the matters mentioned in subsection (1) or (2).

(4)   Nothing in subsection (1) shall affect the recognition or enforcement in the United Kingdom of—

(a)   a judgment which is required to be recognised or enforced there under the 1968 Convention;

(b)   a judgment to which Part I of the Foreign Judgments (Reciprocal Enforcement) Act 1933 applies by virtue of section 4 of the Carriage of Goods by Road Act 1965, section 17(4) of the Nuclear Installations Act 1965, section 13(3) of the Merchant Shipping (Oil Pollution) Act 1971, section 5 of the Carriage of Passengers by Road Act 1974 or section 6(4) of the Merchant Shipping Act 1974.

33. Certain steps not to amount to submission to jurisdiction of overseas court

(1)   For the purposes of determining whether a judgment given by a court of an overseas country should be recognised or enforced in England and Wales or Northern Ireland, the person against whom the judgment was given shall not be regarded as having submitted to the jurisdiction of the court by reason only of the fact that he appeared (conditionally or otherwise) in the proceedings for all or any one or more of the following purposes, namely—

(a)   to contest the jurisdiction of the court;

(b)   to ask the court to dismiss or stay the proceedings on the ground that the dispute in question should be submitted to arbitration or to the determination of the courts of another country;

 (c) to protect, or obtain the release of, property seized or threatened with seizure in the proceedings.

 (2) Nothing in this section shall affect the recognition or enforcement in England and Wales or Northern Ireland of a judgment which is required to be recognised or enforced there under the 1968 Convention.

Appendix 4

CIVIL PROCEDURE RULES

PD 49G   PRACTICE DIRECTION — ARBITRATIONS

This practice direction supplements CPR Part 49 and replaces, with modifications, Order 73 of the Rules of the Supreme Court

PART I

THE OVERRIDING OBJECTIVE
1.   This Part of this practice direction is founded on the general principles in section 1 of the Arbitration Act and shall be construed accordingly.

MEANING OF ARBITRATION APPLICATION
2.1   Subject to paragraph 22.2, 'arbitration application' means the following:
   (1)   an application to the court under the Arbitration Act;
   (2)   proceedings to determine:
      (a)   whether there is a valid arbitration agreement;
      (b)   whether an arbitration tribunal is properly constituted;
      (c)   what matters have been submitted to arbitration in accordance with an arbitration agreement;
   (3)   proceedings to declare that an award made by an arbitral tribunal is not binding on a party;
   (4)   any other application affecting arbitration proceedings (whether instituted or anticipated) or to construe or affecting an arbitration agreement.
2.2   In this Part, an arbitration application does not include proceedings to enforce an award:
   (1)   to which Part III applies; or
   (2)   by a claim on the award.

INTERPRETATION
3.   In this Part:
   'applicant' means the party making an arbitration application and references to respondent shall be construed accordingly;
   'the Arbitration Act' means the Arbitration Act 1996 and any expressions used in this Part and in Part I of the Arbitration Act have the same meanings in this Part as they have in that Part of the Arbitration Act.
   'arbitration claim form' means the arbitration claim form by the issue of which an arbitration application is begun.

FORM AND CONTENT OF ARBITRATION CLAIM FORM
4.1   An arbitration claim form must be in the practice form No. 8A.
4.2   Every arbitration claim form must:
   (1)   include a concise statement of
      (a)   the remedy claimed, and

(b)   (where appropriate) the questions on which the applicant seeks the determination or direction of the Court;

(2)   give details of any arbitration award that is challenged by the applicant, showing the grounds for any such challenge;

(3)   where the applicant claims an order for costs, identify the respondent against whom the claim is made,

(4)   (where appropriate) specify the section of the Arbitration Act under which the application is brought; and

(5)   show that any statutory requirements have been satisfied including those set out, by way of example, in the Table below.

Application made	*Statutory requirements*
section 9 (stay of legal proceedings)	see section 9 (3)
section 12 (extensions of time for beginning arbitral proceedings)	see section 12 (2)
section 18 (failure of appointment procedure)	see section 18 (2)
section 21 (umpires)	see section 21 (5)
section 24 (removal of arbitrators)	see section 24 (2)
section 32 (preliminary point of jurisdiction)	see section 32 (3)
section 42 (enforcement of peremptory orders)	see section 42 (3)
section 44 (powers in support of arbitral proceedings)	see section 44 (4), (5)
section 45 (preliminary point of law)	see section 45 (3)
section 50 (extension of time for making award)	see section 50 (2)
section 56 (power to withhold award)	see section 56 (4)
sections 67, 68 (challenging the award)	see section 70 (2), (3)
section 69 (appeal on point of law)	see sections 69 (2), (4), 70(2), (3)
section 77 (service of documents)	see section 77(3)

4.3   The arbitration claim form must also state:

(1)   whether it is made on notice or without notice and, if made on notice, must give the names and addresses of the persons on whom it is to be served, stating their role in the arbitration and whether they are made respondents to the application;

(2)   whether (having regard to paragraph 15) the application will be heard by a judge sitting in public or in private; and

(3)   the date and time when the application will be heard or that such date has not yet been fixed.

4.4   Every arbitration claim form shall be indorsed with the applicant's address for service in accordance with CPR Rule 6.5(2)

ISSUE OF ARBITRATION CLAIM FORM

5.1   These paragraphs (5.1 to 5.7) are is to be read with the provisions of the High Court and County Courts (Allocation of Arbitration Proceedings) Order 1996 which allocates proceedings under the Arbitration Act to the High Court and the county courts and specifies proceedings which may be commenced or taken only in the High Court or in a county court.

5.2   These paragraphs (5.1 to 5.7) do not apply to applications under section 9 of the Arbitration Act to stay legal proceedings.

5.3   Subject to paragraphs 5.1 and 5.2 above, an arbitration claim form by which proceedings are commenced may be issued:

(1)   out of the Admiralty and Commercial Registry in the Royal Courts of Justice, in which case the arbitration application will be entered into the commercial list;

(2)   out of a district registry where a Mercantile Court has been established, in which case the arbitration application will be entered into the list of that Mercantile Court; or

(3)   out of the office of the Central London County Court, in which case the arbitration application will be entered into the Business List of that court.

(Attention is drawn to the provisions relating to the commencement of proceedings contained in the Commercial Court Practice Direction and the Mercantile Court and Business Lists Practice Direction which supplement CPR Part 49).

5.4   Except where an arbitration claim form is issued out of the Admiralty and Commercial Registry, the Judge in charge of the list into which the arbitration application has been entered shall:

(1)   as soon as practicable after the issue of the arbitration claim form, and

(2)   in consultation with the Judge in charge of the commercial list,

consider whether the application should be transferred to the Commercial Court or to any another list.

5.5   Where an arbitration claim form is issued out of the Admiralty and Commercial Registry, the Judge in charge of the commercial list may at any time after the issue of the arbitration claim form transfer the application to another list, court or Division of the High Court to which he has power to transfer proceedings.

5.6   In considering whether to transfer an arbitration application, the Judges referred to in paragraphs 5.4 and 5.5 shall have regard to the criteria specified in article 5(4) of the High Court and County Courts (Allocation of Arbitration Proceedings) Order 1996 and the application shall be transferred if those Judges so decide.

5.7   in this practice direction 'Judge in charge of the list' means:

(a)   in relation to the commercial list, a judge of the Commercial Court;

(b)   in relation to the list of a Mercantile Court, a Circuit mercantile judge of that court; and

(c)   in relation to the Business List in the Central London County Court, a Circuit Judge authorised to deal with cases in that list,

but nothing in this paragraph shall be construed as preventing the powers of a judge of the Commercial Court from being exercised by any judge of the High Court.

STAY OF LEGAL PROCEEDINGS

6.1   An application notice by which an application under section 9 of the Arbitration Act to stay legal proceedings is made shall be served:

(1)   in accordance with CPR Rule 6.5 on the party bringing the relevant legal proceedings and on any other party to those proceedings who has given an address for service; and

(2)   on any party to those legal proceedings who has not given an address for service, by sending to him (whether or not he is within the jurisdiction) at his last known address or at a place where it is likely to come to his attention, a copy of the application notice for his information.

6.2   Where a question arises as to whether an arbitration agreement has been concluded or as to whether the dispute which is the subject-matter of the proceedings falls within the terms of such an agreement, the Court may determine that question or give directions for its determination, in which case it may order the proceedings to be stayed pending the determination of that question.

SERVICE OF ARBITRATION CLAIM FORM

7.1   Subject to paragraphs 7.2 and 7.4 below and to paragraphs 6.1 and 8.1 to 8.4, an arbitration claim form shall be served in accordance with CPR Part 6.

7.2   Where the Court is satisfied on an application made without notice that:

(1)   arbitral proceedings are taking place, or an arbitration award has been made, within the jurisdiction; and

(2)   an arbitration application is being made in connection with those arbitral proceedings or being brought to challenge the award or to appeal on a question of law arising out of the award; and

(3)   the respondent to the arbitration application (not being an individual residing or carrying on business within the jurisdiction or a body corporate having a registered office or a place of business within the jurisdiction)

(a)   is or was represented in the arbitral proceedings by a solicitor or other agent within the jurisdiction who was authorised to receive service of any notice or other document served for the purposes of those proceedings; and

(b)   has not (at the time when the arbitration application is made) determined the authority of that solicitor or agent,

the Court may authorise service of the arbitration claim form to be effected on the solicitor or agent instead of the respondent.

7.3   An order made under paragraph 7.2 must limit a time within which the respondent must acknowledge service and a copy of the order and of the arbitration claim form must be sent by post to the respondent at his address out of the jurisdiction.

7.4   Where an applicant has made an arbitration application (the first arbitration application) and a subsequent arbitration application arising out of the same arbitration or arbitration agreement is made by a party to the first arbitration application (other than the applicant), that party's arbitration claim form may be served in accordance with CPR rule 6.5 or may be served on the applicant at his address for service given in his arbitration claim form, and on any other party to the first arbitration application at the address for service given in that party's acknowledgement of service in the first arbitration application, and on any further arbitration application the same provisions as to service will apply.

7.5   For the purposes of service, an arbitration claim form is valid in the first instance:

(1)   where service is to be effected out of the jurisdiction, for such period as the Court may fix;

(2)   In any other case, for one month, beginning with the date of its issue.

SERVICE OUT OF THE JURISDICTION

8.1   The Court may give permission to serve an arbitration claim form out of the jurisdiction if the arbitration application fails into one of the categories mentioned in the following table and satisfies the conditions specified.

Nature of application	Conditions to be satisfied
1. The applicant seeks to challenge, or to appeal to the Court on a question of law arising out of, an arbitration award.	Award must have been made in England & Wales. Section 53 of the Arbitration Act shall apply for determining the place where award is treated as made.
2. The application is for an order under section 44 of the Arbitration Act (Court powers exercisable in support of arbitral proceedings). Where the application is for an interim remedy in support of arbitral proceedings which are taking (or will take) place outside England and Wales, the Court may give permission for service out of the jurisdiction notwithstanding that no other remedy is sought.	None.
3. The applicant seeks some other remedy or requires a question to be determined by the court, affecting an arbitration (whether pending or anticipated), an arbitration agreement or an arbitration award.	The seat of the arbitration is or will be in England & Wales or the conditions in Section 2(4) of the Arbitration Act are satisfied.

8.2 An application for the grant of permission under paragraph 8.1 must be supported by an affidavit or witness statement:

(1) stating, or, if the grounds were set out in the application notice, confirming the grounds on which the application is made; and

(2) showing in what place or country the person to be served is, or probably may be found, and no such permission shall be granted unless it shall be made sufficiently to appear to the Court that the case is a proper one for service out of the jurisdiction under this paragraph.

8.3 RSC Order 11, rules 5 to 8 (Schedule 1 to the CPR) shall apply to the service of an arbitration claim form under this paragraph as they apply to the service of other claim forms.

8.4 Any order made on an arbitration application may be served out of the jurisdiction with the permission of the court.

EVIDENCE IN SUPPORT OF ARBITRATION APPLICATION

9.1 The applicant shall file an affidavit or witness statement in support of the arbitration application which sets out the evidence on which he intends to rely and a copy of every affidavit or witness statement so filed must be served with the arbitration claim form.

9.2 Where an arbitration application is made with the written agreement of all the other parties to the arbitral proceedings or with the permission of the arbitral tribunal, the affidavit or witness statement in support must:

(1) give details of the agreement or, as the case may be, permission; and

(2) exhibit copies of any document which evidences that agreement or permission.

REQUIREMENTS AS TO NOTICE

10.1 Where the Arbitration Act requires that an application to the Court is to be made upon notice to other parties notice shall be given by making those parties respondents to the application and serving on them the arbitration claim form and any affidavit or witness statement in support.

10.2 Where an arbitration application is made under section 24, 28 or 56 of the Arbitration Act, the arbitrators or, in the case of an application under section 24, the arbitrator concerned shall be made respondents to the application and notice shall be given by serving on them the arbitration claim form and any affidavit or witness statement in support.

10.3 In cases where paragraph 10.2 does not apply, an applicant shall be taken as having complied with any requirement to give notice to the arbitrator if he sends a copy of the arbitration claim form to the arbitrator for his information at his last known address with a copy of any affidavit or witness statement in support.

10.4 This paragraph does not apply to applications under section 9 of the Arbitration Act to stay legal proceedings.

ACKNOWLEDGMENT OF SERVICE

11.1 Service of an arbitration claim form may be acknowledged by completing an acknowledgment of service in Form No. N15A in accordance with CPR Rule 8.3.

11.2 A respondent who:

(1) fails to acknowledge service within the time limited for so doing; or

(2) having indicated on his acknowledgment of service that he does not intend to contest the arbitration application, then wishes to do so, shall not be entitled to contest the application without the permission of the Court.

11.3 The Court will not give notice of the date on which an arbitration application will be heard to a respondent who has failed to acknowledge service.

11.4 The failure of a respondent to give notice of intention to contest the arbitration application or to acknowledge service shall not affect the applicant's duty to satisfy the Court that the order applied for should be made.

11.5   This paragraph does not apply to:
(1)   applications under section 9 of the Arbitration Act to stay legal proceedings; or
(2)   subsequent arbitration applications.

ACKNOWLEDGMENT OF SERVICE, ETC., BY ARBITRATOR

12.1   An arbitrator who is sent a copy of an arbitration claim form for his information may make
(1)   a request (without notice to any party) to be made a respondent; or
(2)   representations to the Court under this rule,
and, where an arbitrator is ordered to be made a respondent, he shall acknowledge service within 14 days of the making of that order.

12.2   An arbitrator who wishes to make representations to the Court under this rule may file an affidavit or witness statement or make representations in writing to the Court.

12.3   The arbitrator shall as soon as is practicable send a copy of any document filed or made under paragraph 12.2 to all the parties to the arbitration application.

12.4   Nothing in this paragraph shall require the Court to admit a document filed or made under sub-paragraph (2) and the weight to be given to any such document shall be a matter for the Court.

AUTOMATIC DIRECTIONS

13.1   Unless the Court otherwise directs, the following directions shall take effect automatically.

13.2   A respondent who wishes to put evidence before the Court in response to any affidavit or witness statement filed in support of an arbitration application shall serve his affidavit or witness statement on the applicant before the expiration of 21 days after the time limited for acknowledging service or, in a case where a respondent is not required to file an acknowledgment of service, within 21 days after service of the arbitration claim form.

13.3   An applicant who wishes to put evidence before the court in response to an affidavit or witness statement filed under paragraph 13.2 shall serve his affidavit or witness statement on the respondent within 7 days after service of the respondent's evidence.

13.4   Where a date has not been fixed for the hearing of the arbitration application, the applicant shall, and the respondent may, not later than 14 days after the expiration of the time limit specified in paragraph 13.2, apply to the Court for such a date to be fixed.

13.5   Agreed indexed and paginated bundles of all the evidence and other documents to be used at the hearing shall be prepared by the applicant (with the co-operation of the respondent).

13.6   Not later than 5 clear days before the hearing date estimates for the length of the hearing shall be lodged with the Court together with a complete set of the documents to be used.

13.7   Not later than 2 days before the hearing date the applicant shall lodge with the Court:
(1)   a chronology of the relevant events cross-referenced to the bundle of documents;
(2)   (where necessary) a list of the persons involved;
(3)   a skeleton argument which lists succinctly:
   (a)   the issues which arise for decision,
   (b)   the grounds of relief (or opposing relief) to be relied upon,
   (c)   the submissions of fact to be made with the references to the evidence, and
   (d)   the submissions of law with references to the relevant authorities,
and shall send copies to the respondent.

13.8   Not later than the day before the hearing date the respondent shall lodge with the Court a skeleton argument which lists succinctly:
(1)   the issues which arise for decision,
(2)   the grounds of relief (or opposing relief) to be relied upon,
(3)   the submissions of fact to be made with the references to the evidence, and

(4) the submissions of law with references to the relevant authorities, and shall send a copy to the applicant.

DIRECTIONS BY THE COURT

14.1 The rules of the CPR relating to allocation questionnaires and track allocation do not apply to arbitration applications, and the Court may give such directions as to the conduct of the arbitration application as it thinks best adapted to secure the just, expeditious and economical disposal thereof.

14.2 Where the Court considers that there is or may be a dispute as to fact and that the just, expeditious and economical disposal of the application can best be secured by hearing the application on oral evidence or mainly on oral evidence, it may, if it thinks fit, order that no further evidence shall be filed and that the application shall be heard on oral evidence or partly on oral evidence and partly on written evidence, with or without cross-examination of any of the witnesses, as it may direct.

14.3 The Court may give directions as to the filing of evidence and as to the attendance of witnesses for cross-examination and any other directions which it could give in proceedings begun by claim form.

14.4 If the applicant makes default in complying with these provisions or with any order or direction of the Court as to the conduct of the application, or if the Court is satisfied that the applicant is not prosecuting the application with due despatch, the Court may order the application to be dismissed or may make such other order as may be just.

14.5 If the respondent fails to comply with these provisions or with any order or direction given by the Court in relation to the evidence to be relied on, or the submission to be made by that respondent, the Court may, if it thinks fit, hear and determine the application without having regard to that evidence or those submissions.

14.6 Unless the Court orders otherwise, affidavits and witness statements may contain hearsay.

HEARING OF APPLICATIONS: PUBLIC OR PRIVATE

15.1 The Court may order that any arbitration application be heard either in public or in private.

15.2 Subject to any order made under paragraph 15.1 and paragraph 15.3, all arbitration applications shall be heard in private.

15.3 Subject to any order made under paragraph 15.1, the determination of a preliminary point of law under section 45 of the Arbitration Act, or an appeal under section 69 on a question of law arising out of an award shall be heard in public.

15.4 Paragraph 15.3 shall not apply to:

(1) the preliminary question whether the Court is satisfied of the matters set out in section 45(2)(b); or

(2) an application for permission to appeal under section 69(2)(b).

SECURING THE ATTENDANCE OF WITNESSES

16.1 A party to arbitral proceedings being conducted in England and Wales who wishes to rely on section 43 of the Arbitration Act to secure the attendance of a witness may apply for a witness summons in accordance with Part 34 of the CPR to the Admiralty and Commercial Registry or, if the attendance of the witness is required within the district of a district registry, at that registry at the option of the party.

16.2 A witness summons shall not be issued until the applicant files an affidavit or witness statement which shows that the application is made with the permission of the tribunal or the agreement of the other parties.

SECURING FOR COSTS

17.1 Subject to section 70(6) of the Arbitration Act, the Court may order any applicant (including an applicant who has been granted permission to appeal) to provide security for costs of any arbitration application.

POWERS EXERCISABLE IN SUPPORT OF ARBITRAL PROCEEDINGS

18.1   Where the case is one of urgency, an application for an order under section 44 of the Arbitration Act (Court powers exercisable in support of arbitral proceedings) may be made without notice on affidavit or witness statement (before the issue of an arbitration claim form) and the affidavit or witness statement shall (in addition to dealing with the matters required to be dealt with by paragraphs 9.1 & 9.2) state the reasons:

(1)   why the application is made without notice; and

(2)   (where the application is made without the permission of the arbitral tribunal or the agreement of the other parties to the arbitral proceedings) why it was not practicable to obtain that permission or agreement; and

(3)   why the witness believes that the condition in section 44 (5) is satisfied.

18.2   Where the case is not one of urgency, an application for an order under section 44 of the Arbitration Act shall be made on notice and the affidavit or witness statement in support shall (in addition to dealing with the matters required to be dealt with by paragraph 9 and paragraph 18.1(3) above) state that the application is made with the permission of the tribunal or the written agreement of the other parties to the arbitral proceedings.

18.3   Where an application for an order under section 44 of the Arbitration Act is made before the issue of an arbitration claim form, any order made by the Court may be granted on terms providing for the issue of an arbitration claim form and such other terms, if any, as the court thinks fit.

APPLICATIONS UNDER SECTIONS 32 AND 45 OF THE ARBITRATION ACT

19.1   This paragraph applies to the following arbitration applications:

(1)   applications for the determination of a question as to the substantive jurisdiction of the arbitral tribunal under section 32 of the Arbitration Act; and

(2)   applications for the determination of a preliminary point of law under section 45 of the Arbitration Act.

19.2   Where an application is made without the agreement in writing of all the other parties to the arbitral proceedings but with the permission of the arbitral tribunal, the affidavits or witness statements filed by the parties shall set out any evidence relied on by the parties in support of their contention that the Court should, or should not, consider the application.

19.3   As soon as practicable after the written evidence is filed, the Court shall decide whether or not it should consider the application and, unless the Court otherwise directs, shall so decide without a hearing.

APPLICATIONS FOR PERMISSION TO APPEAL

20.1   Where the applicant seeks permission to appeal to the Court on a question of law arising out of an arbitration award, the arbitration claim form shall identify the question of law and state the grounds on which the applicant alleges that permission should be granted.

20.2   The affidavit or witness statement in support of the application shall set out any evidence relied on by the applicant for the purpose of satisfying the Court of the matters mentioned in section 69 (3) of the Arbitration Act and for satisfying the Court that permission should be granted.

20.3   The affidavit or witness statement filed by the respondent to the application shall:

(1)   state the grounds on which the respondent opposes the grant of permission;

(2)   set out any evidence relied on by him relating to the matters mentioned in section 69 (3) of the Arbitration Act, and

(3)   specify whether the respondent wishes to contend that the award should be upheld for reasons not expressed (or not fully expressed) in the award and, if so, state those reasons.

20.4   As soon as practicable after the filing of the affidavits and witness statements, the Court shall determine the application for permission in accordance with section 69 (5) of the Arbitration Act.

20.5   Where permission is granted, a date shall be fixed for the hearing of the appeal.

EXTENSION OF TIME: APPLICATIONS UNDER SECTION 12

21.1   An application for an order under section 12 of the Arbitration Act may include as an alternative an application for a declaration that such an order is not needed.

TIME LIMIT FOR CHALLENGES TO OR APPEALS FROM AWARDS

22.1   An applicant shall not be taken as having complied with the time limit of 28 days referred to in section 70 (3) of the Arbitration Act unless the arbitration claim form has been issued, and all the affidavits or witness statements in support have been filed, by the expiry of that time limit.

22.2   An applicant who wishes:

(1)   to challenge an award under section 67 or 68 of the Arbitration Act; or

(2)   to appeal under section 69 on a question of law arising out of an award,

may, where the time limit of 28 days has not yet expired, apply without notice on affidavit or witness statement for an order extending that time limit.

22.3   In any case where an applicant seeks to challenge an award under section 67 or 68 of the Arbitration Act or to appeal under section 69 after the time limit of 28 days has already expired, the following provisions shall apply:

(1)   the applicant must state in his arbitration claim form the grounds why an order extending time should be made and his affidavit or witness statement in support shall set out the evidence on which he relies;

(2)   a respondent who wishes to oppose the making of an order extending time shall file an affidavit or witness statement within 7 days after service of the applicant's evidence, and

(3)   the Court shall decide whether or not to extend time without a hearing unless it appears to the Court that a hearing is required, and, where the Court makes an order extending the time limit, the respondent shall file his affidavit or witness statement in response to the arbitration application 21 days after the making of the order.

PART II

APPLICATION OF THIS PART

23.1   This Part of this practice direction applies to any application to the Court to which the old law applies and, in this rule, 'the old law' means the enactments specified in section 107 of the Arbitration Act 1996 as they stood before their amendment or repeal by that Act.

23.2   This Part does not apply to proceedings to enforce an award:

(1)   to which Part III of this practice direction applies; or

(2)   by a claim based on the award.

23.3   Reference should be made to the other provisions of the CPR (except Parts I and III of this Part) for the procedure for any application not expressly provided for in this Part.

MATTERS FOR A JUDGE IN COURT

24.1   Every application to the Court:

(1)   to remit an award under section 22 of the Arbitration Act 1950 ; or

(2)   to remove an arbitrator or umpire under section 23(1) of that Act; or

(3)   to set aside an award under section 23(2) of that Act, or

(4)   to determine, under section 2(1) of the Arbitration Act 1979, any question of law arising in the course of a reference,

must be made by the issue of an arbitration claim form under CPR rule 8.6 (a Part 8 claim form).

24.2   Any appeal to the High Court under section 1(2) of the Arbitration Act 1979 shall be made by the issue of a Part 8 claim form.

24.3   An application for a declaration that an award made by an arbitrator or umpire is not binding on a party to the award on the ground that it was made without jurisdiction may be made by the issue of a Part 8 claim form, but the foregoing provision shall not be taken as affecting the judge's power to refuse to make such a declaration in proceedings begun otherwise.

MATTERS FOR JUDGE IN CHAMBERS OR MASTER

25.1   Subject to the foregoing provisions of this Order and the provisions of this rule, the jurisdiction of the High Court or a judge thereof under the Arbitration Act 1950 and the jurisdiction of the High Court under the Arbitration Act 1975 and the Arbitration Act 1979 may be exercised by a judge in chambers, a master or the Admiralty Registrar.

25.2   Any application
  (1)   for permission to appeal under section 1(2) of the Arbitration Act 1979, or
  (2)   under section 1(5) of that Act (including any application for permission), or
  (3)   under section 5 of that Act,
shall be made to a judge in chambers.

25.3   Any application to which this rule applies shall, where there are existing court proceedings be made by the issue of an application notice in those proceedings, and in any other case a Part 8 claim form.

25.4   Where an application is made under section 1(5) of the Arbitration Act 1979 (including any application for permission), the Part 8 claim form or the application notice as the case may be, must be served on the arbitrator or umpire and on any other party to the reference.

APPLICATIONS IN DISTRICT REGISTRIES

26.1   An application under section 12(4) of the Arbitration Act 1950 for an order that a witness summons shall issue to compel the attendance before an arbitrator or umpire of a witness may, if the attendance of the witness is required within the district of a district registry, be made at that registry, instead of at the Admiralty and Commercial Registry, at the option of the applicant.

TIME LIMITS AND OTHER SPECIAL PROVISIONS AS TO APPEALS AND APPLICATIONS UNDER THE ARBITRATION ACTS

27.1   An application to the Court:
  (1)   to remit an award under section 22 of the Arbitration Act 1950; or
  (2)   to set aside an award under section 23(2) of that Act or otherwise, or
  (3)   to direct an arbitrator or umpire to state the reasons for an award under section 1(5) of the Arbitration Act 1979,
must be made, and the Part 8 claim form or application notice, as the case may be, must be served, within 21 days after the award has been made and published to the parties.

27.2   In the case of an appeal to the Court under section 1(2) of the Arbitration Act 1979, the application for permission to appeal, where permission is required, and the Part 8 claim form must be served and the appeal entered, within 21 days after the award has been made and published to the parties. Provided that, where reasons material to the appeal are given on a date subsequent to the publication of the award, the period of 21 days shall run from the date on which the reasons are given.

27.3   An application, under section 2(1) of the Arbitration Act 1979, to determine any question of law arising in the course of a reference, must be made, and the Part 8 claim form served, within 14 days after the arbitrator or umpire has consented to the application being made, or the other parties have so consented.

27.4   For the purpose of paragraph 27.3 the consent must be given in writing.

27.5   In the case of every appeal or application to which this paragraph applies, the Part 8 claim form or the application notice, as the case may be, must state the grounds of the appeal or application and, where the appeal or application is founded on evidence by affidavit or witness statement, or is made with the consent of the arbitrator or umpire or of the other parties, a copy of every affidavit or witness statement intended to be used, or, as the case may be, of every consent given in writing, must be served with the Part 8 claim form or application notice.

27.6   Without prejudice to sub-paragraph (5), in an appeal under section 1(2) of the Arbitration Act 1979 the statement of the grounds of the appeal shall specify the relevant parts of the award and reasons, or the relevant parts thereof, shall be lodged with the court and served with the Part 8 claim form.

27.7   In an application for permission to appeal under section 1(2) of the Arbitration Act 1979, any affidavit or witness statement verifying the facts in support of a contention that the question of law concerns a term of a contract or an event which is not a one-off term or event must be filed with the court and served with the Part 8 claim form.

27.8   Any affidavit or witness statement in reply to written evidence under subparagraph (7) shall be filed with the court and served on the applicant not less than two clear days before the hearing of the application.

27.9   A respondent to an application for permission to appeal under section 1(2) of the Arbitration Act 1979 who desires to contend that the award should be upheld on grounds not expressed or fully expressed in the award and reasons shall not less than two clear days before the hearing of the application file with the court and serve on the applicant a notice specifying the grounds of his contention.

APPLICATIONS AND APPEALS TO BE HEARD BY COMMERCIAL JUDGES

28.1   Any matter which is required, by paragraph 24 or 25, to be heard by a judge, shall be heard by a judge of the Commercial Court unless any such judge otherwise directs.

28.2   Nothing in the foregoing sub-paragraph shall be construed as preventing the powers of a judge of the Commercial Court from being exercised by any judge of the High Court.

SERVICE OUT OF THE JURISDICTION

29.1   Subject to paragraph 29.2,

(1)   any Part 8 claim form whereby an application under the Arbitration Act 1950 or the Arbitration Act 1979, is made, or

(2)   any order made on such an application,

may be served out of the jurisdiction with the permission of the Court provided that the arbitration to which the application relates is governed by English law or has been, is being or is to be held within the jurisdiction.

29.2   A Part 8 claim form whereby permission to enforce an award is sought may be served out of the jurisdiction with the permission of the Court whether or not the arbitration is governed by English law.

29.3   An application for the grant of permission under this paragraph must be supported by an affidavit or witness statement stating the grounds on which the application is made and showing in what place or country the person to be served is, or probably may be found; and no such permission shall be granted unless it shall be made to appear to the Court that the case is a proper one for service out of the jurisdiction under this paragraph.

29.4   RSC Order 11, rules 5 to 8, (Schedule 1 to the CPR) shall apply in relation to any such Part 8 claim form or order as is referred to in sub-paragraph (1) as they apply in relation to any other claim form.

PART III

APPLICATION OF THIS PART

30.1   This Part of this practice direction applies to all enforcement proceedings (other than by an action or claim on the award) regardless of when they are commenced and when the arbitral proceedings took place.

ENFORCEMENT OF AWARDS

31.1   This rule applies to applications to enforce awards which are brought in the High Court and such an application may be made in the Royal Courts of Justice or in any district registry.

31.2   An application for permission under:
   (1)   section 66 of the Arbitration Act 1996;
   (2)   section 101 of the Arbitration Act 1996;
   (3)   section 26 of the Arbitration Act 1950; or
   (4)   section 3(1)(a) of the Arbitration Act 1975;
to enforce an award in the same manner as a judgment or order may be made without notice by use of the practice form referred to in paragraph 4.1.

31.3   The Court hearing an application under paragraph 31.2 may direct that the form (in this Part of this practice direction called 'the enforcement form') is to be served on such parties to the arbitration as it may specify and the enforcement form may with the permission of the court be served out of the jurisdiction irrespective of where the award is, or is treated as, made.

31.4   Where a direction is given under paragraph 31.3, paragraphs 11.1 to 11.5 and 13.1 to 17.1 shall apply with the necessary modifications as they apply to applications under Part I of this practice direction.

31.5   Where the applicant applies to enforce an agreed award within the meaning of section 51(2) of the Arbitration Act 1996, the enforcement form must state that the award is an agreed award and any order made by the Court shall also contain such a statement.

31.6   An application for permission must be supported by affidavit or witness statement:
   (1)   exhibiting
      (a)   where the application is made under section 66 of the Arbitration Act 1996 or under section 26 of the Arbitration Act 1950, the arbitration agreement and the original award or, in either case, a copy thereof;
      (b)   where the application is under section 101 of the Arbitration Act 1996, the documents required to be produced by section 102 of that Act;
      (c)   where the application is under section 3(1)(a) of the Arbitration Act 1975, the documents required to be produced by section 4 of that Act;
   (2)   stating the name and the usual or last known place of residence or business of the applicant and of the person against whom it is sought to enforce the award respectively,
   (3)   stating, as the case may require, either that the award has not been complied with or the extent to which it has not been complied with at the date of the application.

31.7   An order giving permission must be drawn up by or on behalf of the applicant and must be served on the respondent by delivering a copy to him personally or by sending a copy to him at his usual or last known place of residence or business or in such other manner as the Court may direct.

31.8   The order may be served out of the jurisdiction without permission, and RSC Order 11, rules 5 to 8, (Schedule 1 to the CPR) shall apply in relation to such an order as they apply in relation to a claim form.

31.9   Within 14 days after service of the order or, if the order is to be served out of the jurisdiction, within such other period as the Court may fix, the respondent may apply to set aside the order and the award shall not be enforced until after the expiration of that period or, if the respondent applies within that period to set aside the order, until after the application is finally disposed of.

31.10   The copy of the order served on the respondent shall state the effect of paragraph 31.9.

31.11   In relation to a body corporate paragraphs 31.1–31.10 shall have effect as if for any reference to the place of residence or business of the applicant or the respondent there were substituted a reference to the registered or principal address of the body corporate.
Nothing in paragraphs 31.1–31.10 shall affect any enactment which provides for the manner in which a document may be served on a body corporate.

INTEREST ON AWARDS

32.1   Where an applicant seeks to enforce an award of interest, the whole or any part of which relates to a period after the date of the award, he shall file a certificate giving the following particulars:

(1) whether simple or compound interest was awarded;
(2) the date from which interest was awarded;
(3) whether rests were provided for, specifying them;
(4) the rate of interest awarded, and
(5) a calculation showing the total amount claimed up to the date of the certificate and any sum which will become due thereafter on a per diem basis.

32.2 The certificate under paragraph 32.1 must be filed whenever the amount of interest has to be quantified for the purpose of obtaining a judgment or order under section 66 of the Arbitration Act (enforcement of the award) or for the purpose of enforcing such a judgment or order by one of the means mentioned in RSC Order 45, rule 1 (Schedule 1 to the CPR).

REGISTRATION IN HIGH COURT OF FOREIGN AWARDS

33.1 Where an award is made in proceedings on an arbitration in any part of Her Majesty's dominions or other territory to which Part I of the Foreign Judgments (Reciprocal Enforcement) Act 1933 extends, being a part to which Part II of the Administration of Justice Act 1920 extended immediately before the said Part I was extended thereto, then, if the award has, in pursuance of the law in force in the place where it was made, become enforceable in the same manner as a judgment given by a court in that place, RSC Order 71 (Schedule 1 to the CPR) shall apply in relation to the award as it applies in relation to a judgment given by that court, subject, however, to the following modifications:

(1) for references to the country of the original court there shall be substituted references to the place where the award was made; and

(2) the affidavit required by rule 3 of the said Order must state (in addition to the other matters required by that rule) that to the best of the information or belief of the deponent the award has, in pursuance of the law in force in the place where it was made, become enforceable in the same manner as a judgment given by a court in that place.

REGISTRATION OF AWARDS UNDER THE ARBITRATION (INTERNATIONAL INVESTMENT DISPUTES) ACT 1966

34.1 In paragraphs 34.1–34.7 and in any provision of this practice direction as applied by this paragraph:
'the Act of 1966' means the Arbitration (International Investment Disputes) Act 1966;
'award' means an award rendered pursuant to the Convention;
'the Convention' means the Convention referred to in section 1(1) of the Act of 1966;
'Judgment creditor' and 'judgment debtor' mean respectively the person seeking recognition or enforcement of an award and the other party to the award.

34.2 Subject to the provisions of paragraphs 34.1–34.7, the following provisions of RSC Order 71, namely, rules 1, 3(1) (except sub-paragraphs (c)(iv) and (d) thereof), 7 (except paragraph (3)(c)and (d)) thereof), and 10(3) shall apply with the necessary modifications in relation to an award as they apply in relation to a judgment to which Part II of the Foreign Judgments (Reciprocal Enforcement) Act 1933 applies.

34.3 An application to have an award registered in the High Court under section 1 of the Act of 1966 shall be made by claim form under CPR rule 8.6.

34.4 The witness statement or affidavit required by Order 71, rule 3, in support of an application for registration shall:

(1) in lieu of exhibiting the judgment or a copy thereof, exhibit a copy of the award certified pursuant to the Convention; and

(2) in addition to stating the matters mentioned in paragraph 3(1)(c)(i) and (ii) of the said rule 3, state whether at the date of the application the enforcement of the award has been stayed (provisionally or otherwise) pursuant to the Convention and whether any, and if so what, application has been made pursuant to the Convention, which, if granted, might result in a stay of the enforcement of the award.

34.5   There shall be kept in the Admiralty and Commercial Registry under the direction of the Senior Master a register of the awards ordered to be registered under the Act of 1966 and particulars shall be entered in the register of any execution issued on such an award.

34.6   Where it appears to the court on granting permission to register an award or an application made by the judgment debtor after an award has been registered:

(1)   that the enforcement of the award has been stayed (whether provisionally or otherwise) pursuant to the Convention; or

(2)   that an application has been made pursuant to the Convention, which, if granted, might result in a stay of the enforcement of the award,

the Court shall, or in the case referred to in sub-paragraph (2) may, stay execution of the award for such time as it considers appropriate in the circumstances.

34.7   An application by the judgment debtor under paragraph 34.6 shall be made by application notice and supported by affidavit.

Index

Liquidator 95–6
London Court of International Arbitration
  (LCIA) Rules 261, 272
London Maritime Arbitrators' Association
  (LMAA) Terms 261, 272
Loss or right to object
  award 182
  conduct of proceedings 225–6

MacKinnon Committee (1927) 12
Mareva injunctions 152–3
Merchant strangers 2
Mere reference 67
Mere valuation 21–2
Misconduct 8, 234
  acting outside jurisdiction 27
  challenging award for 29–30
  personal 30
  removal of arbitrator for 11, 234
  technical 30
Multiple parties 91–3
  ICC Rules 335, 345

Nema guidelines 196, 198
New York Convention 14, 16–17
  1975 Arbitration Act 16–17
  agreement in writing 294
  commercial disputes 294
  enforcement of award 177, 179, 293,
    294–7
    definition of award 303–4
    in England 303–5
  form of award 170
  formalities 294–5
  parties 274–5
  recognition 293–4, 295, 304–5
  renunciation by contracting State 297
  signatory states 298–9
  treaty obligations under 35
Notices
  absent 307
  appointment, precedent 347–8
  CIMAR 264
  of hearing 250
  ICC Rules 333
  service 232
Notional venue rule 4
Number of arbitrators 102–3, 311

Oaths 253
Offers to settle 210–12
  Calderbank letters 212, 218, 355
  open 210, 211

Offers to settle – *continued*
  sealed 210, 211
  without prejudice 210
Official referees 19
Oral evidence 130
Oral hearing 244, 252, 317, 324
Orders
  failure to comply 17
  interlocutory 13
  peremptory *see* Peremptory orders
  relating to property 150–1

Partial awards 161
Parties
  absent 143–4, 224–5, 337
  administrative receiver 95–6
  administrator 95–6
  age 86
  agents 99–100
  assignee 96–9
  bankruptcy 13, 15
  capacity 86–7, 110–11, 306–7
  choice of procedure 118–19, 121–2,
    125–6, 234–5
    express agreements 235–6
    implied agreement 236
  corporate bodies 86
  costs of 205–6
  Crown 87–8
  death 13, 15
    during arbitration 93–4
    personal representatives 93–4
    prior to arbitration 94
    revocation of written submission 13
  definition 86
  documents in control of 247–8
  failure to comply with orders 17
  foreign States 88
  guarantors 89–91
  indemnifiers 89–91
  international arbitration 274–5
  joinder 263
  liquidator 95–6
  mentally ill person 86
  multiple 91–3, 335
    ICC Rules 345
  partnerships 86, 87
  personal representatives 93–4
  privity of contract 88
  subcontractors 100–1
  surety 89–91
  taking no part in proceedings 224–5
  third parties 88–92